THE
OPPORTUNITY
READER

THE OPPORTUNITY READER

Stories, Poetry, and Essays from the
Urban League's Opportunity Magazine

SONDRA KATHRYN WILSON,

EDITOR

THE MODERN LIBRARY

NEW YORK

1999 Modern Library Paperback Original
Copyright © 1999 by Random House, Inc.

ISBN 0-375-754379-6

Printed in the United States of America

Modern Library website address: www.modernlibrary.com

2 4 6 8 9 7 5 3 1

FOR HARRY BELAFONTE,
WHO COMBINED ART AND HUMAN RIGHTS
TO MAKE A BETTER WORLD

ACKNOWLEDGMENTS

*I wish to thank Manie Barron of Random House
for conceiving the idea of this work and
for his invaluable advice and support.*

I wish to thank the Opportunity *Magazine Publishing Company,
the publisher of the magazine of the National Urban League,
for authorizing the use of these works.*

CONTENTS

Acknowledgments   vii

Introduction by Sondra Kathryn Wilson   xv

Opportunity's *Literary Prize Contest Awards: Charles S. Johnson*   xxiii

PART ONE: POETRY

GWENDOLYN BENNETT
    Heritage   3
    Wind   3
    On a Birthday   4
    Street Lamps in Early Spring   4
    Hatred   5
    Lines Written at the Grave of Alexander Dumas   5

ARNA BONTEMPS
    The Shattering   7
    Golgotha Is a Mountain   7
    Prodigal   9

STERLING BROWN
    When De Saints Go Ma'ching Home   10
    Strong Men   14

JOSEPH S. COTTER [SR.]
    The Wayside Well   17
    A Babe Is a Babe   17
    The Tragedy of Pete   18

COUNTEE CULLEN
    When I Am Dead   21
    I Have a Rendezvous with Life   21
    Uncle Jim   22
    Words to My Love   22
    In Spite of Death   23

ALICE DUNBAR-NELSON
    Of Old St. Augustine   24

Communion 24
Music 25

ANGELINA W. GRIMKE
The Black Finger 26
Dusk 26
I Weep 26
For the Candle Light 26

LESLIE PINCKNEY HILL
Voyaging 28

FRANK HORNE
On Seeing Two Brown Boys in a Catholic Church 29
To a Persistent Phantom 30

LANGSTON HUGHES
Our Land 31
America 31
The Jester 33
To Midnight Nan at Leroy's 34
Dear Lovely Death 34
Aesthete in Harlem 35
Flight 35
Pride 35
Black Seed 36
Negro Servant 36

GEORGIA DOUGLAS JOHNSON
Christmas Greetings 38
The Riddle 38

HELENE JOHNSON
Night 39
Metamorphism 39
Fulfillment 39
The Road 40
Mother 40
Summer Matures 41
Vers de Société 42

CLAUDE McKAY
Africa 43
My House 43
America in Retrospect 44

R. BRUCE NUGENT
  Shadow   45
CLARISSA M. SCOTT
  Solace   46
  Joy   47
H. WALLACE THURMAN
  The Last Citadel   48
  God's Edict   48

PART TWO: FICTION

JOHN AUBREY
  Virginia Idyll   51
ANITA SCOTT COLEMAN
  The Eternal Quest   54
  Cross Crossings Cautiously   57
ARTHUR HUFF FAUSET
  Symphonesque   60
RUDOLPH FISHER
  Dust   73
EUGENE GORDON
  Game   77
ZORA NEALE HURSTON
  Drenched in Light   91
  Spunk   99
  John Redding Goes to Sea   105
  Muttsy   118
CLAUDE MCKAY
  High Ball   131
JOHN F. MATHEUS
  Fog   149
  Clay   158
  Antropoi   167
  Coulèv' Endormi   177
  Nomah—A Story   185
ERIC D. WALROND
  On Being a Domestic   192
  The Stone Rebounds   195
  Cynthia Goes to the Prom   198

Vignettes of the Dusk   202
A Cholo Romance   206
The Voodoo's Revenge   215

DOROTHY WEST
The Typewriter   225

BENJAMIN YOUNG
The Boll Weevil Starts North—A Story   233

PART THREE: PLAYS

MARITA O. BONNER
The Pot Maker   241

GEORGIA DOUGLAS JOHNSON
Plumes   250

FRANK H. WILSON
Sugar Cain   258

PART FOUR: REVIEWS

CHARLES S. JOHNSON
Nigger—A Novel by Clement Wood   277
Some Books of 1924   280

FRANK S. HORNE
Black Verse   284

BENJAMIN BRAWLEY
The Gift of Black Folk   288

ALAIN LOCKE
Color—A Review   291
Welcome the New South—A Review   296

ARTHUR HUFF FAUSET
The Negro's Cycle of Song—A Review   301

STERLING BROWN
Two African Heroines   306

COUNTEE CULLEN
Poet on Poet   314

JAMES WELDON JOHNSON
Romance and Tragedy in Harlem—A Review   317

NELLA LARSEN
Black Sadie   323

PART FIVE: ESSAYS

Personal Essays

JOHN F. MATHEUS
Sand   327

CLARISSA M. SCOTT
A Golden Afternoon in Germany   332

Literary and Cultural Essays

JOHN W. WORK
Negro Folk Song   336

ALAIN LOCKE
Roland Hayes: An Appreciation   343
Max Reinhardt Reads the Negro's Dramatic Horoscope   349

PAUL ROBESON
Reflections on O'Neill's Plays   352

CHARLES S. JOHNSON
Ira Aldridge   355

WILLIS RICHARDSON
The Negro Audience   359
Characters   361

LANGSTON HUGHES
Our Wonderful Society: Washington   364

BRENDA RAY MORYCK
I, Too, Have Lived in Washington   368
A Point of View (An *Opportunity* Dinner Reaction)   378

ELMER A. CARTER
He Smashed the Color Line: A Sketch of Billy Pierce   387

Social Essays

ADAM CLAYTON POWELL [SR.]
The Church in Social Work   390

CASPER HOLSTEIN
The Virgin Islands   392

RAYMOND PACE ALEXANDER
Voices from Harvard's Own Negroes   396
The Negro Lawyer   403

KELLY MILLER
The Practical Value of Higher Education   411

Negro History   416
Where Is the Negro's Heaven?   421

CHARLES S. JOHNSON
Public Opinion and the Negro   430
The Social Philosophy of Booker T. Washington   444

ROBERT W. BAGNALL
The Spirit of the Ku Klux Klan   454

E. FRANKLIN FRAZIER
A Note on Negro Education   460
The Garvey Movement   467

MARY McLEOD BETHUNE
The Problems of the City Dweller   472

A. PHILIP RANDOLPH
The Negro and Economic Radicalism   477

CHARLES H. GARVIN
Immunity to Disease Among Dark-Skinned People   483

IRA DE A. REID
Lily-White Labor   493

J. A. ROGERS
The Negro in European History   502

JOHN HOPE
Trained Men for Negro Business   509

RAYFORD W. LOGAN
Nat Turner: Fiend or Martyr?   515

ELMER A. CARTER
Not in the Headlines: A Story of a Negro Radio Operator   521

Biographical Notes of Contributors   527

Bibliography   539

INTRODUCTION

The story of African Americans, the oldest minority group in this nation, began in 1619. For more than three centuries, black cultural sources and experiential themes have been the chief basis of African-American literature and art. Scholars have noted that this literary tradition was perpetuated because black writers studied the vernaculars, techniques, and themes by earlier writers with whom they felt a kindred spirit. This tradition, handed down from slavery, has always been dependent on its ability to relate to the political, social, and cultural aspects of African-American life. To the extent that Harlem Renaissance writers and writers of today exemplify this purpose is the extent to which they are really successful.

The prosperity of Harlem Renaissance writers like Eric D. Walrond, Alain Locke, James Weldon Johnson, Zora Neale Hurston, and Jessie Redmon Fauset reduced racial barriers and left conditions much more receptive for artists of today like Toni Morrison, Alice Walker, BeBe Campbell Moore, and Walter Moseley. As did their predecessors, today's black writers reflect in their writings the intellectual and cultural history of African-American life. This long-established literary tradition is uniquely significant, because when a race becomes successful in literature and art, that race has achieved one of its greatest guarantees of success.*

---

*See Joanne Braxton's introduction to *The Work of the Afro-American Woman* by Mrs. N. F. Mossell (New York: Oxford University Press, 1988), in the Schomburg Library of Nineteenth-Century Women Writers.

The writings in this volume were first published in the National Urban League's magazine, *Opportunity: A Journal of Negro Life,* between 1923 and 1931. These works exemplify a body of literature that generated the black literary movement of the 1920s known as the Harlem Renaissance.

Founded in New York City in 1910, the National Urban League was incorporated in 1913. The organization was established to service black migrants from rural areas by aiding them in securing sufficient education, employment, and housing. In essence, the Urban League's objective was to help blacks acclimatize to the unfamiliar hardships of urban life. The civil rights organization founded its official organ, *Opportunity,* in 1923. The new journal quickly became an apparatus for jump-starting the Harlem Renaissance. (*The* Crisis *Reader,* another volume in this series, discusses the role of the NAACP's *Crisis* magazine in the birth and development of the Harlem Renaissance.) Scholar David Levering Lewis writes that the Harlem Renaissance was "a somewhat forced phenomenon, a cultural nationalism of the parlor, institutionally encouraged and directed by leaders of the national civil rights establishment for the paramount purpose of improving race relations."[*]

The Harlem Renaissance writer Arna Bontemps divided the black literary movement into two phases. Phase 1 (1921–1924) he deemed the period of black propaganda. Bontemps cited the NAACP's *Crisis* magazine and *Opportunity* as the most important supporters of phase 2 (1924–1931). These two influential journals devoted space to literature and social and political writings. Their efforts must be credited with generating interest in the artistic and intellectual side of Harlem. Phase 2 eventually connected Harlem writers to those members of the white intelligentsia who had access to establishment publishing entities. This connection proved essential in promulgating the Harlem Renaissance.[†]

Prior to the 1920s, barriers based on race prejudice had prevented black artists from attaining the respect of the white publishing establishment. They had often been reduced to publishing either with unscrupulous publishing outfits or out of their own pockets. According to David Levering Lewis, no more than five significant literary writings by African Americans were published between 1908 and 1923: Sutton Grigg's *Pointing the Way* (1908), W.E.B. Du Bois's *The Quest of the Silver*

---

[*] David Levering Lewis, *The Portable Harlem Renaissance* (New York: Viking, 1994), p. xv.
[†] David Levering Lewis, *When Harlem Was in Vogue,* p. 86.

Fleece (1908), James Weldon Johnson's *The Autobiography of an Ex-Colored Man* (1912), Du Bois's *Darkwater* (1920), Claude McKay's *Harlem Shadow* (1922), and Jean Toomer's *Cane* (1923).*

During the first decade of their existence, in the early 1920s, both the NAACP and the Urban League proved effective in their respective arenas. The NAACP waged an unprecedented battle for justice on the political front, while the Urban League aptly addressed the social ills of the day. Notwithstanding the efforts by the two leading civil rights organizations regarding the social and political questions, there was no cultural agenda for African Americans. It was during this time that W.E.B. Du Bois noted that "until the art of black folk compels recognition, they will not be regarded as human." Black literature was a susceptible point for America because it had been malformed, misrepresented, and distributed by an established white literary system; black literature was inauthentic and represented an insolent imitation of an aspect of American literary history. Black leadership had to remedy this invalidity, which had exploited and skewed virtually every external view of African-American life. By the advent of the 1920s, though the NAACP and the Urban League were battling racism on political and social fronts, the time had come for these organizations to make a foray into American culture.

The NAACP and the Urban League, through their respective journals, met the challenge to reclaim through art and literature the status of black Americans by assigning space in *The Crisis* and *Opportunity* for works by writers including Langston Hughes, Zora Neale Hurston, Countee Cullen, and Eric D. Walrond.

The comparable goals of *The Crisis* and *Opportunity* created, on the one hand, a friendly rivalry. On the other, their distinctions rendered virtually impossible any serious competition between the journals. Note that the NAACP's staff was replete with scholar-writers who frequently contributed to *The Crisis:* James Weldon Johnson, W.E.B. Du Bois, Walter White, Jessie Redmon Fauset, William Pickens, and Robert Bagnall. This dominance of talent gave *The Crisis* a clear advantage over *Opportunity*. Even as early as 1919, the circulation of *The Crisis* had reached 104,000, while *Opportunity's* pinnacle circulation by 1928 was only 11,000.

Notwithstanding *The Crisis's* greater prominence, *Opportunity* editor Charles S. Johnson became a premier entrepreneur of the Harlem Renaissance. Langston Hughes wrote that Charles S. Johnson "did more

---

* Arna Bontemps, *The Harlem Renaissance Remembered*, p. 215.

to encourage and develop Negro writers during the 1920s than anyone else." And Zora Neale Hurston contended that the Renaissance "was [Johnson's] work, and only his hush-mouth nature has caused it to be attributed to many others."*

Johnson, a native of Bristol, Virginia, and a graduate of Virginia Union University and the University of Chicago, became the director of the Urban League's Department of Research and Investigations in 1923. This position also made him editor of *Opportunity.* Johnson was widely respected for the militant opinions he articulated in his meticulously researched sociological and economic writings. The noted scholar Arnold Rampersad describes him as "the farsighted manipulative editor . . . trained as a sociologist but sensitive to the power of the arts."†

In the first issue of *Opportunity* (January 1923), Eugene Kinckle Jones, the chief executive officer of the Urban League, asserted that the role of the new journal would be to "depict Negro life as it is with no exaggerations. We shall try to set down interestingly but without sugar-coating or generalization the findings of careful scientific surveys and the facts gathered from research." Charles Johnson did not necessarily disagree with Jones's philosophy for the League's new journal, but he would add another dimension: the literary dimension. In *Opportunity*'s second issue, Johnson wrote, "There are aspects of the cultural side of Negro life that have been neglected."‡

As *Opportunity*'s editor, Johnson was appreciative of black writers like Langston Hughes, Countee Cullen, Zora Neale Hurston, and Eric D. Walrond. Because their writings had appeared mainly in black journals like *The Crisis* and *The Messenger,* he felt that the benefit of their literary efforts was being restricted and was virtually inconsequential to the larger society, and he was quickly losing patience with white America's praise only for Paul Laurence Dunbar, who had "resorted to dialect verse to gain a hearing and then nothing but his dialect verse would be accepted."§

Johnson accepted the challenge of smashing the stereotypes that white America had concocted. According to the writer Robert Hemenway, he "single-handedly made *Opportunity* an expression of 'New

---

* Bontemps, *The Harlem Renaissance Remembered,* p. 215.

† Arnold Rampersad, *The Life of Langston Hughes, vol. 1: I, Too, Sing America* (New York: Oxford University Press, 1986), p. 106.

‡ Bontemps, *The Harlem Renaissance Remembered,* pp. 221–22.

§ Ibid., p. 225.

Negro' thought, and 'New Negroes' made it clear that they would not accept a subordinate role in American society. Art and literature was now the mechanism to prove the cultural and intellectual parity of the race."*

Johnson understood that the art of the Harlem writers was so effulgent that even the most intractable cynic could be convinced. Therefore, he needed only a proper forum in which the Harlem literati and downtown white publishers could coalesce.

The need to unite Harlem writers with the white intelligentsia was threefold. Firstly, the white intelligentsia had ties to establishment publishing entities that were essential outlets for black writers. Secondly, there was a need to connect black and white America through literature and art for the express purpose of contributing to a better understanding between the races. And thirdly, there was a need for full and true self-declaration by black writers.

The idea of hosting a dinner at New York's Civic Club was developed by Johnson as a means to link the two groups. In 1924 he invited such white literary notables as Carl Van Doren, Frederick Allen Lewis, Carl Van Vechten, and William Baldwin. Among the Harlem artists were Countee Cullen, Gwendolyn Bennett, Eric D. Walrond, and Langston Hughes. The purpose of this dinner was to bring literary giants like Carl Van Doren tête-à-tête with black writers like Countee Cullen and to have everyone come away enthralled and highly motivated. This dinner proved to be momentous. During the evening, some black artists secured financial support while others made such impressions that their future funding was inevitable. Although white patrons had been enlightened and awed by the brilliance of Harlem's literati, Johnson was leaving nothing to chance. The relationship between black artists and white patrons had to be crystallized.

In early 1925, he announced the *Opportunity* literary awards contest. He enlisted distinguished persons to serve as judges, including writers Fannie Hurst, James Weldon Johnson, and Carl Van Vechten; editors John Farrar and Carl Van Doren; and dramatic critic Robert C. Benchley. Johnson writes about the significance of the *Opportunity* contest in the following:

It [the contest] hopes to stimulate and encourage creative literary effort among Negroes; to locate and orient Negro writers of ability; to stimulate and encourage interest in the serious development of a body

---

* Robert E. Hemenway, *Zora Neale Hurston: A Literary Biography* (Champaign-Urbana: University of Illinois Press, 1977), p. 9.

of literature about Negro life, drawing deeply upon these tremendously rich sources; to encourage the reading of literature both by Negro authors and about Negro life, not merely because they are Negro authors but because what they write is literature and because literature is interesting; to foster a market for Negro writers and for literature by and about Negroes; to bring these writers into contact with the general world of letters to which they have been for the most part timid and inarticulate strangers; to stimulate and foster a type of writing by Negroes which shakes itself free of deliberate propaganda and protest.*

Although eager to execute his plan for the awards contest, Johnson was faced with financial challenges. Unlike the popular *Crisis* magazine, which was self-supporting, the fledgling *Opportunity* was dependent on the Urban League for most of its provisions.

Opportunity contributor Eric D. Walrond introduced Johnson to Harlem's notorious gambling kingpin Casper Holstein, a native of the Virgin Islands with an insatiable interest in the promotion of black culture. Although his lifestyle was antithetical to the world of Harlem's intelligentsia, he became a major patron of the *Opportunity* contest awards. The awards that proved essential to the promotion of the Harlem Renaissance would not have occurred without the financial backing of one of Harlem's most infamous mobsters.

Between 1925 and 1927 Johnson presided over three contest awards dinners. It is apparent that these events had an invigorating effect on the artists because the dinners hosted the "greatest gathering of black and white literati ever assembled in one room."† And representatives attended from every major publishing house that was interested in black artists, including Alfred A. Knopf, Boni and Liveright, Macmillan, Harper's, and Harcourt Brace.‡

By the mid-1920s, influential whites were patronizing black creative artists. After centuries of struggling, of being cast out, of being scorned, African-American artists were finally gaining their rightful place in America's most sophisticated literary circles. The time had arrived when the white intelligentsia and its publishers were devoting time and resources to black writers. Writings by and about blacks were being published with greater frequency than ever before in American history.

---

*Arna Bontemps, *The Harlem Renaissance Remembered*, p. 227.

† Arnold Rampersad, *The Life of Langston Hughes, vol. 1*, p. 106.

‡ Ibid.

Charles S. Johnson accomplished a twofold objective: he had ingeniously launched an American literary reform that helped to transform race relations, and he had catapulted into publication a comprehensive body of black literature.

Some scholars have denounced the Harlem Renaissance as illusory because it was partially reared by white patronage. The late historian Nathan Irvin Huggins wrote about this generational chauvinism: "Our problem here, is to see men and women of another era in their own terms and not our own. And that will require of us a humanism that will modulate our own ego and self-consciousness enough to perceive theirs."* Moreover, one could readily make the point that, like many American stories, the Harlem Renaissance was anchored in interracial cooperation.

The works presented here reflect America's intellectual and cultural history. This selection of writings is to be valued and preserved as a benchmark for current and future writers. In essence, these works are uniquely significant because they represent our mileposts to the past and our guideposts to the future.

———

EDITOR'S NOTE: The contents of this volume have been reproduced largely as they originally appeared in *Opportunity* magazine. Though some obvious typographical and spelling errors have been silently corrected, most idiosyncrasies of spelling, punctuation, and typography have been preserved.

* Nathan Irvin Huggins, *Harlem Renaissance* (New York: Oxford University Press, 1971), p. 6.

Opportunity's Literary Prize Contest Awards

Opportunity editor Charles S. Johnson instituted the magazine's literary contest. In the following essay, published in September 1924, Johnson explains the parameters of the contest. Ultimately his three literary contests served a major role in jump-starting the Harlem Renaissance.

The contest will include first, second, and third prizes for the following types of writing:

1. Short Story—
First Prize	$100.00
Second Prize	40.00
Third Prize	15.00

2. Poetry—
First Prize	$40.00
Second Prize	15.00
Third Prize	5.00

3. Play—
First Prize	$60.00
Second Prize	35.00
Third Prize	15.00

4. Essay—
First Prize	$30.00
Second Prize	20.00
Third Prize	10.00

5. Personal Experience Sketch—
First Prize	$30.00
Second Prize	20.00
Third Prize	5.00

For the next ten best stories, poems, plays, and essays there will be free criticism by competent authorities in each field of letters.

The winning stories will be published.

Prize winners will be formally announced at a special meeting in New York.

RULES OF THE CONTEST

This contest is designed to stimulate creative effort among Negroes and quite without any notion of discrimination is confined to Negro contestants.

SHORT STORIES

The stories must deal with some phase of Negro life, either directly or indirectly; otherwise there are no restrictions. They may be romantic, realistic, humorous, and will be judged upon their quality as a good short story.

These stories must not exceed 5000 words.

POETRY

No restrictions are placed upon the themes of the poems.

PLAYS

The plays must deal with some phase of Negro life, either directly or indirectly; otherwise there are no restrictions. They may be romantic, realistic, humorous, and will be judged upon their quality as a good play.

ESSAYS

The object here is simply to bid for a much abused type of literary expression, in the hope of finding some examples of recognizable literary merit. The contestant will strive for clarity of diction, forcefulness, and originality of ideas, logical structure, deft and effective employment of language, accuracy of data, and economy of words. The subject may be of the contestant's selection but must relate directly or indirectly to Negro life and contacts, or situations in which Negroes have a conspicuous interest.

These essays are limited to 3000 words.

PERSONAL EXPERIENCE SKETCHES

These sketches must be an actual experience and relate to some incident or situation or circumstance of personal life which makes it possible to understand how one feels and acts in the presence of a particular life problem. The contestant will strive for complete frankness and self-scrutiny, truthfulness, and clarity of expression.

These will be limited to 2000 words.

Any story, poem, play, essay, or personal experience sketch that has already been published is ineligible for this contest.

The contest will close December 31, 1924.

This contest reserves the right to reject all manuscripts in any division if the contributions are deemed below a reasonable standard of quality or insufficient in number.

A complete list of the judges will be published in a later issue. Some of the acceptances are quoted for their expressed interest in the future of creative expression among Negroes. They include the sentiments of leaders of American letters.

John Farrar, Editor, THE BOOKMAN, says:

"I shall be very happy to act as judge in the poetry contest and am honored that you want me to do so. As you know, I am much interested in work of all young writers, and perhaps even more in that of the Negro race."

Carl Van Doren, Editor, CENTURY MAGAZINE, author, writes:

"I shall be glad to serve as one of the judges of your prize contest for short stories by Negro writers if you want me to. Though I have lately declined every other such invitation, on the score of overwork, this one has not caused me a moment's hesitation."

Clement Wood, author, contributor of poems, articles and short stories to magazines, replies:

"I am delighted to serve as one of the judges of OPPORTUNITY's poetry contest for the younger Negro writers."

John Macy, author and editor, says:

"I shall be very glad to act as one of the judges in your contest and to help your work in any way that I can."

Montgomery Gregory, Director, Department of Dramatics, Howard University, states:

"I want to congratulate you upon having taken a step that should do more than anything in the past toward the development of the younger Negro writers. It has been my dream: it is your splendid realization.

"I shall be delighted to serve as one of the judges for plays and I shall, therefore, await further instructions from you. I note that you have made an unusually happy choice of persons to serve as judges."

Robert Hobart Davis, dramatist, Editor, MUNSEY'S, responds as follows:

"I am interested in . . . the work of the Negro writers in this country. I would like to do whatever I can to encourage them in their development."

Dorothy Scarborough, author, book reviewer and short story critic, contributor of short stories, articles and verse to newspapers and magazines, writes:

"I am very much interested in the development of the talents, artistic and otherwise, of the Negroes, and I shall be happy to serve as a judge in the short story contest. I think the plan excellent for arousing interest."

Zona Gale, author, contributor to magazines, says:

"I am very much honored by your invitation to act as one of the judges in the Negro writers' contest. Thank you for thinking of me, and I accept with pleasure."

Edna Worthley Underwood, writer, linguist, author of "The Passion Flower," "The Penitent," writes:

"I am just in receipt of your favor relative to OPPORTUNITY's $500 prize contest. I think it is a splendid plan which you outline to me in your letter and I shall be most happy to serve as one of the judges."

Blanche Colton Williams, editor, author, instructor, Columbia University, accepts as follows:

"Your request honors me and I take pleasure in saying I will gladly serve as judge in connection with the $500 offer of OPPORTUNITY...

"The award that OPPORTUNITY will make in this contest seems to me a happy idea and one that cannot but be helpful to more than one young man and woman."

PART ONE

POETRY

GWENDOLYN BENNETT

Heritage

I want to see the slim palm-trees,
Pulling at the clouds
With little pointed fingers. . . .

I want to see lithe Negro girls,
Etched dark against the sky
While sunset lingers.

I want to hear the silent sands,
Singing to the moon
Before the Sphinx-still face. . . .

I want to hear the chanting
Around a heathen fire
Of a strange black race.

I want to breathe the Lotus flow'r,
Sighing to the stars
With tendrils drinking at the Nile. . . .

I want to feel the surging
Of my sad people's soul
Hidden by a minstrel-smile.

Wind

The wind was a care-free soul
   That broke the chains of earth,
And strode for a moment across the land
   With the wild halloo of his mirth.
He little cared that he ripped up trees,
   That houses fell at his hand,
That his step broke calm on the breast of seas,
   That his feet stirred clouds of sand.

But when he had had his little joke,
   Had shouted and laughed and sung,
When the trees were scarred, their branches broke,
   And their foliage aching hung,
He crept to his cave with a stealthy tread,
   With rain-filled eyes and low-bowed head.

On a Birthday

Angels, craving for a lark
Rubbed the stars to make a spark,
Pelted lake and sea with pearls
Just to see them break in swirls,
Combed the hair of hill-top trees
Just to hear their singing breeze,
Whispered low to birds on wing
Just to hear them trill and sing,
Laughed to see the summer go,
Reveled in the song of snow,
Played with bird and flower and hill
To find their souls were thirsting still.
And then they took the spark of star,
The swirl of sea, the pearls from far,
The song of tree and birds in flight,
The shout of sun, the calm of night,
The urge that makes the Winter pass,
The poetry of sighing grass,
The hush of snow, the laugh of rain,
The ache of joy, the pool of pain,
The sunshine and the shadow, too——
They mixed them well and fashioned you.

Street Lamps in Early Spring

Night wears a garment
All velvet soft, all violet blue . . .
And over her face she draws a veil
As shimmering fine as floating dew . . .
And here and there
In the black of her hair

The subtle hands of Night
Move slowly with their gem-starred light.

Hatred

AWARDED SECOND HONORABLE MENTION—POETRY SECTION

I shall hate you
Like a dart of singing steel
Shot through still air
At even-tide.
Or solemnly
As pines are sobre
When they stand etched
Against the sky.
Hating you shall be a game
Played with cool hands
And slim fingers.
Your heart will yearn
For the lonely splendour
Of the pine tree;
While rekindled fires
In my eyes
Shall wound you like swift arrows.
Memory will lay its hands
Upon your breast
And you will understand
My hatred.

Lines Written at the Grave of Alexander Dumas

Cemeteries are places for departed souls
And bones interred,
Or hearts with shattered loves.
A woman with lips made warm for laughter
Would find grey stones and silent thoughts
Too chill for living, moving pulses . . .
And thou great soul, would shiver in thy granite shroud,
Should idle mirth or empty talk
Disturb thy tranquil sleeping.

A cemetery is a place for shattered loves
And broken hearts . . .
Bowed before the crystal chalice of thy soul,
I find the multi-colored fragrance of thy mind
Has lost itself in Death's transparency.

Oh, stir the lucid waters of thy sleep
And coin for me a tale
Of happy loves and gems and joyous limbs
And hearts where love is sweet!

A cemetery is a place for broken hearts
And silent thoughts . . .
And silence never moves nor speaks
Nor sings.

The poems presented here by Gwendolyn Bennett were published in *Opportunity* in the following issues: "Heritage," December 1923; "Wind," November 1924; "On a Birthday," January 1925; "Street Lamps in Early Spring," May 1926; "Hatred," June 1926; and "Lines Written at the Grave of Alexander Dumas," July 1926.

Arna Bontemps

The Shattering

The pitcher,
Struck by a careless hand,
Is broken at the fountain.
The stone that was so sure
Is cracked at last
By the dip of Spring;
And the song,
Once eagerly proclaimed,
Grown mute in me
At last.

Golgotha Is a Mountain

AWARDED ALEXANDER PUSHKIN POETRY PRIZE

Golgotha is a mountain, a purple mound
Almost out of sight.
One night they hanged two thieves there,
And another man.
Some women wept heavily that night;
Their tears are flowing still. They have made a river;
Once it covered me.
Then the people went away and left Golgotha
Deserted.
Oh, I've seen many mountains:
Pale purple mountains melting in the evening mists and blurring on
        the borders of the sky.
I climbed old Shasta and chilled my hands in its summer snows.
I rested in the shadow of Popocatepetl and it whispered to me of
        daring prowess.
I looked upon the Pyranees and felt the zest of warm exotic nights.
I slept at the foot of Fujiyama and dreamed of legend and of death.

And I've seen other mountains rising from the wistful moors like the
        breasts of a slender maiden.
Who knows the mystery of mountains!
Some of them are awful, others are just lonely.

———

Italy has its Rome and California has San Francisco,
All covered with mountains.
Some think these mountains grew
Like ant hills
Or sand dunes.
That might be so—
I wonder what started them all!
Babylon is a mountain
And so is Nineval,
With grass growing on them;
Palaces and hanging gardens started them.
I wonder what is under the hills
In Mexico
And Japan!
There are mountains in Africa too.
Treasure is buried there:
Gold and precious stones
And moulded glory.
Lush grass is growing there
Sinking before the wind.
Black men are bowing.
Naked in that grass
Digging with their fingers.
I am one of them:
Those mountains should be ours.
It would be great
To touch the pieces of glory with our hands.
These mute unhappy hills,
Bowed down with broken backs,
Speak often one to another:
"A day is as a year," they cry,
"And a thousand years as one day.
We watched the caravan
That bore our queen to the courts of Solomon;
And when the first slave traders came
We bowed our heads.

Oh, Brothers, it is not long!
Dust shall yet devour the stones
But we shall be here when they are gone."
Mountains are rising all around me.
Some are so small they are not seen;
Others are large.
All of them get big in time and people forget
What started them at first.
Oh the world is covered with mountains!
Beneath each one there is something buried:
Some pile of wreckage that started it there,
Mountains are lonely and some are awful.

One day I will crumble.
They'll cover my heap with dirt and that will make a mountain.
I think it will be Golgotha.

Prodigal

I shall come back when dogwood flowers are going
And passing drakes are honking toward the south
With eager necks, I shall come back knowing
The old unanswered question on your mouth.

When frost is on the manzonita shoots
And dogwoods at the spring are turning brown,
There between the interlacing roots
With folded arms I shall at last go down.

"The Shattering," "Golgotha Is a Mountain," and "Prodigal" were published
in March 1926, June 1926, and May 1931, respectively.

STERLING BROWN

When De Saints Go Ma'ching Home

AWARDED FIRST PRIZE—HOLSTEIN POETRY SECTION

(TO BIG BOY DAVIS, FRIEND) IN MEMORIES OF DAYS BEFORE
HE WAS CHASED OUT OF TOWN FOR VAGRANCY.

1

He'd play, after the bawdy songs and blues,
After the weary plaints
Of "Trouble, Trouble deep down in muh soul,"
Always one song in which he'd lose the role
Of entertainer to the boys. He'd say
"My mother's favorite." And we knew
That what was coming was his chant of saints
"When de Saints go ma'chin home . . ."
And that would end his concert for the day.

Carefully as an old maid over needlework,
Oh, as some black deacon, over his Bible, lovingly,
He'd tune up specially for this. There'd be
No chatter now, no patting of the feet.
After a few slow chords, knelling and sweet
Oh when de saints go ma'chin home
Oh when de sayaints goa ma'chin home . . .
He would forget
The quieted bunch, his dimming cigarette
Stuck into a splintered edge of the guitar.
Sorrow deep hidden in his voice, a far
And soft light in his strange brown eyes,
Alone with his masterchords, his memories . . .
        Lawd I wanna be one in nummer
        When de saints go ma'chin home.
Deep the bass would rumble while the treble scattered high
For all the world like heavy feet a trompin' toward the sky.

With shrillvoiced women getting 'happy'
All to celestial tunes.
The chap's few speeches helped me understand
The reason why he gazed so fixedly
Upon the burnished strings.
For he would see
A gorgeous procession to 'de Beulah Land'
Of Saints—his friends—*a climbin' fo' deir wings.*
Oh when de saints go ma'chin home
Lawd I wanna be one o' dat nummer
When de saints goa ma'chin home . . .

2

There'd be—so ran his dream
"Old Deacon Zachary
With de asthmy in his chest
A puffin' an' a wheezin'
Up de golden stair
Wid de badges of his lodges
Strung acrost his heavin' breast
An' de hoggrease jest shinin'
In his coal black hair . . .

An' ole Sis Joe
In huh big straw hat
An' huh wrapper flappin'
Flappin' in de heavenly win'
An' huh thinseled easy walkers
Goin' pitty pitty pat
Lawd she'd have to ease her corns
When she got in!"
Oh when de saints go ma'chin home.
"Ole Elder Peter Johnson
Wid his corncob jes a puffin'
And de smoke a rollin'
Like stormclouds out behin'
Crossin' de cloud mountains
Widout slowin' up fo' nuffin'
Steamin' up de grade
Lak Wes' bound No. 9.

An' de little brownskinned chillen
Wid deir skinny legs a dancin'
Jes' a kickin' up ridic'lous
To de heavenly band
Lookin' at de Great Drum Major
On a white hoss jes' a prancin'
Wid a gold and silver drumstick
A waggin' in his han'.
Oh when de sun refuse to shine
Oh when de mo-on goes down
In Blood
"Old Maumee Annie
Wid huh washin' done
An' huh las' piece o' laundry
In de renchin' tub,
A wavin' sof' pink han's
To de much obligin' sun
An' her feet a moverin' now
To a swif' rub a dub;
And old Grampa Eli
Wid his wrinkled old haid
A puzzlin' over summut
He ain' understood
Intendin' to ask Peter
Pervidin' he ain't skyaid
'Jes what mought be de meanin'
Of de moon in blood? . . .
Wen de saints go ma'chin home . . .

3

Whuffolks, he dreams, *will have to stay outside*
Being so onery.' But what is he to do
With that red brakemen who once let him ride
An empty, going home? Or with that kindfaced man
Who paid his songs with board and drink and bed?
Or with the Yankee Cap'n who left a leg
At Vicksburg? *'Mought be a place, he said*
Mought be another mansion for white saints
A smaller one than hisn' . . . not so gran'
As for the rest . . . oh let them howl and beg.
Hell would be good enough, if big enough

Widout no shade trees, lawd, widout no rain
Whuffolks sho to bring nigger out behin'
Excep'—wen de saints go ma'chin home.

4

Sportin' Legs would not be there—nor lucky Sam
Nor Smitty, nor Hambone, nor Hardrock Gene
An' not too many guzzlin', cuttin' shines
Nor bootleggers to keep his pockets clean.
An' Sophie wid de sof' smile on her face,
Her foolin' voice, her strappin' body, brown
Lak coffee doused wid milk—she had been good
To him, wid lovin', money and wid food.—
But saints and heaven didn't seem to fit
Jes rite wid Sophy's Beauty—nary bit—
She mought stir trouble, somehow, in dat peaceful place
Mought be some dressed up dudes in dat fair town.

5

> *Ise got a dear ole modder*
> *She is in hebben I know*

He sees
> Mammy
> L'il mammy—wrinkled face
> Her brown eyes, quick to tears—to joy
> With such happy pride in her
> Guitar plunkin' boy.
> *Oh kain't I be one in nummer*
> Mammy
> With deep religion defeating the grief
> Life piled so closely about her
> *Ise so glad trouble doan last alway*
> And her dogged belief
> That some fine day
> She'd go a ma'chin
> *When de saints go ma'chin home.*

He sees her ma'chin home, ma'chin along,
Her perky joy shining in her furrowed face,
Her weak and quavering voice singing her song—
The best chair set apart for her worn out body
In that restful place . . .

I pray to de Lawd I'll meet her
When de saints go ma'chin home.

6

He'd shuffle off from us, always, at that,—
His face a brown study beneath his torn brimmed hat
His broad shoulders slouching, his old box strung
Around his neck;—he'd go where we
Never could follow him—to Sophie probably,
Or to his dances in old Tinbridge flat.

Strong Men

The strong men keep coming on.
Sandburg

They dragged you from homeland;
They chained you in coffles
They huddled you spoonfashion in filthy hatches
They sold you to give a few gentlemen ease.

They broke you in like oxen
They scourged you
They branded you
They made your women breeders
They swelled your numbers with bastards. . . .
They taught you the religion they disgraced.

You sang:
Keep a inchin' along
Lak a po' inch worm. . . .

You sang:
Bye and bye
I'm gonna lay down dis heaby load. . . .

You sang:
Walk togedder chillen
Dontcha git weary. . . .
The strong men keep a comin' on
The strong men git stronger.

They point with pride to the roads you built for them,
They ride in comfort over the rails you laid for them.

They put hammers in your hands
And said—Drive so much before sun down.

You sang:
>   Ain't no hammah
>   In dis lan,
>   Strikes lak mine, bebby
>   Strikes lak mine.

They cooped you in their kitchens,
They penned you in their factories,
They gave you the jobs that they were too good for,
They tried to guarantee happiness to themselves
By shunting dirt and misery to you.

You sang:
>   Me an' muh baby gonna shine, shine
>   Me an' muh baby gonna shine.
>   *The strong men keep a comin' on*
>   *The strong men git stronger . . .*

They bought off some of your leaders
You stumbled, as blind men will . . .
They coaxed you, unwontedly soft voiced . . .
You followed a way.
Then laughed as usual.
They heard the laugh and wondered;
Uncomfortable;
Unadmitting a deeper terror. . . .

>   *The strong men keep comin' on*
>   *Gittin' stronger . . .*

What, from the slums
Where they have hemmed you,
What, from the 'tiny huts
They could not keep from you—
What reaches them
Making them ill at ease; fearful?
Today they shout prohibition at you
"Thou shalt not this"
"Thou shalt not that"
"Reserved for whites only"
You laugh.

One thing they cannot prohibit—

The strong men . . . coming on
The strong men gittin' stronger.
Strong men . . .
Stronger . . .

"When De Saints Go Ma'ching Home" and "Strong Men" were published in July 1927 and September 1930, respectively.

Joseph S. Cotter [Sr.]

The Wayside Well

AWARDED FOURTH PLACE

A fancy halts my feet at the way-side well.
It is not to drink, for they say the water is brackish.
It is not to tryst, for a heart at the mile's-end beckons me on.
It is not to rest, for what feet could be weary when a heart at the
    mile's-end keeps time with their tread?
It is not to muse, for the heart at the mile's-end is food for my being.
I will question the well for my secret by dropping a pebble into it.
Ah, it is dry.
Strike lightning to the road, my feet, for hearts are like wells. You
    may not know they are dry 'til you question their depths.
Fancies clog the way to heaven, and saints miss their crowns.

A Babe Is a Babe

O Lord God, we are told
That Thou sleepest not.
Then surely Thou sawest
The little Christ Jesus
In the arms of Mary
On the back of an ass,
Led by Joseph into the Land of the Blacks
That its life might be saved.

O Lord God,
Give us assurance
That Thou hearest the little black babe
In yon cabin in the South,
Crying alone,
Crying all alone,
Because its father's dead body
Is a part of yon charred tree;

Crying alone,
Because its mother is out in the swamps
Calling—"Husband, husband."
And her only answer
Is smoke and sparks and flame,
And the cries of ghoulish men,
Who chock the wheels of time.

O Lord God, Thou sawest,
But dost Thou hear?
A babe is a babe.

The Tragedy of Pete

AWARDED THIRD PRIZE—*OPPORTUNITY* CONTEST

There was a man
    Whose name was Pete,
And he was a buck
    From his head to his feet.

He loved a dollar,
    But he hated a dime;
And so was poor
    Nine-tenths of the time.

The Judge said "Pete
    What of your wife?"
And Pete replied:
    "She lost her life."

"Pete," said the Judge,
    "Was it lost in a row?
Tell me quick,
    And tell me how."

Pete straightened up
    With a hic and a sigh,
Then looked at the Judge
    Full in the eye.

"O, Judge, my wife
    Would never go
To a Sunday dance
    Or a movie show.

"But I went, Judge,
　　Both day and night,
And came home broke
　　And also tight.

"The moon was up,
　　My purse was down,
And I was the bully
　　Of the bootleg town.

"I was crooning a lilt
　　To corn and rye
For the loop in my legs
　　And the fight in my eye.

"I met my wife;
　　She was wearing a frown,
And catechising
　　Her Sunday gown.

"Oh, Pete, O Pete"
　　She cried aloud,
"The Devil is falling
　　Right out of a cloud."

"I looked straight up
　　And fell flat down,
And a Ford machine
　　Pinned my head to the ground.

"The Ford moved on
　　And my wife was in it;
And I was sober
　　That very minute.

"For my head was bleeding
　　My heart was a-flutter;
And the moonshine within me
　　Was tipping the gutter.

"The Ford, it faster
　　And faster sped
Till it dipped and swerved
　　And my wife was dead.

　"Two bruised men lay
　　　In a hospital ward—

One seeking vengeance,
    The other the Lord.

"He said to me:
    'Your wife was drunk,
You are crazy,
    And my Ford is junk.'

"I raised my knife
    And drove it in
At the top of his head
    And the point of his chin.

"O Judge, O Judge,
    If the State has a chair,
Please bind me in it
    And roast me there."

There was a man
    Whose name was Pete,
And he welcomed death
    From his head to his feet.

"The Wayside Well," "A Babe Is a Babe," and "The Tragedy of Pete" were published in June 1925, December 1925, and July 1926, respectively.

COUNTEE CULLEN

When I Am Dead

Love, I would have you weep when I am dead,
Would have you show some sign of grief; be sad,
Despair, lament the joys we two once had,
And wail, regretting, love, that all have fled
With me, your all; and grieve that thorns instead
Of flowers tend your way; say nought can make you glad;
Disband your dreams and name each fancy bad,
When I am gone, to whom your soul is wed.
Yea, I would have you weep, for well I know
Spring comes again with warmth to melt the snow;
And lying there your tears shall water me,
Shall drench my form, my face shall warmly wet,
And then when comes the spring, when you forget,
I'll smile to know *some* tears were shed for me.

I Have a Rendezvous with Life

I have a rendezvous with Life
In days I hope will come
Ere youth has sped and strength of mind,
Ere voices sweet grow dumb;
I have a rendezvous with Life
When Spring's first heralds hum.
It may be I shall greet her soon,
Shall riot at her behest;
It may be I shall seek in vain
The peace of her downy breast;
Yet I would keep this rendezvous,
And deem all hardships sweet,
If at the end of the long, white way,
There Life and I shall meet.
Sure some will cry it better far

To crown their days in sleep,
Than face the wind, the road, and rain,
To heed the falling deep;
Though wet, nor blow, nor space I fear,
Yet fear I deeply, too,
Lest Death shall greet and claim me ere
I keep Life's rendezvous.

Uncle Jim

"White folks is white," says Uncle Jim,
"A platitude," I sneer;
And then I tell him so is milk
And the froth upon his beer.

His heart walled up with bitterness,
He smokes his pungent pipe,
And nods at me as if to say,
"Young fool, you'll soon be ripe!"

I have a friend who eats his heart
Away with grief of mine,
Who drinks my joy as tipplers drain
Deep goblets filled with wine.

I wonder why here at his side,
Face-in-the-grass with him,
My mind should stray the Grecian urn
To muse on Uncle Jim.

Words to My Love

What if you come
Again and swell
The throat of some
Mute bird;
How shall I tell?
How shall I know
That it is so,
Having heard?

Love, let no trick
Of what's to come

Deceive; the quick
So soon grow dumb;
With wine and bread
Our feast is spread;
Let's leave no crumb.

In Spite of Death

All things confirm me in the thought that dust
Once raised to monumental pride of breath,
To no extent affirms the right of death
To raze such splendor to an ancient crust.
"Grass withereth; the flower fadeth," yea,
But in the violated seed exults,
The bleakest winter through, a deathless pulse
That knows spring wipes all sacrilege away.
No less shall I in some new fashion sprout
Again, when death has blown my candles out;
Although my blood went down in shameful rout
Tonight; by all this living flesh holds fair,
Though death should shackle me tonight, I swear
Tomorrow's sun would find his cupboard bare.

These poems by Countee Cullen were published in *Opportunity* in the follow-
ing issues: "When I Am Dead," December 1925; "I Have a Rendezvous with
Life," January 1924; and "Uncle Jim," "Words to My Love," and "In Spite of
Death," July 1925.

ALICE DUNBAR-NELSON

Of Old St. Augustine

Of old, St. Augustine wrote wise
And curious lore, within his book.
I read and meditate, my eyes
See words of comforting, I look
Again, and thrill with radiant hope.
"They did not sin, those white-souled nuns of old,
Pent up in leaguered city, and despoiled
By knights, who battered at the peaceful fold,
And stole their bodies. Yet the fiends were foiled,
They could not harm their stainless, cloistered souls."

O wise St. Augustine, you give
Great joy to those whose earthly form
Is held in thrall. The soul may live
Unscathed—untouched—far from alarm,
True to its cloistered dream—unspoiled.

Communion

This day I dedicated unto you:
I filled each moment of the time with dreams,
Memories, rose-shot, with irridescent gleams.
And now, I find the hours are all too few,
Too soon the lawns are silvered with eve's dew.
A thousand haunting pictures flit—it seems
My mind's a gracious gallery that teems
With exquisite vignettes, forever new.
O rarest day! Your spirit hovering near,
The pressure of your soul upon my own;
None to disturb, no clamoring, petty task!
Your loved whisper breathing past mine ear.
Yourself denied, what better could I ask
Than to commune with memories alone?

Music

Music! Lilting, soft and languorous,
Crashing, splendid, thunderous,
Blare of trumpets, sob of violins,
Tinkle of lutes and mandolins;
Poetry of harps, rattle of castanets,
Heart-break of cellos, wood-winds in tender frets;
Orchestra, symphony, bird-song, flute;
Coronach of contraltos, shrill strings a-mute.
Sakuntala sobbing in the forest drear,
Melisande moaning on crescendic fear;
Splendor and tumult of the organs roll,
Heraldic trumpets pierce the inner soul;
Symphonic syncopation that Dvorak wove,
Valkyric crashes when the Norse gods strove;
Salome's triumph in grunt obscene,
Tschaikowsky peering through forest green;
Verdi's high treble of saccharine sound,
Celeste! Miserere! Lost lovers found.
Music! With you, touching my finger-tips!
Music! With You, soul on your parted lips!
Music—is you!

"Of Old St. Augustine," "Communion," and "Music" were published in July 1925.

Angelina W. Grimke

The Black Finger

I have just seen a most beautiful thing:
Slim and still,
Against a gold, gold sky,
A straight, black cypress
Sensitive
Exquisite
A black finger
Pointing upwards,
Why, beautiful still finger, are you black?
And why are you pointing upwards?

Dusk

Twin stars through my purpling pane,
    The shriveling husk
Of a yellowing moon on the wane,
    And the dusk.

I Weep

Not as the young, pleasurably,
Not as the aged, mistily,
But quietly,—
Drop by drop
The great tears splash upon my hands,
And save you saw their shine,
You would not know I wept.

For the Candle Light

The sky was blue, so blue, that day,
    And each daisy white, so white;

Oh! I knew that no more could rains fall gray,
    And night again be night.
I *knew!* I *knew!* Well, if night is night,
    And the gray skies grayly cry,
I have in a book, for the candle light,
    A daisy, dead and dry.

"The Black Finger," "Dusk," "I Weep," and "For the Candle Light" were published in November 1923, April 1924, July 1924, and September 1925, respectively.

LESLIE PINCKNEY HILL

Voyaging

However hard the winds may blow,
However strong the tides may flow,
Though lightning flash and thunders peal,
We trust the Master at the wheel.

Driven by storms to veer and tack,
He never turns the good ship back,
But rights her keel, and evermore
Fares forward to the distant shore.

Poor children of the human race,
Far voyaging through time and space,
How hard beset, how driven wide
On angry seas by wind and tide!

But high above the streaming years
The faithful lodestar Truth appears,
And thitherwards through tempests still
Trembles the compass of Good-will.

Faith in the Master, and mankind
Some day beyond the flood will find,
When dark and wind and peril cease,
The shining harbor shores of Peace.

"Voyaging" was published in April 1923.

FRANK HORNE

On Seeing Two Brown Boys in a Catholic Church

'Tis fitting that you be here,
Little brown boys
With Christ-like eyes
And curling hair.

Look you on yon crucifix
Where He hangs nailed and pierced
With head hung low
And eyes a' blind with blood that drips
From a thorny crown . . .
Look you well,
You shall know this thing.

Judas' kiss shall burn your cheek
And you will be denied
By your Peter—

And Gethsemane . . .
You shall know full well
Gethsemane . . .

You, too, will suffer under Pontius Pilate
And feel the rugged cut of rough hewn cross
Upon your surging shoulder—
They will spit in your face
And laugh . . .
They will nail you up twixt thieves
And gamble for your little garments.

And in this you will exceed God
For on this earth
You shall know Hell—

O little brown boys
With Christ-like eyes
And curling hair
It is fitting that you be here.

To a Persistent Phantom

AWARDED HONORABLE MENTION—*OPPORTUNITY* CONTEST

I buried you deeper last night,
You with your tears
   And your tangled hair
You with your lips
   That kissed so fair
I buried you deeper last night,

I buried you deeper last night,
With fuller breasts
   And stronger arms
With softer lips
   And newer charms
I buried you deeper last night.

Deeper . . . aye, deeper
And again tonight
'Till that gay spirit
   That once was you
Will tear its soul
   In climbing through . . .
Deeper . . . aye, deeper
I buried you deeper last night.

"On Seeing Two Brown Boys in a Catholic Church" and "To a Persistent Phantom" were published in December 1925 and July 1926, respectively.

LANGSTON HUGHES

Our Land

We should have a land of sun;
Of gorgeous sun,
And a land of fragrant water
Where the twilight is a soft bandanna handkerchief
Of rose and gold,
And not this land
Where life is cold.

We should have a land of trees,
Of tall thick trees,
Bowed down with chattering parrots
Brilliant as the day,
And not this land where birds are gray.

Ah, we should have a land of joy,
Of love and joy and wine and song,
And not this land where joy is wrong.

America

AWARDED THIRD PLACE

Little dark baby,
Little Jew baby,
Little outcast,
America is seeking the stars,
America is seeking tomorrow.
You are America.
I am America
America—the dream,
America—the vision.
America—the star-seeking I.
Out of yesterday

The chains of slavery;
Out of yesterday,
The ghettos of Europe;
Out of yesterday,
The poverty and pain of the old, old world,
The building and struggle of this new one,
We come
You and I,
Seeking the stars.
You and I,
You of the blue eyes
And the blond hair,
I of the dark eyes
And the crinkly hair.
You and I
Offering hands
Being brothers,
Being one,
Being America.
You and I.
And I?
Who am I?
You know me:
I am Crispus Attucks at the Boston Tea Party;
Jimmy Jones in the ranks of the last black troops marching for
         democracy.
I am Sojourner Truth preaching and praying for the goodness of this
         wide, wide land;
Today's black mother bearing tomorrow's America.
Who am I?
You know me,
Dream of my dreams,
I am America.
I am America seeking the stars.
America—
Hoping, praying,
Fighting, dreaming.
Knowing
There are stains
On the beauty of my democracy,
I want to be clean.

I want to grovel
No longer in the mire.
I want to reach always
After stars.
Who am I?
I am the ghetto child,
I am the dark baby,
I am you
And the blond tomorrow
And yet
I am my one sole self,
America seeking the stars.

The Jester

In one hand
I hold tragedy
And in the other
Comedy—
Masks for the soul.
Laugh with me.
You would laugh!
Weep with me.
You would weep!
Tears are my laughter.
Laughter is my pain.
Cry at my grinning mouth,
If you will.
Laugh at my sorrow's reign.
I am the Black Jester,
The dumb clown of the world,
The booted, booted fool of silly men.
Once I was wise.
Shall I
Be wise
Again?

To Midnight Nan at Leroy's

Strut and wiggle,
  Shameless gal,
Wouldn't no good fellow
  Be your pal?

Hear dat music . . .
  Jungle night.
Hear dat music . . .
  And the moon was white.

Sing your Blues song,
  Pretty baby;
You want lovin', . . .
  And you don't mean maybe.

Jungle lover . . .
  Night black boy . . .
Two against the moon
  And the moon was joy.

Strut and wiggle,
  Shameless Nan,
Wouldn't no good fellow
  Be your man?

Dear Lovely Death

Dear lovely Death
That taketh all things under wing—
Never to kill—
Only to change
Into some other thing
This suffering flesh,
To make it either more or less,
Yet not again the same—
Dear lovely Death,
Change is thy other name.

Aesthete in Harlem

Strange,
That in this nigger place
I should meet life face to face;
When, for years, I had been seeking
Life in places gentler speaking—
Before I came to this vile street
And found Life—stepping on my feet!

Flight

Plant your toes in the cool swamp mud;
Step and leave no track.
Hurry, sweating runner!
The hounds are at your back.

No, I didn't touch her.
White flesh ain't for me.

Hurry! Black boy, hurry!
Or they'll swing you to a tree!

Pride

Let all who will
Eat quietly the bread of shame.

I cannot,
Without complaining loud and long,
Tasting its bitterness in my throat,
And feeling to my very soul
Its wrong.

For honest work
You proffer me poor pay.
For honest dreams
Your spit is in my face,
And so my fist is clenched—
Too weak I know—

But longing to be strong
To strike your face!

Black Seed

World-wide dusk
Of dear dark faces
Driven before an alien wind,
Scattered like seed
From far-off places
Growing in soil
That's strange and thin,
Hybrid plants
In another's garden,
Flowers
In a land
That's not your own,
Cut by the shears
Of the white-faced gardeners—

Tell them to leave you alone!

Negro Servant

All day subdued, polite
Kind, thoughtful to the faces that are white.
   O, tribal dance!
   O, drums!
   O, veldt at night!
Forgotten watch-fires on a hill somewhere!
   O, songs that do not care!
At six o'clock, or seven, or eight,
You're through.
You've worked all day.
Dark Harlem waits for you.
The el, the sub.
Pay-nights,
A taxi through the park.
O, drums of life in Harlem after dark!
   O, dreams!
   O, songs!
   O, saxophones at night!
O, sweet relief from faces that are white!

These poems by Langston Hughes were published in the following issues of *Opportunity:* "Our Land," May 1924; "America," June 1925; "The Jester," December 1925; "To Midnight Nan at Leroy's," January 1926; "Dear Lovely Death," "Aesthete in Harlem," and "Flight," June 1930; "Pride," "Black Seed," and "Negro Servant," December 1930.

Georgia Douglas Johnson

Christmas Greetings

Come, brothers, lift on high your voice,
The Christ is born, let us rejoice!
And for all mankind let us pray,
Forgetting wrongs upon this day.
He was despised, and so are we,
Like Him we go to Calvary;
He leads us by his bleeding hand,
Through ways we may not understand.
Come, brothers, lift on high your voice,
The Christ is born, let us rejoice!
Shall we not to the whole world say—
God bless you! It is Christmas Day!

The Riddle

White men's children spread over the earth
Like a rainbow of peace to the drawn-swords of birth;
Uniting the races, soft-tinted, to one—
The World-man, Cosmopolite, Everyman's Son;
Whose blood is the sum of the red and the blue
With deep comprehension transcending the two;
Unriddle this riddle, of outside—in—
White men's children, in black men's skin.

"Christmas Greetings" and "The Riddle" were published in December 1923 and August 1925, respectively.

HELENE JOHNSON

Night

The moon flung down the bower of her hair,
A sacred cloister while she knelt at prayer.
She crossed pale bosom, breathed a sad amen—
Then bound her hair about her head again.

Metamorphism

Is this the sea?
This calm emotionless bosom,
Serene as the heart of a converted Magdalene—
Or this?
This lisping, lulling murmur of soft waters
Kissing a white beached shore with tremulous lips;
Blue rivulets of sky gurgling deliciously
O'er pale smooth stones—
This too?
This sudden birth of unrestrained splendor,
Tugging with turbulent force at Neptune's leash;
This passionate abandon,
This strange tempestuous soliloquy of Nature.
All these—the sea?

Fulfillment

AWARDED FIRST HONORABLE MENTION—POETRY SECTION

To climb a hill that hungers for the sky,
    To dig my hands wrist deep in pregnant earth,
To watch a young bird, veering, learn to fly,
    To give a still, stark poem shining birth.

To hear the rain drool, dimpling, down the drain
And splash with a wet giggle in the street,
To ramble in the twilight after supper,
And to count the pretty faces that you meet.

To ride to town on trolleys, crowded, teeming
With joy and hurry and laughter and push and sweat—
Squeezed next a patent-leathered Negro dreaming
Of a wrinkled river and a minnow net.

To buy a paper from a breathless boy,
And read of kings and queens in foreign lands,
Hyperbole of romance and adventure,
All for a penny the color of my hand.

To lean against a strong tree's bosom, sentient
And hushed before the silent prayer it breathes,
To melt the still snow with my seething body
And kiss the warm earth tremulous underneath.

Ah, life, to let your stabbing beauty pierce me
And wound me like we did the studded Christ,
To grapple with you, loving you too fiercely,
And to die bleeding—consummate with Life.

The Road

AWARDED HONORABLE MENTION—*OPPORTUNITY* CONTEST

Ah, little road all whirry in the breeze,
A leaping clay hill lost among the trees,
The bleeding note of rapture streaming thrush
Caught in a drowsy hush
And stretched out in a single singing line of dusky song.
Ah little road, brown as my race is brown,
Your trodden beauty like our trodden pride,
Dust of the dust, they must not bruise you down.
Rise to one brimming golden, spilling cry!

Mother

Soft hair faintly white where the angels touch it;
Pale candles flaming in her eyes
Hallowing her vision of Christ;

And yet I know
She would break each Commandment
Against her heart,
And bury them pointed and jagged in her soul—
That I may smile.

Summer Matures

AWARDED SECOND PRIZE—HOLSTEIN POETRY SECTION

Summer matures. Brilliant Scorpion
Appears. The pelican's thick pouch
Hangs heavily with perch and slugs.
The brilliant-bellied newt flashes
Its crimson crest in the white water.
In the lush meadow, by the river,
The yellow-freckled toad laughs
With a toothless gurgle at the white-necked stork
Standing asleep on one red reedy leg.
And here Pan dreams of slim stalks clean for piping,
And of a nightingale gone mad with freedom.
Come. I shall weave a bed of reeds
And willow limbs and pale night flowers.
I shall strip the roses of their petals,
And the white down from the swan's neck.
Come. Night is here. The air is drunk
With wild grape and sweet clover.
And by the sacred fount of Aganippe
Euterpe sings of love. Ah, the woodland creatures,
The doves in pairs, the wild sow and her shoats,
The stag searching the forest for a mate,
Know more of love than you, my callous Phaon.
The young moon is a curved white scimitar
Pierced through the swooning night.
Sweet Phaon. With Sappho sleep like the stars at dawn.
This night was born for love, my Phaon.
Come.

Vers de Société

And if I was mistaken—
If your fealty is glossed,
If all your vows were taken
With every finger crossed—

Later I shall be wary,
But later I shall be old.
There is no time to tarry
Since only the young are bold.

Love's an omelette, rum sprinkled,
Set on fire and served while hot,
Puffed to a heavenly fragrance,
Light as a pollen dot.

Be careful it does not fall, dear.
Make haste and have your meal.
Only the dotard is prudent.
Only the dead are leal.

These poems by Helene Johnson were published in the following issues of *Opportunity:* "Night," January 1926; "Metamorphism," March 1926; "Fulfillment," June 1926; "The Road," July 1926; "Mother," September 1926; "Summer Matures," July 1927; and "Vers de Société," July 1930.

CLAUDE McKAY

Africa

The sun sought thy dim bed and brought forth light,
The sciences were sucklings at thy breast;
When all the world was young in pregnant night,
Thy slaves toiled at thy monumental best.
Thou ancient treasure-land, thou modern prize,
New people marvel at thy pyramids!
The years roll on, thy sphinx of riddle eyes
Watches the mad world with immobile lids.
The Hebrews humbled them at Pharaoh's name.
Cradle of Power! Yet all things were in vain!
Honor and Glory, Arrogance and Fame!
They went. The darkness swallowed thee again.
Thou art the harlot, now thy time is done,
Of all the mighty nations of the sun.

My House

For this peculiar tint that paints my house
Peculiar in an alien atmosphere
Where other houses wear a kindred hue.
I have a stirring always very rare
And romance-making in my ardent blood,
That channels through my body like a flood.

I know the dark delight of being strange,
The penalty of difference in the crowd,
The loneliness of wisdom among fools,
Yet never have I felt but very proud,
Though I have suffered agonies of hell,
Of living in my own peculiar cell.

There is an exaltation of man's life,
His hidden life, that he alone can feel.
The blended fires that heat his veins within,

Shaping his metals into finest steel,
Are elements from his own native earth,
That the wise gods bestowed on him at birth.

Oh each man's mind contains an unknown realm
Walled in from other men however near,
And unimagined in their highest flights
Of comprehension or of vision clear;
A realm where he withdraws to contemplate
Infinity and his own finite state.

Thence he may sometimes catch a god-like glimpse
Of mysteries that seem beyond life's bar;
Thence he may hurl his little shaft at heaven
And bring down accidentally a star,
And drink its foamy dust like sparkling wine
And echo accents of the laugh divine.

Then he may fall into a drunken sleep
And wake up in his same house painted blue
Or white or green or red or brown or black—
His house, his own, whatever be the hue.
But things for him will not be what they seem
To average men since he has dreamt his dream!

America in Retrospect

Like vivid scene stamped on a keen child's mind,
Your gorgeous pageants entertain my view;
I see your great all-sweeping lights that blind
Your vision to the Shadow over you.
My thoughts of you are memories of a child,
A healthy child that soon forgets its hurt;
Wistful, I feel no hatred deep and wild,

For you made me a stoic introvert,
I fight with time but for a longer lease
Of those creative hours severe and stern,
Those hours in which I see my purpose plain,
That I may write in freedom and in peace
The accumulations of the years that burn,
White forge-like fires within my haunted brain.

"Africa" was published in May 1924. "My House" and "America in Retrospect" were published in November 1926.

R. Bruce Nugent

Shadow

Silhouette
On the face of the moon
Am I.
A dark shadow in the light.

A silhouette am I
On the face of the moon
Lacking color
Or vivid brightness
But defined all the clearer
Because
I am dark,
Black on the face of the moon.

A shadow am I
Growing in the light,
Not understood
As is the day,
But more easily seen
Because
I am a shadow in the light.

"Shadow" was published in October 1925.

CLARISSA M. SCOTT

Solace

AWARDED FOURTH PLACE

My window opens out into the trees
And in that small space
Of branches and of sky
I see the seasons pass
Behold the tender green
Give way to darker heavier leaves.
The glory of the autumn comes
When steeped in mellow sunlight
The fragile, golden leaves
Against a clear blue sky
Linger in the magic of the afternoon
And then reluctantly break off
And filter down to pave
A street with gold.
Then bare, gray branches
Lift themselves against the
Cold December sky
Sometimes weaving a web
Across the rose and dusk of late sunset
Sometimes against a frail new moon
And one bright star riding
A sky of that dark, living blue
Which comes before the heaviness
Of night descends, or the stars
Have powdered the heavens.
Winds beat against these trees;
The cold, but gentle rain of spring
Touches them lightly
The summer torrents strive
To lash them into a fury
And seek to break them—

But they stand.
My life is fevered
And a restlessness at times
An agony—again a vague
And baffling discontent
Possesses me.
I am thankful for my bit of sky
And trees, and for the shifting
Pageant of the seasons.
Such beauty lays upon the heart
A quiet,
Such eternal change and permanence
Take meaning from all turmoil
And leave serenity
Which knows no pain.

Joy

Joy shakes me like the wind that lifts a sail,
Like the roistering wind
That laughs through stalwart pines.
It floods me like the sun
On rain-drenched trees
That flash with silver and green.

I abandon myself to joy—
I laugh—I sing.
Too long have I walked a desolate way,
Too long stumbled down a maze
Bewildered.

"Solace" was published in June 1925. "Joy" was published in October 1926.

H. WALLACE THURMAN

The Last Citadel

There is an old brick house in Harlem
Way up Fifth Avenue
With a long green yard and windows barred
It stands silent, salient,
Unconquered by the surrounding black horde.

God's Edict

AWARDED HONORABLE MENTION—*OPPORTUNITY* CONTEST

Let the wind-rolled waves tell the tale of the sea,
And the talkative pines tell the tale of the tree;
Let the motored purr of an automobile
Tell the hum-drum tale of power and steel.
Let the blithesome chirp tell the tale of the bird,
And sad, low sounds tell the tale of the herd;
Then enthrone man on the dunce's stool
And let his tale be the tale of a fool.

"The Last Citadel" and "God's Edict" were published in April 1926 and July 1926, respectively.

PART TWO

FICTION

VIRGINIA IDYLL

Published in April 1931, this short story by John Aubrey presents an in-cident depicting the deplorable multilayered by-products of poverty. In this instance the inhumane, intergenerational, emotional, crippling, and in-evitable consequences of deprivation are laid bare in a domestic scene played out by a family already racing toward disaster.

It is a small country kitchen, into which a single window admits the faint light of an early March evening. Two greasy cupboards stand along the wall. In the center of the room is a dilapidated pine table, generously strewn with last year's fly-paper.

Now and then a window-pane rattles, or the fire crackles in a big, wood-burning stove, which is leaning almost against the chimney.

Near the stove a man sits in a chair tilted back against the wall. He is dressed in overalls, which clay soil has dyed a brick-red. His head is bent slightly forward, and he stares straight ahead with a half lazy, half dreamy gaze. There is a banjo in his lap, and as the mood strikes him, he plucks a string, or creaks a tuning-peg. It is the only noise in the room except the crackling of the fire.

The man twists himself so as to bring one foot, encased in its heavy sock, nearer the stove. As he rubs his toasted foot against the other, he grins widely. Soon, however, he compensates for this loss of energy by dangling both feet idly over the sides of the balanced chair.

A woman enters from the adjoining room. She carries a small, lighted lamp, which she places in the center of the table. When she faces the man, her voice bears a challenge.

"Dere ain' no mo' med'cine."

"Yuh? Aw righ'. De doctuh'll come tuhmorruh."

"But we gottuh have de med'cine tuhnight, an' now."

"Well, dere ain' no money in de house, an' Ah ain' goin' out in dis bad weddah, neah ez it is night time. An' de neahest place dat yuh kin git dat med'cine is t'ree miles off, an' back agin."

"De chile gottuh have dat med'cine tuhnight. De doctuh say so, w'en he wuz heah las'."

"Well den, call up de doctuh, an' tell him tuh come on out heah."

"Yuh know damn well ain' no white doctuh comin' out heah tuh see no niggah chile dis time uh night, an' 'sides, de neahes' telephone's at Opal, whuh yuh kin git dat med'cine."

"What yuh gittin' all mad fo', now?"

"Yuh listen to me! Yuh git yo' lazy se'f up outtuh dat chere, fo' Ah break yo' haid, an' go an' git dat med'cine!"

"Wif what?"

"Wif dat wheat we got lef'. Dey'll give yuh money fo' it. Den, go tuh de drug sto'."

"Whuh we gonnuh use fo' braid?"

"Nuffin'. Heah's de bottle. Git out!"

The man slowly puts on his shoes, and shuffles out through the door, mumbling about the "feedin' " he still has to do.

The woman walks over to the fire, and puts on more wood. Then she begins to fry the meat for supper.

The fire has burnt out, and the kitchen is cold and dark. Outside the wind blows in angry gusts.

The kitchen door opens, and the man stamps in, closing the door noisily.

Immediately the woman, bearing the lamp carefully with both her hands, tiptoes hurriedly from the bed-room.

"She ain' doin' well atall. D'yuh git de med'cine?"

"Nuh. De man at de sto' tuk de wheat fo' a bill we had."

"A bill? We ain' have no bill at dat sto'."

"*Ah* had one."

"What fo'?"

"Tubaccy."

"Didn' yuh tell um dat de chile wuz sick? Dat she wuz dyin', maybe? Dat de doctuh wuzn' comin' 'tell tumorruh?"

"Ain' no use tuh tell dat whut man nuffin'.—He wouldn' pay no min', no how. Ah ain' bothuh'd um.—Uh—guess Ah'll go tuh bed, now."

"No yuh ain'! No yuh ain'! Yuh cain' go now! De baby! De baby is dyin', Ah tells yuh! Dyin'! Ah seen um lak huh befo'. She gonnuh *die*! Fo' Gawd's sake, tek sumpin', an' git de med'cine!"

"Dyin'?—Aw-w, woman, yuh is jes' foolin' me. Yuh jes' wannah mek me go out in dat col' again.—Ah ain' goin', do.—Ah'se tiah'd, dammit. Ah'se goin' tuh bed, *now*!"

"No yuh ain'. No yuh ain'! Ah tells yuh de baby is dyin'! Ah'd go my-se'f, but Ah gottuh stay heah. Fo' Gawd's sake! Lord Jesus, make um go!"

"Dere yuh go wif dat stuff ag'in. Git outtuh my way! Ah'm goin' tuh bed. Git—"

"Yuh is goin' tuh ol' man Riley's, an' take dat las' calf we got. Yuh goin' dere, an' tell um yuh wannuh sell de calf. Sell it fo' anythin'. Jes' enuf fo' de med'cine. Yuh heah me? Go tuh ol' man Riley. A' de sto' dey woan tek no calf dis time ob night. Ah wish Ah could go, an' do it right. But yuh got tuh go, or Ah'll—"

"Put dat gun down, woman! Ah'se goin! Ah'se jes foolin!"

The man is shouting hoarsely. He backs clumsily out of the room, knocking over a chair in his excitement.

As the door slams to, the woman's shoulders sag. She places the gun listlessly against the wall, and then walks slowly into the bed-room.

Silence bears down upon the forsaken room. As time passes, the small lamp on the table burns low, and the shadows deepen in the corners of the room. Then, suddenly, the little flame leaps frantically upward. In a moment, however, it chokes to a sickly blue flicker, rallies feebly,—and goes out. The puff of smoke drifts off into the darkness.

There is a long, anguished scream; it seems to quicken even the silence which follows.

After a long time, a figure enters from the bed-room, and slumps heavily into a chair somewhere in the kitchen. The figure remains silent.

At length, the handle of the door rattles. Someone pushes against the door, and stumbles in. He shuffles about the room, and finally scratches a match. Its flame reveals the man, trying to light the lamp. It reveals also the woman, crying silently, her head sunk in her arms, resting upon the table.

"Heah Ah ish, honey. Yash shuh! Heah Ah ish! Yuh know,—ol' man Riley got de besh likah ovah tuh hissh place. An' he sol' me de whole quart fo' dat lil' ca'f. Ah tol' um yuh wouldn' min'. Yuh shee, he gave me shome trial shoshs befo' Ah made de trade—sho's Ah could tell weddah it wash good or no.—But—dere wuz shompin'—dat yuh wanned me tuh do, an' Ah come—all—de—way—home tuh fin' out.—Shompin'—Shompin'—"

THE ETERNAL QUEST

This short story, published in August 1931 by Anita Scott Coleman, lays bare transcendent heights of faith. Coleman demonstrates that in the face of the lyrics of the intellectual or the dialects of the unlettered, providence plays no favorites.

When Evan Given gave up his wife to that grim reaper who holds a mortgage on every man's house and forecloses with or without notice, he turned with a stolid, white-hot passion to his baby, a year-old daughter, for what little comfort he could squeeze from life. The love that he severed with such visible effort from the mother to bestow upon the offspring doubled and trebled in the years during which Polly Given grew up.

At eighteen, she was a sweet flower of a girl. Then, as stealthily as comes the dew at even-tide, the Reaper struck again, deftly, swiftly, and Polly sped forth into the unknown whither Evan dared not follow. And the reason that he dared not was because of a tiny spark that glowed in the very depth of his being—his faith. He believed in life after death, and that the self-destroyer forfeited much if not all of the future existence.

Because Evan Given was one of the foremost surgeons of his day, and dabbled in science as a side-line, it was not altogether incredible, after his burdensome grief, that he elected to give up the one in which he had won fame and fortune for the other, the lesser as a buffer for his sorrow. Quietly, and with no more ado than is usual for a man changing his barber, he dropped all else, and took up the study of science—the science of faith. He closed his house, the palatial dwelling, he had erected for his daughter; cut his London connections, and set himself adrift, as much as it was possible for a man of his standing to do.

What is this thing, faith.... Why does it suffice for some.... Why is it insufficient for others.... Why believing as I do that God is the giver, and therefore has a Divine right to take when and as He wills, am I rebellious because he has bereft me of mine? These were the questions Evan Given sought to solve.

———

No. 60 in ward 400 was one of the strangest cases ever admitted to the county hospital. His was an unique malady and of a far-reaching scope. Plainly it came under the category of cases wherein the great Evan Given had labored so magnificently. It was known that the famous English surgeon was sojourning in the American city. If he could be prevailed upon to grant but an hour of his time, if for no more than a consultation, if only for an observation, anything he might choose to do would be a priceless gift to the medical profession.

At last, when all arguments had failed, someone mentioned that, which seemed to him, the strangest phase of the case in question, that this great hulking giant of a fellow—No. 60 was well over forty—should lay day after day, calling for his mother.

"That," said Evan Given, instantly, "is faith. Wait. I will come."

The span of No. 60's shoulders came near to over-taxing the width of the white iron cot. His massive head pressed against the headpost. His feet protruded through the foot rails. He was easily six foot, ten, and he was delirious when Evan Given saw him first. He was strapped, but yet the strong thongs were proving inadequate, the motions of the man lifted the cot until it tossed about like a frail craft on a windy sea. And always, he screeched the one word, "mom-mer."

"Too late. . . . Nothing can be done!" proclaimed the great man. "At least, he can be made comfortable. Send for his mother!"

"There can be no visitors." Head Nurse of ward 400 voiced a protest, that was curbed at a glance from the Surgeon.

No. 60's mother arrived when he was at his worst. It was the crucial hour. He was seeking with maniacal strength to break his bonds, and screaming fiendishly. The mother, after a brief period with the great London physician, hurried to her son's bedside.

She was a small woman, a tightly, shriveled hard little person, not unlike a black walnut . . . Her timidity fell from her, as she drew near the bed. She became no longer an uneasy visitor among countless strangers, but a mother with her only son, and it was he and she against the world.

The great Evan Given was a close observer of all that passed. This was a pregnant moment to him, in his study of faith.

The mother said quickly and a little shrilly, "Lie down 'dar." Then in firmer tones, and quieter: "Be still. Didn't ah tells you!"

Magically, the huge form upon the bed grew calm.

"What's you a-laying here fo', disturbin' these yere folks, ain't yo mammy done taught yo better'n 'at. . . ." Her voice was crooning. "Ain't yo' shame yo'self. Here's yo mammy done come this long ways to see yo, and yo is lying here yellin' like yo is possessed."

"Mommer." . . .

To the amazement of those watching, the man on the bed was muttering in his turn to the old woman. The mother down on her knees bent her head to hear. Quickly, she stood erect, and called loudly.

"Nurse . . . Doctor . . . somebody come quick and take off dese bindings. My boy wants to die free. . . . Come quick, somebody, quick."

Evan Given came—internes and nurses together removed the straps. No. 60 heaved a great sigh of relief. His head jerked back convulsively, and his eyes rolled wildly towards his mother. "De Lord's done come," he intoned majestically, and fell into his final sleep, peacefully as a babe.

"Faith," jotted Given, mentally.

The old woman sat beside the cot with folded hands. Evan cleared his throat. Surely this was a strange manner in which to meet death, not a tear, in no wise, did she betray regret. "Why-er—why-er," began Evan.

"Blessed lamb. . . . Sweet Jesus, done come and set my po' suff'ring boy, free," chanted the old woman, almost gaily.

"Faith," tabulated Given in his scientific mind.

"What will you do?" he inquired curiously, and not unkindly.

"Do heah this man," exclaimed No. 60's mother, "I's goin'er do muy wo'k." As an afterthought, "I'se got 'er wo'k for sho' now, 'cause dis boy a-lying heah is my sole suppo't. But de Lord will provide."

"Faith," said Evan Given audibly in the voice of a man who talks often to himself. "I must find it."

CROSS CROSSINGS CAUTIOUSLY

Published in June 1930, this quartet of vignettes by Anita Scott Coleman is fairly surreal. Nonetheless, the message she brings makes it clear that caution, thoughtfulness, and practiced judgment are of more value to a black man than trust, simplicity, and kindliness.

Sam Timons rarely thought in the abstract. His thoughts as were his affections were marshalled concretely. His affections were rolled into a compact and unbreakable ball which encircled his wife Lettie and his young son Sammy. His thoughts—he did not think much—but such as his thoughts were, they involved this, if he did a good turn for somebody, somebody else would quite naturally do him or his a good turn also.

Usually Sam was a cheerful creature. Work and love; love and work, that, boiled down to brass tacks is the gist of all life, and Sam possessed both. Even though, at present, he was out of a job.

He walked along the sandy road stirring up miniature dust clouds with every step for his heavy feet shuffled wearily with the burden of his dejected body.

He felt down and out. He was at the end of his rope. One dollar in his pocket. He gripped it in his fingers. All he had. But he could not give up. The ball of his affection, as it were, trundled along before him luring him on. He was "hoofing it" to another town to try again.

"Saw wood . . . clean house, paint barns, chop weeds . . . plow, anything, suh . . . Just so it's work so's I can earn somethin'. I'm a welder by trade, but they don't hire cullud."

Behind him stretched the long, dusty way he had come. Before him a railroad zigzagged his path. As his feet lifted to the incline, he raised his eyes, and met advice from a railroad crossing sign:

CROSS CROSSINGS CAUTIOUSLY

He paused to spell out the words, repeating them painstakingly. Then he went on. A little beyond and across the tracks another huge sign caught his attention.

Soon, he had halted beside this one, letting his eyes sidle up and down and over the gaily painted board. Now he was staring open-mouthed at the glaring yellow lion who crouched to spring, now, at the flashy blond lady pirouetting on a snow white mount. He stood quite still thinking. Wouldn't Lettie and little Sam be wild to see such a show.

—

" 'Lo Mister."

Sam swung around like a heavy plummet loosed from its mooring.

"Gee ... Mister, you 'fraid of me?"

A little girl hardly more than a baby addressed him. She was regarding him with the straight unabashed gaze of the very innocent and of the very wise.

"I want you to carry me to the circus," she announced, when their mutual survey of one another seemed to her enough.

Sam's eyes were fixed on the web-fine, golden hair escaping from two torn places in the child's hat. Already he had seen that the eyes searching his were blue ... He fidgeted. He made a move to go.

"Oh, don't, don't go," beseeched the child. "Mother has to 'tend a meeting, and father is always busy. There is no one else. Mother said I might if only somebody'd take me. See." She thrust out a little smudgy fist—and opening it, revealed a shiny new fifty-cent piece. "This is mine," she said plaintively, "Can't we go?"

—

Mrs. Maximus McMarr was a busy woman. She managed to attend fourteen clubs each week, but that excluded any time to manage Claudia, her five-year-old daughter. Claudia's father considered children woman's responsibility. One advantage or disadvantage this sort of bringing up gave Claudia, she always got what she wanted.

Something about her made Sam do her bidding now.

They were half way between the McMarr place and the circus grounds before he thought about what he was doing. He clutched at the dollar in his pocket. He wanted to laugh, guessed he was nervous. Suddenly, he stopped abruptly—there was another of those signs where the train's right-of-way intersected another dusty country road.

CROSS CROSSINGS CAUTIOUSLY

"Oh do come on," urged the child jerking his hand in an ecstasy of delight and impatience.

Further on a half-grown lad passed them, but stopped and turned to watch them down the road. As the man and the little girl drew out of sight, he faced about and pelted up the road.

The noise of the circus leapt up to meet and welcome Sam and Claudia. The music of the band was sweet to their ears. Sam reveled in it and Claudia's little feet danced over the road. Even the bellowing and roars of the wild animals left them undismayed. It was circus day.

Mrs. McMarr had alighted from a friend's car and remained standing beside it, to talk. Both women observed the runner at the same time. Mrs. McMarr felt her heart skid upward into her throat. Claudia had not appeared. She divined that the messenger tended evil for no other than her precious baby. She made up her mind to swoon even before she received the tidings.

The friend went in search of McMarr who for once allowed himself an interruption. Close-lipped, he tumbled off his harvester and rushed pell-mell across his field.

———

All afternoon, Claudia had been surfeited with care. One after another had tendered and petted and caressed her. Even her father had been solicitous. She curled up, drowsy and very tired, in the big arm chair.

The rain that had threatened to fall all day suddenly commenced like the tat-a-rat-tat of far-off drums. Claudia was wide awake. She sat up. Remembering. The circus band! The monkeys in their little red coats! Her circus man! Something had happened. What?

The impulse to know surmounted the fear she harbored of her father. She slipped over to his chair. He had been very kind today. Perhaps . . . he wouldn't mind telling her . . . Where her circus-man was?

SYMPHONESQUE

In the following narrative, Arthur Huff Fauset suggests the "movements" of a classical musical composition. He explores the wounded mentality of a young black boy and the artlessness of a young female friend of his to exemplify the pain that can be experienced in the transitions of unaided growth and maturation. Awarded first prize in the short-story section, this narrative was published in June 1926.

I
ALLEGRO NON TROPPO
ALLEGRO VIVACE ET CAPRIOSO

The tiny village of Gum Ridge, Texas, fairly hummed under a sizzling white sun that mounted higher and higher in the gray-blue space lately traversed by the stars. Living creatures fled the exposed valley and sought shelter beneath the leafy branches of giant cottonwoods, pecans and maples that studded the sides of the towering hill which lent its name to the village.

The parched fields lay desolate, looking like huge burnt carcasses, and brittle as dead men's bones. They listened to the dull droning of the dust-ridden atmosphere as it quivered under the murderous lashings of the sun, and occasionally to the sonorous hum-m-m-m-m of a solitary bee that braved the death-dealing rays of heat in quest of some petalled haven.

Far down in the blistered valley, within a wretched log cabin, Cudjo, brown youth of seventeen summers, raised himself drowsily from his torn and tattered couch. In a corner of the cabin, Old Ben lay sound asleep. Cudjo knew he was sound asleep by the noise of his snoring, harmonizing ludicrously with the bzz-bzz-bzz of the giant horse-flies that frisked and frolicked about the old man's mouth and from time to time raised huge lumps on his lips and the top of his bald head.

Cudjo stretched and yawned.

He sat down on the edge of his couch and looked about him. The cabin was littered with filth. Rubbish of all sorts was strewn over the floor. Vermin crawled from the bed clothing, from his clothes, and from the newspapers that adorned the walls. Sleek rats darted occasionally across the floor. The smothering rays of the sun, shimmering through long thin cracks in the roof fell with a dazzling brilliance on the nauseating spectacle.

For a moment Cudjo was filled with loathing. Although he had never known any other kind of existence, something within him was not reconciled to this slovenliness. A curious shiver coursed slowly through his body, starting at the base of his spine and trickling out on his lips. Under that burning roof he felt his teeth chattering.

It took but a moment to put on his few fragments of clothing. Then he crept to the door of the shack and started to open it, but of a sudden shut it, exclaiming: "Damn hot . . . Baptism today too . . . Niggahs gonna do dere stuff f' sho' in all dis heat . . . Gotta be dere . . . gotta be dere."

In the corner Old Ben continued to snore profoundly. Cudjo observed him intently for an instant.

"Oughta be up an' gittin' to de ribber, sho's yuh bo'n. Dat's his lil' red wagon ah reckon. Spec' ah bettah let 'um sleep an' tek his rest. If he misses baptism though, be jes' too bad."

He reached for an old black hat hanging off a nail in the door, and pulled it far over his face as he emerged from the cabin.

"Wow, but it's hot," he exclaimed as his bare feet trod upon the sandy road that felt like a bake oven. "Twarn't fo' de damn foolishness ah'd git baptize' m'se'f dis hot day. . . . Somepin' mattah wid mah soul right now an' ah knows it . . . Gotta git dis out O'm' system somehow . . . wonder what's eatin' me?"

He passed old Ebenezer Baptist Church. Standing on a small eminence overlooking the surrounding lands it had the appearance of a smoke-gray lighthouse in an ocean of heat-flame. Cudjo laughed cynically as he stepped by.

"All dis 'ligion ain't gittin' nobody nowheah. All it does, mek yo' all feel good. Mek yo' feel like yo' treading' on soft cushions in Gawd's heb'n. But it ain't gittin' nobody nuffin' ain't gittin' me a damn thing. Dis 'ligion don't keep folks f'um laughin' at me cause ah'm diff'ant f'um dem. Don't kep White Man f'um raisin' hell any time he feelin' dat-a-way. Jes' mek yo' happy dat's all. Mek yo' damn happy. Feel good . . . yea bo'.'"

He looked into the heavens. The sun was a whirling white streak in a hazy gray-blue pattern. His eyes could not stand the glare.

With hands folded behind him he sauntered along as in a dream, thinking, thinking, unmindful of heat or shade. His eyes seemed to be covered with mist. They were nearly closed. He did not have to see. What were feet for? Did they not have ten eyes, as many noses and mouths as well? There was nothing which could be perceived by the ordinary senses that these wonderfully trained friends did not discover even more readily. If he was hungry, they led him to patches of wild blackberries and juicy strawberries. When he was tired and sleepy they carried him gently over rocks and stones, avoiding pits, brambles and poisonous snakes. They knew the east from the west; the quiet lanes that led down to the cool, refreshing brook from the steep stony paths which ascended to the crests of those mighty shaggy turrets that people called hills; those hills from whose tops he delighted to look down on the sleepy villages below and pretend that he was God.

God again!

What was all this talk about God? These niggers and their God! Fools, that's all they were, they and their God.

Did they think that God gave a tinker's damn for them, they in their dirty shacks that bred scorpions, bedbugs and rats, and gave forth a stench that would knock down a polecat! Where was their God when White Man came along at the end of the harvest season and told the niggers they hadn't made enough cotton to pay for their grub to say nothing of their shelter, their clothing, their very liberty!

And what was He doing on that hot afternoon when White Man took Zack Jones and riddled his body with bullets after he had been strung up to a big tree for being in the neighborhood when little "Miss" Dora suddenly took a notion it would be funny to pretend that some nigger had said naughty things to her? . . .

He liked to go up on Gum Ridge in the late afternoon when pale, purple clouds hovered over the tiny villages like a hen over her brood of chicks. It was like being in heaven to be there and hurl a stone high in the air only to watch it fall on some naked roof in the white section of the village; then with fists clenched and arms raised in mighty exaltation to exclaim: "Damn yuh, when ah'm down in de valley yo' all white folks is Gawd. Yeh. Ain't no mo' Gawd when ah'm down dere. But when ah gits up in dese pahts ah'm Gawd. Hyeah me, yo' gawddamned w'ite trash. Yo' all listen to me. Ah'm Gawd. An' one o' dese days ah'm gonna baptize yo' all wif fiah an' brimstone!"

He arrived at the bank of the Tugaloo River, the sluggish, anemic stream that mocking white folks called Ebenezer's Jordan. No other person was in sight. Cudjo lifted himself upon the stern of a small motor launch that lay anchored near the shore, masterfully perched for witnessing the baptismal ceremony.

The sickening sun smote him with its sleep-dispensing rays. He began to feel drowsy. A gentle mist formed over his half-closed eyes; the world commenced to swim from under him.

Pictures flitted across the space in front of him, flickering glimpses of the same slim brown girl who seemed to dance for his pleasure and performed miraculous gyrations like some whirling pinwheel. In a half doze he mumbled to himself: "Damn . . . that's Amber Lee. Sho' is. Amber Lee. Wonder ef she be hyeh today?"

The slim brown figure whirled round and round until it appeared as dazzling as the sun. Cudjo shook himself from sheer dizziness.

"Ah got funny feelin's these days. Don't know whut's wrong wid me. Ah wants to dance an' shout. An' raise hell in gen'ral ah' reckons."

His head nodded. Asleep. Awake. Here, then there, now dead, alive, just enough alive to feel himself crooning an old melody he had often heard Old Ben sing:

> "Hop right! goin' to see mah baby Lou!
> Goin' to walk an' talk wid mah honey!
> Goin' to hug an' kiss mah honey . . .
> Hop right, mah baby!"

He *hopped right* out of his reverie when a party of picnickers, breezing by in a small launch yelled out to him amidst waving of flags and handkerchiefs: "Hello Cudjo! Hello Crazy Cudjo!"

Cudjo's arm shot out with a jovial fling, but ended with a stock gesture, the outstretched fingers of his right hand in close proximity to his nose and yelled back: "Hope t' Gawd yo' all boat turns over!"

There was no more chance to dream. The worshippers were coming down to the river; at first small straggling droves of children; soon after, clustered crowds of men, women and children.

It was hot. The dank water of the Tugaloo smelled like a cistern containing an old corpse. Men and women perspired till the air was filled with a thick pungent odor like soapy stale salt. Old people looked on at the gathering crowd and said little; the young folk laughed and twitted each other. Ebenezer Baptist was on party display. Her women were clad in every description of red, yellow, purple, pink, blue. Many of them wore dresses of brilliant hues woven into Egyptian patterns. They raised gay paper parasols and cotton umbrellas to ward off the scorching sunshine. Young men sported wide trousers with gaudy suspenders or broad brilliantly colored belts. Their belt-furrowed coats made of screaming brown and blue cloth displayed a profusion of buttons, some of them hanging from long tassel-like cords. They wore large brown and black felt hats and glistening derbies.

The congregation grew thicker and noisier. Members found places on odd stacks of lumber that were piled up here and there on the shore; in rowboats which they tied together; on the roofs of sheds and outhouses. Some of the young bucks sat on the trestle of the railroad bridge that spanned the river.

Cudjo viewed the gaudy parade with great glee. He chuckled low to himself and clapped his hands. "Hotdam," he muttered half aloud, "gonna be big doin's in dis man's town dis yere day . . . sho' is . . . Hotdam!"

A loud murmur emanating from the gathering throng attracted his attention to the bank of the river. A cry surged through the congregation. "Uh-uh . . . hyeh dey come . . . hyeh dey come . . . hyeh dey all come'."

II
CRESCENDO
RELIGIOSO FURIOSO

All eyes focused on the preacher, shepherd of the flock who appeared leading his baptismal lambs. He was a tremendous black figure with a large round stomach that almost bulged out of his dark blue vest. As he waddled, his corpulent body seemed like a huge inflated balloon made of thick rubber swaying upon two large resilient pillars.

He wore a white robe that was neither long enough to hide the tips of his blue trousers nor wide enough to cover the heavy gold watch-chain that circled his paunch. A hush came over the ever-increasing throng as the preacher and two deacons prepared a passageway to the river for the baptismal candidates. In their stocking feet they waded out in the smutty brown water and drove two long staves about a yard apart into the soft mud. To the ends of these they fastened ropes which they brought back to the shore and attached to hooks that had been driven into some pilings on the river bank.

The converts, dressed in white, were lined up one behind the other on the shore. Most of them were young girls. Their eyes were red with weeping. Now and then one of them sobbed and fell into the arms of a buxom matron who crooned old Baptist hymns in her ears.

The preacher bustled about, imparting final instructions to his deacons while they waited for a tall brown man, clad in white robes, to make his way through the dense crowd. He was the exhorter.

The ceremony began.

The exhorter discarded the white cap that adorned his head and exposed himself to the excruciating heat. He commenced singing in a high quavering voice:

> "Run away, run away,
> Run away, run away,
> Ain't gonna see you any more."

At the third "run away" the entire congregation echoed the song fervidly. The young candidates took this for a signal to shriek and sob. Their voices rent the sizzling air like screaming sirens in the black of a starless night.

The exhorter continued:

> "Cry some more, cry some more,
> Cry some more, cry some more,
> Ain't gonna see you any more."

Some one in the congregation started to sing:

> "How many done dead an' gone?
> Couldn't have religion I would not be."

The exhorter desiring even more fervor decided that one more song was necessary. Soon the air rang with melody.

> "Ain' we some angels of Jesus, some angels of Jesus,
>   some angels of Jesus,
> Surely He died on Calvary,
> Calvary, Calvary,
> Calvary, Calvary,
> Calvary, Calvary,
> Surely He died on Calvary."

The singing became hysterical. Men and women cried. Some swayed their bodies from right to left; some leapt into the air; others shook themselves up and down like coarse dancers in a burlesque theatre.

Crescendo, crescendo, crescendo. Mighty roar of an ocean tumult. Thunder. Tumult of song that challenges the listening heavens agape.

> "Calvary, Calvary,
> Calvary, Calvary,
> Calvary . . ."

As if by signal the torrent of song diminishes in volume and velocity; step by step, pitch by pitch, it diminishes. Nothing remains but a gentle soft crooning that seems like the pattering of raindrops on the leaves after a storm.

The crooning stops abruptly. The soft voice of the big black preacher wafts its way soothingly over the congregation like an evening lullaby. "Come on chillun, da's 'nough now . . . chillun . . . Gawd done hyard yo' all . . . Gawd sho' hyard his white lambs dat time. Now we gwine ha' prayer by Brother Simpson."

Brother Simpson stepped out from the throng. He threw his battered straw hat on the muddy bank and flung his long black arms toward the sunlit heavens. He spoke slowly at first in low tones that were scarcely audible above the quiet murmuring that wrapped itself around the devout worshippers like a soft blanket. He prays:

"Oh Lawd . . . dis is a prayer to you . . . dis is a prayer to m' father in heb'n, oh Lawdy Jesus . . . yas . . . yas . . . Done turn mah face to de jasper walls so's you kin see de heb'nly sunshine in mah eyes . . . Oh Lawdy Jesus . . . done renounce de flesh an' de debil. . . ."

His prayer grows warmer and warmer. He punctuates each fervent plea with a deep gasp resembling a suffocating man struggling for air.

"Oh, Lawd, Lawdy, u-n-n, hab mercy on dis po' creature of yours, u-n-n, hab mercy on dis thy humble servant, u-n-n oh Lawd, deliber us, u-n-n, f'm de debil's wiles, u-n-n ah holy Lawd Jesus, u-n-n, watch fo' us, u-n-n an' pray, u-n-n, fo's u-n-n, that we be not led, u-n-n, into de temptation ob de wilderness, u-n-n, and fall beneath de prickly feet of dat wicked debil, u-n-n."

The deacon exhorts. He cajoles and laments. He pants, sings, groans and croons. Great clouds of steam fall from his face.

At first the congregation with heads bowed listen in a rhapsody of terror and exaltation. After a little while they too shout and scream as the deacon denounces the wickedness of the devil and depicts the horrors of hell.

From time to time the preacher dips down into the muddy stream with his hands and brings up water to bathe the head of the sweltering deacon and his own as well. After each application he emits a shrill laugh whose fiendish notes resounds on the stifling atmosphere like the midnight cry of a panicky jungle cat. The prayer ended.

The congregation breaks into spontaneous song. Bodies swayed to left and right. Body touched body. A corporate thrill passes through the entire congregation.

Spontaneous song.

> "Oh Lord, thy will be done.
> Oh Lord, thy will be done.
> Our Father which art in heaven,
> Hallowed be thy name,
> Thy kingdom come,
> Thy will be done,
> Oh Lord, thy will be done."

No one was more affected than Cudjo. The scoffer could not help himself. Emotion overcame reason. He laughed and shouted. Tears streamed from his eyes. He pranced in the air, slapping his thighs with the palms of his hands, while his lithe body bent and swayed to the rhythm of the songs.

He sang with tears in his eyes and throat, as if his heart brimmed over with heavenly moisture. Like a drunken man he was reeling in an orgy of emotional rapture, drowning in a warm, rich, overwhelming flood of sensual experience.

An ominous grin spread over his entire countenance. Again his eyes seemed covered with mist. He scarcely knew where or who he was. Uneasiness crept over the members of the congregation who stood by him.

The preacher called for the candidates. Single file they marched through the passageway that led to the living water.

The first was a tender child of fifteen years. She tugged and fought with the leaders as they led her to the stream. Under the scathing sun energies soon flagged and good humors vanished. The preacher was sorely tried. He called out constantly to the congregation to restrain their zeal. Finally he looked in the direction of Cudjo and screamed: "If any yo' niggahs cain't behave yo'se'ves hyeh, yuh kin git out right now ... any you niggahs!"

Water on a duck's back. Cudjo clapped his hands and laughed the more.

Religious frenzy gave strength to the young candidate. It took two deacons and the preacher to immerse her. One took her by the arms while the other two each grasped a struggling ankle. For a moment, the congregation looked on in tense silence. The silence became a dumb shudder. Even the struggling girl, suspended in midair, looked on in dumb wonder as Cudjo rushed down through the surprised throng, and leaping over the ropes made as if to snatch her from the arms of her preceptors. The perspiration gleamed on his face. The muscles of his arms bulged as he tried to tear the girl from the grasp of the amazed preacher.

"You black debil," he shouted to the holy emissary, "you'se a sinner an' a hypocrite. Take yo' orn'ny hands f'um off'n her. De voice ob Gawd speakin' th'oo de clouds f'um he'b'n. Hyeah me, now, hyeah me. John de black Baptis', he hyeah now tellin' me to do all dis. Yo' all baptize wid water but ah baptize . . ." He got no further.

Pandemonium.

Cries of "Lawd Ha' mercy, oh Lawd, Gawd: Save us. . . . Save us, f'um dis debil!"

The candidate still hung suspended in midair, the preacher, two deacons, and Cudjo grasping some part of her. She had fainted and lay lifeless in their hands.

Mad fury swept over the congregation. The baptism was suddenly converted into a scene of near carnage.

"Kill him, kill him, kill the black fool," they all shouted.

Cudjo held on and laughed fiendishly. They swarmed around him and started to crush and pummel him. For a moment he was certain to be killed, but the saner preacher, recovering from his surprise, released the girl and rushed at Cudjo from behind. A dozen stalwart deacons came to his assistance. From the hysterical circle of women and children, flaying him with umbrellas and pelting him with missiles, the outraged deacons bore him clear through the throng out into the open.

Up the banks they ran dragging the interrupter with them. Finally they rushed behind a clump of tall bushes many yards from the scene of the baptism. Like an outcast devil they lifted Cudjo into the air and hurled him as far as they were able. Solemnly they watched him fall in a senseless heap. Then breathless and tired they made their way back to calm the awestruck candidates and to resume the baptism.

III
AGITATO
AGITATO APPASIONATO
SMORZANDO ET TRANQUILLO

Cudjo landed in a thick patch of dry grass. The sudden impact stunned him but aside from painful bruises, he was none the worse for his wild adventure. The merciless rays of the sun beating down upon him seemed more cruel than the scourging crowd, and he crawled to the clump of bushes, grateful for some shade and shelter. There he sat on the hot grass nursing the muscles of his legs. Down by the river he could hear soft music crooned by the congregation, and the rhythmic tread of feet patting on the ground. Gradually the energy of youth returned. He laughed aloud. He looked at his bare feet, burned almost black by the sun; then at his soiled hands. He clapped them together and kicked his heels as high as his sore calves would permit.

He laughed aloud. He cried; he panted. He crooned to himself as if to soothe his torn soul; half speaking, half singing he consoled himself in words of self-pity and encouragement.

"What's matter, ol' Cudjo?" he said. "Cain't yo' all behave yo'se'f? Yo' all done raise 'nough hell fo' one day!"

The echoes of another song wafted over from the river. He heard the congregation crying and screaming, and listened to their stamping and moaning.

> "Take mah Lawd away, Lawd away, Lawd away,
> Take mah Lawd away,
> Not a mumbelin' word did he say,
> Nevah said a mumbelin' word.
> Not a word,
> Not a word,
> Nevah said a mumbelin' word."

Music. Rhythm. Dancing.

Warm bodies swaying like tall sugar cane in an evening breeze. The earth seemed to be swaying beneath him. Unconsciously his own body commenced to sway. A tongue of flame shot from beneath a hidden soul-cloud and set his whole body on fire. Desire possessed his body. He felt an outpouring of white hot desire.

Like a starved beast of the forest who scents game Cudjo sprang erect and poised himself for the leap to the goal of his desire. Savage music tingled in his hot blood. His feet danced away to the mad strains and carried him on and on through the dry grass in long rapid strides.

Gum Ridge lay in the distance. Nearer and nearer his feet took him, then more than half way round, till he could see a cozy green cabin that lay sequestered beneath some maple trees.

Slackening his pace, Cudjo peered intently, while his heart thumped against his chest like angry waters against the shore . . . each thump was a song . . . each song a dance . . . and she who danced . . . was . . . Amber Lee.

Fires within and without.

Cudjo stooped down in some tall bushes that offered protection from the sun. He heard the swarming of insects. He knew they were singing songs to each other. He bent down and listened. And understood.

"I want you. I want you. I'm coming after you my honey. Coming after you and take you. Take you. Hear me my hones. I'm coming to take you. You. You. I'm going to wrap myself around you, all over you, take you, you my honey.... take my honey ... your honey ... I ... want you ... I'm going to take you."

He waited for the answer."

"Come and take me. Come and take me. Take me. But you've got to catch me. I want you to take me. But you've got to catch me. Come and take me. Come take me. Come and wrap yourself all around me and over me and take me. Take my honey, come and take ..."

So this was it!

Cudjo sprang to his feet. He wanted to rush out blindly—to seize her and carry her far off.

The blistering sun brought him back to some realization of earth. He gazed skyward and exclaimed: "Lawd, how come ah nevah know befo' dis? Lawd, ah wants her. Amber Lee dat's what been ailin' me. Lawd, ah wants her. An' Lawd ah gwine to tek her!"

He looked in the direction of the cabin. It stood in a veritable forest of shade. At first sun blindness prevented him from seeing. He peered intently into the open space between the cabin and the trees that sheltered it. She was there. Amber Lee.

Pale straw face brown. Sad face Amber Lee.

Luscious big brown eyes like swelling bays of tears. Pity. Sadness. Hunger. Warmth. Amber Lee. Two warm golden brown breasts soft like young bird's feathers, flaky, soft. Amber Lee. Pale straw face brown Amber Lee. Limbs full and graceful like apple boughs in spring.

Oh, oh, Amber Lee. Amber, Amber Lee. Why did God make you so lovely so lovely down there under the tropical sun where hearts whose passions lie asleep wake overnight throbbing with hot desire—where new seed shoots when the old has scarcely taken root?

Cudjo watched her intently. He lay flat on his belly, hidden in the parched grass while the sun beat down upon him like a burning flail. He only felt a burning sensation from within.

His body was a drum; his heart was the drummer. The flames were passion-music.

And why, dear Cudjo, do you lie there on your belly and hide like a wild beast intent on seizing its prey? Is it not the one—your Amber Lee—the only one in fifty miles who ever understood you and your strange fancies and dreams? It is no new experience for you to hold her in your arms. Remember the day you rescued her from the lake? You have been her friend and playmate. You have done her chores for her.

She has sat at your feet in the dark shadows of the night and listened to you as you told her your dreams and your fantasies.

Why then do you linger in the tall grass and let the relentless sun smite you while you only devour your treasure with your eyes?

Amber Lee.

Amber Lee feels no presence; she sees no person. She feels only herself, her budding self. It is warm, it is hot, it is smouldering. She is warm, she is hot, she is smouldering.

Her heart sings an inward song. She feels but she does not understand. What is this which thunders like a rumbling polonaise and marches through her tortuous limbs on up to the ruddy tips of her swelling breasts?

She hears the song of nature's creatures and feels its echoes quivering through her limbs and breasts.

"Come and take me. Come and take me. Me. But you've got to catch me. Got to catch me. Come and take me. Come and wrap yourself all around me. And over me and take me. Take my honey, come."

But she cannot understand—

The sun had passed beyond the last high curve in the vaulted heavens. Slowly it retreated into the distant west, the pale whiteness of noon absorbed in a vista that grew more and more rosy.

But Cudjo perceived only Amber Lee. Unnoticed were the softer rays of the receding sun, unnoticed the shade which steadily enveloped the fields where he lay hidden. The outer cool only intensified his inner heat. He lay in the grass like a panting beast, his mouth watering for the distant prey.

He could contain himself no longer. Like a tricky savage he quietly bestirred himself. Like a sneakthief in the night he stole his way towards her. The friend and playmate of Amber Lee, twin to her sorrows and longings, stole his way towards her, gliding through the tall grass and skirting the leafy trees like a sneakthief in the night.

Amber Lee.

Gradually she sensed him, sensed a presence. What was it? What was that rumbling through her limbs, her bosom, that quivering in her breasts? What did she want? Want? Want?

Before she knew, even before he could realize, she was in his arms— in Cudjo's warm perspiring brown arms that throbbed and quivered with passion. She looked into his eyes, ravenous flaming eyes that peered out at her as through a silken shade. A chill came over her as she saw those eyes; she became suddenly cold with fright.

She lay in his arms affrighted, like a startled fawn who after she has been pounced upon by a wild beast cowers in silence and stares with an icy stare. She perceived the message of those eyes: "I want you. I want you, you, you. I want you."

Her own which had been so soft and warm responded with terror. The starved beast has his prize. He feasts upon her with his eyes but as he sees her own stricken with terror he can find in them no answering warmth. He has her. She makes no outcry; she offers no resistance. She is his, all his. But she rests in his arms a poor quivering human leaf, her eyes melting into tears of terror and shame.

The fires that had leaped into bursting flame so suddenly, fled as precipitously back to the dark recesses from which they sprang.

Cudjo's eyes filled with tears. Tears of what? He stroked Amber Lee's face and hair gently. "Me, me," he whispered. "Gawd, Amber Lee, it's me. Yo' all know me. Cudjo, ah wouldn't hurt a hair on yo' head. Amber Lee. Amber Lee, m' chile. It's me. Jes' want scare mah lil' Amber Lee, da's all. Lee. Amber, Amber Lee. Un'stan'? Jes' want scare mah lil' Amber Lee."

He placed her gently on the warm grass and did not even kiss her.

She sat upright and looked at him as through a cloud. Limbs quivering, mouth wide open she kept staring at him. All the warm music of her body had ceased; the song in her limbs and breasts had vanished. Once she felt a chill breath steal over her that might have been like death. She quivered.

"Cudjo, Cudjo, you only you. But it wasn't you at first. No, no Cudjo, not you. Only some fierce demon who looked at me with frightful eyes like Satan's. And you rescued me, didn't you Cudjo, just like you saved me in the lake! Oh, Cudjo," she exclaimed, and buried her head in her own bosom.

Cudjo looked down upon her in silence. Far in the west he saw a blood red sun retreating under banks of thick dark cloud. Gum Ridge waned in the distance, a thin shimmering light playing on her crest.

His own body was cool now. The flaming coals of high noon were reduced to barely flickering ashes. His eyelids closed. Without so much as a single look backwards he started towards the towering hill. It seemed far away.

Slowly he mounted its steep sides to the summit. A chill wind had commenced to blow; it was cool there.

He sat on a ledge which jutted out from the very topmost point of the hill and dropped tiny pebbles on the little huts below.

The sinking sun disappeared in the big hollow under the west.

Dust

In this story, Rudolph Fisher crafts a suspenseful incident involving the dangerous mix of youthful impetuousness and fast cars. The high-powered pace of the tale likewise epitomizes the facility with which judgments made by immature minds informed by resentment might end up as a race toward unanticipated tragedy. This story was published in February 1931.

The long, low, black-and-silver roadster overtook a small clutter of cars waiting at a town crossing, snorted impatiently once or twice, and settled into a grumbling, disgusted purr. The people in the other cars stared, conferred among themselves, and stared again.

Pard grinned at the girl beside him. "Kills 'em to see us in a car like this. Know what they're saying?"

Billie smiled back. "Of course. 'Why, my *dear,* they're *colored.*' "

"No," said Pard. "One word: 'Niggers!' Leaves 'em speechless.—Look at that barmaid in the flivver—can't get her mouth shut."

The signal changed, the cars moved forward. Pard said:

"Now, damn it, eat niggers' dust."

Easily the mighty motor swept them in and out past car after car till they were far in the lead.

"Too bad," said Billie.

"What?"

"There isn't any dust."

With open country and a rolling straightaway they settled down to an even forty. A warm breeze sang round the windshield, ruffling the brown girl's hair with gentle fingers—glossy black hair which the low sun touched to a glow. She looked thoughtfully out over the Connecticut landscape. Wide meadows swept past or stretched gently away, lifting into distant hills; the hills dodged behind one another, and the sun dodged behind the high hills. She looked at the proud dark face of her companion, still grim with the joy of outstripping white folks.

"Horrible thing, prejudice," she said. "Does you all up. Puffs you all out of shape."

"Not if you have a safety-valve. This buggy's mine. Take anything on the road. Only fun fays give me."

"It's such bitter fun."

"Deep, though. Satisfying. If hating's their game, I can hate right along with 'em. They hate me—sure. But I out-hate 'em. I hate 'em so much I like it."

"No. You like covering them with dust."

"Sure."

"Even when there isn't any dust."

———

A sudden, loud, almost articulate warning cried startlingly out behind them. Pard instinctively swung over, and a bright yellow sport coupe, of a make as powerful as his own roadster, eased effortlessly past. The interval between the two cars widened rapidly; the other motor's abrupt guffaw dwindled to a receding chuckle.

"Billy, did you see that?"

"He's doing sixty."

"The license-plate, I mean."

"Green and white."

"Georgia."

"Georgia?"

"Georgia—the dirty—"

"Lord protect us now," prayed Billie, knowing what was coming.

"Lord protect him," Pard corrected, his face again grimly bitter. "Hold fast."

His foot went down on the gas; the roadster jumped forward like a cruelly spurred horse then laid back its ears and flattened itself out in a wild, headlong, heedless run.

Already the car ahead was lost around a left bend in the road. Pard took the bend blindly on its inside margin at fifty miles an hour, while Billie closed her eyes. When she looked again the yellow machine was vanishing to the right at the end of a half-mile straightaway. This they clipped off at seventy, taking the next curve, which was luckily shallow, at fifty-five.

The other car re-appeared; the interval had merely been maintained, not diminished. But the road now chose to climb the low ground-rises rather than side-step them so that, save for occasional depressions, it was now visible straight ahead for two miles. And it was clear.

The yellow sport-coupe, unaware of pursuit, maintained its even sixty. Pard's speedometer passed seventy-five. As his fifteen-mile-an-hour advantage devoured the stretch between him and his object, his lips formed rancorous words:

"No damn cracker—do that to me . . . die first . . ."

Billie yelled, "If you mean that, let me out!"

"Lyncher. . . . Atta baby—go get 'im—Red-necked, hill-billy. . . . Ought to run him off the road anyhow—every cracker less is a nigger more. . . . Listen. . . ."

As they drew nearer, the other engine's voice came back to them no longer a decisive chuckle but a deepening, desperate snarl.

"Holler, damn it. Holler and burn—like a black man down in Georgia—"

"Let up, Pard! Sharp curve ahead—"

The Georgia car, now a mere hundred yards in the lead, was slowing around the turn. Pard took the limit of approach before his foot sought the brake; his tires screeched in a straight skid, protesting the sudden change.

The sound seemed definitely to warn the yellow coupe of hostile approach from behind, whereupon it flung off the turn and engaged the next stretch in deadly earnest. This again was long straight highway, flatter than the other and flanked on either side by low, broad pasture-lands level with the road.

"Here we go," said Pard. Billie hung on, praying. The engine roared insanely, the wind whipped harshly past, swiftly, steadily the lead diminished. Perhaps three-quarters of a mile remained of the stretch when Pard, looking beyond the Georgia car ahead, saw the road split in a fork.

"Got to beat him to that fork. Next town's coming."

"And some cars, maybe," said Billie, thanking God for clear roads thus far.

"Come on, baby!" Pard jammed his foot down and held hard with both hands.

Billie squeezed her lids together. The stridor of the yellow car grew, beat painfully in her ears. "Bye-bye, cracker!" An irresistible impulse forced the girl's eyes open to observe impending disaster: Either car was flinging itself precipitately at the fork. Pard's roadster now a length ahead, to the left, both took the left bend of the fork; when, fifty yards ahead, a third car came out of a blind left intersection and stopped dead halfway across the road, startled to a standstill by the mad on-rushing pair.

Both jammed on brakes, Pard bearing right, directly into his competitor's path. The latter swung off the road with a crash into the grassy triangle between the two bends of the fork, managing by the grace of heaven and consummate skill not to flip upside down. Either car came to a standstill, Pard's fifty yards up the highway, the other in the middle of the field.

Billie was trembling. "Pard—go back—he must be hurt—"

No question now of hatred. Pard wheeled and drove back through the grass to the coupe. As they stopped, the yellow door opened, the driver backed stiffly out, and turned to present to their astonished eyes as black a face as ever came out of Georgia.

A deep breath all around. Then, "Are you—hurt?" Billie managed; and, "I'm sorry," from Pard—"I'll pay for any damage—"

A far hill covered the face of the sun, like a hand concealing a grin.

GAME

Eugene Gordon was awarded half of Opportunity's *first prize for "Game." In this story, he adroitly dichotomizes the allegory—grievous wifely privilege up-ends to cruel husbandly payback. This story was published in September 1927.*

As Sam Desmond, porter of the Greater Boston Meat Market, entered that concern's front door, he noticed the deliveryman Roberts returning the telephone to its accustomed place. He noticed also that a mirthful grin was playing havoc with the deliveryman's countenance, breaking its black surface into numberless shining facets. He knew that a message had come for him, and, in the light of many experiences, suspected that it was not a pleasant one. Roberts grinned like that only when there was a possibility of making his colleague uncomfortable.

Sam shuffled the length of the sawdusty aisle of chop-blocks and display cases of a variety of meats to a rear room of the store, where, removing his overcoat and hat, he put on a soiled white jacket, and a skull cap made from the upper portion of a woman's stocking. He knew that Roberts' unconscious love for the dramatic would never permit him to deliver the message before it was asked for, and as he returned to the shop he was resolved to have it out.

"Well, Black Boy," he began, "what's nibblin' at *your* funnybone?"

Roberts carried a basket of meats to the delivery truck at the curb and returned before he had decided to satisfy Sam's curiosity.

"Matter with me, little Snow White? Why, th' ain't nothin' the matter with *me*. Is it, Mr. Bamberger?" Mr. Bamberger was president of the Greater Boston Meat Market, and occasionally revealed his democratic nature by joking and laughing with his colored employees. Now he merely smiled discreetly and continued taking turns about the floor.

"That telephone call," Roberts announced, "came from your better three-quarters, Sam. She want you should tell her how long it take you to eat your lunch. Say ever time she call you up you jus' gone to lunch or jus' gettin' back. Say don't she feed you 'nough? She say——"

Sam held up his hand. "Never mind no more Miller and Lyles, Black Boy. What she wants? That's what I want you to tell me."

Roberts was moving from one clerk to another picking up parcels, and, reading the addresses scribbled on them, arranging them in a basket he carried. He stopped in the midst of this occupation and said impressively:

"What she say, Snow White? She say you better bring her home some game, that's what she say. She say she want a rabbit or a squirrel or a ven'son steak, or somp'n like that: she don't care what, jus' so long's it's game." He delivered his parcels to the truck and, returning, "She say and don't forget somp'n nice for Mussolini," he called, his voice shattering into loud laughter.

The six clerks, Miss Schulte (the cashier) and Mr. Bamberger all laughed at this.

"Damn Mussolini!" Sam was busy now at the big refrigerator, attending to the long-deferred task of top-to-bottom cleansing. "I wish that lousy yaller devil 'ud die or something," he muttered.

"Yeah, damn the cat!" Roberts retorted with gleeful scorn. "Damn Mussolini all you want to, but be mighty particler you don't do it to home. Ef Marguerita ever hear you talk like that 'bout her cat you be lookin' for another place to hang out at."

"Is that so!" Sam threw the scrub brush down, the better to use his hands for gesticulating. "Is *that* so!" He approached the deliveryman, who lolled against a showcase watching a clerk quarter a small pig. "Well, let me tell *you* something, Black Boy. You say she better not catch me cussin' round the house. All right! You watch what I say. She's gonna catch me doin' more than that yet. I'm gettin' sicken tired of bein' bossed round by a woman and a dirty yaller cat. And when I get sicken tired anything I put my foot down and stop it. That aint no hot air; I mean it. You jus' watch, Black Boy; I'm tellin' you."

For a moment he glowered, his runted gnarled little black figure tense and purposeful under the heat of his synthetic anger. Roberts alone laughed, a jeering guffaw that was weighted with scorn and scepticism. "What you think, Mr. Bamberger," he called, pausing on his way to the truck. "When Sam's better three-quarters start naggin' at him old Mussolini join in and spit on Sam. Gee, but that make little Snow White mad." Mr. Bamberger and the clerks immediately donned sober faces. Probably the memory of a tale Roberts occasionally repeated of

Sam's running wild with a cleaver at the Roxbury Market, from which place he had come to Bamberger's, sobered them. They probably thought it wiser—and perhaps safer—to enjoy Sam's discomfiture with straight faces. They had never seen Sam's wife, about whom Roberts had built for their amusement a tradition of pugnacious determination. Roberts admitted that Marguerita had been engaged to him before Sam came along, but insisted that he passed her up because he thought it foolish in a man so black marrying a yaller woman like Rita. They would attract embarrassing attention on the street. Sam said Roberts was a wall-eyed liar.

When he finally heard the spasmodic back-spitting of the delivery truck and saw Roberts scoot with it across the soiled front of the plate glass window, Sam sidled up to Mr. Bamberger, who was talking to Miss Schulte at the cashier's cage. The porter's tone was deeply confidential.

"Mr. Bamberger, I want to get a rabbit or a squ'rrel or a ven'son steak, or some sort of game, to take home to my wife. She's jus' crazy about game, you know, an' she called up an' said——"

"Yes, I know, Sam," interrupted the rotund head of the Greater Boston Meat Market. "I heard Roberts telling you about it. And I said then to myself, I said, 'It's too bad we didn't know sooner,' I said to myself, 'because,' I said, 'I'd like to accommodate Sam.' But there aint any more in the shop, Sam." The small gray eyes were sympathetic. "If you'd just been about a half hour earlier," he appended in a regretful voice. "As it is, Sam, Roberts got the last order of game now delivering it in Brookline. Sorry, Sam. Save you a rabbit tomorrow, if you want me to."

Sam declared that this would be satisfactory, and requested that Mr. Bamberger charge it. "But, Mr. Bamberger, you can give me something for that lousy yaller cat, though, can't you?"

"Sure thing, Sam! Just tell Mike over there . . . O Mike! Fix up some liver or something for Mussolini, will you? . . . Charge that to Sam, Miss Schulte. And tomorrow, Sam, you'll have the game for your wife. We're getting in a fresh supply in the morning, see? . . . Got the refrigerator all cleaned out, eh? Well, finish that up before you go tonight, Sam." He turned and resumed his tete-a-tete with the cashier.

II

Through six years of diligent service to the Greater Boston Meat Market Sam had attained the full confidence of the management and certain prized prerogatives. One of these was the privilege of remaining until every one had gone every night and closing the store. It had been a long time since Mr. Bamberger or Miss Schulte or Mike had locked up. Even when he had an engagement to go out with Marguerite, Sam preferred to exercise his prerogative. Being black offered few enough prerogatives, God knew, and he would be a fool not to grab those proffered him. At home a mere cipher, he felt like a man of some consequence when he was allowed the staggering responsibility of putting out the lights (all except the one over the cash register) and closing and locking the front door. It must have impressed people who passed along Tremont street and saw him. They must have thought him a partner in the concern.

As usual Sam put out the lights, except the one over the cash register, looked about proprietarily to see that everything was all right, and then went out into the cold January night and locked the door. The liver for Mussolini was concealed in an outer wrapper made of a sheet of the Boston *Transcript,* left in the store by a Back Bay customer, and Sam carried it pressed under his arm. Turning north on Tremont Street, he boarded at Northampton a car for Cambridge.

As always when going home he was painfully aware of every step he took from the door of the shop to the car stop, and of each revolution of the wheels of the car from Tremont and Northampton streets to his stop in Cambridge. He was going home after a hard day's work; taking fresh meat to a lousy yaller cat that spit at him to show its contempt; thinking up a presentable lie for a lazy yaller woman. What had he married her for, anyway? Because she was pretty? Well, she was pretty, all right, and no getting away from that. She was a little broad acrosswise and rather heavy on her slippered, slip-slap feet about the small apartment; but pretty, just the same. An ugly little runt like him was lucky to have a woman like Marguerita.... Lucky? Well, he didn't know so much about that. After all, why was *he* lucky? Why wasn't *she* the lucky one? Of course he had a good looking high yaller woman for a wife, but what didn't *she* have? She had a little runt of a black man who would slave for her; somebody who would show up her handsomeness by contrast; somebody who was just crazy about her, and she knew it; somebody she could boss around; somebody who'd continue to slave like a fool the rest of his life for her. That's what she had. And in spite of all this she seemed to love that lousy yaller cat better than she loved him. "What you call him Mussolini for?" he had once asked her. "Because," she had responded, so promptly she must have been thinking about it, "I want to kid myself there's a real man round the house." Of course she loved the cat better than she loved him.

Straight down the middle of his meandering thoughts the car rumbled across the Harvard Bridge, then rattled down Massachusetts Avenue past Technology, and, at Sam's signal, came to a hissing, wheezing, grumbling stop at Lafayette Square. Sam observed the window display of ornate furniture in the store before him as a crazy fantasy. He could feel the complete petering out of his earlier incipient spirit of rebellion. Oh, what was the use, anyway? Straight down Massachusetts Avenue, about two blocks away, lay Central Square. If he had any money . . . He shrugged, then cut across Lafayette Square into Columbia street.

The second-floor-rear window was alight, an indication that Marguerita was in the kitchen. Now what would he say? The truth? Yes, but suppose she wanted to know why he had not gone elsewhere? Bamberger's wasn't the only market on earth, he very well knew. What was the matter with the Manhattan right there in Cambridge? But she knew that he had no penny above his scant allowance.

He removed his hat and overcoat at the top of the stairs. From the kitchen a triangle of yellowish gaslight cut into the darkness of the hallway. There came also the sound of frying meat hissing above that of Marguerita's padded footfalls, and an odor of hot porkchops floating on a haze of gray smoke. He wondered whether she had heard him enter; was certain that she had not, since she had not called for the game. He stood still, trying to decide what to do. Mussolini came out the kitchen door, resembling in his sleek-sided massive bulk a lion cub, and stopped to look Sam over. Then the cat advanced down the hallway toward his mistress' lesser portion, his yellow back arched, his stiff tail standing up like a malignant finger, accusingly. Mussolini rubbed against Sam's legs, almost unbalancing him, sniffed curiously at the parcel of liver, uttering deep throaty supplications.

Sam's reason warned him to observe restraint, yet he disobeyed, and shoved the cat with his foot. It was not a kick, but merely a vigorous push, that made Mussolini sprawl on his side. Immediately the hallway was filled with a yowl of angry protest. Marguerita came hastening from the kitchen, wiping her hands on her soiled apron, slip-slapping glidingly, and peering into the twilight haziness of the hallway. Mussolini ran to meet her, casting backward at his mistress' husband baleful and reprochful glances.

"Wassa matter, Mussolini, darlin'? What's happened to Mother's 'ittle darlin? What——"

Sam stepped briskly forward, as though he had but that moment entered the hallway. His wife was glaring.

"Sam Desmond, what you——"

"Dark out here," he said, rather hurriedly. "Stumbled over him. Guess he smelt his meat. I——"

"I thought 'twas you. Slinkin' round here worse'n Mussolini. What you up to now? I know it's something you ashamed of. I bet you didn't get my game." She waited for him either to confirm or abrogate her suspicion. He was silent, which indicated confirmation. She went on: "That's it, now, aint it? You didn't get my game. You didn't get my game. I knew it. Give me that meat. I knew you wouldn't."

She left him standing miserable in the semi-dark hallway. Mussolini stalked ahead of her into the kitchen. For a moment Sam listened. . . .

"I knew you wouldn't. You never do . . . Come on, Mussolini, and get your dinner, pet. You're the only real male around here . . ." Sam could easily distinguish the part of her address meant for him: "Some day you're going to find yourself looking for another woman . . ." Yes, that was his. He had memorized it years since. He stood motionless, waiting for the rest of it. There it was: "I'm sicken tired of your carelessness. You don't think about doin' nothin' to please me once in a while . . ." Every time he heard this accusation he resented it anew. He felt that it was maliciously untrue. He renounced it with a surging burning resentment. She interrupted his smoldering meditation: "I ask you to bring me——"

"But they didn't *have* any, Rita! You might know they must not've had any if——"

"Oh, that's no excuse! Suppose they *didn't* have any. Is old Bamberger's the only meat market in town? What's the matter with the Manhattan right here at Central Square? No, that aint the reason. You just didn't——"

"But you know I haven't got no account at the Manhattan, Rita. An' I didn't have a pen——"

"Account! Account! Don't make me choke myself laughin'. You haven't got any charge account anywhere, if that's what you mean. Old Bamberger only takes pity on you and lets you have things because he knows you're too dumb to walk out on him and look for a decent job. . . ." He could hear the loud frying of something freshly laid in the skillet. The hissing momentarily blanketed her voice. Presently, however, it broke through: "Account! Account! No, you aint got any account. And *you* aint any account, either."

Making a gesture of resignation to the smoke-filled odor-laden dusk of the hallway, Sam shuffled toward the bathroom. His narrow shoulders drooped lower than usual, and he was angry with himself because he could think of none of the fine set speeches he often rehearsed on the car going home. He closed the bathroom door and lighted the gas. Above the sound of running water he could hear Marguerita's baby talk addressed to Mussolini: "Come on, oo po' 'ittle hung'y kittsy cat, an' get its supper. Come on, dear!"

Mussolini! The lousy yaller beast! Oh, if he could only do something with that cat! Perhaps then his wife would transfer some of these generous affections to her husband. But he did not pursue the notion. It was a will-o'-the-wisp, and not worth pursuit. Mussolini was already twelve years old; he was wiser than most cats of greater age, and as truly an institution of the Desmond household as Marguerita herself. There existed about as much likelihood of his getting rid of that husky feline as there was of his making up to resemble Valentino. Mussolini! The lousy yaller . . . Sam buried his face in the cold water, holding his breath; removed his face and rubbed it with a towel until it glistened in the mirror above the wash basin like polished patent leather. He preferred cold water for his face even in winter, he said, for it soothed his nerves. He studied himself for a moment in the glass, then grimaced.

"So she wishes I wasn't so black, does she?" he muttered, recalling the oft-told tale. "Oh, well, I should worry! I sure don't look like nobody's little Snow-White, 'spite what Roberts calls me."

"Sam, come out that bathroom and get your dinner—if you want any. You must think I'm gonna stay in the kitchen all night."

Sam chuckled grimly as he shambled toward the kitchen. "What a difference when she speaks to me'n when she speaks to that lousy yaller beast."

There being no dining room, they ate in the kitchen, utilizing a folding camp-table which was kept in the kitchen closet between meals. As Sam took his place he watched his wife's face covertly, hoping to determine the extent of her displeasure. She slip-slapped about, jolting the table when her soft ample person made contact with it; filled his plate with bony fried fish, his cup with inky black coffee, and his soul with leaping, shrieking passion for revenge on Mussolini. Why should *he* have to eat fish? He hated it, and Marguerita knew he hated it. He noticed that *her* plate held two browned pork-chops, and suspected that punishment was being visited upon his appetite and stomach for his failure to bring her game. And this angered him, for he had bought those chops with the natural and logical intention of eating one of them himself. He felt resentment swelling, bubbling, in his breast; rising to his throat, and clogging it; to his eyes, making the tears burn beneath his lids; making him blink his eyes rapidly and lower his head as if looking for something under the table.

Marguerita took her place opposite him, scanning him from squinting eyes. Her full fleshy jaw was set, and as she struck back from her moist cheek the vagrant lock of black straight hair, Sam knew that she not only was prepared for a quarrel but would welcome one. He was still reluctant to give her cause, provided she did not think she had cause enough already. There was so far no sound reason for his exploding. If he did, of course, it would be just *too bad*. Yes, he would hold his temper inside. She merely sought an excuse to jump on him; he knew that, and swore that he would give her nothing that even resembled a cue. So he began slowly to thread the fish, picking out with his fingers the innumerable needle-like bones.

The cat sat to one side, regarding them from slitted yellow eyes. Glimpsing what he considered Mussolini's contemptuous regard of the master of the house, Sam sensed a sudden desire to injure it. There Mussolini sat, its great sleek yellow back hunched, its massive head, like a wise old man's, tilted to one side, and a diabolical smirk on its too human features. He wanted to see it squirm in pain, to hear it yowl and spit defiance to no avail. He did not doubt that but for the lousy yaller beast Marguerita would be a better wife.

"You make me sick, Sam Desmond! Here I am all day workin' my head off to make a home for you, an' you can't even do me a little favor."

Sam munched distastefully his fried fish and boiled potato, dropping his eyes from the angry gaze of his wife's; then he looked across at the kingly usurper on the floor. Mussolini, with long, slithering strides, came forward as if once more to demonstrate his priority rights. Crouching slightly, he sprang upon his mistress' lap and thrust his yellow head into her plate. He sniffed about for a moment but, presumably finding nothing to his taste, he sat back with lazy and smug complaisance, almond eyes indifferently fixed on the man opposite.

Then, as if to show further the extent of *his* prerogatives, he lifted a soiled white paw and did what Sam in delirious lapses dreamed of doing but which in sane moments haunted him only sub-consciously:

Mussolini slapped Marguerita's face. With a petulant shove she sent him to the floor. "Get down, Mussolini. I don't feel like playing tonight. I'm mad."

The cat stretched, curled over on the crescent of his back to wash himself, then stalked around the table and sprang upon Sam's lap. For an instant the man shrank in confounded amazement. Why, the damn, lousy, yaller! . . . Why, he'd never dared to do that before! It was downright defiance, that was it; defiance in the presence of his——of *their*———mistress. With a quick, vicious gesture he hurled the cat to the floor. Mussolini made no sound, but stood lashing his tail and looking from the man to the woman; seeming in his attitude to demand the woman's intervention.

The next moment Marguerita had bounded from her seat, nearly upsetting the light table, and had planked Mussolini in Sam's plate. "There, Mussolini," she cried. "And you," she snarled, "Mr. Nice-Nasty, you just touch that cat again if you dare! Just lay your black hands on him again—just go ahead and do it . . . I'm sicken tired of you goin' round here actin' like you was just too disgusted to live under the same roof with me and my cat . . . That's right Mussolini, eat! . . . If you're so disgusted why don't you find somewhere else to stay? You make me . . ." She resumed her seat and glared at him.

With an impatient quirk of the body Sam sent the table skidding against the set tubs. There was a clatter of broken crockery on the floor, the scurrying of heavy footfalls of a frenzied yellow cat, the wide-eyed incredulity of an over-sized yellow woman.

Sam left the scene in silent triumph. It had occurred so suddenly, so instantaneously, that he was confused as to how it had happened. Certainly he had done nothing so radical before in all his married life. Marguerite said nothing. In silence too she took down the folding table and put it into the closet. Then she began to wash the dishes . . . Sam did not often exhibit such temper.

Sam was now in the front room with the radio. He had the earphones on and did not hear his wife's calling until she screeched near his head. He felt that the first round of this fight was his; every detail of her present demeanor seemed to proclaim it. Clearly she was upset. He removed the earphones with methodical slowness and frowned at her, thrilling at the experience.

He heard her say: "Well, why don't you *do* something? Didn't you hear me? He's chokin'!"

She had already turned and slip-slapped quickly back to the kitchen. Muttering, Sam followed. "*He's* chokin'? *Who's* chokin'? What you talkin' 'bout?" He disliked having to admit that her seeming discomfiture at his sudden exhibition of temper was due to something else.

In the kitchen Sam saw Marguerita on her knees with the coughing Mussolini squeezed to her pillowy breast. Tears were on Marguerita's cheek, and she was rocking from side to side as though trying to sooth a fretful child.

"O Sam, Mussolini's got a fish bone in his throat! See if you can get it out. I've tried everything I know," she whined, "an' nothin' don't seem to work. Oh, he's chokin' to death! Oh! Oh!"

Sam straightened his frail shoulders. "Then let the yaller lousy beast choke to death! He can die and go to heaven for all I care." Sam returned to the radio.

For a while he stood holding the earphones in his hands, listening to Mussolini's coughing and Marguerita's baby talk. Then there was silence. Presently he heard his wife coming back, and he hastened to put the phones over his ears and sink into the cushioned armchair. One glimpse of her face told him that she was contrite. He did not like to see her angry or upset. She sat beside him, on the arm of his chair, and pulled his head down against her breast.

He tried to think of Mussolini's recently lying there, but her caresses dulled his senses and exhilerated him. "Naughty boy," she scolded playfully. "Naughty boy, not to bring mama what she wanted. And mama was mad, too; yes, she was. Mama just as mad as she could be." She fondled his head, running her soft fingers through his tight hair. In spite of himself his soothing rebellion cooled under her ministrations. It always did. "Naughty boy! If you had brought mama's rabbit Mussolini wouldn't 've got a bone in his little pink throat, 'cause you've had the chops then, an' . . ."

Sam shook himself free.

"Oh, you still angry with mama, is you, naughty boy? Why you still angry with your mama?"

"You like that lousy yaller cat better than you do me! I'm gettin' sicken——"

"Oh, that's it, is it? Naughty boy jealous of Mussolini!" Her soft deft fingers stroked his cheeks, his throat, his eyelids. He lay back, half listening to the dance music from the Copley Plaza, half hypnotized by the woman's caresses. Resentment was all burned out. He lay back, feeling the throb of her heart beneath the warm soft breast.

"You won't forget tomorrow, will you, Sammy Boy? And you won't be nasty to Mussolini any more, will you?"

His senses were dissolved and merged. "No, never . . . You got the bone out all right? Thas good . . . Tomorrow I'm gonna bring you the nicest, biggest, fattest . . . Les go to bed. I'm all in."

III

The ever-recurrent flare of resentment at Mussolini's presence in the bed flickered for an instant, then glowed angrily thru the rest of Sam's waking hours. The beast lay between him and Marguerita, its warm furry body wedged close. Sam could hear its throaty purr at intervals, like the distant whirr of an aeroplane. Thus was husband separated from wife. He knew that if he moved nearer her Mussolini would challenge him with spitting and scratches; yet, if he lifted the lousy yaller beast by the scruff of the neck and dropped it to the floor, he would suffer verbal attack from Marguerita. His thoughts became an irrational patchwork; he wondered whether she permitted the cat to sleep between them solely to keep him away; speculated dully on ways and means of banishing it forever; listened to his wife's deep regular breathing . . .

Rabbits, squ'rrels, ven'son steak—game; a big yaller cat caressed by a big yaller woman. . . . He slept . . .

His wife, sitting up in bed, was shaking him and calling his name loudly. Through the murk of drowsiness he heard her saying: "That fish bone's still in his throat, Sam! *Please* see if you can't get it out. If we don't do something he'll die! Don't you guess you could call up some doctor now? Mr. Williams downstairs would let you use his telephone. Oh, listen to the poor little darlin'! He's just gaspin' for breath. . . . Sam Desmond, would you lay up there an' let a poor innocent dumb animal suffer? . . . Well, you're even worsen I thought you was. Don't you ever speak to me again, so there!"

She was out of the bed, the cat pressed to her bosom, pulling down the shades, lowering the window, fumbling for matches and the gas jet. There was in her actions all the intense, compact suffering of the mother whose babe lies dangerously ill. Finding it impossible to sleep longer Sam sat up, scratching and rubbing his eyes. The cat was coughing and clawing at its throat. Sam felt suddenly an overwhelming sense of compunction, but before it could move him to action Marguerita had dragged him, cover and all, to the floor.

"What's the matter with you, Sam Desmond? You crazy? I told you to call up a doctor! D you want Mussolini to die?" She tossed her husband his old bathrobe from the foot of the bed. "Put that on and go downstairs and call up a doctor."

But Sam caught up the old garment and hurled it at the choking feline, who, momentarily terrified, wriggled from Marguerita's arms and scampered under the bed. Its coughing had ceased. Sam stood glaring down at it for a moment, then turned to his wife.

"Damn that cat! I'm gettin' awfully tired of so much foolishness, d'you understand? I mean it, Marguerita! I'm sicken tired of playin' butler and chambermaid to that lousy yaller cat. First thing you know you'll wake up some mornin' an' find you aint got no cat nor husband neither. An' another thing," he cut in, raising his hand to check Marguerita's impending retort. "I'm sick of sleepin' in bed with a cat. I'm tired of that nasty beast layin' up there between us. I didn't marry no cat, an' I aint going to sleep with none no more. I mean that, believe me! I think it's about time I put my foot down roun' here."

He scowled at her for a moment, but she stood in stupefied silence, her eyes fixed on his. Then he crawled into bed, dragging the covers with him, and turned his back to her. After a little while he sensed that she had turned out the light. He heard her push up the window and run up the window shade, then get heavily into bed. A flood of exultation overswept him as he realized more fully the prodigious extent of his victory—a victory without bowls. For a long while both lay silent. Presently he heard Mussolini's pat-pat-pat, noted the abrupt cessation of the footfalls, then, before he could speculate on the cat's intention, Mussolini was walking across Sam's head seeking its place between the man and his wife.

With a muttered "damn!" the man sprang up, dragging the covers with him and, seizing the animal, tossed it across the room. It uttered a howling wail of protest, an imprecation, Sam thought, and spit at him. Sam wondered whether in its defiance it would spring at him in the dark. But Marguerita was out of the bed again; pulling down the window and the shade; making a light. Sam hastened to return to the covers. He lay silent and disturbed, his face to the wall. Without a word to her husband Marguerita picked up the cat, crooning brokenly over it; then kissing it noisily, she placed it again in the bed. Sam wondered how much resentment a man's breast would hold before it exploded like an overfilled gas bag. . . .

IV

In the morning Sam heard his wife slip-slapping, slipper-shod as usual, in the kitchen. He rose and went into the bathroom. Above the noise of running water he heard her calling to him: "The cat's still got that fish bone in his throat. I want you to take him to the animal hospital in the Fenway on your way to work. You won't have time to eat no breakfast, but I got you a cup of coffee ready."

Sam found Mussolini caged in an old basket. Marguerita had padded it with clean cloths and covered it with old window screening. Grumbling, his shoulders hopelessly drooped, Sam gulped his coffee, then picked up the basket and left the house. At the hospital examination disclosed nothing more than an inflamed throat. There probably *had* been a bone, it was explained, but certainly there was none now. Sam proceeded to his work, arriving half an hour late.

Roberts observed to the clerical force sometime during the afternoon that "maybe you folks don't know Sam here's Mussolini's nurse maid." "Yeah," he called loudly, from the rear of the store, "Sam nursin' Mussolini now. 'S'wife make him take the cat out to walk when he come to work in the mornin', then walk home with it at night. See that basket Sam bring in here this mornin'? Well, Mussolini's in that. Jus' as nice an' comfy. Aint he, Sam?"

The porter listened in pretended good humor.

The telephone rang, Mr. Bamberger answering it. "Why, yes, Mrs. Desmond, your husband's right here. No, no trouble at all. Just a minute."

Sam was laconic to the point of gruffness. "What's that? Yup! . . . Oh, the cat? Well, it's . . . dead. I said he's dead! Yup, dead. D-E-A-D, dead! Finee! Compree? Expired. Passed out. . . . Yup, at the hospital . . ." He hung up the receiver and turned to the questioning stares of the house. To the proprietor he said: "Never mind the rabbit, Mr. Bamberger. She don't want it now. Lost her appetite, I guess."

Sam swept the floor. He sprinkled fresh sawdust all round, cleaned out the back room, and washed the rear and front windows, inside and out, despite the biting cold! Coincidentally, it was a busy afternoon for the others, too, being Saturday; for which Sam was thankful. He didn't feel like a lot of cheap talk. . . .

It was nearly closing time. Roberts came in from the rear, calling loudly and somewhat excitedly: "Say, Snow White, what's the big idea? Mussolini aint no more dead'n I is. Why——"

"If he aint no more dead'n you, then he's all ready for the embalmin' fluid—an' don't know it. That cat's dead, I'm tellin' you . . ."

Sam closed the shop as usual that night, leaving fully an hour later than the others. He carried no basket, but, instead, a parcel in butcher's wrapping paper, which, in turn, was wrapped within a newspaper; a parcel which may have contained a dressed rabbit or a squirrel or a venison steak. As he waited for a car at Tremont and Northampton streets he grinned into the frigid semi-darkness; then, holding the parcel aloft before his face:

"Why don't you yowl for your mama, you lousy yaller rascal?" he apostrophized, in a low tense voice. "Why don't you spit on me? ... So she wants game, does she? Well, she'll *get* game!"

DRENCHED IN LIGHT

In this story, published in December 1924, Zora Neale Hurston uses the character Isie Watts, a poor and disadvantaged young black girl, to reveal that the sun can shine in every soul, no matter one's worldly achievements.

"You Isie Watts! Git 'own offen dat gate post an' rake up dis yahd!"

The little brown figure perched upon the gate post looked yearningly up the gleaming shell road that led to Orlando, and down the road that led to Sanford and shrugged her thin shoulders. This heaped kindling on Grandma Patts' already burning ire.

"Lawd a-mussy!" she screamed, enraged—"Heah Joel, gimme dat wash stick. Ah'll show dat limb of Satan she kain't shake huhseff at *me*. If she ain't down by de time Ah gets dere, Ah'll break huh down in de lines" (loins).

"Aw Gran'ma, Ah see Mist' George and Jim Robinson comin' and Ah wanted to wave at 'em," the child said petulantly.

"You jes wave dat rake at dis heah yahd, madame, else Ah'll take you down a button hole lower. You'se too 'oomanish jumpin' up in everybody's face dat pass."

This struck the child in a very sore spot for nothing pleased her so much as to sit atop of the gate post and hail the passing vehicles on their way South to Orlando, or North to Sanford. That white shell road was her great attraction. She raced up and down the stretch of it that lay before her gate like a round eyed puppy hailing gleefully all travelers. Everybody in the country, white and colored, knew little Isis Watts, the joyful. The Robinson brothers, white cattlemen, were particularly fond of her and always extended a stirrup for her to climb up behind one of them for a short ride, or let her try to crack the long bull whips and yee whoo at the cows.

Grandma Potts went inside and Isis literally waved the rake at the "chaws" of ribbon cane that lay so bountifully about the yard in company with the knots and peelings, with a thick sprinkling of peanut hulls.

The herd of cattle in their envelope of gray dust came alongside and Isis dashed out to the nearest stirrup and was lifted up.

"Hello theah Snidlits, I was wonderin' wheah you was," said Jim Robinson as she snuggled down behind him in the saddle. They were almost out of the danger zone when Grandma emerged.

"You Isie-s!" she bawled.

The child slid down on the opposite side from the house and executed a flank movement through the corn patch that brought her into the yard from behind the privy.

"You lil' hasion you! Wheah you been?"

"Out in de back yahd" Isis lied and did a cartwheel and a few fancy steps on her way to the front again.

"If you doan git tuh dat yahd, Ah make a mommuk of you!" Isis observed that Grandma was cutting a fancy assortment of switches from peach, guana and cherry trees.

She finished the yard by raking everything under the edge of the porch and began a romp with the dogs, those lean, floppy eared, 'coon hounds that all country folks keep. But Grandma vetoed this also.

"Isie, you set 'own on dat porch! Uh great big 'leben yeah ole gal racin' an' rompin' lak dat—set 'own!"

Isis impatiently flung herself upon the steps.

"Git up offa dem steps, you aggavatin' limb, 'fore Ah git dem hick'ries tuh you, an' set yo' seff on a cheah."

Isis petulantly arose and sat down as violently as possible in a chair, but slid down until she all but sat upon her shoulder blades.

"Now look atcher," Grandma screamed, "Put yo' knees together, an' git up offen yo' backbone! Lawd, you know dis hellion is gwine make me stomp huh insides out."

Isis sat bolt upright as if she wore a ramrod down her back and began to whistle. Now there are certain things that Grandma Potts felt no one of this female persuasion should do—one was to sit with the knees separated, "settin' brazen" she called it; another was whistling, another playing with boys, neither must a lady cross her legs.

Up she jumped from her seat to get the switches.

"So youse whistlin' in mah face, huh!" She glared till her eyes were beady and Isis bolted for safety. But the noon hour brought John Watts, the widowed father, and this excused the child from sitting for criticism.

Being the only girl in the family, of course she must wash the dishes, which she did in intervals between frolics with the dogs. She even gave Jake, the puppy, a swim in the dishpan by holding him suspended above the water that reeked of "pot likker"—just high enough so that his feet would be immersed. The deluded puppy swam and swam without ever crossing the pan, much to his annoyance. Hearing Grandma she hurriedly dropped him on the floor, which he tracked up with feet wet with dishwater.

Grandma took her patching and settled down in the front room to sew. She did this every afternoon, and invariably slept in the big red rocker with her head lolled back over the back, the sewing falling from her hand.

Isis had crawled under the center table with its red plush cover with little round balls for fringe. She was lying on her back imagining herself various personages. She wore trailing robes, golden slippers with blue bottoms. She rode white horses with flaring pink nostrils to the horizon, for she still believed that to be land's end. She was picturing herself gazing over the edge of the world into the abyss when the spool of cotton fell from Grandma's lap and rolled away under the whatnot. Isis drew back from her contemplation of the nothingness at the horizon and glanced up at the sleeping woman. Her head had fallen far back. She breathed with a regular "snark" intake and soft "poosah" exhaust. But Isis was a visual minded child. She heard the snores only subconsciously but she saw straggling beard on Grandma's chin, trembling a little with every "snark" and "poosah". They were long gray hairs curled here and there against the dark brown skin. Isis was moved with pity for her mother's mother.

"Poah Gran-ma needs a shave," she murmured, and set about it. Just then Joel, next older than Isis, entered with a can of bait.

"Come on Isie, les' we all go fishin'. The perch is bitin' fine in Blue Sink."

"Sh-sh—" cautioned his sister, "Ah got to shave Gran'ma."

"Who say so?" Joel asked, surprised.

"Nobody doan hafta tell me. Look at her chin. No ladies don't weah no whiskers if they kin help it. But Gran'ma gittin' ole an' she doan know how to shave like me."

The conference adjourned to the back porch lest Grandma wake.

"Aw, Isie, you doan know nothin' 'bout shavin' a-tall—but a *man* lak *me*——"

"Ah do so know."

"You don't not. Ah'm goin' shave her mahseff."

"Naw, you won't neither, Smarty. Ah saw her first an' thought it all up first," Isis declared, and ran to the calico covered box on the wall above the wash basin and seized her father's razor. Joel was quick and seized the mug and brush.

"Now!" Isis cried defiantly, "Ah got the razor."

"Goody, goody, goody, pussy cat, Ah got th' brush an' you can't shave 'thout lather—see! Ah know mo' than you," Joel retorted.

"Aw, who don't know dat?" Isis pretended to scorn. But seeing her progress blocked for lack of lather she compromised.

"Ah know! Les' we all shave her. You lather an' Ah shave."

This was agreeable to Joel. He made mountains of lather and anointed his own chin, and the chin of Isis and the dogs, splashed the walls and at last was persuaded to lather Grandma's chin. Not that he was loath but he wanted his new plaything to last as long as possible.

Isis stood on one side of the chair with the razor clutched cleaver fashion. The niceties of razor-handling had passed over her head. The thing with her was to *hold* the razor—sufficient in itself.

Joel splashed on the lather in great gobs and Grandma awoke.

For one bewildered moment she stared at the grinning boy with the brush and mug but sensing another presence, she turned to behold the business face of Isis and the razor-clutching hand. Her jaw dropped and Grandma, forgetting years and rheumatism, bolted from the chair and fled the house, screaming.

"She's gone to tell papa, Isie. You didn't have no business wid his razor and he's gonna lick yo hide," Joel cried, running to replace mug and brush.

"You too, chuckle-head, you, too," retorted Isis. "You was playin' wid his brush and put it all over the dogs—Ah seen you put it on Ned an' Beulah." Isis shaved some slivers from the door jamb with the razor and replaced it in the box. Joel took his bait and pole and hurried to Blue Sink. Isis crawled under the house to brood over the whipping she knew would come. She had meant well.

But sounding brass and tinkling cymbal drew her forth. The local lodge of the Grand United Order of Odd Fellows led by a braying, thudding band, was marching in full regalia down the road. She had forgotten the barbecue and log-rolling to be held today for the benefit of the new hall.

Music to Isis meant motion. In a minute razor and whipping forgotten, she was doing a fair imitation of the Spanish dancer she had seen in a medicine show some time before. Isis' feet were gifted—she could dance most anything she saw.

Up, up went her spirits, her brown little feet doing all sorts of intricate things and her body in rhythm, hand curving above her head. But the music was growing faint. Grandma nowhere in sight. She stole out of the gate, running and dancing after the band.

Then she stopped. She couldn't dance at the carnival. Her dress was torn and dirty. She picked a long stemmed daisy and thrust it behind her ear. But the dress, no better. Oh, an idea! In the battered round topped trunk in the bedroom!

She raced back to the house, then, happier, raced down the white dusty road to the picnic grove, gorgeously clad. People laughed good naturedly at her, the band played and Isis danced because she couldn't help it. A crowd of children gather admiringly about her as she wheeled lightly about, hand on hip, flower between her teeth with the red and white fringe of the table-cloth—Grandma's new red tablecloth that she wore in lieu of a Spanish shawl—trailing in the dust. It was too ample for her meager form, but she wore it like a gipsy. Her brown feet twinkled in and out of the fringe. Some grown people joined the children about her. The Grand Exalted Ruler rose to speak; the band was hushed, but Isis danced on, the crowd clapping their hands for her. No one listed to the Exalted one, for little by little the multitude had surrounded the brown dancer.

An automobile drove up to the Crown and halted. Two white men and a lady got out and pushed into the crowd, suppressing mirth discreetly behind gloved hands. Isis looked up and waved them a magnificent hail and went on dancing until—

Grandma had returned to the house and missed Isis and straightway sought her at the festivities expecting to find her in her soiled dress, shoeless, gaping at the crowd, but what she saw drove her frantic. Here was her granddaughter dancing before a gaping crowd in her brand new red tablecloth, and reeking of lemon extract, for Isis had added the final touch to her costume. She *must* have perfume.

Isis saw Grandma and bolted. She heard her cry: "Mah Gawd, mah brand new table cloth Ah jus' bought f'um O'landah!" as she fled through the crowd and on into the woods.

II

She followed the little creek until she came to the ford in a rutty wagon road that led to Apopka and laid down on the cool grass at the road-side. The April sun was quite hot.

Misery, misery and woe settled down upon her and the child wept. She knew another whipping was in store for her.

"Oh, Ah wish Ah could die, then Gran'ma an' papa would be sorry they beat me so much. Ah b'leeve Ah'll run away an' never go home no mo'. Ah'm goin' drown mahseff in th' creek!" Her woe grew attractive.

Isis got up and waded into the water. She routed out a tiny 'gator and a huge bull frog. She splashed and sang, enjoying herself immensely. The purr of a motor struck her ear and she saw a large, powerful car jolting along the rutty road toward her. It stopped at the water's edge.

"Well, I declare, it's our little gypsy," exclaimed the man at the wheel. "What are you doing here, now?"

"Ah'm killin' mahseff," Isis declared dramatically. "Cause Gran'ma beats me too much."

There was a hearty burst of laughter from the machine.

"You'll last sometime the way you are going about it. Is this the way to Maitland? We want to go to the Park Hotel."

Isis saw no longer any reason to die. She came up out of the water, holding up the dripping fringe of the tablecloth.

"Naw, indeedy. You go to Maitlan' by the shell road—it goes by mah house—an' turn off at Lake Sebelia to the clay road that takes you right to the do'."

"Well," went on the driver, smiling furtively, "Could you quit dying long enough to go with us?"

"Yessuh," she said thoughtfully, "Ah wanta go wid you."

The door of the car swung open. She was invited to a seat beside the driver. She had often dreamed of riding in one of these heavenly chariots but never thought she would, actually.

"Jump in then, Madame Tragedy, and show us. We lost ourselves after we left your barbecue."

During the drive Isis explained to the kind lady who smelt faintly of violets and to the indifferent men that she was really a princess. She told them about her trips to the horizon, about the trailing gowns, the gold shoes with blue bottoms—she insisted on the blue bottoms—the white charger, the time when she was Hercules and had slain numerous dragons and sundry giants. At last the car approached her gate over which stood the umbrella China-berry tree. The car was abreast of the gate and had all but passed when Grandma spied her glorious table-cloth lying back against the upholstery of the Packard.

"You Isie-e!" she bawled, "You lil' wretch you! come heah *dis in-stunt.*"

"That's me," the child confessed, mortified, to the lady on the rear seat.

"Oh, Sewell, stop the car. This is where the child lives. I hate to give her up, though."

"Do you wanta keep me?" Isis brightened.

"Oh, I wish I could, you shining little morsel. Wait, I'll try to save you a whipping this time."

She dismounted with the gaudy lemon flavored culprit and advanced to the gate where Grandma stood glowering, switches in hand.

"You're gointuh ketchit f'um yo' haid to yo' heels m'lady. Jes' come in heah."

"Why, good afternoon," she accosted the furious grandparent. "You're not going to whip this poor little thing, are you?" the lady asked in conciliatory tones.

"Yes, Ma'am. She's de wustest lil' limb dat ever drawed bref. Jes' look at mah new table cloth, dat ain't never been washed. She done traipsed all over de woods, uh dancin' an' uh prancin' in it. She done took a razor to me t'day an' Lawd knows whut mo'."

Isis clung to the white hand fearfully.

"Ah wuzn't gointer hurt Gran'ma, miss—Ah wuz jus' gointer shave her whiskers fuh huh 'cause she's old an' can't."

The white hand closed tightly over the little brown one that was quite soiled. She could understand a voluntary act of love even though it miscarried.

"Now, Mrs. er—er—I didn't get the name—how much did your tablecloth cost?"

"One whole big silvah dollar down at O'landah—ain't had it a week yit."

"Now here's five dollars to get another one. The little thing loves laughter. I want her to go on to the hotel and dance in that tablecloth for me. I can stand a little light today—"

"Oh, yessum, yessum," Grandma cut in, "Everything's alright, sho' she kin go, yessum."

The lady went on: "I want brightness and this Isis is joy itself, why she's drenched in light!"

Isis for the first time in her life, felt herself appreciated and danced up and down in an ecstasy of joy for a minute.

"Now, behave yo'seff, Isie, ovah at de hotel wid de white folks," Grandma cautioned, pride in her voice, though she strove to hide it. "Lawd, ma'am, dat gal keeps me so frackshus, Ah doan know mah haid f'um mah feet. Ah orter comb huh haid, too, befo' she go wid you all."

"No, no, don't bother. I like her as she is. I don't think she'd like it either, being combed and scrubbed. Come on, Isis."

Feeling that Grandma had been somewhat squelched did not detract from Isis' spirit at all. She pranced over to the waiting motor and this time seated herself on the rear seat between the sweet, smiling lady and the rather aloof man in gray.

"Ah'm gointer stay wid you all," she said with a great deal of warmth, and snuggled up to her benefactress. "Want me tuh sing a song tuh you?"

"There, Helen, you've been adopted," said the man with a short, harsh laugh.

"Oh, I hope so, Harry." She put her arm about the red draped figure at her side and drew it close until she felt the warm puffs of the child's breath against her side. She looked hungrily ahead of her and spoke into space rather than to anyone in the car. "I want a little of her sunshine to soak into my soul. I need it."

SPUNK

Zora Neale Hurston brilliantly weaves the supernatural into the plot of this short story: Spunk takes Lena from her husband, Joe Kanty; a fight between the two men ensues; and Spunk murders Kanty. Spunk learns almost immediately that "the wages of sin" are losing all prizes. Hurston published this short story, awarded second prize, in June 1925.

A giant of a brown skinned man sauntered up the one street of the Village and out into the palmetto thickets with a small pretty woman clinging lovingly to his arm.

"Looka theah, folkses!" cried Elijah Mosley, slapping his leg gleefully. "Theah they go, big as life an' brassy as tacks."

All the loungers in the store tried to walk to the door with an air of nonchalance but with small success.

"Now pee-eople!" Walter Thomas gasped, "Will you look at 'em!"

"But that's one thing Ah likes about Spunk Banks—he ain't skeered of nothin' on God's green footstool—*nothin'!* He rides that log down at saw-mill jus' like he struts 'round wid another man's wife—jus' don't give a kitty. When Tes' Miller got cut to giblets on that circle-saw, Spunk steps right up and starts ridin'. The rest of us was skeered to go near it."

A round shouldered figure in overalls much too large, came nervously in the door and the talking ceased. The men looked at each other and winked.

"Gimme some soda-water. Sasspirilla Ah reckon," the new-comer ordered, and stood far down the counter near the open pickled pig-feet tub to drink it.

Elijah nudged Walter and turned with mock gravity to the new-comer.

"Say Joe, how's everything up yo' way? How's yo' wife?"

Joe started and all but dropped the bottle he held in his hands. He swallowed several times painfully and his lips trembled.

"Aw 'Lige, you oughtn't to do nothin' like that," Walter grumbled. Elijah ignored him.

"She jus' passed heah a few minutes ago goin' thata way," with a wave of his hand in the direction of the woods.

Now Joe knew his wife had passed that way. He knew that the men lounging in the general store had seen her, moreover, he knew that the men knew *he* knew. He stood there silent for a long moment staring blankly, with his Adam's apple twitching nervously up and down his throat. One could actually *see* the pain he was suffering, his eyes, his face, his hands and even the dejected slump of his shoulders. He set the bottle down upon the counter. He didn't bang it, just eased it out of his hand silently and fiddled with his suspender buckle.

"Well, Ah'm goin' after her today. Ah'm goin' an' fetch her back. Spunk's done gone too fur."

He reached deep down into his trouser pocket and drew out a hollow ground razor, large and shiny, and passed his moistened thumb back and forth over the edge.

"Talkin' like a man, Joe. Course that's *yo'* fambly affairs, but Ah like to see grit in anybody."

Joe Kanty laid down a nickel and stumbled out into the street.

Dusk crept in from the woods. Ike Clarke lit the swinging oil lamp that was almost immediately surrounded by candle-flies. The men laughed boisterously behind Joe's back as they watched him shamble woodward.

"You oughtn't to said whut you did to him, Lige,—look how it worked him up," Walter chided.

"And Ah hope it did work him up. Tain't even decent for a man to take and take like he do."

"Spunk will sho' kill him."

"Aw, Ah doan' know. You never kin tell. He might turn him up an' spank him fur gettin' in the way, but Spunk wouldn't shoot no unarmed man. Dat razor he carried outa heah ain't gonna run Spunk down an' cut him, an' Joe ain't got the nerve to go up to Spunk with it knowing he totes that Army 45. He makes that break outa heah to bluff us. He's gonna hide that razor behind the first likely palmetto root an' sneak back home to bed. Don't tell me nothin' 'bout that rabbit-foot colored man. Didn't he meet Spunk an' Lena face to face one day las' week an' mumble sumthin' to Spunk 'bout lettin' his wife alone?"

"What did Spunk say?" Walter broke in—"Ah like him fine but tain't right the way he carries on wid Lena Kanty, jus' cause Joe's timid 'bout fightin'."

"You wrong theah, Walter. 'Tain't cause Joe's timid at all, it's cause Spunk wants Lena. If Joe was a passle of wile cats Spunk would tackle the job just the same. He'd go after *anything* he wanted the same way. As Ah wuz sayin' a minute ago, he tole Joe right to his face that Lena was his. 'Call her,' he says to Joe. 'Call her and see if she'll come. A woman knows her boss an' she answers when he calls.' 'Lena, ain't I yo' husband?' Joe sorter whines out. Lena looked at him real disgusted but she don't answer and she don't move outa her tracks. Then Spunk reaches out an' takes hold of her arm an' says: 'Lena, youse mine. From now on Ah works for you an' fights for you an' Ah never wants you to look to nobody for a crumb of bread, a stitch of close or a shingle to go over yo' head, but *me* long as Ah live. Ah'll git the lumber foh owah house tomorrow. Go home an' git yo' things together!'

" 'Thass mah house' Lena speaks up. 'Papa gimme that.'

" 'Well,' says Spunk, 'doan give up whut's yours, but when youse inside don't forgit youse mine, an' let no other man git outa his place wid you!'

"Lena looked up at him with her eyes so full of love that they wuz runnin' over an' Spunk seen it an' Joe seen it too, and his lip started to tremblin' and his Adam's apple was galloping up and down his neck like a race horse. Ah bet he's wore out half a dozen Adam's apples since Spunk's been on the job with Lena. That's all he'll do. He'll be back heah after while swallowin' an' workin' his lips like he wants to say somethin' an' can't."

"But didn't he do *nothin'* to stop 'em?"

"Nope, not a frazzlin' thing—jus' stood there. Spunk took Lena's arm and walked off jus' like nothin' ain't happened and he stood there gazin' after them till they was outa sight. Now you know a woman don't want no man like that. I'm jus' waitin' to see whut he's goin' to say when he gits back."

II

But Joe Kanty never came back, never. The men in the store heard the sharp report of a pistol somewhere distant in the palmetto thicket and soon Spunk came walking leisurely, with his big black Stetson set at the same rakish angle and Lena clinging to his arm, came walking right into the general store. Lena wept in a frightened manner.

"Well," Spunk announced calmly, "Joe come out there wid a meatax an' made me kill him."

He sent Lena home and led the men back to Joe—Joe crumple and limp with his right hand still clutching his razor.

"See mah back? Mah cloes cut clear through. He sneaked up an' tried to kill me from the back, but Ah got him, an' got him good, first shot," Spunk said.

The men glared at Elijah, accusingly.

"Take him up an' plant him in 'Stoney lonesome'," Spunk said in a careless voice. "Ah didn't wanna shoot him but he made me do it. He's a dirty coward, jumpin' on a man from behind."

Spunk turned on his heel and sauntered away to where he knew his love wept in fear for him and no man stopped him. At the general store later on, they all talked of locking him up until the sheriff should come from Orlando, but no one did anything but talk.

A clear case of self-defense, the trial was a short one, and Spunk walked out of the court house to freedom again. He could work again, ride the dangerous log-carriage that fed the singing, snarling, biting, circle-saw; he could stroll the soft dark lanes with his guitar. He was free to roam the woods again; he was free to return to Lena. He did all of these things.

III

"Whut you reckon, Walt?" Elijah asked one night later. "Spunk's gittin' ready to marry Lena!"

"Naw! Why Joe ain't had time to git cold yit. Nohow Ah didn't figger Spunk was the marryin' kind."

"Well, he is," rejoined Elijah. "He done moved most of Lena's things—and her along wid 'em—over to the Bradley house. He's buying it. Jus' like Ah told yo' all right in heah the night Joe wuz kilt. Spunk's crazy 'bout Lena. He don't want folks to keep on talkin' 'bout her—thass reason he's rushin' so. Funny thing 'bout that bob-cat, wan't it?"

"Whut bob-cat, 'Lige? Ah ain't heered 'bout none."

"Ain't cher? Well, night befo' las' was the fust night Spunk an' Lena moved together an' jus' as they was goin' to bed, a big black bob-cat, black all over, you hear me, *black*, walked round and round that house and howled like forty, an' when Spunk got his gun an' went to the winder to shoot it, he says it stood right still an' looked him in the eye, an' howled right at him. The thing got Spunk so nervoused up he couldn't shoot. But Spunk says twan't no bob-cat nohow. He says it was Joe done sneaked back from Hell!"

"Humph!" sniffed Walter, "he oughter be nervous after what he done. Ah reckon Joe come back to dare him to marry Lena, or to come out an' fight. Ah bet he'll be back time and agin, too. Know what Ah think? Joe wuz a braver man than Spunk."

There was a general shout of derision from the group.

"Thass a fact," went on Walter. "Lookit whut he done; took a razor an' went out to fight a man he knowed toted a gun an' wuz a crack shot, too; 'nother thing Joe wuz skeered of Spunk, skeered plumb stiff! But he went jes' the same. It took him a long time to get his nerve up. 'Tain't nothin' for Spunk to fight when he ain't skeered of nothin'. Now, Joe's done come back to have it out wid the man that's got all he ever had. Y'll know Joe ain't never had nothin' nor wanted nothin' besides Lena. It musta been a h'ant cause ain' nobody never seen no black bob-cat."

" 'Nother thing," cut in one of the men, "Spunk waz cussin' a blue streak today 'cause he 'lowed dat saw wuz wobblin'—almos' got 'im once. The machinist come, looked it over an' said it wuz alright. Spunk musta been leanin' t'wards it some. Den he claimed somebody pushed 'im but 'twant nobody close to 'im. Ah wuz glad when knockin' off time come. I'm skeered of dat man when he gits hot. He'd beat you full of button holes as quick as he's look atcher."

IV

The men gathered the next evening in a different mood, no laughter. No badinage this time.

"Look 'Lige, you goin' to set up wid Spunk?"

"Naw, Ah reckon not, Walter. Tell yuh the truth, Ah'm a lil bit skittish. Spunk died too wicket—died cussin' he did. You know he thought he wuz done outa life."

"Good Lawd, who'd he think done it?"

"Joe."

"Joe Kanty? How come?"

"Walter, Ah b'leeve Ah will walk up thata way an' set. Lena would like it Ah reckon."

"But whut did he say, 'Lige?"

Elijah did not answer until they had left the lighted store and were strolling down the dark street.

"Ah wuz loadin' a wagon wid scantlin' right near the saw when Spunk fell on the carriage but 'fore Ah could git to him the saw got him in the body—awful sight. Me an' Skint Miller got him off but it was too late. Anybody could see that. The fust thing he said wuz: 'He pushed me, Lige'—the dirty hound pushed me in the back!'—He was spittin' blood at ev'ry breath. We laid him on the sawdust pile with his face to the East so's he could die easy. He helt mah han' till the last, Walter, and said: 'It was Joe, 'Lige—the dirty sneak shoved me . . . he didn't dare come to mah face . . . but Ah'll git the son-of-a-wood louse soon's Ah get there an' make hell too hot for him. . . . Ah felt him shove me. . . .!' Thass how he died."

"If spirits kin fight, there's a powerful tussle goin' on somewhere ovah Jordan 'cause Ah b'leeve Joe's ready for Spunk an' ain't skeered anymore—yas, Ah b'leeve Joe pushed 'im mahself."

They had arrived at the house. Lena's lamentations were deep and loud. She had filled the room with magnolia blossoms that gave off a heavy sweet odor. The keepers of the wake tipped about whispering in frightened tones. Everyone in the Village was there, even old Jeff Kanty, Joe's father, who a few hours before would have been afraid to come within ten feet of him, stood leering triumphantly down upon the fallen giant as if his fingers had been the teeth of steel that laid him low.

The cooling board consisted of three sixteen-inch boards on saw horses, a dingy sheet was his shroud.

The women ate heartily of the funeral baked meats and wondered who would be Lena's next. The men whispered coarse conjectures between guzzles of whiskey.

JOHN REDDING GOES TO SEA

In this narrative, Zora Neale Hurston introduces John Redding, a restless young man who longs to leave his rural village to journey to faraway places "where the sky touches the ground." His travel ambitions are encouraged by his father. However, his self-indulgent and possessive mother attempts to thwart his dream and unknowingly brings down a horrible fate on the family.

The Villagers said that John Redding was a queer child. His mother thought he was too. She would shake her head sadly, and observe to John's father: "Alf, it's too bad our boy's got a spell on 'im."

The father always met this lament with indifference, if not impatience.

"Aw, woman, stop dat talk 'bout conjure. Tain't so nohow. Ah doan want Jawn tuh git dat foolishness in *him.*"

"Cose you allus tries tuh know mo' than me, but Ah ain't so ign'rant. Ah knows a heap mahself. Many and manys the people been drove outa their senses by conjuration, or rid tuh deat' by witches."

"Ah keep on telling yuh, woman, tain's so. B'lieve it all you wants tuh, but dontcha tell mah son none of it."

Perhaps ten-year old John *was* puzzling to the simple folk there in the Florida woods for he was an imaginative child and fond of daydreams. The St. John River flowed a scarce three hundred feet from his back door. On its banks at this point grow numerous palms, luxuriant magnolias and bay trees with a dense undergrowth of ferns, cat-tails and rope-grass. On the bosom of the stream float millions of delicately colored hyacinths. The little brown boy loved to wander down to the waters edge, and, casting in dry twigs, watch them sail away down stream to Jacksonville, the sea, the wide world and John Redding wanted to follow them.

Sometimes in his dreams he was a prince, riding away in a gorgeous carriage. Often he was a knight bestride a fiery charger prancing down the white shell road that led to distant lands. At other times he was a steamboat captain piloting his craft down the St. John River to where the sky seemed to touch the water. No matter what he dreamed or who he fancied himself to be, he always ended by riding away to the horizon; for in his childish ignorance he thought this to be farthest land.

But these twigs, which John called his ships, did not always sail away. Sometimes they would be swept in among the weeds growing in the shallow water, and be held there. One day his father came upon him scolding the weeds for stopping his sea-going vessels.

"Let go mah ships! You ole mean weeds you!" John screamed and stamped impotently. "They wants tuh go 'way. You let 'em go on!"

Alfred laid his hand on his son's head lovingly. "What's mattah, son?"

"Mah ships, pa," the child answered weeping. "Ah throwed 'em in to go way off an' them ole weeds won't let 'em."

"Well, well, doan cry. Ah thought youse uh grown up man. Men doan cry lak babies. You musn't take it too hard 'bout yo' ships. You gotta git uster things gittin' tied up. They's lotser folks that 'ud go on off too ef somethin' didn' ketch 'em an' hol' 'em!"

Alfred Redding's brown face grew wistful for a moment, and the child noticing it, asked quickly: "Do weeds tangle up folks too, pa?"

"Now, no, chile, doan be takin' too much stock of what ah say. Ah talks in parables sometimes. Come on, les go on tuh supper."

Alf took his son's hand, and started slowly toward the house. Soon John broke the silence.

"Pa, when ah gets as big as you Ah'm goin' farther than them ships. Ah'm goin' to where the sky touches the ground."

"Well, son, when Ah wuz a boy Ah said Ah wuz goin' too, but heah Ah am. Ah hopes you have bettah luck than me."

"Pa, Ah betcha Ah seen somethin' in th' wood-lot you ain't seen!"

"Whut?"

"See dat tallest pine tree ovah dere how it looks like a skull wid a crown on?"

"Yes, indeed!" said the father looking toward the tree designated. "It do look lak a skull since you call mah 'tention to it. You 'magine lotser things nobody else evah did, son!"

"Sometimes, Pa dat ole tree waves at me just aftah th' sun goes down, an' makes me sad an' skeered, too."

"Ah specks youse skeered of de dahk, thas all, sonny. When you gits biggah you won't think of sich."

Hand in hand the two trudged across the plowed land and up to the house, the child dreaming of the days when he should wander to far countries, and the man of the days when he might have—and thus they entered the kitchen.

Matty Redding, John's mother, was setting the table for supper. She was a small wiry woman with large eyes that might have been beautiful when she was young, but too much weeping had left them watery and weak.

"Matty," Alf began as he took his place at the table, "Dontcha know our boy is different from any othah chile roun' heah. He 'lows he's goin' to sea when he gits grown, an' Ah reckon Ah'll let 'im."

The woman turned from the stove, skillet in hand. "Alf, you ain't gone crazy, is you? John kain't help wantin' tuh stray off, cause he's got a spell on 'im; but *you* oughter be shamed to be encouragin' him.'

"Ain't Ah done tol' you forty times not tuh tahk dat low-life mess in front of mah boy?"

"Well, ef tain't no conjure in de world, how come Mitch Potts been layin' on his back six mont's an' de doctah kain't do 'im no good? Answer me dat. The very night John wuz bawn, Granny seed ole Witch Judy Davis creepin outer dis yahd. You know she had swore tuh fix me fuh maryin' you, 'way from her darter Edna. She put travel dust down fuh mah chile, dat's whut she done, tuh make him walk 'way fum me. An' evuh sence he's been able tuh crawl, he's been tryin tuh go."

"Matty, a man doan need no travel dust tuh make 'im wanter hit de road. It jes' comes natcheral fuh er man tuh travel. Dey all wants tuh go at some time or other but they kain't all get away. Ah wants mah John tuh go an' see cause Ah wanted to go mah self. When he comes back Ah kin see them furrin places wid his eyes. He kain't help wantin' tuh go cause he's a man chile!"

Mrs. Redding promptly went off into a fit of weeping but the man and boy ate supper unmoved. Twelve years of married life had taught Alfred that far from being miserable when she wept, his wife was enjoying a bit of self-pity.

Thus John Redding grew to manhood, playing, studying and dreaming. He attended the village school as did most of the youth about him, but he also went to high school at the county seat where none of the villagers went. His father shared his dreams and ambitions, but his mother could not understand why he should wish to go strange places where neither she nor his father had been. No one of their community had ever been farther away than Jacksonville. Few indeed had even been there. Their own gardens, general store, and occasional trips to the county seat—seven miles away—sufficed for all their needs. Life was simple indeed with these folk.

John was the subject of much discussion among the country folk. Why didn't he teach school instead of thinking about strange places and people? Did he think himself better than any of the "gals" there about that he would not go a-courting any of them? He muss be "fixed" as his mother claimed, else where did his queer notions come from? Well, he was always queer, and one could not expect the man to be different from the child. They never failed to stop work at the approach of Alfred in order to be at the fence and inquire after John's health and ask when he expected to leave.

"Oh," Alfred would answer, "Jes' as soon as his mah gits reconciled to th' notion. He's a mighty dutiful boy, mah John is. He doan wanna hurt her feelings."

The boy had on several occasions attempted to reconcile his mother to the notion, but found it a difficult task. Matty always took refuge in self-pity and tears. Her son's desires were incomprehensible to her, that was all. She did not want to hurt him. It was love, mother love, that made her cling so desperately to John.

"Lawd knows," she would sigh, "Ah nevah wuz happy an' nevah specks tuh be."

"An' from yo' actions," put in Alfred hotly, "You's determined *not* to be."

"Thas right, Alfred, go on an' 'buse me. You allus does. Ah knows Ah'm ign'rant an' all dat; but dis is mah son. Ah bred an' born 'im. He kain't help from wantin' to go rovin' cause travel dust been put down fuh him. But mebbe we kin cure 'im by disincouragin' the idee."

"Well, Ah wants mah son tuh go; an' he wants tuh go too. He's a man now, Matty. An' we mus' let John hoe his own row. If it's travelin' twon't be foh long. He'll come back to us bettah than when he went off. What do you say, son?"

"Mamma," John began slowly, "It hurts me to see you so troubled over my going away; but I feel that I must go. I'm stagnating here. This indolent atmosphere will stifle every bit of ambition that's in me. Let me go mamma, please. What is there here for me? Why, sometimes I get to feeling just like a lump of dirt turned over by the plow—just where it falls there's where it lies—no thought or movement or nothing. I wanter make myself something—not just stay where I was born."

"Naw, John, it's bettah for you to stay heah and take over the school. Why don't you marry and settle down?"

"I don't *want* to, mamma. I want to go away."

"Well," said Mrs. Redding, pursing her mouth tightly, "You ainta goin' wid *mah* consent!"

"I'm sorry mamma, that you won't consent. I am going neverthe-less."

"John, John, mah baby! You wouldn't kill yo' po' ole mamma, would you? Come, kiss me, son."

The boy flung his arms about his mother and held her closely, while she sobbed on his breast. To all of her pleas, however, he answered that he must go.

"I'll stay at home this year, mamma, then I'll go for a while, but it won't be long. I'll come back and make you and papa oh so happy. Do you agree, mama dear?"

"Ah reckon tain' nothin' tall fuh me to do else."

Things went on very well around the Redding home for some time. During the day John helped his father about the farm and read a great deal at night.

Then the unexpected happened. John married Stella Kanty, a neighbor's daughter. The courtship was brief but ardent—on John's part at least. He danced with Stella at a candy-pulling, walked with her home and in three weeks had declared himself. Mrs. Redding declared that she was happier than she had ever been in her life. She therefore indulged in a whole afternoon of weeping. John's change was occa-sioned possibly by the fact that Stella was really beautiful; he was young and red-blooded, and the time was spring.

Spring-time in Florida is not a matter of peeping violets or burst-ing buds merely. It is a riot of color in nature—glistening green leaves, pink, blue, purple, yellow blossoms that fairly stagger the visitor from the north. The miles of hyacinths lie like an undulating carpet on the surface of the river and divide reluctantly when the slow-moving alli-gators push their way log-like across. The nights are white nights for the moon shines with dazzling splendor, or in the absence of that god-dess, the soft darkness creeps down laden with innumerable scents. The heavy fragrance of magnolias mingled with the delicate sweetness of jasmine and wild roses.

If time and propinquity conquered John, what then? These forces have overcome older men.

The raptures of the first few weeks over, John began to saunter out to the gate to gaze wistfully down the white dusty road; or to wander again to the river as he had done in childhood. To be sure he did not send forth twig-ships any longer, but his thoughts would in spite of himself, stray down river to Jacksonville, the sea, the wide world—and poor home-tied John Redding wanted to follow them.

He grew silent and pensive. Matty accounted for this by her ever-ready explanation of "conjuration." Alfred said nothing but smoked and puttered about the barn more than ever. Stella accused her husband of indifference and made his life miserable with tears, accusations and pouting. At last John decided to bring matters to a head and broached the subject to his wife.

"Stella, dear, I want to go roving about the world for a spell. Would you stay here with papa and mama and wait for me to come back?"

"John, is you crazy sho' nuff? If you don't want me, say so an' I kin go home to mah folks."

"Stella, darling, I do want you, but I want to go away too. I can have both if you'll let me. We'll be *so* happy when I return . . ."

"Naw, John, you cain't rush me off one side like that. You didn't hafta marry me. There's a plenty othahs that would have been glad enuff tuh get me; you know Ah wan't educated befo' han'."

"Don't make me too conscious of my weakness, Stella. I know I should never have married with my inclinations, but it's done now, no use to talk about what is past. I love you and want to keep you, but I can't stifle that longing for the open road, rolling seas, for peoples and countries I have never seen. I'm suffering too, Stella, I'm paying for my rashness in marrying before I was ready. I'm not trying to shirk my duty—you'll be well taken care of in the meanwhile."

"John, folks allus said youse queer and tol' me not to marry yuh, but Ah jes' loved yuh so Ah couldn't help it, an' now to think you wants tuh sneak off an' leave me."

"But I'm coming back, darling . . . listen Stella."

But the girl would not. Matty came in and Stella fell into her arms weeping. John's mother immediately took up arms against him. The two women carried on such an effective war against him for the next few days that finally Alfred was forced to take his son's part.

"Matty, let dat boy alone, Ah tell you! Ef he wuz uh homebuddy he'd be drove 'way by you all's racket."

"Well, Alf, dat's all we po' wimmen kin do. We wants our husbands an' our sons. John's got uh wife now, an' he ain't got no business to be talkin' 'bout goin' nowheres. I lowed dat marrin' Stella would settle him."

"Yas, dat's all you wimmen study 'bout—settlin' some man. You takes all de get-up out of 'em. Jes' let uh fellah mak uh motion lak gettin' somewhere, an' some 'oman'll begin tuh hollah 'Stop theah! where's you goin'? Don't fuhgit you b'longs tuh me.' "

"My Gawd! Alf! Whut you reckon Stella's gwine do? Let John walk off an' leave huh?"

"Naw, git outer huh foolishness an' go 'long wid him. He'd take huh."

"Stellah ain't got no call tuh go crazy 'cause John is. She ain't no woman tuh be floppin' roun' from place tuh place lak some uh dese reps follerin' uh section gang."

The man turned abruptly from his wife and stood in the kitchen door. A blue haze hung over the river and Alfred's attention seemed fixed upon this. In reality his thoughts were turned inward. He was thinking of the numerous occasions upon which he and his son had sat on the fallen log at the edge of the water and talked of John's proposed travels. He had encouraged his son, given him every advantage his own poor circumstances would permit. And now John was home-tied.

The young man suddenly turned the corner of the house and approached his father.

"Hello, papa."

" 'Lo, son."

"Where's mama and Stella?"

The older man merely jerked his thumb toward the interior of the house and once more gazed pensively toward the river. John entered the kitchen and kissed his mother fondly.

"Great news, mamma."

"What now?"

"Got a chance to join the Navy, mama, and go all around the world. Ain't that grand?"

"John, you shorely ain't gointer leave me an' Stella, is yuh?"

"Yes, I think I am. I know how both of you feel, but I know how *I* feel, also. You preach to me the gospel of self-sacrifice for the happiness of others, but you are unwilling to practice any of it yourself. Stella can stay here—I am going to support her and spend all the time I can with her. I am going—that's settled, but I want to go with your good will. I want to do something worthy of a strong man. I have done nothing so far but look to you and papa for everything. Let me learn to strive and think—in short, be a man."

"Naw, John, Ah'll nevah give mah consent. I know yous hard-headed jes'l-ak yo' paw; but if you leave dis place ovah mah head, Ah nevah wants you tuh come back heah no mo. Ef Ah wuz laid on de coolin' board, Ah doan want yuh standin' ovah me, young man. Doan even come neah mah grave, you ongrateful wretch!"

Mrs. Redding arose and flung out of the room. For once, she was too incensed to cry. John stood in his tracks, gone cold and numb at his mother's pronouncement. Alfred, too, was moved. Mrs. Redding banged the bed-room door violently and startled John slightly. Alfred took his son's arm, saying softly: 'Come, son, let's go down to the river."

At the water's edge they halted for a short space before seating themselves on the log. The sun was setting in a purple cloud. Hundreds of mosquito hawks darted here and there, catching gnats and being themselves caught by the lightning-swift bull-hats. John abstractly snapped in two the stalk of a slender young bamboo. Taking no note of what he was doing, he broke it into short lengths and tossed them singly into the stream. The old man watched him silently for a while, but finally he said: "Oh, yes, my boy, some ships get tangled in the weeds."

."Yes papa they certainly do. I guess I'm beaten—might as well surrender."

"Nevah say die. Yuh nevah kin tell what will happen."

"What *can* happen? I have courage enough to make things happen; but what can I do against mamma! What man wants to go on a long journey with his mother's curses ringing in his ears? She doesn't understand. I'll wait another year, but I am going because I must."

Alfred threw an arm about his son's neck and drew him nearer but quickly removed it. Both men instantly drew apart, ashamed for having been so demonstrative. The father looked off to the woodlot and asked with a reminiscent smile: "Son, do you remember showin' me the tree dat looked lak a skeleton head?"

"Yes, I do. It's there still. I look at it sometimes when things have become too painful for me at the house, and I run down here to cool off and think. And every time I look at it, papa, it laughs at me like it had some grim joke up its sleeve."

"Yuh, wuz always imagin' things, John; things that nobody else evah thought on!"

"You know, papa, sometimes—I reckon my longing to get away makes me feel this way.... I feel that I am just earth, *soil* lying helpless to move myself, but *thinking*. I seem to hear herds of big beasts like horses and cows thundering over me, and rains beating down; and winds sweeping furiously over—all acting upon me, but me, well, just soil, *feeling* but not able to take part in it all. Then a soft wind like love passes over and warms me, and a summer rain comes down like understanding and softens me, and I push a blade of grass or a flower, or maybe a pine tree—that's the ground thinking. Plants are ground thoughts, because the soil can't move itself. Whenever I see little whirls of dust sailing down the road I always step aside—I don't want to stop 'em 'cause they're on their shining way—moving! Oh, yes, I'm a dreamer. . . . I have such wonderfully complete dreams, papa. They never come true. But even as my dreams fade I have others."

"Yas, son, Ah have them same feelings exactly, but Ah can't find no words lak you do. It seems lak you an' me see wid de same eyes, hear wid de same ears an' even feel de same inside. Only thing you kin talk it an' Ah can't. But anyhow you speaks for me, so whut's the difference?"

The men arose without more conversation. Possibly they feared to trust themselves to speech. As they walked leisurely toward the house Alfred remarked the freshness of the breeze.

'It's about time the rains set in," added his son. "The year is wearin' on."

After a gloomy supper John strolled out into the spacious front yard and seated himself beneath a China-berry tree. The breeze had grown a trifle stronger since sunset and continued from the southeast. Matty and Stella sat on the deep front porch, but Alfred joined John under the tree. The family was divided into two armed camps and the hostilities had reached that stage where no quarter could be asked or given.

About nine o'clock an automobile came flying down the dusty white road and halted at the gate. A white man slammed the gate and hurried up the walk toward the house, but stopped abruptly before the men beneath the China-berry. It was Mr. Hill, the builder of the new bridge that was to span the river.

Howdy John, Howdy Alf. I'm mighty glad I found you. I am in trouble."

"Well now, Mist' Hill," answered Alfred slowly but pleasantly. "We'se glad you foun' us too. What trouble could *you* be having now?"

"It's the bridge. The weather bureau says that the rains will be upon me in forty-eight hours. If it catches the bridge as it is now, I'm afraid all my work of the past five months will be swept away, to say nothing of a quarter of a million dollars worth of labor and material. I've got all my men at work now and I thought to get as many extra hands as I could to help out tonight and tomorrow. We can make her weather tight in that time if I can get about twenty more."

'I'll go, Mister Hill," said John with a great deal of energy. "I don't want papa out on that bridge—too dangerous."

"Good for you, John!" cried the white man. "Now if I had a few more men of your brawn and brain, I could build an entirely new bridge in forty-eight hours. Come on and jump into the car. I am taking the men on down as I find them."

"Wait a minute. I must put on my blue jeans. I won't be long."

John arose and strode to the house. He knew that his mother and wife had overheard everything, but he paused for a moment to speak to them.

"Mamma, I am going to work all night on the bridge."

There was no answer. He turned to his wife.

"Stella, don't be lonesome. I will be home at day-break."

His wife was as silent as his mother. John stood for a moment on the steps, then resolutely strode past the women and into the house. A few minutes later he emerged clad in his blue overalls and brogans. This time he said nothing to the silent figures rocking back and forth on the porch. But when he was a few feet from the steps he called back: "Bye, mamma; bye, Stella," and hurried on down the walk to where his father sat.

"So long, papa. I'll be home around seven."

Alfred roused himself and stood. Placing both hands upon his son's broad shoulders he said softly: "Be keerful son, don't fall or nothin'."

"I will, papa. Don't *you* get into a quarrel on my account."

John hurried on to the waiting car and was whirled away.

Alfred sat for a long time beneath the tree where his son had left him and smoked on. The women soon went indoors. On the night breeze were borne numerous scents: of jassamine, of roses, of damp earth of the river, of the pine forest near by. A solitary whip-poor-will sent forth his plaintive call from the nearby shrubbery. A giant owl roared and boomed from the wood lot. The calf confined in the barn would bleat and be answered by his mother's sympathetic "moo" from the pen. Away down in Lake Howell Creek the basso profundo of the alligators boomed and died, boomed and died.

Around ten o'clock the breeze freshened, growing stiffer until midnight when it became a gale. Alfred fastened the doors and bolted the wooden shutters at the windows. The three persons sat about a round deal table in the kitchen upon which stood a bulky kerosene lamp, flickering and sputtering in the wind that came in through the numerous cracks in the walls. The wind rushed down the chimney blowing puffs of ashes about the room. It banged the cooking utensils on the walls. The drinking gourd hanging outside by the door played a weird tattoo, hollow and unearthly, against the thin wooden wall.

The man and the women sat silently. Even if there had been no storm they would not have talked. They could not go to bed because the women were afraid to retire during a storm and the man wished to stay awake and think with his son. Thus they sat: the women hot with resentment toward the man and terrified by the storm; the man hardly mindful of the tempest but eating his heart out in pity for his boy. Time wore heavily on.

And now a new element of terror was added. A screech-owl alighted on the roof and shivered forth his doleful cry. Possibly he had been blown out of his nest by the wind. Matty started up at the sound but fell back in her chair, pale and trembling: "My Gawd!" she gasped, "dat's a sho' sign uh death."

Stella hurriedly thrust her hand into the salt-jar and threw some into the chimney of the lamp. The color of the flame changed from yellow to blue-green but this burning of salt did not have the desired effect—to drive away the bird from the roof. Matty slipped out of her blue calico wrapper and turned it wrong side out before replacing it. Even Alfred turned one sock.

"Alf," said Matty, "What do you reckon's gonna happen from this?"

"How do Ah know, Matty?"

"Ah wisht John hadn't went way from heah tuh night."

"Humh."

Outside the tempest raged. The palms rattled dryly and the giant pines groaned and sighed in the grip of the wind. Flying leaves and pine-mast filled the air. Now and then a brilliant flash of lightning disclosed a bird being blown here and there with the wind. The prodigious roar of the thunder seemed to rock the earth. Black clouds hung so low that the tops of the pines were among them moving slowly before the wind and made the darkness awful. The screech owl continued his tremulous cry.

After three o'clock the wind ceased and the rain commenced. Huge drops clattered down upon the shingle roof like buckshot and ran from the eaves in torrents. It entered the house through the cracks in the walls and under the doors. It was a deluge in volume and force but subsided before morning.

The sun came up brightly on the havoc of the wind and rain calling forth millions of feathered creatures. The white sand everywhere was full of tiny cups dug out by the force of the falling raindrops. The rims of the little depressions crunched noisily underfoot.

At daybreak Mr. Redding set out for the bridge. He was uneasy. On arriving he found that the river had risen twelve feet during the cloudburst and was still rising. The slow St. Johns was swollen far beyond its banks and rushing on to sea like a mountain stream, sweeping away houses, great blocks of earth, cattle, trees—in short anything that came within its grasp. Even the steel framework of the new bridge was gone!

The siren of the fibre factory was tied down for half an hour, announcing the disaster to the country side. When Alfred arrived therefore he found nearly all the men of the district there.

The river, red and swollen, was full of floating debris. Huge trees were swept along as relentlessly as chicken coops and fence rails. Some steel piles were all that was left of the bridge.

Alfred went down to a group of men who were fishing members of the ill-fated construction gang out of the water. Many were able to swim ashore unassisted. Wagons backed up and were hurriedly driven away loaded with wet shivering men. Two men had been killed outright, others seriously wounded. Three men had been drowned. At last all had been accounted for except John Redding. His father ran here and there asking for him, or calling him. No one knew where he was. No one remembered seeing him since daybreak.

Dozens of women had arrived at the scene of the disaster by this time. Matty and Stella, wrapped in woolen shawls, were among them. They rushed to Alfred in alarm and asked where was John.

"Ah doan know," answered Alfred impatiently. "That's what Ah'm trying to fin' out now."

"Do you reckon he's run away?" asked Stella thoughtlessly.

Matty bristled instantly.

"Naw," she answered sternly, "he ain't no sneak."

The father turned to Fred Mimms, one of the survivors and asked him where John was and how had the bridge been destroyed.

"Yuh see," said Mimms, "when dat turrible win' come up we wuz out 'bout de middle of de river. Some of us wuz on de bridge, some on de derrick. De win' blowed so hahd we could skeercely stan' and Mist' Hill tol' us tuh set down fuh a spell. He's 'fraid some of us mought go overboard. Den all of a sudden de lights went out—guess de wires wuz blowed down. We wuz all skeered tuh move for slippin' overboard. Den dat rain commenced—an' Ah nevah seed such a down-pour since de flood. We set dere and someone begins tuh pray. Lawd how we did pray tuh be spared! Den somebody raised a song an' we sung, you hear me, we sung from de bottom of our hearts till daybreak. When the first light come we couldn't see nothin' but fog everywhere. You couldn't tell which wuz water an' which wuz lan'. But when de sun come up de fog begin to liff, an' we could see de water. Dat fog wuz so thick an' heavy dat it wuz huggin' dat river lak a windin' sheet. And when it rose we saw dat de river had rose way up durin' the rain. My Gawd, Alf! it wuz runnin' high—so high it nearly teched de span of de bridge—an' red as blood! So much clay, you know from lan' she done overflowed. Comin' down stream, as fas' as 'press train wuz three big pine trees. De first one wuzn't fohty feet from us and there wasn't no chance to do nothin' but pray. De fust one struck us and shook de whole works an' befo' it could stop shakin' the other two hit us an' down we went. Ah thought Ah'd never see home again."

"But, Mimms, where's John?"

"Ah ain't seen him, Alf, since de logs struck us. Mebbe he's swum ashore, mebbe dey picked him up. What's dat floatin' way out dere in de water?"

Alfred shaded his eyes with his gnarled brown hand and gazed out into the stream. Sure enough there was a man floating on a piece of timber. He lay prone upon his back. His arms were outstretched, and the water washed over his brogans but his feet were lifted out of the water whenever the timber was buoyed up by the stream. His blue overalls were nearly torn from his body. A heavy piece of steel or timber had struck him in falling for his left side was laid open by the thrust. A great jagged hole wherein the double fists of a man might be thrust, could plainly be seen from the shore. The man was John Redding.

Everyone seemed to see him at once. Stella fell to the wet earth in a faint. Matty clung to her husband's arm, weeping hysterically. Alfred stood very erect with his wife clinging tearfully to him, but he said nothing. A single tear hung on his lashes for a time then trickled slowly down his wrinkled brown cheek.

"Alf! Alf!" screamed Matty, "Dere's our son. Ah knowed when Ah heard dat owl las' night. . . ."

"Ah see 'im, Matty," returned her husband softly.

"Why is yuh standin' heah? Go git mah boy."

The men were manning a boat to rescue the remains of John Redding when Alfred spoke again.

"Mah po' boy, his dreams never come true."

"Alf," complained Matty, "Why doantcher hurry an' git my boy—doantcher see he's floatin' on off?"

Her husband paid her no attention but addressed himself to the rescue-party.

"You all stop! Leave my boy go on. Doan stop 'im. Doan' bring 'im back for dat ole tree to grin at. Leave him g'wan. He wants tuh go. Ah'm happy 'cause dis maw'nin' mah boy is goin' tuh sea, *he's goin' tuh sea.*"

Out on the bosom of the river, bobbing up and down as if waving good bye, piloting his little craft on the shining river road, John Redding floated away toward Jacksonville, the sea, the wide world—at last.

MUTTSY

Zora Neale Hurston writes in this story about Pinkie, a young girl from rural Eatonville, Florida, who arrives in Harlem and almost immediately falls under the influence of Ma Turner's back parlor. Muttsy, an established gambler, attempts to win Pinkie's hand in marriage. Turning from his gambling addiction proves difficult even for love. Awarded one half of second prize, Hurston published this story in August 1926.

The piano in Ma Turner's back parlor stuttered and wailed. The pianist kept time with his heel and informed an imaginary deserter that "she might leave and go to Halimufack, but his slow-drag would bring her back," mournfully with a memory of tom-toms running rhythm through the plaint.

Fewclothes burst through the portieres, a brown chrysalis from a dingy red cocoon, and touched the player on the shoulder.

"Say, Muttsy," he stage whispered, "Ma's got a new lil' biddy in there—just come. And say—her foot would make all of dese Harlem babies a Sunday face."

"Whut she look like?" Muttsy drawled, trying to maintain his characteristic pose of indifference to the female.

"Brown skin, patent leather grass on her knob, kinder tallish. She's a lil' skinny," he added apologetically, "but ah'm willing to buy corn for that lil' chicken."

Muttsy lifted his six feet from the piano bench as slowly as his curiosity would let him and sauntered to the portieres for a peep.

The sight was as pleasing as Fewclothes had stated—only more so. He went on in the room which Ma always kept empty. It was her receiving room—her "front."

From Ma's manner it was evident that she was very glad to see the girl. She could see that the girl was not overjoyed in her presence, but attributed that to southern greenness.

"Who you say sentcher heah, dearie?" Ma asked, her face trying to beam, but looking harder and more forbidding.

"Uh-a-a man down at the boat landing where I got off—North River. I jus' come in on the boat."

Ma's husband from his corner spoke up.

"Musta been Bluefront."

"Yeah, musta been him," Muttsy agreed.

"Oh, it's all right, honey, we New Yorkers likes to know who we'se takin' in, dearie. We has to be keerful. Whut did you say yo' name was?"

"Pinkie, yes, mam, Pinkie Jones."

Ma stared hard at the little old battered reticule that the girl carried for luggage—not many clothes if that was all—she reflected. But Pinkie had everything she needed in her face—many, many trunks full. Several of them for Ma. She noticed the cold-reddened knuckles of her bare hands too.

"Come on upstairs to yo' room—thass all right 'bout the price— we'll come to some 'greement tomorrow. Jes' go up and take off yo' things."

Pinkie put back the little rusty leather purse of another generation and followed Ma. She didn't like Ma—her smile resembled the smile of the Wolf in Red Riding Hood. Anyway back in Eatonville, Florida, "ladies," especially old ones, didn't put powder and paint on the face.

"Forty-dollars-Kate sure landed a pippin' dis time," said Muttsy, sotto voce, to Fewclothes back at the piano. "If she ain't, then there ain't a hound dawk in Georgy. Ah'm goin' home an' dress."

No one else in the crowded back parlor let alone the house knew of Pinkie's coming. They danced on, played on, sang their "blues" and lived on hotly their intense lives. The two men who had seen her—no one counted ole man Turner—went on playing too, but kept an ear cocked for her coming.

She followed Ma downstairs and seated herself in the parlor with the old man. He sat in a big rocker before a copper-lined gas stove, indolence in every gesture.

"Ah'm Ma's husband," he announced by way of making conversation.

"Now you jus' shut up!" Ma commanded severely. "You gointer git yo' teeth knocked down yo' throat yit for runnin' yo' tongue. Lemme talk to dis gal—dis is *mah* house. You sets on the stool un do nothin' too much tuh have anything tuh talk over!"

"Oh, Lawd," groaned the old man feeling a knee that always pained him at the mention of work. "Oh, Lawd, will you sen' yo' fiery chariot an' take me 'way from heah?"

"Aw shet up!" the woman spit out. "Lawd don't wantcher—devil wouldn't have yuh." She peered into the girl's face and leaned back satisfied.

"Well, girlie, you kin be a lotta help tuh me 'round dis house if you takes un intrus' in things—oh Lawd!" She leaped up from her seat. "That's mah bread ah smell burnin! . . ."

No sooner had Ma's feet cleared the room than the old man came to life again. He peered furtively after the broad back of his wife.

"Know who she is," he asked Pinkie in an awed whisper. She shook her head. "You don't? Dat's Forty-dollars-Kate!"

"Forty-dollars-Kate?" Pinkie repeated open eyed. "Naw, I don't know nothin' 'bout her."

"Sh-h" cautioned the old man. "Course you don't. I fuhgits you ain't nothin' tall but a young 'un. Twenty-five years ago they all called her dat 'cause she *wuz* 'Forty-dollars-Kate.' She sho' wuz some p'utty 'oman—great big robus' lookin' gal. Men wuz glad 'nough to spend forty dollars on her if dey had it. She didn't lose no time wid dem dat didn't have it."

He grinned ingratiatingly at Pinkie and leaned nearer.

"But you'se better lookin' than she ever wuz, you might—taint no tellin' whut you might do ef you git some sense. I'm a gointer teach you, hear?"

"Yessuh," the girl managed to answer with an almost paralyzed tongue.

"Thass a good girl. You jus' lissen to me an' you'll pull thew alright."

He glanced at the girl sitting timidly upon the edge of the chair and scolded.

"Don't set dataway," he ejaculated. "Yo' back bone ain't no ram rod. Kinda scooch down on the for'ard edge uh de chear lak dis." (He demonstrated by "scooching" forward so far that he was almost sitting on his shoulder-blades). The girl slumped a trifle.

"Is you got a job yit?"

"Nawsuh," she answered slowly, "but I reckon I'll have one soon. Ain't been in town a day yet."

"You looks kinda young—kinda little biddy. Is you been to school much?"

"Yessuh, went thew eight reader. I'm goin' again when I get a chance."

"Dat so? Well ah reckon ah kin talk some Latin tuh yuh den." He cleared his throat loudly. "Whut's you entitlum?"

"I don't know," said the girl in confusion.

"Well, den, whut's you entrimmins," he queried with a bit of braggadocia in his voice.

"I don't know," from the girl, after a long awkward pause.

"You chillun don't learn nothin' in school dese days. Is you got to "goes into" yit?"

"You mean long division?"

"Ain't askin' 'bout de longness of it, dat don't make no difference," he retorted, "Sence you goin' stay heah ah'll edgecate yuh—do yuh know how to eat a fish—uh nice brown fried fish?"

"Yessuh," she answered quickly, looking about for the fish.

"How?"

"Why, you jus' eat it with corn bread," she said, a bit disappointed at the non-appearance of the fish.

"Well, ah'll tell yuh," he patronized. "You starts at de tail and liffs de meat off de bones sorter gentle and eats him clear tuh de head on dat side; den you turn 'im ovah an' commence at de tail agin and eat right up tuh de head; den you push *dem* bones way tuh one side an' takes another fish an' so on 'till de end—well, 'till der ain't no mo'!"

He mentally digested the fish and went on. "See," he pointed accusingly at her feet, "you don't even know how tuh warm yoself! You settin' dere wid yo' feet ev'y which a way. Dat ain't de way tuh git wahm. Now look at *mah* feet. Dass right put bofe big toes right togethah—now shove 'em close up tuh de fiah; now lean back so! Dass de way. Ah knows uh heap uh things tuh teach yuh sense you gointer live heah—ah learns all of 'em while de ole lady is paddlin' roun' out dere in de yard."

Ma appeared at the door and the old man withdrew so far into his rags that he all but disappeared. They went to supper where there was fried fish but forgot all rules for eating it and just ate heartily. She helped with the dishes and returned to the parlor. A little later some more men and women knocked and were admitted after the same furtive peering out through the nearest crack of the door. Ma carried them all back to the kitchen and Pinkie heard the clink of glasses and much loud laughter.

Women came in by ones and twos, some in shabby coats turned up about the ears, and with various cheap but showy hats crushed down over unkempt hair. More men, more women, more trips to the kitchen with loud laughter.

Pinkie grew uneasy. Both men and women stared at her. She kept strictly to her place. Ma came in and tried to make her join the others.

"Come on in, honey, a lil' toddy ain't gointer hurt nobody. Evebody knows *me*, ah wouldn't touch a hair on yo head. Come on in, dearie, all th' men wants tuh meetcher."

Pinkie smelt the liquor on Ma's breath and felt contaminated at her touch. She wished herself back home again even with the ill treatment and squalor. She thought of the three dollars she had secreted in her shoe—she had been warned against pickpockets—and flight but where? Nowhere. For there was no home to which *she* could return, nor any place else she knew of. But when she got a job, she'd scrape herself clear of people who took toddies.

A very black man sat on the piano stool playing as only a Negro can with hands, stamping with his feet and the rest of his body keeping time.

> "Ahm gointer make me a graveyard of mah own
> Ahm gointer make me a graveyard of mah own
> Carried me down on de smoky Road"—

Pinkie, weary of Ma's maudlin coaxing caught these lines as she was being pulled and coaxed into the kitchen. Everyone in there was shaking shimmies to music, rolling eyes heavenward as they picked imaginary grapes out of the air, or drinking. "Folkes," shouted Ma, "Look a heah! Shut up dis racket! Ah wantcher tuh meet Pinkie Jones. She's de bes' frien' ah got." Ma flopped into a chair and began to cry into her whiskey glass.

"Mah comperments!" The men almost shouted. The women were less, much less enthusiastic.

"Dass de las' run uh shad," laughed a woman called Ada, pointing to Pinkie's slenderness.

"Jes' lak a bar uh soap aftah uh hard week's wash," Bertha chimed in and laughed uproariously. The men didn't help.

"Oh, Miss Pinkie," said Bluefront, removing his Stetson for the first time, "Ma'am, also Ma'am, ef you wuz tuh see me settin' straddle of uh Mud-cat leadin' a minner whut ud you think?"

"I-er, oh, I don't know, suh. I didn't know you-er anybody could ride uh fish."

"Stick uh roun' me, baby, an' you'll wear diamon's." Bluefront swaggered. "Look heah, lil' Pigmeat, youse *some* sharp! If you didn't had but one eye ah'd think you wuz a needle—thass how sharp you looks to me. Say, mah right foot is itchin'. Do dat mean ah'm gointer walk on some strange ground wid you?"

"Naw, indeedy," cut in Fewclothes. "It jes' means you feet needs to walk in some strange water—wid a lil' read seal lye thowed in.

But he was not to have a monopoly. Fewclothes and Shorty joined the chase and poor Pinkie found it impossible to retreat to her place beside the old man. She hung her head, embarrassed that she did not understand their mode of speech; she felt the unfriendly eyes of the women, and she loathed the smell of liquor that filled the house now. The piano still rumbled and wailed that same song—

> "Carried me down on de Smoky Road
> Brought me back on de coolin' board
> Ahm gointer make me a graveyard of mah own."

A surge of cold, fresh air from the outside stirred the smoke and liquor fumes and Pinkie knew that the front door was open. She turned her eyes that way and thought of flight to the clean outside. The door stood wide open and a tall figure in an overcoat with a fur collar stood there.

"Good Gawd, Muttsy! Shet 'at do'," cried Shorty. "Dass a pure razor blowing out dere tonight. Ah didn't know you wuz outa here nohow."

"Carried me down on de Smoky Road
Brought me back on de coolin' board
Ahm gointer make me a graveyard of mah own," sang Muttsy, looking as if he sought someone and banged the door shut on the last words. He strode on in without removing hat or coat.

Pinkie saw in this short space that all the men deferred to him, that all the women sought his notice. She tried timidly to squeeze between two of the men and return to the quiet place beside old man Turner, thinking that Muttsy would hold the attention of her captors until she had escaped. But Muttsy spied her through the men about her and joined them. By this time her exasperation and embarrassment had her on the point of tears.

"Well, whadda yuh know about dis!" he exclaimed, "A real lil' pullet."

"Look out dere, Muttsy," drawled Dramsleg with objection, catching Pinkie by the arm and trying to draw her toward him. "Lemme tell dis lil' Pink Mama how crazy ah is 'bout her mahself. Ah ain't got no lady atall an'—"

"Aw, shut up Drams," Muttsy said sternly, "put yo' pocketbook where yo' mouf is, an' somebody will lissen. Ah'm a heavy-sugar papa. Ah eats fried chicken when the rest of you niggers is drinking rain water."

He thrust some of the others aside and stood squarely before her. With her downcast eyes, she saw his well polished shoes, creased trousers, gloved hands and at last timidly raised her eyes to his face.

"Look a heah!" he frowned, "you roughnecks done got dis baby ready tuh cry."

He put his forefinger under her chin and made her look at him. And for some reason he removed his hat.

"Come on in the sittin' room an' le's talk. Come on befo' some uh dese niggers sprinkle some salt on yuh and eat yuh clean up lak uh radish." Dramsleg looked after Muttsy and the girl as they swam through the smoke into the front room. He beckoned to Bluefront.

"Hey, Bluefront! Ain't you mah fren'?"

"Yep," answered Bluefront.

"Well, then why cain't you help me? Muttsy done done me dirt wid the lil' pig-meat—throw a louse on 'im."

Pinkie's hair was slipping down. She felt it, but her selfconsciousness prevented her catching it and down it fell in a heavy roll that spread out and covered her nearly to the waist. She followed Muttsy into the front room and again sat shrinking in the corner. She did not wish to talk to Muttsy nor anyone else in that house, but there were fewer people in this room.

"Phew!" cried Bluefront, "dat baby sho got some righteous moss on her keg—dass reg'lar 'nearrow mah Gawd tuh thee stuff." He made a lengthy gesture with his arms as if combing out long, silky hair.

"Shux," sneered Ada in a moist, alcoholic voice. "Dat ain't nothin' mah haih useter be so's ah could set on it."

There was general laughter from the men.

"Yas, ah know it's de truth!" shouted Shorty. "It's jes' ez close tuh yo' head *now* ez ninety-nine is tuh uh hund'ed."

"Ah'll call Muttsy tuh you." Ada threatened.

"Oh, 'oman, Muttsy ain't got you tuh study 'bout no mo' cause he's parkin' his heart wid dat lil' chicken wid white-folks' haih. Why, dat lil' chicken's foot would make you a Sunday face."

General laughter again. Ada dashed the whiskey glass upon the floor with the determined stalk of an angry tiger and arose and started forward.

"Muttsy Owens, uh nobody else ain't to gointer make no fool outer *me*. Dat lil' kack girl ain't gointer put *me* on de bricks—not much."

Perhaps Muttsy heard her, perhaps he saw her out of the corner of his eye and read her mood. But knowing the woman as he did he might have known what she would do under such circumstances. At any rate he got to his feet as she entered the room where he sat with Pinkie.

"Ah know you ain't lost yo' head sho' 'nuff, 'oman. 'Deed, Gawd knows you bettah go 'way f'um me." He said this in a low, steady voice. The music stopped, the talking stopped and even the drinkers paused. Nothing happened, for Ada looked straight into Muttsy's eyes and went on outside.

"Miss Pinkie, Ah votes you g'wan tuh bed." Muttsy said suddenly to the girl.

"Yes-suh."

"An' don't you worry 'bout no job. Ah knows where you kin git a good one. Ah'll go see em first an' tell yuh tomorrow night."

She went off to bed upstairs. The rich baritone of the pianoplayer came up to her as did laughter and shouting. But she was tired and slept soundly.

Ma shuffled in after eight the next morning. "Darlin', ain't you got 'nuff sleep yit?"

Pinkie opened her eyes a trifle. "Ain't you the puttiest lil' trick! An' Muttsy done gone crazy 'bout yuh! Chile, he's lousy wid money an' di-amon's an' everything— Yuh better grab him quick. Some folks has all de luck. Heah ah is—got uh man dat hates work lak de devil hates holy water. Ah gotta make dis house pay!"

Pinkie's eyes opened wide. "What does Mr. Muttsy do?"

"Mah Gawd, chile! He's de bes' gambler in three states, cards, craps un hawses. He could be a boss stevedore if he so wanted. The big boss down on de dock would give him a fat job—just begs him to take it cause he can manage the men. He's the biggest hero they got since Harry Wills left the waterfront. But he won't take it cause he makes so much wid the games."

"He's awful good-lookin," Pinkie agreed, "an' he been mighty nice tuh me—but I like men to work. I wish he would. Gamblin' ain't nice."

"Yeah, 'tis, ef you makes money lak Muttsy. Maybe yo ain't noticed dat diamon' set in his tooth. He picks women up when he wants tuh an' puts 'em down when he choose."

Pinkie turned her face to the wall and shuddered. Ma paid no attention.

"You doan hafta git up till you git good an' ready, Muttsy says. Ah mean you kin stay roun' the house 'till you come to, sorter."

Another day passed. Its darkness woke up the land east of Lenox— all that land between the railroad tracks and the river. It was very ugly by day, and night kindly hid some of its sordid homeliness. Yes, night-ime gave it life.

The same women, or others just like them, came to Ma Turner's. The same men, or men just like them, came also and treated them to liquor or mistreated them with fists or cruel jibes. Ma got half drunk as usual and cried over everyone who would let her.

Muttsy came alone and went straight to Pinkie where she sat trying to shrink into the wall. She had feared that he would not come.

"Howdy do, Miss Pinkie."

"How'do do, Mistah Owens," she actually achieved a smile. "Did you see bout m'job?"

"Well, yeah—but the lady says she won't need ya fuh uh week yet. Doan' worry. Ma ain't gointer push yuh foh room rent. Mah wrist ain't got no cramps."

Pinkie half sobbed: "Ah wantsa job now!"

"Didn't ah say dass alright? Well, Muttsy doan lie. Shux! Ah might jes' es well tell yuh—ahm crazy 'bout yuh—money no objeck."

It was the girl herself who first mentioned "bed" this night. He suffered her to go without protest.

The next night she did not come into the sitting room. She went to bed as soon as the dinner things had been cleared. Ma begged and cried, but Pinkie pretended illness and kept to her bed. This she repeated the next night and the next. Every night Muttsy came and every night he added to his sartorial splendor; but each night he went away disappointed, more evidently crestfallen than before.

But the insistence for escape from her strange surroundings grew on the girl. When Ma was busy elsewhere, she would take out the three one dollar bills from her shoe and reconsider her limitations. If that job would only come on! She felt shut in, imprisoned, walled in with these women who talked of nothing but men and the numbers and drink, and men who talked of nothing but the numbers and drink and women. And desperation took her.

One night she was still waiting for the job—Ma's alcoholic tears prevailed. Pinkie took a drink. She drank the stuff mixed with sugar and water and crept to bed even as the dizziness came on. She would not wake tonight. Tomorrow, maybe, the job would come and freedom.

The piano thumped but Pinkie did not hear; the shouts, laughter and cries did not reach her that night. Downstairs Muttsy pushed Ma into a corner.

"Looky heah, Ma. Dat girl done played me long enough. Ah pays her room rent, ah pays her boahd an' all ah gets is uh hunk of ice. Now you said you wuz gointer fix things—you tole me so las' night an' heah she done gone tuh bed on me agin."

"Deed, ah cain't do nothin' wid huh. She's thinkin' sho' nuff you goin' git her uh job and she fret so cause tain't come, dat she drunk uh toddy un hits knocked her down jes lak uh log."

"Ada an' all uh them laffin—they say ah done crapped." He felt injured. "Caint ah go talk to her?"

"Lawdy, Muttsy, dat gal dead drunk an' sleepin' lak she's buried."

"Well, caint ah go up an'—an' speak tuh her jus' the same." A yellow backed bill from Muttsy's roll found itself in Ma's hand and put her in such good humor that she let old man Turner talk all he wanted for the rest of the night.

"Yas, Muttsy, gwan in. Youse *mah* frien'."

Muttsy hurried up to the room indicated. He felt shaky inside there with Pinkie, somehow, but he approached the bed and stood for awhile looking down upon her. Her hair in confusion about her face and swinging off the bedside; the brown arms revealed and the soft lips. He blew out the match he had struck and kissed her full in the mouth, kissed her several times and passed his hand over her neck and throat and then hungrily down upon her breast. But here he drew back.

"Naw," he said sternly to himself, "ah ain't goin' ter play her wid no loaded dice." Then quickly he covered her with the blanket to her chin, kissed her again upon the lips and tipped down into the darkness of the vestibule.

"Ah reckon ah bettah git married." He soliloquized. "B'lieve me, ah will, an' go uptown wid dicties."

He lit a cigar and stood there on the steps puffing and thinking for some time. His name was called inside the sitting room several times but he pretended not to hear. At last he stole back into the room where slept the girl who unwittingly and unwillingly was making him do queer things. He tipped up to the bed again and knelt there holding her hands so fiercely that she groaned without waking. He watched her and he wanted her so that he wished to crush her in his love; crush and crush and hurt her against himself, but somehow he resisted the impulse and merely kissed her lips again, kissed her hands back and front, removed the largest diamond ring from his hand and slipped it on her engagement finger. It was much too large so he closed her hand and tucked it securely beneath the covers.

"She's *mine*!" He said triumphantly. "All mine!"

He switched off the light and softly closed the door as he went out again to the steps. He had gone up to the bed room from the sitting room boldly, caring not who knew that Muttsy Owens took what he wanted. He was stealing forth afraid that someone might *suspect* that he had been there. There is no secret love in those barrens; it is a thing to be approached boisterously and without delay or dalliance. One loves when one wills, and ceases when it palls. There is nothing sacred or hidden—all subject to coarse jokes. So Muttsy re-entered the sitting room from the steps as if he had been into the street.

"Where you been Muttsy?" whined Ada with an awkward attempt at coyness.

"What *you* wanta know for?" he asked roughly.

"Now, Muttsy you know you ain't treatin' me right, honey. How come you runnin' de hawg ovah me lak you do?"

"Git outa mah face 'oman. Keep yo' han's offa me." He clapped on his hat and strode from the house.

Pinkie awoke with a gripping stomach and thumping head.

Ma bustled in. "How yuh feelin' darlin? Youse jes lak a li'l dol baby."

"I got a headache, terrible from that ole whiskey. Thass mah first und las' drink long as I live." She felt the ring.

"Whut's this?" she asked and drew her hand out to the light.

"Dat's Muttsy' ring. Ah seen him wid it fuh two years. How'd y'all make out? He sho is one thur'bred."

"Muttsy? When? I didn't see no Muttsy."

"Dearie, you doan' hafta tell yo' bizniss ef you doan wanta. Ahm a hush-mouf. Thass all right, keep yo' bizniss to yo' self." Ma bleared her eyes wisely. "But ah know Muttsy wuz up heah tuh see yuh las' night. Doan' mine *me,* honey, gwan wid 'im. He'll treat yuh right. Ah *knows* he's crazy 'bout yuh. An' all de women is crazy 'bout *him.* Lawd! lookit dat ring!" Ma regarded it greedily for a long time, but she turned and walked toward the door at last. "Git up darlin'. Ah got fried chicking fuh breckfus' un mush melon."

She went on to the kitchen. Ma's revelation sunk deeper, then there was the ring. Pinkie hurled the ring across the room and leaped out of bed.

"He ain't goin' to make *me* none of his women—I'll die first! I'm goin' outa this house if I starve, lemme starve!"

She got up and plunged her face into the cold water on the washstand in the corner and hurled herself into the shabby clothes, thrust the three dollars which she had never had occasion to spend, under the pillow where Ma would be sure to find them and slipped noiselessly out of the house and fled down Fifth Avenue toward the Park that marked the beginning of the Barrens. She did not know where she was going and cared little so long as she removed herself as far as possible from the house where the great evil threatened her.

At ten o'clock that same morning, Muttsy Owens dressed his flashiest best, drove up to Ma's door in a cab, the most luxurious that could be hired. He had gone so far as to stick two one hundred dollar notes to the inside of the windshield. Ma was overcome.

"Muttsy, dearie, what you doin' heah so soon? Pinky sho has got you goin'. Un in a swell cab too—gee!"

"Ahm gointer git mah'ried tuh de doll baby, thass how come. An' ahm gointer treat her white too."

"Umhumh! Thass how come de ring! You oughtn't never fuhgit me, Muttsy, fuh puttin' y'all together. But ah never thought you'd mah'ry *nobody*—you allus said you wouldn't."

"An' ah wouldn't neither ef ah hadn't of seen *her*. Where she is?"

"In de room dressin'. She never tole me nothin' 'bout dis."

"She doan' know. She wuz sleep when ah made up mah mind an' slipped on de ring. But ah never miss no girl ah wants, you knows me."

"Everybody in this man's town knows you gets whut you wants."

"Naw ah come tuh take her to brek'fus 'fo we goes tuh de cote-house."

"An' y'all stay heah and eat wid me. You go call her whilst ah set de grub on table."

Muttsy, with a lordly stride, went up to Pinkie's door and rapped and waited and rapped and waited three times. Growing impatient or thinking her still asleep, he flung open the door and entered.

The first thing that struck him was the empty bed; the next was the glitter of his diamond ring upon the floor. He stumbled out to Ma. She was gone, no doubt of that.

"She looked awful funny when ah tole her you wuz in heah, but ah thought she wuz puttin' on airs." Ma declared finally.

"She thinks ah played her wid a marked deck, but ah didn't. Ef ah could see her she'd love me. Ah know she would. 'Cause ah'd make her," Muttsy lamented.

"I don't know Muttsy. She ain't no New Yorker, and she thinks gamblin' is awful."

"Zat all she got against me? Ah'll fix that up in a minute. You help me find her and ah'll do anything she says jus' so she marries me." He laughed ruefully. "Looks like ah crapped this time, don't it, ma?"

The next day Muttsy was foreman of two hundred stevedores. How he did make them work. But oh how cheerfully they did their best for him. The company begrudged not one cent of his pay. He searched diligently, paid money to other searchers, went every night to Ma's to see if by chance the girl had returned or if any clues had turned up.

Two weeks passed this way. Black empty days for Muttsy.

Then he found her. He was coming home from work. When crossing Seventh Avenue at 135th Street they almost collided. He seized her and began pleading before she even had time to recognize him.

He turned and followed her; took the employment office slip from her hand and destroyed it, took her arm and held it. He must have been very convincing for at 125th Street they entered a taxi that headed uptown again. Muttsy was smiling amiably upon the whole round world.

A month later, as Muttsy stood on the dock hustling his men to greater endeavor, Bluefront flashed past with his truck. "Say, Muttsy, you don't know what you missin' since you quit de game. Ah cleaned out de whole bunch las' night." He flashed a roll and laughed. "It don't seem like a month ago you wuz king uh de bones in Harlem." He vanished down the gangplank into the ship's hold.

As he raced back up the gangplank with his loaded truck Muttsy answered him. "And now, I'm King of the Boneheads—which being interpreted means stevedores. Come on over behind dis crate wid yo roll. Mah wrist ain't got no cramp 'cause ah'm married. You'se gettin' too sassy."

"Thought you wuzn't gointer shoot no mo'!" Bluefront temporized.

"Aw Hell! Come on back heah," he said impatiently. "Ah'll shoot you any way you wants to—hard or soft roll—you'se trying to stall. You know ah don't crap neither. Come on, mah Pinkie needs a fur coat and you stevedores is got to buy it."

He was on his knees with Bluefront. There was a quick movement of Muttsy's wrist, and the cubes flew out on a piece of burlap spread for the purpose—a perfect seven.

"Hot dog!" he exulted. "Look at dem babies gallop!" His wrist quivered again. "Nine for point!" he gloated. "Hah!" There was another quick shake and nine turned up again. "Shove in, Bluefront, shove in dat roll, dese babies is crying fuh it."

Bluefront laid down two dollars grudgingly. "You said you wuzn't gointer roll no mo' dice after you got married," he grumbled.

But Muttsy had tasted blood. His flexible wrist was already in the midst of the next play.

"Come on, Bluefront, stop bellyachin'. Ah shoots huy for de roll!" He reached for his own pocket and laid down a roll of yellow bills beside Bluefront's. His hand quivered and the cubes skipped out again. "Nine!" He snapped his fingers like a trap-drum and gathered in the money.

"Doxology, Bluefront. Git back in de line wid yo' truck an' send de others roun' heah one by one. What man can't keep one li'l wife an' two li'l bones? Hurry em up, Blue!"

HIGH BALL

In this tale, Claude McKay offers a clear depiction of life in the fast-moving burlesque stage world of the 1920s. At the same time, he reveals the verity of the adage that "poor judgments, more than chronic disease, is by far more damaging to the human condition." "High Ball" was published in two parts: May and June 1927.

In the early afternoon Nation Roe was seated at the piano practising his latest blues. He was a stout man of about 37 years, clean-shaven, with large hands, thick fingers, and a dark-brown lap of fat bulging over his collar.

Blues, blues, blues! The Dixie blues: the Charleston blues, the Alabama blues, the Tennessee blues. The honeystick blues, the brown boy blues, the fair chile blues, the beautiful blues, the Harlem blues, blues, blues!

Nation's curious alto voice, emphasizing the sudden, quavering variations, and subtle semitones that delighted New York's enthusiastic lovers of syncopation, now filled every corner of his flat, escaping through window and door to tickle the happy ears of his humble Harlem neighbors.

He paused and a voice called from the next room: "Nation, I'm thirsty."

"Want some milk for a change?" he asked.

"Naw, what good's that. I want a gingerale highball."

He opened a cabinet and, taking out a decanter of whisky, went into the adjoining room.

"No ginger ale, Myra dear," he said. "I drank the last bottle when I came in this morning."

The woman sat up in bed and with an irritated smack of her lips said: "Send Esther for some. I forgot to put in an order yesterday. But why did you drink the last bottle when you know I can't do without it?"

He mumbled some excuse and went to call the colored maid. And as he left the room, she said between her teeth: "That black fool!"

"I think I'll take a straight anyhow," she said to herself. And she reached for the decanter and poured out a big drink. She was rather a bloated coarse-fleshed woman, with freckled hands, beet colored elbows, dull-blue eyes and lumpy hair of the color of varnish.

Her husband returned and sat on the edge of a chair.

"Where did you go last night?" she asked him.

"I was out with Lieberman and some more of the fellows."

"Was it a stag?"

"No, there was a few gels there from the Argus. It was pretty good. You should have been there, but I didn't know about it till I was finished at the theatre. And when I tried to phone you, you wasn't here."

"If your gang wanted me, Nation, they'd let me know all right...."

"But they just tho't it up all of a sudden, Myra."

"They can fool you, but they can't fool me. I am one of them. They all treat me mean because I'm married to a black man, but I don't give that much for them."

She snapped her fingers.

"Don't talk like that none at all, Myra. Want me to think my white friends they don't like my having a white wife. If that was so they'd take it out on me. Now, what d'you say about that? You think Lieberman's got any feelings against us, honest now?"

"Oh, I don't mean him," cried Myra. "He and Judith are nice enough. But they pity us, that's what. Can't you see?"

"I ken see many things, but I karn't see any pity for us about George and Judith, nor kan I see anyhow that my friends resent your being my wife, Myra. I know there's lots of prejudice about that, you know—but not among ma friends."

"You're just a big boob. That's why you can't see," she said angrily. "Don't they send you invitations without mentioning me. And when I just made bold and went along with you to that party for Mae Farine— didn't they all treat me as if I was nothing?"

"I didn't notice no such thing. They were polite...."

"Yes, like a roomful of pokers."

The maid knocked at the door and brought in the gingerale. She was about twenty-two years old, soft-skinned and chestnut-complexioned. Myra poured herself a highball.

"Come, dress and let's go to the 'Skipper' for eats, Myra. You drink too much."

"Leave me alone," she retorted. "I'm sick of that old Skipper. They don't like me there either. Guess because I'm your wife."

"For Christ's sake, Myra. What's the matter with you? You say my white friends against you and you imagine the colored ones are too."

"I'm right about it too," she insisted. "I think I'll eat at home."

Nation knew, of course, that respectable Negroes, especially the women of his race, resented intermarriage between white and black. That did not worry him. What did worry him was Myra's constant hints that his white friends slighted her because she was his wife. He did not want to believe that.

From a colored cabaret in Baltimore to the glory of Broadway. That was Nation's achievement. It was a perpetual nine-days wonder in Harlem. It gave Nation a unique place in New York's theatrical circles.

A freak of chance brought the thing about. An actor-manager had an evening in Baltimore. He had no means of amusing himself in that town. He took a curious walk down Druid Hill Avenue, the street of the Afro-American aristocracy. He had asked for the Belt and was directed there: Druid Hill Avenue disappointed him. The atmosphere of conscious decency was more austere than that of Park Avenue. The actor-manager turned off into a side street. He saw a pink flare of light which advertised a Negro cabaret. It was a cheap singing-and-drinking joint. Buck-dancing and trap-drumming, too.

Nation was singing when the curious visitor entered. The regular customers eyed him furtively. It was unusual. A well-dressed white man dropping in at their joint. Nation sang with all his heart, as he always did when a personage came to the cabaret. He sang his own songs, blues, that he made up himself in bad grammar and false rhymes. Shrewd comments and sidelights on American life from a Negro's point-of-view. And that very night the actor-manager made a contract with him.

During his first year on Broadway, Nation's manager had enough trouble with him. It was the sort of trouble that his manager had never expected when he contracted with Nation.

The Metropolitan writers had praised his technique extravagantly. But Nation had become one of the big men of the Belt. He possessed the right of entry to the Belt's best homes. The Negro journals said that Nation was among the few living men of the race who served as an example and incentive to all Afro-Americans. But those very journals also said that Nation's bad grammar and false rhymes were not interpretative of the modern spirit of the Negro. . . . Nation was persuaded to put rhyme and grammar in his songs but they failed to get across to his audiences as his earlier things did. At last Nation's manager put a firm foot down on all academic improvements.

*   *   *   *

Nation found a friend in George Lieberman, a successful black-face actor. One day when he was half blacked up George said he wished he had been born colored. To which Nation at once answered: "You wouldn't never ha' said that so easy at all of you'd known what it meant to live colored."

George retorted that he knew what it was to live as a Jew.

"It aint the same thing, though," said Nation smiling broadly and good naturedly shaking his great curly bean. "It ain't the same, I tell you, brother: you ken be one of the crowd when I kaint never."

George introduced Nation to a group of his colleagues to whom real merit was a thing considered above color or condition. And in that group Nation found himself. He gained needed confidence in himself. Among those free, friendly and serious artists, Nation came to an understanding of the subleties that critics call artistry. He became certain of the finest accents of his voice, qualities that he always possessed, but of which he was never surely aware.

Nation's artistic contacts helped to give his voice a wider range and greater power. His audiences grew bigger. His pay also. And his manager smiled.

Nation's white friends invited him to parties in the downtown district.

In the earlier days of his career his walnut-brown wife from Baltimore often went with him to those parties. The first Mrs. Roe was a slim little home wife. She had drum-stick legs, but the lines of her shoulders were perfect, and white women liked her style of plaiting her fuzzy hair and making it look like a turban.

Mrs. Roe always said very little at those parties. She really had very little to say at any time. Even to Nation at home. But she enjoyed the parties. And Nation's white colleagues were nice to her. They liked her because she possessed the quality of simple charm. But Nation on his side acquired a critical attitude toward his wife. All the girls at the down-town parties were gossipy and brightly entertaining. And Nation began wishing that he had a brilliant-talking wife like one of the white actresses. . . .

—

At a Negro cabaret in the Belt, Nation met Myra Peck. Myra did not belong to the circle in which Nation's white friends moved. Her set was made up of jockeys, bookmakers, successful salesmen and cabaret actors—people who read the *Morning Telegraph* when it is hawked around in the first hours of a new day. It was a set that patronized certain notorious cabarets in the Belt, cabarets where the proprietor, the musicians, the singers and waiters were colored and the patrons almost all white. Colored persons were not made welcome at those cabarets. The few who were welcomed were known in the Belt as "Big Money" Negroes. At those cabarets white and colored people drank, chatted and danced together in a happy atmosphere.

When Myra heard who Nation was, she made strenuous, obvious efforts to attract him. Perhaps he might have been flattered and over-softened by any other white girl who went after him with as much determination as Myra. For, until his success on the stage, he had never moved freely and naturally among white people. He knew that white people were generally hostile towards him because of his color. And he always regulated his public life in anticipation of the hostility of the whites.

Even when success brought him white appaluse and new associates he was never quite sure of his ground among his white friends. Often in their company he felt instinctively that there were some things left unsaid, some things left undone, that would have been said and done if a Negro had not been among them.

But Myra showed herself to him wide open in every way. She brought the alien white world close to him. The commonplace in her turned his head because to him the commonplace had always been strange. He felt a mysterious charm in Myra's putty-colored skin; he saw a golden foam in her lumpy straw-colored hair. He divorced his Baltimore wife. He married Myra.

———

Nation himself had noticed no change in the attitude of his white associates since his second marriage. But when Myra began worrying him with her bitter resentments, he reluctantly began to notice it. At the café where they usually met down-town, his friends were very cordial, and at any special affairs he stood out as Nation Roe, the singer. He was always called upon to make a speech, often the principal speech.

He was forced to admit, however, that his white friends did not visit him very often in Harlem now. They used to before his second marriage. And they used to ask his little brown wife to visit them. But now it seemed that they managed to ask him without including Myra. He was so wrapped up in Myra, so much in love with her, that he had been blind to the slights of his friends. . . .

A little hatred began stirring in him now for all of them. What business was it of theirs if he chose to marry a white girl? And if they resented that, why should they make his wife suffer for it.

They are nice to me only because I am successful. White folks care for fame and fortune only. I won't let them start any trouble between me and Myra.

III.

Myra sat with her fat arms laid out unceremoniously on the table, a lavendar scarf arranged over her shoulders. She always began eating with gingerale highball and finished with it. Her days were filled and running over with highballs. But to Nation that did not matter. Some days when she could not get up for luncheon or when she had to put ice on her forehead and temples, he suggested that she might try milk in the mornings for a change. But Myra stuck to her highball. Sometimes she became very angry with him and he would always blame himself and bring home peace offerings of candies in the evenings.

"When I see George today, Myra, I'm going to look him square in his eyes and ask him if they'se got anything against we two."

"What's the good of saying anything to that old dumb-bell?"

"He's true blue, Myra. Would never go back on me. George and Judith are A number 1 sports. They don't mind coming up here to see us."

"It's good business for him to keep in right with you."

"I'm sure they like us, Myra. Don't be sore on George and Judith because the other p'raps. . . ."

"I'm not sore on anyone. . . . I don't care if none of those down-town snobs ever come here."

Myra hated George Lieberman and his wife. Myra said that George liked Nation because he could learn useful things from him to further his career as a blackface comedian. Nation defended George and Judith. His simple mind made him see things clearly despite his blind infatuation for Myra. He could not understand, of course, that Myra was afraid of George and Judith, that she was afraid of their obvious superiority. George and Judith really loved each other in a simple, beautiful way and Myra hated to see them together. She hated to sit down at a table and see them look at each other. And she felt almost hysterical when Nation said tender things to her before them.

"But, Myra, if you're nice to George he could fix things up. I was going to put the whole business before him."

"I don't care about them. . . . But I would like to go to some of those down-town parties."

"They're mostly stags, though. . . ."

"Stags," she sneered, "*you* men! Don't mind about me, Nation. In fact, I really don't want to go to those affairs. Honest, I don't. It's just some sort of jealousy. I don't care about anybody, as long as Dinah sticks to me."

"And me?" asked Nation. "What about me?" he laughed.

"Oh you know! I don't mean you. I mean Dinah compared to those down-town snobs."

"You're a strange mixture, Myra. I kaint tell just what you want. I wish I could, for I want to please you always."

She drank another highball.

"Don't mind me, Nation. It's nothing really. I think I want things that I really don't want, but I have to want them because my friends think I should have them. I don't want anything and I want everything."

"That's beyond me, Myra, like something outa big heavy books." And he went to his room to dress.

He returned tall, big, heavy, in his blue chinchilla overcoat. The bell rang and Dinah D'Aguilar came in. She kissed Myra affectionately with a great deal of fuss and cried, "Hello, Nation," at him in a very offhand manner.

Nation hated Dinah. She was the only white person that stirred up an instinctive feeling of aversion in him. That night when he first met Myra, at the cabaret Dinah was with her. And when he married Myra, Dinah became a permanent visitor to their flat. Dinah and Myra were everlastingly embracing and kissing each other and swilling highballs. And Nation sometimes felt that Myra was more affectionate towards Dinah than she was towards him.

Moreover he had a suspicion that Dinah was laughing at him always. In her eyes, in her voice, in her attitude, he saw mockery. When he went along to parties Dinah and Myra went together to cabarets where they caroused with their old friends. Myra was forever talking about her dear Dinah. Whatever could she do without dear Dinah. Dinah went with her shopping. Dinah went with her to the cabarets of the Belt. Dinah accompanied her to down-town places of amusement where Nation was not admitted. Myra was always giving presents to Dinah. And they were costly enough presents.

Dinah was tall and black-haired, sharp-featured and snub-nosed. Her arms were uncommonly long. Her nails were manicured to sharp and exceedingly long points. Her lips were carmine—excessively rouged. And she affected black dresses with a touch of red, black velvet slippers and purple stockings. She used to act in burlesque shows. But that was long ago. She managed to marry well, divorced her husband, got some money and now she lived without working.

Nation's dislike of her was increased by one incident which filled him with burning hate whenever he remembered it. And he remembered it very often, indeed, every time he saw her.

The incident occurred when they were all three of them dining at Skipper's Restaurant on Seventh Avenue. They had been drinking and joking and Myra said they ought to find another person and go and dance. Nation said to Dinah: "Why don't you get you'self a permanent partner?"

Dinah answered: "I didn't get rid of a dumb-bell to pick up a millstone."

"All of us ain't dumb-bells and millstones," retorted Nation.

"Well you're a good old skate all right," said Dinah. "But there aren't many like you."

"I'll look out for a good chappie for you," laughed Nation.

"Thanks," answered Dinah, "but I don't like prunes." She clapped her hand on her mouth almost before the word was off her tongue. And she added, red and embarrassed: "I don't mean you, Nation. Hope you don't mind it."

But he was terribly offended. He explained that he had really meant that he would find Dinah a friend among his white associates. And the thing was only a joke after all. Dinah agreed that the whole incident was a joke and therefore Nation shouldn't try to explain anything. If she didn't like prunes, she didn't like onions either, she said, making an awkward effort to set things right.

But Nation was raging inside of him. He kept thinking and wondering if Dinah always referred to Negroes as prunes among her white friends. Perhaps she had even said it to Myra, his own dear wife. And perhaps they had laughed together over "prunes." And he was a "prune". . . . He laughed and told Dinah it was all right. Yet he could never forget.

Buttoning up his overcoat and readjusting his brown derby on his head he kissed Myra goodbye. His hand was on the door knob when Dinah said:

"Say what about the Stunts Annual, Nation? I heard some girls talking about it last night at Fearon's Cabaret. Of course you and Myra are going. Can't you try and wheedle a ticket out of somebody for me? I'd love to go."

"I don't know that I ken. I'll try though and...."

"It would be awful nice of you, Nation. I've never been to one of their affairs."

"Nor I," said Myra. "I hear they're awful swell and funny and awfully free."

The Stunts Annual was the great yearly event of a group of actors of which George Lieberman was a leading spirit. Nation had attended last year's celebration with his first wife. They had both a very happy night of it. Walking towards the subway station Nation recalled how specially welcome Ethel was made there. Somebody had called upon her for a speech and when she wouldn't budge, everybody cried: "Speech! Speech! Speech! Mrs. Roe" amid waving of glasses and clapping of hands. And Ethel got up timid, smiling and said: "It's a great pleasure to be here among Nation's friends, but I must leave the stage entirely to him."

That made a great hit with the revellers and Nation was happy that Ethel did her simple part so well.

The feeling of his white friends for Ethel had been genuine. But Myra.... It hurt him to think that his white friends should be concerned about his marrying a woman of their race. He did not want to believe that that was true. Why should they mind about his private life? If Myra pleased him.

IV.

George Lieberman was seated in a large comfortable leather chair, indolently looking at the photographs in the *Theatre News* when Nation greeted him. George's club was perhaps the only one frequented by white people in New York where a man of Nation's complexion could be received decently. George was delighted to see Nation. His delight shone frankly in his brown eyes and roundish face. He was a compact, round-shouldered, hair-fellow-well-met-type. Nation sat down on the other side of the news-paper-strewn table. Two other actors came in. One leaned against Nation putting his elbow on his shoulder.

"Let's go round to Cruse's for a drink, fellows," he suggested.

"Excuse me, brother," said Nation. "I have a personal message for George."

George got up. And he and Nation went out together. They knew a quiet café in West Thirty-Ninth Street. The roar of the Sixth Avenue

Elevated Train drove them toward Broadway. The crowd of the great thoroughfare drove them into a taxi-cab.

The mechanically pleased face of the bartender beamed a genuine welcome to his distinguished customers. He made them a gin-fizz each.

"George," said Nation, "I am worried a tall lot about some'n. And you sure ken tell me what I want to know about this business. Don't imagine that I minds hearing the truth, even if it's a hard dose to swallow. I'd like to know just how things stand."

"Well," asked George, "What is it?"

"It's about Myra, my wife. . . ."

He hesitated, took a sip of his fizz and twirled his gold chain.

"A fight?" asked George expectantly and in a joyful tone.

"Oh Lord no!" exclaimed Nation. "It's . . . Have you fellows anything against me 'cause I'm married to a white girl?"

He said it hastily as if he were spitting a nasty fly out of his mouth.

"Gracious! No, Nation. . . . Aren't we all just the same to you?"

"To me, sure you're all right, you all are. But youse different with Myra. The Fellows don't come up to Harlem any more. And I don't seem to get any invites out with her. Mind you, I didn't notice the change myself. Myra did. And when she spoke I saw it sho'nough."

"I don't think it's anyone's business who your wife is," said George dryly. "And if we—if any of us fellows resented your marriage to a white woman—don't you think you would feel it, old man?"

"I think that too," Nation said in a low half-ashamed voice. "But Myra says I'm blind. She sees everything clear as daylight."

"Perhaps she does see something. . . ."

Nation finished his fizz and asked for another. He had been hoping that there was nothing in Myra's allegations after all and that he could go home and tell her so. In his big body there was the sensitiveness of a child. He wanted to live in simple peace, to sing his songs perfectly at each performance, chum with his white friends and go home to the exotic bosom of his Myra reeking of Pall Malls and gingerale highballs. But George's "Perhaps she does see something" made Nation ask pointedly:

"Well, is there anything against Myra herself?"

George hesitated to answer.

"Tell me, you ken tell me the truth," urged Nation, "and I don't mind. Honest to God, George, I won't mind. It'll make me feel better."

"It's nothing, really," said George guardedly, "except that your wife doesn't belong with our crowd, doesn't fit in at our affairs. But nobody holds anything against you for that. How could we?"

"I see," said Nation, "least ways I'm trying to see. But why kaint she come in with the bunch same as me?"

"Well, I'll tell you what one of the chaps thinks about it and that was exactly how the crowd felt . . . if you won't be offended."

"No, I tell you again. It's better I hear. Let's have it."

"It was put like this," said George. "If we were talking about a fish Myra would want to gut it right on the table; if it was about pigs she'd bring in the slops from the pen; if it was the sewer, she'd want to crawl into it. . . . That's awful strong talk, Nation, but you said you wanted to hear. It isn't anything really. And Myra couldn't fit in like you. Lots of the fellows don't bring their women around and the women have sense enough not to want it either."

Nation winced.

"Who was it said that about Myra, George," he asked.

"Gracious, Nation! Don't ask me that. You've just said you wanted to know the truth, but only in a general way. Myra is your wife after all and I hate the idea of me sitting here discussing her with you."

"All right, Georgie. Don't mind me, thanks," Nation said putting his hand on his friend's shoulder. "It was a bonehead question. Honest, I really don't want to know who said it!"

George asked Nation to have dinner with him at home. . . .

The table was laid for five persons. Judith Lieberman's cousin, Joseph Hyman, with his wife, was dining with them.

When they were seated around the table Nation thought to himself that it would be a nice party if his Myra were there.

Judith was a pleasant hostess. She was pretty with her shiny, short, black hair and plump peach-colored cheeks. Nation liked Judith for her simple, free manners. He liked the way in which she talked to the mulatto maid who served the dinner. She spoke in a natural, easy yet dignified manner. He thanked God Judith had not thought it necessary to introduce the maid to him and say: "Perhaps you've heard the great singer of your race," or, "She's a very intelligent girl, Mr. Roe, and she gives such excellent service."

Judith asked about Myra.

"I left Dinah with her. They have a date for this evening, I guess. Some cabaret or other. Dinah is crazy about cabarets."

"I don't care now for cabarets, since I got married," commented Judith.

"I like them sometimes," said Nation.

"Me too," agreed George. "Remember, Judith, we first met in a cabaret."

"And after that I had no reason to go any more," laughed Judith.

"I should like to go to a cabaret sometimes," said the sweet, soft, contented Mrs. Dr. Hyman. "But Joe won't go further than the theatre. He's so busy with his practice, he can't stay up late."

"You could go with my brother," said her husband. "He goes to all the dens and dives."

Mrs. Hyman pretended not to hear.

"I should think actors have a swell time of it spending all their life in theatres and cabarets," she said.

The others laughed, even her industrious husband.

"We spend a little time at home, too," said George. "But you should see some real cabaret life, Mabel. Sometimes it's just a little more tiresome than a church. What about getting up a party one of these nights?"

"I'm game if Doctor,—"

"Sure, Doc, you've got to run away from your patients one night. . . . let them live, Doc."

"Why not come to Harlem," suggested Nation. "And I'll show you all of the news that the colored jazz-hounds are putting on."

"A good idea," agreed Judith. "Last time I was up your way Dinah told me she didn't have any more time for down-town cabarets. Only the colored ones have the real spirit, she says."

"I think she's right," agreed George. "Harlem has all the real hot stuff."

Nation was feeling glad that he had turned the cabaret talk Harlemwards when Judith said:

"Why not let's go to one of these down-town places tonight after the theatre. Joe can't excuse himself out of it now. We'll just keep him here. I love to go off on a party like that without planning beforehand. It's such fun."

"All right," agreed George, "and some night we'll make up a big party for Harlem."

"That's fine!" Mrs. Hyman clapped her hands and nodded and smiled like a nice bird at her Husband.

"Nation," said Judith, "you'd better telephone Myra now and tell her to meet us after the theatre with Dinah."

Nation looked embarrassed and did not answer. George, remembering their talk in the cafe, said:

"Come on, Nation, phone Myra, and we'll have a real night of it among ourselves."

"But I couldn't go," said Nation helplessly.

"Why not!" asked Mrs. Hyman.

"Oh come on, Nation," insisted George. "It will be good fun."

"But you know I can't go," said Nation in a vexed and hurt tone, "Because . . . because I'm Negro." He blurted that out almost angrily.

The others grew red and confused. Nation excused himself to get his cigarette case from his overcoat. "It's a shocking shame!" he heard Mrs. Hyman say as he went along the hall.

It was, indeed. He shrugged his heavy shoulders. He had been placed in similar embarrassing positions, and had heard those identical words so often, that the phrase had grown trite and meaningless for him. He knew that George and Judith were the most humanly considerate persons in the world, yet they had messed him up like this tonight.

Nation knew that his friends suffered. He knew that they resented the petty limitations to which he was subjected. Yet sometimes in a burning wave of resentment he felt that his white friends made cruel blunders that bit into his flesh like this because they had never suffered so deeply.

Their way of ordering their life of work and love and play was based upon hundreds of years of tolerant tradition among themselves. It had become a commonplace routine to them and they could not accustom themselves to imagine the position of a Negro in the pattern of that frame. High imagination is the child of deep suffering, and his friends did not suffer enough.

They all went into the sitting-room for coffee and smoking. And a little later George and Nation left for the theatre. They strode along in silence. George desired to say something soothing to Nation, knowing that he was hurt, but he could not find a precisely appropriate phrase. Nation apprehended George's mood. He preferred that nothing further should be said about the incident, so he talked a great deal about nothing.

At Broadway and Forty-third street they parted a little awkwardly, each one going to his own theater.

V.

Ten o'clock in the evening. Myra, stumpy and panting, wearing a broadish maroon hat and overcoat to match, waddled lazily up the stairs. Dinah, slim, lizardlike, crept after her. Reaching the third floor Myra looked in her red leather handbag for her Yale key, inserted it in the lock and opened the door. Nation was sprawling half-dressed against the piano.

"Aren't you gone yet?" asked Myra in a loud raw voice.

"No, I don't know that I should...."

"Why not? What's the good lying around the house like this? It's so trying."

"I don't care about going without you, Myra," said Nation despondently.

His voice grated on her nerves like a saw against a nail.

"Oh shucks! What's the good in talking like that? I should have liked to go and Dinah, too, if you'd gotten the invite for us. But it's not any fault of your'n that we didn't. And why shouldn't you go and enjoy yourself? I'm not selfish."

"I won't enjoy the damned ole show at all without you.... of course most of the fellows aint taking their women...."

Dinah had seated herself and listened to the dialogue with a contemptuous and bored expression.

"You'd better finish dressing and skate along, Nation," said Myra. "I couldn't grudge you a little fun like that. Look at all the places I can go to when you can't."

"I don't want to hear none a that, Myra. I don't like it. It woulda been better we two went everywhere together, or stays home together. That would make me feel a whole lot happier."

"We can't have everything just as we want," she said. "You go on along to the Stunts. You can't afford to miss such things if you want to hold your place on the stage. Don't mind me at all. I can look after myself."

Two hours before they had quarreled and Myra had flung herself out of the flat raging. She had thought Nation would be gone by the time she returned, and she was intensely annoyed to find him still at home. She thought that sitting there so dejected, he looked ever so much like a stupid black stump of a tree, spoiling the landscape of her life.

Nation went out closing the door. Dinah, standing behind Myra's chair, put her long slim arms, enveloped in tight black satin sleeves, around her friend's fat, freckled neck. Myra put her hands up to her breast and squeezed Dinah's pretty hands.

"Darling," murmured Dinah, "sometimes I get a feeling that you really like that great big plug-ugly."

"Oh Lord, Dinah! What makes you think that way? I've got to nag at him, and be discontented, you know, acting superior-like. For he must never get it in his head that I'm like any of the cheap nigger women he's been used to."

"You clever dear," Dinah kissed Myra.

"He's a good-natured old thing, though, Dinah. Better than any hard-fisted brute of a white male."

"I should say he is," agreed Dinah.

"He pays the bills without asking any questions. And I do use up gallons of gingerale highball. He's all right as a reliable stand-by, even if I've got to shut my eyes sometimes and imagine he's somebody else."

———

Nation had been very upset when George gave him the invitation and Myra was not included in it. He almost felt that it was an insult.

"And Myra," he protested, "Myra. . . ."

"I know," said George, "I understand. Judith isn't going either nor Bert Roach's wife. It's nothing personal why Myra isn't invited."

George explained to Nation that they had taken in many new members in the course of the year and that it had been a problem to hold the party down to the usual size so that it should keep its old intimate and friendly atmosphere. For that reason the Committee had decided to have as guests only a few people actively connected with the stage and many friends and relations had been left out.

George was angry with himself for having lied. Yet he could not tell Nation that the Committee had barred Myra because she was undesirable. Now he would have to ask Anna Roach and Judith to stay away from the party. George wondered if he could persuade Anna! The Roaches did not understand and feel about Nation as George and Judith did.

As George walked away he thought how dreadful it was that Nation should be burdened with Myra. Good God! How could a man with such a beautiful voice put up with such a coarse cow. I wonder if something is always lacking in Negroes the way they say? Was Nation blind? Had his discriminating faculties deserted him when he entered upon his career? He had sung his way into the heart of the great white public. How could he forget about his race? Forget that he was a living lifelong problem and pick up the burden of a Myra on top of that problem?

Nation received a warm ovation when he walked into the reception room of the Stunts Annual. Ferns, palms and evergreens were ranged against the walls. The Platform was banked with a profusion of large white chrysanthemums, pink carnations and red geraniums. Half-hidden behind the flowers were the Negro musicians from the Harmony Club. The banqueting table was crowned with three green baskets filled with American Beauties. A Stars and Stripes was suspended like a vast bowl over the platform. Buntings of blue, white and red zig-zagged around the ceiling, and paper streamers, hung low, ran diagonally across. The evening's surprise, planned by the Recreation Committee, was the tiny pennants hearing the name of his theatre that each actor found beside his plate. The pennants were in various colors and very pretty under the rainbow-striped Chinese lantern that hid the electric globe.

The attendants were white. They wore light green uniforms. The actors dressed as they pleased, some in Tuxedo coats and soft white shirts and some in dark sports suits. There was a sprinkling of Pierrots and some Harlequins. But it was the women that were radiant and oh so fascinating in all the warm tropical colors that women alone can wear!

Nation was seated between George and the petite sunny-haired Mae Farine, the clever actress of sentimental comedies, whose skin was white and sweet like the petal of an apple blossom. Opposite were the Roaches. Anna smiled intimately at Nation and he wondered that she was there and remarked it to George.

"She came in just a little before you with a message for Bert," George explained, "and the fellows wouldn't let her go. . . . You know how it is when they're stewed a little."

Nation also noticed a sprinkling of gay girls that he knew were not connected with the stage. But Judith at any rate, was conspicuously absent. Nation felt confident that George had not hoaxed him.

The cocktails were very dry and worked rapidly. And before the rich plum cake and the tutti frutti ice cream were served, the champagne had already reduced everyone present to a happy playful state of relaxation. The green-uniformed servitors were having their own high time downstairs, you could tell that by the way they lifted up their feet and by the hot color of their ears. Those black boys behind the white chrysanthemums were getting their share too. You knew that they were by the gleam of their teeth.

A crazy-love-warmed boy tossed a tangerine at Mae Farine's golden head and immediately a little war was on. Bits of biscuits, candies, American Beauties—everything was commandeered and sent flying at ducking heads amid cascades of laughter. Seats were exchanged, seats were left vacant, window sills were invaded.

And Nation forgot everything and entered wholeheartedly into the fun. Down in one corner of the room, Anna Roach and a group of girls had tied a red silk handkerchief over his eyes and were playing Blind Man's buff with him. It was past midnight when he was yelled at to do some special thing. To sing a little song or make a little speech before the dancing began.

And in the midst of the whistling and hand-clapping for Nation, Judith walked in wrapped up in a fortune of furs. She said her taxicab was waiting outside. She was passing and dropped in to say a word to George. Some one cried: "You should have been here long ago!" Mae Farine shrilled: "Send the taxi away!" Judith was surrounded and divested of her furs. She was beautiful in a fine-fitting cerise frock and a string of pearls.

Nation's thoughts darkened. Surely he had been fooled. Judith's coming at that hour was not accidental. George had planned it. Nation's head was heavy from champagne but his faculties were working all right enough. The party became a rotten and cheap affair for him. "I won't stand this cussed crowd any longer," he thought.... "Trying to make a fool baby of me because I'm black and lonely. Myra is as good as any of them here. Why should they have any objection to her? Myra is a good sport. If there's any difference between her and these here women I kain't see it. Myra was right. They despise me because I'm married to a white woman...."

"Speech, speech, Nation!".... "Ho, Nation, sing us the Brownboy Blues".... "No, let's have the Harlem Blues".... "No! No! Not Harlem. ... The Charleston!" "The Charleston! The Charleston!" cried a chorus of voices. "The Charleston, Nation."

Nation's head reeled. He gripped the table.... "Leave me be, you crackers. Youse all a gang of damned peckaround hypocrites."

The revellers were struck-dumb with amazement: shocked into soberness.

Horrified, George rushed up to Nation and took hold of his arms. But Nation shook him off with an angry gesture. He felt like a wild bull. He dashed from the room. The green-uniformed Greek in the cloakroom helped him into his overcoat. He took the first taxicab for Harlem.

"I don't care.... I don't care.... I don't care," he kept on repeating to himself. "I don't care for stupid gaiety and a cheap bunch of hypocritical friends. All I want is Myra, nothing more than Myra...."

When Nation let himself into the apartment house he heard an unusual noise. And as he mounted the third floor sounds of laughter and intermittent chords from the piano came from his flat.

Myra must have gotten lonely and asked a few friends up to amuse herself. Poor Myra! I'll enjoy this better than the Stunts.

His hand was on the doorknob when he heard Dinah say: "Here's your highball, Myra. Let's all drink to the success of the good old prune."

There was a general clinking of glasses and a typsy young male voice cried: "Here's to prune, prune, prune, our nation. . . . al prune."

Nation recognized the voice as that of a pretty young habitue of Fearon's cabaret who often went dancing with Dinah. He was nicknamed Lord Percy.

Nation stood stone still, dropping his head. He heard Myra call imperiously precisely as she used to call him: "Hand me another drink. . . . God damn you, Percy, I don't want a straight. I want a . . ."

Perhaps, Nation's spirit blazed so fiercely that the flames reached through to Myra inside. For without visible reason she staggered over to the door and opened it and saw Nation standing there. She backed and fluttered heavily away into the center of the room like a frightened duck.

Nation walked into the midst of them. Myra's guests glanced at his dark face and sneaked away as quickly as they could.

But Dinah remained.

"Get out!" cried Nation.

Dinah fled.

"And you, too," he exclaimed, jerking his thumb at Myra.

"Me! I can't leave here like this . . . My things. . . ."

"You'll find them on the sidewalk tomorrow."

"But what have I done? Where can I go! I am—am I not—ain't I married to you . . . your wife?"

"Look a here, white woman . . . Go on away from me *right now.* Leave me alone with God!"

She had never before heard his voice like that. She looked into his eyes and cleared out.

Nation looked around the room at the glasses half-filled with red and yellow liquor. It seemed as though a crowd of white insects were still sitting there and screaming "Prune! Prune!! Prune!!!"

He had a sharp thought of George Lieberman and the friends he had so grossly insulted. He remembered his colored wife, Ethel Roe. She could never have said "prune" and made it hurt him.

He quivered. His heavy frame shook. He knelt down against the liquor stained piano and bellowed like a wounded bull.

Fog

Published in May 1925, this story was awarded first prize. John F. Matheus writes about people of various races who are traveling by bus and a near-fatal incident occurs. Matheus brilliantly shows how such a common undergoing can obliterate the narrowly perceived chasms.

The stir of life echoed. On the bridge between Ohio and West Virginia was the rumble of heavy trucks, the purr of high power engines in Cadillacs and Paiges, the rattle of Fords. A string of loaded freight cars pounded along on the C. & P. tracks, making a thunderous, if tedious way to Mingo. A steamboat's hoarse whistle boomed forth between the swish, swish, chug, chug of a mammoth stern paddle wheel with the asthmatic poppings of the pistons. The raucous shouts of smutty speaking street boys, the noises of a steam laundry, the clank and clatter of a pottery, the godless voices of women from Water Street houses of ill fame, all these blended in a sort of modern babel, common to all the towers of destruction erected by modern civilization.

These sounds were stirring when the clock sounded six on top of the Court House, that citadel of Law and Order, with the statue of Justice looming out of an alcove above the imposing stone entrance, blindfolded and in her right hand the scales of Judgment. Even so early in the evening the centers from which issued these inharmonious notes were scarcely visible. This sinister cloak of a late November twilight Ohio Valley fog had stealthily spread from somewhere beneath the sombre river bed, down from somewhere in the lowering West Virginia hills. This fog extended its tentacles over city and river, gradually obliterating traces of familiar landscapes. At five-thirty the old Panhandle bridge supported by massive sandstone pillars, stalwart, as when erected fifty years before to serve a generation now passed behind the portals of life, this *old* bridge had become a spectral outline against the sky as the toll keepers of the *new* bridge looked northward up the Ohio River.

Now at six o'clock the fog no longer distorted; it blotted out, annihilated. One by one the street lights came on, giving an uncertain glare in spots, enabling peeved citizens to tread their way homeward without recognizing their neighbor ten feet ahead, whether he might be Jew or Gentile, Negro or Pole, Slav, Croatian, Italian or one hundred per cent American.

An impatient crowd of tired workers peered vainly through the gloom to see if the headlights of the interurban car were visible through the thickening haze. The car was due at Sixth and Market at six-ten and was scheduled to leave at six-fifteen for many little towns on the West Virginia side.

At the same time as these uneasy toilers were waiting, on the opposite side of the river the car had stopped to permit some passengers to descend and disappear in the fog. The motorman, flagged and jaded by the monotony of many stopping and starting waited mechanically for the conductor's bell to signal, "Go ahead."

The fog was thicker, more impenetrable. It smothered the headlight. Inside the car in the smoker, that part of the seats nearest the motorman's box, partitioned from the rest, the lights were struggling bravely against a fog of tobacco smoke, almost as opaque as the dull grey blanket of mist outside.

A group of red, rough men, sprawled along the two opposite bench-formed seats, parallel to the sides of the car, were talking to one another in the thin, flat colorless English of their mountain state, embellished with the homely idioms of the coal mine, the oil field, the gas well.

"When does this here meetin' start, Bill?"

"That air notice read half after seven."

"What's time now?"

"Damned 'f I know. Hey, Lee, what time's that pocket clock of yourn's got?"

"Two past six."

There was the sound of a match scratching against the sole of a rough shoe.

"Gimme a light, Lafe."

In attempting to reach for the burning match before its flame was extinguished, the man stepped forward and stumbled over a cheap suitcase of imitation leather. A vile looking stogie fell in the aisle.

"God! Your fee're bigger'n Bills's."

The crowd laughed uproariously. The butt of this joke grinned and showed a set of dirty nicotine stained teeth. He recovered his balance in time to save the flaring match. He was a tremendous man, slightly stooped, with taffy colored, straggling hair and little pig eyes.

Between initial puffs he drawled: "Now you're barkin' up the wrong tree. I only wear elevens."

"Git off'n me, Lee Cromarty," growled Bill. "You hadn't ought to be rumlin' of *my* feathers the wrong way—and you a-plannin' to ride the goat."

Lake, a consumptive appearing, undersized, bovine eyed individual, spat out the remark: "Naow, there! You had better be kereful. Men have been nailed to the cross for less than that."

"Ha! ha!—ho! ho! ho!"

There was a joke to arouse the temper of the crowd.

A baby began to cry lustily in the rear and more commodious end of the car reserved for nonsmokers. His infantine wailing smote in sharp contrast upon the ears of the hilarious joshers, filling the silence that followed the subsidence of the laughter.

"Taci, bimba. Non aver paura!"

Nobody understood the musical words of the patient, Madonna eyed Italian mother, not even the baby, for it continued its yelling. She opened her gay, colored shirt waist and pressed the child to her bosom. He was quieted.

"She can't speak United States, but I bet her Tony Spaghetti votes the same as you an' me. The young 'un 'll have more to say about the future of these Nunited States than your children an' mine unless we carry forward the word such as we are going to accomplish tonight."

"Yeh, you're damned right," answered the scowling companion of the lynx-eyed citizen in khaki clothes, who had thus commented upon the foreign woman's offspring.

"They breed like cats. They'll outnumber us, unless——"

A smell of garlic stifled his speech: Nich and Mike Axaminter, late for the night shift at the La Belle, bent over the irate American deluging him with the odor of garlic and voluble gutteral explosions of a Slavak tongue.

"What t' hell! Git them buckets out o' my face, you hunkies, you!"

Confused and apologetic the two men moved forward.

———

"Isn't this an awful fog, Barney," piped a gay, girlish voice.

"I'll tell the world it is," replied her red-haired companion, flinging a half smoked cigarette away in the darkness as he assisted the girl to the platform.

They made their way to a vacant seat in the end of the car opposite the smoker, pausing for a moment respectfully to make the sign of the cross before two Sisters of Charity, whose flowing black robes and ebon headdress contrasted strikingly with the pale whiteness of their faces. The nuns raised their eyes, slightly smiled and continued their orisons on dark decades of rosaries with pendant crosses of ivory.

"Let's sit here," whispered the girl. "I don't want to be by those niggers."

In a few seconds they were settled. There were cooings of sweet words, limpid-eyed soul glances. They forgot all others. The car was theirs alone.

"Say, boy, ain't this some fog. Yuh can't see the old berg."

" 'Sthat so. I hadn't noticed."

Two Negro youths thus exchanged words. They were well dressed and sporty.

"Well, it don't matter, as long as it don't interfere with the dance."

"I hope Daisy will be there. She's some stunnin' high brown an' I don't mean maybe."

"O boy!"

Thereupon one began to hum "Daddy, O Daddy" and the other whistled softly the popular air from "Shuffle Along" entitled "Old-Fashioned Love."

"Oi, oi! Ven I say vill dis car shtart. Ve must mek dot train fur Pittsburgh."

"Ach, Ish ka bibble. They can't do a thing without us, Laban."

They settled down in their seats to finish the discussions in Yiddish, emphasizing the conversation with shrugs of the shoulder and throaty interjections.

In a seat apart to themselves, for two seats in front and behind were unoccupied, sat an old Negro man and a Negro woman, evidently his wife. Crowded between them was a girl of fourteen or fifteen.

"This heah is suah cu'us weather," complained the old man.

"We all nevah had no sich fog in Oklahoma."

The girl's hair was bobbed and had been straightened by "Poro" treatment, giving her an Egyptian cast of features.

"Gran'pappy," said the girl, "yo' cain't see ovah yander."

"Ain't it de troot, chile."

"Ne' min', sugah," assured the old woman. "Ah done paid dat 'ployment man an' he sayed yo' bound tuh lak de place. Dis here lady what's hirin yo' is no po' trash an' she wants a likely gal lak yo' tuh ten' huh baby."

———

Now these series of conversations did not transpire in chronological order. They were uttered more or less simultaneously during the interval that the little conductor stood on tiptoe in an effort to keep one hand on the signal rope, craning his neck in a vain and dissatisfied endeavor to pierce the miasma of the fog. The motorman chafed in his box, thinking of the drudging lot of the laboring man. He registered discontent.

The garrulous group in the smoker were smouldering cauldrons of discontent. In truth their dissatisfaction ran the gamut of hate. It was stretching out to join hands with an unknown and clandestine host to plot, preserve, defend their dwarfted and twisted ideals.

The two foreign intruders in the smoker squirmed under the merciless, half articulate antipathy. They asked nothing but a job to make some money. In exchange for that magic English word job, they endured the terror that walked by day, the boss. They grinned stupidly at profanity, dirt, disease, disaster. Yet they were helping to make America.

Three groups in the car on this foggy evening were united under the sacred mantle of a common religion. Within its folds they sensed vaguely a something of happiness. The Italian mother radiated the joy of her child. Perhaps in honor of her and in reverence the two nuns with downcast eyes, trying so hard to forget the world, were counting off the rosary of the blessed Virgin—"Ave, Maria," "Hail, Mary, full of grace, the Lord is with thee; blessed art thou among women."

The youth and his girl in their tiny circle of mutual attraction and affection could not as in Edwin Markham's poem widen the circle to include all or even to embrace that small circumscribed area of humanity within the car.

And the Negroes? Surely there was no hate in their minds. The gay youths were rather indifferent. The trio from the South, journeying far for a greater freedom of self expression philosophically accepted the inevitable "slings and arrows of outrageous fortune."

The Jews were certainly enveloped in a racial consciousness, unerringly fixed on control and domination of money, America's most potent factor in respectability.

The purplish haze of fog contracted. Its damp presence slipped into the car and every passenger shivered and peered forth to see. Their eyes were as the eyes of the blind!

At last the signal bell rang out staccato. The car suddenly lurched forward, shaking from side to side the passengers in their seats. The wheels scraped and began to turn. Almost at once a more chilling wetness filtered in from the river. In the invisibility of the fog it seemed that one was traveling through space, in an aeroplane perhaps, going nobody knew where.

The murmur of voices buzzed in the smoker, interrupted by the boisterous outbursts of laughter. A red glare tinted the fog for a second and disappeared. La Belle was "shooting" the furnaces. Then a denser darkness and the fog.

The car lurched, scintillating sparks flashed from the trolley wire, a terrific crash—silence. The lights went out. Before anybody could think or scream, there came a falling sensation, such as one experiences when dropped unexpectedly in an elevator or when diving through the scenic railways of the city amusements parks, or more exactly when one has nightmare and dreams of falling, falling, falling.

"The bridge has given way. God! The muddy water! The fog! Darkness. Death."

These thoughts flashed spontaneously in the consciousness of the rough ignorant fellows, choking in the fumes of their strong tobacco, came to the garlic scented "hunkies", to the Italian Madonna, to the sisters of Charity, to the lover boy and his lover girl, to the Negro youths, to the Jews thinking in Yiddish idioms, to the old Negro man and his wife and the Egyptian-faced girl, with the straightened African hair, even to the bored motorman and the weary conductor.

To drown, to strangle, to suffocate, to die! In the dread silence the words screamed like exploding shells within the beating temples of terror-stricken passengers and crew.

Then protest, wild, mad, tumultuous, frantic protest. Life at bay and bellowing furiously against its ancient arch-enemy and antithesis—Death. An oath; screams,—dull, paralyzing, vomit—stirring nausea. Holy, unexpressed intimacies, deeply rooted prejudices were roughly shaken from their smug moorings. The Known to be changed for an Unknown, the ever expected, yet unexpected, Death. No! No! Not that.

Lee Cromarty saw things in that darkness. A plain, one-story frame house, a slattern woman on the porch, an overgrown, large hipped girl with his face. Then the woman's whining, scolding voice and the girl's bashful confidences. What was dimming that picture? What cataract was blurring his vision? Was it the fog?

To Lafe, leader of the crowd, crouched in his seat, his fingers clawing the air for a grasping place, came a vision of a hill-side grave,—his wife's—and he saw again how she looked in her coffin—then the fog.

"I'll not report at the mine," thought Bill. "Wonder what old Bunner will say to that."

The mine foreman's grizzled face dangled for a second before him and was swallowed in the fog.

Hoarse, gasping exhalations. Men, old men, young men, sobbing. "Pietà! Madre mia!—Mercy Virgin Mary! My child!"

No thoughts of fear or pain on the threshold of death, that shadow from whence all children flow, but all the Mother Love focused to save the child.

"*Memorare*, remember, O most gracious Virgin Mary, that never was it known that any one who fled to thy protection, implored thy help and sought thy intercession was left unaided."

The fingers sped over the beads of the rosary. But looming up, unerasable, shuttled the kaleidoscope of youth, love, betrayal, renunciation, the vows. *Miserere, Jesu!*

> "Life is ever lord of Death
> And Love can never lose its own."

The girl was hysterical, weeping, screaming, laughing. Did the poet dream an idle dream, a false mirage? Death is master. Death is stealing Love away. How could a silly girl believe or know the calm of poesie?

The boy crumbled. His swagger and bravado melted. The passionate call of sex became a blur. He was not himself, yet he was looking at himself, a confusion in space, in night, in Fog. And who was she hanging limp upon his arm?

That dance? The jazz dance? Ah, the dance! The dance of Life was ending. The orchestra was playing a dirge and Death was leading the Grand March. Fog! Impenetrable fog!

All the unheeded, forgotten warnings of ranting preachers, all the prayers of simple black mothers, the Mercy-Seat, the Revival, too late. Terror could give no articulate expression to these muffled feelings. They came to the surface of a blunted consciousness, incoherent.

Was there a God in Israel? Laban remembered Russia and the pogrom. He had looked into the eyes of Fate that day and watched God die with his mother and sisters. Here he was facing Fate again. There was no answer. He was silent.

His companion sputtered, fumed, screeched. He clung to Laban in pieces.

Laban remembered the pogrom. The old Negro couple remembered another horror. They had been through the riots in Tulsa. There they had lost their son and his wife, the Egyptian-faced girl's father and mother. They had heard the whine of bullets, the hiss of flame, the howling of human wolves, killing in the most excruciating manner. The water was silent. The water was merciful.

The old woman began to sing in a high quavering minor key:
"Lawdy, won't yo' ketch mah groan,
O Lawdy, Lawdy, won't yo' ketch mah groan."
The old man cried out: "Judgment! Judgment!"
The Egyptian-faced girl wept. She was sore afraid, sore afraid. And the fog was round about them.

Time is a relative term. The philosophers are right for once. What happened inside the heads of these men and women seemed to them to have consumed hours instead of seconds. The conductor mechanically grabbed for the trolley rope, the motorman threw on the brakes.

The reaction came. Fear may become inarticulate and paralyzed. Then again it may become belligerent and self-protective, striking blindly in the maze. Darkness did not destroy completely the sense of direction.

"The door! The exit!"

A mad rush to get out, not to be trapped without a chance, like rats in a trap.

"Out of my way! Damn you—out of my way!"

Somebody yelled: "Sit still!"

Somebody hissed: "Brutes! Beasts!"

Another concussion, accompanied by the grinding of steel. The car stopped, lurched backward, swayed, and again stood still. Excited shouts re-echoed from the ends of the bridge. Automobile horns tooted. An age seemed to pass, but the great splash did not come. There was still time—maybe. The car was emptied.

"Run for the Ohio end!" someone screamed.

The fog shut off every man from his neighbor. The sound of scurrying feet reverberated, of the Italian woman and her baby, of the boy carrying his girl, of the Negro youths, of the old man and his wife, half dragging the Egyptian-faced girl, of the sisters of Charity, of the miners. Flitting like wraiths in Homer's Hades, seeking life.

In five minutes all were safe on Ohio soil. The bridge still stood. A street light gave a ghastly glare through the fog. The whore houses on Water Street brooded evily in the shadows. Dogs barked, the Egyptian-faced girl had fainted. The old Negro woman panted, "Mah Jesus! Mah Jesus!"

The occupants of the deserted car looked at one another. The icy touch of the Grave began to thaw. There was a generous intermingling. Everybody talked at once, inquiring, congratulating.

"Look after the girl," shouted Lee Cromarty. "Help the old woman, boys."

Bells began to ring. People came running. The ambulance arrived. The colored girl had recovered. Then everybody shouted again. Profane miners, used to catastrophe, were strangely moved. The white boy and girl held hands.

"Sing us a song, old woman," drawled Lafe.

"He's heard mah groan. He done heard it," burst forth the old woman in a song flood of triumph.

> "Yes, he conquered Death and Hell,
> An' He never said a mumblin' word,
> Not a word, not a word."

"How you feelin', Mike," said Bill to the garlic eater.

"Me fine. Me fine."

The news of the event spread like wildfire. The street was now crowded. The police arrived. A bridge official appeared, announcing the probable cause of the accident, a slipping of certain supports. The girders fortunately had held. A terrible tragedy had been prevented.

"I'm a wash-foot Baptist an' I don't believe in Popery," said Lake, "but, fellers, let's ask them ladies in them air mournin' robes to say a prayer of thanksgiving for the bunch."

The Sisters of Charity did say a prayer, not an audible petition for the ears of men, but a whispered prayer for the ears of God, the Benediction of Thanksgiving, uttered by the Catholic Church through many years, in many tongues and places.

"De profundis," added the silently moving lips of the white-faced nuns. "Out of the depths have we cried unto Thee, O Lord. And Thou hast heard our cries."

The motorman was no longer dissatisfied. The conductor's strength had been renewed like the eagle's.

"Boys," drawled Lake, "I'll be damned if I'm goin' to that meetin' tonight."

"Nor me," affirmed Lee Cromarty.

"Nor me," repeated all the others.

The fog still crept from under the bed of the river and down from the lowering hills of West Virginia—dense, tenacious, stealthy, chilling, but from about the hearts and minds of some rough, unlettered men another fog had begun to life.

CLAY

John F. Matheus's obvious firsthand knowledge and proficiency in description of "nature" of his story's locale are strong contrasts to the unlettered dialect of his characters. He deftly labels them "marionettes of clay pulled by the strings of chance in the hands of destiny." His circuitous fable and symbolism show that, contrary to intentions and the minds of humankind, there is neither discrimination nor mercy in the clay, in the storm, or in other works of the Divine Order. This story was published in October 1926.

A maroon ox, broad chested and thin of flank, was munching leisurely of the spare wire grass, which struggled for two feet from the paved street before succumbing finally to the hard, red clay of the town market. An anemic, hatchet face cracker woman—her stringy, mud colored hair plastered down over her round head, was sitting on a rough pine board in the front of a cart behind the munching ox. She was selling salted mullets to a fat, black woman, clad in a pink shirtwaist, spotted with purple polka dots, a white and red calico skirt, brown stockings wrinkling over thick ankles, and low shoes run down at the heels. A rusty spring balance glittered in splotches from incrustations of dried fish scales, scintillating in the sun.

Rank, fetid smell of gray mullets, flounders, trout, fresh-water bream struck the nostrils. A buzz of flies, big, bluebottle flies, vied with the persistent hum of mosquitoes. Goading gnats flitted with impunity in the eyes of man and beast.

A few yards away, across a clay aisle, a brown youth, tall and thin, with drooping moustache, was selling bloody beef.

Clumps of cushaws, watermelons, early yams, okra pods, ghastly onions with withered ends made lackadaisical appeal to wary, hungry buyers.

The air was languid. The relentless heat beat upon oxen, mules and men. The indifferent bargainers were stifling. Ants, darting hither and thither, diabolically thorough, were darkening chunks of flesh, tugging at bits of grain, quite oblivious of the human ants tugging less industriously in the world above them. Straggling chickens scratched and picked in piles of dung. Dirty daubers, local name of the mud Wasp, with hunks of oozy clay in their long hind legs, skimmed over the market square toward mud houses they were building somewhere to harbor new generations of dirty daubers.

This plebeian insect seemed to mirror the lives of these poor people, white and black, shuttling back and forth through the curb market of the quaint and insipid Dixie town, typical of the far South. Worn-out farmers, hook-worm, malaria and pellagra victims, robbed by landlords, impoverished by taxes, boll weevils, corn worms, fruit lice and potato bugs, had dug so long in plots of clay land that their drawn and lusterless faces had become stamped with clay, with the brand of clay. They were of the "earth earthy," primitive in their wants and in ways and means of satisfying them, crude, brutal, emotional in their religious practices, dulled brothers of the soil, peasants of the clay hills and muck lands.

Unlike the dirty daubers they went about the business of living with no direct assurance, with none of the dispatch that seems to say: "I know where I am going and I must hasten there."

"Wha' yo', boy?" said the fat, black woman, looking about her.

"Hyah me, mammy," answered a ragged, snotty-nosed urchin, whose nappy head was covered with cotton burs.

"Tote dese hyah fishes tuh yo' pappy ovah yandah an' tell'm tuh put 'em in de caht."

"Yassum," said the offspring, combining action with affirmation.

The Saturday crowd grew larger. Dilapidated Ford trucks appeared, rattling and back firing audaciously, as if, being more aristocratic than the miscellany of wheeled vehicles that had preceded them to the market, they had a right to arrive later, demand the best stands and get them.

In one truck, newer than the others, appeared a load of brown earthen jugs, labeled, "CANE SYRUP."

"The las' o' las' yeah's crap," lamented the best shouldered white man, driver of the truck and vendor of the stuff.

"An' the best," he continued, shifting a cud of tobacco from his right to his left cheek.

"Wal, gimme a pint," muttered an evil looking, hard fisted man, whose face, red and bloated, leered in perpetual scowl.

"Am a gunnin' this mo'nin', Jim, fo' a niggah wut stole a caow o' mine."

"Naow look heah, Dick Rivers, don't staht no fuss head. Let us boys tek kere o' it fo' yo'."

"Nope—this here's mah business an' ah reckon mah job."

" 'Scuse mah, sah, 'scuse mah," whined a voice apologetically, "but, bu-but Mistar Singlereed don' sont mah hyah fo' er jug an' he tol' mah Ah mought have a pint, he did, for' mahself."

"Wait a minute, ol' niggah. Don' yo' see he's talkin' tuh a *white* man," interjected the scowling countenance.

" 'Scuse mah, sah." The thin voice died away into inaudible air.

"Tha's ol' Jarvis Singlereed's niggah," whispered the syrup seller.

"Wal, tuh hell with him, too. He's no frien' to a po' white man. Hard as his coffin nails," sputtered the angry man, shaking his fist in the direction of a two-story, squat, brick building, which rose, abruptly across the paved street, opposite the market square.

"JARVIS SINGLEREED
LIVERY AND UNDERTAKING ESTABLISHMENT"

The black letters of the huge sign leaped at one from the whiteness of the background, dazzling in the sun.

The "syrup" vendor looked nervously around. Then he slipped a flask into the hip pocket of the irate iconoclast of the curb market.

"Naow don't spile mah business, Dick Rivers. Remember what ah done tol' yo'."

Dick Rivers turned his evil face, as he stealthily hid the unexpected boon, and shambled away toward the munching ox and the hatchet face cracker woman.

"Howdy, Miss Ma'y Jane," he muttered, towering above the wheel of the cart in vain essay of kindly tone.

"Howdy, Dick. How's yo' fam'ly. Yo' ol' woman an' chillun, Ah mean."

"Po' ez Job's turkeys with niggahs stealin' ouah caows."

He whispered something to her. She looked up quickly.

"Ain't that him ovah thar?"

He glanced across the intervening aisle of clay.

The babble of bargaining had drowned the lazy humming of the insect world. The Negro vendors were in the other side of the dividing clay line where scowling Dick was peering. Negro buyers suffered no segregation. Less drawn than the whites in their broad features, more like the maroon ox, the Negroes bore, nevertheless, the indelible mark of the clayey land.

Clay was the symbol of their livelihood. Stamped on their gnarled, plowman fingers, ground in the spreading toes of their ebon women, wide hipped and shaking bosomed, with band and turbans and snuff between their teeth, clay colored snuff, the soil seemed to reach up like some giant earth octopus and suck them into itself. The very children, unkempt and unlettered, cane syrup caked and smeared on their winsome faces, seemed too but an inseparable part of that mud monster.

The emaciated, narrow-chested hill billies, with no power in their lungs to cut off the interminable drawl of their talking, their women flat-breasted and hungry-eyed, their children puny and spindle-shanked, lounged and relaxed from the fierce struggle of a meaningless existence.

Puppets they were all, marionettes of clay, pulled by the strings of chance in the hands of destiny. Today the sun was baking the land, burning their scanty crops, of black and white alike. To-morrow perhaps it would rain and liquify the clay, this same clay, ploughed and tilled by the dwellers there of hill and dale, rewarding or thwarting without benefit of favor. The gamble was understood by all; the stakes at best were meager, a mere, gaunt sustenance. That was the one unfailing certainty. All else was hazard.

Old wiseacres, adept in nature's lore felt a weather change approaching.

"Too hot an' steamy," they croaked.

The tree frogs joined them and the rain birds shrieked.

The tragedy happened quickly as such things occur. Dick Rivers had pushed his way through the sweating crowd. The tall, brown youth was cutting the bloody beef, a stew for the fat, black woman. His back was turned to the crowd, his strong muscular fingers were red with coagulating beef gore. The long, slim knife sped through the flesh.

A curse, hoarse, staccato, shot through the air.

"Yo' thievin' skunk, you stole mah caow. Don't deny it," shrilly challenged the voice. "I traced the blood to you' niggah nest."

The crowd drew back before the white man, outraged, terrible in his wrath. The Negro turned deliberately fingering the knife.

" 'Twas mah beef," he retorted. "Yo' beat Ike Jimeson out o' his land' an' his wages, but you'll not beat Ike Jimeson's son. Lemme alone."

More oaths.

"Ah'll puncture yo' lyin' black hide," yelled the white man, reaching for his revolver.

A flash of brown fingers, a whizzing knife, a muffled stroke, an outcry, a dull thud—the body as it struck the clay.

Nobody moved. Not a sound. Black faces turned ashen.

The Negro backed against the beef stand, stumbling. His forehead was covered with cold sweat.

Then bedlam broke loose.

"Kill 'im, hang 'im, burn 'im."

The hatchet-faced cracker woman screamed, the fat, black woman screamed, children yelled, black men recoiled, white men bellowed, gathered brick bats, drew guns and revolvers. A deputy sheriff, risen up from God knows where, attempted to reach his prisoner.

Two shots simultaneously exploded. Without a word the drooping moustache drooped lower, the brown face grimaced, the body crumpled and fell. The thirsty clay was drinking blood.

Old man Jarvis Singlereed, hearing the noise looked out of his office window from the second floor of his livery and undertaking establishment. He had often peeped thus upon the Saturday market crowds. In his heart he despised all the common throng. He counted them with his mules, these niggers and crackers. They all labored for him directly or indirectly. They worked his plantations for a pittance. Misanthrope and hypocrite, he loaned them money. From patrician forebears he had inherited an almost equal disdain for Negroes and poor whites. Yet the prestige of this inheritance of aristocracy had carried him ahead. He was the political leader and big man of the section.

The whistle of the cotton gin down by the Sea Board yards was blowing for the end of the noon hour when Jarvis Singlereed looked upon his little world. Two men were writhing in their Golgotha. Now it was all over for them. The clay had claimed them. Its obliterating matrix would hide them forever. Clay brothers they were who knew not each other's maternity.

"Oh God, what is man that Thou are mindful of him?"

Jarvis Singlereed had often heard the Baptist minister quote this and he, Jarvis, used to whisper to himself, "then why should I be mindful of him?"

But now, suddenly he was mindful. A latent terror, inherited too, from slave holding ancestors, descended upon him of the second generation, the dread of black rebellion, black usurpation, black self assertion.

"By God!" his own cracked voice startled him. "My God!"

Excitement seized him. He forgot his bad heart and high blood pressure, forgot that he must keep calm and collected on pain of sudden death. He ran, precipitately he ran, through halls, down stairs, into the morgue. Breathless he met the press.

They laid Dick Rivers' corpse on the morgue slab.

"How grotesque. Dick Rivers dead? That mortgage—his wife—she will never pay it—the children. Well twenty more clay acres are mine. Dead! A nigger killed him!" Jarvis Singlereed trembled in his soliloquy.

He looked again at the dead man. The frown of hot distrust and bravado had frozen upon the set face.

"He hated me," thought Jarvis Singlereed.

The crowd outside the morgue muttered and growled.

"Let's burn the black carcass," some one ejaculated.

"Let's git some of them young bucks," another interpolated.

"Back, step back a bit boys," the deputy sheriff commanded.

The coroner had arrived. His broad felt hat could not completely overshadow the importance of his inquest.

He looked at the dead white man with tightening lips.

"Wha's the niggah?"

The crowd made way. The representative of the law, her emissary in time of unnatural death, pushed the body of the dead Negro with his booted foot.

"We're figurin' on barbecuin' him," someone ventured.

"He's dead, ain't he? Ah reckon you'd bettah barbecue some of these breathin' bucks."

A sneaking cur, so starved that the outline of every rib stood out, smelled at the blood that seeped from the gaping wound in the Negro's head.

"Not in here. Not in here, I say," cried Jarvis Singlereed with an oath.

Two frightened Negroes, commandeered to carry the body, vacillated with their grewsome burden.

A slouching individual stepped out from the whites and whispered something to Singlereed.

"Well I'll be—do you mean—capital idea," sputtered Singlereed. "Put that dead niggah ovah theah, you."

The two Negroes responded with alacrity, carrying the body into the morgue and laying it on the slab beside his victim.

"You niggahs stay with us. We got work fo' you to do."

Derision and ridicule echoed in the jeering guffaws.

The clay of the market place had become dust an inch thick from the tramping of many feet. The jugs labeled "Cane Syrup" had all disappeared. Brooding wrath lowered.

When unnoticed, rawboned mules with quivering underlips were surreptitiously ridden away by black masters. Wagons and carts with crinkly heads bobbing from springless beds vanished in the distance.

Three o'clock struck from the jail house tower. The last vestige of breeze had subsided. A suffocating humidity began to wilt the mob, already stifling in the blazing heat of violent passion.

The sun was still an unblinking eye of flame. Heat waves danced before the arching gaze. A tense understanding sped among the poor white farmers. A sudden secret word was whispered. "To-night—at seven—the sign will be given—at seven."

Grapevine telegraph or what not the news was circulated likewise in black town. Uncertainty, consternation and blind fear reigned.

"Bong! Bong! Bong! Bong!" The jailhouse clock was striking.

But for the dead in Jarvis Singlereed's morgue there was no time.

In the lull Jarvis Singlereed had gone back to his office to finish counting his money. Crouching in his swivel chair, pursing his vulture lips, with bald head, beaked nose and scrawny neck, he looked as he was, a giant bird of prey, counting his toll, fingering his toll.

The temperature mounted, mounted. The torrid swelter became unbearable. Mopping his fevered brow, wiping his moist wrist until his handkerchief was soaked, Jarvis Singlereed again looked out of his office window.

A slight breeze was stirring in the tree tops. A shadow was stealing over that burning furnace, the sun. Immediately a chill filled the air. Spirals of dust and debris gyrated. Birds, twittering uneasily, fluttered in and out of the tree tops, swaying now more and more vigorously. Bold blue jays, thieving crows, chipping sparrows, red feathered cardinals, ricebirds, vied with the sound of the gathering breeze; then they were drowned in the onrushing thunder of a tremendous wind.

Jarvis Singlereed glimpsed excited farmers scurrying after their beasts, cars, wives, children. Then he saw nothing but the fury of the descending storm. He heard nothing but the sough of the wind. Nature, the old master, played upon the strings of the tempest, whistling, moaning, sobbing, scolding, roaring, defying, crashing.

The hurricane leaped through the window at Jarvis Singlereed and he slammed down the rattling glass, panting, amidst flapping curtains, falling calendars and flying papers. Hot rage throbbed in his temples, a vague anger at the importance of human clay in the face of the invincible Unseen.

The lightning blinded him, the peals of thunder rasped his nerves. His money lay uncounted. His papers were topsy-turvy. Disgusted, he rushed into the hallway, stumbled, cursing, down the stairs and into his deadhouse. That drear chamber was forsaken. Only the dead lay there.

He called stable boys, cab drivers, chauffeurs, all his retinue of hands. Never an answer. Either they had absconded or the storm had engulfed his feeble cries. It had inundated him. He felt tentacles reaching, feeling, severing him from the thoughts of the living, drawing him to those forms about to disintegrate.

Greater wrath smote him. He would cut that black carcass into pieces. That was what the hillbilly had whispered in his ear and he had promised.

"Ha! Ha! Ha! Ha! How the niggers will skuttle to their holes when pieces of carrion are flung through their windows—to their holes, like—like cockroaches."

Now he was fumbling in a cupboard for scalpel and knives. How dark it was! The sound of tearing clothes. More lightning. He stood, knife raised high. More thunder. Oaths. He paused before the blow fell.

"God!"

"This is a white man! This is Rivers!"

All clay is shadowed in the twilight, so little difference is there between white and black. So little difference is there in the grave.

Whiskey! Whiskey! This sickness in the pit of his stomach must be halted. The moonshine liquor gurgled, then the "Cane Syrup" labeled jug, slipping from his trembling fingers, smashed.

The gloom thickened, while the dead faces showed more ghastly at each lurid flash.

"Jarvis Singlereed, old Jarvis Singlereed, what have you done to us?" they seemed to say.

And Jarvis Singlereed cast sheets over their glassy eyes. The wind stole in through tiny crevices and cranny, blowing aside the mortuary coverings. Clammy fingers were exposed, dead fingers, that had no color, but pointed, pointed. At every turn they assailed, warned, menaced.

The gale whined, like a sick dog. Rigor Mortis had come to life. He lurked in the corners of the spreading shadows. He stalked along the outer edges. He leered at Jarvis Singlereed, and that proud man felt a coldness in his veins, as he dwindled down into utter nothingness.

That was not the lightning cracking? No. It was the scourging lashes of the whip of Fate, castigating, cudgeling, herding cattle beneath the clay, feeding flesh to that giant troll Clay.

Were the fingers beckoning? Were the stiff fingers opening, closing?

"Oh God, if there is a God, where are you?"

In his throat Jarvis Singlereed felt his heart swelling, choking. Fear pounced upon him like a wolf. He hobbled, groping for the door, the door that would not open, running from a Something that stared and rattled, a Something that was reflected in his bursting eyes and echoed in his wind pipe.

The rain was dropping from the eaves, like clay falling on a coffin. On so many coffins he had heard the clay falling.

Then Rigor Mortis jumped from the shadow and Jarvis Singlereed fell, struggling.

When the mob came at seven with heavy feet find no light in the morgue, to hear no sound. The vanguard entered and flashed lanterns in the funeral chamber. The body of Jarvis Singlereed was lying huddled near the door, his hands over his face, as if to shut out the sight of the monstrous Unknown.

The frigidity of Death mingled with the chill of the aftermath of the tempest. Some had come reluctantly, their ardor cooled by the fierce convulsion of the storm. They were willing to let vengeance rest with the dead, for they had caught some of the terror in the sightless eyes.

They laid Jarvis Singlereed on his own marble death slab, beside Dick Rivers and young Ike Jimeson. Softly they stole away in the night to break the news.

The sun shone brightly the next day, drying up traces of the rain. On Saturday the maroon ox was munching the wire grass that still struggled against the hard, red clay. The hatchet face cracker woman was selling her salted mullets to fat black women. Ants were tugging at bits of grain, their flooded hills repaired. Dirt daubers flew over the market place, carrying in their long hind legs little hunks of clay to build mud houses for future generations of dirty daubers.

ANTROPOI

In this short story, John F. Matheus paints a verdant landscape that serves as a backdrop for the physical and emotional growth and maturation within one generation of dichotomous families. He adroitly depicts the "warp and woof" with which he weaves a human tapestry exemplifying the potential for beauty, synchronicity, and mutual respect among men rather than the enmity, bitterness, and lack of understanding that is often the by-product of difference. This story was published in August 1928.

There were visible several shades of green—the deep verdure of the trees on the West Virginia hill-sides, the bright green of the trees, lighted by the noon sun on the Ohio shore, then the dull, oily green of the river and the green, differing from all, that shone in the grey eyes of Bushrod Winter—the green of envy and exasperation.

Bush Winter had long held bitter feelings against Demetrius Pappaniasus. The latter had come from Greece by way of the Latin Quarter of Paris, where he had drudged for months in a tailor shop on the Boulevard Raspail until he had garnered enough francs to pay for steerage passage to New York. Wandering about like his famous countryman of classical times he drifted West and finally settled down in the Tri-State Valley, where the Ohio river touches Pennsylvania, West Virginia and the commonwealth which is that river's namesake.

Bush Winter was an American of African descent. Born in Ohio in the last year of the Civil War he had grown up in a free and friendly atmosphere, a tradition handed down from the establishment of the Northwest Territory. He had gone through the grammar school and had acquired quite early an argumentative interest in public activities which developed into petty leadership among his group in local politics.

Demetrius Pappaniasus was an undersized, swarthy, black haired Greek.

Bush Winter was an oversized, swarthy, black haired mulatto.

When Bush Winter first knew the Greek the men and boys around town called him John, a general appellation then coming into vogue among native Americans of the eighteen-nineties to designate the foreigner. Bush was driving a dray for a living. It was a big dray pulled by powerful Percheron horses. He was an expert in moving heavy objects, iron safes and pianos. Daily he drove up Market street to meet the Panhandle trains and daily he was greeted from all sides in hale small town intimacy, "Hello, Bush. How goes 'er?"

In those days Bush had not been long married and he found much joy in coming back to town on Saturday nights to buy groceries and gossip in the "Equal Rights Barber Shop" where black and white could have their tonsorial needs attended to. Sometimes he would drop in Pappaniasus's boot-black stand on the corner of Market and Westmoreland Avenue and pay him a nickel to shine his broad shoes. And the little man shined them well, bending over his task with the finesse of an artist, rubbing the paste in with his fingers, gnarled and dirty with blacking under the nails.

Pappaniasus lived then on Water street with his brown-skin Syrian wife. All the newly arrived wops and hunkies lived on Water street: Croatians, Poles, Bohemians, Italians, Greeks, Syrians. They were piled up in little racial clumps and there lumped together by the town's old residents with out the least regard for age old feuds and demarcations.

Their children had already begun to multiply whereat his wife was glad, since these swarthy babies were coming in free America, where people did not live in hovels and had hydrant water right in the yard.

When Pappaniasus took out his first naturalization papers he shortened his name to Pappan. It was better so for business, because the Americans always protested against dago names that were more than two syllables long.

By the time Pappaniasus had reduced his name to Pappan he had saved enough nickels to open a little restaurant on Market street. There anybody who would come could buy cheap, filling food; beans, baked and boiled, buttermilk, ham sandwiches, hot coffee, hot soup and so the rounds of cheap and wholesome menus. And Pappan continued to save money, learning the English language and absorbing American customs.

When he was able to add a candy kitchen and a soda water counter he had become naturalized and adept in imitating the slangy banter he heard in his restaurant. He moved his family from Water street into a house on Eighth street, a neighborhood being invaded by the more prosperous of the Greek colony. He had the house all alone for his family save for two boys who flunkied for him in the restaurant. But it still smelled of garlic.

It so happened that Bush Winter lived on Eighth street too, on the higher, hillier section of that street. From his upstairs window could be seen the Ohio river meandering through the hazy valley in lazy curves, the trains, puffing across the Panhandle bridge, the boats, with hoarse, raucous steam whistles, slipping down stream to Cincinnati and Louisville.

On Sundays he enjoyed watching this placid scenery and sometimes in the afternoon he would go down town and hire a buggy for two dollars and hitch up one of his draught horses and give his wife and boy and girl the treat of a drive along the river bank. The Greeks never did this, not a bit more than they would buy chicken for dinner or spend their money for fine clothes.

Bush believed in good clothes for the adornment of the body. He always had an account at Bergstein's Emporium or at some of the gentile establishments. On the other hand styles meant nothing to the Pappans. Clothes had but one function for their point of view—the prime function of covering the body.

These were the little details which led Bush Winter to think of Pappan with the patronizing air of the rest of the native born members of the community. It never occurred to him to ponder upon what was Pappan's attitude toward him, not even when they were exchanging crude, bluff jokes. But he found out unexpectedly.

On a certain sultry August Sunday in the midst of the heat of dog days Bush brought his family into the inviting coolness of the Pappan Ice Cream Parlor for the refreshing pleasure of some cold carbonated drink.

"Hello, John," shouted Bush with brisk joviality, "give us something cold to drink."

One of the boy flunkies darted forward obligingly. He was gathering up the red bottles, sweating cold drops of condensed vapor as the hot air struck the frigid glass.

Pappan was standing near, stretching his face in a forced smile and rubbing his hands together nervously, as though he were washing them in the humid air. He said something in the Greek language to his clerk, rapid, guttural words.

"No can drink him here," said the boy.

Pappan bowed politely.

Bush did not grasp what it was all about, but his quicker witted wife sensed the meaning immediately.

"He doesn't want us to drink his pop in here, Bush."

"What—what do you mean?" roared Bush.

"Me no can help. My beezness—these 'leukoi'—these I mean other Americans, they no like black. You all right, Bush, but eet is beezness."

He continued rubbing his hands, a mimicry of helpless Pilate.

"Why you dirty—," began Bush, reaching for one of the bottles, the cold drops dripping down his coat sleeve; but his sensible wife grabbed his uplifted arm and the glass smashed on the tile floor.

So began their feud. And Bush stood green with impotent rage and exasperation. He had lived to see the day when an Esau had stolen his birthright. He would seek redress in the courts. He could do that. Thinking such thoughts, he turned on his heel and stalked out, his family behind him.

He consulted a lawyer on Monday morning. After hearing the facts, the attorney doubted the wisdom of his bringing suit, since there had been no refusal to sell or denial of service, save the request to drink outside of his parlor.

"There is a technicality that may beat you," observed the lawyer.

———

The weeks slipped by. Bush worked hard, rising early and turning in late, endeavoring to offset the competition of a rival who had bought a truck. His wife had urged him to sell his horses and purchase a truck too, but he was hard to convince because the initial investment was high and their home had not been completely paid for.

Demetrius Pappan in the meantime flourished like the green bay tree. His trade grew. He had to enlarge his quarters. In the front of his restaurant now appeared the sign—WHITE.

Bush winced when he saw it, as he jostled down Market street, perched on the lofty front seat of the heavy dray.

Worry over the effrontery of Pappan, fuming and fretting about the unfairness of it all, was becoming an obsession with Bush. His children took it up. They had heard their father berate the "dirty dagoes" so much, and their mother's indignant agreement had penetrated so deeply in their consciousness, that they involuntarily began to vie with Pappan's son and daughter in the local High School.

Mary Pappan was quite as dark as Edith Winter and there was a shade of color in favor of Bush's son, Bush Winter, Jr., when the critical High School students compared him with young Demetrius Pappan.

"Mary Pappan is as black as a nigger!" whispered some of the girls behind her back and when some tattler told Mary, the girl was beside herself with rage.

But anyway the native born Americans began to concede a grudging respect for the thrifty Greek. He was a good business investment. That was why the Savings Trust Company had loaned money to Pappan for his project to open a moving picture theatre that would monopolize the amusement business in the little valley town. So much was it worth to have inherited acumen, handed down from the sharp practices of ancestors who matched wits with the Turk, the Armenian and the Jew of the Levant.

The opening of Pappan's Palace Theatre was widely advertised, especially in the local Republican and Democratic papers. They agreed that the theatre would eclipse all others in the valley, become the center of the community's entertainment.

Pappan knew how to spend his money.

The opening was quite an event. Bush had made reluctant promise to his children to allow them to go, after admitting that he did not believe in cutting off the nose to spite the face. So on inauguration night they were in the crowd. Bush hurried to buy a ticket.

Mary Pappan was the ticket seller. Bush waited. She did not notice him. He knocked impatiently with his hard silver money on the smooth glass counter.

"Ticket, please."

She pointed to a sign. He had not noticed it. He read, "We do not cater to the Ethiopian race."

The Ethiopian race? What had he to do with the Ethiopian race. Her renegade father was as black as he was, and wasn't Mary Pappan the color of his quadroon wife and daughter?

But she held out and would not sell him a ticket.

He had a clear case against him now, and he lost no time in bringing suit for damages. He hired a lawyer, one Solomon Lavinsky, who in turn subpoenaed the needed witnesses.

The case came to trial in the Mayor's Court. Lawyer Lavinsky reviewed the history of the case, stressing the violation of the Civil Rights Law of the State of Ohio that was involved, and its infringement of democratic principles in general.

The attorney for the defendant argued that his client had been within his legal rights, that he was in no way responsible for the state of public opinion and should be protected in making such rules as would defend his business from unwarranted losses.

Of course the race issue was drawn in with all of its nasty complications. But there could be no denial of the clear violation of the Civil Rights Law.

Bush Winter was given one dollar damages and Pappan was ordered to remove the offending sign.

A lot of publicity was given the decision. Bush considered the award a victory, for he was contending for the principle involved and not for pecuniary damages. His sense of triumph was further exhilarated by the news that was brought home from High School, that his son had won highest honors in scholarship.

But this triumph was shortlived. Adroit lawyers have so many clever suggestions to foil the laws. News came that the Pappan Palace Theatre was drawing a line in seating. He hoped somebody would test the ugly discrimination. But nobody did.

"I will test it," he said.

He went alone this time, seeking to save his family humiliation. He was not refused a ticket, but there they were all huddled together in the most undesirable section of the balcony. He called the usher.

"Get me another seat."

He went away and came back shortly.

"All sold out, mister," he said bumptiously.

Then he went himself. The ticket seller made the same excuse and then sold a man a ticket in the section he had asked for.

Now he was to learn the intimate secrets of the court, the law's delay and the wearing sacrifice of the fight. His suit was lost this time.

The old obsession was growing. He was outraged. He took the matter to his lodge and then to his church. He preached boycott. But no money came, for some of the dark skinned folk said, "Humph! Serves him right. Tryin' to be white."

Others were interested and willing to help but their fate was hard enough already. They were poor and exhausted with their daily struggle for sustenance.

So Bush Winter became a bitter man, complaining against his lot and communicating his disgust to his children.

———

Then came the great Alembic of the War, into which the sons of the families of the Nation were fed. Bush Winter and Demetrius Pappan both gave theirs. But Fate was merciful to them both, for the sons were returned unharmed and the fathers were glad to tears to behold them once again.

"Now," said Pappan, "I can do what I have planned. Turn my business over to him while I go back to my native heaths once more before I die and enjoy with my wife a bit the fruit of long years of toil."

"If I could only give my boy a college education," grieved Bush Winter, but how could he? Bad luck had overtaken him.

While moving a safe he had strained himself severely. The rope had slipped and he had to bear the load for a while or be crushed. The doctor told him to stop all work if he wanted to live.

And so he had been compelled to rent out his dray and depend upon haphazard and untrustworthy hirelings to bring in what they chose.

———

Edith Winter had inherited her father's pessimistic discouragement. She had finished High School, but never had been able to adjust herself to the blow her pride had received when Mary Pappan had been able to secure at once a position as stenographer in the Savings Trust Company's offices, while she, who had made better marks had been offered nothing but a kitchen job.

But young Bush Winter had opened his eyes in the army and taught himself to think. Away from the smug ways of his valley home he began to study things as they were. He saw clearly the futile strivings of his father, seeking redress in the courts from a usurper of what was there for him to get. He pictured old man Pappan forsaking his native ties and emigrating to America with the flaming spirit of the pioneer. He saw it all clearly and determined that he would study this secret mastery of the purse strings. If only he had capital he would build up his father's business. He would get power and erect his own theatre and then he could determine where people should sit.

He broached the difficult subject to his father but could find no solution for the broken man had to confess his poverty.

"All that you say is mighty fine, son, but they are a young fellow's dream. It takes money to buy trucks and do all you want, and—and—the house is already mortgaged."

———

Those were trying days after the War. Foolish laborers, who never looked beyond their noses were not prepared for the sudden slump in wages and for the unemployment which followed the closing of the munition factories. Yet prices soared, while statesmen wrangled and passed the dastard word, "profiteering", in councils of state and nation. And there were charges and counter charges.

People of the age of Bush Winter and his wife and the Pappans wondered if the younger generation were going to the dogs. The safe old moorings had all been swept away and there seemed to be no stakes to which the drifters could be anchored.

Edith Winter and her set were caught in the vortex of this moral maelstrom. Mary Pappan and her younger sister lost their heads. The fathers and mothers worried and begged, cajoled and threatened without avail. Bobbed hair, short skirts, loose language, suggestive dances—and behold, the flapper appeared.

Young Bush Winter and young Demetrius Pappan, returned home, leaving that long isolation from currents of home thought, found themselves entangled in the meshes of a baffling reaction.

So it happened one autumn night after a day of fruitless worry, feeling that the bottom had fallen out of things, young Bush Winter followed his sister to the Idle Dream Hall where the boys and girls of their group toddled to the strains of jazz. Across the street one square below in the Knights of Columbus Hall, white youth were swaying in the same unbridled revelry, body to body beneath the reddish glare of low burning lights.

Resentment at first welled up in the harassed spirits of the young ex-soldiers and each in his set upbraided his sister in the stinging chastisement of a protecting brother who is worldly wise. But what the use? The blandishments of passionate music bring surcease of trouble. They had paid and paid, they had suffered and why refuse this little fling? Let us all throw the barriers down and drink life, feel life, for yesterday was hell, and to-morrow. . . .

—

Sudden sound of shooting, muffled detonations and dancers stopped and music ceased. Eager, curious faces pressed against window panes, jumping for some new excitement. The Ku-Kluxers were burning a cross on the hill above the town, the fiery cross, casting sinister shadows against the sky, and many remembered veiled, unfounded rumors. Aftermath of War!

That lowing, composite roar of crowds gushed down the street, now mounting loudly, now fading to a whisper. A great throng was in procession, automobiles with flying flags, men in long white robes and cone-shaped hoods.

Young Demetrius Pappan led the gang that rushed from Knights of Columbus Hall, hatless, breathless, in the mood for anything. In one piercing glance he sensed it all, the automobile leading the way, fluttering flag of his country on the hood. A white wave of anger swept over him and young Demetrius Pappan stepped boldly before the honking machine, arms upraised, a dramatic figure in the blinding glare of the headlights.

"Stop," he cried. "Take down that flag. I didn't fight in France to see it desecrated by cowards who hide behind a mask. Why don't you take off your masks, I say?"

He grabbed the flag and broke the fragile stick that fitted into the ornament on top of the hood.

———

"A riot! A riot!" echoed in the hall where Edith Winter danced. Young Bush Winter tried to find his sister in the stampede for the door.

Hats were thrown away; overcoats forgotten.

"Git off o' my arm, girl," somebody yelled. "This ain't no time to faint."

Clatter down the stairs. Confusion in the streets. Shots are fired. The police are coming—the Fire Department clangs out, throwing water on the squirming mass.

After the fight a wreck of automobiles, punctured tires, broken glass, wasted gasoline and Demetrius Pappan's son, beaten half to death, unconscious on the ground.

He lay many days in the Valley Hospital, hovering between life and death. During those trying days old man Pappan's form grew bent and deep wrinkles seared his brow. He thought as he never thought before, walking silently through the streets.

Bush Winter saw him one evening, pottering before his house—his enemy, his grudge of years in person, the obsession of agonizing meditations.

"How-do, Bush," greeted Pappan.

"How-do, John," grunted Bush.

"Ah, I have much troubles."

"How is your boy, Pappan? I was sorry to hear of his being hurt."

"Ah—what can I say? The doctors, they don't say. And your boy—he's fine feller, too. You can be proud of heem."

And in the talk that flowed a rapprochement grew.

"Tell your girl it ees a good beesness head on her shoulders. My Mary will help her get trade. Shurr—there ees no Beauty Parlor een thees town," he confided as he sauntered slowly on.

They understood each other, these old, worn fathers, after all.

And many an evening they talked and Bush was glad to review his hopes and Pappan listened, comprehending.

"Such a life," commented Pappan. "You because you not white must suffer and I because I be born in Greece. Your son he can fight, but mine, maybe he die."

———

But he did not die. His strong young vitality would pull him through and the next day after the doctors had pronounced their verdict. Demetrius Pappan came pottering to Bush's house.

"I want see you," he said.

Bush took him upstairs to his room where they could see the river's yellow stream in the fading light. Pappan pulled out his check book, coughing uneasily and speaking brusquely.

"How much money your boy want to buy them truck and open garage. 'Tis good beesness head he hev. Fine feller that boy."

"No, no!" he waved to Bush's wild-eyed protest. "I like mek invest. Take it from me. Bush, when I see beesness, I know beesness."

"That's what my wife always said," assented Bush.

"An' my old woman, too," laughed Pappan.

———

Old Bush Winter out of his window saw the deep verdure of the trees on the distant West Virginia hillsides, the brighter green of trees on the Ohio shore, lighted by the last rays of the evening sun, and the shimmering, oily green of the river, but the reflected emerald in his eyes gleamed with tears.

COULÈV' ENDORMI

This story, published in December 1929, is set in the waterfront "night-pleasure" area of Port-au-Prince, Haiti. John F. Matheus reveals the situation ruminations and reflections of a collection of emigrés, foreign visitors, and Haitians in a bar on a rainy evening. While Matheus provides colorful detail of their range of reactions to the shared experiences there, he sharply demonstrates the verity of such pearls of wisdom as "things are rarely what they seem," or "that which is beauteous and fair need not thereby be good," or "that formed from nature so colorful and comely man, in reality, be a sleeping serpent."

The rain had scattered prospective dancers and cooled the ardor of the few who still remained lolling in the stuffy, rectangular hall of the Cabaret Ba-Ta-Clan. A couple of North American traveling salesmen, sucking Chesterfields, bought at Laurie's down town for twice what they cost in the States, were fingering between them what they could not legitimately buy at home, a bottle of Haitian rum. Two empty glasses and two glasses filled with water in which floated rapidly disappearing chunks of ice, completed such a study in still life as Cezanne would be delighted to have immortalized.

A couple of sportily attired Haitian youths of the upper class lounged near the door, conversing in an undertone of gliding French. A Syrian sat at a table by himself, evidently waiting impatiently for some one, for he frequently pulled out a watch and peered intently at it, frowning the meanwhile. Three girls, voluptuous blends of Latin and African blood, giggled together in a corner of the portion of the room roped off for dancing. They also were smoking, long cigarettes of strong Haitian tobacco rolled in Port-au-Prince.

The black piano player had taken advantage of the lull to go behind the counter and ask the bartender for a drink. The latter, a big, black mustached Belgian, was preparing him a Martini.

The French proprietor, who knew his Montmartre and how the tourists fall for alcohol and a show of the exotic female was silently cursing his luck. He had counted on this night to bring him some needed money. A Dutch Line boat, New York bound, had docked that afternoon, while the ANCON of the Pan American Line was expected to depart in the morning for the Canal Zone.

It was always this way in Port-au-Prince—a port for the Prince indeed! The Prince of Devils! Such rains, pouring the water in sheets into the inadequate sewers, making the unpaved middle of the street in front of the Cabaret a messy mud hole.

But maybe it would clear up. Maybe. The Americans stared at the bar and blinked their eyes before the colossal red letters which spelled out the ancient Indian name of the island. Q-U-I-S-Q-U-E-Y-A. The letters hung from the ceiling and were decorated with gaudy tinsel bought from a German importer from the Fatherland.

Automobile brakes creaked as a big car pulled up with a jerk and a quiver at the curb, splashing water over the concrete squares of the sidewalk and almost wetting a pair of bedizened and sleepy-eyed creatures who were talking Dominican Spanish with gushing dash and clatter. Natty in their khaki uniforms, two American officers flung themselves through the swinging doors, bought drinks, flipped real United States money on the bar and pranced out in a hurry to attend the dance at the American Club, where no dark skin was allowed to appear.

The taciturn proprietor had overheard their conversation for he had learned to understand English well, even if he spoke it with difficulty. The knowledge only served to increase his bad humor, since, even if it cleared up, his tourist trade would probably prefer the American "hop." But after it was over, then, maybe.

The traveling salesmen wore white duck suits, as did the other men for that matter, and from time to time languidly struck at moths, bugs, gnats, persistent flying insect nuisances, finding refuge from the rain in the Ba-Ta-Clan.

"An aftermath of last week's hurricane," continued the blond salesman with a Dixie accent and face burned red by a fiercer heat than even Louisiana knows. "And that hurricane has ruined business fo' faiah in the South."

He looked contemplatively at the amber liquor he had just poured into the empty glass.

"I found things about the same at the Cape. Practically no damage done." The trim, cold blooded New Englander with his North of Boston accent and unwinking blue eyes, ran muscular fingers through black hair.

"Jeremie's a mess. Roads impassible. It took eight hours to come from Jeremie to Cayes."

"Papers up here have been filled with news about the terrible 'degat.' Red Cross sending aid, even the President is reported to have contrib—tri—tri—."

His sentence ended in an explosive cough as the attempt to talk and drink Haitian rum refused to cooperate. He took a hurried sup of water. The last bits of ice jingled in the glass.

"That's the trouble," commented the other. "Too much time wasted gettin' the help. Could have saved much suffering, but my God, in an undeveloped country like this a hurricane can paralyze business for months. Crops destroyed, no work and all that."

He pressed the blackened end of his cigarette hard against the side of the bottle of rum.

"I'll be damn glad to get out of it all for a while," he of the red face resumed.

"Where do you go?"

"Make Cristobal and Panama."

"Thank Heavens, I'm bound for New York. My first trip to the tropics. Always had a hankerin' for the Romance of the thing, but I've found no Romance, nothing, nothing, but bad roads, stinking joints, and—"

"And 'wowzy' niggahs, if you know what I mean," laughed his companion.

One of the Haitian youths lounging in the doorway, caught himself in the middle of a sentence and said something to his friend in the Creole patois of the country people.

The Syrian, drumming more impatiently than ever on the table, beckoned to the bartender, who called sharply, "Ti-Jean."

A half grown black boy darted in from somewhere in the cavernous rear.

"*Allez vite. M'sieur vlé boire,*" commanded the bartender in Creole. "Quick! The gentleman wants something to drink."

"*Oui, oui, oui, oui.*"

It seemed he was going to string out his eager affirmatives without end.

"*Un cocktail,*" snapped the Syrian.

Then as the boy started to go with the celerity of one of those little lizards, that were probably at that very minute catching bugs, somewhere up in the creepy looking ceiling, the Syrian seized him by the arm and shouted, "*Attendez.*" Lowering his voice he asked, "Where is she?"—*Coté été li?*

"*Li va vini toute-a-l'heure.* She will come in a little while."

An undersized, precocious urchin sauntered in from the outside, one of the polyglot tribe of gamins found in port cities everywhere, who can pick out nationalities with uncanny surety and address them in their own vernacular.

"Shine, meestair," he whined, shaking the water from his cap.

"No. Get out," and the blond haired American waved him away.

"*Cirer les soulier-ou?*" He approached the Haitians.

The taller put out his foot.

The boy dropped his box at once. Resting his right foot on the wooden form, the youth nonchalantly continued his conversation.

"*Comment elle est belle!*" His words rang with the fervor of a poet, or of a religious devotee before his Deity's shrine. *How beautiful is she!*

"But listen, Felix, think of your father, your family, your position. An infatuation, well that could be tolerated, but to want to marry her. What do you know of her past? And her present!"

"Ah, but wait. You haven't seen her yet."

"But there are plenty pretty girls in Haiti."

"Yes, but this one, Ah, this one! *Mon Dieu,* she is a reincarnation of Cleopatra, the serpent of the Nile."

"Ha! Ha! The serpent of the Artibinite."

"Wait," was the cold reply.

The speaker moistened dry lips with feverish tongue, and shifted his left foot for the bootblack to clean.

Outside the clouds had drifted from the sky overhead. The stars began to shine. A cooler breeze blew from the harbor. The proprietor began to think better of his fate and ordered the piano player back to his job.

A fat-headed, yellow youth came in from the back and took seat beside the piano player.

Immediately they began to make music. They played that enticing and rhythmical product of the Haitian clime, that combination of Spanish salt and African fire, called the "*méringue,*" because it is just that, a mixture.

The girls who had been loitering outside now came in, each with a man, sailors from some Norwegian freighter in harbor, a pudgy man of that shade of brown which is called in Haiti "*griffe,*" and two sailors who spoke to each other in Dutch. The man walked to the bar and gave a *gourde,* or twenty cents, for the pleasure of dancing with their frowsy partners. They each received a dirty, dog-eared ticket, bearing the legend, "*Pour danser,*" which they handed over to an old hag who had now stationed herself in the entrance to the roped-off enclosure.

The couples began to dance with wonderful grace and rhythm of movement.

"Niggahs can suah dance, the world ovah."

"A clever step that."

A rounding bosomed mulattress, dressed in red, lips rouged in Cupid's bow, turned toward the Haitians, who were paying the boot-black.

"*Bailez, senor?*—You do not know Spanish. *Ah, dansez avec moi?*"

"*Va-t-en!* Get out!"

With lifted eye brow and disdainful shrug of an over plump shoulder she undulated by.

The music drew others. Sailors, hungry for shore and all that it holds, hurried in, some dripping still from rain, others spick-and-span.

Some black girls with sparkling eyes and earrings negotiated with a group of sailors in broken English.

"Oh, get the heck out o' here!"

"Oh, ice cream you mean! Do they sell it in this joint?"

"Don't try to *savez* me now."

The musicians changed to the whining blues of world encircling American Jazz. The crude building began to shake with the vibration of the pounding feet.

"Not much different from the niggahs back home."

"Yes, but they tell me the other families are quite different."

"Ah, I don't know. The mongrels ought to be—"

"They say the French and Germans are quite willing to marry the upper class daughters, rich, beautiful, well educated."

"Well, no American white man would."

"No!" after an interval of reflection.

There was a lull in the music. The dancers now warming up to the glories of the night rushed for the tables, some for cold drinks, some to guzzle strong beverages that would whet their mounting passions. A babel of languages ascended, as tangible, as the reeking tobacco smoke, as the cheap perfume and cosmetics of the women, as the smell of beer, wines and whiskey. A riot of color and shades face to face, cheek by jowl, meeting upon that one world-flung plane of humanity, beyond caste and race, creed and social barriers, inevitable, indefinable.

The atmosphere was surcharged with unexpressed thought and latent desire, that seemed to stifle for composite expression, to seek an articulate and incarnate manifestation. And it came! It came suddenly and surprisingly for the newcomers, but chafingly anticipated by the frowning Syrian, by the Haitian youths and even by the big, mustached Belgian. It came or rather *she* came gliding from the darkness behind the dancing enclosure, a symphony in shimmering green and crimson under an ebony clip of gold and silver spangles that flashed under the low-powered electric bulbs like the scales of the rainbow-colored fish in the blue bay when the rays of the noon sun reflect in the opalescent waters like the scales indeed of Lucifer before he crawled out of Eden's garden.

And when that motley throng beheld her face there was a spontaneous murmur of praise and envy, envy from her less gorgeous competitors. Her skin was of the color of rich cream in a blue enameled bowl into whose smoothness some drops of coffee accidentally may have fallen, *"crème au café,"* or perhaps it was more like that rare old ivory that Oriental art carves into delicate beauty. Her hair was a lustrous glory, as blue black as a raven's wings. She smiled and eyes, lips and teeth intoxicated. There was withal an inscrutable stamp upon her face, a composite mark of Asia, Africa and Europe. There was the Mongolian slant of her eyes, the Eastern hair, the bit of African impigmentation, the untrammeled Negro abandon, the sophistication and masked hardness of white ancestry.

The black piano player left his keys and pulled forth a drum and began to beat a frenzied spasm. The lovely vision that seemed to have sprung into being from the thoughts of them whose eyes were riveted upon her began to dance age old rhythms. Her eyes were closed. For the nonce she appeared to have been lulled to sleep by the witchery of the drum. Then up, wide awake with a sudden start she spun around, gliding, in serpentine revolutions, as though suspended upon fluttering wings.

The Syrian sat panting, transfixed, transfigured. Tense, pale the Haitian boy looked at her as upon a vision. A puzzling wonder was on the countenance of his friend.

"And where did she come from?" gasped the salesman from New England.

"Where?" echoed his countryman.

"Comment je t'aime, je t'aime," the Haitian sighed.

"A dancer in a baudy cabaret in this place! Why, if she were in New York—imagine Hammerstein, Ziegfeld seeing this."

"A beauty I declah! To be ogled by blacks—why—something ought to be done about it. But she's probably got some niggah blood. I've seen 'em as white in Louisiana, but they're descended from the quadroons. You've heard about them of co'se."

Boom! The last beat fell. The dance was over. The Syrian sprang nervously to his feet. The Haitian was trembling. The men applauded again and again. She returned. The cords of the spell drew tighter. She wound in and out, sinuating, curving, more and more tantalizing until she stopped amid ringing salvos of applause.

She disappeared. The black boy returned to his piano and the sailors to their girls whose splendors had been temporarily eclipsed.

The proprietor strolled over behind the table occupied by the Americans.

"How do you like?"

"Merveilleux," said the Louisianian, muttering his French.

"Fine!" replied the other. "Where does she come from? What's her history?"

"I do not comprehend eet her history. But she ees dancer ver' excellent. That man indicating the Syrian, he come evair day jes' to see 'er dance and look, look. I theenk he go *fou,* ah, what you call crazy.

"She is fine for yo' business."

With a shrug of his shoulders he hastened to serve an order. A clap of thunder echoed. The rain was falling again. It could be heard splashing on the cement pavement.

After a time the couples began to disappear. The raucous cacophony of rough talk subsided. Pessimism descended its gloom upon the wretched proprietor. The Americans bought another drink and rose to go. They glanced at the Syrian still sitting at the table, his head now buried in his hands.

Out into the street they stepped, sniffing the fresh air with decided relish. A dilapidated four-wheel carriage drawn by one horse and driven by a nodding driver was passing the corner.

"Pst! Pst!" they hissed in good Haitian fashion to call the driver to take them to the hotel. Rushing past a narrow hallway they glimpsed the silhouette of the dancing girl and a man reflected on the drawn curtain over a door.

"Tell him to wait," said the New Englander. "My curiosity is aroused. I must see who is with her."

Creeping up to the door he heard the voice of the Haitian talking French. Impatient he hurried out and beckoned his companion to come. "Tell the fellow to wait.—— What is he telling her?"

"How much he loves her," summarized the Louisianian.

Then they heard the woman's voice—for the first time. She was speaking with great effort.

"Well, well," muttered the interpreter. "She says for a great wrong done her by a marine who left her and her child she has sworn vengeance upon all men. She hates—hates—all men—her heart is dead, or gush to that effect."

They crept out again into the air. The door opened almost behind them. The tall Haitian youth walked out with drawn face and disappeared in the direction of the National Bank, his white trousers slowly vanishing in the engulfing darkness.

In the doorway *she* stood and watched him out of sight. Turning her face toward the two men they saw she was weeping. Evidently she had not noticed them before. Becoming suddenly self-conscious she gave a little cry and ran into the house.

"*Qui été femme-la?* Who was that woman?" asked the Southerner in Creole of the driver of the vehicle.

"*Li été coulèv' endormi.* Ah! She is the sleeping serpent. They call her that. She takes the heart and sets men crazy—many have died in the crazy house after—after—she has charmed them. *Ah! Oui!* She is the sleeping serpent."

"That is the native peasant name for a species of boa-constrictor found in the island," commented the man from Louisiana, as they jogged along the uneven stones toward the hotel.

NOMAH—A STORY

John F. Matheus crafts a spiraling tale in the following story, which, through its mystical maze of intergenerational effect, reminds us that we are truly children of the earth conceived in the "Garden of Eden"—out of Adam and Eve—ever in need of redemption. This story was published in July 1931.

All Monrovia knew that somebody had died in Kru Town. The sun had barely dropped in the snarly sea, slapping down abruptly night's blanket of darkness over the Liberian shores, when the sound of wailing rose, a weird, inimitable ululation, echoing the lamentation of generations of jungle-dwelling forebears, who centuries before had gone down to the West African sea. It ascended like the beating of the waters against the sandy bars that are the streets of sprawling Kru Town, above the beehive houses, above the low stretch of barren beach to the top of Cape Mesurado and beyond, an unforgettable, palpable moaning. There were pauses, when the voices ceased and even those at a distance who strained their ears could detect the sharp staccato of the calabashes filled with pebbles shaken in unison by the strong arms of sturdy black women. And always the background of this sound picture was the thud of drums.

The sea, implacable enemy, had claimed a veteran fisherman. His little dug-out had drifted ashore that morning after a night of terrific rain and wind. Daybreak beach wanderers had stumbled over it, partly filled with sea water, and recognizing the battered dug-out had pulled it past the clawing reach of the angry waves. Then excitedly they had gone to tell the news.

Now the white traders, the business men, looked at each other over their whiskies and sodas, the missionaries muttered prayers, all accepted the inevitable tragedies of the rainy season, which come in Liberia like the heat, the fever and the mosquitoes, remorseless and unpreventable. The Liberians shrugged drooping shoulders, bowed by the burdens of sky, malaria and the hard facts of existence and went to sleep.

But there was no sleep in Kru Town.

In the house of Kadah Watu there was mourning and his daughter, Nomah, would not be comforted.

"Ah wah! Ah woe! To think this should be his end. Death must come to us all, sooner or later, but not to be able to see his body, whence Kadah Watu had fled into the waters, the air, the earth, who knows? To feed the belly of the shark—quite probably they never would find so much as a bone.

"So many years battling with the waves, for so many years. That was why he could not prevail against the tempest, that was why. He was too old, his strength, like his eyesight had begun to fail and who has mercy for the old or pity, save their children?

"But the sea is older than many men or generations of men, yet never does the sea wear out, nor become enfeebled, but swallows, swallows even the land itself.

Batee, batee, prayers! His daughter was not remiss. Her body was stocky and solidly made and could endure long vigils without tiring. Amidst the endless ceremonies which the missionaries said were heathen, Nomah thought of the Christian God, *Nyeswa,* and of his Son, *Ju, Yesu Kristi.* She would pray that He might bring back her father's body. That wasn't much. She did not dare hope to ask that her father himself be returned, but only his dead body.

That night of mourning ended and others like it. The "civilized" people when they heard the shaking of the gourds, the throbbing of the drums, the chanting, forgot whether it was for joy or for sorrow.

But Nomah, daughter of Kadah Watu, never forgot. Her trouble rested heavily upon her. She thought but seldom now of Gbanga, good-looking youth who paid her court, nor did she have patience even to listen to the whinings of that old fool, Kufu, though he were headman of the rowing crew for the English Line and had many goats and British shillings. Neither could relatives divert her melancholy.

Their grief, she said, was shallow, but *she,* well she remembered, recalled every wakening minute the teachings of her father, his companionship, how he took her out to fish on calm days, instructing her in the art of selecting bait, of casting the line, of pulling in, how he liked her way of cooking salt fish with rice, seasoned with hot peppers. She was proud of her cooking and of her secret of keeping the palm wine from fermenting too much, a secret learned from her mother buried in the Catholic Mission plot in the Monrovia cemetery.

Like her mother, Nomah too was Catholic. That is, she had formed the habit of going occasionally to the Catholic Mission on the hill, had been baptized and sometimes went to confession. She was, the other Krus said, *kre Katri Coce,* in the Catholic Church.

Probably she would not have been married according to the queer ceremonies of the Catholic faith, with its preliminaries and much ado, but would have accepted the proffers of her ardent suitor, Gbanga; whom she liked very much and upon whom she secretly longed to bestow her favors. That old pest, Kufu, had more shillings, every steamer increased his bulging wealth, but he was too old, too ugly, impotent, while she was young and virile. She also remembered now with an enhanced gratitude, that her father had not tried to force her, as he had right to do, for according to tribal custom, baldly stated, girls in the family went to the highest bidder. But he had been kind, so generous, so considerate, and with wise prescience had encouraged the suit of the younger man, Gbanga. If her father had not been thus ruthlessly snatched away, she and Gbanga would now have been happily mated.

The city Krus in Monrovia privately thought Kadah Watu a fool, a man in his dotage, with no eye to his later years. Kufu had bags of silver shillings with the palm tree on one side and the great English King's face on the other, while the shiftless Gbanga, although he worked hard, unloading and loading the boats, bought shoes to wear, a watch and other silly adornments. However, because Nomah did not approve he no longer bought trade gin, but spent his money for brightly colored silk and cotton dressgoods to be made into turbans and to be wrapped tightly around her plump and undulating figure.

Kufu gave better gifts than these, but Nomah turned up her nose at them and laughed in his homely face, so that Kufu went into the bush to buy him a love charm.

But now all was suddenly changed. Her little world was turned topsy-turvy. A daughter's first duty is to her father. His spirit could not rest with no word said in his memory, no holy ceremony to give peace to his soul.

Then a happy thought struck her. She wondered why it had not come to her before. She would go to confession and ask the priest if he would not give her father proper burial rites, a Christian burial; that she was sure would satisfy him and allay his troubled spirit. The more she reviewed the plan, the more eager was she to carry it out.

The bread fruit was turning yellow on the bread fruit trees. Nomah observed them, as a passing breeze shook them a bit and they spattered water over her plump black shoulders, bare of clothes, as she made her way in the early morning to the little mission with the white cross on the top of its roof. Her bare feet hit with a saucy smack the hard reddish laterite drying off after the latest rain. The imprint of her toes was left in the occasional soft spots of the road.

The priest's "boy" responded to her timid knock. He was a Bassa and stupid, but she made him understand that she must see his employer at once. The priest appeared after an interval, an old man, wearing glasses, behind which twinkled kindly eyes. He was venerable, patriarchal, with his flowing robes and white beard.

"Massa, I want palaver one time," she began eagerly in the jargon which the Germans call "Neger Englisch."

"Yes." The old man lifted heavy eyebrows. "You want to talk to me in box, to confess?"

She nodded.

He was an understanding priest of the humble people he had labored among for many years. He heard her patiently—how her father had been lost at sea—the dug-out floating sinisterly to shore with the sea water in its bottom—how the days had become weeks and yet no service had been said for his poor soul and she feared, feared that he was not at rest.

"We shall say mass for your father, my daughter," answered the priest, crossing himself. "That will give him peace and restore peace to you, my daughter."

Nomah hesitated. Who was she, poor maiden, to dare tell the august father what to do, but she steeled herself.

"No, massy, no. He must be buried. He must."

"But we do not have his body. It matters not where the body lies."

"Massy 'no savvy. Gwine have cemetery palaver."

No argument could change Nomah's mind and the old priest thinking of the day he was blessed in Rome, of his subsequent visit to Florence and the Church of Santa Maria Maggiore, where he saw the figure of a little African boy in the intricate mosaics of the entrance, bowed his head and promised to "give palaver" in the cemetery the next day.

Happy, Nomah went at once to the undertaker's to buy a coffin. In this dread chest she had seen the dead of Monrovia borne to their last resting place. It was to her more than the symbol of Death. It was the epitome of proper interment, the acme of respect for the dead, preceding that final gesture, that of the benediction of religion.

She left the undertaker's downcast, overwhelmed. He must have ten pounds, 200 shillings. Impossible! Why she could not sell herself for that much. And become a pawn? Ten pounds! Her father's happiness in the other world was worth it, but—

She staggered at the thought as if struck.

Slowly she turned homeward. That was the only solution. The more she pondered it, the surer was she that it was the proper one. She would marry Kufu if he would furnish the money.

Surrender Gbanga, fresh, the elemental male, strong, kind, who loved her? She trembled, tucked the upper flare of her skirt more snugly about her waist, and made the irrevocable resolution.

The relatives at first were averse to participating in any such insane enterprise. Never in the history of Kru Town had a coffin been buried without a body. But if Nomah had won over the priest how could the relatives withstand her entreaties. It was settled. Kadah Watu would have his funeral, civilized fashion. All Kru Town approved. A dutiful daughter was Nomah.

At three o'clock in the afternoon the sun is still too hot for Europeans to venture out without helmets and colored glasses, unless they were long inured to the climate as was the priest. Then, too, it was the rainy season and the clouds were always over the sky. This day was a rare one, when the sun broke through the gray overhanging mist and the water puddles began to steam the earth and the life thereon.

Six strong Kru men carried the empty coffin, fellows whom old Kadah Watu had taught to swim, to fish, to dive, to load and unload the ships. Then followed on foot Nomah, the priest, Kufu, smug, triumphant, vainly endeavoring to simulate a sorrow which his foxy, shifty gaze constantly belied. The other relatives and friends brought up the rear. Gbanga looked on from the side, his eyes hazy, red from drinking gin.

These kinsfolk, unversed in the ways of "Katri Coce," burst forth into a wild Kru lament for their dead, the unsophisticated requiem of the tribe.

> Kadah Watu, a Kruman is dead.
> Honor him, honor him.
> His prowess on the sea was great:
> He knew no fear.
> O Kadah Watu rest.

The little procession slowly crept up the hill from the water front and made its way across town to the lugubriously shaded tract of the burial ground.

Bare-headed they stood before the open grave.

Silent now, they allowed the "civilized" to have their way.

"*Sum* . . . resurrectio . . . I am the resurrection . . .", chanted the priest mechanically.

Never had such a light coffin been lowered in that burial ground.

"Earth to earth. . . . Requiescat in pace."

Kufu took Kadah Watu's place in Kadah Watu's house, only he was husband as well as father. Generous with his shillings before their marriage, he now became miserly and parsimonious. Nomah could not understand the change.

"I've paid for you once," he would say. "Don't ask me for money. Keep mouth shut."

Then Nomah looked about her for ways to make some pennies. She might sell peanuts in the market, make balls of cassava for a penny each or like her father catch fish. Hadn't he taught her all the art? But she would not let Kufu know. He would take her money.

So the next time the hoarse whistle of the ship was heard in the harbor and Kufu took his tool chest and went to unload the freight, Nomah slipped off to the water's edge.

In a seldom frequented spot she found the dug-out that had been washed ashore and dragged that first morning beyond the greedy reach of the insatiable waters. Neither she, the fishermen, her friends, not even the children of the tribe would touch the boat after that. The taboo of the dead was upon it, the curse of evil luck.

But now anger and desperation gave her determination to examine this fatal conspirator with the elements which had connived at her father's death. Her strong arms turned over the dug-out to drain the remaining water, residue of the sea and the recent heavy rains. The bottom covered with the white sand, dazzled her eyes, made her shut them quickly and tightly or avert her gaze. The water dripping from the boat ran a short distance around her bare feet and soon sank in the thirsty gray grains, leaving only a dark spot to mark its passing.

Finally Nomah turned the canoe right side up and climbed inside to look it over before dragging it again to the water. Her blue skirt bunched up behind as she squatted to scrutinize with the air of an expert the sea-worthiness of the craft. Her examination became suddenly more alert. What was this? The bottom showed a honeycomb of many little holes, at first concealed by the sand. Were they devastation of some bugs or worms? They were too uniform, too different from worms and their craft. In frantic nervousness she bent closer and began to wipe out the holes with a bit of palm leaf that the caprice of some breeze had blown. They showed identical marks of some small boring instrument. Each aperture revealed an almost imperceptible series of indentations of the same pattern. The bottom of the dug-out was a sieve.

Nomah was dazed by this discovery. Could some one have played a foul trick upon her old father? Who could have profited by his death? She went home with brow wrinkled, head down.

When Kufu had eaten his full of salt fish and rice seasoned hot with pepper and exhausted by the day's hard labor and gorged with food, had fallen in heavy sleep, Nomah searched among his tools and found an ancient gimlet-like instrument. She grasped it firmly in her muscular fingers and slipped away in the moonlight.

Again all Monrovia knew that somebody had died in Kru Town. The sound of lamentation once more rose from the sandy shores of that teeming section. The rattle of the calabashes, the voices of the mourners, the insistent tones of the drums proclaimed the passing of another soul.

Ugly old Kufu had died suddenly after eating heartily of his favorite dish, salt fish and rice. He was buried at night, Kru fashion. No civilized rights for him. It was whispered that old Kadah Watu's coffin is not as empty now as it was when lowered first into the red Liberian earth.

On Being a Domestic

In this story, published in May 1923, Eric D. Walrond gives a more-than-explicit rationale for the "spirit-wounds" implicit in the work of the black domestic worker of his era. He also sets forth a potential motive for the lack of hope for upward mobility among most domestics.

" 'Ousman?" he asked.

"Yes", I replied, dodging a cataract of saliva.

"Work the blazes out of you, too. Last nigger they had quit the very day they took him on."

"That's fair enough."

"Nearly worked him to death. That housekeeper—she's a pippin. Work—work—they'll kill you with work in this place. Why, nobody stays here longer than three days."

"I'll quit if they work me too hard", I retorted.

"Well, you're sure—you're bound to quit".

And I did, really. Surely a laborer—a galley slave—has that much left to him. The prerogative of quitting! The ease, the luxury, the beautiful freedom of it!

Still, it wasn't for the reason put forward by my voluble pearl diver. It was this—simply this.

It was morning. The housekeeper, a fragile lady—herself an inflated galley slave—wrote and ladled out memos as she talked.

"Run up", she flung at me, "to 301 and tidy it up. And when you get through go to 303—307—309—411—633—714—."

Up to 301 the elevator shot me. On the door I rapt.

"Who is it?"

"Houseman."

"Come back in about an hour. I am not ready for you yet".

I went to 303. I swept and dusted and mopt and scrubbed and threw at times a misty eye at the poet at the sun-baked window, tugging at his unruly brain. Surreptitiously I sipt of the atmospheric wine. At least he would let me stay—and live. So unlike that other place on the top floor where I had forgot my pail. I went back for it. The lady, the lady of the scenarios, on opening the door and depriving me of the aesthetic privilege of at least hearing her voice, poised on the threshold like an icily petrified thing—and pointed with Joan-of-Arc-like fingers at it—my pail—nestling under the writing table. Audibly, loudly her fingers articulated, "There it is! Come and get—you coon!"

In bewilderment I groped my way back to earth—and reason.

II

Back to 301 I went.

"Who is it?"

"Houseman."

Follows a pause. Then, briskly the door opens. The lady, horn-eyed, street attired, is cross, crimson, belligerent.

"I told you to come back over two hours ago. I can't waste my time waiting on you. Why didn't you do as I told you? I told you to come back in an hour. Why, I've been out almost two hours. And now I return, and the place is still dirty. You go in and clean up and lock the door when you come out. I am going out for lunch now and I won't be back for an hour, so you'll have plenty of time to clean up. I don't want to be alone in the room with you while you're cleaning up—."

I am tongued-tied. I drop the broom and the pail and out of eyes, white with the dust of emotion, watch the figure chastely going down the steps. Aeons of time creep by me. It is years before I come to. But when I do it is with gargantuan violence. There rises up within me, drowning all sense of reason and pacification, a passionate feeling of revolt—revolt against domestic service—against that damnable social heirloom of my race.

It is low, mean, degrading—this domestic serving. It thrives on chicanery. By its eternal spirit-wounds, it is responsible for the Negro's enigmatic character. It dams up his fountains of feeling and expression. It is always a question of showering on him fistfuls of sweets, nothings, tips,—"With us, it matters not that you are colored. We don't care what color you are. Our firm opens its arms to everybody. Why, who knows, we might in time put you in charge of a bench. Who knows?" Only when the crucial moment comes, the usual aftermath—subterfuge is

"Yes, niggers are so doggone lazy. They won't work! They expect as much consideration as white people."

Or—

Now that colored fellow was all right, but I couldn't make him shipping clerk. Porter to shipping clerk! Ridiculous! Imagine me doing that. Why, it'd ruin my business. It'd break up the morale of my help. I told him so, but he said he'd quit just the same—let him quit. I can't help it. I'll get another one like him in the morning."

Or, again, this,—taken from the NEW YORK TIMES, May 27, 1923——". . . . If they (the Negroes) have worked a few days, they lay off and loaf until their money is exhausted. They shift from place to place in the slightest cause or pretext . . ."

And still they wonder why. Still, but what's the use?

It is hell, I say, to be a domestic!

THE STONE REBOUNDS

Eric D. Walrond offers a first-person narrative of a self-styled progressive young white man in search of "blackness." The young man discovers that reactions to color may be strong and off-setting on both sides of "the divide." This story was published in September 1925.

It is night. I am in dark Harlem. I am walking along Seventh Avenue, in company with a Negro playwright. I had met him at a radical forum downtown. I pride myself on being an intellectual anarchist; I haven't any prejudices. I am interested in the Negro problem. Interested in it the same as I am interested in Russia and India and Korea. I want to see Society take on a different shape. I am a radical. I stick to my Negro friend. I take him around with me. I run the risk of being ostracized. I remember once I took him to Barrett Manor. Barrett Manor is an art colony. Flappers and broken-down celebrities hang out there. It is a nice place. It is full of Dore's illustrations. I like it. Always I am lionized by the crowd. Of love and death, poetry and pragmatism, sex and the eternal will—of all these things I would talk. They would hang around and anticipate the words as they came from my lips, especially the girls. I was such a favorite there. Then I took my Negro friend there. Why not? My friend is more intellectual than I. I realize it. I am big enough to admit it. In the old days as soon as I opened the wire-screened door they would all flock to greet me—but that day, I shall never forget it. I let my friend in first. I went in afterward. What a change! I was no longer the idol, the master conversationalist; no, I had fallen. Fallen from grace; fallen like Lucifer. That entire day I felt a pang of remorse at what it was to be white. Earl, superman that he is, did not seem to notice it. Why should he? It was his first visit there. But it galled me. I have tabooed Barrett Manor. I haven't been there since.

I think of all these things as I swing up the avenue. And my confession! As much as I had tried, I couldn't conceal it. At first I used to blame it on the bourgeoise; but Earl was wise. I could see it in the way he'd smile. Smiling out of the corner of his mouth!

So I decided to tell him. I laid my cards on the table. It is useless, I said, trying to run up against a stonewall—a Gibraltar of prejudice. Useless! I didn't have any difficulty bringing him to my point of view. Yes, he said, he had felt it all along—at the restaurant, the theatre, on the bus, in Greenwich Village; yes, it had followed us, like a starving wolf. But my friend, non-combatant that he is, suggested a way out. Why not let us meet up in Harlem, Black Harlem? Surely——. No, I hadn't any objection, I hastily assured him. Truth is, the idea thrilled me. I long wanted to visit the place. I had heard so much about it.

"It is in here."

I am jerked out of my reverie. I am on a dark, maple-shaded street. I don't know how Earl manages it, but I suppose he knows the place very well. I follow him. It is down in a basement. A sheet of purple is over everything. Dimly I make it out. Witch-like silhouettes belt it. Over the fireplace is a white peacock. A majestic-looking bird. On the wall, over the piano, is a girl sitting on the bough of a huge cypress, playing a harp. Sunset shines thru the branches. Beside the piano is a bookcase, and on the center table is a medieval lamp. Its chimney is daubed with Oriental flowers. Quaint as can be. At once I take to it. I like the atmosphere. But the people in it! At a jut-like table is a girl, I don't know whether she is white or colored, talking to a man. I can not see his face—it is away from me. But his neck I can see. It is black. I am being introduced around. I can not always see their faces. The place is so romantically dark. It is a long time before I adjust my sight to the light. I am invited to a seat at the center table, and talk—group chatter—is resumed. A girl with pomegranate cheeks is on my right, and at my left is Earl. The girl is saying something to me.

"Well, Mr. Kraus, how do you like it up here?"

"Oh, I think it is great," I whisper dreamily. "It is so—Bohemian."

The girl has creole eyes and I feast on them; but they are not magnetic enough to arrest the functioning of my other self—my subconscious self. I can hear Earl's soft musical voice as he leans over and talks to the lady with the cossack hat, at his left.

"No, he isn't colored. Jewish—a friend of mine. What? No, I don't think so. Kraus is a poet, not an anthropologist."

"What is he doing up here, then?"

"He just came along with me, that's all."

"Humph, that is funny."

"What's funny?"

"This white man coming up here—I don't understand it."

"Oh, don't be silly, Daisy. I thought you always say you haven't any prejudice."

I am talking to the dark-eyed girl at my elbow. Of course, it is about the race question. Everyone seems to be talking about it these days. I ask her what are her views on that eternal bugaboo—social equality.

"Well, it is this way," she begins, knocking the ash off her cigarette. "I am colored, and self conscious. Very much so; I can not get over it. It is part of me. I believe it ought to be so that if I want to marry a Dutchman, I can. I am of age, and I think I know what is best for me. More than the ignorant mob out on the street. Yes, I believe in social equality—if by social equality you mean inter-marriage, and that is what it means nowadays."

I don't know what sort of look has crept into my eyes, but it must be an alarming one.

"Understand me clearly!" She hastened to add, "By that I do not mean that *I* personally wish to marry a white man. Get that straight."

I am conscious of an enveloping silence. I drink the tea that is put before me and try to think up clever things to say. I can not explain it. It is sepulchral—the silence. Even the girl beside me is taken up with the string of Spanish beads around her neck. Occasionally I would glance over at the woman on Earl's right. She is toying with the Japanese ash tray on the table. But I am sure now and then she emits a grunt. Something ugh-ish. I am sure of it. I look around. On me a houseful of eyes is cast. I do not feel out of place. I rejoice in the reaction. I know why they are staring at me. I am white.

Cynthia Goes to the Prom

Eric D. Walrond's tale examines the motive and mission of a popular and bright young black girl who finally learns that once past the "age of innocence" color does matter, unequivocally. This story was published in November 1923.

In the city where I live, Cynthia is singled out as a girl with "nerve." It is this very ennobling quality which gets her everything she wants. Her sister, for instance, who is older than she, is a school teacher; but Elmira gets very little enjoyment out of life. In fact, she lives a very cloistered life—always dreaming or brooding over something. Some of the girls say it is because she hasn't got a fellow. Others, because she was balked in her attempts to get the job she had prepared herself for—that of teaching French in a high school.

Not so Cynthia. Much prettier, Cynthia is the madcap of the family. In school she is popular—very, very popular. In the "gym" the white girls would stand back aghast at the way she'd put her "soul" into her dancing. Scholastically she always came out on or very near the top. In her senior year, that eye-opening year of hers, she was elected to the Arista.

Yes, Cynthia was the best known colored girl at ————. The girls forgot the color of her skin. The boys, at first shy and undemonstrative, stared askance at the ebony locks that adorn her bronze temples; then, before you knew it, "took" completely to her. In short, Cynthia, a comely black girl, stylish, "up-to-date," brilliant, at a school where Irish, Jew, Italian, Anglo-Saxon mixed, was a favorite. The girls flocked to her. Arm in arm they'd be seen tramping through the corridors with her. All of which, to a sensitive soul like Cynthia, led the girl to pout her lips when her dad, a compositor who was born in the West Indies, and who never had a steady job the twenty-two years he has been in America, although he belongs to the union, etc.—upbraided her for not reading the armfuls of colored papers he weekly brought home.

"I can't see the sense of it," Cynthia would say, "this race-conscious business. I can't see it." In this way Cynthia developed a complex that is characteristic of the Negroes of East New York.

Six days ago Cynthia, her eyes as big as saucers, came to me. She had been crying. Unlike the fiery creature I had known she was broken in spirit, ready to give up the ghost.

"I want to go to the prom and I can't get anyone to go with me," she snuffled. "All the boys I know throw up their hands in despair, saying, 'I ain't going to no white folks' ball. I don't want to get put out.' Like it isn't our ball too!

"I am bent on going because the last dance the school had I didn't go—and some of the girls bawled me out. Said it was all right and it didn't make any difference to them. And I don't want to come out of high school and say I didn't go to the prom. And it is to be given at the McAlpin, besides.

"Last year Girls' High had its prom at the St. George and a few of the colored girls got up a party and went and, as you know, there was a big to do about it in the papers. Since then the colored boys in East New York have got cold feet. You can't make 'em see the point."

"I'll go," I said. And we went—all eight of us.

In the lobby of the McAlpin I timidly asked a white-haired orderly to show us where —— was having its prom. Instead of answering me, he looked over my shoulder at the gowned Cleopatras in silk and velveteen and darted over to the desk. I heard, after a little wait, an abrupt, "Oh, just high school kids. Let 'em up." The orderly, whose face had now turned white, came and without a word, pointed a finger at the elevator.

"Twenty-fourth floor."

At least the elevator man hadn't any prejudice. Some of us expected the car to stop midway and refuse to budge. Car trouble comes that way, you know. Yes, come to think of it, that elevator man must have been a Negro passing for white, or a radical, or a socialist, or——.

At the landing a stately lady in flickering mauve who acted as hostess—I think she was the principal's wife—turned first scarlet and then her back on us.

"Let's check our coats."

"Ask one of those girls where the lady's cloak room is."

News spreads fast. In half a second the three hundred odd guests knew we were there. They all trotted out to see what we looked like. Yet, we were not confused. We did not ask anybody questions. We did not smile. Nor did we turn white in the face. Yes, we were silently composed.

Somebody espied the gents' cloak room. We separated, each of us grinding his or her teeth—inwardly boiling, outwardly steaming. We squeezed through the curious crowd. Nobody stumbled over the carpet. Nobody tripped. In fact, I think I saw a look of disappointment on some of our spectators' faces. Some of them had come for a good hearty lung-expanding laugh. But they didn't get it.

The man in the men's cloak room smiled and eagerly served us. That done, we started to rejoin the girls. Around the corner at the ladies' cloak room Cynthia and the other girls still had their coats on.

"Can't you get your coats checked?"

"No, she hasn't any more hooks left so she says she'd have to put our coats on the floor."

"What?"

I looked at the lady in charge of the cloak room. Her face barked at me. Her green eyes spat fire. She was ready to fight, to fly at our throats. It was evident she was having a difficult time endeavoring not to look pugnacious.

I looked over her head at the coat rack. I saw a whole row of vacant hooks. "What is the matter with those hooks there?" I said to her.

"Another party—there's another party across the hall and I'm saving 'em for them."

Ah, so that was it. Other ladies came to Cynthia's prom but they didn't have to put their coats on the floor and have them "carelessly" walked over.

"I heard a woman say to her as I got off the elevator, 'No room. No room!'"

Into the ball room we went. They quietly made way for us. Our shoes must have creaked or something. Or one of us must have looked like a scarecrow. But decidedly everything was dropped to stare at us. Stare! Can't they stare? They are past-masters in the art.

"Don't you know any of these people?" I said to Cynthia.

"Do I?"

"You'd think they'd even nod to you."

"Why, you see that girl there in blue—that's so and so. In school we are like that. But you wait; let her come asking me anything about geometry again———."

"Well," I said to Cynthia as the taxi started to cross Brooklyn Bridge, "what do you think of social equality now?"

"Not much. I tell you one thing, though—whenever I get a chance I'm going to these affairs. They've got to get used to us! They must!"

Which, from a disciple of passivism like Cynthia, was astounding, to say the least.

VIGNETTES OF THE DUSK

Published in January 1924, this piece by Eric D. Walrond offers five tales that demonstrate the truism that levels of color (shade or tint), country of birth, economic status, education, and vocational orientation cannot withstand the vagaries of racial discrimination.

It is lunch time. I am in the heart of America's financial seraglio. It is a lovely day. Spring. Oceans of richly clad people sweep by me. In my pockets I jingle coins of gold. Gold! I am tired of eating at Max's Busy Bee. The fellows who dine there are so—so—rough sometimes. Still it is the most democratic eating place I know. There is no class prejudice; no discrimination; newsboys, bootblacks, factory slaves, all eat at Max's.

Today I am "flush" and I think I ought to blow myself to a decent meal. My courage is bolstered up. Rich, I am extravagant today. I rub elbows with bankers and millionaires and comely office girls. Of seraphs and madrigals I dream—nut that I am. I look up at the sparkling gems of architecture and marvel at the beauty that is America. America!

I almost ran past it. There it is, the place with the swinging doors and the chocolate puffs in the show case. Myriads of Babbitts and elfin girls pour into it. Tremblingly I enter. It reminds me of a mediaeval palace. Mirrors, flowers, paintings, candelabra; waiters in gowns as white as alabaster; and at the table a row, two deep, of eager, bright faced youths and maidens.

I stand back in bewilderment. How efficient these waiters are! Don't they ever make mistakes? Don't they ever give wrong change? Don't they ever serve a frappe for a temptation, a soda for a sundae? Don't they ever—

The waiter's inquiring eyes are on mine. He has got round to me. I whisper my order to him.

"Oyster salad—and vanilla temptation."

I put both hands in my coat pockets and think of the beauty and romance to be found in this place. Up my sleeve I laugh at your intellectual immigrants who howl about the barrenness of America. To me it offers exhaustless possibilities. It opens up entirely new and unexpurgated editions to life. Yes, I say to myself, I must come back again. It is weirdly enchanting. The cuisine is so good. And the people here are such refined eaters! So unlike Max's, where everything is bolted down at a gulp!

Oh, why does he put himself to all that trouble? Couldn't he just hand it to me over there instead of having to come all the way round the counter to make sure that it gets into my hands? Couldn't he have saved himself all that trouble?

He is at my side. Stern and white-lipped he hands me a nice brown paper bag with dusky flowers on it. He holds it off with the tips of his fingers as if its contents were leprous.

"Careful", he warns farsightedly, "else you'll spill the temptation." I do not argue. Sepulchrally I pay the check and waltz out. It is the equivalent of being shoed out. And, listen folks, he was careful *not* to say, "No, we don't serve no colored here."

II.

In 1918 he came to America. That means he is still a foreigner. He is not a citizen—yet. But he is going to be. It is going to be the Big Adventure of his life. But wait—

Sometimes he stops and thinks. He is a Negro. He is a foreign Negro. Every day he reads of lynchings in the South. He is besieged on all sides by vicious soul pricks. No, they'd say to him, you mustn't go South; you won't like it down there. In some places, like Texas, you can't stand up under the same roof with a white man unless you take off your hat. You would rebel against it. You, with your white man's point of view (don't you know, the white nurse woman who attends his wife once told him, as she cocked her red head on one side and shut one of her ugly cross eyes, "I think English Negroes are more like white people in their point of view, don't you think so? They're so fine—and not so race conscious.") You, they say to him, you with your white man's ways and outlook will not stand for it. They'd string you up on a tree! They'd. . . .

"But I must go", he screams back at them. "I must! I can't be an American unless I am able to go South! I've got to go."

He thinks of his friend Williams. Williams is a Jamaican. But he is thoroly, spiritually, euphistically American. Some dusky folks, mistaking him for a native, so perfect is his philological assimilation—I am referring to those Afro-Americans who speak of West Indians as "monkey chasers"—come to him and say, "You know, Bill, dem monkey wimmin is de dummest—"

But Williams, who owns a lovely home in Jersey, and has a pretty wife, a jewel of one of the best colored families of Baltimore, is not a citizen. And he doesn't intend to be one. He has been here twenty years. "America is all right", he'd say, "but I ain't taking no chances!"

III.

I am a listening post. I am anchored in the middle of life's gurgling stream. It is a stream that is anthropologically exotic. Up in the Negro belt.

I am at a chop house on Lenox Avenue. It is a rendezvous for Negro Bohemians. I am amazed at the conglomerateness of it. Quadroons, octoroons, gypsies, yellows, high and low browns, light and dark blacks, of all shades and colors of shades.

"Well, what do you think of this young Negro generation? Think they'll amount to anything?"

"Oh, they'll fizzle out like all the rest. Wind up as porters.... elevator men.... janitors...."

Silence.

IV.

I am thinking, thinking, thinking. Of white supremacy; of the Nordic Renaissance....

And again I don the armor of the listening post.

Right of me is a Negro, a very black Negro clarionetist, who, as I take my seat, rises to go out. At the table from which he rose two other men sit. One is a mulatto; the other is fair, very fair, almost white. He of the golden hair and thin lips leans back in his chair and looks at the young man about to go out.

"Say", he whispered, "kin—kin ah come along?"

The other played with it. Slowly he took the tooth pick out of his mouth and wagged his head decisively.

"Nope", he said, "I can't take you along, old top. Where I'm going the folks don't like no yalla men."

V.

Out on the street. I whine at the whirl of dust and dirt the wind blasts up on me. I am slowly going down the avenue. In front of me is a jet black trollop. Her hair is bobbed. I snort at the bumps—barber's itch— I am forced to see on the back of her scraped neck. Ugh! Glass bottle!

I stop at Archie's. I always stop at Archie's on the way down. Out on the steaming boulevard he is, as usual. Myriads of men—please don't tell me they all work at night—talk to him about horses, horses, horses. Coming up the avenue is a woman, an anthropological metamorphosis. . . .

"May God strike me dead if I ain't telling you the truth", Archie is trying to convince a skeptic of something. "Eight years, I tell you. After me for eight long years. But I didn't bother. And talk about pretty, she was a dream. Her father was one of the richest colored men in Virginia. And she had a lovely bungalow on the South Side. Oberlin graduate too. But I didn't marry her. And I didn't have anything against her. . . . She was so fine and thoughtful. . . . Come any time at the house. I'll show you the little cuff links . . . things like that. . . . I didn't have anything against her. . . . Not a thing. Only thing she was too white. Her hair was a bit too much like old gold. . . . She was too white. . . ."

Coming up the avenue is the anthropological metamorphosis.

"Sure she ain't white, Archie?"

"Ah don't know . . . ."

"Seems lek she . . . ."

Goes the mystery by. Then . . . .

"Naw", Archie spits, "she ain't white. Can't you see her neck?"

A CHOLO ROMANCE

In this fable published in June 1924, Eric D. Walrond shows off his facility with dialects. While doing so he utilizes four short chapters to exemplify the apparent chinks in the sensitivity and emotional armor between males and females in any language—Spanish, English, and even black dialect.

"Enrique!" exclaimed Maria. "Enrique, look!"

Before I could get away from her she had grabbed me by the arm, a winsome smile on her half-Indian, half-African face.

"Vex with Maria?" she pouted, her face close to mine. "No—no—likee me no more?"

There was something wistful about this Cholo girl. Her face was round, moon-like if you wish, with dainty black freckles all over it. Her hair was done up in a slip-shod fashion—plaited in two and coiled in a lump on her head. Around her oily neck she wore a bright silk bandanna. The calico skirt she wore resembled very much the festival costumes of the dark beauties of Martinique.

"Come, Enrique. Come see Chineeman."

I hesitated.

"Enrique!" The nostrils of her straight Roman nose dilated—dilated furiously. There was an unutterable command in the way she threw back her head, arms akimbo, her eyes, like bits of amethyst, flashing at me. I followed her down the stairs. About midway she stopped and leaned over the bannister.

"Look, Enrique!" she cried.

Below, wrapt in a veil of smoke, we could see into the kitchen of a Chinese ghetto restaurant. "Melican," or Li Fung, the proprietor, was stirring a row of pots on the fireplace of his dark, ill-smelling kitchen. One contained the remnants of yesterday's lima beans, the other of a white, soul-less thing that went for rice, and the third of what was served to the starving Asiatic coolies as beef stew.

"Iguana-soup!" Maria whispered.

The Chinaman, instead of washing the pots, poured fresh peas over the stale peas, fresh rice on top of the stale rice, and scraps of meat on the rotting stew. After that he poured into each pot about a pint of boiling water, stirred it, and added coals to his fire. This was done every day in the year, and the only time they got a washing was when he took them to the tin-smiths to be re-soldered.

"You!" yelled Maria.

The Chinaman looked up.

"Diablo! Sung fy-ee-ah, dlyam lascal too. Slut up!" And he ran for a fire poker. With leaps and bounds we ran up the steps, Maria dying with laughter in one breath, and in another exhausting her already limited vocabulary of pidgin English on a sermon that: would have done justice to the Medicine-Man of Pasadena.

Suddenly, from around the corner, we heard the dragging of slippers, of the chug-chug of Mme. Chili's fat self, coming in our direction. Mme. Chili, a fat, Basque woman with a flabby, vermicelli face, seamed and canaled with a map of prairie-like lines, was formerly the wife of a local wine merchant. Originally from Barcelona, she had tried, in her painful way, to introduce in her social set all the charms and graces of Castillian society. Not that she was in any sense a member of Aspinwall's Four Hundred. Far from it. Be it said, however, that it was her desire to be linked up with the Ariases and the Arosemenas, the Galindos and the Arcias—the first families of the Republic. She cultivated tastes that amounted to prejudices. Around her three room flat she erected a fence—a very physical fence. It was unheard of for anyone living in the house, lodger or otherwise, to enter unasked that part of it. Five years ago, so the story ran, she had adopted a little moon-faced Indian girl whom a Mache trader had left with her. The girl, she figured, was to grow up as brilliant as any of the *senoritas* of the land, and Maria, with an inherent dignity of carriage, fitted right into her mistress' plans. At times, however, she would break away from the conventions of her rigorous bringing up and stray into the company of one whom Mme. Chili had told her she must despise as a *Chumbito.*

"Maria!" cried Mme. Chili, staring through her pince nez. "Maria!"

"Senora!"

Swinging around the corner with a paroquet perched on her forefinger, she swept past me like a whirlwind. As she passed, Mme. Chili, staring at me down the end of the hall, palavered so rapidly in the Mache dialect that I was forced to turn away my face. It hurt me to think that I had been the cause of the girl's castigation. So many times had I heard her utter the word *Chumbito.*

After getting as much fun as it is possible to get out of watching a wet canary dry itself in the sun, I stuck my head between the leaves of a Dick Turpin yarn. Black Bess had just jumped off one of London's tallest skyscrapers, and Dick, eluding his captors, was Johnny-on-the-spot as the shining steed landed on its feet. With his usual dash he leaped into the saddle and in a jiffy was lost from view!

In a moment she returned, a flower-painted vase of orchids in her hands. She went to the cesspool, filled the vase with fresh water and started to go back, humming a barbaric native *plena*. Half-way she stopped. "Oh!" Turning, she came and sat beside me, gazing at the lurid picture on the back of a London Tid-Bit.

"Enrique," she whispered, "me no vex-y por you. Me like por you berry, berry much. But Mme. Chili, she tell por me no likee you. You no good, she tell por me. You *Chumbito*, she say; but me no like Mme. Chili. She too big, too much-ee de lady por me, me no like. . . . You no vex por me, Enrique? No?"

"Why should I, Maria?"

"Next week me go marry por you, Enrique, and then we go tell Mme. Chili—"

"Maria!"

"Senora!"

She was gone.

II.

One day a wooden-legged man by the name of Baxter called and sat at the top of the stairs talking in soft, earnest tones to Maria. He was a tall, bearded man, as black as the ebony lignum vitae he carried, and a more ragged creature I had never seen before. There was something familiar about that man. As I looked at him I was sure I had seen him somewhere before. Vainly I ransacked my brain trying to "place" him. Finally, a few days later, as soon as he had left her, I asked Maria who he was.

"My father," she promptly told me. Her father? That black, rare-lipt creature? I was inclined to think not. Moreover, the man spoke English—perfect English. There wasn't the slightest trace of either Spanish or Indian in him. Black as tar, there was no question as to his ethnic oneness. As I sat and thought it over I mentally concluded that it was one of the multiple mysteries to do with this gay Cholo girl.

The next day, while strolling down the waterfront, I ran into an old gold-digger from Berbice. Here was a man who had spent the greater part of his life ore-hunting, a man known at half a dozen sea-ports on the Caribbean. In him was personified the very spirit of wanderlust. This time, he confided, he had just come up from the Valley of the Cauca in the interest of an archaeologic expedition.

"But I am anxious to go to Darien. I had a long talk with an engineer who has been up there and he tells me there is an army of prospectors bound for the interior. Then, there is this here Pearl Island. I have got to get a peek at that. Between these two surely I ought to find enough to interest me until the *Husaco* comes along."

"Perhaps," I said, "but you can't lay too much stress on these crazy rumors. There is a great deal of gold in Panama, but as long as I have been here I haven't heard of anyone who has found any of it."

"Well, that is true, but you never can tell, my boy."

"Yes, they say—"

"Say," he interrupted, looking down the street. "Well, if that isn't Br'r Goat."

"Who?"

"Br'r Goat. Don't you remember him? That is he, all right. Well, well, to think that that old son-of-a-gun is down here. I wonder how he got here."

In the white hot sun at the entrance to the Royal Mail wharf there was Br'r Goat, the man who Maria told me was her father. Far back in my boyhood days I recalled a sordid picture of this freak of nature. On the banks of the Essequibo. I had heard a lot about him and his relations with the East Indians who infested the East Coast. Once he was implicated in the disappearance of a "coolie" princess, but that was neither here nor there. From that time the pseudonym by which he had become known stuck to him. But many a Rod Street school boy had his "mud-head" broken if his legs did not carry him fast enough from the scene of jumping Br'r Goat.

"Let's go down and talk to him," suggested Sanford. "I'd like to hear what the old beggar has to say for himself."

Before I could raise a finger in protest, he had started and the only thing to do, I suppose, was to trot along. At the gate Br'r Goat had stopped ostensibly to light his pipe. That he had seen us I had not the slightest shadow of a doubt, and as I looked into the smouldering depths of his lurking black eyes I am certain I was right. I don't think I ever saw such terrible, cat-like eyes in all my life. They ate into one's soul, saw beyond every act, interpreted every gesture. Eyes that tore the veil from one's inmost thoughts, eyes that saw in terms of motives, not actions. Of everything else I was oblivious. The color of his skin, the shape of his nose, his eyelids, his mouth, his chin, all these I saw and saw not. Only one thing stuck in my brain and that was the way those eyes bored into me, how they actually mesmerized me. I dared not look away. During all the talk that followed he never once took his eyes off mine. . . . Yes, he had shipped out on a schooner at Trinidad, stopping at Santa Cruz and Curacao. He had come to the isthmus bent on getting a job with the Commission at Gatun or as a railroad hand in Cristobal. Yes, he liked the place all right, although the rain brought back his old backaches. Those awful rheumatic-pains laid him up for days some times. No, he hadn't been there very long, and he was getting to like the place pretty well. Very few friends from Majica he had met during his stay on the isthmus, and these didn't interest him. Where did the old folks he knew back home hang out?

III.

"Enrique," said Maria to me the next morning, "Enrique, me—me—me—want-y por spikkoty you."

I was taken back at the look I saw in the girl's flushed face. Eyes red, lips swollen, Maria had been crying—crying her heart out. Alarmed, I jumped out of my hammock, knocked the ashes out of my pipe, and prepared for something desperately out of the ordinary. She sat on the goat-upholstered bench beside me, clasped her knee in her beaded hands, and looked up into my face.

"Tell me, Maria," I said, "tell me, what is the trouble?"

"Me no want-ee por go back to the mountains. San Blas too far from Colon. In Colon jew have nice dress, nice music in de park, el teatro, el carnival, and," she added slyly, "Enrique. Mme. Chili, she no know 'bout this. Suppose she know," and she shrugged her shoulders feebly, "suppose she know she go fret, maybe she go beat me."

"But who is taking you back to the mountains, Maria?"

"My padre, he go take me back, *manana*."

"*Manana?*"

"*A las siete por la manana.*"

That white-slaver of a father of hers, I suspected, was up to some of his old dirty tricks!

"Listen, Maria, how is it that this man, Br'r—Baxter, I mean—how is it that he is your father—and he is so different, so unlike you?"

"Me no know, me no know." She shrugged her slender shoulders indifferently. "Mme. Chili, she tell me he fuh my papa, but what do I know?"

"But surely you must have some recollection of your past, Maria. Don't you know where you were born, and who your parents were?"

"Me no know," she used the first thing that came to her mouth, "me no know."

"Try, try and go back a bit. Tell me, where did you first come to know this Baxter—your father?"

"Oh, not berry, berry long. Let me see, me think—"

"I think, Maria."

"Yes, I—I—think it was a little before you came por live here. One day I went to the market por buy *pescow* por Mme. Chili, and as I go 'cross Bolivar Street dis man come to me and say 'Maria, Maria!' Me look, and him say, 'You no know fuh you papa, Maria?' and started por cry. I no notice him and 'im follow me home. Him come and spikkoty Mme. Chili, then Mme. Chili call por me and say 'Maria, dis por yuh papa.' Me no know no more."

"I am going straight to Mme. Chili and ask her," I decided impulsively. "I am sure there is a misunderstanding somewhere."

"Please, Enrique," Maria entreated, "please, no go to Mme. Chili, she go beat me."

Right. Moreover, very little was to be gained by taking the bull by the horns at this early stage of the game.

"Never mind, Maria," I assured her. "Never mind, Enrique go fix por you."

A wave of hope swept over her brown, primitive face. Impulsively she caught my hand, and sloth that I was, had fastened a kiss on it before I could prevent her.

As I started to go down the steps I saw Mme. Chili, clad in utmost black, hurrying down in front of me. Ever since I had been a lodger in the house I had not once seen her in street attire, and the mere fact of her going out was in itself an event. But clad in black, and acting as nervously and as mysteriously as she did, made the matter all the more important. Should I follow her? So far I had no definite plan as regards the predicament in which Maria was placed, and, curiosity-bound, I decided to trail her just for the fun of it. The good *senora*, heavily veiled, kept close to the side of the buildings as she sped along. At Eighth Street she turned in the direction of the Cosmopolitan Hotel. As it so happened, Sanford was stopping there and I had a pretty good reason, I felt, in entering it. The Cosmopolitan Hotel is one of those places in Latin America which boast of being built under the "European plan"—whatever that is. Its rooms are separated by walls so thin that it was possible to sit in one room and hear all that went on in the next. At any rate, I was just in time to see Mme. Chili enter one facing Front Street. Now if my friend from Berbice had had his right next to it, I could have entered, and by reason of its "European construction" listened to all that was said in it. But, alas, no such fortune was in store for me, and all I had to do was to trot up and down the porch for a full half hour, practically helpless. One thing I found out, though, and that was that the room Mme. Chili had entered was occupied by a wooden-legged man by the name of Baxter!

IV.

Desperate, I ran down the street. Two things I was firmly convinced of. Baxter was not Maria's father, and Mme. Chili knew it!

It was a busy day for the merchants. Scores of American tourists and horn-eyed "scientists," en route to New Zealand, had brought a harvest to the city. The bazaars and jewelry stores and places where curios and canal stones and sharks' teeth were bought drew the largest crowds. Out of the conglomeration of Duque ticket vendors and tourists and inquisitive bystanders, I recognized a man I wanted to see more than anyone else in the world—Julio Jiminez.

"Hello, Julio," I cried, "what are you doing for yourself these days?"

"For cry sake, Sr. Martin! I wanted to see you very badly the other day. Where are you living now? I was up at the Arjona Club the other night and I proposed you for membership, just as I told you I was going to. Dr. Arjona is bound to loom big in the coming election, as the people are sick and tired of the vacillating policies of Pobras and Lefevre. We want a man who is going to interpret the will of the people and not be afraid to express it, a man to tell the gringoes they must live up to the provisions of the treaty and not overrun our cities with hostile marines."

The same old Julio. A violent patriot, he was ever yelping about the Imperialism of the United States, of the child-like leadership of the Republic's statesmen, dreaming of the time when the young radicals would overthrow the "capitalist traitors" and send him to Paris or Rome with the rank of Ambassador Extraordinary. As I looked at his diminutive figure, his mulatto face, his immaculate duck and spotless shoes, I wondered whether he had become so bigoted, so pig-headed, as to be beyond the reaches of my plan.

"Yes, we missed you badly," he continued. "We wanted you to be on that *Junta* that went to the capital a few days ago to wait on His Excellency. This is going to be a big year for the Liberals, I tell you, and we want you to come around. The other night he had a *baile* and we missed you very much. Those Burgo girls were there and they were asking about you."

"I tell you, frankly, Julio, I have been so dog gone busy these days I haven't been able to go anywhere."

"Yes, I imagine so. For cry sake, man, I saw in *La Estrella* where you had taken over Banton's cocoanut interests around the coast, and I suppose that is enough to keep anybody busy."

"Say, Julio," I cried at last, "I want you to do me a favor—a pretty big favor."

"Well, that is what I've been willing to do for a long time. I shall never forget that you once got me out of a serious hole, and I always insisted I owe you a debt of gratitude. As I told you once before, I am at your command—always."

I looked at him, noted the firmness of his mouth, the steady glitter of his eyes, the sincerity with which he said it.

"But this," I frowned, "is a pretty big thing to ask of any man, and I wish you'd see your way to do it. Julio, I am up a tree. I know a little Cholo girl who is about to be sold into slavery by a man posing as her father. The lady she is living with is in a measure implicated in it, and the only way out as far as I can see is to marry the girl. Marry her off to some responsible man who will protect her. Julio—will you do it?"

The boy's eyes flew open. I hated to think I was making capital out of a debt he felt he owed me, but what else could I do? *I myself was out of the running!*

"But I've got to have time to think it over. For cry sake, man, you must not forget that I and Helena have been going together for some time. Give me about a day or so."

"No, I am sorry, Julio, but I've got to have your decision within the hour."

"For cry sake."

"I know it's tough, Julio. It is a pretty serious thing to ask of any man, but that girl is practically friendless, and that white-slaver is going to take her away tomorrow at sunrise. Let us go and take her to the *alcalde* and get a license. I don't think you will like the girl, but for pity sake help me to shield her a while until this skunk is convinced she is in safe hands. Then, of course, we will see if we can't get you out of it."

"From anybody else this would be preposterous," he snapped, "but I am with you. Let's go."

Jumping in a coach, we rode to the boarding house on Bottle Alley. As we got into it a strange premonition stole over me. Suppose Baxter had anticipated us? With quick steps we ran up the stairs, and, disregarding the rules of the place, I raced to the entrance to Mme. Chili's, raising my voice in a loud, "Maria." No answer. Presently I heard a shuffle of feet, as if someone were coming to meet us. Were my ears deceiving me? Surely Maria didn't walk that way. Nor Mme. Chili. That peg-step sounded like Br'r Goat's! No sooner had that thought come to me than his black, shining disk shone before us, like a spectre out of the night.

"Come, Maria is inside. Go and see her."

For the first time I entered the Chili apartment. Inside a curious sight awaited us. Mme. Chili, the proud, beautiful mistress of the house, had the little Indian girl clasped to her bosom, smothering her with kisses and words of love.

"Oh, my own dear child," she wept, "my own darling Maria."

Struggling out of her mother's arms, Maria espied us, and at once ejaculated, "Enrique!"

"I have brought you a redeemer, Maria," I murmured so that the others could not hear, "a hero who is willing to risk life itself so that you won't have to go back to the mountains."

"No necessaire, Enrique, no necessaire. Me no go to San Blas no more. Mme. Chili, she my mama, Baxter he my papa *en realidad*. You know? Me go stay in Colon and go to the park on Sunday night, and hear the nice music, and *el teatro* and el carnival, and see the nice ladies and everything. Let me hug por you, Enrique, por next week me wantee por marry por you."

"Maria!"

"Senora!"

She was gone.

THE VOODOO'S REVENGE

This narrative reveals Eric D. Walrond's expansive knowledge of tropical French West Indies locales and seaports. In the following story, he details a quintet of personae for trader-editor Villaine, who manages to find solutions to several dilemmas through obeah assistance. Walrond published this story, awarded third prize, in July 1925.

At the edge of Faulke's River a fleet of cayukas lay at anchor. It was a murky slice of water front. Half Latin, it was a rendezvous for those French creoles who had left the service of the Americans to go into business for themselves as liquor dealers, fishermen, coal burners, black artists, etc. On the side of it facing the muddy rivulet with its coral islets and turtle shoals, were the usual cafes, dance halls and fish markets. Behind these stretched a line of "Silver" quarters—cabins of the black Antillian canal diggers.

One ran across in this part of the Silver City Negroes who spoke *patois*—black and brunettes from St. Lucia and Trinidad and Martinique. Fronting their quarters a road meandered, dusty on sunny days and a lake of mud and slush on rainy ones, up to Monkey Hill.

Along Faulke's River folk gathered each morning to buy up the offerings of the fishermen and the pearl divers who had come in the night before. In the group of traders one saw pretty Negresses from the isles of the Caribbean who wore flame-colored skirts and East Indian ear-rings and heavy silver bangles reaching up to their elbows. Some, those of "higher caste," wore in their bosoms cameos and pearls and Birds of Paradise feathers to ornament their already gorgeous head dress. In those days short skirts were foreign to the women of the tropics—and one saw long beautiful silk dresses, a faint echo of Louis Quinze, trailing behind the dusky grand dames as they went from stall to stall and with bamboo baskets bought dolphins and pigeon peas and guinea birds. For hours, as the tropical sun beat down upon them, these lovely angels of Ethiopia would shop and dye their lips with the wine of luscious pomegranates and talk lightly of the things on sale. With them it was a Spring rite. They made a holiday out of it. And far into the morning cayukas full of coral and oranges and yam-pies would come swinging up out of the dark tremulous bowls of the lagoon beyond, to empty themselves upon the wharf while the *patois* men would stand by and fill their pipes, chin, and oft-times steal away in soft bits of voodoo melody.

> *Zoomie maca le*
> *Maca le la*
> *Le a le a le*
>
> *Zoomie tell me*
> *Pape say kiss*
> *'Am a' ready*
>
> *Tell me mama say wahlo . . .*
>
> *Zerry wuz a mambe*
> *Zerry.*
> *Wahlo, wahlo, wahlo.*
>
> *Zamba le a le a le a*
> *Zoke! Zoke! Zoke!*

A queer lot these men. Huge, gigantic, black as night, each grew a mustache or a grizzly beard. In them one saw a transplantation of the ancient culture of Europe. In the oil Maiden Islands one saw big hairy black ship chandlers and fishing boat men who walked with the grace and majesty of university professors. And in these silent old witch-worshipping seamen on Faulke's River, unlike the voluble Maches and Spaniards who infested the clumbling wharves along Limon Bay, was a lingering strain of those heroic men who set out at the beginning of the Nineteenth Century to conquer in the name of France the tropic isles of the Caribbean.

Night in the tropics is an erotic affair. As it flung its mantle over the shining form of the lake the fishermen along it would sit on the bottoms of upturned cayukas and for hours dream of far off weird things. Dreaming; dreaming; dreaming. That is all they seemed to do. For it was difficult to penetrate the mind of a *patois* man. He spoke little. He preferred solitude. He preferred to smoke his cow-dung pipe for days in silence. But he never slept. The fire in his lustreless eyes never went out.

One of these *patois* men was a robust son of the soil who still went by the name of Nestor Villaine. Certainly it had been a comparatively easy thing for him to get in, jabber a few mouthfuls of broken French, and live as an *obeah* man. Up in the hills, he lived the life of a hermit, ate *bobo* fish and iguanas and corn cakes and grew up as hardy and as hairy-chested as the oaks and mahogany he tore down to burn his coal. Away from the society of men and the endearments of women Nestor grew to be a stern son of the jungle. Hard, cold, relentless, he hated the sight of human beings.

Villaine plotted revenge!

II

Caught in the maelstrom of local politics Editor Villaine of the *Aspin-wall Voice* drew a breath of righteous indignation as he was jostled into the *alcaldia*. Alongside him was a crouching bit of humanity—a short, brown-skinned stranger whose immaculate duck, white and tan shoes, jippi-jappa hat, branded him an enemy; in all probability in the pay of the reactionary Ex-Governor Tejada. One of his arms was in a sling; a bit of plaster adorned his left temple. His nose was cut. Dark spots, of ink, soiled the *caballero's* otherwise white suit.

As if they were made by sharply pointed finger nails, gashes and bruises covered his copper-coloured face. His eyes threatened to close up. His lips hung unbeautifully. Not only an arm was in a sling, but tied about his head was a red neckerchief. Unlike his fistic antago-nist he had on workmen's clothes. Ink stained his jacket. Dust and dirt disfigured his already ink-stained trousers. Indubitably Nestor was not at his best.

In walked the alcalde. He was a tall, finely built man. Former Deputy Salzedo was one of the handsomest men in the Republic. Friend and foe admitted that. It had an added significance, especially when one is brilliant and fearless and something of a radical. That was what he was. He was the hope of the Liberal Party. He had been swept into office, a few weeks previous, on the crest of a mighty wave of re-bellion. In the coastal provinces he was hailed as a Messiah, a man to lead the people out of the chaos brought on by the Tejadistas.

"*Orden!*"

The *tinterillos* came to a verbal halt. The *alcaldia* was full of them. They sat in the best wicker chairs. They buzzed around it like a nest of hungry bees. Out at the door Pablo, the black porter, who belonged pathologically to the leper asylum as Palo Seco, kept order with an *agente's* baton. Leaning up against the newly papered wall was the dean of the *tinterillos,* the celebrated Dr. Cecilio Rhodes, a West Indian Negro. As the alcalde entered, and malleted for order, Rhodes, dragging the tooth pick out of his mouth, yelled to his colleagues engulfed in the soft wicker chairs to "Rise, in respect to His Excellency, el Senor Alcalde!"

The *tinterillos* rose with one accord out of respect to His Excellency El Senor Alcalde.

Alcalde Salzedo gazed at the prisoners. Editor Villaine and the truculent *extranjero* with the white and tan shoes.

"Well, what is the trouble with you two?"

The *agente* testified. At high noon, as the labor train had emptied its freight and had started on its way back to the round house, he had been standing in front of the kiosk at the corner of Sixth and Bolivar Streets when a shrill cry attracted his attention. Seizing his baton he raced in the direction whence it had come. In the middle of the block, in the offices of the *Aspinwall Voice,* he found the prisoners wrestling and throwing rolling pins at each other. After a terrific struggle in which he lost a button off his coat and a bit of skin off the third finger of his left hand, he had succeeded in arresting the scoundrels and there they were. . . .

"Now, what have you got to say for yourself?" asked His Excellency as the *agente* retired.

Villaine bristled. Ah, to hear his master's voice? To be able to look into his mentor's dusky eyes and tell him the story of his love and fidelity to him! To relate, by a striking tale of primordial lust, just how far he was willing to go for the Liberal Party! To do that! For years, as a fly-by-night pamphleteer, he had longed for an opportunity to show these native leaders, like Salzedo, just how loyal a "Chumbo"—that is, a black from the English colonies—could be. For Nestor was a native of Anguilla who had come to the isthmus as a "contract laborer" to dig the canal. But he didn't want to do that; he had ideas, big, earthquaking ideas. So when the *Magdalena,* the ship on which he had arrived, docked, he managed, as the laborers disembarked, to slip out of the line and secrete himself behind a bale of merchandise in front of the wharf. When the car in which the men were sardined began to pull out, he had raced across the railroad tracks and had joined the carnival of folk which swept leisurely up Front Street. Dusk found him safely ensconced in a Chinese lice-ridden rooming house on Bottle Alley.

But that was six years before.

"Nothing to say?" the alcalde inquired impatiently. He was annoyed at the glow in Villaine's dreamy black eyes.

"Ah," he breathed, "I was—way—this brute came in my office and without provocation at all began to abuse the Liberal Party, began to swear at Alcalde Salzedo—vilely—criminally! And when he did that I got red in the eyes, and I—well, I went after him, that's all!"

"And you?" inquired the alcalde, turning to the other.

"*Nada!*"

All right then, sixty days, both of you.

Madre de Dios! Villaine staggered under the weight of the sentence. Sixty days—sixty days—

Naively, very naively, he went up to the desk, put his black ink-stained hands on it, and faced his gaoler.

"Surely," he smiled eagerly, "surely, you do not mean me?"

"Yes, you too. Both of you. Next."

The *tinterillos* began beseiging the *alcalde* with their preposterous requests. Pablo with his baton hopped in and escorted the prisoners to the cuartel, which was nearby.

Villaine was in a psychic stupor. It took a long time for it to sink into him. He couldn't understand it. It was a nightmare, a hideous dream. His head ached.

On a cold, wet slab he sat in the cuartel, staring at the crumbling ceiling. Why, he had been fighting Salzedo's battles! He fought for him! He was—get away you—rat! Yes, come to think of it he had been Salzedo's champion right along. *The Aspinwall Voice* was willingly and freely his. It boosted him. It came to be known as the Liberal Party's keenest weapon of satire.

Still . . . ah, the fleas in this place! Still Salzedo, on his magisterial throne, had sentenced him to sixty days in jail as if he were a common felon. His body was sore. It was full of cuts and bruises. Cuts and bruises that he had suffered while fighting his jailer's battles.

Revolution surged through him. And at night when the prisoners conspired to break through the walls of that terrible inquisition Nestor Villaine, the "Chumbo" *herido* would be plotting, plotting.

At Porto Bello, where he broke rocks, he was gruff and brooding. His fellow prisoners avoided him. The *guardias* chucked the food at him and had as little dealings with him as possible. Plainly Villaine had something on his mind.

III

One of the show places of the river front was a cafe with a brothel in the rear. Here the *patois* men drank goblets of anisette and vermouth and met their women. It was the prototype of Sablo's Baron Bolivar Street. But this nameless rendezvous also served a deadly purpose. It was here that the black artists met "their" cooks and servant girls who worked for the white Americans—folk of the "Golden City"—and gave them for a pittance tips on secret poisoning through vegetable alkaloids, etc. And here it was one dark still night Nestor agreed to meet a young St. Lucian by the name of Sambola.

As the clock struck twelve the boy flung aside the dingy curtain and stepped into the room. Except for Nestor, alone at a table with a glass of green liquor, it was deserted. Squeezing through a network of demi-johns the boy came and sat at Nestor's table. Silently the man pushed the bottle over to him and pretending to take a puff at his pipe threw out a haze of smoke to hide the flames that had leapt into his eyes. Sambola poured out a drink and dashed it down his throat. Nestor lowered his eyes in assurance.

Yes, this boy was just the one for it. He came from a family that wallowed in *obeah*. His brother, who was a time-keeper on the Zone, which was a big job for a grammar-school boy to hold, had kept his job there all three years by virtue of it. His other brother, the one all of whose front teeth were capped with gold, steered clear of dagger-gemmed combs and senorita's vials simply because his old witch-stricken mother sat of nights and burned *obeah* for the dusky ladies with whom he consorted in *El Barrio Rojo*.

"Now, look a here," he dashed the pipe away, "I don't wan' no bunglin', *oui?*"

"Non," Sambola dared not blink, so potent was the power Nestor exerted over him.

"You must hide it safely in yo' pocket till the men begin fo' get sleepy—till it is late. Lissen out fo' de polise wissle fo' one o'clock. Pape is likely fo' go a bit early, you say? But that don't matter. Be sure you get it in *his,* though . . ."

Far into the night the older man talked to the boy. He talked to him with the petulance and the nervous gestures of an Oriental. But the thing was Nestor's life balm. For ten long years he had been cherishing it. And there it was—within his grasp!

"Here, take this, and don't lose it, *oui?*"

"Non!"

He took the green vial and tucked it safely in his bosom. Nestor gleamed at him fiendishly. Drink after drink he made the boy swallow. Thru the curtain of the night came the sound of fish splashing in the molten river. From atop the undulating *cordilleras* in the distance a lion howled.

About four o'clock in the morning Sambola slipped out.

Later in the day, as the dusky folk flocked to the waterfront to gobble up the oysters and cayukas of venison, among the things offered for sale was the big yellow cayuka of the trader Villaine.

IV

"Sambola, don't forget the Chess Club meets tonight. And I want you to run over to Calavaggio's and get some of that Jamaica rum he's got."

Mr. Newbold, the manager of the West Indian Telegraph Company, was a social climber. A mulatto, he was something of a mogul. In a small place like Aspinwall, it was easy to know and talk with the mayor and the governor and the agents of the steamship lines that plied to the city. Born in the Cayman Islands he had been to Liverpool, Calais, Bremen. He was a cosmopolitan. In Aspinwall, where life is more precarious than it is elsewhere, white men found time to cultivate one another. On the native side Mr. Newbold was well liked. Alcalde Munoz and Governor Salzedo were great friends of his. And at the governor's reception he was one of the principal guests. Moreover, his wife, a dark brown woman from one of the islands, passed as a shawl-swept *senora*. And his idea of a chess club had originated with Mr. Newbold. A few men in the Republic played it, and he was bent on popularizing the game. It was too good to limit to a straggling few.

In Sambola, the West Indian office boy, he had a faithful and obedient servant. Sambola was a good boy. Unlike the others Mr. Newbold had had he never smoked or whistled or stayed out late at nights or read "Old Sleuth," "Dick Turpin" or "Dead Wood Dick." He hadn't any imagination. That, Mr. Newbold felt, was good for him. He would sit, out there in the front office, and watch Mr. Newbold's collie lying on the hot sun-drenched pavement growl and snap viciously at the flies on his nose.

"You know, Sambola," said Mr. Newbold as the boy returned, "I want you to put on a white apron—like a regular waiter. I was thinking of that the other day. Serving drinks to such a distinguished assemblage in your working clothes looks a bit out of place, don't you think?" So that night Sambola had on a white apron to serve the liquers.

The chess club met upstairs in Padros' Bar, facing Slifer's Park. On Friday nights the park band did not play. In consequence the park was deserted—shrouded in darkness. It was a good night for chess.

Sambola got there first. He opened the door, turned on the gas, and arranged the table. The place was in ship shape for Mr. Newbold always saw to it that Sambola clean and tidy it up the day after each game. In one corner was an ice box. Opening it Sambola examined the array of liquers, and again closed it. A moment later Mr. Newbold arrived.

"Well, Sambola, how's tricks? Are all the bottles there?" He went to the icebox, poked a nose in, and took out a bottle of champagne. He took down a glass.

"Don't drink, eh Sambola?" he asked as he filled the glass and put it to his lips.

"No, sir."

"Not even champagne?"

"No, sir."

"That's a good boy."

A few minutes later Herr Pape, the agent of the Hamburg American Line, blond, grey-eyed, a pipe in his mouth, entered. Following him Sir Winfield Baxter, the agent of the Royal Mail Steam Packet Company, a flippant, youngish old man, a perpetual twinkle in his cat grey eyes; Vincent Childers, the British Vice-Consul, hoarse, humpbacked, anaemic, and dribbling at a brown paper cigarette. Lastly came the Governor and Mayor Munoz.

The years of triumph had heightened the charms of the populist idol. Salzedo wore the usual duck, the same long French shoes with the narrow instep and pointed toes, the same gold and brown peacock charm at his watch, the same fascinating light in his eyes.

"Well, gentlemen," said Mr. Newbold, "this is our club's first anniversary. Let's drink to its health."

After which, the game began. Herr Pape and Mr. Newbold, Governor Salzedo and Sir Winfield, Alcalde Munoz and Vice-Consul Childers.

Thus it was for hours. Between times the men were served sherry and ice, whiskey and soda, coca cola. Silently Sambola served the drinks, got a check signed, and stole softly back to his stool out on the porch to watch the shadows of barques and brigantines and big ocean liners tied to their piers. Below, in the dusky shadows, he saw, too, brown boys and girls spooning. And Sambola grew reminiscent. For down in the Silver City he also had a girl, a yellow beauty from one of the isles, A'Minta, who went with him to the *parque* on Sunday evenings. . . .

Hours he sprawled on the balcony, the vial clutched to his bosom. . . . Ah, Pape was going. He always left early.

"Good luck, gentlemen, I've got to run along. Big day before me tomorrow."

Another hour slipped by. The policeman downstairs blew a long owlish wail. Once, twice, thrice. Twelve o'clock. Somewhere on the roof Sambola heard the unmistakable snarl of a lust-bound boar cat. He dimly glimpsed a yacht in the bay.

One more drink he served. Ensued a long sleeping spell . . . a sleep in which he dreamt of a shark tugging at his gizzard and of being washed up on the ebony shores of Faulke's River.

"Sambola!"

Sir Winfield wanted his glass refilled. He hadn't had anything for an age. The others also wanted theirs refilled. Alert, on the job, a wonderful host, Mr. Newbold also saw it.

"Here, Sambola, fill up the glasses. Why, governor, yours is quite empty."

"Oh, let me see, I'll take vermouth."

Unemotional as a clam, Sambola went to the ice box and began pouring out the liquers. As if he had forgotten something he turned to make sure. No, no one was looking at him. They were deeply engrossed in the game. The boy took the vial out of his bosom and uncorked it. Odorless. Colorless. He put three tiny drops in the governor's anisette. It scarcely created a ripple.

V

The next day the Republic was thrown into a paroxyism of grief over the strange death of Governor Manual Salzedo. The physicians said it was due to heart failure. Others privately attributed it to a vendetta in *El Barrio Rojo.* Donna Teresa demanded an autopsy. But it did not reveal anything. The newspapers, in dealing with it, threw a cloak of still further mystery over it. They hinted at assault by the ousted Tejadistas. *El Dario* went so far as to dig up or fabricate a parallel in the Republic's bloody history.

But no one ever got to the bottom of it. Not even the enterprising reporters of the fictional press—not one of them ever thought of link-ing the governor's death with the finding a few days later of a Negro's shark bitten body fished up out of the black lagoon on Faulke's River.

Soon, like everything else, it died down. And if you asked any of the old residents about it they'd say, "Ah, that is one of the legends of this legendary country. Like the failure of the French."

Yet Sambola, as meek as before, continued to serve liquers on Friday evenings to the members of Mr. Newbold's Chess Club. Only sometimes a strange, smoky gleam would creep into his eyes. On nights when he'd go to that brothel on the banks of the river by the Silver City there were those who couldn't help but compare it with the cat-like light they had often seen in the eyes of the old grouchy trader, Nestor Villaine. As a matter of fact, folk oftimes, for no reason that they could explain, referred to Sambola as Nestor Villaine.

THE TYPEWRITER

Dorothy West earned half of the second prize for this story, which depicts the limited but prideful aspirations of an ordinary "cullud man." Though his happiness and dreams approach their zenith, it is apparent that he may never have been understood, appreciated, or loved. This story was published in July 1926.

It occurred to him, as he eased past the bulging knees of an Irish wash lady and forced an apologetic passage down the aisle of the crowded car, that more than anything in all the world he wanted not to go home. He began to wish passionately that he had never been born, that he had never been married, that he had never been the means of life's coming into the world. He knew quite suddenly that he hated his flat and his family and his friends. And most of all the incessant thing that would "clatter clatter" until every nerve screamed aloud, and the words of the evening paper danced crazily before him, and the insane desire to crush and kill set his fingers twitching.

He shuffled down the street, an abject little man of fifty-odd years, in an ageless overcoat that flapped in the wind. He was cold, and he hated the North, and particularly Boston, and saw suddenly a barefoot pickaninny sitting on a fence in the hot, Southern sun with a piece of steaming corn bread and a piece of fried salt pork in either grimy hand.

He was tired, and he wanted his supper, but he didn't want the beans, and frankfurters, and light bread that Net would undoubtedly have. That Net had had every Monday night since that regrettable moment fifteen years before when he had told her—innocently—that such a supper tasted "right nice. Kinda change from what we always has."

He mounted the four brick steps leading to his door and pulled at the bell; but there was no answering ring. It was broken again; and in a mental flash he saw himself with a multitude of tools and a box of matches shivering in the vestibule after supper. He began to pound lustily on the door and wondered vaguely if his hand would bleed if he smashed the glass. He hated the sight of blood. It sickened him.

Some one was running down the stairs. Daisy probably. Millie would be at that infernal thing, pounding, pounding. . . . He entered. The chill of the house swept him. His child was wrapped in a coat. She whispered solemnly, "Poppa, Miz Hicks an' Miz Berry's orful mad. They gointa move if they can't get more heat. The furnace's bin out all day. Mama couldn't fix it." He said hurriedly, "I'll go right down. I'll go right down." He hoped Mrs. Hicks wouldn't pull open her door and glare at him. She was large and domineering, and her husband was a bully. If her husband ever struck him it would kill him. He hated life, but he didn't want to die. He was afraid of God, and in his wildest flights of fancy couldn't imagine himself an angel. He went softly down the stairs.

He began to shake the furnace fiercely. And he shook into it every wrong, mumbling softly under his breath. He began to think back over his uneventful years, and it came to him as rather a shock that he had never sworn in all his life. He wondered uneasily if he dared say "damn." It was taken for granted that a man swore when he tended a stubborn furnace. And his strongest interjection was "Great balls of fire!"

The cellar began to warm, and he took off his inadequate overcoat that was streaked with dirt. Well, Net would have to clean that. He'd be damned—! It frightened him and thrilled him. He wanted suddenly to rush upstairs and tell Mrs. Hicks if she didn't like the way he was running things, she could get out. But he heaped another shovelful of coal on the fire and sighed. He would never be able to get away from himself and the routine of years.

He thought of that eager Negro lad of seventeen who had come North to seek his fortune. He had walked jauntily down Boylston Street, and even his own kind had laughed at the incongruity of him. But he had thrown up his head and promised himself: "You'll have an office here some day. With plate-glass windows and a real mahogany desk." But, though he didn't know it then, he was not the progressive type. And he became successively, in the years, bell boy, porter, waiter, cook, and finally janitor in a down town office building.

He had married Net when he was thirty-three and a waiter. He had married her partly because—though he might not have admitted it—there was no one to eat the expensive delicacies the generous cook gave him every night to bring home. And partly because he dared hope there might be a son to fulfil his dreams. But Millie had come, and after her twin girls who had died within two weeks, then Daisy, and it was tacitly understood that Net was done with child-bearing.

Life, though flowing monotonously, had flowed peacefully enough until that sucker of sanity became a sitting-room fixture. Intuitively at the very first he had felt its undesirability. He had suggested hesitatingly that they couldn't afford it. Three dollars the eighth of every month. Three dollars: food and fuel. Times were hard, and the twenty dollars apiece the respective husbands of Miz Hicks and Miz Berry irregularly paid was only five dollars more than the thirty-five a month he paid his own Hebraic landlord. And the Lord knew his salary was little enough. At which point Net spoke her piece, her voice rising shrill. "God knows I never complain 'bout nothin'. Ain't no other woman got less than me. I bin wearin' this same dress here five years, an' I'll wear it another five. But I don't want nothin'. I ain't never wanted nothin'. An' when I does as', it's only for my children. You're a poor sort of father if you can't give that child jes' three dollars a month to rent that typewriter. Ain't 'nother girl in school ain't got one. An' mos' of 'ems bought an' paid for. You know yourself how Millie is. She wouldn't as' me for it till she had to. An' I ain't going to disappoint her. She's goin' to get that typewriter Saturday, mark my words."

On a Monday then it had been installed. And in the months that followed, night after night he listened to the murderous "tack, tack, tack" that was like a vampire slowly drinking his blood. If only he could escape. Bar a door against the sound of it. But tied hand and foot by the economic fact that "Lord knows we can't afford to have fires burnin' an' lights lit all over the flat. You'all gotta set in one room. An' when y'get tired settin' y'c'n go to bed. Gas bill was somep'n scandalous last' month."

He heaped a final shovelful of coal on the fire and watched the first blue flames. Then, his overcoat under his arm, he mounted the cellar stairs. Mrs. Hicks was standing in her kitchen door, arms akimbo. "It's warmin'," she volunteered.

"Yeh," he was conscious of his grime-streaked face and hands, "it's warmin'. I'm sorry 'bout all day."

She folded her arms across her ample bosom. "Tending a furnace ain't a woman's work. I don't blame your wife none 'tall."

Unsuspecting he was grateful. "Yeh, it's pretty hard for a woman. I always look after it 'fore I goes to work, but some days it jes' ae's up."

"Y'oughta have a janitor, that's what y'ought," she flung at him. "The same cullud man that tends them apartments would be willin'. Mr.

Taylor has him. It takes a man to run a furnace, and when the man's away all day—"

"I know," he interrupted, embarrassed and hurt, "I know. Tha's right, Miz. Hicks tha's right. But I ain't in a position to make no improvements. Times is hard."

She surveyed him critically. "Your wife called down 'bout three times while you was in the cellar. I reckon she wants you for supper."

"Thanks," he mumbled and escaped up the back stairs.

He hung up his overcoat in the closet, telling himself, a little lamely, that it wouldn't take him more'n a minute to clean it up himself after supper. After all Net was tired and prob'bly worried what with Miz Hicks and all. And he hated men who made slaves of their women folk. Good old Net.

He tidied up in the bathroom, washing his face and hands carefully and cleanly so as to leave no—or very little—stain on the roller towel. It was hard enough for Net, God knew.

He entered the kitchen. The last spirals of steam were rising from his supper. One thing about Net she served a full plate. He smiled appreciatively at her unresponsive back, bent over the kitchen sink. There was no one could bake beans just like Net's. And no one who could find a market with frankfurters quite so fat.

He sank down at his place. "Evenin', hon."

He saw her back stiffen. "If your supper's cold, 'tain't my fault. I called and called."

He said hastily, "It's fine, Net, fine. Piping."

She was the usual tired housewife. "Y'oughta et your supper 'fore you fooled with that furnace. I ain't bothered 'bout them niggers. I got all my dishes washed 'cept yours. An' I hate to mess up my kitchen after I once get it straightened up."

He was humble. "I'll give that old furnace an extra lookin' after in the mornin'. It'll las' all day to-morrow, hon."

"An' on top of that," she continued, unheeding him and giving a final wrench to her dish towel, "that confounded bell don't ring. An'—"

"I'll fix it after supper," he interposed hastily.

She hung up her dish towel and came to stand before him looming large and yellow. "An' that old Miz Berry, she claim she was expectin' comp'ny. An' she knows they must 'a' come an' gone while she was in her kitchen an' couldn't be at her winder to watch for 'em. Old liar," she brushed back a lock of naturally straight hair. "She wasn't expectin' nobody."

"Well, you know how some folks are—"

"Fools! Half the world," was her vehement answer. "I'm goin' in the front room an' set down a spell. I bin on my feet all day. Leave them dishes on the table. God knows I'm tired, but I'll come back an' wash 'em." But they both knew, of course, that he, very clumsily, would.

At precisely quarter past nine when he, strained at last to the break-ing point, uttering an inhuman, strangled cry, flung down his paper, clutched at his throat and sprang to his feet, Millie's surprised young voice, shocking him to normalcy, heralded the first of that series of great moments that every humble little middle-class man eventually experiences.

"What's the matter, poppa? You sick? I wanted you to help me."

He drew out his handkerchief and wiped his hot hands. "I declare I must 'a' fallen asleep an' had a nightmare. No, I ain't sick. What you want, hon?"

"Dictate me a letter, poppa. I c'n do sixty words a minute.—You know, like a business letter. You know, like those men in your building dictate to their stenographers. Don't you hear 'em sometimes?"

"Oh, sure, I know, hon. Poppa'll help you. Sure. I hear that Mr. Browning—Sure."

Net rose. "Guess I'll put this child to bed. Come on now, Daisy, without no fuss.—Then I'll run up to pa's. He ain't bin well all week."

When the door closed behind them, he crossed to his daughter, con-jured the image of Mr. Browning in the process of dictating, so arranged himself, and coughed importantly.

"Well, Millie—"

"Oh, poppa, is that what you'd call your stenographer?" she teased. "And anyway pretend I'm really one—and you're really my boss, and this letter's real important."

A light crept into his dull eyes. Vigor through his thin blood. In a brief moment the weight of years fell from him like a cloak. Tired, bent, little old man that he was, he smiled, straightened, tapped im-pressively against his teeth with a toil-stained finger, and became that enviable emblem of American life: a business man.

"You be Miz Hicks, huh, honey? Course we can't both use the same name. I'll be J. Lucius Jones. J. Lucius. All them real big doin' men use their middle names. Jus' kinda looks big doin', doncha think, hon? Looks like money, huh? J. Lucius." He uttered a sound that was like the proud cluck of a strutting hen. "J. Lucius." It rolled like oil from his tongue.

His daughter twisted impatiently. "Now, poppa—I mean Mr. Jones, sir—please begin. I am ready for dictation, sir."

He was in that office on Boylston Street, looking with visioning eyes through its plate-glass windows, tapping with impatient fingers on its real mahogany desk.

"Ah—Beaker Brothers, Park Square Building, Boston, Mass. Ah—Gentlemen: In reply to yours of the seventh instant would state—"

Every night thereafter in the weeks that followed, with Daisy packed off to bed, and Net "gone up to pa's" or nodding inobtrusively in her corner, there was the chamelion change of a Court Street janitor to J. Lucius Jones, dealer in stocks and bonds. He would stand, posturing, importantly flicking imaginary dust from his coat lapel, or, his hands locked behind his back, he would stride up and down, earnestly and seriously debating the advisability of buying copper with the market in such a fluctuating state. Once a week, too, he stopped in at Jerry's, and after a preliminary purchase of cheap cigars, bought the latest trade papers, mumbling an embarrassed explanation: "I got a little money. Think I'll invest it in reliable stock."

The letters Millie typed and subsequently discarded, he rummaged for later, and under cover of writing to his brother in the South, laboriously, with a great many fancy flourishes, signed each neatly typed sheet with the exalted J. Lucius Jones.

Later, when he mustered the courage, he suggested tentatively to Millie that it might be fun—just fun, of course!—to answer his letters. One night—he laughed a good deal louder and longer than necessary—he'd be J. Lucius Jones, and the next night—here he swallowed hard and looked a little frightened—Rockefeller or Vanderbilt or Morgan—just for fun, y'understand! To which Millie gave consent. It mattered little to her one way or the other. It was practise, and that was what she needed. Very soon now she'd be in the hundred class. Then maybe she could get a job!

He was growing very careful of his English. Occasionally—and it must be admitted, ashamedly—he made surreptitious ventures into the dictionary. He had to, of course. J. Lucius Jones would never say "Y'got to" when he meant "It is expedient." And, old brain though he was, he learned quickly and easily, juggling words with amazing facility.

Eventually he bought stamps and envelopes—long, important-looking envelopes—and stammered apologetically to Millie, "Honey, poppa thought it'd help you if you learned to type envelopes, too. Reckon you'll have to do that, too, when y'get a job. Poor old man," he swallowed painfully, "came round selling these envelopes. You know how 'tis. So I had to buy 'em." Which was satisfactory to Millie. If she saw through her father, she gave no sign. After all, it was practise, and

Mr. Hennessey had promised the smartest girl in the class a position in the very near future. And she, of course, was smart as a steel trap. Even Mr. Hennessey had said that—though not in just those words.

He had got in the habit of carrying those self-addressed envelopes in his inner pocket where they bulged impressively. And occasionally he would take them out—on the car usually—and smile upon them. This one might be from J. P. Morgan. This one from Henry Ford. And a million-dollar deal involved in each. That narrow, little spinster, who, upon his sitting down, had drawn herself away from his contact, was shunning J. Lucius Jones!

Once, led by some sudden, strange impulse, as an outgoing car rumbled up out of the subway, he got out a letter, darted a quick, shamed glance about him, dropped it in an adjacent box, and swung aboard the car, feeling, dazedly, as if he had committed a crime. And the next night he sat in the sitting-room quite on edge until Net said suddenly, "Look here, a real important letter come to-day for you, pa. Here 'tis. What you s'pose it says," and he reached out a hand that trembled. He made brief explanation. "Advertisement, hon. Thassal."

They came quite frequently after that, and despite the fact that he knew them by heart, he read them slowly and carefully, rustling the sheet, and making inaudible, intelligent comments. He was, in these moments, pathetically earnest.

Monday, as he went about his janitor's duties, he composed in his mind the final letter from J. P. Morgan that would consummate a big business deal. For days now letters had passed between them. J. P. had been at first quite frankly uninterested. He had written tersely and briefly. Which was meat to J. Lucius. The compositions of his brain were really the work of an artist. He wrote glowingly of the advantages of a pact between them. Daringly he argued in terms of billions. And at last J. P. had written his next letter would be decisive. Which next letter, this Monday, as he trailed about the office building, was writing itself on his brain.

That night Millie opened the door for him. Her plain face was transformed. "Poppa—poppa, I got a job! Twelve dollars a week to start with! Isn't that *swell*!"

He was genuinely pleased. "Honey, I'm glad. Right glad," and went up the stairs, unsuspecting.

He ate his supper hastily, went down into the cellar to see about his fire, returned and carefully tidied up, informing his reflection in the bathroom mirror, "Well, J. Lucius, you c'n expect that final letter any day now."

He entered the sitting-room. The phonograph was playing. Daisy was singing lustily. Strange. Net was talking animatedly to—Millie, busy with needle and thread over a neat, little frock. His wild glance darted to the table. The pretty, little centerpiece, the bowl and wax flowers all neatly arranged: the typewriter gone from its accustomed place. It seemed an hour before he could speak. He felt himself trembling. Went hot and cold.

"Millie—your typewriter's—gone!"

She made a deft little in and out movement with her needle. "It's the eighth, you know. When the man came to-day for the money; I sent it back. I won't need it no more—now!—The money's on the mantelpiece, poppa."

"Yeh," he muttered. "All right."

He sank down in his chair, fumbled for the paper, found it.

The Boll Weevil Starts North–
A Story

This story, written by Benjamin Young, clearly reveals the feeble intent of an aged yet hardy southern farmer who was inspired to begin a trip to see his son in Cleveland, Ohio, but is besieged by a series of personal calamities. After a final blow by failed luck and unfortunate circumstance on the train, the old man is led to turn back and terminate his hope for a northern sojourn before he is even halfway to his destination. Would a boll weevil choose to shrivel in familiar climes rather than in those unknown? This story was published in February 1926.

Before me was a trip to Cincinnati and back twenty-seven hours each way from New Orleans. Such a journey in a day coach calls for fortitude. At Greenville, in the heart of Alabama's Black Belt, more migrants came aboard, ranging in complexions from black through brown to a saddle color. Last of the lot was an old man, rather dressed-up in over-sized clothes. He took the seat directly across from me and began fanning himself with his new felt hat which had covered a head of bristly white hair. "Not a day under seventy," I silently surmised, "yet hardly fifty to look at his firm ebony face."

"Lands sake," he blew off in relief, looking about the coach at the same time. His glance passed over me. "Ain't that Sumpter over dare?" he questioned out to someone to my rear.

"Yas-sir," came a drawl answer. "How's you, elder Scott?"

"Sumpter, what you doin' on here? Is you goin' North too?"

"Naw-sir—well, yas-sir, after I's staid in Birmingham a while. How's the folks all?"

"Dey's all about left an' gone on ahead—now I'm followin'. Y'know ev'ry thing got mighty punk, farmin's gone to beggar weeds. 'Tain't what hit use' to be. Sumpter, hit's been nigh five years since I's seen you. Where you-all been?"

"Pensacola mostly—an' Mobile some," admitted the younger man.

"Sumpter, is you staid out'n jail much? Back home you boys didn't never come to church for skinnin' an' playin' crackaloo on Sundays. Yer mammy was a pilar of the church, but you taken after old man Sump. Lak pa lak son, you is."

The old man had slowed down with his fanning and was wiping his face in a ponderous blue handkerchief. The train was moving off to a wrangling bell. Already the conductor, followed by his colored *attache*, the porter, was headed through taking up tickets. When they reached the old man he fumbled in his hip-pocket and brought forth a worn, bulky wallet from which he fished a long green ticket.

"Uncle, it's a mighty long ticket for you—trying to follow all these young darkies North?" spoke the conductor as he scanned the strip. "Cleveland—you hold this train 'til you reach Cincinnati, then you change to the Big Four for Cleveland." He tore off a part of the ticket and, followed closely by his man Friday, passed on to the next passenger. "Umph, I ain't chasin' 'hind these young niggers," informed the old man while carefully placing the ticket in his inside coat pocket. "No sitch thing—dey's goin' North fur freedom, fur privileges, fur to be treated white, dey claims. But I ain't wantin' sitch. Done lived most of my life here an' got 'long ver tol'rable wid you devilish white folks. Dese young bucks lak Sumpters wants North'n free air. Hit doan mean nothin' to me.

"In fact, I's goin' north 'cause my luck run out; been under a sort of hoodoo ev'ry since nineteen-nineteen when I kilt 'at air old brindle cat. Stuck a pitch-fork plumb through her covered in some hay." He stopped automatically as if puzzled why he was talking so loud. The conductor, the target of his sputtering, had passed on to the next coach.

However, having earned the attention of the other passengers, he was determined to finish his story. "Seems lak ev'ry thing that's got four legs been 'ginst me. Up 'til the las' minute—even the ole mule got hisself stuck in the mud an' lak'd to cause me to miss my train. If an automobile hadn't come by an' unpulled us I'd never made hit." He had settled himself and was talking directly across the aisle to Sumpter, most attentive of all his auditors.

"Dey told me I was superstitious by that cat," he kept on; "an' fur a long while dey all laf'd at me, sayin' seven years hard luck was 'pon me. An' not less than a week after I had stuck that cat when a swarm of bees lit on my ole mare and stung her so she ran away an' tore up my buggy an' injured by internals. I was flat on my back three weeks."

"Well, I jes' declared," supplemented Sumpter, "was hit that same little blaze-face mare named Minnie?"

"Yeah—she's dead now. An' soon after along comes another calamity—my cows got loose an' wandered over on Sampson Jackson's place. You heard 'bout Sampson bein' on the gang, didn't you? Dey finally got 'im fur bootlegging. Well, my six head of cows got in some of his mash an' come home walkin' on their hind legs, fallin' 'round an' actin' lak demons. Four of 'em died that week an' the other two ain't never been no good since. Dey all told me I ought have sued Sampson Jackson, but what was the good wid 'im on the chain gang. An' anyway, my fool cattle was trespassin' on his premises. 'Twas 'jes that 'air cat luck on me I well knowed.

"Come next the boll weevil, an' the furst year dey didn't do so much, but the next year—dey ain't, left me 'nough cotton for a garden patch. Folks all said get some guineas an' turn 'em loose in the cotton an' dey would clean out the weevil, but dem guineas acted lak a cotton field was hoodoo'd. After a while along come a Gov'ment man an' says poison 'em, but hit only made the weevils fatter so dey could work harder on the bolls. An' den I heard about the Argentina ants that would jes' run the weevils lak the Yanks did the Rebels, but all the Argentina ants done was to move 'way nearly half my smoke-house. So I saw 'twas nothin' but the old cat on me, an' I decided to care' hit to the Lord in prayer. But the Lord, He ain't never had a chance to answer, 'cause jes' as I got 'pon my knees an' says, 'Hebenly Father,' a boll weevil disturb me right dare in the church on a Sunday morning. 'Fore I got off my knees I made up my mind to leave, 'cause when the Lord can't get a chance to he'p you hit's movin' time."

"Elder Scott, boll weevils done run a lots of farmers away from Calhoun County," commented Sumpter by the way of filling the gap. The old man had told his jeremiad in a credulous way, and to have seen his frank expression and childish intonation would have added to the sincerity of the situation. One would have had no doubts that he was being driven away from his home by the machination of animated Fate.

"That's why I'm goin' North," he concluded, "sold out ev'rything an' wrote my son in Cleveland I was comin'. I ain't heard from 'im, but I's good directions whar, he's livin' at. No, I ain't goin' up North fur freedom, I's goin' out of the way of that cat's four legged bad luck."

A long, mourning whistle from the engine came as a sort of benediction. It was a signal for another station, this time a little more than a cross road. To Montgomery we were "running local" the porter told me; from there on we would make a faster schedule. So many were going North that all passenger trains were compelled to do local work through this district.

From Montgomery we made good time, making a flying stop at Clanton and a brief stay at Calera, a junction. Here there was much commotion on the outside. Up and down by my window antagonistic voices clattered, not like that of the city newsies, for Calera is no city. Maybe a dozen business places scattered around the station, including a combination drug store post office. From my window I discovered that the excitement came from lunch vendors, men and boys of color. They were working rapidly and with fervor; our train would not tarry long.

"Get yer red-hot chicken lunches—two fur a quarter."

"Heah, hea's the bes' fried chicken—no wings, no necks."

"Fresh fish sandwiches—fresh fish, one dime."

As they passed under the window barking the merits of their eatables they brandished big trays piled with lunches wrapped in oiled paper. And not to be left out of the scene, not to be unheard or unnoticed, the local station razorbacks were chanting their grunts of industry.

Station hogs in the South are an institution; they thread in and out under the trains with rare unconcern, never losing so much as a tail. And in Calera these forever rooting creatures were a hustling lot. They investigated every thing that resembled a discarded remains of a lunch.

There was the call of "board" and the engine bell began its warning wrangle. The lunch vendors increased their sale talk to a last chance plea. We were leaving Calera to get over its own routine excitement until the next passenger train came in.

"An' I didn't have no change," the old man came down the aisle explaining. "Got off to get me a snack and had to give that boy a bill out'n my pocket-book, an' den he come near not havin' time to make change."

"Tickets—get your tickets ready." The conductor and the porter were headed through again. Their advance cleared the old man out of the aisle. From the smoking compartment a thrumming rondo of a guitar was welling through the car like some weird jungle rhapsody with now and then a plaintive voice of:

"Riding in de day-coach wid no Pullman on my mind,
I'm riding to my sugar an' the train's on time."

Our next stop was Birmingham where we lost an appreciable number of passengers, including Sumpter and the sleepy-eyed guitar player. Night had caught us and the city was bedecked with incandescence. Cincinnati was still sixteen hours away and knowing the run by the way of several previous trips I made early preparations for passing the night by renting a stuffy white pillow from the porter. So to speak, I retired early.

But even in a Pullman, unless one is a habitue, sleep comes in snatches. Hardly had I embedded my head in my pillow when someone touched me. It brought my sleep-courted head around to face a scene. The conductor was standing in the aisle by my seat, while the porter was searching with his lantern under the seat opposite mine.

"Seven hundrd an' forty dollars, an' all I've got in the world! I jes' know that trifling Sumpter stole hit—I jes' know hit was him, 'cause he come an' sit awhile wid me." It was the old man down behind his seat helping the porter in his search. The whole coach was upset; comments were flying, heads peering down the aisle.

"Well, uncle, you ought'n had all that money on you," spoke the conductor. "It's a wonder any of you boll weevils ever get past Birmingham. Good thing you've got a through ticket, else them slicks would pick you clean before you'd get out of Cincinnati." And he passed on down the aisle.

"Can't find it, uncle," declared the porter after his boss had moved along. "Sorry fur you, but I's seen the same thing happen a dozen times already. There's a band of slicks that rides this road and they finds good pickings."

The old man was mumified, his tongue was locked and he sat down mopping his dampened brow. He was, all of him, a bronze study of Old Age Baffled. For perhaps twenty minutes he sat in a stupor. No words of sympathy or questions about how it happened from his fellow passengers moved him. He just sat there, holding the blue handkerchief in his trembling hand, with a swipe at his sweaty brow at intervals.

Gradually I got my mind off the tragedy and again 'turned in' on my pillow. Sleep came stingily, often interrupted by that haunting twanging of the afternoon before, "Riding in de day-coach wid no Pullman on my mind——"

When I awoke we were bearing upward through the chill of a Kentucky morning. Weary and grimy I stretched myself, in the midst of which I became aware that the ill-fated old traveler's seat was empty and his wicker suitcase gone from the rack. No where in the car of drowsing passengers was he to be seen.

"Old man got off last night at Decatur," the porter told me. "Said he was going back to Birmingham an' get that guy what stole his pocketbook. An' that pocketbook may be right on this train, yet still and likely, the one what hooked hit dumped off in Birmingham."

"I wonder what'll become of him," I thought aloud.

"Oh, he'll make hit back to the farm from where he come—this is done cured him of traveling North. Anyway, there's too many of them boll weevils movin' North," concluded the porter as he passed to the baggage car just ahead.

A week later I was on my trip back. At Nashville I looked for my friend the porter but another crew was on. At Birmingham I had no expectancy except for a moment's thought anent the outcome of the old man's search for his lost fortune.

Late that afternoon when we reached Granville I inquired from my window of a truck handler about Elder Scott who had left for Cleveland a week before. The man only took time to inform me that he had seen an old man who resembled him get off there two or three days before. And that was all I ever heard about the old man, except for something I learned that day before reaching Greenville.

Just before the train had pulled out of Birmingham in came that same man with the guitar. He passed on back to the smoking compartment. As I recognized him a premonition raced through my train-racked brain.

Soon there came a vanguard of vagrant chords. Just a handful of them and a pause, then the starting of a strain only to ebb away. We road on to the singing of the guitar and the intervaled blowing of the engine's whistle.

And on to Calera, the lunch burg. Here the man of the charmed guitar unboarded; and I, in a half-subconsciousness and a desire to stretch, filed out behind him.

The lunch vendors were putting on their usual strenuous show up and down the sides of the coaches. All amongst them were the gruntling, scuffling hogs, investigating every scrap of paper. Up ahead the express was being transferred to trucks for another train. The man with the guitar was standing idly on the gravel walk as if waiting for the train to pull off. I strolled aimlessly by him and stood watching the unloading.

"Hey, there, Music Man, where've you been?" came a greeting from one of the lunchboys.

"Howdy, Roscoe, why ain't Sandy selling today?" asked the returned musician.

"Sandy got lucky, Music Man, got lucky."

"Boys' ain't had a big game on, is they?"

"Naw. He found hisself a fortune—found one of these hogs chawing hit up. Pocket-book had 'round seven hundred bones in hit by my countin'. He done left here on Number Four for Chicago las' Sunday. Some rich tourist dropped hit an' that old bobbed-tail sow under there was trying to make vituals out'n hit——"

There I was, standing and listening while my train was actually moving off.

" 'Board——all aboard here, mister," the porter was yelling at me when I realized my dumbness. With a few strides I swung nervously on the end of the coach and tottered back to my seat.

PART THREE

PLAYS

THE POT MAKER

In the following play, self-styled preacher Elias Jackson practices for his first sermon. He uses pots as a metaphor. In an ironic twist of fate the pots mirror his own destiny. This play by Marita O. Bonner was published in February 1927.

SETTING:

See first the room. A low ceiling; smoked walls; far more length than breadth. There are two windows and a door at the back of the stage.— The door is between the windows. At left and right there are two doors leading to inner rooms.

They are lighter than the door at back stage. That leads into the garden and is quite heavy.

You know there is a garden because if you listen carefully you can hear a tapping of bushes against the window and a gentle rustling of leaves and grass.

The wind comes up against the house so much aswash—like waves against the side of a boat—that you know, too, that there must be a large garden, a large space around the house.

But to come back into the room. It is a very neat room. There are white sash curtains at the window and a red plaid cloth on the table. Geranium in red flower pots are in each window and even on the table beside the kerosine lamp which is lit there. An old-fashioned wooden clock sits on a shelf in the corner behind the stove at the right. Chairs of various types and degrees of ease are scattered around the table at center.

CHARACTERS:

> The Son—"called of God," Elias Jackson
> His Wife, Lucinda Jackson
> His Mother, Nettie Jackson
> His Father, Luke Jackson
> Lucinda's Lover, Lew Fox

As the curtain is drawn, see first the mother; a plump colored woman of indeterminate age and an indeterminate shade of brown, seated at the table. Luke, the father whose brown face is curled into a million pleasant wrinkles, sits opposite her at the left.

Lew stands by the stove facing the two at the table. He must be an over-fat, over-facetious, over-fair, over-bearing, over-pleasant, over-confident creature. If he does not make you long to slap him back into a place approaching normal humility, he is the wrong character for the part.

You must think as you look at him: "A woman would have to be a base fool to love such a man!"

Then you must relax in your chair as the door at right opens and Lucinda walks in. "Exactly the woman," you will decide. For at once you can see she is a woman who must have sat down in the mud. It has crept into her eyes. They are dirty. It has filtered through—filtered through her. Her speech is smudged. Every inch of her body, from the twitch of an eyebrow to the twitch of muscles lower down in her body, is soiled. She is of a lighter brown than the mother and wears her coarse hair closely ironed to her head. She picks up each foot as if she were loath to leave the spot it rests on. Thus she crosses the room to the side of Elias who is seated at the window, facing the center of the room.

It is hard to describe Elias. He is ruggedly ugly but he is not repulsive. Indeed you want to stretch out first one hand and then the other to him. Give both hands to him. You want to give both hands to him and he is ruggedly ugly. That is enough.

ARGUMENT:

When you see Elias he is about to rehearse his first sermon. He has recently been called from the cornfields by God. Called to go immediately and preach and not to dally in any theological school.

God summoned him on Monday. This is Wednesday. He is going to preach at the meeting-house on Sunday.

SCENE I

As the curtain draws back, expectation rests heavily on every one. The mother is poised stiffly on the edge of her chair. Her face and her body say, "Do me proud! You're my son! Do me proud."

The father on his side rests easily on his chair; "Make all the mistakes you want. Come off top notch. Come off under the pile. You're my son! My son."

That sums them up in general too. Can you see them? Do you know them?

ELIAS *(rising and walking toward the table),* "You all set back kind er in a row like." *(He draws chairs to the far end of the room at right)* "There, there, Ma here! Pa there! Lew——" *(he hesitates and Lew goes to Lucinda's side and sits down at once).* (This leaves Elias a little uncertain but he goes on.) "Now——*(he withdraws a little from them)* "Brothers and sisters."

MOTHER, "M-m-m-m, 'Lias can't you think of nothin' new to say first? I been hearin' that one since God knows when. Seems like there's somethin' new."

ELIAS, "Well, what'll I say then?"

MOTHER, "Oh——'ladies and gent'mun'; somethin' refined like." *(At this point, Lew and Lucinda seemed to get involved in an amused crossing of glances)* "But go on then, anything'll be all right." *(The mother stops here and glares at Lucinda to pay her for forcing her into back water. Lucinda sees Lew.)*

ELIAS *(continuing),* "Well Brothers and Sisters! There is a tale I'd like for to tell you all this evening, brothers and sisters; somethin' to cheer your sorrowing hearts in this vale of tears."

LUCINDA, "What if their hearts ain't happen to be sorrowing?"

FATHER, *(cutting in)* "Boun to be some time, chile! Boun' to be!" *(The son flashes thanks to father. He appears to have forgotten the jibe and to be ignorant of the look of approval, too. He is a delightful mutual peacemaker.)*

ELIAS, "A tale to cheer your sorrowing hearts through this vale of tears.—This here talk is about a potmaker what made pots."

LUCINDA *(laughing to herself—to Lew),* "Huh, huh; Lord ha' mercy."

MOTHER *(giving Lucinda a venomous glance and rising in defense),* "Look here 'Lias, is that tale in the Bible? You is called of God and He aint asked you to set nothin' down He aint writ himself."

ELIAS, "This is one of them tales like Jesus used to tell the Pharisees when he was goin' round through Galilee with them."

MOTHER, "Jesus aint never tol' no tales to Pharisees nor run with them either! Onliest thing He ever done was to argue with them when He met them. He gave 'em good example like."

ELIAS, "Well this'n is somethin' like——wait you all please! Once there was a man what made pots. He lived in a little house with two rooms and all that was in those rooms was pots. Just pots. Pots all made of earthenware. Earthenware. Each one of them had a bottom and a handle just alike. All on them jes' alike. One day the man was talking to them pots——."

LUCINDA *(just loud enough to be disagreeable),* "What kinder fool was talking to pots?"

ELIAS *(ignoring her),* "An' he says, listen you all. You all is all alike. Each on you is got a bottom to set on and a handle. You all is alike now but you don' have to stay that away. Do jes' as I tells you and you can turn to be anything you want. Tin pots, iron pots, brass pots, silver pots. Even gold." "Then them pots says——."

MOTHER "Lias, who the name of God ever heard tell of a minister saying pots talked. Them folks aint goin' to let you do it."

ELIAS "Ma! Then the pots said; 'what we got to do?' And the man he told them he was goin' to pour something in them. "Don't you all tip over or spill none of the things I put in you. These here rooms is goin' to get dark. Mighty dark. You all is goin' to set here. Each got to set up by hisself. On his own bottom and hold up his handle. You all is goin' to hear rearin' and tearin.' Jes' set and don't spill on the ground." "Master, I got a crack in me," says one of them pots, "I got a crack in me so's I can't hol' nuthin." "Then the man took a little dirt and he spit on it and put it on the crack and he patter it—just as gentle like! He never stopped and asked 'How'd you get that crack and he patted it—just as gentle like! He stooped right down and fixed the crack 'cause 'twas in his pot. His own pot. Then he goes out."

"Them rooms got so dark that a million fireflies couldn't have showed a light in there." " 'What's that in the corner?' says one of the pots. Then they gets scared and rolls over on the ground and spilled."

LUCINDA "Uhm" *(she sees only Lew again).*

ELIAS *(still ignoring her),* "It kept getting darker. Bye 'n bye noises commenced. Sounded like a drove of bees had travelled up long a elephant's trunk and was setting out to sting their way out thoo the thickest part. 'Wah, we's afraid,' said some more pots and they spilled right over.

For a long time them rooms stayed right dark and the time they was dark they was full of noise and pitchin' and tarin'—but pres'n'y the dark began leaving. The gray day come creepin' in under the door. The pot-maker he come in; 'Mornin y'all, how is you?' he asks.

Some of them pots said right cheery, 'We's still settin' like you tol' us to set! Then they looked at their selves and they was all gol.'

Some of them kinder had hung their heads but was still settin' up.

The pot-maker he says, 'Never min', you all, you can be silver. You aint spilled over.'

Then some of the pots on the groun' snuk up and tried to stand up and hol' up their heads. 'Since you all is so bol' as to try to be what you aint, you all kin be brass!"

An' then he looked at them pots what was laying on the groun' and they all turned to tin.

Now sisters and brothers them pots is people. Is you all. If you'll keep settin' on the truth what God gave you, you'll be gol.' If you lay down on Him, He is goin' to turn you to tin. There won't be nothin' to you at all. You be as empty as any tin can" ...

FATHER, "Amen, amen."

ELIAS, "Taint but just so long that you got to be on this earth in the dark—anyhow."

"Set up. Set up and hold your head up. Don' lay down on God! Don' lay down on Him! Don' spill on the groun.' No matter how hard the folks wear and tear and worry you. Set up and don' spill the things He give you to keep for him. They tore him—but He come into the world Jesus and He went out of it still Jesus. He set hisself up as Jesus and He aint never laid down." *(Here, Lucinda yawns loudly and gives a prolonged Ah-h-h-h-h!)*

ELIAS, "Set up to be gol' you all and if you ever feels weak tell God; 'Master I got a crack in me.' He'll stoop down and take and heal you. He wont ask you how you got cracked. He'll heal you——the pot-maker done it and he warn't God. The pot maker he didn't blame the pots for bustin.' He knows that pots can bust and God knows that it wouldn't take but so much anyway to knock any gol' pot over and crack it an' make it tin. That's the reason He's sorry for us and heals us.

Ask Him. And set. Set you all. Don't spill on the groun'. Amen."

There is a silence. The father looks along the floor steadily. Elias looks at him. Lucinda sees Lew. The mother sees her son. Finally Elias notes Lucinda has her hand in Lew's and that they are whispering together. But Lew releases her hand and smiles at Elias, rising to his feet at the same time.

LEW *(in a tone too nice, too round, too rich to be satisfactory)* "Well, well folks! I'll have to go on now. I am congratulating you, sister Nettie, on such a son! He is surely a leadin' light Leadin' us all straight into Heaven." *(He stops and mouths a laugh)* "I'll be seein' you all at the meetin'—good night" *(he bobs up and down as if he were really a toy fool on a string)* "Ah—Lucinda—ah—may—I—ask—you—for—a drink of water if—ah——it do not bother you?"

(The tone is hollow. There will be no water drunk though they may run the water. Lucinda smiles and leaves behind him giving a defiant flaunt as she passes Elias. This leaves the other three grouped beside the table.)

FATHER "That is a right smart sermon, 'pears to me. Got some good sense in it."

MOTHER "But them folks aint goin' to sit there and hear him go on to tell them pots kin talk. I know that."

A door bangs within the room in which Lucinda and Lew have disappeared. Lucinda comes out, crosses the stage, goes into the room at right. A faint rustling is heard within.

MOTHER *(calling)*, "Cinda what you doin' in that trunk? Taint nuthin' you need in there tonight." *(The rustling ceases abruptly—you can almost see Lucinda's rage pouring in a flood at the door.)*

LUCINDA *(from within)* "I aint doin' nothin"—— *(She appears at the doorway fastening a string of red beads around her throat.)*

MOTHER, "Well, if you aint doin' nothin' what you doin' with them beads on?"

LUCINDA *(flaring)* "None of your business."

MOTHER "Oh it aint! Well you jes' walk back in there and rest my best shoes under the side of the bed please, ma'am."

FATHER, "Now Nettie, you women all likes to look———."

MOTHER, "Don't name me with that one there!"

ELIAS "Ma don't carry on with 'Cinda so."

MOTHER "You aint nothin' but a turntable! You aint got sense enough to see that she would jam you down the devil's throat if she got a chance."

LUCINDA "I'm goin' long out of here where folks got some sense." *(She starts off without removing the shoes).*

MOTHER "Taint whilst to go. I'm goin' callin' myself. Give me my shoes." *(Lucinda halts at the door. There are no words that can tell you how she looks at her mother-in-law. Words cannot do but so much.)*

LUCINDA *(slinging the shoes)* "There."

Elias picks them up easily and carries them to his mother.

She slips them on, and, catching up a shawl, goes off at back followed by her husband. Lucinda stamps around the room and digs a pair of old shoes up from somewhere. She slams everything aside that she passes. Finally she tips one of the geraniums over.

ELIAS *(mildly)* "Taint whilst to carry on so, Lucinda."

LUCINDA "Oh for God's sake shut up! You and your 'taint whilst to's' make me sick."

(Elias says nothing. He merely looks at her.)

LUCINDA "That's right! That's right! Stand there and stare at me like some pop-eyed owl. You aint got sense enough to do anything else."

(Elias starts to speak. Lucinda is warmed to her subject. What can he say?)

LUCINDA *(even more rapidly),* "No you aint got sense enough to do anything else! Aint even got sense enough to keep a job! Get a job paying good money! Keep it two weeks and jes' when I'm hoping you'll get a little money ahead so's I could live decent like other women—in my house—You had to go and get called of God and quit to preach!"

ELIAS *(evenly),* "God chose me."

LUCINDA "Yas God chose you. He aint chose you for no preachin.' He chose you for some kinder fool! That's what you are—some kinder fool! Fools can't preach."

ELIAS "Some do."

LUCINDA "Then you must be one of them that does! If you was any kind of man you'd get a decent job and hold it and hold your mouth shut and move me into my own house. Ain't no woman so in love with her man's mother she wants to live five years under the same roof with her like I done."

(Elias may have thought of a dozen replies. He makes none.)

Lucinda stares at him. Then she laughs aloud. It is a bitter laugh that makes you think of rocks and mud and dirt and edgy weather. It is jagged. "Yes you are some kinder fool. Standing there like a pop-eyed owl—*(there follows the inevitable)*. The Lord knows what I ever saw on you!"

ELIAS *(still evenly)*, "The Lord does know Lucinda." *(at that Lucinda falls back into her chair and curses aloud in a singsong manner as if she were chanting a prayer. Then she sits still and stares at him.)*

LUCINDA "Elias—aint you never wanted to hit nobody in your life?"

(Before he can answer, a shrill whistle is heard outside the window at left. Lucinda starts nervously and looks at the window. When she sees Elias has heard the sound she tries to act unconcerned.)

LUCINDA "What kinder bird is that whistlin' at the window?" *(She starts toward it. Elias puts out a hand and stops her.)*

ELIAS "Taint whilst to open the window to look out. Can't see nothin' in the dark."

LUCINDA "That aint the side that old well is on is it? That aint the window is it?"

ELIAS "You ought to know! Long as you been livin' here! Five years you just said." *(There is a crackle of bushes outside the window close to the house. A crash. Then a sound of muttering that becomes louder and louder. A subdued splashing. Lucinda starts to the window but Elias gets there first. He puts his back to the wall.)*

LUCINDA "Somebody's fallin' into that well! Look out there!"

ELIAS "Taint whilst to."

LUCINDA "Taint whilst to! Oh God—here um calling! Go out there! Taint whilst to!" *(She tries to dart around Elias. They struggle. He seizes her wrist drags her back. She screams and talks all the time they struggle.)* "Call yourself a Christian! The devil! That's what you is! The devil! Lettin' folks drown! Might be your own mother!"

ELIAS "Taint my mother!—You know who it is!"

LUCINDA "How I know? Oh, go out there and save him for God's sake." *(The struggles and the splashing are ceasing. A long-drawn "Oh my God" that sounds as if it comes from every portion of the room, sifts over the stage. Lucinda cries aloud. It is a tearing, shrieking, mad scream. It is as if someone had torn her soul apart from her body. Elias wrenches the door open——)* "Now Cindy, you was goin' to Lew. Go 'long to him." "G'long to him," he repeats.

LUCINDA, *(trying to fawn at him)*, "Oh! No! Elias, Oh Master! Ain you no

ways a man? I aint know that was Lew! I aint know that was Lew—
—Oh, Yes I did. Lew, Lew." *(She darts past Elias as if she has forgotten him. You hear her outside calling),* "Lew, Lew." Full of mad agony, the screams search the night. But there is no answer. You hear only the wind. The sound of wind in the leaves. Elias stands listening. Then he closes the door. All at once there is the same crackling sound outside and a crash and a splash. Once more Cindy raises her voice—frightened and choked. He hears the sound of the water. He starts toward the door. "Go 'long to Lew," he shouts, and sits down. "You both is tin." But he raises himself at once and runs back to the door. "God, God, I got a crack in me too!", he cries and goes out into the darkness. You hear splashing and panting. You hear cries. "Cindy give me your hand! There now! You is 'most out." But then you hear another crash. A heavier splashing. Something has given away.

One hears the sound of wood splitting. One hears something heavy splashing into the water. One hears only the wind in the leaves. Only the wind in the leaves and the door swings vacant.

You stare through the door. Waiting. Expecting to see Elias stagger in with Lucinda in his arms perhaps. But the door swings vacant. You stare——but there is only wind in the leaves.

That's all there will be. A crack has been healed. A pot has spilled over on the ground. Some wisps have twisted out.

PLUMES

This one-act play by Georgia Douglas Johnson, published in July 1927, was awarded first prize in Opportunity's *play section. Johnson brilliantly crafts a plausible intrigue emphasizing the power of a mother's instincts.*

CAST OF CHARACTERS

Charity Brown, *The Mother*
Emmerline Brown, *The Daughter*
Tildy, *The Friend*
Dr. Scott, *Physician*

SCENE:

The kitchen of a two-room cottage. A window overlooking the street. A door leading to street, one leading to the back yard, and one to the inner room. A stove, a table with shelf over it, a wash tub. A rocking chair, a cane bottom chair. Needle, thread, scissors, etc., on table.

A groaning is heard from the inner room. Scene opens with Charity Brown heating a poultice over the stove.

CHARITY—Yes, honey, mamma is fixing somethin' to do you good. Yes, my baby, jus' you wait I'm a coming.

(Knock is heard at door. It is gently pushed open and Tildy comes in cautiously.)

TILDY *(whispering)*—How is she?
CHARITY—Poorly, poorly. Didn't rest last night none hardly. Move

that dress and set in th' rocker. I been trying to snatch a minute to finish it but don't seem like I can. She won't have nothing to wear if she—she——

TILDY—I understands. How near done is it?

CHARITY—Ain't so much more to do.

TILDY *(takes up dress from chair, looks at it)*—I'll do some on it.

CHARITY—Thank you, sister Tildy. Whip that torshon on and turn down the hem in the skirt.

TILDY *(measuring dress against herself)*—How deep?

CHARITY—Let me see now. *(Studies a minute with finger against lip)*—I tell you—jus' baste it, cause, you see—she wears 'em short, but—it might be——*(stops)*

TILDY *(bowing her head comprehendingly)*—Eughhu *(meaning yes)* I see exzackly *(sighs)* You'd want it long—over her feet—then.

CHARITY—That's it, sister Tildy. *(Listening)* She's some easy now. *(Stirring poultice)* Jest can't get this poltis hot enough somehow this morning.

TILDY—Put some red pepper in it. Got any?

CHARITY—Yes. There ought to be some in one of them boxes on the shelf there. *(Points)*

TILDY *(Goes to shelf, looks about and gets the pepper)*—Here, put a plenty of this in.

CHARITY *(Groans are heard from the next room)* Good Lord, them pains got her again. She suffers so, when she's wake.

TILDY—Poor little thing. How old is she now, sister Charity?

CHARITY—Turning fourteen this coming July.

TILDY *(Shaking her head dubiously)*—I sho hope she'll be mended by then.

CHARITY—It don't look much like it but I trusts so— *(looking worried)* That doctor's mighty late this morning.

TILDY—I expects he'll be long in no time. Doctors is mighty oncon-cerned here lately.

CHARITY *(Going toward inner room with poultice)*—They surely is and I don't have too much confidence in none of 'em. *(You can hear her soothing sick girl)*

TILDY *(listening)*—Want me to help you put it on, sister Charity?

CHARITY *(from inner room)*—No, I can fix it. *(Coming back from sick room shaking her head rather dejectedly)*.

TILDY—How's she restin' now?

CHARITY—Mighty feeble. Gone back to sleep. My poor little baby. *(Bracing herself)* I'm going to put on some coffee now.

TILDY—I'm sho glad. I feel kinder low spirited.

CHARITY—It's me that's low spirited. The doctor said last time he was here he might have to operate—said she *might* have a chance then. But I tell you the truth, I've got no faith at all in 'em. They takes all your money for nothing.

TILDY—They sho do, and don't leave a thing for putting you away.

CHARITY—That's jest it. They takes every cent you got and, then you dies jest the same. It ain't like they was sure.

TILDY—No, they ain't sure. That's it exzactly. But they takes your money jest the same, and leaves you flat.

CHARITY—I been thinking 'bout Zeke these last few days—how he was put away——

TILDY—I wouldn't worry 'bout him now: he's out of his troubles now.

CHARITY—I know... But it worries me when I think about how he was put away... that ugly pine coffin, jest one shabby old hack and nothing else to show—to show—we thought somethin' about him.

TILDY—Shoo... hush, sister, don't you worry over him. He's happy now anyhow.

CHARITY—I can't help it... then little Bessie.... We all jest scrouged in one hack and took her little coffin in our lap all the way to the graveyard. *(Breaks out crying).*

TILDY—Do hush, sister Charity. You done the best you could. Poor folks have to make the best of it. The Lord understands.

CHARITY—Yes. I know... but I made up my mind when little Bessie went that the next one of us what died would have a sho nuff fun'ral—plumes! So I saved and saved and now—this doctor——

TILDY—All they think about is cuttin' and killing and taking your money. I got nothin' to put 'em doing.

CHARITY *(Goes over to wash tub and rubs on clothes)*—Me neither. Now here's these clothes got to get out. I needs every cent.

TILDY—How much that washing bring you?

CHARITY—Dollar and a half. It's worth a whole lot more. But what can you do?

TILDY—You can't do nothing—— Look, sister Charity, ain't that coffee boiling?

CHARITY *(wipes her hands on apron and goes to stove)*—Yes, it's boiling good fashioned—come on, let's drink it.

TILDY—There ain't nothing I'd rather have than a good strong cup of coffee. *(Charity pours Tildy's cup).*

TILDY *(sweetening and stirring hers)*—Pour you some. *(Charity pours her own cup).* I'd been dead too long if it hadn't been for my coffee.

CHARITY—I love it but it don't love me, gives me the shortness of breath.

TILDY *(finishing her cup, taking up sugar with spoon)*—Don't hurt me. I could drink a barrel.

CHARITY *(drinking more slowly, reaching for coffee pot)*—Here, drink another cup.

TILDY—I shore will. That cup done me a lot of good.

CHARITY *(looking into her empty cup thoughtfully)*—I wish Dinah Morris would drop in now. I'd ask her what these grounds mean.

TILDY—I can read 'em a little myself.

CHARITY—You can? Well, for the Lord's sake look here and tell me what this cup says. *(Offers cup to Tildy. Tildy wards it off)*.

TILDY—You got to turn it round in your saucer three times first.

CHARITY—Yes, that's right, I forgot. *(Turns cup round counting)* One, two, three. *(Starts to pick it up)*.

TILDY—Eughn nhu *(meaning no)* Let it set a minute. It might be watery. *(After a minute while she finishes her own cup)* Now let me see? *(Takes cup and examines it very scrutinizingly)*.

CHARITY What you see?

TILDY *(hesitatingly)*—I ain't seen a cup like this one for many a year. Not since—not since——

CHARITY—When?

TILDY—Not since jest before ma died. I looked in the cup then and saw things and . . . I stopped looking.

CHARITY—Tell me what you see, I want to know.

TILDY—I don't like to tell no bad news——

CHARITY—Go on. I can stan' any kind of news after all I been thru.

TILDY—Since you're bound to know I'll tell you. *(Charity draws nearer)* I sees a big gethering!

CHARITY—Gethering, you say?

TILDY—Yes, a big gethering—people all crowded together. Then I see 'em going one by one and two by two. Long lines stretching out and out and out!

CHARITY *(softly)*—What you think it is?

TILDY *(awed like)*—Looks like *(hesitates)* a possession.

CHARITY—You think it is?

TILDY—I know it is.

(Just then the toll of a church bell is heard and then the steady and slow tramp, tramp of horses' hoofs. Both women look at each other).

TILDY *(in a hushed voice)*—That must be Bell Gibson's funeral coming way from Mt. Zion *(gets up and goes to window)* Yes, it sho is.

CHARITY *(looking out of window also)*—Poor Bell suffered many a year; she's out of her pain now.

TILDY—Look, here comes the hearse by!

CHARITY—My Lord, ain't it grand. Look at them horses—look at their heads—plumes—how they shake 'em! Land O'mighty! Ain't it a fine sight?

TILDY—That must be Jeremiah in that first carriage, bending over like, he shorely is putting her away grand.

CHARITY—No mistake about it. That's Pickett's best funeral turnout he got.

TILDY—I bet it cost a lot.

CHARITY—Fifty dollars, so Matilda Jenkins told me. She had it for Bud. The plumes is what cost.

TILDY—Look at the hacks *(counts)* I believe to my soul there's eight.

CHARITY—Got somebody in all of 'em, too—and flowers—— She shore got a lot of 'em.

(Both women's eyes follow the tail end of the procession, horses' hoofs die away as they turn away from window).

(The two women look at each other significantly).

TILDY *(significantly)*—Well——

TILDY *(significantly)*—Well—— *(They look at each other without speaking for a minute). (Charity goes to the wash tub)*—Want these cups washed up?

CHARITY—No, don't mind 'em. I rather you get that dress done. I got to get these clothes out.

TILDY *(picking up dress)*—Shore, there ain't so much more to do on it now.

(Knock is heard on the door. Charity answers knock and admits Doctor).

DR. SCOTT—Good morning—how's my patient today?

CHARITY—Not so good, doctor. When she ain't asleep she suffers so, but she sleeps mostly.

DR. SCOTT—Well, let's see—let's see. Just hand me a pan of warm water and I'll soon find out just what's what.

CHARITY—All right, doctor, I'll bring it to you right away. *(Bustles about fixing water).*

(Looking toward dress Tildy is working on) Poor little Emmerline's been wanting a white dress trimmed with torshon a long time—now she's got it and it looks like—well—

TILDY—Don't take on so, sister Charity—The Lord giveth and the Lord taketh.

CHARITY—I know—but it's hard—hard——— *(Goes to inner door with water. You can hear her talking with the doctor after a minute and the doctor expostulating with her—in a minute she appears at the door, being led from the room by the doctor).*

DR. SCOTT—No, my dear Mrs. Brown. It will be much better for you to remain outside.

CHARITY—But, doctor———

DR. SCOTT—No. You stay outside and get your mind on something else. You can't possibly be of any service. Now be calm, will you?

CHARITY—I'll try, doctor.

TILDY—The doctor's right. You can't do no good in there.

CHARITY—I knows, but I thought I could hold the pan or somethin'. *(Lowering her voice)* Says he got to see if her heart is all right or some-thin'. I tell you———

CHARITY *(softly to Tildy)*—Hope he won't come out here saying he got to oparate. *(Goes to wash tub).*

TILDY—I hope so, too. Wont' it cost a lot?

CHARITY—That's jest it. It would take all I got saved up.

TILDY—Of course if he's goin' to get her up—but I don't believe———

CHARITY—He didn't promise tho—even if he did, he said maybe it wouldn't do any good.

TILDY—I'd think a long time before I'd let him operate on my chile. Taking all your money, promising nothing and ten to one killing her to boot.

CHARITY—This is a hard world.

TILDY—Don't you trust him. Coffee grounds don't lie!

CHARITY—I don't trust him. I jest want to do what's right by her. I ought to put these clothes on the line while you're settin' in here, but I hate to go out doors while he's in there.

TILDY—*(getting up)*—I'll hang 'em out. You stay here. Where your clothes pins at?

CHARITY—Hanging right there by the back door in the bag. They ought to dry before dark and then I can iron tonight.

TILDY *(picking up tub)*—They ought to blow dry in no time. *(Goes toward back door).*

CHARITY—Then I can shore rub 'em over tonight. Say, sister Tildy—hist 'em up with that long saplin' prop leaning in the fence corner.

TILDY *(going out)*—All right.

CHARITY *(standing by table beating nervously on it with her fingers—listens—and then starts to bustling about the kitchen). (Enter doctor from inner room).*

DR. SCOTT—Well, Mrs. Brown, I decided on the operation——

CHARITY—My Lord, doctor—don't say that!

DR. SCOTT—It's her only chance.

CHARITY—You mean she'll get well if you do?

DR. SCOTT—No, I can't say that. It's just a chance—a last chance. And I'll do just what I said, too, cut the price of the operation down to fifty dollars. I'm willing to do that for you.

CHARITY—Doctor, I was so in hopes you wouldn't operate—I—I—— And you say you ain't a bit sure she'll get well—even then?

DR. SCOTT—No, I'm not sure. You'll have to take the chance. But I'm sure you want to do everything——

CHARITY—Sure, doctor, I do want to—do—everything I can do to—to—— Doctor, look at this cup. *(Picks up fortune cup and shows doctor).* My fortune's been told this very morning—look at these grounds—they says—*(softly)*—it ain't no use, no use a tall.

DR. SCOTT—Why, my good woman, don't you believe in such senseless things. That cup of grounds can't show you anything. Wash them out and forget it.

CHARITY—I can't forget it, doctor—I feel like it ain't no use. I'd jest be spendin' the money that I needs—for nothing—nothing.

DR. SCOTT—But you won't, tho—— You'll have a clear conscience. You'd know that you did everything you could.

CHARITY—I know that, doctor. But there's things you don't know 'bout—there's other things I got to think about. If she goes . . . If she must go . . . I had plans . . . I had been getting ready . . . now . . . Oh, doctor, I jest can't see how I can have this operation—you say you can't promise—nothing!

DR. SCOTT—I didn't think you'd hesitate about it—I imagined your love for your child——

CHARITY *(breaking in)*—I do love my child. My God, I do love my child. You don't understand . . . but . . . can't I have a little time to think about it, doctor . . . it means so much—to her—and—me!

DR. SCOTT—I tell you. I'll go on over to the office and as soon as you make up your mind get one of the neighbors to run over there and tell me. I'll come right back. But don't waste any time now, every minute counts.

CHARITY—Thank you, doctor. Thank you. I'll shore send you word as soon as I can. I'm so upset and worried I'm half crazy.

DR. SCOTT—I know you are . . . but don't make it too long . . . say within an hour at longest. Remember—it may save her.

(Doctor exits).

CHARITY *(goes to door of sick room, looks inside for a few minutes, then starts walking up and down the little kitchen first holding a hand up to her head and then wringing them). (Enter Tildy from yard with tub under her arm).*

TILDY—Well, they're all out, sister Charity—what's the matter?

CHARITY—The doctor wants to oparate.

TILDY *(softly)*—Where he—gone?

CHARITY—Yes—he's gone, but he's coming back—if I send for him.

TILDY—You going to? *(puts down tub and picks up white dress and begins sewing)*

CHARITY—I don't know—I got to think.

TILDY—I can't see what's the use myself—he can't save her with no oparation—coffee grounds don't lie.

CHARITY—It would take all the money I got for the oparation and then—he can't save her—I know he can't—I feel it . . . I feel it . . .

TILDY—It's in the air . . .

(Both women sit tense in the silence. Just then a strange strangling noise comes from the inner room).

TILDY—What's that . . .

CHARITY *(running toward and into the inner room)*—Oh, my God!

(Tildy starts toward inner room. Stops. Sighs, and then walks slowly back to chair).

(Charity is heard moaning softly in the next room, then she appears at doorway. Leans against jam of door).

CHARITY—Rip the hem out, sister Tildy.

(Curtain)

SUGAR CAIN

In this play by Frank H. Wilson, the character Sugar Cain is burdened by a secret that jeopardizes the life of the man she loves. Published in June 1926, it was awarded first prize in Opportunity's *play section.*

CHARACTERS—Paul, Martha, Sugar Cain, Fred, Howard, Ora.

SCENE—Room at the Cain Homestead, Waynesboro, Georgia.

TIME—Present.

CURTAIN RISES SHOWING—Small room in an old-fashioned frame house, the wall hung with cheap wall paper, some of it hanging down in long strips. The wooden floor is covered with a torn, and dilapidated rug. In the center of the room stands a small wooden table covered with cheap oilcloth. An old oil lamp sits in the center of table, shedding a faint glow throughout the room, two hand-made wooden chairs sit at each end of the table. Back up against the wall center, is an old couch, with broken springs—hanging up on the wall are several religious pictures and mottoes—over on the left side is an old bureau, cheaply covered and with many trinkets and glasses upon it. Down left front is the door leading into the spare room. Up right rear are steps leading up stairs to the rooms above. Down right the door leads out through the kitchen to the back yard. At the foot of the stairs is a small window, with a broken pane of glass in it. Cheap curtains hang from the top of the window. The whole room gives the appearance of honest, but poor people. There is a small cuspidor down along side one of the chairs.

Pause.

Sugar enters from spare room. She is a young dark brown skin girl about 23 years old, comely and well built. She closes the door quietly as if not to disturb someone asleep therein, she then moodily crosses the room, and goes out through the kitchen door.

Paul comes down the stairs as Sugar is crossing the room. He is an old-fashioned Negro, about 62 years old, with grey beard, eyebrows and hair, walks and moves somewhat feeble from hard work. Watches Sugar as she crosses room and goes out through kitchen.

Martha enters from kitchen, wiping her hands on her old apron. (She is a small dark complexioned old lady of about 55 years, with kindly face and disposition.)

MARTHA—Wat yer want Paul?

PAUL—What's de matter wid Sugar?

MARTHA (coming in)—I don aknow, why?

PAUL—She's bin actin mouty funny dese las few days.

MARTHA—Funny—how?

PAUL—Well she's walkin roun hear lak she's in a trance.

MARTHA—Mebbe she's think bout dat Howard Hill.

PAUL (Angrily coming down from stairs)—Doan mention dat black guard's name in mah house. I tole yer'.

MARTHA—Oh, Paul, scuse me. I fergot yo ain't got no use fer him.

PAUL (coming down)—Ain't got no use fer him, nor fer anny buddy fum up North (pause). Dat's wot's de matter wid Sugar. Dat's why she's havin dem quiet spells, case she's worried bout her troubles (going over to chair left of table). All comes o' yo' lettin dat Northern nigger stay hyer. I tole yo I didn't want him in de furst place.

MARTHA (pleadingly)—Oh, Paul, please doan go over all dat agin. I admit it was mah mistake, wot mo kin ah do?

PAUL (sitting in chair)—I know, but it makes me mad ebery time I think of it.

MARTHA (timidly)—Goin' ter church ter-night?

PAUL (taking out his pipe)—No.

MARTHA—Why, not?

PAUL—Case I don't feel lak it.

MARTHA—Ye ought ter go ter church mo, Paul. Mebbe yo'd feel better.

PAUL—Feel better nothin. Think I'd go down there among dem ole gossippy an back biten brothers, dey done scandelize our name all over de town.

MARTHA—No dey didn't.

PAUL (lighting his pipe)—Doan tell me ooman. De minnit dat Hill boy started stoppin hyer dey started talkin, en wen he lef an dey heard about Sugar's baby, de talked fer sho den. *(Pause.)* I wish yo had taken mah advice an not let him stay hyer. But you so hard headed. Wouldn't lissen ter me.

MARTHA—Sugar says twarnt him.

PAUL—Sugar lies, who else could it be?

MARTHA (her feelings hurt, goes back into the kitchen).

PAUL (turns, sees that Martha has walked out on him spits in cuspidor and grunts)—Humph.

FRED (enters from kitchen—he is husky young Negro, about 24 years old. He is dressed in soft blue shirt, open at the throat, blue overalls, tan shoes and black felt hat)—Hello, Pop.

PAUL (grunts)—Umph.

FRED (coming in)—Jist met our fren—Lee Drayton.

PAUL—Whar?

FRED—Goin' down de road towards his house, gwine ter pay his mother her usual weekly visit I reckon. *(Pause.)* He goes away some time and stays months.

PAUL—I reckon Miss Mary generally knows whar he is.

FRED—No, she don't.

PAUL—How you know?

FRED—She tole me so her sef, she did an'——— (Paul grunts and continues to smoke his pipe.)

FRED—It's queer ter me how a good woman lak Miss Mary kin have sich a son.

PAUL (spits again)—Yo des doan understan him—dat's all.

FRED—Ha ahm goin ter understan him, wen his own mother don't?

PAUL—De boys wile lake all yo youngsters.

FRED—He's mo den wile.

PAUL—I know he's a lil ruff and gruff in his talk.

FRED—An actions.

PAUL—But wot kin yer spec. His ole man befo him was dat away. He ain't no wurse den any of de res ob dese white folks down hyer.

FRED—Oh, yes he is, Pop. Dere's some fine white folks down hyer I know. But Lee Drayton ain't one of em.

PAUL (spits disgustedly)—He may not be alright ter people lak dat Hill boy fum up North—who doan know ha ter act wen he gits in dis part ob de country, but ter we folks down hyer who understans dese white folks—Lee Drayton is alright. (Puffs on his pipe.)

FRED (looks at Paul for a minute)—Pop, you puts too much faith in dese white folks.

(Paul gives him an angry look.)

FRED (taking a seat)—Yo's too willin ter believe eberything dey say. Yo seems ter have mo faith in dem den you hab in God.

PAUL (quickly and angrily)—Wot if I has?

FRED—Yer ought ter believe a lil mo in you own race—git a lil mo race pride.

PAUL (spits angrily)—Whard yo git all dat foolishness, fum dat northern nigger—Hill, I reckon.

FRED—No, pop, I didn't git it fum nobody, but since I bin gitten a lil older Ahm trying ter think fer ma sef, these white folks bin thinking fer me long enuf.

PAUL—Yes, and if dey hadn't bin thinkin fer yo, whar would yo be now—running round in Africa half naked, an yo wouldn't knowed B fum Bull frog. *(Pause.)* Who's got everything down hyer—white folks, ain day?

FRED (reluctantly)—Yes.

PAUL—An who's got nothin'—we has, ain't we?

FRED (shakes his head yes).

PAUL—Alright—now we wants what de white man's got—or some of it.

FRED (quickly)—We wants our share.

PAUL (settling himself back in chair)—Well, ha yo goin ter git it? Take it away fum him, I specs?

FRED (fails to find an answer to this question).

PAUL (spits)—Yo upstart youngsters know so-o-o much an we ole folks dat libed fer years among dese people doan know nothin. *(Pause.)* If a man's goin ter fight yo and he's gotta gun, and yo ain't got nothin— what you goin ter do?

FRED (quickly)—Fight him.

PAUL—An git killed, dat's wot de Indians done wen de white man come ter dis country—fought him—dat's the reason Indians are so scarce now days.

FRED (anxiously)—But de respec him mo for it.

PAUL (impatiently)—I ain't lookin fer no respec. *(Pause.)* I'm lookin fer sumphin dat going ter feed me and my family. *(Pause.)* Dis house hyer whar yo an Sugar was born an raised—it's mine, ain't it?

FRED (quietly)—Yes, sir.

PAUL—It may not be no palace, but it's MINE jist de same. (Points out window.) So is dat patch ob farmland out dere—all mine. How you reckon I got it, by fightin dese white folks down hyer. Humph—I guess not.

FRED—But dey thinks dey better den we are, Pop.

PAUL (in exasperation)—Wot if dey does. It ain't going ter hurt em ter think is it? (Pointing his pipe at him.) As long as I can fool dese white folks outer dere money an land, by lettin feel dat deys better dan I am, dat's wot ahm goin ter do. (Spits.) Lissen, son—I got money an I got property. I could buy an sell some o dees white folks roun hyer—but I ain't goin ter let dem know it. I could fix dis shack up and live in grand style if I wanted to—but de minnit I did dat dese folks would git curious and wanter say dat I didn't know mah place, an dat I was tryin ter act lak white folks—fus thing yo know I'd have a lot ob trouble on mah hans—an I couldn't stay hyer—so I fools em. Ah banks mah money, keeps mah mouth shut, an makes believe ahm a poor ole Nigger, and dat deys de cock o de walk. And I kin git dere shirt. I know em. An I didn't learn dat in no school neither. I ain't bin livin in de southlan all dese years fer nothin.

FRED—But, Pop, do you think dat's right ter—

PAUL (emphatically)—Yes, it's right. Yo all talk bout race pride, you'd better get a lil race sense. Dese Niggers round hyer ain't got nothin ter give yo—nothin. (Imitating.) Niggers talk about "aw dey kaint do dat ter us—we kin do dis, and we kin do dat—Niggers kaint do nothin—NOTHIN." White folks got ebery thing—an ahm going ter git some of it.

FRED (rises dispondently, and goes up to window).

PAUL (takes a puff at his pipe)—Yo bin gittin all dese low down notions fum Hill.

FRED (turning quickly)—I ain't got no mo use fer Hill den you has.

PAUL (turning to him)—Stop lyin'.

Pause.

FRED (looks at his dad for a minute, and then turns and looks out the window).

PAUL—I know wot yer bin doin, yo bin round town shootin off yo mouth dat you was gittin tired of de souf, dat you wuz goin up North ter live so yo could git a education. Whar else did you git dat but fum Hill.

FRED (looking down at Paul)—Well, I do think I could stand a lil mo learnin'—both me an Sugar.

PAUL (rising)—Well, if you wants learnin' yo'd better git it down hyer, case I ain't got nothin fer up North ter do. Dis is mah home, whar I wuz bred an born, an its whar I wants ter be buried wen I die—I doan care if I never see any buddy fum up North—and if I ever lays mah hans on dat skunk Hill—I'll kill him.

PAUL (stands glaring at Fred).

FRED (does not answer).

PAUL (exits into kitchen).

FRED (takes letter from his pocket, then looks at it).

MARTHA (enters from kitchen)—Fred, yo goin ter church wit me ter nite, ain't yer?

FRED (still looking at letter)—Yessem.

MARTHA—I kaint git yer father to go.

FRED—I wuz jist tellin Pop bout Lee Drayton.

MARTHA—Wots the matter wit him?

FRED—Pop says he's alright.

MARTHA (kindly)—A man wit sich a fine mother lak Miss Mary must hab some good in him. Yo know wot she say de odder day? She say, "Martha, I'm sick an kaint git about so good, an yo all mus come down an see me often. We's all brudders and sisters in de sight ob de Lord. We got ter live tergether in Heaven, so we mought well git used ter it down hyer on earth."

FRED—Yeh, I know Miss Mary's alright, but dat ain't her son.

MARTHA—Oh, he's des young.

FRED—Umph, de oney one dat seems ter think he's low down is me an Hill. (Shows Martha letter in his hand.)

MARTHA—Wot's dat?

FRED—Dat's a letter fum Hill.

MARTHA (surprised)—Howard Hill?

FRED—Yes, I got it yestiddy. He sent it ter me, sayin he wuz comin down hyer ter make a surprise visit, an ter see dat Sugar wuz home.

FRED—I bin holdin it secret, scared ter say anything, yo know how Pop is wid Hill.

MARTHA—Yes Lord, doan let him see dat—wen is he comin?

FRED—Ter day, I think. (Looks at letter). Yes, Sunday.

MARTHA—Mebbe he's comin back ter (hesitates) marry Sugar.

FRED—Do you know, Mom, I ought ter hate dat boy, but I don't.

MARTHA (looking apprehensively toward kitchen)—I lak him, Fred. (Lowers her voice.) He didn't do zactly right by Sugar wen he ran off dat away. But we all makes mistakes.

FRED—I lak him, cas he's got learnin. But I wonder why Sugar protects him?

MARTHA—Case she loves him.

FRED—Wot do you think bout it?

MARTHA—He's de father ob dat chile, alright. But Sugar's afraid ter ammit it, for fear I'll git down on him. She knows her dad's on to him already.

SUGAR (enters from kitchen door).

MARTHA—Whar's you father?

SUGAR—Sitten out in de yard.

MARTHA—He's kinder cranky dis evening.

SUGAR—He's cranky every evening.

MARTHA—Fred, Son, get dressed fer church.

FRED—Yessem.

(Fred goes upstairs.)

MARTHA (looks at Sugar a minute, then speaks)—Fred jist got a letter.

SUGAR—From who?

MARTHA—Howard Hill.

SUGAR (gives a slight start)—Wot does he say?

MARTHA—Fred said dat he wanted it kept fum yo'—but ah reckon I'd better tell you.

SUGAR—Wanted wot kept from me?

MARTHA—The fac dat he wuz comin down hyer.

SUGAR (greatly alarmed)—What?

MARTHA—Yes.

SUGAR—Wot's he comin down hyer fo'.

MARTHA—Ter see yo.

SUGAR (stands as if in a daze).

MARTHA—Ah frightened stiff. Yo father threatened ter kill him on sight, now wot are we gwine ter do?

SUGAR (as if in a daze)—Wen is he comin?

MARTHA—Ter day—or ter nite de letter said. (Calls.) Fred!

SUGAR (quickly)—Doan call him.

FRED—What is it, Mom?

SUGAR (in a whisper)—Doan call him.

MARTHA (looking at Sugar)—Ne'mine gettin ready fer church.

SUGAR—Wot shall I do?

MARTHA—Fergive him, Sugar. I'm sho he'll make you a fine husband.

SUGAR (almost to herself)—I wonder if he'll ever forgive me?

MARTHA—Fergive yo—yo ain't done nothin.

SUGAR—Yes I have.

MARTHA—Wot have yo done!

SUGAR (her voice choking with emotion)—I—I——

FRED (coming down stairs, dressed for church)—Ready for church, Mom?

MARTHA—Yes, an you had better come along, Sugar.

(Fred goes to window and looks out.)

MARTHA—Whars Ora?

SUGAR (points to door left).

MARTHA—Asleep?

SUGAR—Yessem.

MARTHA—She'll sleep until we get back, come on.

SUGAR—I'm afraid dey church bell might frighten her. When it rings she always wakes up. I'm goin ter stay hyer.

FRED (to Martha)—Did yo tell her?

MARTHA—Yes—I thought it would make her feel kinder glad, but she's a giten scart.

SUGAR—Din yo say dat Pop wuz goin ter kill Howard if he came down hyer?

MARTHA—He'll be glad enuf ter see de man come back if he does de right thing.

SUGAR—I'm goin ter stay hyer an meet him.

FRED—Church time, Mom.

MARTHA—Well, if yo won't go ter church, I'm goin ter pray fer yo both. Yo and yo father's goin ter let people's tongues keep yo outer Heaven. (Starts for door.)

FRED—Goes out kitchen door.

SUGAR (quickly)—Mom.

MARTHA (stopping)—Wot's de matter?

SUGAR—Let Fred go ter church alone. I wanter talk ter ye.

MARTHA (yelling off to Fred)—Fred!

FRED (voice off)—Mam?

MARTHA—Go long ter church. I'll be there presently.

SUGAR (stands looking pitiously at Martha).

MARTHA (coming back)—Talk fas. I doan wanna miss dat Sermon.

SUGAR (goes over, puts her arms about Martha's neck and starts crying).

MARTHA (caressing her)—Wot is it, Sugar?

SUGAR—Howard's comin.

MARTHA—I know dat.

SUGAR (now holding down her head)—But there is something else ye don't know.

MARTHA (pointing towards room)—I know dat's his chile in dere.

SUGAR—No, Mom——

MARTHA—Wot?

SUGAR—Dat ain't his chile.

MARTHA—Yo still sticks ter dat story wen we knows different?

SUGAR—Yo de oney one I can trust, Mom. I've got ter tell yo dis.

MARTHA—Tell me de truf den, dat Howard Hill wuz de man.

SUGAR—No.

MARTHA—Ain't it enuf ter bring disgrace down on your poor ole mother and father?

SUGAR (goes over to chair, sits down and weeps).

MARTHA (her heart softening)—Who's de guilty one, Sugar? Tell me (goes over to her). I laked Howard an I wuz willin ter stand fer dis, but fum no odder man livin. Tell me who de scamp wuz so I kin put him in jail.

SUGAR (without looking up)—Lee Drayton.

Pause.

MARTHA (stands as if petrified).

SUGAR (sits, afraid to move).

MARTHA—Wot's dat yo said bout Lee Drayton?

SUGAR (speaking slowly)—Lee Drayton is the father.

MARTHA (frightened)—Stop. Gal shut yo mouth——

SUGAR—It's the truth, Mom.

MARTHA—How—wen did it——

SUGAR—Wen yo sent me down there with Miss Mary's clothes——

MARTHA (forcefully)—I doan believe it.

SUGAR—He would'n let me go. He would'n let me go—he threatened the whole family in case I tole any buddy—he said he'd bring the clan down on us—I feared fer you, Pop an Fred—I did'n dare tell you the truth bout who it wuz.

MARTHA (sinks helplessly in chair)—If you had oney spoken en tole me——

SUGAR—I wuz afraid, I wanted ter tell you dat Howard wuz innocent, but you might question me too close, and fine out the truth——

MARTHA—What could we do——

SUGAR—Fred's so hot headed—Wot am I going ter do—Howards comin——

MARTHA (after thinking a minute)—I doan know—I'm goin ter church, an do the oney thing I kin do—Pray—Yo'd better come along wid us——

PAUL (enters from kitchen, goes toward stairs, stops and looks at them both)—Wot's the matter, you all ain't gwine ter church?

MARTHA—Yes—come on, Sugar.

SUGAR (shakes her head, no).

PAUL (gives Sugar a curious glance, then goes upstairs, and off).

MARTHA (looks at Sugar—tries to speak, words failing her, she goes on out).

SUGAR (looks toward bedroom, apparently listening, then comes slowly down and sits in chair).

Pause.

HOWARD (peeks in through window, he looks about room until he spies Sugar, he then smiles and leaves the window quietly).

SUGAR (buries her head in her arms, leans on table and groans).

HOWARD (enters kitchen door quietly; he is a fine looking, well dressed young Negro, about 24 years old, speaks with a clean and pure diction)—He steals softly toward Sugar—his straw hat accidentally drops from his hand.

SUGAR (turns to him with a quick start).

HOWARD (stands looking at her, smiling).

SUGAR (rises from the chair and quickly backs around to the other side of the table).

HOWARD—Celia—I wanted to surprise you. I sent word to your brother, Fred.

SUGAR (stands with a frightened look, staring at him).

HOWARD (pause)—Noticing her actions. Aren't you glad to see me?

SUGAR (smiling sickly)—Yes, Howard——

HOWARD—You don't look it——

SUGAR (looks fearfully toward stairs)—Let's go outside (starts toward kitchen door).

HOWARD (unable to restrain himself, takes her in his arms)—Celia, my Celia Cain, called Sugar for Sweet, I told you I'd come back after I graduated. Three years is a long time—but I'm happy now. All I need is your mother and father's consent to our marriage.

SUGAR (struggles free from his grasp)—Please, Howard—don't— (staggers weakly back against table).

HOWARD (astonished)—Celia——

SUGAR (leans heavily against table).

(Church bell is heard tolling nearby.)

SUGAR (a look of fear coming to her face, stares at bedroom).

HOWARD (stands non-plussed).

ORA (voice heard off in bedroom)—"Ma, Ma"—"Ma, Ma."

HOWARD (looks toward bedroom door).

ORA (enters quickly in her night dress; she is a little brown baby, about 2 years old)—"Ma, Ma"—I fraid—(runs to Sugar, holding up her arms to be taken up).

HOWARD (looks from Sugar to Ora).

SUGAR (frightened, holds baby close to her side).

HOWARD—Who—who is this——

SUGAR (struggling to suppress her emotions, picks Ora up in her arms)—My baby.

HOWARD (stands dazed at this confession).

Pause.

PAUL (comes quietly downstairs—sees Howard—a look of intense hatred comes to his face, his eyes riveted on Howard, he goes stealthily upstairs again).

HOWARD—You—tell me this is your child?

PAUL (comes downstairs quickly, looking at Howard, he has a loaded shot gun in his hand)—Yo dirty Varmit (points gun at Howard).

SUGAR (screams and rushes in between them holding Ora in her arms).

PAUL (angrily)—Git one side Gal till I blow this snake ter hell——

SUGAR—No Pop.

PAUL (coming down with gun raised)—One side I tell you, you and his brat.

HOWARD (steps out from behind Sugar).

SUGAR (quickly jumps in front of him)—No Pop, you wrong, this aint his, it's Lee Drayton——

PAUL—Wot?——

HOWARD (looks at her at the name of Lee Drayton).

SUGAR—Ora is Lee Drayton's child.

PAUL—Ye lie gal—What are yer tryin' ter do, save him—Come out fum behind there Nigger.

HOWARD—Mr. Cain——

PAUL—Mister nothin'—Sugar move I tell yer.

SUGAR (pleading)—No, Pop—it wuz Lee Drayton I tell yo——

HOWARD (to Sugar)—Do you mean to tell me that this is—is—(points at Ora).

SUGAR—Yes, Howard, I——

HOWARD—I'll get him—(darts quickly out of room).

SUGAR (calling after him)—Howard.

PAUL—Runnin' away, eh—Well, I'll git him fo he gits outer town—

SUGAR—Pop——

PAUL (angrily)—Git outer ma sight, fo I does yo bof harm, yo an Ora—

SUGAR (crying puts Ora in the bed room, fearing Paul in his frenzy might harm them—she locks the door taking the key herself).

PAUL—It aint enuf fer yo ter disgrace me wid dat kid—but yo got dat nigger hangin roun hyer—well, he'll never go north again—I'll—(A shot is heard off toward Drayton's house).

SUGAR (screams)—Howard—Howard, Pop, he's innocent, he's bin killed!

PAUL (lowering his gun)—Hope he has—serves him right—mebbe Fred got him.

HOWARD (enters kitchen door, all out of breath, with a revolver in his hand)—I got him!

PAUL (turning to Howard)—What?

SUGAR (quickly wrenches gun from Paul).

PAUL—Gimme dat gun gal——

SUGAR (running toward stairs)—No!

PAUL (comes back to Howard)—Yer got who?

HOWARD—Lee Drayton!

SUGAR AND PAUL—Lee Drayton?

HOWARD—Yes—I met him just as he was coming out of the house, he knew I was after him, for the minute he saw me he drew his gun and fired but missed—

SUGAR (prayerfully)—Thank God!

HOWARD—I closed in on him before he could fire again, and we grappled. In the struggle we both fell, he was underneath, his head struck a large rock, he lay motionless. (Quietly) God Almighty placed that rock there to save me from being a murderer.

PAUL—Yo mean ter tell me yo killed Lee Drayton?

HOWARD (starts to speak).

(There is a loud roar from the direction of Drayton's house, of many excited yells, and roars—shouts, and murmurs.)

SUGAR (frenzidly)—There comin' Pop, the mob they are comin' after us—(comes down from stairs.)

PAUL—Gimme mah gun——

HOWARD—Don't give it to him—until I find out why he threatens me.

SUGAR—It's my fault——

(Voices seem to be getting nearer.)

HOWARD (listening)—Mr. Cain, this mob's coming down here after me—and I'm going to fight, are you fighting with me, or against me?

PAUL (angrily)—I'm against yo tooth and toe nail, this gal's lyin ter perteck yo, dats all. She can't fool me—I opened mah door ter yo before, and yo done me dirt—an now yer done come down hyer, an stirred up dese white folks—Git outer mah house!

HOWARD (tensely)—You try and put me out—

PAUL (turning angrily to Sugar)—Gimme dat gun I tole yer.

SUGAR (runs up and throws shot gun out of the window, breaking the glass and tearing down the curtain in doing so—)

PAUL (in a rage)—Yo impudent hussy——

(Noise of crowd is still heard much louder.)
(A red glow shines in through the broken window.)

PAUL (rushes up to window to look for gun, sees the reflection of the glow, and looks down towards Drayton's house)—Fire!

SUGAR AND HOWARD (look up at window bewildered).

PAUL (still looking out window)—Fire—it's Miss Mary's house.

SUGAR (in alarm)—Miss Mary!

PAUL (looking at Howard)—Yo done this.

MARTHA (comes in hastily)—Paul! Paul!—Miss Mary's house is on fire.

PAUL—I know it——

MARTHA—Fred's gone down ter save Miss Mary——

PAUL AND SUGAR—Wot?

MARTHA—We saw the glow fum de church. Fred rushed on down there (crying, crying). Oh, poor Miss Mary, wot can we do?

SUGAR—They'll kill him.

MARTHA—Kill who?

SUGAR—Fred.

MARTHA (looks bewildered).

PAUL (pointing at Howard)—This man killed Lee Drayton.

MARTHA—Good, he——

PAUL (surprised)—Wot——?

FRED (voice off)—Mom! Mom!

SUGAR (somewhat relieved at his voice)—It's Fred——

MARTHA (turns toward door).

FRED (rushes in, his clothes slightly burned, his face scorched, and his hand cut)—Miss Mary's safe—She wasn't hurt a bit—des a lil frightened, some of the folks are teken her to de hospital in dere machines.

MARTHA (sees his hand)—Fred—son, yo's hurt——

FRED—Just a lil cut ah got while smashin' mah way frew de back winder.

HOWARD—What about the mob?

FRED (looking at Howard for the first time)—Oh, hello Hill——

HOWARD—Where's the mob?

FRED—Wot mob?

HOWARD—Wasn't there a gang coming down this way?

FRED (sits in chair)—No——

PAUL—Wot wuz all dat noise?

FRED—Dat wuz de crowd cheerin' when I saved Miss Mary——

PAUL, SUGAR AND HOWARD (breathe a sigh of relief).

FRED—All I fergot ter tell yer, Lee Drayton is dead——

PAUL—Yes—dis man——(points at Howard—)

FRED—Dey des dragged his body frum de fire.

SUGAR—What——?

FRED—Almos' burned ter a crisp.

MARTHA (in horror)—Oh! dis blow wit kill Miss Mary——

HOWARD—Did you say they dragged Lee Drayton's body from the house?

FRED—Yes, saw it wid mah own eyes.

SUGAR—Yo said he fell in de yard, Howard.

HOWARD (speaking to Fred)—I guess he was only stunned; when he fell in the yard, he came to, saw the fire, and rushed in to save his mother—

MARTHA—An wen he got in de house, God punished him fer his sins.

PAUL—Wot sins?

MARTHA—His sins—gainst yo an me—an Sugar.

PAUL—Den yo believe that he——

MARTHA—Yes—I believe mah Sugar all de time.

FRED—Gee, dis han hurts—must ter burnt me mo den I fought.

MARTHA—Come on in de kitchen, Fred, till I put somfin on it (exits into kitchen).

FRED (rising)—Do yo know, folks, ah feel lak ah done sumfin, savin Miss Mary today—She's a woman wurth savin—(goes out into kitchen).

Pause.

PAUL (goes up by window, and stands looking out in a depressed manner).

HOWARD (stands down right, looking into space, thinking deeply).

SUGAR (stands, looking doubtfully at Howard).

HOWARD (picks up his hat from the floor).

SUGAR (turns her head slowly, sees Paul, goes up to him, weakly lays her hand on his shoulder).

PAUL (without even looking at her, goes dejectedly up stairs).

SUGAR (wavers for a minute by the window, hardly able to stand, and then falls limply on the stairs, sobbing and crying).

Pause.

HOWARD (stands thinking deeply, hearing Sugar's sobs, he turns, looks at her for a minute, then walks up slowly looking down at her, his heart softens. He kneels down beside her, lifts her gently up, and holds her to his bosom, as she sobs and crys broken heartedly).

(The church bell tolls dismally.)

Pause.

(Ora's baby is heard behind the bedroom door crying and beating her little hands upon the door.)

HOWARD (looks toward the door, hearing the child's voice).

(As Howard is looking toward door, Sugar reaches up appealingly, and puts her arms about his neck———.)

HOWARD (turns tearfully to Sugar and holds her to his bosom, as———)

The Curtain Falls.

PART FOUR

REVIEWS

NIGGER

A NOVEL BY CLEMENT WOOD

This novel was reviewed by Charles S. Johnson in the first issue of Opportunity, *January 1923.*

Scientific treatises on the relations of white and black in this country are more accurate, but a novel if it is in the least plausible and interesting, gets under the skin. Unlike the meteoric vogue of H. A. Shands and T. S. Stribling who flashed into public notice with poorly written novels of Negro life, interesting only for their novelty, Clement Wood is an author with a reputation established apart from the race issue.

"Nigger" is a tragic tale of three generations of a Negro family. Beginning in slavery they are carried down to the present thru a series of paralyzing handicaps, the common lot of their race in the South, and landed sixty-five years later still wandering confusedly, hopeless and cast down, looking for an emancipation which they seemed never likely to realize.

The story begins with Jake, non-descript slave boy, early left parentless. The establishment of his family is a record of births and deaths, the heavy toll of ignorance and the death-dealing malaria of the black swamp. He married Phoebe, a mulatto from "Cunn'l Clopton's place." They begat five children all of whom died but one, Isaac the oldest. Isaac took a bride and they begat seven more. Both of the parents died shortly after the arrival of the last child leaving seven children on the grand parents. Jake, a philosophical old codger, wanted his charges to be "ejjicated" that they might find the emancipation which their elders had been given but could never enjoy. Jim Gaines, a ne'er-do-well neighbor, was less optimistic. "What's the use?" he asked. "Do readin' make yo' skin white? Do writin' gib yo' de vote? Do cipherin' mop out de black?" A mob killed Jim and his pregnant daughter, and the rest of his family fled to Mobile.

Of Jake's seven charges, all of whom had been sent to school, one son had been killed while robbing box cars in Birmingham, another paralyzed for life by a bullet on the same escapade, a third was killed in the war, and the fourth, after many disheartening disappointments fitted himself into the uninteresting routine of the rolling mill. Of the three girls, one took up life in a house of prostitution (for whites only), a second settled down to domestic drudgery with a lazy husband, and the third became the mistress of a white man.

In spite of the very manifest effort of the author to avoid the usual pit falls of over sentimentality one way or the other, "Nigger" is an example of the difficulty of telling a story of a race by following the experience of a family. The effect of fairness is achieved by a sort of balancing of evils. That the castigations of the author on such manifest wrongs as lynching, disfranchisement, and other forms of oppressive over-lordship may not be regarded as evidence of his pro-Negro bias, he weights these down with an equal proportion of the stereotyped "Negro traits" like stealing, crap shooting, immorality, ignorance and vice, all of which may have been true in the case of this family, but certainly are not representative of the Negro race, nor even a typical Negro family, if such a thing exists.

There are delicate touches, however, which show an apt understanding of certain of the simpler forms of behavior, and deftly tell a story in themselves. The family, for example, "walked to the front end of the railroad platform and climbed aboard." This is the only reference to the "Jim Crow" transportation arrangement thru which countless other hardships are endured. Or again, passing an open square they did not go in because they saw no Negroes there. Behind this casual observation is a long history of exclusion from common privileges. To avoid insult or perhaps physical injury they must take no chances.

The dialect is reasonably faithful. Tho occasionally strained and distorted it can be understood, and that is a great deal. Much of the talk commonly paraded as Negro dialect is a silly gibberish unintelligible even to the Negroes who are supposed to speak it.

Tragedy must be relieved with occasional dashes of humor, and this the author all too frankly tries to do. Almost without exception, however, this humor turns out to be a re-hash of some time-worn joke about the Negro. And herein lies what is perhaps the most serious weakness of the story. The author has undoubtedly observed many Negroes, heard them talk, perhaps listened to anecdotes about them, and read about them in the newspapers. All this is objective, and interpretation therefore, is purely a matter of speculation. His sympathies have carried him a long way, but he could not make his characters live, feel, think and act. The same current superstition about what goes on in a Negro lodge, for example, finds expression in one of his outstanding incidents, altho not so fearsomely treated. Most white persons, especially those living in the South entertain the dire belief that Negroes take advantage of their one occasion for a closed meeting to hatch rebellions. In the same category are the naive assumptions that the *Elite* of the Negro race spend their leisure time at chitterling and watermelon parties, that mulattoes are outwardly ashamed and inwardly proud of their white blood; that education means redemption from hard work; that the church organist is also the piano player in some bawdy-house; and that Negro church meetings begin with a barbecue and have nine hell fire exhorters, all of whom are ignorant. Is this to be regarded as typical? The author steps out of his story on one occasion to assure his readers that it is: "What was said around the kerosene lamp on the Lowe's pine dining-table" (page 158), "was said around tens and hundreds and thousands of other tables in the Negro homes of Birmingham."

If Stribling in the novel "Birthright" made an unnatural person of an uneducated Negro, Clement Wood practically denies the existence of such a being. What we see is the happy-go-lucky Negro whose lot is unfortunate, but whose puny aspirations help bring on their tragedy. Jake's boys learned to read and write and went out looking for office jobs. There isn't much tragedy in their failure to get them. Those for whom such a setting would be more appropriate, Negroes qualified by all the tests save that of color, looking for work and a career, have no place in his book.

But the story is serious, honest and tremendously impressive—a real tragedy. The Negro is pictured as a human being capable of some aspirations and standards enough to feel his disappointment over failure to attain them. This is a long step. The poignant criticism of the demoralizing practices of the South in some measure compensates for some of his sins of commission and omission on the side of the Negro. A race drama involving highly controversial issues between the white and Negro population of the South is not easy to write. "Nigger" from this point of view is a triumph of the novelist's skill.

SOME BOOKS OF 1924

Charles S. Johnson writes about recently published books on or about African Americans that to some extent reveal the diversity and interests of the race. This essay was published in February 1925.

Mr. Arnold Mulder, in an article in the *Independent,* in which he voices a hope that out of the vast, rich depths of Negro life would come forth a novelist to tell the world "something vital" about this race, makes the observation, quite incidentally, but with ample warrant, that a "magazine nowadays without a Negro story is hardly living up to its opportunities." If he had been talking about science or sociology, or economics or politics rather than fiction his comment would have been no less pertinent. Nothing more powerfully expresses the changing attitude of this generation on the Negro than the amount and type of discussion which has centered about him during the past year. In a static society discussion is needless. Only when the seeds of restlessness and unbelief begin to sprout do we get in print the doubts which assail men's consciences,—the explosion of their fears and desires; solutions, palliatives, analysis, and, perhaps what is most hopeful, a general curiosity for some approximation to truth through it all. A candid reviewer in the *Springfield Republican* caught and expressed the note of this new interest at the very beginning of the year in his comment on the anthology of verse by Negro poets prepared by Dr. Robert E. Kerlin under the title "Negro Poets and their Poems." "He is to be thanked," this writer declares, "for giving us something which all too few of us know anything about, let alone enough."

From North Carolina came another anthology of Negro verse prepared by Dr. N. I. White, Professor of English at Trinity College, and W. C. Jackson, Vice President of North Carolina College for Women, with unusual care and judgment. The *American Mercury* precipitated a mild furore when it published "All God's Chillun Got Wings" by Eugene O'Neill, the tragedy of a mixed marriage. It was produced on the stage and published in book form amid fearful warnings of riot and conflict which, strangely enough, never came. Ronald Firbank's "Prancing Nigger" was an ultra-sophisticated novel based on Negro life in the West Indies, "obliquely visual, seen with aloof, yet discerningly selective eyes," says the *New York Times.* Two English writers, Llewelyn Powys and F. Brett Young, did much during the year to remake Africa for us into something a bit more real than the long tradition of the imperialists, missionaries and European ethnologists. "Black Laughter" a second book on Africa by Powys is filled with "biting realistic sketches which stick close to the concrete truth, and yet have artistry enough to bring out all the color and exotic glamor of the jungle." "Woodsmoke," by Young, shows the possibility of Africa as a background for fiction. Another volume of striking merit is "African Clearings," by J. K. Mackenzie. From France came the "The Long Walk of Samba Deouf," by Jerome and Jean Tharaud, a story of life among the Senegalese in West Africa, which the *New York Times* calls "as much of an anthropological study as a novel." Two novels involving the more or less intimate contact of white and black appeared in England: "Gone Native" by Asterisk, author of "Isles of Illusion," and "God's Step Children" by Sarah Gertrude Millin. The first is an excellent English counterpart of "The White Cargo" now in its second year of stage production in New York. The English reviews think it "very touching, whimsical and depressing," the American reviewers that it brings clearly to the surface all the nastiness hidden under the beauty of the South Sea "Isles of Illusion." "God's Step Children" is a (race) problem-novel and quite comes up to expectation in being "pathetic, tragic and unreal."

Most significant among the year's offering are the books by Negroes themselves. Jessie Redmond Fauset's novel, "There is Confusion," is probably the first full fledged novel by a Negro woman. It is a quite competent reflection of the life among the educated class of Negroes. The *Boston Transcript* calls it a work of high merit. Walter F. White's "The Fire in the Flint," a story of the trials of a refined Negro family in the south proved a terrific indictment of the civilization of that section. The book met a most favorable reception among the critics above the "line" and in at least one case was responsible for the disinheriting of a liberal Georgia critic living in New York who said Mr. White was substantially right on his facts. Henry Joshua Jones, living in Boston, released his novel of the race problem which he called "By Sanction of Law." Another book by W. E. B. DuBois, "The Gift of Black Folk," which is both history and art, adds sturdiness and charm to the year's contribution by Negroes. A new edition of William Picken's "Bursting Bonds" appeared. In the field of history the valuable work of the Association for the Study of Negro History, directed by Carter G. Woodson, begins to flower. Through the Associated Publishers, appeared in 1924 "The Negro in South Carolina During Reconstruction" by A. A. Taylor, a revealing account; "The Everlasting Stain" by Kelly Miller, a writer whose trenchant decisive style is remembered from his "Race Adjustment" and "Out of the House of Bondage" (in this is a splendid introduction by Alain Locke); and a third edition of "The Negro in Our History" by Carter G. Woodson, revised and enlarged.

Out of the South have come books which are a quiet revolution in themselves. Julia Peterkin's "Green Thursday" is one of them. A refined South Carolina woman, isolated on a plantation, she writes about the Negroes around her with a penetrating sympathy. Her characters are neither crap-shooters nor hilarious clowns, but field hands,—black men, women and children faced with problems of life, love and death. A ponderous tome, "The Negro from Africa to America," is another such unusual book from the pen of W. D. Weatherford. "Harrowing, instructive, interesting," it is called by the *Boston Transcript.* Between the extremes of criticism by Hershell Brickell of the *New York Evening Post* that it "leaves little to be learned" and that of Dr. DuBois that it is "poorly balanced" it will be found to be a significant contribution during the year. The success of Negro stories probably prompted the Gullah tales from South Carolina. "With Aesop Along the Black Border" and "The Captain: Stories of the Black Border" by A. E. Gonzales, while amusing, are heavily freighted with the tradition of the plantation, a sort of dead past.

"The Southern Oligarchy" by William H. Skaggs, a white Alabamian, smashes many cherished myths about the Negro's chicanery by telling with calm, scholarly assurance supported by documents more of the facts about the rest of the South. Frank Tannenbaum arrives at something of the same results in his "Darker Phases of the South," a vivid analysis of certain economic and social problems through the fabric of which the Negro is interwoven. Probably because he suspected that he would not be believed, he documented his statements heavily.

We may credit religious bodies with at least four serious and eminently worth while contributions to the science of race relations during 1924. The editor of the *International Review of Missions,* J. H. Oldham, attempted the difficult task of convincing our Christian nation that racial antipathy "is not instinctive or inborn." His "Christianity and the Race Problem" is an admirable study. So also is the English attempt at the same thing, "The Clash of Color, a Study in the Problem of Race," by Basil Matthews, published by the Missionary Education Movement. Robert H. Speer makes a plea for the spirit of Christianity in his "Of One Blood" which carries its argument in its title. The Council of Women for Home Missions is responsible for this volume, and the Christian Way of Life movement for that most unusual collection of stimulating incidents and experiences published under the title "And Who Is My Neighbor?"

More of Lafcadio Hearn's delightful "Creole Sketches" came near the close of the year, posthumously published; and another volume by R. E. Kennedy, "Black Cameos" added much rollicking humor for those who like to laugh at the antics of those Negroes whom Mr. Kennedy says he knows and loves so completely. And for the further delight of those interested in this admittedly distorted but popularly entertaining comedy we may add to the list Robert McBlair's "Mister Fish Kelly" and Octavius Roy Cohen's "Come Seven."

As a much needed antidote for Charles Conant Josey's "Race and National Solidarity" and Lothrop Stoddard's further hysterical utterings in his "Racial Realities in Europe," another edition of Jean Finot's "Race Prejudice" appeared. Two books on the Ku Klux Klan also have a place among the books of interest on the race question. One of these, by Miss S. L. Davis, was a rather belated justification of the first hooded order, the second a more scholarly discussion of the causes back of the development of the present invisible empire by J. M. Mecklen.

This does not pretend to be a statistically complete list. But it covers the high spots and, as must be evident, reveals the extent and diversity of interest now current on our much dissected race question.

BLACK VERSE

The volume Anthology of Verse by American Negroes *was edited by Newman Ivey White. Frank S. Horne offers the following review, published in November 1924.*

"*. . . And do not ask the poor man not to sing, For song is all he has.*"
                                                    —ROBERT NATHAN.

From the Trinity College Press, Durham, North Carolina, comes an "Anthology of Verse by American Negroes," edited by Newman Ivey White, Ph.D., Professor of English at Trinity College, and Walter Clinton Jackson, Vice President of the North Carolina College of Women, with an introduction by James Hardy Dillard, Ph.D., L.L.D., President of the Jeanes Foundation and the John F. Slater Fund.

We have here something more than just another anthology. It distinguishes itself, on the one side, by coming from the heart of the Southland, by its utter impartiality, and its scholarly completeness; on the other, by its lack of direction in development, absence of personality, and faultiness of viewpoint.

The professors have been most diligent. There is evidence of concentrated application and profound probing into obscure poetical sources. The book is redolent of the South, the schoolroom, and the professorial dictum. The work is scholarly, and the treatment is both critical and sympathetic to some degree. It at least demonstrates that these two southern scholars have looked upon this definite body of literary production, and deemed it worthy of their recognition. But for all that, the anthology is sluggish; it lacks distinction and verve. It possesses neither the vigor and raciness of Professor Talley's folk lore col-

lection, nor the poetical finesse and judgment of James Weldon Johnson's "Book of American Negro Poetry." The book lacks, in a sense,
personality. To a student of the subject, the work is undeniably a worthy contribution; but to the reader of verse, it is a volume he can as
well get along without.

In an effort to achieve completeness, the authors have included several worthy features. There is a more or less critical and historical general "Introduction"; brief biographies of the authors accompanying
the selections; and a mass of "Bibliographical and Critical Notes" at
the end. We shall consider them each in turn. The general "Introduction" is truly more historical than critical. The professors, not being
poets, lack the poetical judgment and the insight that is so evident in
James Weldon Johnson's "Essay on the Negro's Creative Genius"
which serves so aptly as an introduction to his own admirable collection. In essence the two viewpoints stand sharply contrasted when it
comes to the question of the ultimate contribution of the Negro to
American poetry. The professors, after correctly stating that the constant themes of religion and race in Negro poetry contribute nothing
new, go on to say: "There is, however, a kind of Negro humor that deals
in a distinctively racial manner with the Negro's love of music, talk,
animals, meetings, dancing, loafing and fishing, and is best exemplified
in the poems of Dunbar, Allen, and Davis. In this direction, the Negro
is perhaps likely to make a purely racial contribution to American poetry. Otherwise, his contribution is apt to be individual and not racial
in character." And there you have it! The compilers of this volume appear to believe that the "loud guffaw and the wide grin" are the paramount expressions of Negro aesthetics. At this point, I join the
company of Johnson, Braithwaite, and DuBois, and vehemently dis-
sent. The Negro poet has long since forsaken the jester's tatterde-
malion. His contribution is more subtle and pregnant; more sensitive
to the adventures of his own harassed soul. And in support might be offered such examples as "Self-Determination", by Leslie Pinckney Hill;
"When I Die", by Fenton Johnson; "Fifty Years", by James Weldon
Johnson; "And What Shall You Say", by Joseph Cotter, Jr.,—I offer you
William Stanley Braithwaite, Jessie Redmond Fauset, and Claude
McKay—and I offer you the youngest voices, Countee P. Cullen,
Gwendolyn B. Bennett, and Langston Hughes. With the work of such
as these already significant, the dictum of the professors need not be
taken too seriously.

The brief biographies of the authors accompanying the selections
are adequate and interesting. The critical and bibliographical notes at

the end of the volume are indispensable to the student, and add much to the value and completeness of the volume.

As for the body of the poetry included, there is little new or distinctive. The verse up to the time of Dunbar is below any real critical standard. It is to be marveled at, that in this period of sordid darkness, even voice was found to essay song. Its essence is a whimpering prayer for the Balm of Gilead to ease these mortal wounds. From Dunbar on, slowly but surely, the expression takes on form and virility, growing sophistication, and in enlivened interest in the life to be lived here and now. There comes the realization that the life of the Negro is a many sided adventure, worthy of recording.

The authors note that it was lack of education that impoverished earlier Negro poetry. They go on to say that this same lack of education perhaps accounts for the almost total absence of free verse from the mass of Negro poetry. This statement is open to considerable doubt. In the first place, the Negro is essentially lyrical. And the subtle rhythm of the best free verse, it might be urged, is not sufficient for the fullness of his song. From the mass of so-called free verse floating about that has been my lot to read, one might be inclined to express little regret if the Negro never gets educated in that direction. A decided and unmistakable progress in Negro verse, however, is graciously admitted as the compilers conclude that the quality of the poetry has depended generally upon the cultural opportunities of the poets. England took three centuries after the Norman Conquest to produce her first great poet; the Negro has been hardly that long out of Africa! Period for period, we have developed as fully and as rapidly. They see no reason, nor do we, why Negro poets will not reach as ultimate a peak of expression as has ever been or will ever be attained.

After much has been said on either side, we can conclude that the book justifies its existence for us, if only because it includes a selection by Countee P. Cullen. This man, though still very, very young, pens lyrics that already sing. Twice, successively in the last two years, his work has gained second place in the Undergraduate Poetry Contest of the Poetry Society of America; most all of the better magazines have included him in their pages; his sonnets have often topped F.P.A.'s "Conning Tower" in the New York *World;* the *American Mercury* will soon carry something like a hundred and ninety of his lines. He steps with a sure tread, and we expect him to go far.

So set to, makers of black verse. We have already shown that we can write their music, give them their dance, make their money, and play their games. Your task is definite, grand, and fine. You are to sing the attributes of a soul. Be superbly conscious of the many tributaries to our pulsing stream of life. You must articulate what the hidden sting of the slaver's lash leaves reverberating in its train,—the subtle hates, the burnt desires, sudden hopes, and dark despairs; you must show that the sigh is mother of the laugh they know so well. Sing, so that they might know the eyes of black babes—eyes that so sadly laugh; that they might know that we, too, like Shylock, cry when we are hurt, but with a cry distinctive, and subtly pregnant with overtones, and fraught with hidden associations. Sing, O black poets, for song is all we have!

THE GIFT OF BLACK FOLK

The Gift of Black Folk was written by W. E. B. Du Bois. The following review by Benjamin Brawley was published in December 1924.

Mr. DuBois' new book deals with one of the most important and far-reaching questions that a thoughtful citizen of the United States can ponder—that of the relation and contribution of a distinct racial element to the body politic as a whole. A reader might well wonder how it is that no enterprising publisher has previously stood sponsor for a series along the line represented by "The Gift of Black Folk". Some of our mission study clubs and agencies have from time to time been attracted to the idea, and have indeed acted upon it; but in general the makers of books have passed it by. The series now advanced by the Knights of Columbus in a large way meets the theory of the Ku Klux Klan that the Anglo-Saxon element in the population is the only one on which the nation's strength depends, and that other elements, such as the Celtic, the Jewish, and the Negro, are sources of weakness. Whatever the motive, the main conception of the "Racial Contributions to the United States" is sound, and the result is a contribution to American historical study.

Dr. Edward F. McSweeney contributes an introduction which in itself is a thesis and which serves to present not only the immediate work but the series as a whole. He reviews the history of immigration, shows that in the course of time there will be in the country practically no people of Mayflower descent, and brands recent immigration laws as "haphazard, unscientific, based on unworthy prejudice, and likely, ultimately, to be disastrous in their economic consequences." One may or may not agree with the conclusions, but he will undoubtedly find informing the review of facts, especially those affecting the Irish people.

As for the main part of the book, one of the first impressions that one bears away from it is that it must have been composed very rapidly. Occasionally there are typographical errors that can easily be corrected at the next printing; but there are also other things that show that the author has not had the time or has not taken the time to give the book the finish that he unquestionably knows how to give to any such production. The quotation at the bottom of page 109 is hardly clearly introduced; *asking* (page 123, line 9) is very evidently intended for *asked;* in the quotation from Pennington (page 257, line 23) *American* should be *America;* and *Mitchell* at the bottom of page 303 is for *Williams.* All these things, however, are secondary. The book may have been written under pressure; but it is still a book by Dr. DuBois and one of the most interesting that the distinguished author ever wrote.

"The Gift of Black Folk" has nine full chapters on such subjects as Negro Explorers, Negro Labor, Black Soldiers, the Freedom of Womanhood, and the Gift of the Spirit. The chapter on the Explorers summarizes more fully than has ever been done before the part that the Negro played in early American exploration. That on Labor, with its review of the Negro as an economic factor and as an inventor, is alone worth the price of the book; and the treatment of such more familiar topics as the Negro Soldier and Negro Art and Literature also holds the reader. The most powerful section, however, and the longest, is the one entitled "The Reconstruction of Freedom". It is no accident that this is the middle chapter, for it is a genuine climax. Calling to his aid his study of the Freedman's Bureau of some years ago, and adding to this his experience in more public service in recent years, the author undertakes to show "how the black fugitive, soldier, and freedman after the Civil War helped to restore the Union, establish public schools, enfranchise the poor white, and initiate industrial democracy in America." "The North, being unable to free the slave, let him try to free himself. And he did, and this was his greatest gift to the nation." Dr. DuBois handles in independent fashion the whole matter of the Negro's citizenship in the United States, and is especially strong in his consideration of the rise of the new industrial mastership in the South in the generation after the Civil War.

At every turn the book touches upon some vital subject, and again and again one comes upon an arresting page. One of the most frank discussions is that of racial intermixture—not only the infiltration of Anglo-Saxon blood into the Negro race, but also that of Negro blood into the white race; and a page is given to the ancestry of Alexander Hamilton. The influence of Haiti on liberty in America, the suggestion for the employment of Negroes in the Confederate armies, the careers of Negro men in Congress, recent achievement in music and other forms of art, the spiritual contribution of the race to America—all these things and many others are brought back to mind, not always with the fullness of detail that the author is unquestionably able to give them, but certainly with the straightforward and popular treatment that the aim for the series demands.

Two things we note with special pleasure. No work that the author has written can be said to surpass, or even to equal, "The Souls of Black Folk" in literary quality; yet in its optimistic temper, its constructive spirit, and its catholicity of interest, we know of no book of his that can equal the present. Moreover, at this time when in every field the race is forging to the front, and when in many ways rivalry is keen, the generosity and urbanity of the author—his readiness to accord recognition wherever it is due—furnish a model for all who may come after him. With the example of this book before us, we should by all means feel henceforth that the chief thing is not who does the work, but that the work is done, and that the race and the country shall have the benefit of every effort that might help toward the enthronement of truth, a better understanding, and a patriotism both exalted and sincere.

COLOR

A REVIEW

Color, a volume of poetry, was written by Countee Cullen. Alain Locke's *review was published in January 1926.*

Ladies and gentlemen! A genius! Posterity will laugh at us if we do not proclaim him now. COLOR transcends all the limiting qualifications that might be brought forward if it were merely a work of talent. It is a first book, but it would be treasurable if it were the last; it is a work of extreme youth and youthfulness over which the author later may care to write the apology of "juvenilia," but it has already the integration of a distinctive and matured style; it is the work of a Negro poet writing for the most part out of the intimate emotional experience of race, but the adjective is for the first time made irrelevant, so thoroughly has he poetized the substance and fused it with the universally human moods of life. Cullen's own Villonesque poetic preface to the contrary, time will not outsing these lyrics.

The authentic lyric gift is rare today for another reason than the rarity of poetic genius, and especially so in contemporary American poetry—for the substance of modern life brings a heavy sediment not easy to filter out in the poetic process. Only a few can distill a clear flowing product, Housman, de la Mare, Sara Teasdale, Edna St. Vincent Millay, one or two more perhaps. Countee Cullen's affinity with these has been instantly recognized. But he has grown in sandier soil and taken up a murkier substance; it has taken a longer tap-root to reach down to the deep tradition upon which great English poetry is nourished, and the achievement is notable. More than a personal temperament flowers, a race experience blooms; more than a reminiscent crop is gathered, a new stalk has sprouted and within the flower are, we believe, the seeds of a new stock, richly parented by two cultures. It is no disparagement to our earlier Negro poets to say this: men do not choose their time, and time is the gardener.

Why argue? Why analyze? The poet himself tells us

> Drink while my blood
> Colors the wine.

But it is that strange bouquet of the verses themselves that must be mulled to be rightly appreciated. Pour into the vat all the Tennyson, Swinburne, Housman, Patmore, Teasdale you want, and add a dash of Pope for this strange modern skill of sparkling couplets,—and all these I daresay have been intellectually culled and added to the brew, and still there is another evident ingredient, fruit of the Negro inheritance and experience, that has stored up the tropic sun and ripened under the storm and stress of the American transplanting. Out of this clash and final blend of the pagan with the Christian, the sensual with the Puritanically religious, the pariah with the prodigal, has come this strange new thing. The paradoxes of Negro life and feeling that have been sad and plaintive and whimsical in the age of Dunbar and that were rhetorical and troubled, vibrant and accusatory with the Johnsons and McKay now glow and shine and sing in this poetry of the youngest generation.

This maturing of an ancestral heritage is a constant note in Cullen's poetry. *Fruit of the Flower* states it as a personal experience:

> My father is a quiet man
>   With sober, steady ways;
> For simile, a folded fan;
>   His nights are like his days.
>
> My mother's life is puritan,
>   No hint of cavalier,
> A pool so calm you're sure it can
>   Have little depth to fear.
>
> And yet my father's eyes can boast
>   How full his life has been;
> There haunts them yet the languid ghost
>   Of some still sacred sin.
>
> And though my mother chants of God,
>   And of the mystic river,
> I've seen a bit of checkered sod
>   Set all her flesh aquiver.

> Why should he deem it pure mischance
> A son of his is fain
> To do a naked tribal dance
> Each time he hears the rain?

> Why should she think it devil's art
> That all my songs should be
> Of love and lovers, broken heart,
> And wild sweet agony?

> Who plants a seed begets a bud,
> Extract of that same root;
> Why marvel at the hectic blood
> That flushes this wild fruit?

Better than syllogisms, *Gods* states the same thing racially:

> I fast and pray and go to church,
> And put my penny in,
> But God's not fooled by such slight tricks,
> And I'm not saved from sin.

> I cannot hide from Him the gods
> That revel in my heart,
> Nor can I find an easy word
> To tell them to depart:

> God's alabaster turrets gleam
> Too high for me to win,
> Unless He turns His face and lets
> Me bring my own gods in.

Here as indubitably as in Petrarch or Cellini or Stella, there is the renaissance note. What body of culture would not gladly let it in! In still more conscious conviction we have this message in the *Shroud of Color:*

> Lord, not for what I saw in flesh or bone
> Of fairer men; not raised on faith alone;
> Lord, I will live persuaded by mine own.
> I cannot play the recreant to these;
> My spirit has come home, that sailed the doubtful seas.

The latter is from one of the two long poems in the volume; both it and *Heritage* are unusual achievements. They prove Mr. Cullen capable of an unusually sustained message. There is in them perhaps a too exuberant or at least too swiftly changing imagery, but nevertheless they have a power and promise unusual in this day of the short poem and the sketchy theme. They suggest the sources of our most classic tradition, and like so much that is most moving in English style seem bred from the Bible. Occasionally one is impressed with the fault of too great verbal facility, as though words were married on the lips rather than mated in the heart and mind, but never is there pathos or sentimentality, and the poetic idea always has taste and significance.

Classic as are the fundamentals of this verse, the overtones are most modernly enlightened:

> The earth that writhes eternally with pain
> Of birth, and woe of taking back her slain
> Laid bare her teeming bosom to my sight,
> And all was struggle, gasping breath, and fight.
> A blind worm here dug tunnels to the light,
> And there a seed, tacked with heroic pain,
> Thrust eager tentacles to sun and rain.

Still more scientifically motivated, is:

> Who shall declare
> My whereabouts;
> Say if in the air
> My being shouts
> Along light ways,
> Or if in the sea
> Or deep earth stays
> The germ of me?

The lilt is that of youth, but the body of thought is most mature. Few lyric poets carry so sane and sober a philosophy. I would sum it up as a beautiful and not too optimistic pantheism, a rare gift to a disillusioned age. Let me quote at the end my favorite poem, one of its best expressions:

THE WISE

> Dead men are wisest, for they know
> How far the roots of flowers go,
> How long a seed must rot to grow.
>
> Dead men alone bear frost and rain
> On throbless heart and heatless brain,
> And feel no stir of joy or pain.

Dead men alone are satiate;
They sleep and dream and have no weight,
To curb their rest, of love or hate.

Strange, men should flee their company,
Or think me strange who long to be
Wrapped in their cool immunity.

WELCOME THE NEW SOUTH

A REVIEW

The Advancing South was written by Edwin Mims. Alain Locke's review of the volume was published in December 1926.

It has been said—and well said—that it takes more courage to be liberal than to be radical. Here at last is an adequate and convincing portrayal of the progressive and enlightened liberalism which is working out what has been aptly phrased as the "second Reconstruction" in the South. With the cautiousness of tact rather than of timidity, Professor Mims has given a graphic picture of the struggle for agricultural and industrial progress and for social and educational reform in the Southland, and as well a dramatic view of the issues of personalities in the conflict now waging there for academic, religious and cultural freedom. Essentially *The Advancing South* is a book addressed to the South itself—an attempt to consolidate the front of Southern liberalism and win the South over to its better self through the agency of dramatic percept and the tactful medium of self-criticism. And should the book attain, as we hope it will attain, this purpose, it will be historically pivotal and important in its influence on the movement it so encouragingly describes. But even as it is, a significant accomplishment already stands, the old Bourbonism has been signally challenged by its own scions, the enlightened minority has at least one hand on the bridle and one foot in the stirrups; the *New South* states its claim to the saddle.

This book should be widely read in the interest of the wider American understanding that must come before democracy is truly realized among us. There is, regrettably, as counterpart to the "professional Southerner," the professional Northerner—and more understandably, but just as obstructively, the professional Negro. *The Advancing South* will have to face the antagonism, misunderstanding and distrust of all of them. But how any of these biases can survive the reading of this book I, for one, cannot see. With none of the selfish, ostrich-headed sectionalism of Grady and Gardner Murphy—with none of the professional reformism of Weatherford and Woofter, we have there a convincing, sane and forward-looking liberalism that ought to enlist the practical interest of all friends of human progress. Especially should all intelligent Negroes read the book, not merely for the broadening of their inevitably narrowed vision of the South, not merely for the possible gains of a possible alliance with these auspicious new forces, but for the important realization that the race problem cannot be isolated from the other social problems of the Southland, and that a policy of isolation, either in thought or public interest or public action, is fatal under the circumstances of the present generation. Our best tactics for the future will be to join the common causes of public enlightenment and welfare, to regard reactionism in politics, religion and public thought as more, or at least as much of an enemy as race prejudice, and to make the practical demands of our enlightened effort focus upon that prejudice which limits or excludes our practical participation in the progressive movements that are now under way. The attitude of Southern liberals and progressives has not been tested by practical advances—our contacts and loyalties have been too much for and with the ancient regime. We have really been in many indirect and unenlightened ways party to the dominance of the Old South. Even in our protests, the South we have helped advertise is the South of the Tillmans, Vardamans, Hoke Smiths, Heflins and Tom Watsons: a South that has protracted its natural lease of life and power by bluff and circus tactics. We should know and help to the center of attention the South that this book reveals—the progressive South of Dr. Knapp and Captain Walker, of Curry, Aycock, and McIver, of Tompkins, Hertz and George Gordon Crawford, of Presidents Chase and Poteat, of Mrs. Munford, Mrs. Hammond and Martha Berry, of Howard Odum, Paul Green and Gerald Johnson, of John Eagan, Ashby Jones, Will Alexander, and Julian Harris. It is names like these that should be our household words; agricultural, educational, industrial reform in the Southland have a vital meaning for the progress of the Negro, and until class freedom, sex freedom, cultural freedom and religious freedom are in some measure attained, rights and liberties for Negroes need not be expected. These movements and the constructive efforts they represent should therefore have not only the moral support of our intelligent sympathy but the practical help of our active participation.

It should be one of the articles of faith of the young Negro movement to believe in the New South.

The *New Negro* and the *New South* have more than interesting parallelisms, they have many ideals, loyalties and objectives in common. Each seeks an emancipation from the old obsessions of the Southern traditions—a revolution of mind and social attitude sought as a necessary preliminary to any really vital reform; each demands a change of leadership based on concrete, constructive programs and a philosophy and policy of class cooperation and mass education; each is economically and not politically pointed; each strives to raise a stagnated but richly endowed folk tradition to the level of free-flowing and creative expression; each hopes to freshen and purify brackish group emotions through new, dynamic processes of cultural and spiritual release. Art for the minority, education for the masses, self-direction, self-criticism, self-determination in both, are the common creed and common spirit of these two movements; which only the most enlightened on either side will be able for a half generation or so to see and recognize. History, however, will see them as definitely the products of the same social forces of our time, and as inevitable collaborators in the new social order. Success for one means success for the other.

It is equally true of both the Negro and the South that as long as they were incapable of self-criticism they were incapable of self-leadership. Fortunately both have now attained this fine pre-requisite of rapid progress. No one can be taught in a mood of resentment and protest or reformed in an attitude of self-justification. As with the younger generation Negro, the significance of the situation as reported by Professor Mims' book is that what is said and done is being said and done by Southerners for Southerners. It is Walter Hines Page with his challenge to the arisen South: "We must look forward to a golden age that we may surely help to bring about, not back to one that never was," with his dictum that the South must educate all or stagnate, must forget the past or perish. It is the native vision of Lanier that sees the redemption of the South in "the village library, the neighborhood farmers' club, the amateur Thespian society, the improvement of the public schools, the village orchestra, and all manner of betterments and gentilities and openings out into the universe." One rampant sectionalism cannot cure another. It is Clarence Poe who is quoted as saying: "The whole tragic system in the South is the outgrowth of our idea that labor is degrading—we must either have the Negro trained or we must not have him at all—our economic law knows no color-line." An official survey of the welfare projects of the great Tennessee Company's system reports: "What pleased us most was that the company disregards racial lines and aims in its home and housing provisions to provide the same comforts and surroundings for the Negroes as for the whites." The new intellectual South that has attempted at last at Chapel Hill to make good the Southern boast that the South knows the Negro best, is a significant development; it should be assisted toward its goal and made, if possible, the basis of a new contact of the educated minorities on either side. The inter-racial movement, halting and cautious as it has been, is nevertheless full of fine future potentialities—it is the only possible constructive basis of practical reform. And while Mims' treatment of this subject of the color question comes nearest of any of his chapters to temporism and apologia, he here comes nevertheless nearest to indicating a way out—cooperation. And if the formula is in any sincere spirit followed for even a half generation, what he aptly calls "the ebbing tide of color" will make way for a rising tide of general progress.

As Charles S. Johnson has already pointed out in an editorial in OPPORTUNITY, perhaps the most striking and significant feature of the whole situation is the independent discovery of the same cultural program by the newer schools of Negro and Southern art. The substitution of the vital assertiveness of self-realization as over against the sentimental and forlorn defeatism of the past generation is recognized by all these younger artists as the only way of personal and group salvation. Donald Davidson's brilliant article on "The Artist as Southerner" (*The Saturday Review of Literature*, May 15, 1926) with his statement: "In sum, the Southern character, properly realized, might display an affirmative zest and abandon now lacking in American art" has its counterpart in the creed of the young Negro artist, and the Harlem school has cultural cousins at Chapel Hill, Nashville and Oklahoma. OPPORTUNITY and *The Journal of Social Forces* are part of the same vision, Paul Green's plays and The Carolina Folk Players, counterparts of the Ethiopian Art Theatre, the Howard Players and the Krigwa Guild; and the decade that produces Stribling, Clement Wood, Ellen Glasgow, Du Bose Heyward, John Crowe Ransom, Frances Newman, Julia Peterkin and the rest has given us Walter White, Claude McKay, Rudolph Fisher, Langston Hughes and Countee Cullen. We make no pretense at being over-optimistic on either side; each of these efforts toward overcoming the cultural inertia and narrowed perspectives common to the South and the Negro has great loads to carry and hard obstacles to batter down or overleap. Neither can succeed without being consistently courageous, frank and objective, and as well;

convinced to the point of inspiration of their own intrinsic resources and possibilities. Both need particularly at this time not merely the drive of their creative impulses, but the clear-sighted guidance of sober and enlightened criticism. Cultural autonomy must not be a stalking horse for rancorous sectionalism or rampant racialism. What Paul Green says of the South is equally true of the Negro: "The trouble with Southern writers is that our emotions have lacked the chastening and subduing control of reflective thinking." A poised criticism becomes as vital then for their success as a soaring impulse and ambition. But for each a new cultural elevation and outlook are possible— and out of it an opportunity at least of a new self and mutual understanding. Let the New Negro, therefore, welcome the New South in the confident hope that the New South will welcome the New Negro.

THE NEGRO'S CYCLE OF SONG

A REVIEW

The Negro and His Songs *was edited by Howard Odum and Guy B. Johnson. Arthur Huff Fauset's review was published in November 1925.*

I'm goin' to heaven on eagle's wing,
All don't see me, goin' to hear me sing.

The pity of it is that all who read this splendid volume must content themselves with the mere seeing. Negro song is not something to be looked at; to appreciate it and understand it you must hear it.

Odum and Johnson, the compilers of the volume, both heard and saw; better than that, they devoured what came across their paths, and apparently made a good meal of it. Seldom have we had the pleasure of encountering such perfect comprehension of the Negro on the part of white investigators. For say what you will, the Negro is a difficult "problem." Like the Irishman's flea, it's hard to put your finger squarely upon him. Sometimes he seems to defy analysis.

His songs, like himself, are a problem. As I stated above, they must be heard to be fully appreciated and understood. In cold type they are words, ofttimes—and what crude vehicles are words for suggesting the pulsations, the quiverings, and the trippings of the soul! Sometimes in the case of these songs they approach the inanity of nonsense-syllables.

Small wonder. They have arisen from every conceivable condition of mind and body, and from circumstances innumerable. The wonder is not that they are as they are, but that they even exist. What right have Negroes to be singing anyhow! . . . But that's the whole secret.

The songs have their own general characteristics, of course, which make their origin very apparent, but as to classification, they simply defy any method of classifying.

They scan and they don't.

They are full of sense and they are so much nonsense.

They are sad and droll at the same time.

They contain evidences of profound philosophical reflection couched in expressions which have no parallels for naivete.

Depending on your point of view, they might be everything, nothing, more than anything, less than anything.

Now, can you beat that?

This is a choice sample:

> *I got de blues, but too damn mean to cry.*

The epitome of dolefulness. Nevertheless I laughed when I read it. Take this:

> *When I git to heaven gwine to ease, ease,*
> *Me an' my God goin' do as we please,*
> *Settin' down side o' holy Lamb.*

Or this:

> *Of all de beastes in de woods,*
> *I'd rather be a tick;*
> *I'd climb up roun' my true love's neck,*
> *An' there I'd stick,*
> *Jus' to see her roll dem snow-white eyes.*

The following is certainly a jewel:

> *Someone stole a chicken in our neighborhood,*
> *They 'rested me on suspicion, it was understood.*
> *They carried me fo' a jury—how guilty I did flee.*
> *'Cause my name was signed at de head, de jury said was me.*

But then, why try to analyze and classify Negro songs? As well attempt to analyze a spirit. It isn't the words, nor the length of the lines; it isn't even the rhyming—on which Odum and Johnson lay more than necessary stress, I think—none of these are the Negro's song. That song, sir, is an indefinable something which makes you feel it. Negro song . . . feeling . . . that's Negro song. The Negro feels it, you feel it, that's the song. You get the same indefinable something in the glint of a Negro's eyes, the gleam of his teeth, the sway of his body, the lilt of his feet. These are the Negro and his song, and they tell you that the Negro is the soul of his music.

What is the need of dissecting such a stanza as this:

> *Hop right! goin' to see my baby Lou.*
> *Goin' to walk an' talk wid my honey,*
> *Goin' to hug an' kiss my honey,*
> *Hop right, my baby!*

No mere words make you feel this; it is far from poetry in the conventional sense of that term. But some power from within unquestionably expresses itself in such a song which any man who has ever thought of going to kiss and hug and walk and talk "wid my honey" cannot fail to appreciate.

The song just referred to is among those which Odum and Johnson call Social Songs. In the chapter dealing with these the compilers have the following remarks which very likely will stir up some lively debates:

"It is to be regretted that a great mass of material cannot be published because of its vulgar and indecent content. These songs tell of every phase of immorality and vice and filth; they represent the superlative of the repulsive. Ordinarily the imagination can picture conditions worse than they are, but in the Negro songs the pictures go far beyond the conception of the real. The prevailing theme is that of sexual relations, and there is no restraint in expression. In comparison with the indecency that has come to light in the vulgar songs of other peoples, those of the Negro stand out undoubtedly in a class of their own."

A pretty bald statement and a bold one. Evidently Odum and Johnson have made careful comparisons of the contents of social songs of various peoples. The sympathetic treatment rendered in the whole body of the present work lends weight to the belief that these remarks are not made in the spirit of prejudice against the Negro. At the same time the book has a scientific air about it which suggests, to say the least, that this is not snap judgment. It is up to the Negro to prove his own case based on scientific evidence of the facts.

It is not a pleasant duty to prolong discussion of an already unpleasant topic, but certainly the scientific investigator must be prepared to give an explanation of this situation in the event that Odum and Johnson have presented the case correctly. The logical question following from such a conclusion as the compilers have come to is this: "Why is this so?" Perhaps the compilers' explanation that "it must be constantly borne in mind that this collection of songs is representative only of what may be called the Negro lower class," is the answer.

I believe we can say this with safety: the Negro is never more himself than in his songs. Through them all, religious songs, work songs, social songs, the Soul of Black Folk marches on, restless, dolorous, blithesome, bedewed as with heavenly dew, "sometimes...up...sometimes...down..."

Perhaps you are acquainted with the Negro in this mood:

> *Sinner, what you goin' to do*
> *When de devil git you?*
> *What you goin' do*
> *When de devil git you?*
> *What you goin' do*
> *When de devil git you?*
> *Lord, I'm on my way.*

Or in this frame of mind:

> *I was bohn in a mighty bad lan*
> *For my name is Bad-lan' Stone,*
> *I want you all fer to understan'*
> *I'm a bad man wid my licker on.*

Certainly you haven't missed him as he thus pictures his attitude towards life:

> *Rich folks worries 'bout trouble,*
> *Po' folks worry 'bout wealth.*
> *I don't worry 'bout nuthin';*
> *All I want's my health*

But if you want to get down to the real soul of the Negro, the part of him that makes all others wonder, wonder about that peculiar faculty of his of being happy when he's sad (or sad when he's happy—which is it?)—ponder over these lines, lines which must have surged more than once through the breast of every Negro who has any sense of the great injustice which he suffers for a "crime" over which he had no control:

> *Ain't it hard, ain't it hard,*
> *Ain't it hard to be a nigger, nigger, nigger?*
> *Ain't it hard, ain't it hard,*
> *For you can't git yo' money when it's due.*

> *Well, it make no difference*
> *How you make out yo' time;*
> *White man sho bring a*
> *Nigger out behin'.*

Nigger an' white man
   Playin' seven-up;
Nigger win de money——
   Skeered to pick 'em up.

If a nigger git 'rested,
   An' can't pay his fine,
They sho send him out
   To the county gang.

A nigger went to a white man,
   An' asked him for work;
White man told nigger;
   Yes, git out o' yo' shirt.

Nigger got out o' his shirt
   An' went to work;
When pay-day come,
   White man say he ain't work 'nuf.

If you work all the week.
   An' work all the time,
White man sho to bring
   Nigger out behin'.

Song is the Negro's mother. She nurtures him, soothes him, pacifies him, glorifies him. She keeps his heart cheered when the weight of an oppressive world would bend his body to the sod. She exalts him when others would see him abased, and draws his eyes upward to realms of higher achievement when the scoffs of men would crush him and force him into the role of stone-hewer.

Many will be inclined to laugh as they read the words which Odum and Johnson have recorded so faithfully and interpreted with such evident carefulness. Some will call it gibberish. And nonsense much of it is if naked, cold, physical eyes do the measuring. But visions quickened by a sense of things spiritual cannot fail to perceive that the soul which underlies and permeates these songs of black folk is the same one which in latter years has burst forth into the luxuriant, mellifluous outpourings from the hearts of such children as Dunbar, DuBois and Countee Cullen.

TWO AFRICAN HEROINES

Sterling Brown's review of these two novels, The Sailor's Return *by David Garnett and* Mambu, et Son Amour *by Louis Charbonneau, was published in January 1926.*

We have in these two novels, development of what has been hinted, here and there, by writers such as Powys, the *Tharauds,* Pischitari, and Coudenhove. We are shown qualities of the African scene other than savagery, bestiality and predestined malignance. Black Laughter here is no mockery at man's puniness, no hysterical half witted taunt. It is rather genial; not raucous, but sincere; not mocking, but sly, perhaps; warming the heart's cockles, rather than chilling the heart.

A quieter Africa is depicted and quieter folk symbolize it. It is an Africa where still, beside the fierce jealousies and spites and lusts and orgies, here is place for the peaceful, the tender, the delicate, the reticent. It shows the lyric that all along one had suspected somewhat near the 'roaring, epic, ragtime tune.' After Lindsay's

"Blood," screamed the whistles and the fifes of the warriors.

"Blood," screamed the skullfaced lean witchdoctors,"
and the frequent variations on the theme, one felt that to be true to his heritage, he had to go 'a headhunting,' to burn his books, and take to beating the tom-tom; in other words to ape the Nordics of our Southland. We learn otherwise here. Mambu and Tulip weren't savage beyond recognition, nor were their African companions. And in Garnett's book the savagery springs from England, from English forerunners of the Ku Klux Klan of this Age of Our Own Enlightenment.

It is not at all that Africa has become effete in these books. It is not yet what certain Garveyites seem to think it, a place of hot water heating and Associated Drug Stores. In *The Sailor's Return* we have such episodes as the death dealing elephant-hunt; in *Mambu* the heavy storms, the impenetrable forests, the vast distances, the marches, whence wretched sicknesses are dragged. There are the venomous crab-spiders, the gaudy birds, the alligators who devour Mambu's winning protegée. Africa has lost none of the wonted grandeur, or color, or danger.

But though Africa is still sullen and picturesquely terrible the stress is laid on the characters in the foreground, rather than on the tragic background. And these characters are not so much African, as human. They show that Africa has its kindliness. One has been so often reminded of its inhumanity. Obviously, as any other vast land, it has both.

In Garnett's other two tales, *Lady Into Fox, A Man In the Zoo,* he employs a realistic technique to bolster a somewhat flimsy major assumption. Here the technique is still as realistic, although the initial improbability is far less. And that improbability, Targett's marriage with Tulip is never overgreat, and dwindles throughout the plausible tale, even if it does not disappear on meeting Tulip, whose 'savage bones were small and delicate.... light as a bird's, and like a bird's bones filled with air ... The features were regular; the nose short, but straight and thick; the nostrils and lips spreading like those of a child pressed against the panes of a village sweetshop; but the mouth itself was small and the teeth were fine, regular and white as sugar ...'

Targett's first appearance with his African princess is humorous, simple and in its way, perfect. We have Tulip, except for earrings disguised as a man, the baby in a basket, whence he is revealed 'lying upon his back with his eyes open, diligently sucking the first two fingers of his left hand' ... The quiet humor persists through the story of Targett's setting up a public house. "The Sailor's Return," on Tulip's dowery, his experiences, genial with his customers and lady love, and galling with his implacable sterilized-Nordic sister Lucy. And this quietness goes to the end, making of the last scene a tragedy without a false note, and honestly moving.

Without the grimness of the one, or savagery of the other, Garnett's nineteenth century England seems as real as that of Hardy or T. F. Powys. It has a mask of joviality, aptly described, under which lurk stupidity, conventionalism, cruelty. We have the merriment of winter evenings over blazing hearths and ale, and the sombreness of other evenings when the natives of Dorset feel a religious need to torment human beings different from them.

Among the characters intimately sketched are the Targett brood (with whose womenfolk only, is Tulip unpopular); Tom Madgett, solid and loyal bartender; Eglantine Clall, charwoman etched real in a half dozen scattered lines; Cronk, the puzzled Shepherd, insistent on getting an unwanted black lamb into the fold; and the chorus of villagers, heavy with beef and ale and Nordic envies. But far above these portraits are those of the Targetts, William and Tulip.

William is the type of mariner England must have had in the last century; simple, hardworking, sensible as honest as the ale he sells, as robust as a squire in fielding. He brings a paganism, a reasonable animality to bear on daily complexities. The conventions of the hidebound notwithstanding, he lives with his Tulip, expansively, happily, *'taking his ease at his inn.'* They coolly startle the villagers and seem not to know it. Let us see them returning from a morning swim after a night of African jigs, 'Tulip with a jacket hanging loosely in folds round her naked body, and her wet woolly head shining,' and Targett, giving each shocked *Frau* a cheerful good morning. When questioned about his love for Tulip he fails to understand Harry's stupidity,

"Lose Tulip for a stinking pothouse, Harry? By God, do you take me for a weevil? .... Send away my Tulip? It is clear, Harry that you have never loved a woman."

And when he discovers that all needful is that he shall marry, he roars out his laughter until he cries. And so he is married again to Tulip, the African rite having a different rubber stamp. He has a humorous imperviousness to slight insult. But to insults not answerable by jesting, William is ready with his fists. He snips splendidly a carter who has maltreated his wife when he was away. He is hard hitter, and fair. But as so many other good men, his fair hard hitting cannot avert his tragedy.

And as for Mrs. Tulip Targett, she is unforgettable. Coming from a kingdom 'where women are the more equals of the men than here in England' she is self contained, capable, admirable. At her wooing, she listens to Targett's sincere offers, and the king, her father's verbosity, and still puzzling over a thorn in her foot answers their piled up questions with 'I must first get this broken thorn out of my foot, father.' Then looking Targett up and down. 'Yes I will have him. You are a very big man, Captain William to be my husband; otherwise I like you well enough as I think you must know already.'

And just as William fell in love with her, so do Harry and Francis Targett, and Tom Madgett. She is a witching minx with her great wisdom, and her great bewilderment. Her religious education, entrusted to William is amusing—if precarious; her distracting fears of the bap-

tism slated to 'wash her boy whiter than snow,' and her relief on finding baptized Sambo, as back as ever, are utterly delightful. Her petty
quarrels with William, her reconciliations show her the woman; her
mastery of trouble, (while white savages storm the front, she has been
composedly filling water buckets at the rear) her fearlessness, her plan-
nings show her the princess. Her sorrows, of which there are many, tes-
tify not only to tenderness but to stoicism. She is wise when she grows
distressed at Puritan, straitlaced, joyless England; so different from her
Africa. There is little of the sentimental in her. Her modesty is sincere,
if strange; her consciousness of breeding is touching. This little black
Hausfrau is a perpetual delight.

But stealthily grief stalks the happy pair. Over the *Sailor's Return*
shadows lengthen. The birth of Sheba, little gray sister of Sambo
seems ominous. She dies shortly of pneumonia, leaving William sad-
dened, and Tulip desolate. Tulip's slimness grows heavier, although
her native grace is not all gone. 'Soon it would vanish, and then no one
would believe that William had called her Tulip because she had
seemed to him like that brilliant flower, swaying upon its slender,
green, cylindrical and sappy stalk. . . .'

And in quick order, disasters follow. There is the rising spirit of the
yokels, their attempt at roasting the darker Targetts. And William,
avenging these wrongs is decoyed into a fight, and unfairly slugged. He
died soon after.

Tulip, wretched, is at a loss. She still has Sambo, however, and her
own money, which the family magnanimously allows her (since to do
otherwise would be illegal). She packs her things, fingering again the
silks and satins, and ruining them with sudden deluges of tears. And
then she makes a bonfire of them.

Then she seeks to shake the hateful alien dust from her feet. Her be-
seeching and scheming to get passage to Africa are vain and the picture
is sheerly tragic. She does succeed in parcelling Sambo to her cousin.
Having taken farewell of her boy, unknowing his fate, and the boy unknowing what separation means, she wanders aimlessly awhile, until
her feet lead her wearily back to *The Sailor's Return,* once bought and
renovated with her money. Here she takes up the sort of drudgery so
well known to women of her race.

And when the questioner seeks to find her savage joy at news of the
hanging of her husband's murderer, "I have seen so many deaths, I do
not care about them any more," said Tulip.

There is scarcely a page in this book without its burden of irony, its
muted overtone of pathos and of humor, strangely combined. And yet

one feels that as it should be, the tale is the thing. If it reverts to Fielding in its robustness, to Swift in its irony, in artistry it is Gallic. It is clear, sprightly, swift, consistently excellent. The dedication to George Moore is significant if one is considering the style.

Like the prefixed woodcut of Tulip, *The Sailor's Return* epitomizes the simple, the delicate, the sensuous and the healthy.

Louis Charbonneau charts the hidden ways of the heart in this novel, *Mambu, et Son Amour,* with a finesse rightly awarded, one would think, by the *Prix Coloniale.* The narrative never drags. But the successful tradings of Libono, his trade depots, his cornerings of oil, his prospectings, his governing of the natives, all merely serve as a realistic setting to another story of the way of a man with a maid—and, a maid with a man.

To add to the illusion of reality, Libono tells the story in diary form. Obviously enough from the very first appearance of Mambu, the little black heroine, the core of the telling is to be the wooing and winning of this 'vraie perle.' Of sufficient interest perhaps, would be the sketches of the numerous characters, native to the place, where French Equatorial Africa and the Belgian and Portuguese Congos meet. Books ere this have been written merely to show travellers' familiarity with such as Zan, the farcical cook in his cemented kitchen, dancing around, spanking the bread to make it rise, defending his mistreatment of it; Casserole, 'fat of cheeks and belly,' who works hardest at eating; the 'artist' passionately fond of his brush, who is busy painting from morning to evening, as well as whitewashing and coal tarring; the 'salad man,' or gardener; and the chicken man who grumbles about the new fangled incubator.

Of sufficient interest too might be the French slants at questions treated already by English and American writers and alarmists. (I use and advisably.) Hell's playground is not at all paradisal in this portrait, but it is not vastly unlike any other community. And while there is still hell in the climate there is not so terribly much in the folks. Pedro, the mulatto half brother of Mambu is not at all one of God's truculent stepchildren. He happens to be in a surrounding where he can develop his shrewdness (which once at least, approximates intuition) and honesty and geniality. His different standards do not seem to alter his character overmuch.

And of sufficient interest to America's Babbittry, devouring the fables of men who succeed commercially over great odds, might be Libono's business dealings. But all these things are subordinated to the story of the amour. And whatever else Libono brought from Africa, surely the experience with Mambu was the finest, surely the memory of her is the most precious.

The first night after he has met the little lady, Libono remembers an old *fiote* proverb, 'If one follows a thread of water he finishes at the sea.' This refrain threads its own way through the story. One sees a tiny thread of respect, widening—to keep up the allegory—into desire, and rushing headlong into love.

Libono is no half baked adolescent suddenly set in Hell's Playground. White women and natives had both taught him sufficiently of woman's excellencies and her limitations, for him to possess a sane cynicism. There had been, among the natives, he muses more or less philosophically, Tianga, heavy and curious; Tagourou; Dionga, who had been to Rouen, and wanted a white child; Tuano, the beautiful mercenary, who wanted enough money out of the transaction to open a cafe. The gift of these women had been their bodies. And here is Mambu, scornful of such paltriness.

For Mambu insists that she is no *Cabinda*. She is willing to be his housekeeper, but other relations, she lets him know, are distasteful. Only his commands, and they will be disagreeable, will change her. Libono used to different languages from whites and blacks, is startled from his three-ply Gallic cynicism into something near respect.

And thus starts the idyll; in no Arcadian pastures, but in the lush vegetation of Congo forests, and among the whitewashed cabins of the Luali depot. Nor are the characters sentimental abstractions in some 'cold pastoral'—but rather of warm flesh and blood. Their idyll begins as a strange duel, Mambu defiant, scorning any advances, Libono piqued, although too fairminded to command of her. But the Fiote proverb dins in his ears; and we are sure that Mambu shares the wisdom of her people.

Mambu becomes civilized by degrees, and in turn humanizes the Frenchman. She is a good housekeeper, keeping her bounds, delighting childishly in serving tea or coffee, believing whatever she is told. Libono writes 'In any case, my home is admirably kept, and if, at times, Mambu help herself to my cologne, I am sure that, unlike my last boy, she will not use my toothbrush, or my razors.'—She loves to accompany Libono about the place, losing her staid primness before the flock of pigeons, and the poultry. The incubator is unfailingly mysterious to her.—And all of the time, the place becomes dear to her, and Libono;—and she, ever inaccessible becomes dearer to him.

Africa, malevolent to such happiness strikes Mambu with a wearying fever, like the sleeping sickness. Libono begins to see how attached he is 'to that tiny morsel of bronze called Mambu. . . . Not especially pretty—but thoroughly charming. . . .'

Jealousy ends the duel between these strange lovers. Another woman, 'a Cabinda' whom Libono has merely spoken to; absence from the ménage overnight; the tagends of a fatiguing sickness—and Mambu blurts her confessional. Libono is as proud to leave his proud perch. And the two become lovers.

Mambu, mistress of *her own* household is quite as charming. Indeed as an observer notices to Libono—'You and your Negress are certainly not bored.' It is just because Mambu is not 'his Negress' that the delight continues. Mambu adopts a filthy little scullion, scrubs her a week or so, feeds her nearly as often, and adds another to this gallery of pleasing, domestic Africans. And learning from this child, she herself becomes chubby and rounded and healthy—and a pagan content shines in her face. It is noticeable that the adjective she uses oftenest in these days—is *'content'*—with its various meanings of happy, tranquil, satisfied, at peace. Even the *Mother* from the Mission cannot persuade her that her contentment is precarious, or that her pagan pride in physical beauty is wrong. She has her own wisdom, and the words of Libono.

Nor does Mambu flinch when in straits. The feverish Libono, against whom the ceaseless rains, and the swift climatic changes have ably conspired—recovers health more than once because of her untiring, sensible care. Mambu, the nurse, in spotless white pagne, is worth thinking on. The death of Moana brings out the finest womanliness.

And although Mambu dies of heartbreak, on hearing that her lover, at the time in France, will never come back to her; she is no weakling even in this great giving way. Never too robust, her lack of interest now leaves her all to open to the lurking diseases of Africa. Her old enemy, the sleeping sickness drags her off, to a sounder sleep, unbroken even by the cries for Libono.

Marie Louise, mulatto friend of Mambu, is responsible for the false report and thereby for Mambu's death. Her stupidity, apparently unmotivated is one of the very few artistic blemishes on the work. And this is more than repaid by the quiet beauty of the close.

Strange parallels might be drawn between Will Targett, old wayfarer, strong and shrewd, and Louis 'Libono' Charbonneau, bronzed prospector, human and cynical, both 'civilized' by two little African ladies; stranger might be drawn between these ladies. For Mambu and Tulip are much alike, both childish, gay, surprised at prudery, contemptuous of those 'less disciplined,' healthy, kindhearted, vain, amusingly stupid, and at the same time wiser than their husbands—in ways that women are and should be wiser.

But the French portrait is delineated more at length, and occupies more of the canvas. Mambu, vain as an African pheasant, and warmhearted; maliciously coquettish, and self forgetful; pagan and puritan; Mambu teaching Moana, scrubbing the little scallywags, cooking for Libono's friend the bluff English captain, hoarding her silks, and wearing white cotton—Mambu is sensitively pictured—and she is worth the care.

Outside of strictly Colonial literature—there are at least two other works in French literature like it. One, Chateaubriand's *Atala* tells of a love, designed to be as ill-starred, in an exotic setting. But the Indian maiden Atala is not as easily understood as Mambu, and her romantic tragedy is superhuman. Mambu's, being simple, strikes nearer home. While there is less lamentation, there is more despair; deeper maybe for its brevity. Lotis' *Madame Chrysantheme* is the second. But whereas there may not be the strange exotic beauty of setting here, there is the greater beauty of character under the stress of finer emotion. There is a vast difference between the chill artistry of Lotis' casting the pink lotus petals on the Yellow Sea, while Madame Chrysantheme coldly and correctly examines her dollars to a tuneless song, and this other parting—

"Sleep, little Mambu. . . . if your spirit hovers about your grave, it will be happy to have seen me. Sleep on, in front of that sea which did not bring you in time that which you were waiting for."

These two books seem important to the reviewer because they bring home, not uncertainly, recognition of fundamentals in all human nature. Their two authors, clear eyed, keen minded, are able to discover something deeper than pigmentation. They do this without gush, without hysteria, without the martyr-like mien of the sole defender of a losing cause. They have ably tabulated their findings for those who think. It is up to this counting minority to investigate these findings.

POET ON POET

The Weary Blues, *a volume of poetry by Langston Hughes, was reviewed by poet Countee Cullen in February 1926.*

Here is a poet with whom to reckon, to experience, and here and there, with that apologetic feeling of presumption that should companion all criticism, to quarrel.

What has always struck me most forcibly in reading Mr. Hughes' poems has been their utter spontaneity and expression of a unique personality. This feeling is intensified with the appearance of his work in concert between the covers of a book. It must be acknowledged at the outset that these poems are peculiarly Mr. Hughes' and no one's else. I cannot imagine his work as that of any other poet, not even of any poet of that particular group of which Mr. Hughes is a member. Of course, a microscopic assiduity might reveal derivation and influences, but these are weak undercurrents in the flow of Mr. Hughes' own talent. This poet represents a transcendently emancipated spirit among a class of young writers whose particular battle-cry is freedom. With the enthusiasm of a zealot, he pursues his way, scornful, in subject matter, in photography, and rhythmical treatment of whatever obstructions time and tradition have placed before him. To him it is essential that he be himself. Essential and commendable surely; yet the thought persists that some of these poems would have been better had Mr. Hughes held himself a bit in check. In his admirable introduction to the book, Carl Van Vechten says the poems have a *highly deceptive air of spontaneous improvisation.* I do not feel that the air is deceptive.

If I have the least powers of prediction, the first section of this book, *The Weary Blues,* will be more admired, even if less from intrinsic poet-

ical worth than because of its dissociation from the traditionally poetic. Never having been one to think all subjects and forms proper for
poetic consideration, I regard these jazz poems as interlopers in the
company of the truly beautiful poems in other sections of the book.
They move along with the frenzy and electric heat of a Methodist or
Baptist revival meeting, and affect me in much the same manner. The
revival meeting excites me, cooling and flushing me with alternate
chills and fevers of emotion; so do these poems. But when the storm is
over, I wonder if the quiet way of communing is not more spiritual for
the God-seeking heart; and in the light of reflection I wonder if jazz
poems really belong to that dignified company, that select and austere
circle of high literary expression which we call poetry. Surely, when in
Negro Dancers Mr. Hughes says

> *Me an' ma baby's*
> *Got two mo' ways,*
> *Two mo' ways to do de buck!*

he voices, in lyrical, thumb-at-nose fashion the happy careless attitude,
akin to poetry, that is found in certain types. And certainly he achieves
one of his loveliest lyrics in *Young Singer.* Thus I find myself straddling
a fence. It needs only *The Cat and The Saxaphone,* however, to knock me
over completely on the side of bewilderment, and incredulity. This
creation is a *tour de force* of its kind, but is it a poem:

> *EVERYBODY*
>
> *Half-pint,—*
> *Gin?*
> *No, make it*
>
> *LOVES MY BABY*
>
> *corn. You like*
> *don't you, honey?*
> *BUT MY BABY* . . . .

In the face of accomplished fact, I cannot say *This will never do,* but
I feel that it ought never to have been done.

But Mr. Hughes can be as fine and as polished as you like, etching
his work in calm, quiet lyrics that linger and repeat themselves. Witness *Sea Calm:*

> *How still,*
> *How strangely still*

> *The water is today.*
> *It is not good*
> *For water*
> *To be so still that way.*

Or take *Suicide's Note:*

> *The Calm,*
> *Cool face of the river*
> *Asked me for a kiss.*

Then crown your admiration with *Fantasy in Purple*, this imperial swan-song that sounds like the requiem of a dying people:

> *Beat the drums of tragedy for me,*
> *Beat the drums of tragedy and death.*
> *And let the choir sing a stormy song*
> *To drown the rattle of my dying breath.*
>
> *Beat the drums of tragedy for me,*
> *And let the white violins whir thin and slow,*
> *But blow one blaring trumpet note of sun*
> *To go with me to the darkness where I go.*

Mr. Hughes is a remarkable poet of the colorful; through all his verses the rainbow riots and dazzles, yet never wearies the eye, although at times it intrigues the brain into astonishment and exaggerated admiration when reading, say something like *Caribbean Sunset:*

> *God having a hemorrhage,*
> *Blood coughed across the sky,*
> *Staining the dark sea red:*
> *That is sunset in the Caribbean.*

Taken as a group the selections in this book seem one-sided to me. They tend to hurl this poet into the gaping pit that lies before all Negro writers in the confines of which they become racial artists instead of artists pure and simple. There is too much emphasis here on strictly Negro themes; and this is probably an added reason for my coldness toward the jazz poems—they seem to set a too definite limit upon an already limited field.

Dull books cause no schisms, raise no dissensions, create no parties. Much will be said of *The Weary Blues* because it is a definite achievement, and because Mr. Hughes, in his own way, with a first book that cannot be dismissed as merely *promising*, has arrived.

ROMANCE AND TRAGEDY IN HARLEM

A REVIEW

Carl Van Vechten's novel Nigger Heaven *caused quite a stir because of its title, especially within the black community. This review by James Weldon Johnson was published in October 1926.*

From its intriguing prologue to its tragic end, here is an absorbing story. Whether you like it or dislike it you will read it through, every chapter, every page. Mr. Van Vechten is the first white novelist of note to undertake a portrayal of modern American Negro life under metropolitan conditions. Mr. Van Vechten is also the only white novelist I can now think of who has not viewed the Negro as a type, who has not treated the race as a unit, either good or bad. In *NIGGER HEAVEN* the author has chosen as his scene Harlem, where Negro life is at its highest point of urbanity and sophistication, and there the entire action of the story is played out. The economy of stage Mr. Van Vechten imposes for himself enables him to gain in dramatic intensity but it does not limit him in the scope of the action. The story comprehends nearly every phase of life in the Negro metropolis. It draws on the components of that life from the dregs to the froth.

It was inevitable that the colorful life of Harlem would sooner or later claim the pen of Carl Van Vechten. He has taken the material it offered him and achieved the most revealing, significant and powerful novel based exclusively on Negro life yet written. A Negro reviewer might pardonably express the wish that a colored novelist had been the first to take this material and write a book of equal significance and power. Mr. Van Vechten is a modernist. In literature he is the child of his age. In *NIGGER HEAVEN* he has written a modern novel in every sense. He has written about the most modern aspects of Negro life, and he has done it in the most modern manner; for he has completely discarded and scrapped the old formula and machinery for a Negro novel. He has no need of a *deus ex machina* from the white world either to involve or evolve the plot. There is, of course, the pressure of the white world, but it is external. The white characters are less than incidental. The story works itself out through the clashes and reactions of Negro character upon Negro character. Its factors are the loves, the hates, the envies, the ambitions, the pride, the shamelessness, the intelligence, the ignorance, the goodness, the wickedness of Negro characters. In this the author pays colored people the rare tribute of writing about them as people rather than as puppets. This representation of Negro characters in a novel as happy or unhappy, successful or unsuccessful, great or mean, not because of the fortuitous attitudes of white characters in the book but because of the way in which they themselves meet and master their environment—a task imposed upon every group—is new, and in close accord with the present psychology of the intelligent element of the race. The only other full length novel following this scheme that I can recall at this moment is Jessie Fauset's *THERE IS CONFUSION.* It is a scheme for the interpretation of Negro life in America that opens up a new world for colored writers.

There are those who will prejudge the book unfavorably on account of the title. This was the attitude taken by many toward Sheldon's *THE NIGGER,* perhaps, the finest and fairest play on the race question that has yet been successfully produced in New York. This attitude is natural, but it is probable that the reaction against the title of the novel will not be so strong as it was against the title of the play which was produced sixteen years ago. Indeed, one gauge of the Negro's rise and development may be found in the degrees in which a race epithet loses its power to sting and hurt him. The title of Sheldon's play was purely ironic, and the title of *NIGGER HEAVEN* is taken from the ironic use of the phrase made by the characters in the book. But whatever may be the attitudes and opinions on this point, the book and not the title is the thing. In the book Mr. Van Vechten does not stoop to burlesque or caricature. There are characters and incidents in the book that many will regard as worse than unpleasant, but always the author handles them with sincerity and fidelity. Anatoles and Rubys and Lascas and number kings and cabarets and an underworld there are as well as there are Mary Loves and Byron Kassons and Olive Hamiltons and Howard Allisons and Dr. Lancasters and Underwoods and Sumners and young intellectuals. There are, too, Dick Sills and Buda Greens, living on both sides of the line, and then passing over. It is all life. It is all reality. And Mr. Van Vechten has taken these various manifestations of life and, as a true artist, depicted them as he sees them rather than as he might wish them to be. But the author again as a true artist, deftly maintains the symmetry and proportions of his work. The scenes of gay life, of night life, the glimpses of the underworld, with all their tinsel, their licentiousness, their depravity serve actually to set off in sharper relief the decent, cultured, intellectual life of Negro Harlem. But all these phases of life, good and bad, are merely the background for the story, and the story is the love life of Byron Kasson and Mary Love.

Mary is a beautiful, golden-brown girl who works as an assistant librarian in one of the New York public libraries. She is intelligent, cultured and refined. She is sweet, pure and placid until she meets Byron; she remains sweet and pure, but her placidity is shattered, the emotions which she sometimes feared she did not possess are stirred to the depths. Byron, bronze-colored, handsome, proud, impetuous and headstrong has just been graduated from the University of Pennsylvania. At college he had made a literary reputation in the university periodicals; his professors had encouraged him; so he comes to Harlem to make writing his profession and to conquer New York. He and Mary first meet at a gay week-end house party given by a wealthy woman of the smart set at her country home on Long Island—a house party at which Mary is sadly out of place. They meet again at a dinner given by the Sumners, one of the well-to-do, cultured colored families of Harlem. Byron calls to see Mary at her home, and the beginnings of love burst into a flame. The author makes an idyl of the awakening of love in Mary's heart. Byron starts out buoyant and sanguine. He receives a small monthly allowance from his father, but he must work to supplement that sum while he makes his way as a writer. He smarts under the rebuffs he meets with in trying to find work he considers in keeping with his training. He grows bitter and cynical under failure. He finally takes a job as an elevator boy, but this job he fails to hold. In the meantime he is devoting such time as the distractions of New York leave him to irresolute efforts at his writing. But there is something wrong with his stories, he sends them out and they regularly come back. Byron begins to slip. Mary tries to give him the benefit of her intelligent opinion and her knowledge of literature but his pride will not let her. His pride also keeps him from going for assistance to the Sumners and other influential friends to whom his father had given him letters; he does not want to be "patronized" by them. Byron cannot adapt himself, he cannot bend the bars of his environment to accommodate his own needs and desires. He has already failed, but he is not yet lost.

Mary's love is what he needs to keep him steady, but the very fullness of her love raises for him a wall which his rebellious nature will not permit him to get over or through. Mary's love has developed in a two-fold manner, passionately and maternally; she jealously wants her handsome young lover wholly for herself, and she wants to watch over him and guide and protect him as she would a child, which in many respects he is. Byron is irritated by her jealousy and her attitude of guardianship he resents. He realizes that he is a failure compared to the young intellectuals and professional men of Mary's acquaintance and he feels that she, too, is pitying him, is patronizing him; and he will not be patronized. He begins to think of the fascinating, exotic Lasca Sartoris, whom he had met and danced with at a big charity ball. Her wit and beauty had amazed him and the talk about her purple past had stirred his imagination. He compares the tender, solicitous Mary with this superb woman, Lasca, who tramples all conventions under her shapely feet, who recognizes no limitations, who takes what she wants. Why couldn't he know intimately such a woman? That would be life— that would be inspiration.

One day Byron receives a letter from Russett Durwood, the editor of a great magazine, asking him to call regarding a story he had sent in. It is the story that carries all of Byron's hopes, his great story. He forgets all about Lasca. He rushes as fast as his feet can carry him to Mary. It is Mary to whom he wants to break the good news. He is again the buoyant, sanguine and the lovable Byron. He is sure of success now, he has regained his self-confidence and self-respect, Mary's love and solicitude are now grateful to him. The outcome of the interview is a lecture from the great editor on the defects of the story. He has sent for Byron because he is interested in Negro literature and Negro writers. He has seen from parts of Byron's story that he has talent and ability and can write. But "why in hell" doesn't he write about something he knows about? Negro life—Harlem—West Indians, Abyssinian Jews, religious Negroes, pagan Negroes, Negro intellectuals all living together in the same community. Why continue to employ the old clichés that have been worked to death by Nordics? Why not use this fresh material before a new crop of Nordics spring up and exploit it before Negro writers get around to it? Byron is stricken dumb, he can make no answer. He drags himself out of the building and makes his way to Central Park. Through whirling emotions of disappointment and heartbreak there surges a flame of fury. He will go back to the editor and tell him what he thinks of him; he will not stand to be treated as a Nigger. But he does not; instead, he sinks upon a park bench discouraged, disheartened, beaten. He hears a woman's voice calling him, he raises his head to see Lasca beckoning him from her luxurious limousine, Lasca, who takes what she wants. She takes Byron. She showers him with all the fragrance, the beauty, the wild ecstacies, the cruelsweets of love that her perfect body and her lawless soul know. Byron, now, has not only failed, he is lost. And yet his is a fate before which self-righteousness should take no occasion to preen itself. One must, indeed, be much of a prig not to make some allowances for youth caught in the circle of the lure of Lasca, the courtesan supreme. Lasca keeps Byron for a period, then, as she had done others before, she throws him out, banishes him wholly, and takes Randolph Petijohn, the number king. From here on Byron's journey downward is steep and fast. His moral disintegration is complete. He pleads, he raves, he broods. He becomes obsessed with the desire for revenge; and he procures a revolver and haunts the cabarets, lying in wait for the two objects of his hatred. One night in the Black Venus, drunk to the point of irresponsibility, he sees the number king enter. While Byron is trying to bring together his dissolved will for the accomplishment of his purpose a shot rings out and Petijohn falls dead. The shot had been fired by Anatole, the Scarlet Creeper, who also had a grudge against the number king. Byron, playing his futile role in the drama out to the end, springs up, stands over the prostrate form and is emptying his revolver into the dead body when the law lays its hands upon him. An absorbing, a tragic, a disquieting story.

Byron is at many points a symbol of the tragic struggle of the race thrown as it is in an unsympathetic milieu and surrounded by fateful barriers. But Byron's story is especially true as an individual story. It is a true story—and an old story. It is the story of many a gifted and ambitious young colored man who has come up to New York as the field for success, and has been sucked in and down by the gay life and underworld of the great city. It is the story of talent and brilliancy without stamina and patience. The theme has been used before. Paul Dunbar used it in a measure in *THE SPORT OF THE GODS,* and I myself skirted it in a now forgotten novel. But never before has it been so well and fully used.

The book is written with Mr. Van Vechten's innate light touch and brilliancy, but there is a difference; Van Vechten, the satirist, becomes in *NIGGER HEAVEN* Van Vechten, the realist. In every line of the book he shows that he is serious. But however serious Van Vechten may be, he cannot be heavy. He does not moralize, he does not over-emphasize, there are no mock heroics, there are no martyrdoms. And, yet—Mr.

Van Vechten would doubtless count this a defect—the book is packed full of propaganda. Every phase of the race question, from Jim Crow discriminations to miscegenation, is frankly discussed. Here the author's inside knowledge and insight are at times astonishing. But it is not the author speaking, he makes his characters do the talking, and makes each one talk in keeping with his character. If the book has a thesis it is: Negroes are people; they have the same emotions, the same passions, the same shortcomings, the same aspirations, the same graduations of social strata as other people. It will be a revelation, perhaps, a shock to those familiar only with the Negro characters of Thomas Nelson Page, Thomas Dixon and Octavius Cohen. It is the best book Mr. Van Vechten has done, and that is saying a good deal when we remember *PETER WHIFFLE*.

NIGGER HEAVEN is a book which is bound to be widely read and one which is bound to arouse much diverse discussion. This reviewer would suggest reading the book before discussing it.

BLACK SADIE

Black Sadie was written by T. Bowyer Campbell. This review by Nella Larsen was published in January 1929.

Black Sadie—what a title! Great, isn't it? Unfortunately the book, which is the story of a Negro dancing girl's rise to popularity, isn't.

The tale opens in the south with a rape and closes in New York with a murder. Every strangeness, every crudity, every laxity, which by ancient superstition has been ascribed to the black man, Mr. Campbell has incorporated into this story—and some others. In this way he has managed to produce an effect of difference with traits and habits which every intelligent person knows to be utterly usual, by throwing into exaggerated relief characteristics found in some degree in all human beings, and in themselves commonplace. The result is clever but inaccurate.

It must, however, be admitted that the white characters are not more kindly handled than the black. But, they are not set down as thieving, sexually immoral, and brutal. The method which the author uses for their outlining is ridicule and heavy-handed sarcasm. What he does is not so much grin as to grimace.

Black Sadie is an awkwardly written and disorderly book. Mr. Campbell seems not to have learned the art of selection and arrangement. And there are certain peculiarities of style that after a while become tedious, the too frequent repetition of the same phrases and words. Though this is a deliberate mannerism, it is none the less tiresome.

Nevertheless, in spite of its twaddle concerning the inherent qualities of the Negro, in spite of its affectations of style, the book is worth reading. Sadie, a handsome black wench, is an interesting and forceful character, which no one interested in modern Negro fiction can afford to ignore. She is absolutely without subtlety and her ways of obtaining the things she wants are rude and often terribly direct. But she *is* successful. And her personality leaves its impression not only on all the other people in the book, but on the reader as well.

In some of its episodes *Black Sadie* is brutal, stark, gruesome almost. Some of the drama is pitiful. But Sadie herself is a delightfully sunny person. And often its very inaccuracies make much of the book very amusing—especially to the Negro reader.

Don't miss it.

PART FIVE

ESSAYS

SAND

This essay, published in July 1926, earned John F. Matheus first prize for personal experience sketch. In it, Matheus shows off his expansive imagination. By way of creative exposition, he pilots our thoughts through minefields of perception that show the infinitesimal and tenuous nature of man's existence on an earth of whose true age we still are not fully aware.

I feared to count the years. Like some woman trembling for the perpetuity of her vanishing youth and knowing absolutely that the charms which once attracted are fading, I began to dread time. From seventeen to thirty-five. So long from seventeen to thirty-five, so short from thirty-five to seventeen!

And what about the accomplishments, the great deeds, the wonderful record? Thus I thought as I walked the boards of Atlantic City's great pageant way. I saw the whitecapped waves rushing nonchalantly to the shore—ceaselessly. The blue water stretched away and away forever.

Then I remembered the bathers on the beach. Great crowds of humanity, men and women of all races, creeds and conditions, Jews, Italians, Negroes, Japanese—why enumerate?

And on the board walk an ever moving river of humanity, passing by. It was a visualization of Bergson's philosophy that life moves on like a river, vitalized into motion by an irresistible "élan vital."

Young men, ogling the shapes of women; old men, roués, madly rioting in the forms of girls; women, watching the dresses of other women; men in clerical garb and grave demeanor thinking perhaps of the evils of dress, fit subject for a Sunday text. There are fun makers, enjoying holiday. Gay youths, lustless, enthralled by the contagion of the frolic. Children, playing at ball and jumping the waves or covering themselves in the sand.

There were beautiful girls with ravishing lips and eyes, covered by the white, clean sand; there were old women with flabby cheeks and dull, bored eyes, covered by the sand; there were young men with shining hair and smooth-as-baby faces, hiding their glistening muscles in the sand, and old men, with bald heads and fat pounches, hiding their shriveled muscles in the sand. The irrepressible giggle of shop and office girls on vacation festivity, the mirthful shout of little children, the hoarse bass of joking men, rise from bodies concealed in the warm white sand.

A few days, a few years, and how many of these same atoms of human life will be hidden in the warm bosom of the dark earth forever? But what a joy killing thought! Yet why ignore it? Why drink the drug of pleasure to forget the great Reality? The bodies shall be hidden and life, will it find a brighter shore, a cleaner, whiter sand?

On the board walk the parade goes on. A sea of humanity, waves of faces, gazing restlessly on the Atlantic ocean; waves of water never resting. How transient, how futile and puny the human sea! How grand, how immeasurably and inexpressibly wonderful that fitful sea, the salt sea, turbid, everlasting! Yes, it will be roaring when all that mortal ocean is melted into nothingness and I am gone.

Up above the board walk tower the hotels. Their lofty pinacles, like young mountains, piece on piece, form the jagged sky line of that city of pleasure. Piles upon piles of dollars they represent and toil. Their furnishings are the last word of luxury. Their velvet rugs and damask hangings, their downy couches and regal trimmings enfold beauty and splendor, loveliness and glory of the flesh. Sometimes they hide woeful ugliness of soul, debauchery, bawdy, fornication, adultery.

Should I with my brown skin knock for admittance at those gilded doors, the scorn of the assembled guests would mount higher than their pyramiding roofs. Should I come with uncounted wealth to buy a night's lodging, the outraged clerk would kick me into the street, or not understanding, he would show me the way to the rear where the kitchen odors dwell.

"Servants are hired in the rear," he would say.

And yet, and yet, any Hindoo, Japanese, Chinaman, Malay, Arab, Turk, stained with Christian blood, Indian, from his wigwam in the West, can buy there a lodging for the night.

Let me walk by the shining places where food is served. I am hungry. I have walked a long way. The salty smell of the sea has filled my lungs and strengthened me. I am hungry. I have money in my pocket. I enter. The evening lights have begun to glimmer on the polished silver and the costly linen. I seat myself. I wait. The eager patrons come and go. I wait. The busy servants rush back and forth, back and forth. I wait. I am hungry. I look about me. Hot indignation wells up like a typhoon wave. I seek somebody, headwaiter, cashier, proprietor.

"Make 'em serve you," leers the first.

"I only take the money," comments the second.

"I don't serve niggers," frankly snorts the third.

I am hungry. I will seek self-service, where no white hand will be sullied with serving me. The Automat! God bless that capitalistic entrepreneur whose get-rich-quick brain first conceived the Automat! I gather together cup and saucer and pour in the steaming liquid coffee. I slide a nickle here and a dime there. I am served. I am satisfied.

I leave the clean tile and the gleaming mirrors. Crash! What is falling behind my footsteps? What clattering breaking-to-pieces of crockery is that?

"Ah I know. I know. The Greek bus boys are throwing my dishes on the tile floor! One by one, breaking my dishes on the tile floor."

I am glutted, cloyed and hungry of soul.

O God! I will forget it. I will drown it all in the raging waves of the Atlantic. Better the raging waves of syncopated Jazz. The famous colored review is showing at the Bright Light Cabaret. Their names are echoing in all the theatrical journals, the Billboard features them, the dramatic critic praises them. Forsooth I am proud of my brothers in black. I will see them. The crowd is surging through the swinging doors. The mammoth letters blink and wink in electric glory above the doorway, "Baker and Hudson—Colored Review." Their pictures are featured in the lobby. I will buy a ticket. I approach the window.

"Sold out!" says the ticket seller.

"Sold out!" I echoed and added, "But others are buying."

"They have engaged seats by telephone," she says.

"You lie," I retort.

The ushers come. The manager fumes.

"We cater to the Caucasian race," he apologizes.

"Why your entertainers are Negroes," I storm.

"Our entertainers, yes."

"I will call down the law upon your cowardly, un-American heads," I threaten.

"But this is not a public theatre, sir. It is a private affair, sir. Do your damnest, sir."

I hear the tinkle of glasses and the wailing buffoonery of a saxophone, moaning the "Aggravatin' Papa Blues."

Then I go down by the sand. The moon comes up silent over the restless sea, eternally restless, beating against the imprisoning bars of land, like some he-lion in his cage. The sands slip and slide under my weary feet.

"And the beating sea will encroach upon my standing place," I think, "even as it swept over that mystical Atlantis of the dim, Greek legend. Then it will retreat and leave the sand, white and dry, like the desert of Sahara, white and dry, like the stretches beyond Salt Lake City, burying civilizations of forgotten men."

"And the sea shall rave on somewhere. It has roared and laved the retreating and advancing shore before there was a human face, when colossal beasts washed themselves in its shallows. It shall be roaring when other atoms of men and women will stand to watch its ebb and tide, even as I, and fling themselves in its mad, mad bosom."

Suddenly I am sleepy. I fall upon the soothing sands. I dream.

"Lullaby—lullaby," I hear my mother's voice again. "The sand man is throwing sand in your eyes, my boy—throwing sand in your eyes, my boy."

"Who is the sand man, mother?" I pray.

There arises before my vision a mighty and panoplied figure, whose back is broad with sinewy strength, whose projecting arm is knotted with muscles, like ropes, whose brow is high, whose eye is piercingly hard and pitiless, whose voice is raucous and deep and coarse.

"I am the Sand Man," he bellows. "I am White Civilization. I hate Black. I crush Black. He who serves me may survive, but he who would equal me must die. This land is mine, these board walks, these shops, yonder hotels and theatres, all the wealth and power of the City behind the breakers. I am White Civilization—Invincible. Nothing can break me."

His words smote upon me like sand in my eyes. They blind me. I stagger in my dream and in my dream fall down again.

Comes then a great wave rolling from the myriad billows of the ocean and covers me from head to foot. I gasp for breath. I feel the cold wetness on my face and in my eyes.

The wave rolls back from whence it came. The water has washed the sand from my eyes. I see clearly.

A greater figure looms behind the mighty one of the doughty arm. No definite shape has the hooded form. Just clinging folds of shadowy stuff blending with the night. A voice speaks like the chiming of silver bells with golden clappers. At the sound of the first vibration my heart leaps up, for I see emanate a pale, penetrating luminosity, a glow such as shines neither on land nor sea.

"I am Spirit," the voice atones. "I am the Spirit of the Sea and the Sand, of all things and men. I am Truth. Than me there is nothing greater. When civilizations forget me, my sea and sand have buried them. I am abiding. I never die."

The armed and mighty Sand Man vanishes, as though he were a man of sand.

"Lullaby," pleads my mother's voice so long unheard.

Then I awake. I stand up.

Behind me rises the untiring din and cacophony of the City's endless pageantry. I turn my back upon that modern Babel of Pandemonium. In front of me the waves are rising and falling in the moonlight as far as the eye could see.

A Golden Afternoon in Germany

This personal essay by Clarissa M. Scott describes her visit and experiences at the home of the Walter von Ruckteschell family in Munich. Frau von Ruckteschell, after having lived in and absorbed much of the culture of Africa, expresses her feeling that she and her husband had finally reached "a space of quiet breathing" and convinced Scott that she was "a person to whom racial difference is no barrier and for whom spiritual values are the only real values." This essay was published in December 1925.

Africa, old as eternity, mysterious as the future; her people one with the earth, now laughing in the sunshine, now silent and sad as the deep gloom of their forests and the throbbing blackness of their nights has drawn to herself people of many lands. They come on many errands and remain held by an irresistible fascination, or leave only to feel again and again an aching nostalgia.

One would not expect to find in German people a deep response to the spirit of African people. And yet there can be no keener sensing of the beauty of the African nature than one finds in Walter von Ruckteschell and his wife.

We were in Munich for a time, and on finding in our frequent consulting of the map that Dachau, the home of the von Ruckteschell's was near at hand, decided to get in touch with them as we bore a letter from the editor of OPPORTUNITY. Whereupon we essayed the mysteries of the German telephonic system and talked to Frau von Ruckteschell, who told us that her husband was in Hamburg, but that she would be happy to have us come out to Dachau and spend the afternoon with her.

It was Sunday, and the people of Munich were streaming out of the city, auf das Land; the men in their picturesque hiking suits, the women in full skirts and blouses, and all looking sturdy and sunburned and one with the sunlight and the air. We walked through the shaded streets of the little village where many artists live, stopping ever so often to ask the way, until at last we reached a white bungalow.

We were warmly greeted by Frau von Ruckteschell, whose personality immediately reached us. She is Swiss, of medium height, robust in build, strong of face—with steady, searching honest eyes, and a firm hearty handclasp. We sat under the trees in the garden that Sunday afternoon drinking tea—but talking of many things. How rich in experience her life and that of her husband has been, how much of pain and suffering, of joy in creation! She told us simply, wholly without emphasis, of their stay in Africa, of their climbing the great mountain Kilimanjara, which is 20,000 feet above sea level, of the outbreak of the war and the necessity of her husband's joining the colonial troops, since he held an officer's commission, of her enlistment as a nurse, of her husband's illness and their separation for three years with no news of each other. Behind her simple statement of events and facts, there was unbounded suffering and unforgettable memories.

And then we saw her husband's studio and his plans for the Altar of Good-Will, which is being made for Swarthmore College. There are to be figures representing the different peoples of the earth and different cultures. "But my husband has broken with his old method and he cannot do work in the Gothic style", said Frau von Ruckteschell. "So thoroughly has Africa taken a hold on him that he wants to work only with African subjects and in the style which he gradually came to use for that material".

Their house is beautiful; beautiful with objects which they have made; with the wondrous woodcarvings, two of which the Stadtgalerie in Munich wished to buy, but which he would not sell, so dear they are to him; with gay textiles from Africa, with gorgeous pottery which Frau von Ruckteschell has made. As we looked at the drawings of a mother and father and child, she said, "So often those groups seemed to my husband to be a sacred family."

One magnificent woodcarving, a torso of an African, Frau von Ruckteschell said her husband had carved from a tree trunk which he found lying beside the road while resting from a day's march. Once he came to see the beauty in the African face, the brooding sadness, the haunting melancholy, the look which closeness to elemental things brings to the human face, he had a feverish desire to put on paper, to carve in wood, his impressions of these people. In expression, in gesture, in movement, in repose, they are different from white people, and Walter von Ruckteschell has caught this difference and expressed it in a fluid line suited to his subject.

We talked on about America, about the color problem there, about the curious contradictions in the American nature on this question which her husband found so difficult to understand when he was in the United States. And then, because we did want to know, we asked her about the German attitude toward the Colonial troops on the Rhine, placed there by the French.

"We do not feel race prejudice," she said, "but we do feel the resentment which any cultured nation feels at having people of a lower culture thrown in intimate contact with them. Many tropical diseases which our doctors do not know how to treat have been introduced into the country. Many families, highly cultured families, have had to open their homes to a rough, rude people who have no appreciation of the atmosphere which surrounds them." She spoke with feeling, though with nothing of racial hostility, only admission of the difficulties created by bringing into close contact peoples of such different cultural development.

There is on the side of the house a frescoe of an African St. Christopher and an African Christ-Child, a powerful painting it is, sweeping in line, vigorous. This identification of the African family group, of the African figure and character with the sacred family and religious subjects which have long interested European painters, shows a tenderness in Walter von Ruckteschell's attitude towards the spirit of the African, a recognition of soul, of spirituality in the African, more moving because it is unconscious.

Walter von Ruckteschell is finding it difficult to continue his work in the African vein. It is impossible for him to get the beautiful wood from Africa which lends itself so well to carving, but more than that, he is far from the source of his material, from the people which he and his wife love so deeply. They feel that they must go back some day to the land in which they spent such full, such rich years, years of artistic and spiritual development.

Many of his wood carvings, paintings and drawings were lost during the war. An officer could not carry much excess "luggage" with him, and a prisoner of war none. So it was that many of his best pieces were destroyed; some were found in a Swiss railroad station lying under debris unclaimed and unknown. At the Glaspalast's Secession exhibit there is one of his carvings, a powerful head. This exhibition, which represents the most recent work of the modern German painters, shows a definite trend toward the African motif.

Although it was our interest in Walter von Ruckteschell, the artist, that brought us to Dachau, it was Walter von Ruckteschell, the man, as seen through the eyes of his sympathetic wife, that made so strong an appeal to us. Not every man has had bestowed on him the gift of so strong, so comradely, so understanding a woman. "Although I do ceramic work and have exhibited several times, I feel now that I have no greater work than that of creating for my husband an atmosphere in which he can create, and in giving my two children a real start in life, a start with no physical, mental or spiritual handicaps," she said. "I do not feel as many American women do, that my own career comes before my husband's or the training of my children." And just this attitude of hers makes her the complete woman that she is, wife, comrade, mother, artist, elemental, and yet completely cultured.

Frau von Ruckteschell walked with us to the station, across a rolling meadow. A blessed calm was over all the sun-soaked landscape, white clouds floated in a blue, blue sky, a fresh earthy fragrance permeated the air, and a goose maiden drove her flock along a winding path.

"Here is peace for one," she said. Behind these words lay a great weariness of struggle and a sense of joy at having found a space of quiet breathing after such tumultuous years.

We last saw her from the train window, standing with her children and their maid in the deep rich meadow in the glory of the afternoon sunshine, waving us goodbye. It was a moving moment, that. Suddenly we had as complete a glimpse and realization as will probably ever be vouchsafed us, of a person to whom racial difference is no barrier and for whom spiritual values are the only real values.

NEGRO FOLK SONG

In the following essay, John W. Work writes about the Negro spirituals as the only distinctive American folk song form and their significance as the basis and inspiration for other forms of American music. This essay was published in October 1923.

After Dvořák had made a thoro study of music in America, he pronounced the Negro Folk Song "original and American", adding that if America ever had a national music, it must be based upon the songs found among the southern Negroes. Confident in the hope that it would be the beginning of the national music, he composed his "New World Symphony", employing thematically and characteristically the Negro Folk music as a basis and inspiration.

The "Second Symphony" by Chadwick, the "Sunny South Overture", "Rural Symphony", "Sonata" for piano and violin by Schoenefeld, and the "Ten American Sketches" by Kroeger, are all based upon the Negro Folk music.

Besides his peculiar scale, his peculiar rhythm, and his peculiar syncopation, there is another peculiar quality,—the text of his song. It is Virtue. He sings of courage, patience, humility, faith, hope, endurance, Joy and Love, and in all the hundreds of songs we know, there is not the slightest hint of any such sentiment as bitterness, hatred or revenge. In the sublimity of ideal, this music is original and unapproached by the folk music of any other people.

If this music which the Negro believes is his, and feels is his, is not his, but only an imitation of some other peoples, where is its prototype? What music antedating the Negro Folk Song is stamped with such resemblance, such similitude, as to make possible any just claim of "imitation"? Henry T. Finck, in the New York *Evening Post* of June 2, 1923, states that Booker T. Washington writes in the preface to a collection of "Negro Melodies", made by Coleridge-Taylor, that his race realizes that "Apart from the music of the red men, the Negro Folk Song is the only distinctive American music." "This," continues Mr. Finck, "is the almost universal belief to-day, among the whites of this country, too,—yet it is about as unspeakably absurd as anything could possibly be." In reply it ought to be stated, first, that Coleridge-Taylor never made a collection of Negro Melodies, but merely made transcriptions of certain Negro Folk Songs which had been collected and published in America; to this edition Dr. Washington wrote the preface; second, Mr. Finck can not disprove Dr. Washington's statement by his bare assertion, "This is about as unspeakably absurd as anything could possibly be", for Dr. Washington stated a fact, supported by such authorities as Dvořák and Krehbiel and further by the proof that no other distinctive American music has been discovered.

Mr. Finck quotes with much satisfaction and approval, from a letter written to him by Colonel Dangerfield Parker in which this statement occurs: "The so-called Negro music has been composed by white men, Foster and others." Does he mean that "Swing Low, Sweet Chariot", "Roll, Jordan, Roll", and thousands of other "Negro Folk Songs" were composed by white men? Surely not. Or is he or Mr. Finck acquainted with the folk music of the Negro? The origin of many of these songs we definitely *know*—and there is no trustworthy evidence that any race, save the Negro race, had anything to do with their production. Now what of the songs of Foster? As beautiful as they are, and as deeply as they touch our hearts, they are merely imitations of the Negro Folk Songs. They were doubtless inspired by the songs which Foster heard among the Negroes. They are *not Negro Folk Songs!* They are the very best imitations of the Negro Folk Music. The composer caught something of the Negro spirit, much of his beautiful melody, much of his smooth rhythm, nothing of his syncopation, and in "Old Folks at Home" and "Massa's in the Col', Col' Groun'", he practically used the Negro scale.

This music excels any of the secular Folk Songs of the Negro, but it does not approach the spirituals. "He received the inspiration for many of his Negro songs in the humble cabins of the darkies and wove into his music many of the melodies which he heard in such places." According to Mr. Finck, Richard Wallashek, upon examination of slave songs collected by Miss McKim and H. C. Spaulding, was surprised to find them "ignorantly arranged; not to say ignorantly borrowed from the national songs of all nations—from military signals, well known marches, German student songs, etc."

The writer is not acquainted with these collections of slave songs, consequently he does not know what they are; but he certainly knows what they are *not* (if Wallashek's description of them is accurate). They are *not* the slave songs we know as "Negro Folk Songs" or "Spirituals".

American History and Encyclopedia of Music states: "While the songs of the American Indian are of questionable value musically, those of the Negro, another peculiarly *American* product, are of undoubted worth."

"The Negro's music isn't ours", says Dr. Damrosch, "it is the Negro's. It has become a popular form of musical expression and is interesting, but it is not ours. Nothing more characteristic of a race exists, but it is characteristic of the Negro, not of the American race."

"The songs of the slaves", writes Dr. Krehbiel, "are practically the only American product of their kind which meet the scientific definition of Folk Song."

American History and Encyclopedia of Music states: "While not strictly of American origin, they have undoubtedly gone to form the foundation of such Folk Song literature as this country possesses."

Can this music be the basis and inspiration of an American National Music? Some Americans say, "No"—others say, "Yes".

What do facts, evidence, and conditions answer? Facts answer that this music is American. It expresses a phase of American life in its literature and a broader scope in its ideal. Southern life from 1619 to 1863 is narrated in Negro Folk Song. Religious and social customs are clearly described therein. "Steal Away to Jesus", "Swing Low, Sweet Chariot", "Great Camp Meeting", "I'm Troubled in Mind", "You May Bury Me in the East", "Every Day Will Be Sunday", "Rise, Shine", and hundreds of others, tell interesting stories. Both in sentiment and in melody there is the ideal approaching the sublime. The poetry contemplates Virtue; its spirit is the spirit of Right. It is epitomized in that matchless song "I Want To Be Like Jesus". In the melody of this music there is clearly the ideal of perfection. "There Is A Balm In Gilead", "Roll, Jordan, Roll", "Couldn't Hear Nobody Pray", "Were You There", are illustrations of this ideal.

It seems incredible that in the face of such clear evidence, there could be in the mind of any one any doubt concerning the origin of that music known as "Plantation Melodies", "Jubilee Songs", "Negro Spirituals", and "Folk Songs of the American Negro". Yet, every now and then, some one comes forward with the statement that this music is not original with the Negro, but is nothing more than an imitation of the white man's music. It is sometimes advanced that this music is *not* American, and can form no part of American music.

No one who gives due thot to this subject can arrive at any other conclusion, than that this music is original with the Negro, and that it is genuinely American.

Let us look into the nature of Folk Song. It is the musical expression of the feelings of a people as a whole. It is primitive and simple; spontaneous and sincere. It is natural and portrays the crudities of an undeveloped condition. It is the product and possession of the whole people and a history of their racial life.

Let us consider briefly the peoples who settled America, and the conditions surrounding them: The Englishman, the Scot, the Spaniard, the Dutch, the Swede, and the Portuguese, all came from civilizations fully developed. They were all beyond the stage of folk song creation, for civilization atrophies those conditions from which folk songs grow.

The Negro was the only immigrant to this country who was capable of producing Folk Song. He was in a primitive state, untouched by the folk-song-atrophying influences of civilization, emotional, of a musical temperament and naturally expressing himself in song.

The new world was a wonderland to the immigrants, and especially to the African. All the newness, strangeness and vastness; the mountains, rivers, and bays; the climate and the people; all these were overwhelming. They gave him new experiences which had to be expressed.

No wonder he sang! Rather would it have been wonderful if he had not sung and produced a Folk song; for all the necessary and appropriate forces and influences worked together in complete harmony to create the Folk Song of the American Negro.

The musical vehicle thru which he conveyed these first new experiences was indeed simple. It was a scale of only five notes, the pentatonic scale, 1, 2, 3, 5, 6. This was purely and wholly African, and has been taken as a basis for argument to prove that the Negro's music is not American. But such argument is futile and valueless because it is the spirit which must determine whether or not this music is American. *Does this music express America, or any part of American life?*

The Negro expressed in his music that part of America that he knew, the South; and that character of American life of which he was a considerable part—bondage.

"Steal Away to Jesus" was a protest against a master's prohibition against religious services; it was a declaration of adhesion to that commandment, "Thou shalt have no other God before Me"; a declaration of a perfect belief in that pronouncement of the Christ, "He who is ashamed of Me before men, of him will I be ashamed before my Father in Heaven."

> "No mo' peck of meal for me,
> No mo', no mo',
> No mo' peck of meal for me,
> Many thousands gone."

That song tells its own story. So do they all tell their stories—even the melodies tell their stories.

What could be more expressive of the easy, smooth, luxurious southern life than such melodies as "Swing Low, Sweet Chariot", "Roll, Jordan, Roll", "O Freedom", "Balm in Gilead", and hundreds of others? Music like this is found no where in all the world except in the Southern States of the United States of America.

Some decades after his arrival here, the Negro changed his scale from the pentatonic to sexatonic, from a five tone to a six tone scale. Thus he created an entirely new scale, no longer African but American, and original with himself. This was accomplished thru the addition of flat 7—a note expressing complete surprise. After this new creation the Folk Song was generally expressed in this scale.

The best known songs which illustrate this original American scale are "Great Camp Meeting", "Roll, Jordan, Roll". There can be no doubt that the flat 7 is the expression of consummate surprise. It is quite credible that this surprise struck the African thru the newness, strangeness and suddenness of the new world which broke upon his vision. The note expressing all this is the flat 7 and is the note that evolves the African into the American scale—which is 1, 2, 3, 5, 6, flat 7. This flat 7 is not an accidental, but a natural.

This scale is *original* with the American Negro, and is *American*. The evolution of the pentatonic (African) into the sexatonic (American) scale was contemporaneous with the evolution of the African into the American.

The rhythm and highly developed syncopation of this music are peculiarly its own. Any violation of these two qualities destroys the character and the individuality of the music. So intense was his love for perfection in rhythm that the creator of this music resorted to original inventions, where the text of the song was lacking in word or phrase, meeting the demands of rhythm.

> "Judg-*a*-ment, Judg-*a*-ment,
> Judg-*a*-ment day is *a*-rollin' aroun'

Judg-*a*-ment, Judg-*a*-ment,
O how I long to go."

"Good News!   The chariot's *a*-comin'
Good News!   The chariot's *a*-comin'
Good News!   The chariot's *a*-comin'
An' I don't want *a* leave *a*-me behin'."

There are hundreds of songs that employ this invention, showing abhorrence of faulty or indifferent rhythm.

When Dvořák began his quest for some character of music to furnish a basis and an inspiration for an American National Music, and in the course of his investigations began the study of the Negro Folk Music, what struck him more forcibly than any other quality was syncopation. It was a kind of musical expression quite new to him. He had met it nowhere, except in America, and to him it was a very interesting subject for study.

Evidence answers that this music is already being employed as a basis and inspiration of American music, such as we have. American History and Encyclopedia of Music says: "The Negro has exerted an influence in the history of Music in America, not only by means of his own song, but indirectly thru the efforts of the Negro minstrel, whose inspirations were derived from Negro sources.

"America owes much to the Negro in the creation and development of its popular music, for a large part of such music is due directly or indirectly to Negro sources."

The influence of this music is also to be observed in our Gospel hymns of to-day, as well as in our distinctive American national product—Ragtime. Melody, Rhythm and Syncopation are employed to the point of irresistibility. Such composers as Burleigh, Dett, White, and Diton, have used this music thematically and have produced works that are truly American.

Thematically this music is of boundless wealth. Such melodies as "Go Down, Moses", "Nobody Knows the Trouble I See", "Deep River", "Listen to the Lambs", "Somebody's Knocking at Your Door", have certain possibilities of development. That these Folk Songs have the possibility of Art Music development has been clearly demonstrated by Dvořák, Chadwick, Schoenefeld, Burleigh, F. J. Work, Dett, and Coleridge-Taylor.

Conditions point to the plain truth that, since the Negro Folk Song is the only American Folk Music that meets the scientific definition of Folk Song, since it is so rich in theme and in the beauty of its melody, since it is so comprehensive, so strikingly original and so strong in its appeal, it is the only natural basis and inspiration for American National Music.

In the building of her National Music, America will surely follow Nature and Truth.

ROLAND HAYES: AN APPRECIATION

Concert singer Roland Hayes (1887–1977) was born in Curryville, Georgia. He became the first African American to sing in Boston's Symphony Hall. In the following essay, published in December 1923, Alain Locke discusses Hayes's artistic talent, his triumphant concerts in European capitals, and his perseverance in the face of racism.

One of the most accepted of the Viennese musical critics writes in a recent issue of the *Mittag-Zeitung:* "Roland Hayes, heralded before his first concert as a sensation and artistic curiosity because of his color, had already before this last one quite disillusioned the curiosity-seekers and chastened the gossip-mongers. Not as a Negro, but as a great artist, he captured and moved his audience. And our prophecy of April last, that he would always be welcomely heard in Vienna, was fulfilled yesterday. An audience that filled the Konzerthaus to capacity was again enthralled by the magic of his really wonderful mezza voice, was once more astounded by the matchless diction and interpretation of his German songs, and was made to realize the deep religious inspiration and poetic feeling of the Negro spirituals. Indeed, these admirably simple but unfortunately not too happily harmonized songs were among the best that the artist had to offer."

By the time this article is in print, Mr. Hayes will have sung as soloist with the Boston Symphony Orchestra and will be in the midst of a concert tour of America that will be epoch-making with regard to the recognition by the general American public of a Negro singer. As outstanding and commendable as this is as an artistic achievement, it has still more considerable significance—it should serve—it will serve—two timely purposes: it will educate the American public out of one of its worst and most unfair provincialisms (and in this respect, we must remember that the native-born and native-trained artist, white or black, has had great handicaps in America); and then too it will mark a very singular vindication of indisparagable ambition and courage, which would not accept the early rewards of the double standard so often temptingly imposed upon Negro talent by well-meaning but short-sighted admirers of both races. For these reasons, I write this comment—though of course, artistically, racially, and personally I was happy that the circumstances of travel made me a companion and witness of Mr. Hayes' almost triumphant recent tour of Austria, Hungary, and Tzcheco-Slovakia.

Vienna is the music-capitol of Europe—the Viennese critics are the most exacting and the Viennese public one of the most musically enlightened bodies in the world. The acclaim of Vienna is therefore the ambition of the greatest artists, and the tradition of success here opens all doors; especially that which leads to the historical recognition of posterity. It is perhaps not becoming for a friend to chronicle overlaboriously the details of such a success—I mention as mere suggestions, that the audience cheered about the stage in semi-darkness for quite a half-hour after the regular program; that several critics missed Jeritza's annual leave-taking of the Opera to attend; that Madame Arnoldson Fischoff, the prima-donna who has sung with the greatest tenors of two musical generations from Tamango to Bathstini, requested an Italian aria as an encore and declared it "perfectly sung"; that the creator of the role of Parsifal declared very generously that he would have given half his career for such mastery of the mezza-voice; that occasional Americans of the foreign colony spoke with pride of "our American artist" whom until recently they could never have heard without condescension and in some parts of our country, proscription and segregation. How shall we best appraise this triumph—as personal, as artistic, or racially? In each of these respects, it is significant and exceptional.

Personally, it represents the triumph of a particularly high and far-sighted ambition. Just when his admirers in America were on the verge of flattering him into the fatal success of mediocrity, Mr. Hayes began in a fresh field to study and conquer the higher interpretative technique of his art. Indefatigable work, a large part of it is the cultural background so often neglected by musicians, has made a seasoned artist out of a gifted, natural-born singer. We have as a group more artistic talent and fewer artists than any other; nature has in music done too much for us—so that in this musical generation we have produced but two artists whose equipment can challenge the international standard—Roland Hayes and Hazel Harrison. There will be many more when the lesson of their careers is sufficiently impressed upon the younger generation of race talent. Race talent in all fields is in the quicksands of the double standard—our own people through short-sighted partisanship and pardonable provincialism, white Americans through sentimental partiality or through haughty disparagement, make it doubly difficult. The turning point of Mr. Hayes' career was when he refused to accept an assured success of this sort, and risked failure for the single standard of musical Europe. Success there has opened doors otherwise closed in America, not only for Mr. Hayes but for all qualified talent in the future. As he himself told me, "I hope to leave open behind me every door that I open—my ultimate intention in coming to Europe, in appealing to European judgment, was eventually to widen opportunity for the Negro artist in America." So an Acropolis has been captured by the shrewd strategy of a flank attack.

Artistically Mr. Hayes, through the very intelligent pedagogy of Mr. Hubbard of Boston and Dr. Lierhammer of London, has cultivated his voice on its own pattern. It is not an imitation of other models, however great; but an intensive cultivation of a voice that had its natural limitations—especially that of medium volume. Through building up the intrinsic resources of the voice, there has been produced a lyric song-tenor of unique quality and flawless technique—a voice that would really be over-refined and too subtle except for the peculiarly fine rhapsodic flow which Mr. Hayes has taken over from the primitive race gift in the art of song. The combination has created a rare medium which satisfies the most critical and sophisticated, without losing the primary universal appeal of simplicity and directly apprehensible beauty. So that a critic can say, "This Negro singer adds a new contribution to the tenor-mystery in producing sensuous effects. It is old traditional culture taken hold of by a new temperament."

Without losing its individuality, the voice adapts itself to every language, to all schools and periods—because of its essential naturalness and freedom. Critical France is satisfied with the interpretation of its best modern music, and the German school with the interpretations of Bach, Schumann, Schubert, Strauss and Wolf, whereas the Italian literature, especially of the older seventeenth and eighteenth centuries, is sung with a flow that qualifies according to the best traditions of *bel canto*. "Perhaps it comes through the deeper naturalness of tone-expression", suggests the same critic—no less than the dean of Viennese critics, Korngold, "that from each phrase, though technically perfectly rendered, a primitive sort of feeling wells up." No better artistic lesson can be taught than that of escaping from the limitations of one school and style of singing by the arduous endeavor to be sincere, genuine, and original—in other words, to be throughout all oneself and wholesomely natural. Refined but unaffected, cultivated but still simple—it is a voice of artistic paradoxes, and for that reason, unique.

Racially? Is there race in art? Mr. Hayes attributes his success to his racial heritage, which fortunately he cannot disown, if he would. Contrary to the general impression, it has not been an easy matter to make musical Europe accept and understand upon an art-plane the Negro spirituals which Mr. Hayes has always insisted upon as part of his program. Accompanists have often failed to interpret them properly, critics have been condescending toward them while nevertheless wholly favorable to other classical numbers, orchestrations have had to be expressly made and orchestral traditions broken to allow them as part of several programs. That which might have been expected to make Mr. Hayes' career easier upon the basis of a novelty has really, to my knowledge, been a difficult crusade, that but for tact and insistence would have failed. The result has been of peculiar value in giving a new cultural conception of the Negro to important circles of European society—a work that has made the artist a sort of ambassador of culture in our behalf. At first they excite only curiosity and the reaction—why does he sing them? Then a few catch the seriousness of the interpretation and eventually the few understand. "Mr. Hayes sang the spirituals with dignity, penetrated by his mission," says one. "We should not forget that of the three wise men who were guided by the star on their quest, one was a Negro, and that the Negro today is able in the cool, peculiar beauty of these spirituals to tell of Him so vividly and touchingly that one might forget much that, had the wise men lived long enough to experience, might bitterly have disappointed them", says another. And not to rest upon the testimony of others, I will venture the opinion that here in this side of Mr. Hayes' work, we have had an artistic missioner of the highest effect and importance— a racial vindication and appraisal that could not have come in any better way, being all the more effective through being expressed through the international speech of melody and insinuated into the mind through the channels of feeling and the heart. The Negro as a group has lived Christianity in a peculiar way and exceptional degree. It has saved him—saved him in this world—saved his heart from corrosion under the acid of persecution, enabled him to survive through optimism and hope when despair and cynicism would have added the last sinking ounce of weight—and in this near future of racial vindication, it is to be one of the most potent mediums of interpretation and vindication.

"The highest tribute we can offer Mr. Hayes is to say that while singing these, he might have been a statue shaped by the hands of his own race through long centuries, for the ultimate purpose of transmitting the soul of the race. It was the soul of his race which sang through him in these childlike yet tragic spirituals; sang of barbarities committed and endured, and of a faith running like a golden thread through the gloomy web of wrongs." [*The New Age,* May 5, 1921] To have elicited such recognition from the stranger is a tribute to interpretative art of the highest character. A similar impression was no doubt made upon the sensitive mind of Mr. Evon Philpot, whose portrait of *Roland Hayes Singing* is more the expression of a race symbol than of an individual—the attempt to translate a spiritual message and give the social rather than the personal note in art. The effect is, in every such instance, reciprocal; the people gain through the art; the art gains in vitality and in spirituality from its background in the people.

Mr. Hayes has given this racial material a balanced background by which it has commanded more respect than when separately and over-exploited as has been the case with many other European presentations of our songs. "I will never sing spirituals without classics, or classics without spirituals, for properly interpreted they are classics,"—this is Mr. Hayes' artistic platform—and he is right and will be eventually justified. From this challenging comparison with other classical song material has come not always an admission of equal value— that could not be expected—but always there has been conceded a seriousness of purpose and mission and loyalty to self that has commanded admiration and respect.

No better instance of the soundness of this procedure can be given than the transfer from these simple folk-songs to Bach, through an affinity of religious feeling, of a religious quality which makes Mr. Hayes' interpretation of Bach songs a delight to all connoisseurs of that great master. And then, finally, their inclusion has demonstrated to the very apprehending the true school of Mr. Hayes' art. It has folk-parentage—it is the mother-art that through intense and sincere and quite religious feeling has given rare capacity in evoking the spirituality which lies back of all great music, but the sense of which comes not so much from the technique and discipline of art, but from the discipline of life itself, and most often from that side of it which we racially have so deeply tasted under the necessities of hardship. To capitalize these spiritual assets, especially in and through art, ought to be one of the main objectives and missions of the younger, more happily circumstanced, generations.

Max Reinhardt Reads the Negro's Dramatic Horoscope

Max Reinhardt, one of the foremost theatrical producers of the day, spoke to Alain Locke, and in the following essay, published in May 1924, Locke relates Reinhardt's sentiments on blacks in drama and their possibilities for the future.

Max Reinhardt has always been a prophet in the theatre,—and the things which he has foreseen and helped come to realization have matured so quickly and vigorously as to make his own work of ten or fifteen years back almost old-fashioned in comparison with the advanced contemporary art of drama which, we must always remember, his work has so largely made possible. Perhaps no one could have a more pronounced "sixth sense" with respect to drama or a more dependable knack of finding new veins of dramatic possibilities. When, therefore, we learned that Director Reinhardt of "The Miracle" had expressed keen interest in the work of the Negro actors whom he had seen in his visit to New York last season, we were naturally most anxious to have a first hand opinion. Max Reinhardt must be interviewed. The opportunity was missed at Salzburg; and again, by the accidents of travel, at Vienna; and the trail eventually led back to New York and the second season. From the beginning it was not the usual interview. Charles Johnson and I found our subject too willing to be in any sense the usual victim. It was not a tribute to us so much as to the subject in which we were interested that this rather busy and inaccessible man was anxious to talk with us. Indeed, our first engagement was excused on the ground that there wasn't sufficient time to talk over so important a subject adequately. A second visit found us very much in the predicament of the fisherman who catches other fish than he was fishing for: obviously we ourselves were about to be interviewed. And we were,—but that is not our story. Then the springy, inquisitive, experimental mind of the man came back at us,—with what he apologetically called "mere impressions," but what the reader will instantly recognize as penetrating and quite prophetic observations.

"Yes, I am very interested,—it is intriguing, very intriguing, these musical comedies of yours that I have seen. But, remember, not as achievements, not as things in themselves artistic, but in their possibilities, their tremendous artistic possibilities. They are most modern, most American, most expressionistic. They are highly original in spite of obvious triteness, and artistic in spite of superficial crudeness. To me they reveal new possibilities of technique in drama, and if I should ever try to do anything American, I should build it on these things."

We didn't enthuse. What Negro who stands for culture with the hectic stress of a social problem weighing on the minds of an over-serious minority could enthuse? Liza, Shuffle Along, Runnin' Wild! We had come to discuss the possibilities of serious Negro drama, of the art—drama, if you please. Surely Director Reinhardt was a victim of that distortion of perspective to which anyone is liable in a foreign land. But then, the stage is not a foreign land to Max Reinhardt. He has the instinct of the theatre,—the genius of the producer who knows, if anyone knows, what is vital there. So we didn't protest, but raised brows already too elevated perhaps and shrugged the shoulder that carries the proverbial racial chip. Herr Reinhardt read the gestures swiftly.

"Ah yes, I see—you view these plays for what they are, and you are right; I view them for what they will become, and I am more than right. I see their future. Why? Well, the drama must turn at every fresh period of creative development to an aspect which has been previously subordinated or neglected, and in this day of ours we come back to the most primitive and the most basic aspect of drama for a new starting point, a fresh development and revival of the art,—and that aspect is pantomime,—the use of the body to portray emotion. And your people have that art—it is their forte—it is their special genius. At present it is prostituted to farce, to trite comedy,—but the technique is there, and I have never seen more wonderful possibilities. Yes, I should like to do something with this material. If I knew more about it I certainly would do something with it. Somebody must demonstrate its fresh artistic value. Now it is exploited, when will it be utilized?"

Now we understood. Baronial hotel arm-chairs moved as lightly and as instinctively as ouija-boards. Understanding made a circle, and the interview was ended though the conversation continued thrice as long.

"No, not the story, not the acting in the conventional sense, not the setting, not even the music, and certainly not the silly words; but the voices, the expressive control of the whole body, the spontaneity of motion, the rhythm, the bright emotional color. These are your treasures—no, not yours only,—these are American treasures."

"But how, Mr. Reinhardt, are we to develop these,—especially in the face of exploitation?"

"Only you can do it, you yourselves. You must not even try to link up to the drama of the past, to the European drama. That is why there is no American drama as yet. And if there is to be one, it will be yours. That is my advice, that is my feeling about this. I would gladly help. I would gladly do something just to show what can be technically developed out of such material. But I would have to saturate myself with the folk-spirit, and really this requires the Negro dramatist eventually."

" 'Eventually,'—why, we have already many plays of Negro life, some promising Negro playwrights, several attempts at a Negro theatre, a college department of dramatics."

"That is interesting, most interesting—but I am afraid of that sort of a thing. It is too academic. I fear there is too much imitation in it. My last word is, be original—sense the folk-spirit, develop the folk-idiom,—artistically, of course, but faithfully; and above all, do not let that technique of expression which is so original, so potential, get smothered out in the imitation of European acting, copied effects.

"With such control of body, such pantomime, I believe I could portray emotion as it has never been portrayed,—pure emotion, almost independently of words or setting. It is really marvelous. You are perhaps too near to see it."

We terminated the interview in deference to Mr. Reinhardt's engagements,—he was still talking, still "intrigued," as he kept putting it. And to our "Thank you's," his reply was: "Not at all, gentlemen. On the contrary, I must thank you for an opportunity of expressing an opinion about the possibilities of Negroes and for an occasion to learn more of what is actually being done toward developing these fine resources of American art." So when it was reported by the *N. A. A. C. P. Press Service* that "Max Reinhardt, one of the foremost theatrical producers of Germany, who recently staged a monster production of 'The Miracle' in New York, has recently praised the art of the American Negro, in an interview, cabled to the *Chicago Daily News*," two amateur but ardent race journalists had the exhilaration of having been "backstage" on that.

REFLECTIONS ON O'NEILL'S PLAYS

Paul Robeson starred in two of Eugene O'Neill's plays in 1924: The Emperor Jones and All God's Chillun Got Wings. Because of its miscegenation theme, All God's Chillun Got Wings opened on Broadway surrounded by opposition and threats. Nonetheless, Robeson writes in the following about the unique opportunity to have appeared in both plays. This essay was published in December 1924.

All this seems so very strange to me—writing about the theatre. If, three years ago, someone had told me that I would be telling of my reactions as an actor I would have laughed indulgently. Even now the whole chain of events has a distinct dream-like quality. To have had the opportunity to appear in two of the finest plays of America's most distinguished playwright is a good fortune that to me seems hardly credible. Of course I am very, very happy. And with these things there has come a great love of the theatre, which I am sure will always hold me fast.

In retrospect all the excitement about "All God's Chillun" seems rather amusing, but at the time of the play's production, it caused many an anxious moment. All concerned were absolutely amazed at the ridiculous critical reaction. The play meant anything and everything from segregated schools to various phases of intermarriage.

To me the most important pre-production development, was an opportunity to play the "Emperor Jones," due to an enforced postponment. This is undoubtedly one of "*the* great plays"—a true classic of the drama, American or otherwise. I recall how marvelously it was played by Mr. Gilpin some years back. And the greatest praise I could have received was the expression of some that my performance was in some wise comparable to Mr. Gilpin's.

And what a great part is "Brutus Jones." His is the exultant tragedy of the disintegration of a human soul. How we suffer as we see him in the depths of the forest re-living all the sins of his past—experiencing all the woes and wrongs of his people—throwing off one by one the layers of civilization until he returns to the primitive soil from which he (racially) came. And yet we exult when we realize that here was a man who in the midst of all his trouble fought to the end and finally died in the " 'eighth of style anyway."

In "All God's Chillun" we have the struggle of a man and woman, both fine struggling human beings, against forces they could not control,—indeed, scarcely comprehend—accentuated by the almost Christ-like spiritual force of the Negro husband,—a play of great strength and beautiful spirit, mocking all petty prejudice, emphasizing the humanness, and in Mr. O'Neill's words, "the oneness" of mankind.

I now come to perhaps the main point of my discussion. Any number of people have said to me: "I trust that now you will get a truly heroic and noble role, one portraying the finest type of Negro." I honestly believe that perhaps never will I portray a nobler type than "Jim Harris" or a more heroically tragic figure than "Brutus Jones, Emperor," not excepting "Othello."

The Negro is only a medium in the creation of a work of the greatest artistic merit. The fact that he is a Negro Pullman Porter is of little moment. How else account for the success of the play in Paris, Berlin, Copenhagen, Moscow and other places on the Continent. Those people never heard of a Negro porter. Jones's emotions are not primarily Negro, but human.

Objections to "All God's Chillun" are rather well known. Most of them have been so foolish that to attempt to answer them is to waste time. The best answer is that audiences that came to scoff went away in tears, moved by a sincere and terrifically tragic drama.

The reactions to these two plays among Negroes but point out one of the most serious drawbacks to the development of a true Negro dramatic literature. We are too self-conscious, too afraid of showing all phases of our life—especially those phases which are of greatest dramatic value. The great mass of our group discourage any member who has the courage to fight these petty prejudices.

I am still being damned all over the place for playing in "All God's Chillun." It annoys me very little when I realize that those who object most strenuously know mostly nothing of the play and who in any event know little of the theatre and have no right to judge a playwright of O'Neill's talents.

I have met and talked with Mr. O'Neill. If ever there was a broad, liberal-minded man, he is one. He has had Negro friends and appreciated them for their true worth. He would be the last to cast any slur on the colored people.

Of course I have just begun. I do feel there is a great future on the serious dramatic stage. Direction and training will do much to guide any natural ability one may possess. At Provincetown I was privileged to be under the direction of Mr. James Light. I'm sure even he thought I was rather hopeless at first. I know I did. But he was patient and painstaking, and any success I may have achieved I owe in great measure to Mr. Light. I sincerely hope I shall have the benefit of his splendid guidance in the future.

What lies ahead I do not know. I am sure that there will come Negro playwrights of great power and I trust I shall have some part in interpreting that most interesting and much needed addition to the drama of America.

IRA ALDRIDGE

A leading nineteenth-century Shakespearean actor and a descendant of African nobility, Ira Aldridge received international acclaim particularly for his interpretation of Othello. In the following essay, published in March 1925, Charles S. Johnson writes about the artistry of Aldridge.

There was something sadly prophetic about the almost unvarying English press announcements of Ira Aldridge, called the African Roscius, who more than seventy-five years ago was internationally famed as an interpreter of Shakespeare's masterpiece, "Othello". Always these announcements began: "*As he is the only actor of Colour that ever was known, and probably the only instance that may ever again occur . . .*"

The English who were extravagant in their praise of his talent, who with their King and a formidable array of royalty packed the theatres, greeting him thunderously when in his prime he overshadowed every other interpreter of the difficult role of Othello, thought of the sheer infrequency of genius, particularly among a race not generally countenanced in the exercise even of common intelligence. A keen clairvoyance it would have required to trace through the years to come with such blunt directness the subtle evolutions of racial feeling to the very moment, when un-blackened Othellos, whatever their competence or claims to art are savagely unbeseeming and not at all to be countenanced.

Nevertheless Ira Aldridge, dark, bewhiskered, of unequivocally African features, graceful proportions and genteel manners, was a phenomenon worthy to be recalled as the Negro forges again into the glare of the footlights, stripped in part of the clown's regalia and slap sticks; as the play itself, through the courage of Walter Hampden, is brought back to Broadway after ten years neglect.

Aldridge was a descendent of a prince of the Fulah tribe in Senegal, West Africa. His grandfather, a humane ruler, in the face of a common practice of selling captives into slavery, preferred to exchange them. As a result of this humanity he incurred the enmity of his chiefs and in a *coup d'etat* he was murdered, together with his family and attendants. One son only survived who, under the protection of a missionary, fled to America. This son was the father of the great actor. He was trained as a minister of the gospel and accomplished some distinction in this profession. But still restless and anxious for his tribe, and freshly inspired to regain rule and propagate the religion he had embraced, he married an American Negro woman and returned to Africa. Civil war resulted, his adherents were defeated and again he fled for his life. At this crisis Ira Aldridge was born and for nine years lived concealed with his fugitive parents in Africa. They escaped to America and the education of the son began. Youth was spent in Bel Air near Baltimore and among the Germans of Western Maryland where he learned to speak the German language with ease and fluency. Although intended for the ministry the boy was from the beginning "dazzled and fascinated by the stage." Early he studied the part of Rolla in Pizarro and ventured an amateur performance with a Negro cast. Later he haunted the old Chatham Theatre in New York City, nightly taking his stand behind the "wings," having secured entree through some trivial service. But his father, unable to reconcile the stage with the ministry, bundled him off to Schenectady College for his theological studies. Thence he was sent to Glasgow University where, incidentally, he achieved a notable scholastic record, winning several premiums and a medal for Latin composition. He met the renowned Edmund Keen, a great actor, who became interested in him and both whetted and abetted his zeal for the stage. Finally, in 1826, after a long struggle against the barriers to his color he made his first appearance in Othello at the Royalty Theatre in London. Acceptance was immediate and enthusiastic. Thence to Coburg to a Theatre of higher pretensions. Encouraged, he added to his repertoire Oroonoko, the story of a royal slave, still another play, *The Slave,* in which he took the part of Gambia, and other lighter productions. His rapid rise brought the obligation of further study, and withdrawing for a while he returned for a tour which encompassed all the important cities of England and Scotland. Without exception his reception was most flattering. Dublin alone persisted against his color. At his own expense he went and convinced the managers, performed and was acclaimed a great sensation. It was at this point that the invaluable offices of his friend and helper, Edmund Keen, served him well. In Ireland Keen played Iago to his Othello and he Abaon to Keen's Oronooko. Later he began his appearances on the continent. It is reputed that the King of Prussia was so deeply impressed with his appearance in the role of Othello at Berlin, that he sent him a congratulatory letter and conferred upon him the title of Chevalier. In St. Petersburg his acting was so realistic that in the midst of a scene a young man stood up and cried: "She is innocent, Othello, she is innocent." A correspondent in *Le Nord* at that time wrote:

"The success of the Negro actor, Ira Aldridge, has been wonderful. At his debut, people were curious to see an Othello who needed neither crape nor pomade to blacken his face. Many expected tears of laughter rather than tears of emotion, when they learned that Iago and Desdemona would reply to him in German. (The absence of an English troupe forced him to play with German actors.) Those who counted on this were strangely deceived. From his appearance on the stage the African artist completely captivated his audience by his harmonious and resonant voice, and by a style full of simplicity, nature and dignity. For the first time we had seen a tragic hero talk and walk like common mortals, without declamations and without exaggerated gestures. We forgot that we were in a theatre, and followed the drama as if it had been a real transaction.

"The scene in the Third Act, when the sentiment of jealousy is roused in the ferocious Moor, is the triumph of Aldridge. At the first word of the wily insinuation you see his eye kindle; you feel the tears in his voice when he questions Iago, then the deep sobs which stifle it; and finally, when he is persuaded that his wretchedness is complete, a cry of rage, or rather a roar like that of a wild beast starts from his abdomen. I still seem to hear that cry; it chilled us with fear and made every spectator shudder. Tears wet his cheeks; his mouth foamed and his eyes flashed fire. I have never seen an artist identify himself so perfectly with the character which he represents. An actor told me he saw him sob for some moments after his exit from the scene. Everybody, men and women, wept. Boileau was right in saying to actors: 'Weep yourselves, if you would make others weep.' Rachel, in the fourth act of Les Horace, is the only artist who ever produced so great an effect. At the first representation the poor Desdemona was so horror-stricken at the terrible expression of the Moor, that she sprang from the bed and fled, shrieking with fright.

"In spite of his stony nature, Aldridge can contain himself to those scenes which require calmness and subdued passion. In Shylock, to see him trembling with fear and indignation before the tribunal which is endeavoring to force Christianity upon him, makes one of those impressions which are never effaced."

"An American negro, named Ira Aldridge, has been performing at the Imperial Theatre in several of Shakespeare's pieces, and has met with great applause. His principal character, of course, is Othello, and he portrays the jealous African with such truth and energy that even those amateurs who recollect our great Russian tragedian, Karatugin, acknowledge the superiority of his sable successor. In Shylock, too, he shows unusual dramatic power; and, painted and tricked out for the stage, he passes very well by lamplight for 'the Jew that Shakespeare drew.' "

Lady Wrixon Beecher, then a great actress, said of him: "During my professional as well as private life, I never saw so correct a portraiture of Othello amidst the professional luminaries of my day." He had the distinction of restoring to the stage *Titus Andronicus* which, prior to 1851, had not been acted for two centuries. The press showered the loftiest econiums upon him. In France he was the associate of the leading litterateurs, among whom was Alexander Dumas, who always hailed him as *mon Confrere*. In Prussia he received the medal of Art and Sciences, from the Emperor of Russia he received the Cross of Leopold, and at Berne a Maltese Cross. In America he was no less a triumph when he appeared in New York and Baltimore. The American critics accepted him with a most astonishing disregard of his color.

The correspondent of the *New York Herald* says:

Aside from the role on which his fame rests he took leading parts in a large stock of plays, some serious, others light:

Le Docteur Noir, Bertram (a pirate play), *Lovers of Bourbon, Virginian Mummy, Merchant of Venice, Capt. Ross, Zanga, the Moor, Savage of the Rocks, Law of Java, The Padlock, The Unknown, Macbeth, Black Eyed Susan, Zembuca, Revenge, Karfa, the Slave, Ali Pacha, Massaroni, Opossum Up a Gum Tree, Castle Spectre, Pizarro, Sicilian Pirate, Father and Son, Obi* and others. He was twice married, his first wife an English woman, his second a Swedish Baroness. There were two daughters, one of whom became a musician of great talent and a collector of folk songs. He died August 7, 1867, at Lodz, Poland, as he was making preparations to fill a new American engagement. He was given a great civic funeral and the decorations conferred upon him by various continental monarchs were borne on a State cushion.

"A Child of the Sun—his soul of fire made genius burn more bright . . ."

THE NEGRO AUDIENCE

Playwright Willis Richardson writes in the following essay that the human portrayal of life is a major objective of drama. Nonetheless, certain African-American audiences find the dramatization of their race's true life experiences distasteful. Richardson published this essay in April 1925.

It is my opinion that the average Negro audience seldom goes to the theatre to hear a Negro play with open mind. They seem to think the Negro character should be portrayed on the stage as an angel. I distinctly remember the great howl that was sent up a few years ago by some of these audiences when Eugene O'Neill's "The Emperor Jones" was played by the Howard University Players. Some wondered why the University would stoop to allow its students to give a performance of a play in which the leading character was a crap-shooter and escaped convict. One went so far as to say that O'Neill had no standing as a playwright. This last seemed rather strange to me in the face of the fact that O'Neill is the internationally admired American playwright at the present time, and the greatest ever developed in this country; but after reconsidering the matter I came to the conclusion that, although the person who made this strange statement was a respected teacher of English, he was somewhat uninformed concerning the development of the modern drama.

I had an amusing experience one night while listening to my own humble effort, "The Chip Woman's Fortune." Every time the dialogue would fall from the perfect English (and it fell generally) a lady in front of me would make the correction in undertones to her companion. When Mr. Kirkpatrick playing Silas Green said "Ah aint," she whispered to her friend, "I'm not," and when the same actor took off his shoes on the stage she was totally scandalized.

This is the state of affairs. These average audiences do not generally like dialect, they do not like unpleasant characters and endings, and the most important thing of all they forget, if they ever knew, that the main business of the drama is the portrayal of human characters. Those characters may be beggars or kings, prostitutes or queens; that part of it should not matter. Some of the things which should matter are: whether the characters are well drawn, whether the dialogue is natural, whether the ending is consistent and whether the whole thing is interesting and logical. These are some of the things Negro audiences must learn if the Negro drama is to prosper and become "a thing of beauty and a joy forever." And I think it will prosper although its beginning is doubtful and filled with disappointment and pain as was the beginning of the often mentioned and justly admired Moscow Art Theatre, whose members have worked together for nearly a quarter of a century, and after overcoming hardships and criticisms merited and unmerited have developed the greatest of all dramatic organizations.

I, for one, truly expect this Negro drama finally to come into its own, "Not with a riot of flags and a mobborn cry," but rather with great labor, and quietly win the hearts of the people. For as Bjalmar Bergstrom says at the ending of "Karen Borneman": "It seems to be almost a law of life that nothing new can come into the world except through pain."

CHARACTERS

This essay was published in June 1925 by Willis Richardson, who discusses why characters in plays that portray African-American "peasants" might be more interesting in contrast to cultured African-American characters.

One of the first questions every person who is seriously interested in the drama asks, is why melodrama, musical comedies and mere shows so far outnumber what Shaw calls higher dramas. And by higher dramas it is my opinion that he means plays which deal more with the souls of men and women than with their bodies, plays which are serious rather than foolish, plays which are logical rather than unreasonable, and above all, plays which are clean in the treatment of their subject matter rather than plays which are dirty.

In attempting to place the blame for so much that is bad in our theaters, some blame the authors who write purely commercial plays, others blame the producers who place these plays before the public, while still others blame the audiences who support what these purely commercial authors and producers offer them for their entertainment. It is the opinion of many that authors cannot support themselves by writing serious plays; and these same people hold that the producer who attempts to entertain the public with what is commonly called higher drama will at most performances play to vacant seats. Those who are tempted toward this same opinion ought to think of Eugene O'Neill and be convinced that this opinion is wrong.

Any discussion of this question will make those people who are particularly interested in the Negro race wonder if Negroes would willingly accept serious plays in those theatres they support. All of us know they accept the blackface comedian with his painted lips and crude jokes, accept him with wild applause, and go to see him perform the same insanity time after time, whether he be bootlegger, thief, crapshooter, or criminal of whatever kind. So long as he grins and cracks a laughable joke he may be their hero forever. But for one moment wash the burnt cork and paint from his face and let him be a bootlegger planning seriously to become wealthy by this illegal practice and he is at once taboo, they will have none of him. It is because he has discarded his grin that they object to him, or is it because he plans seriously to do something outside the law? Has it narrowed down to the fact that as a fool a Negro character may do anything he wills and gain applause while one error on the part of a Negro character as a man will make the whole race throw up its hands in horror?

We hear that the desire is for Negro characters of refinement and culture. This is all very well. All of us know that there are thousands of refined and cultured Negroes, but what shall the Negro character in the drama be? Shall he be like Hamlet of Denmark, refined, cultured, and a Prince of the blood, but harboring revenge in his heart? Shall he be like the Macbeths committing murder, or like our own Othello, a leader of men, listening to the slanderous lies of a scoundrel and strangling a faithful wife? All these characters are refined and cultured, but look what Shakespeare has done with them.

No, it is not necessary for your leading character to be a criminal, but it is very necessary for him to be interesting and distinctly a Negro type. In order for him to be interesting he must either do something or have something done to him; and in order for him to be a distinct Negro type he must be distinctly different from the white man. How much difference is there between the cultured Negro and the cultured white man? White men and Negroes of the same cultured plane use the same language, have the same manners, and their desires are very nearly the same; so nearly the same that one cannot tell them apart by hearing their voices, reading their letters, knowing what they eat at meals, or learning how they wish to spend their summer vacations. Judging by these things and thousands of others one can easily see that the cultured Negro is so much like the cultured white man that he is seldom interestingly different enough to be typical of the whole Negro race. So to write a play about cultured Negroes is very nearly to write a play about cultured white people; and unless it should be a propaganda play the average audience would hardly call it racial.

Of course the thing is not impossible to do; but if it is done the play that comes out of it will not have the strength of those plays written around the peasant class of the Negro group. That trite saying about the weakness of the link measuring the strength of the chain may be fitted here, for I suppose those less fortunate among us who are sometimes called the lower class do form the weakest link in this chain of Negro life; but I imagine, though I may be wrong, that it is rather our duty to strengthen that weak link than to be ashamed of it. And after everything is said and done the fact remains that that part of the race we call the weak link is after all different and interesting which two things are of great importance in the theater of today. Also I would say to those who would leave them out as being too unpleasant for our coming drama what Wordsworth said in pleading for his beggar:

> "But deem not this man useless.—Statesmen! ye
> Who are so restless in your wisdom, ye
> Who have a broom still ready in your hands
> To rid the world of nuisances; ye proud,
> Heart-swoln, while in your pride ye contemplate
> Your talents, power, and wisdom, deem him not
> A burthen to the earth!"

Our Wonderful Society:

Washington

As a young man, Langston Hughes visits Washington, D.C. Hughes had formed a laudatory opinion of middle- and upper-class black Washingtonians before he arrived in the city, but after a while he sees nothing that he deems substantive behind many of the opulent lifestyles. This essay was published in August 1927.

Washington Society, both white and colored, with its diplomatic, academic, and governmental circles producing niceties of social status that do not occur to the same extent in any other section of the land, represents an anomaly in the national and racial social life. In the most remote sections of the country Negroes speak, sometimes with awe and envy, as often with ill concealed intolerance, of high society life among the colored denizens of the national capitol. It is our feeling, then, that we are stirring, if not so formidable a thing as the hornet's nest, at least a fracas toward which all who love a good intellectual or emotional bout will turn with interest and a loud, Hear! Hear! And we offer you no mean, ill-matched combatants. Langston Hughes, proclaimed many times over the poet of the masses of his people, severely takes to task those aspects of Washington against which it is natural for his soul's bent to rebel; while Brenda Ray Moryck, a writer well-known to our readers, with years of residence in Washington to give point to her objections, endeavors to call the poet's attention to some views of Washington he may have missed . . . Editor's Note.

As long as I have been colored I have heard of Washington society. Even as a little boy in Kansas vague ideas of the grandeur of Negro life in the capital found their way into my head. A granduncle, John M. Langston, had lived there during and after the time of colored congressmen and of him I heard much from my grandmother. Later, when I went to Cleveland, some nice mulatto friends of ours spoke of the "wonderful society life" among Negroes in Washington. And some darker friends of ours hinted at "pink teas" and the color line that was drawn there. I wanted to see the town. "It must be rich and amusing and fine," I thought.

Four or five years passed. Then by way of Mexico and New York, Paris and Italy, through a season of teaching, a year at college, and a period of travel, I arrived at Washington. "Of course, you must meet the best people," were almost the first words I heard after greetings had been exchanged. "That is very important." And I was reminded of my noble family ties and connections. But a few days later I found myself a job in a laundry, carrying bags of wet-wash. The dignity of one's family background doesn't keep a fellow who's penniless from getting hungry.

It was not long, however, before I found a better place in the office of a national Negro organization. There I opened up in the morning, did clerical work, took care of the furnace, and scrubbed the floors. This was termed a "position," not a "job." And I began to meet some of the best people. The people themselves assured me that they were the best people,—and they seemed to know. Never before, anywhere, had I seen persons of influence,—men with some money, women with some beauty, teachers with some education,—quite so audibly sure of their own importance and their high places in the community. So many pompous gentlemen never before did I meet. Nor so many ladies with chests swelled like pouter-pigeons whose mouths uttered formal sentences in frightfully correct English. I admit I was awed by these best people.

Negro society in Washington, they assured me, was the finest in the country, the richest, the most cultured, the most worthy. In no other city were there so many splendid homes, so many cars, so many A. B. degrees, or so many persons with "family background." Descendants of distinguished Negroes were numerous, but there were also those who could do better and trace their ancestry right on back to George Washington and his colored concubines: "How lucky I am to have a congressman for grand-uncle," I thought in the presence of these well-ancestored people.

She is a graduate of this . . . or, he is a graduate of that . . . frequently followed introductions. So I met many men and women who had been to colleges,—and seemed not to have recovered from it. Almost all of them appeared to be deeply affected by education in one way or another, and they, too, had very grand manners. "Surely," I thought when I saw them, "I'll never be important unless I get a degree." So I began to spend ten cents for lunch instead of fifteen,—putting the other nickle away for college.

Then I met some of the younger colored people, sons and daughters of the pompous gentlemen and pouter-pigeons ladies, some of them students at Northern colleges or at Howard. They were not unlike youth everywhere today,—jazzy and loud. But, "They are the hope of the race," I was told. Yet I found that their ideals seemed most Nordic and un-Negro and that they appeared to be moving away from the masses of the race rather than holding an identity with them. Speaking of a fraternity dance, one in a group of five college men said proudly, "There was nothing but pinks there,—looked just like 'fay women. Boy, you'd have thought it was an o'fay dance!" And several of the light young ladies I knew were not above passing a dark classmate or acquaintance with only the coolest of nods, and sometimes not even that. "She's a dark girl but nice," or similar apologies were made by the young men for the less than coffee-and-cream ladies they happened to know. These best young people had, too, it seemed, an excessive admiration for fur coats and automobiles. Boasts like this were often to be heard! "There were more fur coats in our box at the Thanksgiving game than in anybody else's." Or concerning the social standing of a young lady: "Her father owns two cars." Or of a sporty new-comer in town: "He's got a racoon coat just like a 'fay boy." Or as the criterion of success: "He's one of our leading men. He has a Packard and a chauffeur."

But cars or fur coats or fine houses were not more talked about, however, than was culture. And the members of Washington society *were* cultured. They themselves assured me frequently that they were. Some of those who could pass for white even attended down town theatres when "The Scandals" or Earl Carrol's "Vanities" came to town. But when a concert series of Negro artists including Abbie Mitchell and other excellent musicians, was put on at a colored theatre, the audiences were very small and most of the members of cultured society were absent.

I knew that Jean Toomer's home was Washington and I had read his book "Cane" and talked about it with other readers in New York and Paris and Venice. I wanted to talk about it in Washington, too, because I had found it beautiful and real. But the cultured colored society of the capital, I mean those persons who always insisted that they were cultured, seemed to know little about the book and cared less. And when the stories of Rudolph Fisher (also a colored Washingtonian) appeared in *The Atlantic Monthly,* what I heard most was, "Why didn't he write about nice people like us? Why didn't he write about cultured folks?" I thought it amazing, too, that a young playwright of ability and three or four poets of promise were living in Washington unknown to the best society. At least, I saw nothing being done to encourage these young writers, for the leading women's clubs appeared to be founded solely for the purpose of playing cards, and the cultured doctors and lawyers and caterers and butlers and government messengers had little concern for poets or playwrights. In supposedly intellectual gatherings I listened to conversations as arid as the sides of the Washington monument.

There appeared, also, to be the same love of scandal among the best folks as among the lower classes. Sometimes I heard how such-and-such a pompous gentleman had struck his wife or how this or that refined couple had indulged in physical combat,—all of which was very amusing but hardly compatible with a society which boasted of its gentility. Such consciously nice people ought never to let down the bars, I thought, but they did.

———

Washington is one of the most beautiful cities in the world. For that I remember it with pleasure. Georgia Douglass Johnson conversed with charm and poured tea on Saturday nights for young writers and artists and intellectuals. That, too, I remember with pleasure. Seventh Street was always teemingly alive with dark, working people who hadn't yet acquired "culture" and the manners of stage ambassadors, and pinks and blacks and yellows were still friends without apologies. That street I remember with pleasure. And the few fine and outstanding men and women I met who had seemingly outgrown "society" as a boy outgrows his first long trousers, those men and women I remember with pleasure. But Washington society itself,—perhaps I am prejudiced toward it. Perhaps I had heard too much about it before hand and was disappointed. Or perhaps I didn't really meet the best society after all. Maybe I met only the snobs, and the high-yellows, and the lovers of fur coats and automobiles and fraternity pins and A. B. degrees. Maybe I'm all wrong about everything.—Maybe those who said they were the best people had me fooled.—Perhaps they weren't the best people,—but they looked tremendously important. Or, perhaps they *were* the best people and it's my standard of values that's awry . . . Well, be that as it may, I have seen Washington, of which city I had heard much, and I have looked at something called "society" of which I had heard much, too. Now I can live in Harlem where people are not quite so ostentatiously proud of themselves, and where one's family background is not of such great concern. Now I can live contentedly in Harlem.

I, Too, Have Lived in Washington

Brenda Ray Moryck attempts to contradict Langston Hughes's disapproving opinion of black Washington society (see the previous essay). Moryck describes a Washington that is much less pompous and hollow than Hughes's description. She sees a more intellectually vibrant black Washington society. This essay was published in August 1927.

"What went ye out into the wilderness to seek? A reed shaken with the wind?— But what went ye out for to seek?"

Fully aware that in quoting Biblical Scripture, I am exhibiting that behaviorism the learned Caucasian psychologists note as being peculiarly typical of the Negro,—"a naturally religious trend of thought sub-lying all material consciousness," I nevertheless take delight in setting down the text by means of which I begin my response to Mr. Langston Hughes, youthful and sometimes charming poet, for the moment turned critic of the world in general, (for all the world lives in Washington,—at least through some representative), while resting from his opportunism. But since I am neither ashamed nor afraid of being a Negro, I offer no apology for flaunting the badge of my race in turning to my use the rhetorical phrases of Jesus Christ.

There is an ancient oriental saying, subtle and double-charged as were most of the maxims born in the far east in early times, which has come down to us through the ages until we fancy it but a common slogan of our own day, which reads, "We seek what we find,—we see what we look for."

We do.

———

I, too, have lived in Washington, and I have seen the sun setting over Virginia hills across Potomac waters,—the red sun, resplendent in immeasurable glory, sinking behind green hills,—reflected, until the last soft afterglow has melted into a purple dusk twilight, on the marble grandeur of the Lincoln Memorial Temple; I have seen the miracle of America,—the Japanese cherry blossoms in bloom around the Tidal Basin, exquisite and delicate—divinely beautiful,—fairyland on earth for a span; I have seen the sparkling waters of Rock Creek Park rushing over crags and stones between sun-spattered banks; I have seen children at play in the squares in Spring; I have seen from the enchanting great height of that granite shaft, the Washington Monument, all the beauty and the loveliness of design that is this nation's capital and all the open country and hills and rivers round about; I've viewed the Unknown Soldier's tomb and stood beside that dazzling, gleaming amphi-theatre which marks a people's tribute to their hero-dead. I have seen Art in the Corcoran Galleries, and Science at the Smithsonian Institute; I've seen, in the halls of Congress, law in the making,—men rising to betray the sacred trusts borne by them, and not ashamed,—scheming to shape some evil end for their own and not the people's good, and other stalwart champions arising to denounce and crush out the poison weed ere it take root and flourish into treachery; I've seen the President and the First Lady, and their collies. . . . and Paulina—; I've glimpsed some Swedish Royalty, and received a blinding flash of Roumanian Marie, her children and her retinue; I've seen ambassadors and their regalia; I've viewed the embassies and their elegance; I've seen the relics of the last war, maimed and wounded and blinded at Walter Reed; I've watched the crippled babies on their hospital porch in their pitiful attempts at play; I've seen the shops and buildings, the ceremonies and the people,—and—I've seen the Negroes.

What went I out to see in Washington?

———

Yes,—I've seen the Negroes.———I've seen the "best people,"—those "persons of influence,"—whom the young poet's trenchant pen has presented,—"men with some money, women with some beauty, teachers with some education,—pompous gentlemen, quite audibly sure of their own importance,—ladies swelled like pouter-pigeons, whose mouths uttered formal sentences in frightfully correct English,—persons who knew they were the best people," although they never assured me of the fact,—no doubt respecting my riper years too much to presume to tease my credulity in the same manner that ensnared the gullible Langston. I've seen "the splendid homes, the many cars," read "the many A. B. degrees, and three of the five Ph.D's belonging to colored women in this country, on programmes and pamphlets without number,—though not with scorn, (for is not the striving to attain the world's general standard of education a laudable endeavor?) The figures,—125,000 college students in the United States in 1903, 438,000 in 1922 and today nearly 600,000 seem to argue that it seems a worthwhile pursuit to an ever increasing many; and I've talked with "the many persons with family background," legitimate and *á main gauche.*

Some of the younger colored people too, "sons and daughters of the pompous gentlemen and pouter-pigeon ladies," called "the hope of the race," says Mr. Hughes, although I did not know that they were, having heard quite the contrary from many of their despairing and disgusted parents, have come within my ken. And I heard a youth, dropped down from New York, speaking of a fraternity dance there, use those same "pink" and "o'fay" terms which Mr. Hughes gives as the language of his Washington character. (No doubt the New Yorker set the mode, since not to do as the Harlemite does is to place one's self beyond the pale of intelligent comprehension.) I've also passed "the several light young ladies" whose pseudo-Nordic ideal prohibited their public recognition of a swarthy-skinned friend,—in New York, Boston, Philadelphia, Cleveland, Buffalo, and Baltimore, as well, but somehow or other the blind spot in my eye has always had a sudden simultaneous way of appearing to obscure my sight the instant my fair friends' vision begins to fail and I have not been able to recognize them either, thereby bringing down upon my own distinctly Negroid head, a similar charge of "passing," particularly if I happened to be in the company of genuine Caucasians when I so unfortunately went blind. (For four years while I was at college, I "passed"—so I am told now-a-days. For what, I haven't been able to ascertain, but I could not have been one Negro among fourteen hundred white girls,—impossible!)

Dark girls, when they have lacked "charm" (to imitate Helen Hayes) 'tis true have sat against the walls of the dance hall all evening while the fair belles occupied the center of the floor, here as elsewhere, but at least they have been extended the courtesy of an invitation. New York has long since eliminated that problem by the surgeon's method.

Admiration for fur coats and automobiles among the younger generation of Washington I've likewise seen, although I cannot concede the adjective excessive," deemed necessary by Mr. Hughes, since all young people everywhere in this age must have a fur coat or an automobile or both, and some of us older ones can't be happy without them either, but if this is a particularly silly Washington weakness why will not the New Yorkers attend the Thanksgiving game at all unless they can come gorgeously garbed in coats of the latest and most expensive furs to display in their Washington friends' boxes, and motor down in elegant and dazzling high-powered cars in which to park before these same friends' doors? And can it be that I read in a New York weekly in the society column only a month or so ago that Mr. and Mrs. So-and-So "were sporting a new Marmon on Seventh Avenue the other afternoon;" Dr. So Gross "was seen stepping on the gas of his new Pierce-Arrow, on 135th Street," and Miss Self-Important "departed for Atlantic City in her 1928 model Packard," while the Stay-at-Homes' "latest Lincoln sedan was seen parked in front of the Cotton Club?"

Absurd!—but true.

Again I have seen, but not heard, of Washington "culture," not at all unlike the "culture" of every city and every race the world over,—a cheap tinsel substitute for the realities of life,—a sham blind to protect vacuity,—the artificial barrier erected to deceive and dazzle the striving,—and I have seen—Washington culture,—"Georgia Douglas Johnson conversing with charm and pouring tea on Saturday nights for young writers and intellectuals,"—a dark working man on Seventh Street, "who had not yet acquired 'culture' and the manners of stage ambassadors," tenderly herding his slightly less dark little family into an early evening film showing of Rin-Tin-Tin; "pinks and black and yellows," their heads bent together in "friendly fashion without apology" in a common attempt to solve a common problem at an interracial meeting; "the few fine outstanding men and women, who had seemingly out-grown 'society' as a boy outgrows his first long trousers." I have seen the snobs and the strivers, the fools and the clowns, the simple and the weak, the frail and the evil,—and then—I have seen Washington Society.

———

"Your actions speak so loudly, I cannot hear what you say," was the homely but pithy sentence by which one wise man damned up the explanatory flow of his companion's language ere it had clouded honest penetration, and if Mr. Hughes had uttered the same remark in time, he might have been the recipient of more wholesome and sane treatment at the hands of even the "elite" whom he mistook to represent Washington. In that fortunate event, he would have had the necessary leisure to discover who is who and why, as I did.

When I came to reside in Washington, less than three years ago, I was not totally unknown, having visited there two or three times during my childhood, and occasionally afterwards, but my acquaintanceship did not extend beyond a very few now facetiously termed "cave dwellers" and their retiring daughters and sons, so my circle was very limited at the start. I had no ancestry, distinguished or otherwise, born, reared or careered in the capital, or even near it, so I had no preconceived notions of how things ought to be. I had heard, of course, as who has not?—of the grandeur of that earlier day when colored Congressmen, orators, statesmen and eminent divines held splendid sway, and was duly impressed with what had been, in like manner as was Mr. Hughes, for despite his scorn and scoffing and skepticism, he is impressed. Else why does he call to notice his famous ancestor and bear with pride his honorable name if the sterling worth of those great men who placed the first bricks above the corner-stone laid by Abraham Lincoln for the civic, economic and political progress of the Negro is all a myth?

Unlike Mr. Hughes, however, being slightly older than he, I know that "the old order changeth" and I was quite prepared to meet the new whatever it might be.

Instead of going forth in search of it, I remained at home and after many days, one symbol of it came to me in the form of an invitation from, to employ the parlance of the society editor, "one of the city's most prominent young matrons," a "pink" whom I had known long ago while summering in the mountains as a child, and who had paid me one fleeting call upon my arrival. It asked me to a supper party at her home.

I went—went into as exquisite a home as it has ever been my good fortune to enter, and since in my varied experience, it has been my privilege to cross the thresholds of the nouveau riche, time-worn aristocrats, and the mellow wealthy, I have seen some fine houses. But no one called my attention to the solid silver, the priceless linen, the Persian rugs or the old mahogany, nor the quantity and quality of the food.

There were, among the small group present, three well-known and successful lawyers, one of them on his way to the Judge's bench, but nothing was said of the fact. I knew neither their profession nor their standing until afterwards, when I made personal inquiry concerning each.' There was ease, there was fun, there was hospitality, and though I felt culture in the invitation, refinement and prosperity in the home, intelligence in the conversation, and knew my hostess to be a very charming modern edition of an old family with solid background, these things were not even whispered on the air. Yet the party lasted from eight in the evening until two the next morning,—ample time to hear anything, especially in the loquacious precincts of fine drinks!

A guest whom I met at that supper, understanding me to be a

stranger in town next asked me to a dance. I went, I saw, I enjoyed,—a gathering brilliant in its assemblage, gorgeous in its gowns and setting,—rich in its jewels and furs and cars. Was it mere oversight that no one troubled to announce the figure of his bank account to me, nor name his degree, nor point out his automobile, nor inform me of his importance in the community? Was I snubbed? Or were we all having too jolly and interesting a time to be bothered by such idiocy?

Next, followed a card party—a breath-taking revelation to me, for the stakes were high and the prizes purchased at prohibitive prices. Moreover, the women played with the tense seriousness of the seasoned gambler and played to win—those magnificent prizes, yet it was at this same party that I heard, as did several others,—a Washingtonian, an elderly lady,—gentle and elegant and formal rebuke another who had recently returned from the metropolis for bringing back the idle rumors rampant there.

Said the returned visitor in answer to a question put concerning the welfare of two prominent people: "Why they're about to separate. He's about to sue her for divorce."

General consternation and immediate interest on the part of everyone near.

"Why, did you expect anything else? This is the third time they've nearly broken up."

Still incredulity.

"Why that's common talk,—in New York,—the way she's behaved,—everybody knows it."

Spoke the lady: "Yes, you are right, it *is* common talk,—the talk of the common,—cheap, common talk, and no self-respecting woman will repeat such rubbish."

And no one did thereafter. The card-playing was resumed.

Then followed other pleasures and privileges—never talked about,—simply extended and granted and gradually intimacies sprang up,—as charming and as sound as any ordinary friendships on earth can be, so that I came to know rather well a goodly number of people who lived well, dressed well, entertained elegantly and constituted Society, if "the more cultivated portion of a community in its social relations and influences"* constitutes Society anywhere in the world.

Mr. Hughes claims that everywhere people were eager to impress him. My experience was quite the contrary. Everywhere, *I* was impressed. Born, bred and schooled among cultivated Caucasians, I had lost the last shred of illusion concerning the idealism and nobility of the majority belonging to the sophisticated classes, and I confess I was utterly unprepared for what I met. I went to dinner at the lovely home of a very prominent and able woman who occupies a high position in the educational world and is almost weekly feted and honored by some great college or university, and was altogether humbled at the simplicity of her reception and her constant and courteous attention to my every trivial need although the friend with whom she resides was my hostess rather than she.

In this same extraordinary charming retreat, I was again startled into humility by the long reticence concerning European residence of my friend, when after many visits, we fell into conversation about foreign books, the remark was casually made in passing comment. It is in this exquisite company too, that I learned that more was to be gleaned in five minutes concerning the worth-while activities of the world, particularly literary pursuits, than could be heard in several hours in the New York that I know, yet the only sign of all this erudition is visible not audible,—books in every crevice and cranny,—books on every shelf and table,—books, well-used.

Informal luncheon in the spacious homelike home of a man of world renown brought me face to face with the other side of a so-called society-mad family. The mother, a gracious, middle-aged lady is a great card-player, as are both her gay young daughters, and frequently the three capture all the prizes at party after party, yet on the warm summer afternoon that I made so delightful a visit among them, the mother had dismissed the maid that she might attend a picture show, and herself prepared the luncheon for fourteen people, herself, her distinguished husband, her five children, her son's wife, her two grandbabies, two nieces, and a nephew who were visiting there, and myself, and then sat down to preside charmingly over a family as jolly and happy, yet as loving and deferential as I can possibly conceive, and my imagination is most elastic when there is need.

After dinner, the great man took me into his garden which he himself finds recreation in keeping, and instead of discoursing to me upon the solar system or his vast importance or even his latest book, he pointed out the marvelous magnolia tree which Charles Sumner planted in a corner of the yard during the time that the distinguished ancestor of the present cynical Mr. Langston Hughes occupied the house, and then passed on,—not to cabbages and kings, but cabbages and beets and carrots and lettuce and hollyhocks and nasturtiums and pansies.

Later in the day, the "society-mad matron" sat in the hammock and rocked a grand-baby to sleep (old-fashioned, isn't she?) while one flapper daughter lovingly embroidered a waist for her and the other cut the grass.

Now-a-days, I drop into that home often at any hour, any day, because I love it, and I find always the same happy, serene, well-ordered tone,—a gracious mother as chatateine, the chum of her children, yet their respected authority and guide, and six joyous, wholesome young folks,—for the married son and his wife and babies spend as much time with the mother and are as welcome there as in their own home.

Again, I formed an attachment for a very distinguished woman whose personality I admired as much as her great distinction and achievements. She graciously entertained my advances, and though tremendously busy at all times following her profession, and in much demand socially because her very presence dignifies any function, she yet found time to make me cordially welcome in her home whenever I chose to call, which was frequently. Everywhere, there was abundant evidence of refinement and cultivation and financial ease, yet mention of anything beyond the topics of the day, current literature, in which she is greatly interested, the decline of genuine scholarship, and trivialities (she is a great lover of fun and a good joke) was never made.

It was after more than a year of our fine acquaintanceship, though I had long known of the fact before, that she reluctantly talked of her trips abroad and sojourn in Europe, and it was not until I somewhat rather lately made the discovery for myself that she acknowledged her father to be the author of an eminent book I found reposing obscurely on a shelf in her library. She and her family entertain, quietly, without ostentation, but frequently and elegantly, and all the world is happy when he or she receives a bid to come.

The block in which I reside, where a representative group of Society have their home, is known by the envious who can't find a house left to get into, as "Strivers' Row," but God forbid that it should derive its name from any similarity to certain other "Strivers' Rows" that I know of, which might with more exactitude be termed "Strifers' Rows." On it, there live an important Bishop of the Methodist Church,—in the world, a towering, powerful and dominant figure,—in his home, a simple, genial, kindly, cordial man, full of the love of his fellowmen and devoted to his family and his neighbors; a Judge,—pleasant, neighborly, quiet, minding his own business and nobody's else, who never yet has come and gone in his judicial robes and never will; the Recorder of Deeds,—an able and efficient man in office, in "the row" the lover of little children and his dog,—ever ready with a cheery greeting and hopeful comment for any and all who pass his way, a Secretary-Treasurer of a large university,—smiling, thoughtful,—a man invincible in the harness,—after-hours, happy, strolling in the company of his youngest son; two physicians, whose offices in another section of town, make them glad to return to the beauty and serenity of their home ground,—to be seen any evening cuddling a baby or their young children on the lawn as they relax before the night shift; four prominent lawyers,—one, a very young man, whose scholastic record, academic honors, and subsequent achievements would have turned the head of any mortal with a less choice spirit than his, yet whose leisure hours are spent in earnest endeavor to bring about better educational facilities for young aspirants to the bar less fortunate than he, and in making more attractive for small boys' recreation at the Y. M. C. A.! two pharmacists, one with a flourishing drug-store which he is too modest to discuss; a young dentist, several business men, teachers, and an architect, all constituting Washington Society. The "caterers, butlers and government messengers," I have not met, but then, unlike Mr. Hughes, I have not seen anything in Washington, nor even in my block, which by the way, I will tell on him—is the same in which he lived while here!

For solidarity and neighborliness, there is nothing like the charm of "Striver's Row," of a spring or autumn twilight when between the children's going to bed and preparation for the evening's pleasure in or out of the home, there comes a pause in individual occupation and the residents meet casually in little informal groups before this or that one's fine home or stop to sit on the hospitable seats on the tiny lawns to chat for a moment of the day's history.

New York knows nothing of it,—the human side of human life. It cannot even conceive it, cramped, jaded, restless, striving, sophisticated, cynical as it is. When it reads of pretty little Mrs. So and So, the wife of Dr. X, at this function tonight, that, tomorrow afternoon, the Country Club tomorrow night,—a luncheon the next noon, it does not know how sweetly she has played with her adorable young children all day long, how carefully she is training them,—how she tucks them in at noon and again at night before she goes forth to her own pleasure, and how tenderly she cares for her mother. How can it? How can anybody outside her intimate friends? Yet she is one of the younger matrons who form the society of Washington spelled with a capital S.

It is not hollow—Washington Society—although its outer shell may be brittle, for I have touched and probed its mettle and not found it wanting. Society,—not "society" for I have neither the time nor the patience to be concerned with the latter, offered me, a stranger to many, entree to its pleasures. If I have seemed sometimes of late to cherish them little, it is not because they lack intrinsically something higher that I would have and so stand aloof in my condemnation, but merely because the woods and trees, sunlight and water, books, writing and the contemplative life make the greater appeal to me now, while for my kind, gay friends, constant indoor frivolity is more satisfying.

Like Mr. Hughes, I too, had heard of Washington ere I arrived,—longer than he, because I am older, and much more because I am a woman, but fortunately for me I did not plunge from the sea-green perfection of a world tour or the sun-kissed vista of Mexican hills into a city as civilized and sophisticated as ultra-sophisticated New York. I came by way of Baltimore,—but an hour's ride from the capital, where resides a group of cultured not "cultured" (an eminent writer has recently drawn the fine distinction) colored people whose parallel is not easily to be found in any city—fine, intelligent, intellectual, home-loving, hospitable people with families,—not large, but a child or two apiece as an earnest of their good intentions at wedlock, who, though they follow the daily round of worldly fashion,—bridge, teas, luncheons, stags, poker and dances, yet find time for friendships and ideals, for kindness and sincerity, gentleness and consideration,—for love, loyalty and beauty, and the permanent good of life, as well as for current events, scandal along with Lindbergh's flight and the threatened British-Russian War and the Chinese situation and *God's Trombones,* (for like the rest of the great human family, they too, share the common failings.)

Perhaps if Mr. Hughes had trod the training ground for a season as I did for several, he would have learned to skim off the froth from the cup which he would examine and look beneath for the essence to quaff. Diamonds and precious metals were never discovered on the crust of the earth. If one would seek for pearls, he must dive deep—and he who would have gold must not be satisfied with the first handful of dross which he scoops up when on his quest.

Mr. Hughes has been hasty,—for I, too, have lived in Washington.

And though I long for the privilege of being near New York—hunger for the zest and stimulation, inspiration and freedom and life that is New York,—for the shops, the theatres, the concerts, my club,—go there at every possible opportunity, I still live contentedly here.

A POINT OF VIEW
(AN *OPPORTUNITY* DINNER REACTION)

In this essay, published in August 1925, Brenda Ray Moryck argues that the entire history and literature of African Americans have been predicated on the experiences of Caucasian life. As Americans, blacks have intermingled with whites of all levels. Moryck points out that black American writers, contrary to the advice of some, should feel free to handle varied classes and races of people if they desire to do so.

"Irvin Cobb and Octavus Roy Cohen,—recognized experts in the field of the short story of ebony hue and chocolate flavor? Why, I thought they were white men!"

"I thought so too."

"But they can't be!"

"Why not?"

"Because they write Negro stories."

"Well,—suppose they do."

"Then they must be Negroes themselves. We are told that people can only write very well of their own race because they know that race best."

"Indeed."

The foregoing bit of conversation was recently overheard in a Southern city.

And there you have it,—the Caucasian, with his facile pen, sketching life, wherever he finds it, excelling in any field to which he turns his art, while he recommends with sincerest sophistry that his darker brother keep within the narrow and prescribed area of his own racial precincts.

A paradox,—a white man may be an expert in his treatment of a theme on black folk, but a colored man, and I say "colored" advisedly, is not to be encouraged to emulate his example by reciprocation. Strange, too, when colored people always have known, and always will know, as long as white people continue to depend upon them for the most intimate personal services one human being can render another, far more about them individually and collectively than they will ever know about the black race.

Yet one of the most popular arguments advanced by modern critics, to convince the Negro writer of the wisdom of curtailing whatever free play he might care to allow his imagination in the treatment of any and all themes is the one which states that he knows best about his own people. Granted that he does, is it not possible that in the range of his varied experiences he may not, through intimate contact with other peoples, come to know them equally as well, even as Thomas Nelson Page, Ruth McEnery Stuart, Joel Chandler Harris and others, not omitting the estimable Messrs. Cobb and Cohen, have come to know and understand a certain type of Negro? I venture to say that a Negro writer living North could excel some of his present peers in the handling of an Irish or Jewish or Italian or Polish or even upper-class Caucasian theme if he were to try, for living and attending school for the most part, as he does, among the heterogeneous type of Americans, native, or foreign-born, contemptuously classed as "poor white trash," and either working for or with,—no matter which, so the daily contact is there, a better class Caucasians from clerks to royalty, he runs the gamut of the social scale in his daily existence and may be presumed to have direct knowledge of all classes of white people.

Then, too, his schooling, whether little or much, if academic training is as valuable as it is purported to be, should have contributed vastly to his understanding of white people. Whether or not the Negro writer has attended mixed schools or colored schools, been tutored by white or colored instructors, or by both, is of scant importance. The essential point is that his entire history and literature courses have been built up almost exclusively about the geneology, character, growth, development, and achievements of the Caucasian race. Where more than a passing reference to Negroes or Mongolians has been made in a school text, it has been by way of some dry-as-dust anthropological treatise intended to draw the attention of an esoteric few. The daily newspapers with exception of those few Afro-American sheets which recently became so popular with both blacks and whites, are journals of Caucasian customs, manners, habits, pursuits, enterprises and engagements. The intelligent Negro lives in a white world perforce, for since he is outnumbered ten to one according to the census count, he can not ward off this daily enlightenment as to how the other nine-tenths live, even if he would. He begins the a b c of knowledge of the white race with his first academic studies, and does not take his final degree in "Caucasianology" until the hour of his death, frequently being ministered to by a white physician during his passing, by which time he merits every award given for high attainment and proficiency in a prescribed course. His natural endowment of curiosity renders him an apt pupil in the school of life.

If then, familiarity with the subject is the first requisite for intelligent writing about it, the educated Negro possesses the proper basic material in a pre-eminent degree. Pause but a moment and think of the beautiful and appealing love lyrics of the Negro *poet*,—on his haunting and wistful nature poems, so devoid of any reference to color,—so charmingly free of all race consciousness. Consider "Fog," as a prose example, the story which took first prize in a recent literary contest inaugurated to discover Negro talent. With a masterly and impersonal stroke, the author has handled varied classes, types and races of people,—the Negro element in his theme, sketched in evidently to make it conform to the rules of competition, being the weakest part. The Negro poet has long since discarded the bonds of Negro dialect as the sole vehicle of his expression and gloriously transcended themes purely subjective in character. His fancy wanders where it lists. Why not the Negro writer of fiction?

I am not, however, advocating that he direct his talent to delineating Caucasian character to the utter exclusion of his interest in his own race. My intention is merely to point out his ability to write freely on any subject, should he elect to do so, contrary to the advice of his well-wishers and critics.

There is a danger, it seems to me, in confining a writer to certain limits. His vision is narrowed, his imagination is dwarfed and warped, and his theme is robbed of its universality of appeal if he must forever be bound to the task of depicting racial reactions peculiar to the Negro. The Negro race as a whole now differs from the white race in externals only. "Death and the mysteries of life, the pain and the grief that flesh and souls are heirs to, the eternal problems that address themselves to all generations and races, produce in the soul of the Negro the same reactions as in any other individual," says Robert T. Kerlin in his essay on Contemporary Poetry of the Negro. Granted that intrinsically the Negro of pure African stock is more emotional, has greater depth of feeling, larger capacity for enjoyment, vaster appreciation for sensuous beauty than his white brother,—is essentially more of the artist,—more of the poet,—and also more of the buffoon, still he exhibits his atavistic traits after three hundred years of cultivation and adulteration only in proportion as he is removed from modern civilized culture. The individual differences so avidly hit upon by contemporary writers are found only in a certain type of Negro—a very captivating colorful creature of swiftly changing moods, and unexpected humorous or sad reactions it is true, but one type only, nevertheless.

The writer who wishes to confine either his realism or his imagination to the still primitive groups, groups, whose precinct is Seventh Street or Seventh Avenue, Chicago or Alabama, will find an unfailing wealth of marketable material whose novel appeal can not be denied. And the author who would make the prose literature of his race, can not afford to discount the valuable contribution which a study of any people still in the elementary stages of American civilization furnishes. Myra Kelly has given us those charming stories, "Little Citizens" and "Little Aliens," Kathleen Norris, with her delightful gift for portraying Irish humor and Irish pathos still paints the Americanized descendants of Ireland's emigrants; O. Henry offered us young America of the gutter and the curbstone, and I am told, upon excellent authority that "Little Afro-Americans" is now in the process of being manuscripted.

Further still, the Negro writer must delve into the past and steep himself in all the tragic lore of the South prior to the Civil War, adding to his present invaluable memory-store of slave history and slave legend, those poignant episodes of Negro life so replete with the very essence of reality, and with his native capacity for relishing the dramatic,—the sad as well as the gay, interpret them for the World, as only he can, if he would complete and enrich the racial literature which will some day be held precious.

But when he has finished this task of painting tragic history, albeit history embellished by the imagination,—when he wearies of the grotesque and the humorous in his race, when his pen lags over the delineation of those superstitions and credulous characters once so numerous in the south but now fast disappearing; when he is done with slush and maudlin sentimentality, to what shall he turn his attention?

There still remains a rich unexplored field if he must continue the study of his own race,—the vast domain of the colored *hoi polloi*—the middle class Negro, neither unintelligent nor yet cultured,—and the realm of the highly cultivated few,—few, not in numbers, but by comparison. Jessie Fauset, in "There is Confusion", has sketched both classes, and Walter White, with another motive than that of pure entertainment, has presented us the problems and difficulties daily faced by the ambitious, educated groups of Negroes in his book "The Fire in the Flint." Other writers may follow their lead with similar works, but such stories, estimable though they are, do not represent purely creative art. They are both, more or less, propaganda novels, conceived for the purpose of presenting to a white audience certain faces and conditions concerning Negroes. They are not the charming impersonal themes so ably handled by many of the best Caucasian writers and not always the best either, but the most widely read.

Let the young writer try his hand at this sort of writing for the sole purpose of entertaining. He will discover before very long, when he writes of life as he finds it, and so will his audience and his critics, that he is writing not of Negroes but of just people,—people no different in standards, customs, habits and culture from any other enlightened American groups,—merely American people. I say American, because the Negro is now American thoroughly so,—having through amalgamation of blood,—there is no denying it when one views the ever increasing Nordic features and coloring appearing among the so-called blacks,—through assimilation of ideas and ideals and conscious and unconscious imitation, absorbed every iota of the good and bad in American life.

Undoubtedly, if he had been allowed to remain in his native land, Africa, and his black blood had never known the taint of many nations diffused through it in honorable and dishonorable ways, he would still have been as distinctly different in character as the Mongolian or Jew alienated from other peoples either by physical, political, or racial barriers, and developing in isolation a distinct race consciousness. Or, if, having been brought to America, he had been huddled into a pale or ghetto, there to develop solely among his own kind, we should still see among all classes, traits and characteristics peculiarly individual to him. We should then probably have had a black Tolstoi writing of a dusky Anna Karenina.

But the Negro, for a large part, is no longer a Negro. He is an American, or living abroad, an Englishman, a Frenchman, or a German, according to his present place of abode, with *sometimes* a dark skin and sometimes a skin not so dark. Contrary to the premise submitted by many so-called scientists that one drop of Negro blood makes a man a Negro, the black blood is not strong, but weak, and when once permeated by the Caucasian complex, the Negro becomes a Caucasian in all but his physique and frequently even in that. He sheds his peculiarly different African heritage with the ease with which a chameleon changes its colors and dons a new garment which, in the fifth and sixth generation of American civilization,—the heritage which many Negroes can now boast, has become his skin.

How long has the Jew or any other immigrant remained racially different once he has become a part of America? Only so long as he has been forced to keep to himself and has not been assimilated in the great melting pot. Once he has acquired money and grappled to himself those advantages which he came seeking, he emerges from racedom, just as an American citizen. Witness the upper class Jew in any community or study the high-born Mongolians numerous in diplomatic circles in Washington or on the Pacific Coast. Seldom, if ever, are their reactions in any way peculiarly racial once they have become Americanized. They differ only as any other people differ according to both and breeding. That too when both races have carefully preserved their racial integrity.

In any untutored people, we find emotionalism, unrestraint and novel and unexpected responses to the experiences of life, hence the naivete of the masses of Negroes, who have long fascinated the white public and recently have begun to charm their own people. In any peoples just emerging from a long period of subjugation to a dominant group, we find greater depth of feeling, more intense religious fervor, a more serious and challenging outlook on life, than in the chosen few, who are the lords of the earth. The ordinary Negro is but a part of the great human family.

Likewise does he run true to form in the upper strata of society. He has on the one hand, all the airs, graces, superficialities and hypocrisies of the white race; all the shallowness, the meanness, the irreverence for holy things, the insatiable thirst for pleasure, the irritation at restraint, the envy, the jealousy; the contempt for the weak, the repudiation of the idea that he is his brother's keeper and the rejection of the Golden Rule which have ever characterized the over-sophisticated and too successful since the days of Babylon's glory, while on the other hand, he possesses in the same degree as all other representatives of a high degree of civilization,—the tampering of his white, forbears is responsible for the present degree—noble ideals, lofty thought, keen intellect, sane philosophy, sound judgment, hunger for knowledge, and a craving for all that is finest and best in life.

Prejudice against his color, when he shows any, has greatly hampered his progress as far as his material desires are concerned. But in spite of Fate, the mass Negro, the financially successful Negro and the cultured Negro as a whole, parallel their Caucasian complements in all but monetary wealth.

A story of any one of these types can be worked up into a purely Negro theme of course, by depicting the tragedies and disappointments wrought by discrimination, and injustice, common occurrences in the daily lives of colored people—but at best such works are morbid. Yet any other attempt to portray the normal ordinary pursuits of the classes of Negroes just described, unless spattered with constantly repeated references to color or to race, becomes at once, simply an account of individuals, not of Negroes as such.

Konrad Bercovici, in a recent article published in the Harlem number of the *Survey Graphic,* argues that the Negro should preserve his racial heritage even as the Jew has held fast to his. The cases are not analogous, even in the instances where Jews are found to be true to the original type. Their ranks were closed against all modifying and assimilating influences of their religion. Now that their orthodoxy is somewhat weakening in this country, even they are becoming more and more like any other Americans. "The Good Provider" an undeniably true picture of prosperous American Jewish life gives patent evidence of that fact. "Humoresque" likewise a gripping portrait of the Jew, represents his gradual change in character in proportion to his contact with the broadening influences of life. The high class young Jews found in private schools and colleges are exactly the prototype of other American youth.

Granted, however, that the Negro should wish to emulate the Jew, in his earlier stages of development in America, it is too late. He was robbed forever of his opportunity of remaining a distinct group people long, long ago by his white ancestors. He is now from one-sixteenth to nine-tenths Caucasian and if he preserves any racial characteristics at all they must be of a Janus nature.

Mr. Bercovici likewise points out that in his study of Negro groups gleaned from intimate Harlem contacts with all classes of colored Americans, he found among them distinct differences of character and thought, peculiarly individual to the Negro.

I beg to differ with his findings.

Because I have discovered so few people whose opinions I value, to agree with me on this subject, and can quote no significant authorities, I must be intensely personal in what follows, offering my own experiences and those of others well known to me to support my contention. I therefore ask my readers' indulgence.

If Mr. Bercovici were to leave off his exquisite word-painting of gypsy and Roumanian life and write a story of his colored friends—a certain well-known Negro actor and his clever wife,—a chemist of recognized ability in her line,—would he find, I wonder, when that comedian had doffed the robes of the "Emperor Jones" or when Mrs "Emperor Jones" had returned to her tiny New York apartment, or any of the others of the little Harlem group, anything especially different in their habits of life or manner of thought which would be a startling revelation to a jaded world fast learning how the other half lives? I think not.

Yet, not alone, either, are Konrad Bercovici and the other Caucasian critics, in staunchly advocating the idea that a Negro writer must forever write of Negroes, first because he lacks the necessary knowledge for any other sort of writing and second, because portrayal of the Negro character offers something new and refreshing. They are warmly seconded by many of the ablest men of letters of the darker race. At a dinner not so long ago, I heard a prominent Negro, distinguished in a certain field of literature, eloquently argue for this same prescribed idea—he—a man of distinctly Caucasian features, and soft, straight hair, whose only identity with the race is his color and his wish,—whose wife is a highly cultivated young woman, charming and beautiful after the Spanish pattern, whose fair-skinned babies—four of them, two of them fair-haired also, gambol about their inviting playroom, just as any babies do, scrapping, hitting, pounding, banging, crying, only to don quickly their company manners and smile and curtsey adorably or offer a pink-dimpled hand when guests appear, just as any other well-bred infants do the world over, exhibiting in no-wise those peculiarly different characteristics attributed to the Negro and argued for by their father.

For pastime, I recently wrote an intimate study of an eminent Negro author and his lovely wife and submitted it to a number of personal friends for their diversion. Except for the use of names and a passing reference to the color and features of a child, no one recognized it as a "colored story." There was nothing in the scholarly elegance of the man nor in the gracious charm of the woman nor in the cunning capers of the three children to brand them as Negroes, although in reality this couple very ardently and energetically identifies itself with the black race.

These are but a few examples. A panoramic view of cultured American Negro life will reveal many, many others of the same cast all over the country. The colored schools are filled with the children of such parents, the large southern cities abound in their number,—not always with quite the same cultural attainment, as the very privileged few,—but with a background as fitting and an outlook as sane and devoid of emotion as any of their compatriots of the same level of society, whose ancestors have enjoyed some little education and certain additional advantages.

Without stressing the unpleasant and dismal element of race-prejudice and its cursed results, it would be impossible to construct a Negro theme as such, from the daily tragedies and joys and ordinary pursuits of colored people, except of those belonging to the untrained and inexperienced groups, who through continued lack of enlightenment and contact with refining influences have reverted or remained true to the African type, which I frankly and readily admit is peculiarly different from all other race types.

Above that class, the Negro becomes just a person, differing from all other persons in color, according to the amount of Negro blood in his veins,—in dress, tastes and habits, according to the degree of his cultivation, in manner of living, according to wealth. Proof of this fact may be found in the thousands of so-called colored people who yearly sever themselves with such ease from the race to which the laws of Virginia and South Carolina and a few other states, grown hysterical over what they once started and can not now control, have assigned them, to become lost in the milieu of an immigrant crowded white world. If he were inherently different, the peculiar racial characteristics supposedly his would be as apparent in the white-skinned Negro as in the black.

If then, a survey of colored American life reveals the fact that people are people, white or black, the Negro prose writer with safe assurance may invade with his pen, any world he desires, for by merely knowing his own race people, he knows in addition all other people of his country not alone through study and observation but *per se*. Freedom of range of idea, unhampered by race consciousness or smothered by race pride, he as well as the poet must have, if the latent gift of creative art recently uncovered to the public is to reach the ripe fulfilment of its rich promise.

Not only then will he produce a great Negro literature, but beyond that in time, he too, will be added to that list of honored men, which bears the names of the makers of the creative literature of the world.

HE SMASHED THE COLOR LINE:

A SKETCH OF BILLY PIERCE

In this essay about Billy Pierce, Elmer A. Carter describes Pierce as a man who overcame the barriers of race to establish one of the foremost dance studios of his time. This essay was published in May 1930.

When you enter the dancing studio of Billy Pierce on 46th Street the roar of Broadway still lingers in your ears, but not for long. Hardly have you stepped across the threshold when another sound, at first faintly audible and then growing more distinct and clear envelops you. It is a sharp staccato sound which seems to issue from the ceiling, the floor, the very walls. Tap-tap-tap-tap-tap above you, beneath you, around you everywhere. Unconsciously you find yourself mentally following the regular measure of this tapping; its rhythmic beat gets into your blood.

A glance at the walls of the office of Billy Pierce's studio is sufficient to establish his position in the world of the contemporary theatre. Every available niche and corner is covered with photographs for the most part of beautiful women; women whose names are in huge electric lights a half block away on Broadway; women whose grace and beauty and dancing have placed them at the very top of the theatrical profession. A close examination of these photographs reveals in every instance a fine sentiment expressed in the handwriting of the donor; an expression of appreciation and gratitude to Billy Pierce for his patience and skill in teaching the intricacies of tap dancing.

Here on these walls there is a photographic directory that is a veritable Who's Who of the American Theatre. And in the class rooms, which are crowded from early morning until late at night, are the budding stars of tomorrow. Behind the closed doors one may hear the broad "a's" of New England, the nasal twang of the west, the gentle drawl of the far South.

From every section of the country they come, more often than not young women, the prize beauties of their communities anxious to seek fame and fortune on the stage. It is a strange experience for some of them to find that Billy Pierce is a Negro. Solicitous mothers at first eye his rather stern countenance with apprehension, which, however, soon gives way to utter confidence when they come to realize that Billy Pierce is as anxious as they are for their daughters to reach the heights of stardom. His courtesy and tact are completely disarming. And many who enter for the first time with suspicion and prejudice have become his staunchest friends and most enthusiastic admirers.

From Virginia where he was born about forty years ago, Billy Pierce, after completing a common school education and matriculating at Storer College at Harpers Ferry, went to Washington, D. C., for the purpose of studying a profession at Howard University. He didn't stay there long. Wünderlust, the urge to see and know the great world beyond the confines of the campus, drove him forth in search of adventure. To the accumulated experience gained from years of travel and work in Europe, in the far East, along the African West Coast and in every part of the United States, Canada and Mexico, Billy Pierce ascribes his success. During these years he learned to discount the handicaps, real or imagined, of color and race. He learned that the similarities in men, black, white, yellow or brown were greater than their differences.

It is difficult to get Billy Pierce to talk about himself. He is naturally taciturn. From his casual conversation, however, he reveals himself as a man endowed with exceptional tenacity. Without this he must have succumbed long ago to the pitiless competition of Broadway. Every street that intersects Broadway in the theatrical district has its dancing schools and studios, and the great "White Way" itself is literally lined with them. It is no easy task for a white man to "make the grade" in a field already filled to the point of saturation. For a Negro it is little short of miraculous.

During his first year he suffered reverses that would have deterred most men. No pupils came to his door. His scanty funds soon were exhausted. Each month it became increasingly difficult for him to pay the rent of his studio. But he refused to quit. He went to the owners of the building and asked for the job of night janitor. He got it. And then night after night he scrubbed the offices and halls of the building where now he leases two whole floors. When Billy Pierce speaks of this, there is no indication that he considers his efforts particularly praiseworthy. There is no hint of braggadocio. He merely smiles and says: "All of those tiles belong to me. I have counted them one by one."

The stamp of the Billy Pierce Studio is unmistakably imprinted on every one of his pupils. He gives them something other teachers cannot give. It is something of Negro abandon, enhanced and yet partially concealed by exquisite grace and a perfect sense of rhythm. The shrewd producers of Broadway send him promising young women and men in whom they see possibilities of future greatness. Few dance studios can boast of such a distinguished clientele of stage and screen stars as that which includes: Betty Compton and Evelyn Hoey, Ramon Navarro, Louise Brooks, Ann Pennington, Adele Astaire, Frances Williams, Mary Eaton, Ruth Fallows, Libby Holman, Clifton Webb, Jack Buchanan, Paula and Dorothy Stone, Anita Loos, Ruby Keeler, Bessie Love, Ed Wynn, Barbara Newberry, Ada May, Irene Delroy, Lily Damita, Zelma O'Neil, Bobby Agnew, Queenie Smith, Jack Hulbert, Marie Saxon. These are but a few of those who have come under the tutelage of Billy Pierce.

When you speak of the color line to Billy Pierce, he is apt to smile and say: "Well, you wouldn't take me for anything but a colored man, would you? And my secretary, Miss Jackson, is colored and my staff of instructors under Buddy Bradley is colored."

And you have to admit as you listen to the tap-tap-tap-tap-tap and let your eyes wander around the walls of his office that Billy Pierce has beaten the color line.

THE CHURCH IN SOCIAL WORK

This essay was published by Adam Clayton Powell, Sr., in January 1923, when he was senior pastor of Abyssinian Baptist Church in Harlem. He writes that the church must not only meet the spiritual needs of its members, but it must enlarge its activities to meet the social needs of the community as well.

The church must enlarge its religious activities if it is to retain the respect and support of intelligent men. Christianity is more than preaching, praying, singing and giving; it is all of these but a great deal more. The purpose of the Christianity of Jesus as revealed in the New Testament is to supply man's social as well as spiritual needs. The church is being called upon to give the world a Christianity of deeds as well as a Christianity of creeds. Very few people ask any more "What the church believes?" but "What the church is doing for the amelioration of the condition of mankind?" The majority of people care very little about church doctrines. They are looking for a translation of the spirit of Jesus Christ in the everyday life of his professed followers. The church will never draw and hold the masses by essays on faith, but by showing her faith by her works.

The church has not discharged its obligations when it has hired a man to stand up twice one day in seven, and piously ram the Bible down the throats of the people. It must go into the highways and hedges during the week caring for the sick, the wounded, the distressed and all that are needy, and then on Sunday they will hear us and believe us when we tell them of "Jesus, the Mighty to save."

The Abyssinian Baptist Church of New York City is planning to carry out this larger program of applied Christianity. A $300,000 Church and Community House is being erected in Harlem, the most densely populated Negro Center in the world. This Church will be a kind of an intellectual go-between for the public schools and the higher institutions of learning. Thousands of Negroes are coming to Northern cities each year who are too old to be reached by the public schools and too poorly informed to enter universities. This large group has in it tremendous undeveloped possibilities. Thru the classes in English, Reading Circles and Lecture Courses that will be provided, there will be not only a vision of the great world in which we live, but a means by which they may helpfully relate themselves to a movement for world betterment.

The Church should be the social center of the community in which it is located. Man seeks the fellowship of other human beings, as surely as water seeks its level. If he cannot find the fellowship he craves with good men he will find it with bad ones. The majority of people who go to disreputable places do not go because they desire to do wrong, but for fellowship. The Church should cease criticising and abusing people for spending their evenings in questionable places until it has given them a place to socialize in a wholesome environment. The Church which will grip and hold men in the future will be the Church that vitally relates itself to every problem of the masses. This does not mean that emphasis will be shifted from man's spiritual to his social needs. It is the paramount duty of the Church to Christianize the social order. The Church, therefore, which undertakes to carry out a large social program must be more spiritual than the one which deals simply in emotional religion. The world has gone wild like an uncaged beast of the jungle and there seems to be no power in science, politics, diplomacy, or economics to gird it. Only the social reign of God can bring order out of man's social confusion.

THE VIRGIN ISLANDS

The American government purchased the Virgin Islands for twenty-five million dollars in 1917, and the United States Navy took over their administration. Casper Holstein, a native of the islands and the author of the following essay, writes about the neglect and mistreatment of the Virgin Islands by the American government. This essay was published in October 1925.

The tourist in search of romance can find its footprints in the Virgin Islands of the United States. The grim walls of Bluebeard's Castle on the heights overlooking the town of Charlotte Amalia in St. Thomas, recall the days when the black flag with its skull and crossbones threw terror into the hearts of peaceful merchants and other travellers. The Salt River plantation still stands at the mouth of a lagoon, up which tradition says that Columbus sailed on St. Ursula's Day, when he named the group of islands in honor of St. Ursula and her eleven thousand virgins.

It was in the little town of Bassin, or Christiansted, in St. Croix, that the boy Alexander Hamilton grew up and labored as clerk, under Nicholas Kruger, and first exhibited those remarkable powers that took him through what is now Columbia University in New York at the age of sixteen and made him the active genius and "father of the American Constitution". It should be said here that the natives of the Island of St. Croix raised the funds to send the young Hamilton to New York by popular subscription. The tomb of his mother, Rachall Fawcett Levine, may still be seen by the inquiring tourist at the Grange Estate in St. Croix.

On the same Island slavery was abolished by the slaves themselves after a bloody uprising in 1848. But long before this, the fierce love of freedom characteristic of the Danish Negroes had blown a spark over the mainland where, in 1822, one of them, by the name of Denmark Vesey, organized a slave-revolt in Charleston, South Carolina, which all but succeeded. And since that time the Virgin Islands have sent many famous sons to mingle their blood, brains and initiative with those of their brethren under the Stars and Stripes on the mainland. It is an interesting list which includes such names as Hamilton, Blyden, Roberts, Harrison, Benjamin Banneker, Jackson and many others. It is an outstanding fact testified to by the American rulers of the Islands, that illiteracy in the Danish West Indies when they were taken over, was less than 5 per cent, and as the editor of *The New York World* put it: "That is more than we on the mainland can boast of."

Under Danish rule the islanders were more or less happy and contented. It is true that the decline of the sugar industry in the West Indies brought the pressure of poverty into the scheme of things in every West Indian Island, including those of Denmark. But the source of this pressure was economic rather than bureaucratic. Today, after eight years of American rule, the population is discontented, clamoring for changes in the fundamental law under which they are governed, and in the personnel of the governing body. What is the cause of this disastrous change? The answer will be found in the following brief narration of the events which have transpired since 1917. In that year the American Government bought the islands for twenty-five million dollars as the first point in the strategic defense of the Panama Canal. Soon after the islands were taken over we entered the war against Germany. At that time it was necessary to establish what Mr. Lloyd George described as a "practical dictatorship." During our dictatorship most of the functions of Congress were taken over by the Executive. It was perfectly natural, therefore, that the Government then set up in the Virgin Islands should have followed the fashion of autocracy. And it did. The government has been administered by the Navy Department—which is the first instance in our History, or that of any other Colonial power, of putting the government of a tropical dependency (not acquired through conquest) under a war making branch of the government. Against this brutal anomaly the common-sense of the Virgin Islanders cries out.

In the beginning the government in the islands quite frankly described itself on its seal and official letter-head, "The Naval Government of the Virgin Islands." When the democratic agitation of the Virgin Islands Congressional Council began to make headway on the mainland, the Navy's officials quickly changed the legend on the seal and letter-heads and have been declaring ever since that there is no naval government in the Virgin Islands. In the eight years since the transfer there have been six naval governors, each one taken from active duty in the Navy Department. But, as it was recently and wittily put by *The Nation*, "It is not a change of governors, but a change of government that the Virgin Islands need." Their objection to the rule of the Navy Department is based not only on the fact that it is anomalous and undemocratic but also on the policies which the Navy's personnel have promulgated. American race-prejudice, from which the islands had been free, has been officially introduced by the Department's officials. While Mr. Woodrow Wilson's government, backed by some weak-kneed "liberals," was dealing out ferocious hanging sentences to the Negro soldiers who shot in defense of their lives at Houston, Texas, white marines were rampaging in the islands and shooting up the inoffensive black citizens in their peaceful homes. For these light diversions hardly any official punishment has been meted out. On the higher levels, naval judges have used their power to pay off personal scores and the Navy officials in the islands have deported and imprisoned editors and other critics of their misconduct.

In the meantime the islands have suffered both from official neglect and official unconcern. As is well known, the bay-rum industry has been the main-stay of the island of St. Thomas, together with the coaling and provisioning of the numerous ships that entered the harbor in the days before the Volstead disaster. But the application of the 18th Amendment and a new Port Law have almost wiped out the bay-rum industry and the income from the ships which now go elsewhere for coal and provisions. That this is either ill-will or deliberate indifference appears from the fact that the rest of the United States Constitution—and especially those parts which guarantee the right of full manhood and womanhood suffrage—are kept in abeyance by the Naval officials in the islands, who declare that the United States Constitution does not apply to the Virgin Islands. And, in many instances there has been glaring disregard of that great document. As Mr. George Washington Williams, District Judge of the Virgin Islands, in conversation with a high government official of Porto Rico, said: "What is the Constitution among friends?"

The Islanders may very well ask why apply the recent 18th Amendment to their detriment while withholding the application of the 14th and 15th, which, with some others, would be to their benefit?

To this simple reasoning Naval officials, like Judge George Washington Williams (of Baltimore), who is the chief exponent of naval rule in the islands, reply that they are enforcing *a Danish law*. This law deprives nineteen-twentieths of the population from exercising the franchise. But when this law is examined, it is found that it went into effect in 1906 and that it provides explicitly that the restrictions on the franchise were to be revised ten years later. *But in 1917 the American Navy took over the administration of the islands!* So it is evident that this continued limitation of the franchise is the product of an American policy rather than a Danish intent—as Lieut. Commander Wm. S. Zane, of the Navy, Executive Secretary, while representing the Governor at a recent meeting of the Colonial Council in St. Croix, said: "We have broken the laws so long we may as well break them a little longer." But it is quite in keeping with the purpose of the Navy Department to keep these darker nephews and nieces of Uncle Sam forever on the outside of Democracy's backyard.

For the removal of this and other disabilities the Virgin Islanders are looking forward confidently to the next session of Congress and are putting forward their claims for consideration on grounds of patriotism, justice and democracy. They want a decided change in their present status, which is neither that of citizens nor aliens. They want to be happy and contented citizens of the United States, and since the present naval regime stands as an absolute bar to that, they are seeking the *abolition* of Naval Rule and the *establishment* of civil government.

Voices from Harvard's
Own Negroes

In the following essay, Raymond Pace Alexander calls into question Harvard's tradition of fairness when the university bars African-American matriculating freshmen from living in the university's dormitories. Harvard president A. Lawrence Lowell defended the issue by citing the prejudices of the university's southern students that cannot be disputed. This essay was published in February 1923.

Philip Kerr, until recently private secretary to Lloyd-George, who sat with the latter at the many international conferences during the past few years, himself an authority on international affairs, said, at a recent lecture before the Harvard student body, "one can hardly appreciate the difficulties involved in solving international problems. They are in a large measure due to the differences in race of the various representatives and the ancient prejudices and antipathies between the races such as the French, Germans, Belgians and Austrians. In addition to this we were confronted with another and a greater difficulty in the recent conferences and that was arbitrating questions involving races of different *color*.* *On these questions nations become irrational.*"

The audience did not sit amazed, neither did it express any surprise nor was this unfortunate confession challenged or inquired into during the time allotted to questioning the speaker.

Could a more damaging confession fall from the lips of so able a statesman? Could it have been better timed to fall upon the ears of those who but a few days before had announced to the world in unflinching terms their going on record to arbitrarily exclude from certain otherwise compulsory features of college life at Harvard a certain racial group because they were "of different color"?

---

* The speaker had reference to the English Indian problem, Japan and the Shantung controversy and the French use of Colonial soldiers.

Was Harvard, speaking thru its learned President A. Lawrence Lowell, in prohibiting Negro students from living in the Freshmen Dormitories more rational than the council of nations dealing with their questions or as irrational? Certainly it was not so confessedly irrational. If it was more rational, which is a violent supposition, by what process of reasoning could it have reached such strange results and what factors and elements were considered as the basis of this reasoning? Finally, why in the world can't men, nations or whatnot be rational when a little bit of color is thrown into an issue? Is it possible that the question becomes so onesided?

For a proper treatment of this question it would perhaps be better to sketch briefly the history of the exclusion policy as recently adopted by Harvard.

In the fall of 1921 five colored youths applied for admission to the freshman class, all of them having taken the examinations successfully, were admitted. Three applied for rooms in the freshmen dormitories, which place was a compulsory living quarters for out-of-town freshmen, being optional with local students. These boys were Bertram C. Bland of Newark, N. J., Cecil Blue, Washington, D. C., Pritchett Klugh, Boston, Wm. J. Knox, Jr., New Bedford, Mass., and Edward W. Wilson, Boston. Those requesting dormitory residence were Bland, Blue and Knox, the latter alone being successful. He made application from, and took his examinations in New Bedford, and he was assigned to a room in Standish B. 32, and sent a porter's card to admit his bags and belongings. It happened that one subject, chemistry laboratory, had to be taken in Cambridge for which he appeared in person. This was the beginning of all the trouble. He was "spotted" at once, being brown in complexion (incidentally the darkest of the five), found to have been assigned to a room in the exclusive dormitories and by an artful method was made to give it up, in this way. Immediately he was sent a telegram to the effect that there was some error in assigning him to B. 32 in Standish concluding, "will you please return your porter's card so that this error might be adjusted," signed by Dean Chase of the college. Knox, a native of New Bedford and having lived there all his life, never having been outside of the state of Massachusetts, innocent and unsuspecting, freely complied with the request. Each day he awaited correspondence of equal dignity advising him of his new assignment, but none came. Finally, the light dawned in the nature of a letter of explanation from the Dean stating that "the ruling of the President is that no Negro students shall hereafter be permitted to live in the Freshmen Dormitories." Can anything more depressing be imagined on the mind of this youth than these events, especially in light of the manner in which he was deprived of his assignment?

Knox and a Negro graduate of Harvard of that year, Edwin B. Jordain, Jr., immediately journeyed to Boston. Jordain is also a native of New Bedford, and is a son of a prominent attorney of the same name of that city, and lived in the Freshmen Dormitories in 1917 without the least friction, living in the same room with white boys, and eating at the same table. Later he was a member of the same track team that boasted of the famous Gourdin. They interviewed Dean Chase who has always been a very fair man, and who cannot now be impeached, but his position was uncompromising, being bound by the orders of President Lowell. It was then thought best to see the President, which was done, Jordain alone making the interview. President Lowell was a very pleasant person to talk to, but was immovable in his convictions, giving as his reasons, without deliberating in their forthcoming, the following, which is the gist: The southern element in the school is becoming increasingly large while the Negro element is very small, less than one per cent of the entire matriculation. That the southern students have very pronounced prejudices, cannot be disputed, the most acute being their dislike of anything that approaches, or savors of, social equality. *Ergo,* since living in the Freshmen Dormitories is compulsory upon *all* students which would throw southerners in contact with Negroes to their discomfort, and since it is not our policy to compel artificial social contact between Negroes and whites, it is thought that the best policy is to forbid the Negro students this privilege.

The mere assertion of such a statement would raise in the mind of even the untrained a glaring *non sequitur.* Does it follow that because a University enforces a rule that it thought fit and just for all students at its inception which might incidentally mean that a colored student will have to live in the same dormitory with southerners that the University is forcing a sort of social equality between the two types of students, or forcing the southern students to accept the Negro in his social circle, or forcing him to have any social relations with him other than sleeping under the same roof separated by four strongly partitioned walls, and probably some flights of stairs? Does it follow that there is some artificiality in even this most harmless contact, and at the same time legitimate contact, legitimate because the *rules* make it so? Does it follow that because the southern element is increasingly large, and the Negro body very small, that this great institution, which has never been known to suffer from a shortage of students or a boycott because of a policy, must restrict the operation of this rule, enacted for all races, in order to satisfy any racial or geographical element? Does it follow that the only way to meet such an issue as this is to summarily dispose of the question by putting a bar against all further admission of Negroes to the Freshmen Dormitories? Since this question involves a deep principle of ethics, justice, and fairness, would not the most logical and wholesome policy be unqualifiedly to admit the Negro students, and let those objecting make the next move? Would not the "therefore" clause stand with better logic on this ground? All these questions save the last seem to answer themselves in the negative, and we are faced with our original question: "Whether Harvard was any more rational or as irrational in its pronunciation of policy as was the Council of Nations at Versailles?" We submit to the latter that it was.

The present Negro student body of Harvard is particularly proud of the type and bearing of the young Negroes who are entering this University, and those against whom this policy was announced. It would probably be not too much to conclude that a great deal of the public sympathy with the Negro on this issue, and popular support, may be directly traceable to the fact that the students were treated in such manner came from very representative Negro families. A word or two concerning them would not be out of place.

Cecil Blue's father is a graduate of Queens College, British Guiana, and the medical school of Howard University, Washington, D. C., and is at present a successful physician of that city. The Reverend Doctor David Klugh, the father of Pritchard Klugh, a prominent Boston clergyman, is a graduate of Yale, and Butler R. Wilson, Esq., a member of the Boston bar, is a Harvard Law School graduate and a successful attorney. And now we add to these the name of Roscoe Conkling Bruce, Jr., the son of Roscoe Conkling Bruce, '02 Harvard, class orator, and Phi Beta Kappa man, grandson of Blanche K. Bruce, United States Senator from Mississippi in 1875, Register of the Treasury under President Garfield in the early eighties. To use the words of a reflecting white student, . . . "He certainly picked out most unfortunate cases to start with," would not be amiss.

It is probably fair to conclude that no half dozen men picked at random among the Harvard freshmen class could present any better family history or training in a comparative sense, than these young Negroes. It reflects the advent of a new element of Negroes to our colleges and universities; sons of graduates of these larger institutions as distinct from "the first generation educated" that formed the pioneers among Negro men of letters and science. Not only are these youths better prepared than their fathers were, but their parents have ample means in most cases with which to support these boys in the proper style and comfort. Irrespective of this social progress of the Negro students, we are faced with this pernicious policy of discrimination which strikes at the very source of entrance into the University.

The natural question to ask is what are the aims and underlying purposes of this sudden departure from the great Harvard tradition of fairness and justice to all, irrespective of race or color. Is there an ulterior purpose with its object an immediate limitation in the Negroes attending Harvard and in the future the total exclusion from all departments? One cannot dismiss this question lightly, and rest too assured that Harvard traditions and principles will not allow such when all of its principles, traditions and everything else were freely tossed to the winds in this present affair. One cannot overlook the great significance of this policy, restricted as it is to the Freshmen Dormitories, and the effect that it will have on Negro matriculation. It has already had its effect! In September, 1921, there were six Negroes in the freshman class (one was too fair to be affected by this policy) all of whom were registered before the enunciation of this rule. Last September only one Negro applied for admission to the Harvard freshman class, and he is the son of the Hon. William H. Lewis, noted Harvard football star centre of all time, and an ex-Assistant United States Attorney General. The latter would not be satisfied under any circumstances with another college for his son because his Harvard training has meant too much to him, not to mention his contribution to Harvard, and in this respect, he is not unlike scores of other Negro graduates of Harvard, and hundreds of other parents who want their sons to study under the Harvard system that they themselves were unable to experience.

Young Lewis made no effort to get into the Freshmen Dormitories because his parents live in Cambridge. But was not the apparent desire of the officials fulfilled, with not one Negro requesting to live in the Freshman Dormitory in 1922, and only one Negro in the entire class? It might be asked why is it that the Freshmen Dormitories are indispensable for the quartering of Negro students or why is it that the colored youths do not live with private families. The answer is plain enough. In Cambridge, the colored population, with very few exceptions, is made up of the middle or working class of people with small, modest homes situated some distance from the campus, not too well adapted to lodging college men because of their small, incommodious quarters, inadequate lighting and heating facilities and the utter impossibility of getting board at one's lodging place, or in the one or two instances where board can be got the striking lack of unwholesomeness of the food and culinary art in its preparation. Those persons of the so-called leading families do not make a practice of taking lodgers of any kind, as is true among the upper class of whites.

All things considered the Negro student body is faced with a more momentous question than one readily appreciates and it is only given its full significance when one begins to wonder what will be the next move? Will Harvard next adopt the Yale policy and announce that "because of the growing southern element (sentiment?) and their displeasure at the possibility of coming in contact with Negroes in the voluntary dormitories, it is thought that the best way to preserve the comity of race relations is to hereafter forbid Negroes from living in any of the dormitories." The next most logical step would be to bar them from the college altogether because of the contact in the class-rooms! The bare possibility of this registers a shudder and thrill in the heart and soul of the present Negro students; but this is not at all unlikely if one reflects on the significance of the present policy.

"Dormitories or no dormitories, Negroes will always go to Harvard" is the cry of some; but this is not meeting the issue squarely. Moreover, it is a bare conjecture based on a false assumption if the current freshmen Negro number is at all a fair criterion. The issue must be met by constructive effort on the part of many groups, by the Negroes themselves, i. e., the Negro alumnae and present student body, by pressure brought to bear on the General Alumnæ Association, support from the influential members of the faculty who are fair and impartial, circularizing the white undergraduates or in some manner presenting them with the truth of the situation as herein attempted to be outlined, for their reflection asking for an expression of opinion on their part, finally, by acquainting the Board of Overseers with the magnitude of the significance of their acts on the race in its strides for higher education of its young men, to develop the proper type of leadership, and the psychic effect it will have on the white student body and the citizens of this section of the country in bringing to their minds the fact that *Harvard* realizes that there is an "eternal, fundamental, and inescapable difference" between the two races. No better time affords itself for approaching these groups and working among them than the present, while the matter is still fresh in the minds of the people, and when the press of the country has in a large majority of cases given our cause such great support. It will be of no little interest to state that at present there are movements under way by two of the above groups that stand in a powerfully strategic position. First, there is an organization of white students which is canvassing the undergraduate body in the effort to get a prevailing sentiment against the policy of the President and to present him with a petition, on his return from Europe, to reconsider his stand and revoke the rule on the ground that, "the very persons who would be affected by the admission of Negroes into the dormitories, do not find such a state of affairs objectionable". Secondly, there are reports, not yet verified, that certain members of the faculty are forming a petition to the President and the Board of Overseers, to reconsider such action stating that "any form of racial discrimination is a serious departure from true Harvard principles, and would violate very precious Harvard traditions" substantially the stand of President Emeritus Charles W. Eliot. It is submitted that these two movements, if carried through in full, will have an incalculably great effect.

Harvard does mean something to the Negro. We cannot but look with pride at the list of America's outstanding Negroes and feel an indescribable love for the institution that has honored such men, that has given them their training, industry and resourcefulness, that stamps them as men of calibre, ability and integrity; men who by their deeds have gained the respect and admiration of an entire race, indeed, of the whole country. The University that has cast such men as Greener, W. E. B. DuBois, William H. Lewis, Carter G. Woodson, Archibald Grimke, and the host of others including Marshall, Matthews, Bruce, Morton, Jackson, and Pope; that honored Booker T. Washington with a degree for his great achievements, cannot hold only a passive interest for the Negro.

There is much to be gained at Harvard; there is overwhelmingly much to be lost by Harvard closing its doors to our boys, not alone from the loss of the privilege of studying within its walls; but from the loss of the priceless inspiration from the heritage of able Negroes who passed on before, and the ruthless destruction of the significance of their deeds and accomplishments by their own Alma Mater.

THE NEGRO LAWYER

At the time this essay was published in September 1931, Raymond Pace Alexander was a prominent Philadelphia lawyer. He had been president of the National Negro Bar Association formerly, and the following essay is an excerpt from an address he made to that organization. Alexander contends that African-American lawyers have a unique opportunity to make a lasting contribution to American jurisprudence.

In the State of New York, we read a few years ago with great interest the attempt of a wealthy son of an old and distinguished New York family to have the Courts of New York declare void his marriage to a mulatto girl, whose features and color were that of an Anglo-Saxon, because at the time of the courtship and marriage he alleged he believed the girl to be white and that this concealment of her racial identity (this is stating it very liberally) was the withholding of a material fact which was tantamount to deceit; and the Court, as a matter of law, he alleged, should declare the marital contract null and void. The Courts of New York, however, took a different view and held both in the lower and the Appellate Court that this did not amount to deceit and refused to disturb the relationship. This case is familiar to us as *Rhinelander* vs. *Rhinelander*.

In Chicago recently a wealthy white man, a Yale graduate, past 70 years of age, married his colored housekeeper who had been his most loyal, kind companion during the 20 years that he had been a widower. Immediately, some of his disappointed kinsmen took legal proceedings to declare him of unbalanced mind and to have a guardian placed over him on the ground that his estate would be jeopardized and squandered by the enterprising colored woman who had been his constant source of happiness and companionship since the death of his wife! The Cook County Courts, after hearing the petition, clearly interpreted its intent and refused to molest the man in his quest for full domestic happiness.

In California, twenty years ago, a colored man, born in Virginia of colored parents, he however, being very light in complexion, married a well-to-do white woman without labelling himself "colored" and afterward made a fortune in the brokerage business. His wife was independently wealthy and, in addition, inherited a large sum of money from her parents. She pre-deceased her husband, leaving the bulk of her estate to the latter. Just before he came into possession of it his brokerage house became involved in the use of the mails to defraud and he was sentenced to the penitentiary. His colored relatives, some of whom reside in Philadelphia, reading of this in the papers, put in appearance for his defense. Upon the kinsmen of the deceased wife learning of the racial identity of the husband, they took proceedings to declare the original marriage null and void under a particular California remedial statute. The California Courts supported the petition and allowed the annulment which had the effect of disinheriting the husband from taking any part of his wife's estate.

During the last year, in the same jurisdiction, a Portuguese, one Louis Gomez, living in San Francisco, was described in "The Daily News" of that city as "Louis Gomez, a Portuguese Negro," and immediately brought suit in the Supreme Court of California, in the City of San Francisco, for damages, charging a libellous publication, on the mere printing of these words. The Supreme Court, after reviewing the authorities, mostly from Southern States, which would allow an action for damages for the mere mistaken description of a white person, designating him a Negro, said: "In reference to a publication of the character here complained of, the effect must depend very largely upon the condition, sentiment and sectional feeling of the particular community, and the moral, intellectual and social standards of both the colored and white population.... The colored residents of San Francisco are as a class progressive, self-respecting and law-abiding ... such as would not justify a Court in declaring as a matter of law that a publication describing a white person as a Negro as ... libellous per se ... since it imputed no crime or moral turpitude."

The foregoing illustrations of actual cases in our Courts showing in three widely separated sections of our country attempts to put into our law books decisions that reflect adversely upon an entire race of people, are instances of a positive nature that the Negro in today's social order is not in a position to be envied. The illustrations are pernicious in their bold and insulting purpose. Yet, one can see somehow that the motivating force behind most of the cases with the possible exception of the last cited case, was the customary American greed for gold and in the Rhinelander case it would seem that this was an attempt on the part of the proud Nordic family to prevent the mulatto girl from enjoying or possibly inheriting the wealth of the family of her white husband.

Not only are we faced with humiliation of the type described above but anywhere in our large cities where there are large numbers of colored residents, we find creeping up all about us, under our very eyes, a definite trend in the direction of infringing and restricting the very basis of our social liberties and rights to enjoy free society. This is not alone perpetrated on those of us who happen to be of the laboring class, but it has happened, very probably, to all of us who may read this article. Just one square from my office in Philadelphia a few months ago I was refused service at a soda fountain of the United Cigar Stores because of my color, the clerk at the soda fountain informing me that he received orders not to serve colored people at the fountain. On another corner, one square distant from my office, in one of the Stanley Playhouses, my wife, also a member of the Philadelphia Bar, was refused a seat on the lower floor of an ordinary motion picture house. These acts have given rise to litigation in our Courts.

During the Christmas holidays one of the Assistant Professors at Howard University School of Fine Arts, a graduate of the University of Pennsylvania, came to Philadelphia on a brief visit and stopped at one of our chain restaurants for luncheon, just two squares from the Pennsylvania Railroad Station. He cautiously selected a cafeteria, or a self service restaurant, of the Horn and Hardart chain, because of the fear of not being given service at one of the tables where there were waiters. He stood in line with his tray amid a group of white men of questionable stamp, all of whom were served, and when Assistant Professor Hilliard Robinson asked for his food the cafeteria counter man stood mute, declined to give him service. On appeal to the manager he was told that colored people were not served in that cafeteria.

The problem that faces the Negro in his social relations is increasingly difficult and the duty that faces the Negro attorney, his responsibility to society and to his race, seems to be not only very clear and definite, but is a challenge that must command his immediate attention.

It is not enough that we are to be embarrassed and humiliated by the periodic attempts of ill-willed legislators of many States in their efforts to have made part of their State laws acts to prohibit marriage between colored and white people. This we are accustomed to. We are constantly confronted with litigation of the nature before discussed that must serve to awaken the Negro Bar of the country to a renewed sense of public and race responsibility in our efforts to advance the general cause of the Negro in his relations to the American people and thus gain for him the respect that he is entitled to and that should be his by right as a people proud of his race and its accomplishments.

As lawyers we are members of an ancient and honorable profession. We are called the ministers of justice, yet we are constantly brought face to face with such acute problems in the administration of law that we, as lawyers of color, ponder and wonder if justice, as defined at the head of the Institute of Justinian as "the constant and perpetual willingness to render to everyone his right," actually exists as far as the Negro is concerned.

We lawyers are the conservators of the law. We owe the law more than merely using it as a means of making a livelihood. We owe to our people, who, more than any other people are in need of our services, a duty to see that there shall be a quick end to the discrimination and segregation they suffer in their everyday activity, and the continual infringement of their rights to enjoy a free and intramingled existence the same as any other American citizen. And who, may I ask is more able to guard against further and more dangerous encroachments of the rights of the Negro than a body of well-trained and well-organized lawyers?

The Negro lawyer in the future cannot any longer rest on his laurels and divest his mind of deep responsibilities that he owes to his race, if he is to be progressive and a leader among his people. We have too long brought ridicule upon ourselves and engendered lack of confidence by our spirit of aloofness from those problems that confront the very people to whom we are responsible for a living and whose problems are none the less our own and which confront us in every walk of life and in our daily activities.

The intolerant spirit in America today, next to the grave question surrounding the enforcement of law, is America's most perplexing question. The Negro finds intolerance his most difficult problem; intolerance socially, economically and politically. The actual cases cited are typical of the intolerance he feels in his social relations, and these exist in matters where the contact with his white brothers is so impersonal as hardly to be classed within the sphere of social relations.

We find today, however, a type of discrimination where the Negro seeks employment in industry and the manufacturing trades, in the service occupations, such as hotel and restaurant workers, in general domestic service occupation in the homes of well-to-do families that is more dangerous and far-reaching in effect than any kind we have heretofore experienced and which, unless checked, will bring the most disastrous results. This is especially true in the Northern and Eastern states.

We are faced with changes in the economic world as regards the Negro, which must be considered a problem to be faced not only by the established social, welfare and advancement agencies working in the interest of the colored people, but as a challenge to the attention of the American Negro lawyer because such a vital problem is one that attacks the fundamental right to work, free from race influences; it is one that strikes at the very root of our existence. It is only too clear that we are gradually finding it a thing of the past to expect certain types of employment to be given colored people because of tradition. The hotel services, trades, such as waiters, bell-men and maids; employment in large buildings such as elevator operators, janitors, etc., and even employment in the maintenance of way departments of our large railroads and in our municipal corporations; employment in many of the low wage scale jobs in our large industries is no longer considered the type of employment that a Negro can expect without competition from his white brothers who now eagerly seek such employment.

Recent occurrences in the political world have given rise to profound thought among Negro lawyers everywhere as to what should be their future political activities. We look with amazement upon the inglorious treatment given the traditional Negro Republican voter as the result of the policies of the Republican National Committee during the last Presidential campaign. We review in our mind the attempt of the Republican organization to refuse the seating of Negro delegates from Mississippi, Georgia, Florida and other Southern states at the Republican Convention in Kansas City in 1928, and their attempt to discredit Negro Republican National committeemen and committeewomen from Mississippi and Georgia to the extent of either unmercifully ignoring and embarrassing them out of the Republican National Committee or prosecuting them for alleged misdemeanors while in office in order to force their resignations. We further view with concern the dispensing of patronage throughout the South to white Republicans and ignoring colored Republican leaders who have for years been the bulwark and strength of the Republican Party in the South. Finally, we saw a more bold attempt to bid for a "Lily White" Republican Party in the South by the nomination of a man for the Supreme Court of the United States, one Judge Parker of North Carolina, who by his own admission made public addresses, stating unequivocally that he did not believe the Negro had advanced to a position in society either to understand or appreciate the responsibilities of government or to be capable of holding public office.

It is incredible to believe that all qualified candidates for office, that all appointees to office, that all persons who are appointed to fill public positions on the basis of their capabilities, can be of one race only, the white race. We have demonstrated that if the Negro is given an equal opportunity to show his merit on the same basis of qualification as his white brother, the results will be equal in a given number of cases, and it is also eminently true that usually one can find a Negro of much better qualifications and training for a given position than the white man because the opportunities are fewer for the Negro and there is a greater number of trained Negroes who will accept such positions than white applicants.

Because of such treatment at the hands of the Republican Party we naturally look for another way to turn politically and wonder what our future course should be. We at once think of the second great political party and see the beneficial results of Democratic allegiance as demonstrated in New York and Massachusetts. We see in New York Negro appointees to high positions in the city and state governments. We see the election to the bench of two Negro judges, men of standing and ability, in the recent state-wide elections. We view with interest equally good results in the City of Boston. But, in the same picture we see positive laws enacted by our Federal Government designed to prevent discrimination of the Negro's right to vote in primary and general elections in either party, such as the 15th Amendment and enforcement acts such as Section 20, Chapter 3 of the Federal Criminal Code hurled to the winds and ignored. We see the Federal officials in Texas telling the Federal Government in Washington by actions, the same thing that Coleman Blease of South Carolina said in words "To hell with the constitution" when a Negro in Texas attempts to vote the Democratic ticket. We simply *cannot* vote in the Democratic primary in many parts of the South, principally in Texas, Nixon vs. Herndon, 273 U. S., 536 and U. S. vs. Moseley, 238 U. S., 383, to the contrary, notwithstanding. When we appeal to the Federal District Attorney in Texas for relief he refuses to grant a writ of injunction. The Federal Attorney General tells you he is powerless to act except through his District Attorney in Texas and if they won't we are denied our constitutional rights by the actions of the Federal Judges appointed to protect and guarantee such rights. (See actions of Federal District Judges Duval West and Joseph Henderson at Southern District [Houston, Texas] and Western District [San Antonio] during the Democratic

Primary Election cases in 1928). One liberal and fair-minded young Democratic judge who granted such a writ in 1919 in Waco, Texas, was not only defeated for re-election, but was so severely ostracized and criticized, reduced in position in society, because of his liberal actions, that he later committed suicide, leaving a memo to the effect that his friends had killed him. He said his people did not appreciate a good lawyer and an honest judge.

We are forced by circumstances to adopt the position that we shall cast our ballot, not by virtue of traditional allegiance, not because the Republican Party was the party of Lincoln, but shall vote for the man—for the party that offers opportunities to the men and women of color to participate in the affairs of government by appointing to public positions of responsibility and credit and by endorsing and supporting Negro men and women to high elective or appointive offices.

The political future of our race should intimately concern the Negro lawyer, if he hopes to meet the problems that confront his race and himself, which retard the development of his people and his own development. The progress of events in the few years just passed have taught us the vital need of greater education of the Negro, the urgent need of the freedom of learning and the need to avail ourselves of the results of scientific investigations in our three spheres of human relationships, our social relations and our economic and political activities. The assurance of the future lies in the education of the masses and the development of a new and more liberal public opinion resting on the broad liberal culture within our group which will reflect a greater appreciation by the white people of the merit and accomplishments of the Negro race.

The future of the Negro lawyer, notwithstanding the difficulties he will face, is nevertheless, very bright. It depends, however, not so much on the future of American institutions as we know them or the future of society if we wish to call it that, as it does upon the men and women themselves who make up the Negro Bar. Our problems are distinctly different from those of our white brothers at the Bar. Not only are we faced with all the popular distrust of the laymen for the attorney, the lack of his faith in the machinery of justice and even his disbelief in the honesty and integrity of our Courts, but in addition his native disbelief in the integrity and ability of his Negro brother as an advocate before the Courts. He has a commonly accepted belief that the lawyer is one who by skillful and cunning manipulation can "put over" a certain result largely through politics and graft rather than honesty of purpose and ability.

Our courses of study, our course of apprenticeship, our course of conduct at the Bar will determine our future. We are cognizant of the fact, however, that we do not have the opportunity to learn from practice and from contact with the old, long established law firms the rules of conduct, of practice and the practical ethics of the profession. This is a limitation we face that is difficult to overcome. We cannot boast of long established firms. Those we do have are limited in size and cannot care for the young men who seek and should have, whether the law provide for it or not, legal internships—or a period of apprenticeship. The graduate may stand at the head of his class at the leading law school of the country but he will find no large and well established law firm of the white race that will accept him.

We Negro members of the Bar of America face the unusual opportunity of making a lasting contribution to American Jurisprudence not yet attained by our white brothers and that is the cultivation of respect for the written law and by our actions, forcing our white contemporaries into a more tolerant and indulgent attitude with respect to the laws designed for the protection of our rights which are now ignored but which we can in this manner make them respect.

THE PRACTICAL VALUE OF
HIGHER EDUCATION

At the time this essay was published in February 1923, Kelly Miller was a dean at Howard University in Washington, D.C. Miller discusses the need for African-American educators to be motivated by a sense of racial responsibility. He argues that "the quickening power of racial motive" is the great challenge before black educators. He concludes by offering a practical and essential challenge for black educators.

In the February number of the Dial, Bertram Russell, the mathematical sociologist or the sociological mathematician, has an informing article on "Freedom in Education: A Protest Against Mechanism." We read, "machines are admirable servants, but until we have made them *mere* servants we shall not reap the benefit of their service."

There are two wide apart theories of education. The one claims that man should be educated for his worth, the other that he should be trained for his work. The one aims to produce a *man* working, the other a *working man*. The highest expression of the former is in terms of manhood, of the other of mechanism. One contends that the metal should be toughened and tempered regardless of the end to which it is to be put, the other maintains that the crude material should at once be shaped into the desired implement of service. One school believes that acquired discipline and culture can be translated into any mode of service, the other denies that formal discipline and culture have any value.

To educate the head, the hand and the heart is but to educate the man in spots. The wiser policy is to educate the *man*, of whom hand and head and heart are but component faculties. That education is of most worth which enlightens the nature in all of its parts and powers. In this practical age there is little tolerance for abstract doctrine and fruitless theory that do not immediately translate themselves into the actualities of things. The whole world has been profoundly influenced by this tendency. The stress of educational emphasis has been shifted from the passive to the active voice. To be somebody is less praiseworthy than to do something. It is meaningless to be a man unless the manhood is manifested in practical workmanship.

This tendency towards the practical aim in education is greatly accentuated when applied to the colored race. The higher educational institutions for the Negro are still on an altruistic foundation. During the last forty years the trend of Negro philanthropy has been running towards the concrete and the practical. The supporting race is reverting to the old belief in the mechanical function of the Negro in the white man's scheme of things. The Negro was regarded as a good hand, just as one speaks of a good ox or a good ax. His highest value and virtue consisted, not in his quality as a man, but in his utility as a tool.

The World War has shattered most of our revered ideals, and substituted no others in their place. Some one has said that the only thing that America gained from the war was prohibition and the "flu"; if we add the Ku Klux Klan the quota of gain will be complete. How shall we reshape our shattered educational ideals? still remains an unanswered query. No educator or educationalist has yet successfully essayed to restate these older aims in terms of the new conditions. To restate the case in terms of the peculiar and especial needs of the Negro is hardest of all.

Any discipline that purifies and ennobles the nature and imparts the right impulse towards the issues of life should be considered of the highest form of practicability. When the test is applied to the Negro, however, it usually resolves itself into what he shall eat, what he shall drink and wherewithal he shall be clothed.

I will make my own definition of a practical education, to operate within the limits of the present discourse. That education is practical which makes the Negro a better man and a better citizen, and renders him a more effective instrument of service to his race. I will not waste while attempting to differentiate between the several types of education. The futility of such contention is demonstrated by the fruitless controversy of the last half generation. Any form of education whether it pushes up from the bottom or pulls up from the top is working towards the same objective of race uplift and reclamation.

The chief aim of what I constrained to call the higher education is to produce an efficient leadership. Any segregated or semi-segregated group is doomed unless it develops and sustains its own leadership and wise self-direction. The Catholic priesthood with its high standards of intelligence and consecration is the salvation of the non-Protestant foreigners who flock to our shores. The Jewish Rabbi with his high cultural and ethical aims is the light of Jewry in all parts of the earth. The laboring world struggled in vain against the overlordism of capital until it began to raise up a set of instructed leaders who understand the intricate issues of capital and labor as well as the adversary against whom they contend. The red Indian has gone the way of all weak peoples who fail to develop an enlightened leadership. Unless the Negro falls under wise and instructed guidance out of his own group he will be doomed to a like fate. No white man can guide him within the limits of the area of his circumscribed life and opportunity.

The present temper of the American people assigns the Negro to separate social areas and segregated limits. How permanent these limits are to be is largely a matter of abstract speculation. They exist today and will continue for the time with which we are now concerned. The decision of the Supreme Court upholding the validity of the Fifteenth Amendment will not give a single additional vote to the Negro in the state of Mississippi. The nullification of the segregation ordinances has no perceptible effect upon the growth of Harlem. The Negro of the immediate generation with which we are concerned must qualify to exploit racial and segregated opportunities. The segregation of the Negro makes it necessary that his professional and higher needs be met by professional men of his own race. The Negro teacher, preacher, doctor, lawyer, editor, writer and social worker become a social necessity. Hence the importance of the Negro college and University to train men and women of this blood for the high offices to which they are assigned by our social scheme. Just in proportion as the spirit of segregation increases the demand for internal leadership becomes intensified. All will agree that professional workers should have about the same degree of education regardless of the social advantages or disadvantages of the field to which they may be called to labor. The arrogant and exclusive attitude of the white race effectually bars the white worker from this field regardless of his personal disposition. No race, even through its most sacrificing members, can furnish intimate guidance for a despised people where existing regulations make it obligatory for them to eat at separate tables, to ride in separate coaches and to walk the streets apart. The function of the Negro college is to prepare the choice men and women of the race to fill the high places of intellectual, moral and spiritual authority as guide philosopher and friend of their less fortunate brethren. The people perish for want of vision as well as for want of provision. The blind cannot lead the blind less they both fall into the ditch.

To give concrete illustrations of the practical value of the higher education of the Negro, I would mention: 1. To prepare Negro youth for the sacred office of the Christian ministry. The great religious estates have already been prepared by those who have gone before. There exist religious denominations with over four million members demanding fifteen thousand highly educated and consecrated men to command the pulpit. Our colleges today are lamentably failing in their highest practical function, in that they are not inspiring the youth with the moral and spiritual ardor for this high and holy task. If the pulpits of the race might be manned and commanded in the next half generation by the best mind and heart and conscience of the race, all of our complex problems would be well on the way to solution. If on the other hand our churches are to fall into the hands and under the manipulation of the poorly equipped and illy prepared, the general life will sink to a lower level, whatever our achievements in other directions.

2. We need thirty thousand teachers to enlighten the youth according to the standard of modern pedagogic requirements.

3. The field calls for ten thousand physicians to take the place of those now in practice as they may be eliminated by time and to meet the growing demands of the healing profession. The standard of school of medicine have been formulated so that no one can become a licensed practitioner who has met at least one-half of the requirements of a college degree.

4. There is need for several thousand lawyers to protect the life and property of their people. There are fundamental principles of human rights and legal interpretation which the lawyer must fathom and unfold. The white jurist lacks the stimulus of actual and acute needs of his constituents for such insistence. The rights of no people or group will be long vouchsafed unless they develop out of their own midst jurists with the interest and learning to safeguard them.

5. Hundreds of editors, writers, scholars and thinkers are required by the needs of the masses whom they are to lead and enlighten, guide and direct.

6. There is springing up a new profession of social service calling for increasing numbers of men and women of the requisite impulse and motive, and with the specific training for this new field of service.

Collegiate education furnished the necessary stimulus for the higher aims of industrial and mechanical pursuits. Engineers, agriculturalists, architects, and leaders in the practical arts can be prepared for their function only thru the agency of the higher education.

These as well as other lines of endeavor, not here enumerated, impose upon the Negro college as responsible a burden as that borne by any portion of the educational world. No one of these callings can be adequately or efficiently fulfilled without a goodly measure of the training and equipment which the higher education is calculated to impart.

Our higher educational institutions today are in a sad pathological condition. The power of the philanthropic impulse imparted by the good missionaries from the north has all but died away. The old knife has grown dull and needs newness of blade and keenness of edge. The technical letter increases while the quickening spirit grows feebler. Our intelligentsia does not effectually grasp the actualities of racial life and uplift as the founders of our colleges hoped they would do. How to reinvigorate our collegians with the sense of racial responsibility and the quickening power of racial motive is the great task that devolves upon us. There is no problem that is more practical and pressing than this.

NEGRO HISTORY

When this essay was published by Kelly Miller in March 1926, the significance of collecting and preserving African-American history had not yet become a recognized priority among many in the black community. Nonetheless, a number of organizations were making attempts to research the history of black Americans. Miller writes in this essay about Carter G. Woodson's Association for the Study of Negro Life and History. According to Miller, the association proved incalculable in its value to scholars. Called the "Father of Negro History," Woodson devoted much of his energy to publishing and promoting books on the history of his race.

The Association for the Study of Negro Life and History has just completed its tenth anniversary. During the past two decades a number of movements have arisen among Negroes with the aim of improving and advancing racial welfare in distinctive fields of endeavor. The older type of organization with universal scope to better the condition of the race "morally, educationally, spiritually, financially and socially," has given way to more definite lines and specific spheres. Among these may be mentioned the Young Men's Christian Association, the Young Women's Christian Association, the Urban League, the National Association for the Advancement of Colored People which wisely limits its activity to civil rights, The National Medical Association, the Negro Year Book and the Association for the Study of Negro Life and History. The last two are distinctive in that they are wholly concerned with research in the field of racial knowledge and the publication of statistical and historical data.

The Society for the Study of Negro Life and History was born in the brain of Carter G. Woodson. Its conception, inspiration, growth and development are the outgrowth of his personal genius and energy. Mr. Woodson, by his own unaided effort and undaunted endeavor, pushed his way up from the coal mines of West Virginia, through Berea College, and then through the University of Chicago, winding up with the doctorate from Harvard University. He gained a wide and varied range of teaching experience in his native state, in the Philippine Islands, in the public schools of Washington, in Howard University. The restrictions of the school room did not furnish free scope to exploit his specialty implied in the degree "Doctor of Philosophy in His History." In the meantime his life purpose was taking shape and direction in his mind. His dominant purpose was to turn his historical training and preparation to the best racial account. "The Education of the Negro Prior to 1861" was his first attempt at publication in his chosen field. The sharp limitations of the treatise implied in the title is indicative of the accuracy and thoroughness of his method. This volume is the only treatise which covers the field marked out with adequate research and scholarship. Several other historical works attest his indefatigable industry, scholarly accuracy as well as his modern method of treating historical material.

Ten years ago, while still engaged in teaching, Dr. Woodson organized the Association for the Study of Negro Life and History and launched the *Journal of Negro History*, as the official organ to publish the output of its research. The Journal is a quarterly scientific magazine which publishes carefully selected and accurately treated topics of historical character concerning the Negro people. Forty numbers of this Journal have already been issued which have found their way into every important library in the United States and indeed in many foreign countries. The Association for the Study of Negro Life and History has already more than justified its existence and should it wind up its affairs with its tenth anniversary, Dr. Woodson's historical contribution would stand as his enduring monument.

The literature of the race problem abounds mainly in propaganda based upon opinion and argumentation. The importance of collecting and collating exact and accurate material has not yet received the recognition which it deserves. We are so anxious to solve the race problem, that we do not take time to study it. Infallible assumption and passionate dogma take the place of carefully ascertained fact and calm analysis. The largest measure of our admiration is due to the Negro who can divest himself of momentary passion and prejudice and, with self detachment, devote his powers to searching out and sifting the historical facts growing out of race relationship and present them to the world, just as they are, in their untampered integrity.

The Association for the Study of Negro life and History is furnishing the material which will be of incalculable value to students and scholars of race relations, not only in the immediate future but in the remoter years to come. This organization possesses what might be termed a strategic timeliness. America is just acquiring the scientific method of handling historical material. Dr. Woodson is, I believe, the first member of his race to receive complete university training and equipment for scientific historical inquiry. The facts involved in the contact of the African with the Western World are scattered throughout many sources which are growing less and less available as the years go by. Like the Sibyline books, the value increases as the volumes decrease. Many private libraries contain irreparable material, which will be disseminated or destroyed unless it is utilized during the life time of the compilers. Much invaluable material is now confirmable by living memory, which, within a few years, will pass beyond reach of consultation. Now is the time of all times to gather up the documents and to collect and collate the racial material which they contain.

Dr. Woodson has made every possible sacrifice for the cause to which he is devoted. In the beginning of the movement he beggared himself that the work might succeed. The work of the Association for the Study of Negro Life and History soon approved itself to the historical scholars of the country. Dr. Woodson had studied both at Chicago and Harvard. The historical departments of both of these great universities at once recognized the importance of what he was endeavoring to do. The great philanthropic foundations began to find out what was being accomplished and furnished substantial assistance. Among those making personal donations to the cause we find such well known philanthropists as Jacob H. Schiff, William G. Wilcox, Morefield Storey, James J. Storrow, Frank Trumbull, Cleveland H. Dodge, Morton D. Hulland and Julius Rosenwald.

Largely through the good offices of Dr. James R. Angell, then President of the Carnegie Corporation, now President of Yale University, an annual grant of five thousand dollars was secured for five years beginning in nineteen twenty-one. The Laura Spelman Rockefeller Memorial, at the same time, awarded a grant of five thousand dollars for five years, to be used specifically for the study of the Free Negro prior to the Civil War and the Negro in the Reconstruction of the Southern States. Upon the basis of these grants and other private donations, the Association has been enabled to accomplish worth while work which speaks for itself.

The project has gone far beyond the ability of one man to operate. Dr. Woodson has on his staff several carefully trained Negro students in present day historical method through whom, under his direction, much of the research work is accomplished. It is to be hoped that the grants and donations to this work will continue with increased largess. Philanthropy can hardly be bestowed more efficiently or upon a more deserving cause, in its immediate and ultimate bearing upon the tangled issue of race relationship. In the meantime, the colored people have contributed according to their modest means to this important enterprise, and show a disposition to stand back of Dr. Woodson and uphold his hand in the accomplishment of this important feature of race well-being.

The social importance of history, or perhaps, I had better say, the importance of social history, has become but recently appreciated. As a school boy, I used to read in the text books that history was a record of the deeds and doings of important personages and people. Distinguished achievements and spectacular performances monopolized the entire field of recorded human action. The ordinary deeds and doings of ordinary people did not rise to the level of the historian's concern. But in more recent time we are beginning to recognize that any performance, individual or *en masse*, which influences the course of human progress or retrogression is deemed a contributory factor to history. If no single slave ever rose above the benumbing drudgery of hewing wood and drawing water, nevertheless, slavery and the slave could not be omitted from any trustworthy account of the civilization of the South, and indeed, of the nation. Dr. Woodson has somewhere made a sharp distinction between the history of the Negro and the Negro in history. Too often the artist makes the mountain peaks suffice for the whole landscape. The infinite smaller eminences and depressions are apt to be ignored by the painter bent on exploiting dominant features. But not so with the scientific historian. The battle may be lost for the want of the horse shoe nail as well as for lack of the imperious general. It is said that the loss of the Battle of Waterloo, which turned the tide of European history, might have been attributable to the careless cook whose tough beef steak affected Napolean's usual alertness and enabled the Duke of Wellington to take advantage of his momentary dullness. Henson, the black attendant, accompanied Peary to the North Pole. The menial part played by this sable attendant was an important and essential part in polar discovery. Dr. Woodson is concerned in digging out every significant role which the Negro has played in the American drama. This makes American history, not only full and complete, but true to the actualities of historical happenings.

The Negro is often forced to feel that there is a conspiracy of silence to ignore his best deeds and to exploit his imperfections. If a Negro athlete takes the world's sprinting record, the feat is exploited, while his race is ignored. But if a Negro commits a crime its heinousness is enhanced by reason of the color of the criminal. The reputation of the race suffers seriously by the exploitation of its vices and the suppression of its virtues. The true historian holds the balance true between good and evil. To him the deeds of Judas are as full of historical meaning as those of John. His function is "to smoke out the facts."

The Negro's pride of race is humiliated when he contemplates the great drama of this continent and finds that he is accorded no honorable part in the performance. The tendency is always to glorify the white man and to debase the Negro. The effect upon the spirit of the Negro is deplorably oppressive. If he must forever dwell upon a picture in which all worthwhile deeds are ascribed to white men and none to his own race, whence can he derive spirit and inspiration? So strong has been the tendency towards race belittlement, that even Negroes affect to disdain their own contributions. Some are even ashamed to study about themselves and the doings of their Negro students have been known to feel ashamed of the songs which welled from the heart of their race as the trill from the throat of the bird. How much more ennobling they feel to read about "how Achilles injured the Greeks" than recount the lesser exploits of their own blood? But thanks to Dr. Woodson and the Association for the Study of Negro History, all of this is being changed. The story of ones own blood and breed is naturally of keener interest and zest than the story of an alien. Every Jewish boy's heart feels a little bigger when he reads of the part his race has played in the drama of mankind. Not a single fact creditable to Jewry is ever allowed to escape his attention. See how the women delight to extol the part played by their sex; how the Catholics exploit the achievements of their co-religionists; and so the Negro must learn to know his own story and to love it.

WHERE IS THE NEGRO'S HEAVEN?

Harlem Renaissance white patron Carl Van Vechten's novel Nigger Heaven *(1926) caused quite an emotional sensation within the African-American community because of its title. Kelly Miller lived in Washington, D.C., at the time this essay was published in December 1926. In it, he writes that Van Vechten portrayed a Harlem that lacks seriousness—a place of frolic and fun. Miller offers sociological evidence to rebut the rapidly crystallizing theory that Harlem represents the apex of black culture, and he explains why Washington is still the "Negro Heaven."*

Senator John Sherman, of Ohio, noticing the exceptional advantages and advancement of the colored people of the national capital before the Emancipation Proclamation, called Washington the Negro Heaven. The title has been undisputed until quite recently when New York laid claim to the proud distinction. But Washington is not willing to yield the palm without requiring her rival to prove her claim. Up to the census of 1900, Washington city contained the largest Negro population of any municipality in the United States, if not in the world. The tide of Northern migration, stimulated by the World War, has rapidly swollen the number of Negroes in Northern cities, shifting Washington to the third or fourth place as to the Negro population. According to the census of 1920, New York contained 152,467 Negroes, Philadelphia, 134,229, Washington, 109,966, and Chicago, 109,458. The estimated figures for 1925 greatly increase the lead of the Northern cities and throw Washington still further in the rear.

New York has at present an estimated Negro population of over two hundred thousand, three-fourths of whom are segregated in the Harlem District, which constitutes the so-called Negro Heaven. Undoubtedly the most interesting and spectacular phase of the Negro problem is now presented in Harlem. The Negro's problems grow out of his presence. Such a mass of Negroes suddenly transplanted from Southern towns and villages and from the open country and thrust into the midst of the greatest and most progressive city in the world, partaking of its industrial life and general opportunities, sharing the energy of its rushing current, a part of, and yet apart from the surrounding social scheme, excites the liveliest social interest and attention. The outcome of this field of racial adjustment is bound to be watched with a degree of social attention which no other point of race contact can at present command. The New Negro, of whom we have recently heard so much is nothing but the old Negro exposed to the Harlem environment.

Carl Van Vechten, the well known critic and author of the realistic school has recently published a novel entitled *Nigger Heaven*, which is merely an artistic portrayal of the Harlem Negro, in his gayer mood for joy and jazz.

The mad quest for "kicks" and thrills, the saturnalia of song, dance and wine, the revelry of the cabaret are merely outbursts of Negro nature which would break forth at any place and time under like provocative conditions. The so-called Negro art is merely the Negro soul turning itself wrong side out for white people to weep over and laugh at. The Negro life in Harlem is mainly effervescence and froth without seriousness or solid supporting basis. The riot of frolic and frivolity is characteristic of Babylon on the verge of destruction rather than of Heaven, the blissful abode of tradition.

The Washington Negro occupies a unique place in the scheme of race relationship which gives this group a peculiar and far reaching social significance. While New York, Philadelphia and Chicago have a larger number of Negroes counted by themselves, yet as a percentage of the total population they are practically negligible. Two hundred thousand Negroes of New York in the midst of six million whites have no more relative significance than a single apple in a half bushel basket. On the other hand, the Negroes in Washington constitute one-fourth of the total population, and necessarily color and complicate every feature of the community life. The great metropolitan city plods its accustomed way unconscious of the relative handful of Negroes and unconcerned about them, except in their restricted, segregated area. If every Negro should withdraw over night from the greater New York, nothing would be missed except the jazz and the blues. But with Washington, it is otherwise. The atmosphere and attitude of the national capital is the resultant of many sectional and local components. Here the North and the South meet. The race feeling is the complex of the two. If the population might be likened unto a triangle, it could be said to have a Southern base and a Northern altitude. Socially the Negro is treated according to the formula of the South; while politically, he is dealt with after the notion of the North. In order to establish a plausible basis of political equality, both races were reduced to a political null—on the theory that all zeroes are equal.

In Washington the Negro labors under the same social disabilities or disadvantages as in the South, with the exception of the fixity of law. The federal government cannot afford to vitiate the integrity of the law to meet the exactions of local prejudice and proscription. The silent force of custom and tradition obviates that necessity. There are no jim-crow laws on the federal statute, but there are jim-crow practices under federal connivance. Separate schools exist in the District of Columbia rather by common consent and acceptance than by categorical congressional enactment. There are no separate cars, although sundry futile attempts have been made to this effect. There are no laws forbidding the intermarriage of the races; and yet the two races rarely intermarry. But comprehensively speaking the Negroes of the national capital occupy the same sort of separate social existence as in the South. In public functions involving semi-social contact, the line of demarkation is sharply marked and understood. Occasionally a Negro official falls in line to call on the President at a public levee. Negroes are not accepted as guests in hotels or as patrons in restaurants, barber shops, theaters, or places of amusement, except on the basis of separate assignment of seats and accommodation. The federal government has taken on the spirit and method of local proscription. Negroes in the civil service are segregated, either by separate assignment of rooms, or by being given separate desk assignment in the same room. Mr. William Monroe Trotter, the intrepid editor of the *Boston Guardian,* greatly embarrassed President Woodrow Wilson by confronting him to his face with the charge of segregating federal employes on the ground of race and color. The press of the country sided with Mr. Trotter that the practice was undemocratic, un-American and wrong in principle. But the exposure had little effect upon the practice. Notwithstanding forced explanations, evasions and semi-denials of bureau chiefs and heads of department, segregation continues under Republican and Democratic administrations alike. The writer was a member of a delegation headed by Mr. Trotter to protest the continuance of the invidious practice under President Coolidge. Racial segregation of federal employes was reprobated in principle. Cautious assurance was given that practice would be checked, as it could be prudently done, with hope of its ultimate elimination.

The question of residential segregation is now raging in every city with a considerable Negro contingent, from Atlantic City to Los Angeles, and from New York to New Orleans. The District of Columbia has become the fountain head of this agitation. Attempts to fix legal boundaries of racial habitation have been estoped by decision of the Supreme Court of the United States. In all of the large cities of the country the two races occupy separate residential areas. Public sentiment always finds a way to enforce its feeling as effectively without the law as with it. There are no discriminatory laws on the statute books of New York state, and yet Harlem is as sharply delineated, as if pencil drawn and knife cut. The Negroes are being relegated to the land of Goshen in all our great cities, which as completely pens them in to themselves as were the Jews in the land of Egypt, in the days of the Pharoahs.

The Negro has a habit of falling heir to the fairest portions of the cities in which he dwells. This is certainly true of the capital of the nation. The colored population occupies fully a square mile in the Northwest quadrant, the most favored section, overlooking the Capitol, Washington Monument and the principal public buildings with the Potomac River on the rim of the dim horizon. This section is within easy reach of the business heart by the city and is traversed by the principal arteries of travel and trade. The interlacing broad streets and avenues are lined with choice shade trees planted in the early years of the city's development in harmony with the original design. The beautiful parks, squares and triangles scattered throughout express the last word in municipal landscape planning. The whites are now seeking residence in apartment houses and in remoter suburban subdivisions; but they must needs traverse the Negro section in going and coming from business portions of the city or the public offices. Palatial residences built by the most wealthy and fashionable element a generation ago are now occupied by Negro owners or tenants.

Thus the Washington Negro, unlike his New York rival for the heavenly title, is not crowded into seven-story apartment houses, where normal home life and wholesome social intercourse become all but impossible.

Washington is the only city in the country that has a Negro elite of sufficient size to make it a worthwhile social entity. All social distinction, among black folks as among white, according to the traditional conceit, is based upon occupation. The Negro learned from slavery to look down on people who must needs work with the hands and to idolize and extol those whom circumstances or good fortune lifted above the necessity of manual toil. His contempt for the poor white man who must work for a living the same as himself is deep seated and abiding. The black man's fondness for seizing upon meaningless forms of distinction and of exploiting them to a ridiculous degree is well known. The Negroes of the national capital before the Civil War were mainly free persons. They were a hard working lot with no more social distinctions among them than might be expected among a peasant class. They all worked as waiters, coachmen, barbers, and attendants upon families of wealth. Besides a few school teachers and preachers, there were no Negroes in the so-called higher pursuits such as they are understood today. Colored society with all of its airs and pretensions was created during the days of reconstruction. These were days of sudden and swift transformation among black folk. Lucky Negroes were translated from the corn field to Congress. Negro senators, congressmen, legislators and officials sprung up like magic. Washington was the center of the display of all of this suddenly acquired glory and glamor. The newly made Negro gentility imitated all of the dress and fastidious manners of the master class from whose sway they had recently been released and were easily prone to better the instruction. There used to be a saying in the South: "if you want a thing run into the ground, let the Negro get a hold of it." The whole population of the national capital began to look up to and imitate these artificial standards.

For the first time colored men were given clerkships in the federal government. These positions became at once a badge of social distinction. At the same time a system of public schools was inaugurated which imported Negro teachers from all points in the North where good educational advantages had existed. Picked colored men and women were drawn from all parts of the land by the political and educational attractions of the national capital. For the first time, since Jamestown, there were assembled a considerable body of Negroes who were lifted above the level of manual labor and domestic service. This group constituted what was known far and wide as the Washington colored society.

Upon the overthrow of the reconstruction governments in the South, the political "lame ducks" flocked to the national capital to secure berths in the clerical service of the government. Practically every Negro of distinction sought residence or sojourn here. Frederick Douglass, Senator Bruce, John M. Langston, Governor Pinchback were among the celebrities who helped to give dignity and tone to the newly formed social group. At that time Washington had no rival to the title of "Negro Heaven."

This sudden political influx and the pretentious regime which it inaugurated, produced a chasm in the Negro population which two generations of temperate judgment and good sense have hardly been able to efface. Although under the democratizing effect of the public schools, these arrogant distinctions are gradually fading away, still the social breach between the masses and the classes of Negroes in Washington is more pronounced than in any other city of the country.

It requires a pyramidal ordering of society to give exclusiveness beyond the reach of the multitude. Those who reach the top are looked up to with admiration, jealousy, covetousness and despair by the masses below, who finding themselves hopelessly excluded from the charmed circle, console themselves with the philosophy of the fox who always describes the high hanging grapes as sour. This bad eminence may rest upon blood and birth, as in the South, upon culture and tradition, as in New England, or upon ostentatious wealth among the parvenues of recent riches. But with the New York Negroes there is no traceable line of differentiation. The bootblack, the bootlegger, the gambler, the dancer, the songster, the woman of good looks and glad rags—whosoever will, may come.

The Washington Negro has the only complete school system in the country practically under his own control. Three out of nine members of the Board of Education are assigned to the colored race, who are supposed to see to it that the colored branch of the system suffers no disadvantage in comparison with the whites. The schools are divided into two grand divisions—white and colored in harmony with the understood and accepted policy of the community. The superintendent is a white man under whose general supervision both divisions are operated on equal footing and along parallel lines. The first colored Assistant Superintendent is in charge of all colored schools and has complete original jurisdiction in appointment, promotion and assignment of eight hundred teachers and officials. The colored teachers and officials have the same rank and pay as do the whites of corresponding grade and work. The courses of study and standards of instruction are uniform throughout. In providing for school buildings, appointments and facilities, there is supposed to be absolutely no discrimination. There is an understanding in Congress that the colored schools shall receive their full proportion of appropriations for school purposes. Fifteen thousand Negro children sit at the feet of these eight hundred teachers. The Washington public school system is justly famous throughout the country. The Negro division contributes its full share to this national distinction. The colored high and normal schools enroll over three thousand pupils above the eight grade level. This number of secondary pupils cannot be approximated in any other city—not even New York, Philadelphia and Chicago, with a much larger total Negro population. The faculties of these high and normal schools are recruited by graduates from Harvard, Yale, Columbia, and indeed from every college and University in the North and West which does not limit the opportunity for education and culture to considerations of race and color. There are four women doctors of philosophy from Yale, Harvard, Chicago and from the Sorbonne of Paris, France, in the number. I believe that these are the only Negro women doctors of philosophy from institutions of the highest standing, in the United States.

The annual competitive drill where a thousand male cadets under fifty Negro officers display their military skill before the assembled city constitutes a social event, not paralleled in America, if in the world.

Howard University, the largest and best equipped institution for the higher and professional education of the colored race, is located at the national capital. This institution has over two thousand students drawn from all over the United States and from foreign lands pursuing courses which will fit them to stand in the high places of leadership and authority. The faculty of this institution comprises one hundred and fifty professors and instructors mainly of the colored race who along all lines of the arts and sciences as well as in the technical and professional pursuits dispense wisdom and technique to this multitude of ambitious youth who hunger and thirst after knowledge, Howard University and the public schools together center about the city of Washington the cream of the intelligentsia of the Negro race.

The Freedmens Hospital, acknowledged to be the most complete and best equipped institution of its kind between Baltimore and New Orleans is in close physical juxtaposition and professional relationship with Howard University. This institution is in charge of a colored surgeon-in-chief with a highly skilled staff of assistants under him.

A residuum of the by-gone political glory still lingers in the national capital. Washington is still the headquarters of the Negro politician, although like Othello, he finds that his occupation is all but gone. A few officials are still left, with many more who call but are not chosen. The tradition of senators, representatives, registers, recorders, and other high officials is still here. There are many thousand Negroes on the federal pay roll, which of itself, aligns them with the preferred class among the race.

The Negroes of Washington have reached the point of complete professional self sufficiency. Howard University has turned out an army of physicians, lawyers, teachers and clergymen, who never leave the city as long as there is the slightest likelihood of local need of their services. A white physician of Negro patients is almost as unusual as a white minister of a Negro parishioner. Negro lawyers in the main look after the needs of the Negro client, while the preacher and the teacher have a complete monopoly.

To these may be added an increasing number of successful business men who are beginning to see and to seize the immense business opportunity wrapped up in the needs and necessities of so great a mass of Negro flesh and blood.

So great a body of Negroes, lifted by occupation above the level of ten-fingered service constitute an element of social importance which neither New York nor any other community can hope to approximate.

Washington has the fault or the misfortune of all groups of Negroes everywhere. There is no middle class. The connecting link is missing. There are no local productive industries in the District of Columbia. Realtors and local merchants constitute the sum total of business men. The Negro only in limited numbers enters these lines. The great bulk, except the favored persons above described, are common laborers or domestic servants. The social maladjustment between the upper and the lower levels of position and occupation frustrates concerted action and greatly retards the common progress.

But in Washington, as in New York, the proletariat must be entertained. Theaters, movie houses, dance halls and cabarets are springing up everywhere. There is no lack of facilities for enjoyment on the part of any social element. There is little or no race friction here, of which any considerable portion of the community is conscious for any considerable proportion of the time. Once in a great while some outbreak or agitation arouses the people to self-consciousness; but like a hasty spark, they straightway grow cold again. There is nothing that interferes with the uniformity of a good time among all classes.

The Negro race in every mood is prone to the enjoyment and the delights of life. Moments of grave reflection over the hardships and ills of his lot are quickly forgotten in anticipation of a good time.

Washington is the social capital of the Negro race. Social celebrities from all parts of the country find fulfilment of their highest ambition to shine at some great function in the national capital. Every four years a president of the United States is inaugurated. The occasion is usually featured by an inaugural ball. Although the Negroes may have little cause for jubilation over the incoming administration, they usually have two or three inaugural balls, whereas the whites are satisfied with one. The minor inaugural receptions are too numerous to enumerate. On such occasions, the Negroes usually take option on every available dance hall or place of amusement, placing the whites at a great disadvantage. The writer recalls that on the very night when the fate of the Dyer Anti-Lynching Bill was hanging in the balance in the Senate Committee, the Negroes were fiddling and dancing the time away in every dance house in Washington in celebration of the Thanksgiving festivities. At the time of President Coolidge's inauguration, I counted twenty placards within a few blocks announcing as many different inauguration receptions. I have even seen the announcement of a dance in an undertaker's window. Who says the Negro feels that his is an oppressed race?

The capital city furnishes the best opportunity and facilities for the expression of the Negro's innate gayety of soul. Washington is still the Negro's Heaven, and it will be many a moon before Harlem will be able to take away her scepter.

PUBLIC OPINION AND THE NEGRO

This essay was an address delivered at the National Conference of Social Work in Washington, D.C., on May 23, 1923, by Charles S. Johnson. It was published in Opportunity *in July 1923. Johnson relates some commonly held opinions about African Americans and offers some insights into the origins of these stereotypical views.*

In the study of the influence of public opinion on race relations we are dealing with three important and highly sensitive elements: the facts upon which this opinion rests, the theories about these facts, and most important of all, the actions based on the theories. There are certain physical facts that do not change. It is not the purpose here to deny or make apologies for the existence of them, whatever they are. But with respect to these there is a disposition to assume that the theories about the facts are as unchanging as the facts themselves; to deny the fact when it contradicts the theory; and to see facts when they do not exist because the theory demands them. There are again, generalizations and theories built upon these assumed and actual facts that do change as society develops, and as false statements are refuted and new facts come to light. It is on these theories that the layman is most frequently confounded. Yet upon these as a basis he is constantly acting.

Let us consider the nature of some of the beliefs commonly met in public opinion, and at the same time examine their origins and justifications. Although prejudice and matters of sentiment figure largely in race relations, it is not only possible but necessary to study the origins of these beliefs in a purely objective manner. The growth of feeling in the United States on the question of the Negro is a natural process. No one seriously believes that the conduct of the two races in relation to each other is inspired by moral depravity or mere calculating meanness. No other relations are to be expected on the present background of beliefs, the one race about the other. The greatest difficulty in objectively analyzing these beliefs lies in the fact that we quite generally and naturally regard our views and beliefs, whatever they are, as founded on eternal and unchanging principles. It is not often that we care to question the origin of our most firmly rooted convictions. As James Harvey Robinson points out: "We like to continue to believe what we have been accustomed to accept as true, and the resentment aroused when doubt is cast upon any of our assumptions, leads us to seek every manner of excuse for clinging to them. The result is that most of our so-called reasoning consists in finding arguments for going on believing as we already do." Only within recent years have we begun to study our own thinking processes, and the conditions and tendencies of our social life. Only recently have we ceased to bow down with unquestioning acquiescence to the locally familiar as the universal intention of nature and the ordinance of God. In his attack upon the particular justifications, theories, explanations, and philosophies which, wholly without substantial reason, held women in subjection, John Stuart Mill makes an observation which applies without a single modification, to the question of the Negro:

"When there is feeling mixed with an opinion, it tends to gain rather than lose by having a preponderant weight of argument against it. If accepted as the result of argument, the refutation of the argument might shake its foundation; but when it rests on feeling the worse it fares in argumentative contact, the more persuaded its adherents are that their feeling must have some deeper ground which arguments do not reach, and while the feeling remains, it is always throwing up new entrenchments to repair the old."

The analogy between the struggle of women for status and that of the Negro population, is suspiciously close. Anatomically, mentally, and by an alleged special act of God, both have been arranged in the scheme of creation a little lower than supreme man of the particular race making the comparison. Less than seventy-five years ago women were held unfitted for college education. Governor Winthrop of Massachusetts thought such training would certainly induce insanity. Scientists are still saying, but with a perceptibly weakened sense of conviction, that women measure five ounces less brain matter than men and lack reasoning capacity. It is more than an historical accident that Negro suffrage and woman suffrage were proposed and fought for at the same time. The facts about woman, as for example, that she is different from man had not changed in 1920 when universal suffrage was granted. The theories about the fact, however, had undergone an almost complete revolution.

Some of the familiar and, perhaps, less serious stereotypes of the Negro will be quickly recognized. For example, that they are boisterous, over-assertive, lacking in civic consciousness, that they usually carry razors, shoot craps habitually, are inordinately fond of red, and of watermelon, are afraid of ghosts and graveyards. Mr. H. L. Mencken in "The American Credo" has caught up other points: a Negro's vote may always be readily bought for a dollar. Every colored cook has a lover who never works and she feeds him by stealing the best part of every dish she cooks. Every Negro who went to France with the army has a liaison with a white woman and won't look at a colored woman any more. All Negroes can sing. If one hits a Negro on the head with a cobblestone the cobblestone will break. All Negroes born South of the Potomac can play the banjo and are excellent dancers. Whenever a Negro is educated, he refuses to work and becomes a criminal. Every Negro servant girl spends at least half of her wages on preparation for taking the kink out of her hair. All Negro prize fighters marry white women and then afterwards beat them. All Negroes who show any intelligence are two-thirds white and the sons of United States Senators. The minute a Negro gets eight dollars he goes to a dentist and has one of his front teeth filled with gold. A Negro ball always ends up with a grand free-for-all fight in which several Negroes are mortally slashed with razors.

Jokes about Negroes, news stories, anecdotes, gossip, the stage, the motion pictures, the Octavus Roy Cohen, Hugh Wiley and Irvin S. Cobb type of humorous fiction repeated with unvarying outline, have helped to build up and crystallize a fictitious being unlike any Negro. Usually one of two things happens when a Negro fails to reflect the type: Either he is considered an exception, or he is "out of his place." The sources of information covering this group that might be useful in dispelling many of these notions are most unfortunate. Few white people read Negro periodicals, and they come in contact with only a few Negroes, usually their servants, whom they often seem to regard as omniscient on the aims, individuals and incidents of the race.

It is this mass of ideas about the Negro, accumulated through experience, passed on through tradition, embedded in the mores and absorbed even without conscious attention, with which this paper deals. These are the background of recognition of classification, and of behavior itself. This body of ideas, compounded of time-saving generalizations, stereotypes, myths, conventions, dogma—what Walter Lippman in his excellent volume on PUBLIC OPINION calls "the picture within our heads"—determine our attitudes, our way of interpreting facts, our way even of seeing facts. To quote this author: "Except where we deliberately keep prejudice in suspense, we do not study a man and judge him to be bad," ... "We see a bad man."

False notions, if believed, false preconceptions, may control conduct as effectively as true ones. The moral eruptions observed in the reckless unrestraint of the mob mind, are from one point of view merely an acute phase of the same opinion held by those who condone even while not actually participating in the unpleasant work of the mobs. The "hoodlums", those members of the public least able to sublimate their impulses or restrain their resentments, however acquired, are merely the executioners of prevailing sentiment. The judgment is passed by the community. The riots in Washington, Atlanta, Chicago, East St. Louis, and Omaha are striking examples of the accumulated resentments, unchallenged mutual beliefs, the one race about the other. If these beliefs can be made accessible for examination, there is hope that many of them may be corrected.

There are three cardinal beliefs that may be said to control in one form or another most of the thinking about Negroes: first, that they are mentally inferior; second, that they are immoral; and third, that they are criminal. The alleged innate mental inferiority of the Negro was once held to be due to a difference in species, then again to a more recent emergence from primitive life, and finally to backwardness in ascending the scale of civilization. A natural deduction follows: the mind of the Negro cannot be improved beyond a given level, so quite logically adapting his education to his capacities, he is taught mainly to use his hands. It is most common to hear it advanced as an argument against the entrance of Negro workmen to skilled trades that they are not capable of performing tasks which require sustained mental activity.

On this same theory a Chicago school principal, finding that "colored children are restive and incapable of abstract thought and must be continually fed with novel interests and given things to do with their hands," altered her curriculum to teach them handicraft instead of arithmetic and singing instead of grammar. Again, this theory provides one of the strongest objections to expenditures for Negro education in states where there are separate schools for Negroes—they are uneducable.

Tracing the origin of this theory we find that the first Negroes brought to this country were bond servants on the same footing with indentured white servants, but it soon developed that permanent servitude and the slave traffic were highly profitable. The holding of slaves by a Christian nation demanded some kind of justification—a conscience balm. If it were ethically wrong for one human being to enslave another conscience could best be eased by proving that these slaves were less than human. Accordingly, Biblical arguments founded on Noah and the ark and his three sons, one of whom was cursed, have conveniently supplied support for the unscientific. Charles Carroll wrote a book to establish from Biblical texts the fact that man was created in the image of God, and since God, as everybody knows, is not a Negro, it follows that the Negro is not a man. John C. Calhoun, at a time when Negro slaves were everywhere by intention deprived of the elements of education, with most unbecoming illogic for a statesman, ventured that if he could find a Negro capable of giving the syntax of a Greek verb, he would be disposed to call him human. Thomas Jefferson observed that a Negro could scarcely be found who was capable of tracing and comprehending the investigations of Euclid. This was probably true, but does this justify the formulation of theories that would place this limitation upon Negroes for all time?

Science helped to bolster up the theories. In 1870, Dr. Jeffries Wyman of Harvard discovered that the Negro afforded the point "where man and brute most nearly approached each other." A. H. Keene, author of an anthropology still used found that the black and white human types had no sanguinary affiliation, and that the black was inferior because it registered a lower cranial capacity. Dr. Vogt, an eminent German scientist, deduced the inferiority of the Negro race from the examination of a single Hottentot woman. In 1906, Dr. Bean, who is quoted in most discussions on the intelligence of Negroes, seized upon a theory advanced by Spitzka that brain weights determined genius, and applied it to 150 white and 150 Negro brains. He announced that he had found constant and important variations according to race. Under remarkable circumstances, the accuracy of his findings was tested by Dr. Franklin P. Mall, an associate, who used the same brains, more precise instruments, and concealed the racial labels until the measurements were made. Dr. Mall announced that almost invariably the Negro brains had been underweighed by Dr. Bean, and the white brains overweighed. His final result showed no such "differences" as Dr. Bean reported.

Sir Francis Galton, scientist and the father of Eugenics, based a rather remarkable conclusion concerning the mentality of Negroes upon accounts he had read and heard of the stupidity of Negro servants in America. Such an unscientific basis would have been rejected for any of his other conclusions. E. B. Tyler, author of a text-book on anthropology, assumed from the accounts of European teachers of children of backward races, that after the age of 12 the mentality of colored children is arrested: G. Stanley Hall fixed 14 as the age at which it comes to a partial standstill. Another queer assumption connects their arrested mentality with sexual over-development, thus combining two popularly accepted traits. A few months ago, before a meeting of the Eugenics Education Society in England, Dr. A. F. Tredgold, M.D., F.R.S., Edinburgh, in an address on the inheritance of mental qualities cited as his sole proof of the racial difference in potentiality for development along educational lines, a comparative racial study made by Dr. M. J. Mayo in the public schools of New York City. This study was taken as a fair test because the black and white races were educated side by side. This study has also been quoted in most discussions of Negro intelligence. Whatever the facts are, Dr. Mayo's study could not possibly have discovered them. In the first place, his study was made from records which had to be classified according to race by the memory of the teachers extending back as much as four years. The gradings by which they were measured were largely subjective with the teachers and admitted by the investigator himself to be unscientific. Many of the Negro children were from immigrant families from grossly inferior Southern schools, which might as reasonably be offered as an explanation of their retardation. And finally, as evidence of the subjective character of the gradings, the Negro children made their lowest scores in English and their highest in Mathematics where biased grades are less possible. In spite of all this the difference between Negro and white children finally amounted to no more than four per cent.

Then came the army intelligence tests, which a new school is insisting are a measure of innate intelligence. Again the Negroes have been consigned to their familiar station. They were needed in largest numbers as laborers and fewest in the higher branches of the service; and by admitted design the lowest classes among whites were freely eliminated. The Surgeon General's instructions to the Psychology Division explicitly state that "in the examination of Negro recruits camp procedure should be determined by the practical needs of the army, and the collection of scientific data always incidental to this main purpose." Yet the results are being used by some as the primarily scientific.

Moreover, before judgment can safely be passed upon the finality of the army intelligence tests in determining the inherent mental inferiority of Negroes, the following seldom mentioned facts must be accounted for: (1) The Negroes in most camps were marched in a body to the Beta tests designed principally for non-English speaking recruits; this was done in spite of the objection of practically all the camps that these tests unnaturally limited Negroes. Specifically 65.6 per cent. of the Negroes as compared with 24.7 per cent. of the whites were given the Beta tests. (2) Discrimination was further shown when it came to re-examination, only 20 per cent. of the Negro failures were re-examined, in spite of the fact that 86.9 per cent. of these improved their score anywhere from 3 to 30 per cent. (3) The intelligence gap between Southern Negroes with practically no schools and Negroes living in the North with better educational facilities is eight points greater than the difference between native whites and Negroes. (4) When the native white population of Northern and Southern states, presumably of the same stock, are compared, a similar difference is found: for instance, Connecticut with only a 35 per cent. native white population, registers 30 points higher for white recruits than North Carolina with a 99 per cent. native-born white population. This is a difference greater by 50 per cent. than that shown between the native whites and Negroes. (5) When the factors of bad schools, mass handling, and to a large extent, examiners with a prescience concerning Negro mentality are eliminated, as in the case of Camp Lewis, in a Northwestern section, Negroes register a median score superior to the white recruits in Camp Gordon in the South. And finally, (6) the Negroes recruited from New Mexico registered a score equivalent to the highest rank of whites—the officers.

During slavery when it was the policy to keep Negroes ignorant, and for a period after emancipation when over 90 per cent. of the Negro population was illiterate, it could easily be believed that their illiteracy was unescapable and eternal. But now educability has been demonstrated: illiteracy has been reduced to 25 per cent.; thousands have graduated from standard universities; and thousands have entered the professions. In spite of such facts as these and in spite of its questionable support, the belief in the innate mental inferiority of the Negro persists. It tends to crush the Negro's hope of improvement through education; it insists that Negro education is useless; it distorts honest ambition into a desire to avoid hard work, all effort at honest thinking into impertinence and radicalism, and poise into arrogance and smartness.

The second cardinal belief to be considered concerns the constitutional immorality of Negroes. They are sometimes in charity called unmoral. Frederick L. Hoffman, after a pretentious array of figures concluded that "all his facts proved that education, philanthropy, and religion have failed to develop (among the Negroes) an appreciation of the stern and uncompromising virtues of the Aryan race." A prominent member of this Conference, in a volume published in 1910, gave the stamp of his authority to the belief that "their minds are filled with that which is carnal, their thoughts are most filthy and their morals generally beyond description." He had made his observation in the most disadvantaged sections of the South, among a group of Negroes living in enforced ignorance, whose lack of standards, assuming the accuracy of his observations could be explained by the same circumstances of environment that account for this lack among mountain whites and among mill workers of certain sections.

Not long ago, a professor in an Eastern college made the statement that less than 3 per cent. of the Negro women are virtuous. It got credence in spite of the fact that it is as impossible of proof as a similar statement about any other race. A writer in a prominent sociological magazine a few months ago, after a study of sixteen cases of desertion in Negro families, deduced a philosophy about the family life of 12,000,000 Negroes.

The statistical evidence of immorality consists largely of figures on illegitimacy. Records here are meagre and when found tend to shield those with greater means of secrecy and knowledge of birth control—the number of illegitimate mulattoes and the prevalence of venereal diseases, however, point to a lack of restraint not wholly Negroid. Pure blacks do not propagate mixed breed and venereal diseases were unknown among the Negroes imported to this country. But there is a theory to explain the mulatto population in what is called the "biological urge" of females of inferior races to mate with males of the superior race. This places the latter quite innocently on the defensive. There can be no honest objection to the statement that there are immoral Negroes, in fact, many such. The rub and the real danger come in the assumption that this immorality is the result of a constitutional laxity which is peculiar to Negroes as a race. Here, again, a belief whose foundation is uncertain, tends to cut off all hope of improvement, and place a scarlet letter upon those Negroes who *are* moral when measured by the sternest code. Here, again, revision of theory will reduce the passionate hatred, suspicion and jealousy entertained in many sections by white wives and mothers toward Negro women, and lessen the hazards and actual insults endured in silence and fear by Negro girls who are lumped together in the assumption against their morals.

The third cardinal belief is closely allied with the foregoing, that Negroes are criminal by nature. An alleged peculiar emotional instability predisposes them to crimes of violence, particularly sex crimes, and a constitutional character weakness addicts them to petty thefts. In practically every city with a large Negro population their crime rate exceeds their proportion in the population. There *are* Negro criminals and they are condemned without apology or excuse. But the bugaboo of the *criminal nature of Negroes* is unnecessarily severe. A constitutional criminal nature would most certainly have shown itself during the Civil War when the protective hand of the master was withdrawn from his family and the Negro slave stood guard. Yet not a single case is recorded of the betrayal of that trust. Figures on Negro crime rarely escape factors completely vitiating for comparative purposes. Thus, judges, prosecuting attorneys and jury foremen testified before the Chicago Commission on Race Relations that in Chicago, a northern city, the unvarying tendency was to arrest and convict Negroes more readily and on less evidence than whites and give them longer sentences. The police officers, jurors and court officials are members of the public and mold the common beliefs about Negro traits. These Negroes, further, have less money to fight their cases, to escape detection, to pay fines or even, so far as records go, to bribe officials.

In one part of New York City, to take one example, there were in one year, 9 more white persons *indicted* for rape in the first degree than there were Negroes even *accused* of the crime throughout the United States in four years—and more evidence is required by a New York jury than by a lynching mob. Or put it this way: a predilection for sex crimes can scarcely in fairness be assigned to a race with an average population of eight million, of which number six hundred and seventy-five have been charged with the crime in a period of thirty years. Yet this belief, deepened by its association with the most elemental of human passions, prompts constant and innumerable perversions and absurdities of conduct. A woman screams and a race riot brews; a lurid story in the press even when the criminal is in jail, and the nation's capitol is in the hands of a mob, murder bent. This sex motif ran with more or less prominence through each of the riots.

Although these three cardinal beliefs are the most dangerous—there are others, less important, but worth questioning at least: (a) That the Negro race is physically repulsive—one encyclopedia states that they "emit an odor similar to that of a goat." This is entertained less by those whose children were reared by Negro "mammies" than by those who read about Negroes or are expecting this peculiarity. (b) That they are constitutionally incapable of resisting the ravages of white man's diseases—dying out irredeemably from tuberculosis and venereal diseases—thus making programs of health improvement hopeless, although by a little effort their mortality has been reduced 21 per cent. in 11 years. (c) That they are "happy-go-lucky" and "thriftless" although they own farm lands valued at more than two and a half billion, nearly two million are insured in one large insurance company alone, and one of every four families owns its home.

Now, what of the Negroes themselves? What are the effects of all these beliefs upon them? They cannot escape being assailed on every hand from early childhood to the end of their lives, with a pervading intimation of their own inferiority. From the beginning they are "saturated in a tradition of their own incompetence." This is a poison, as one writer puts it, at the very centers of growth. They grow up in the system inferior not only to the other race, but to their potential selves. They are in the midst of an advanced social system, of definite cultural influences, but denied full participation. They may never escape the insistent implications of their status and race. Attention and interest are centered upon themselves. They gradually become race conscious. Opinions and feelings on general questions must always be filtered through this narrow screen that separates them from their neighbors. Their opinions are therefore largely a negative product—either disparagement of difficulties or protest. This enforced self-consciousness has developed strange distortions of conduct, in many, increasing sensitiveness to sights and fabricating compensations for their inferior station. Natural impulses and desires are balked. Their conduct becomes unintelligible. The processes of thought by which opinions are reached and translated into action are as a result of their isolation, concealed from outsiders. It has been observed for example, that the "old-time darky" is passing. This is probably but another way of putting the very real fact that rapidly developing industrialism, increased literacy, mobility, and means of communication, and the irresistible trend of present-day forces that are upsetting the old order and creating new desires generally, has affected the Negro as they have all others. A writer in the *Century* magazine makes an apt observation when he says that the "peaceful co-existence of rules and ruled is possible only where relations between classes remain static for long periods of time." This condition is favorable to the growth of traditions, the love of common things and the manifestations of kindliness and loyalty. This country's static conditions were broken up by the Civil War. Those who picture the Negro of that regime forget that he is being swept along by the same tide that wrecked the institution of slavery and increased the tempo of our whole rational life. He is, indeed, not the same and it is inconsistent to expect him to be. The World War brought about another jolt of traditions, and simultaneously a different outlook on life from Negroes. Their new desires and behavior are regarded as peculiar and dangerous. The only reaction is increased measures of restraint which neither destroy nor change the attitudes.

The back to Africa movement among Negroes is a dramatic demonstration of their attitude towards their status. This rather absurd dream, to which more than a million Negroes are contributing funds, is more than a gesture to escape America. It is a movement of the class lowest down to fabricate a background and a racial self-respect, to compensate for the prestige and power they have habitually lacked. The extravagant titles of the movement like those of the K. K. K. help to clothe little men with the importance and prestige they otherwise would not have.

The movement is significant further not because of any possibilities of realization, but because it provides at least a mental relaxation for hundreds of thousands of Negroes in the picturing of a complete escape from the constant and unrelenting embarrassments under which they must live and while living present the air of contentment and of happiness.

A second effect registers in the mass movements of Negroes from south to north. Over a half million have moved within the last six years. Probably 100,000 have moved in the last year. The motives have been both economic and sentimental. Both desires are evidences of dissatisfaction and unrest, and these dissatisfactions are in large part the result of changing standards among the Negroes.

A third effect is flight of quite a different sort. It is that of leaving the Negro race entirely—"crossing over" it is called. When a person of partial Negro descent who is to all appearances indistinguishable, elects to class himself as a Negro, he voluntarily assumes all of the limitations placed upon that group. But he is an equal and an eligible to all forms of association with whites so long as he forgets the black twig on his family tree. Dr. Hornell Hart estimates this forgetfulness to be occurring in about 25,000 new cases each year. The subject does not yield itself readily to statistical treatment and the estimate is probably overstated, but it is a fact that as the ring around the Negroes grows tighter it is squeezing out many who can easily escape, and thus beginning a process which the most zealous upholders of the American dogma have declared could never occur and which they are most anxious to prevent.

Now it is important to recognize that the most serious clashes of interest come in that vague and intangible world of feeling where reason ceases to function. Attitude and opinions have been set and ground into tradition. Demand for reasons is absurd and infuriating, because they are perhaps the least important and least convincing factors in a confirmed attitude. Where there is general agreement on the premises they are unnecessary but where, as in the case of a less prejudiced person, the premise is questioned and it is necessary to support one's attitude, there is a temptation, rarely avoided, to compensate for deficiency in fact by embellishing it to fit the feeling. A Negro becomes a "burly Negro." Objection to their presence in public meetings is based on smell. Instead of smiling they "grin" or "expose a gleaming row of ivory from ear to ear." The French Military Mission stationed with the American Expeditionary Army circulated and withdrew under protest of the French government a clear-cut example of this disposition. It read in part:

> "American opinion is unanimous on this (the Negro question) and permits no discussion of the matter. The kindly spirit which exists in France for the Negro profoundly wounds Americans who consider it an infringement of their national dogmas.... We should not sit at the table with them and they should not be too warmly praised, especially in the presence of Americans.... The vices of the Negro are a constant menace to the American who has to repress them sternly. The black American troops in France have by themselves given rise to as many complaints for attempted rape as all the rest of the Army. The black is constantly being censored for his lack of intelligence and discretion, his lack of civic and professional conscience...."

Here is a classic example of the effort, rather becomingly covert, to do something obviously difficult in the absence of a similar cultural inheritance.

Added to this situation which makes exaggeration necessary is the fact that this intangible world of feeling holds subjects in which there is a most pronounced taboo. This not only powerfully intensifies the feeling itself, but protects it from the assaults of reason and contradictory fact. When the president of a Woman's State Federation of Clubs says, "you all know what we have to fear from Negro men," no one questions her. Each is more likely to think of the worst possible cause of fear. And it does her women hearers perhaps a very little injustice to say that with such a presupposition against these men, they could neither interpret nor relate accurately their conduct of any description. Thus goes the vicious circle.

There are just two instances of the peculiar working of opinion upon the Negro to which attention will be drawn because while most pervading and subtle in their effect, they are most frequently overlooked. Negroes have no more historical continuity than the millions of American whites who have blended into the American stock from an uncertain origin. This is the only culture they know or have ever been exposed to. The circumstances of their lives make it necessary for them to share it and contribute to it. They know no other in spite of the theories concerning survivals of African traits. They read the same papers and books, and in many instances, attend the same schools. They are familiar with the professed ideals of our nation. It is decidedly difficult on the background of the same mental content to avoid having the same or at least similar habits of thinking and similar desires. They have no such autonomy as makes possible the development of a special culture. It cannot be improper to inquire how it can ever be possible for them to follow the advice of many of their friends and advisers to develop here in America a "culture of their own", "to be the best possible Negro rather than an imitation of the white man," however delightful the expression sounds as a solution of the problem. Their culture must be the same or its chances of survival will be small. The state of affairs in our democracy that would follow the independent development of a special culture by each racial group in our population can be well imagined. Where evidences of it have appeared they have been put down with a stern hand. The program of Americanization was designed to prevent just such tendencies as are recommended for the Negroes.

Another is just a different shade of the same problem from the point of view of the Negroes. In the measurement of genius and attainment in which the Negro population so frequently is pointed out as deficient, the fact is often ignored that the standards of comparison are set by the dominant group and at the same time the Negro group is definitely restricted to a narrower circle of effort. There are few Negro captains of industry because they may not often break out of the rank of unskilled labor, and are definitely excluded from supervisory positions. There are no Negro Napoleons because they may not in the first place be generals.

On the basis of prevailing beliefs race discriminations are faultlessly logical. When the practices vary it is because the beliefs vary. No sensible person would insist that morons should be accorded by society the liberties of normal individuals. But the fact that it has been found of temporary convenience to attribute to Negros the mental and moral qualities of morons is no warrant for permitting the belief to go unchallenged.

This paper has no intention of denying any clearly demonstrable fact concerning the Negro population; the questions raised are solely upon the theories about existing fact which, questionable in themselves, have blinded the eyes of observers to factual contradictions and prompted hallucinations of fact to support the theory.

This body of beliefs compounded of this mixture of truth and fiction, self-interest and passion, forms the structure of public opinion on the question of the Negro. These beliefs unchallenged not only magnify themselves and breed others, but react upon the Negro group, distorting its conduct. This distortion provokes in turn a sterner application of these beliefs and so on indefinitely, and with each step the isolation increases, each group building up its own myths and stiffening its own group morale. If the myths can be dissolved, if indeed the beliefs can be honestly questioned, many of our inhibitions to normal, rational and ethical conduct will be removed.

THE SOCIAL PHILOSOPHY OF
BOOKER T. WASHINGTON

Booker T. Washington (1856–1915) advocated a conciliatory philosophy on race relations. Washington's critics pronounced his philosophy, particularly his educational philosophy, as a rationale for perpetuating a racial caste system. In this essay, Charles S. Johnson argues that those African Americans who objected most vehemently to Washington's philosophy were generally the best educated and perhaps needed it the least. This essay was published in April 1928.

It has now been thirteen years since Booker T. Washington died, and thirty-five years since a lightning flash across the brooding South illumined the social philosophy which made him great. The battle of the two "schools of Negro thought" waged bitterly and long, has had the effect of reducing the tenets of both to commonplace politics and rhetoric, and of obscuring, at least for the present generation, the vast interplay of social forces of a period just past, which are so interesting now to the student of race and of societies. The case of the "leaders" who insist upon prompt and unqualified recognition of Negroes upon an equalitarian basis, is relatively simple, and can be established by the Declaration of Independence, the Constitution, the principles of Christianity and abstract ethics. In this country, perhaps the only qualifying condition in the principles sustained has been the fact that the protagonists have been, by the very nature of things, the articulate ones who have not themselves been wholly certain whether they meant to include all Negroes or merely all Negroes sufficiently well educated and cultured to argue for their rights. And while the aspect of race and rights held by the resisting white population has been of the unpalatable mass, that of the indignant Negroes has been most frequently of those Negroes merely who were indignant. Their course has been more direct, requiring less strategy, tolerance and patience, and indeed, less compromising, temporarily or permanently either with ideals or with the ordinary privileges of citizenship. But this does not yield the story of the battle of cultures in that section of the country where most of the Negroes have been and still are; where emotions, by no means favorable to the ultimate doctrines of the equalitarians, have been whirling at white heat; and where traditions required to be dismantled in the same orderly manner that they were built up. In this setting Mr. Washington was important, not because he became a great man, or a great Negro, or rose from slavery, but because he embodied the survival elements of the Negro race in an environment hostile to its ultimate objectives.

The strategies which he employed, consciously or unconsciously, are only now finding their most pronounced effect in the self-concern of Negroes and in the attitudes of white persons with respect to them. His social philosophy, where it has been recognized at all, has been taken too personally. Inevitably the ones who objected to it most were the articulate Negroes who needed it least, and who have merely seen the directness of his principles without considering the logic of their implications. It is possible, with a great freedom, to view this philosophy in the light of the very nature of human nature.

If the coldly dispassionate judgment of a philosopher or social psychologist, with no racial theories at stake, were sought in advice as to the calculating diplomacy required to establish a submerged group of former slaves on a plane of equality with their former masters, who both hated and despised them, he would quite reasonably argue thus:

In the first place, passions cannot be argued with; the meeting of defiant passion with resistant passion never brings peace but conflict which ends inevitably without conviction.

Beliefs disparaging to the weaker group which have grown up over hundreds of years until they crystallized into traditions, cannot be swept away by mere assertions of their falsity, however false they may be. They must be proved objectively, and this proof can best proceed when the emotional resistance to proof is diverted.

When there is fear that the weaker group will destroy the integrity of the stronger or threaten its self-interest if freely admitted to equality with it, this fear more than any other passion, will lead to desperate measures, and no movement of the weaker group, however exalted in its principles can succeed rapidly until the fears are by some means quieted, or entirely dissipated.

This philosopher would probably advise, as a first step, the allaying of these fears by any means at hand which did not compromise manhood. He would advise taking hold of those strangely effective "symbols" and "myths" which have been most potent in promoting an aggressive racial solidarity in the stronger group, stripping them of their most horrid features when these features are not immediately required, and retaining those features which are required, to give them most acceptable content. A force is a force by whatever name it is called. And if to the stronger group "social equality" in its most obnoxious sense means a matter of eating together, and to the weaker group means the acquirement of a status which if carried out would make eating together a simple matter of course, it is the surer wisdom to expend energy on the status and let human nature take its inevitable course. This philosopher would reasonably argue that since men hold passionately to opinions which are founded upon intangible emotions, the wiser strategy would shift proof from a subjective to an objective plane, from immaterial belief to visual reality. Such a diplomacy would select from the "emotional clusters", the most favorable features and extend their implications, and it would spare itself the energy of combatting unfavorable features futilely by the expedient of pointing out, to the strong group, the self-destructive qualities inherent in them. It would as frequently as possible divert unpleasant attention from itself, by directing attention to greater "menaces". It would deprive the stronger group of the satisfaction it might get through insults, by developing the defensive coating of a sense of humor; it would rid the inferior position of that debasement which engenders scorn, by deliberately rationalizing this position into one which gave its enemy no satisfaction. It would constantly divert attention from abstract and undefinable theories while it laid an unmoveable foundation at the base of this scorn.

And of what should such a foundation consist:

1. Security in the possession of land
2. Security in the possession of wealth
3. Security in the possession of skill
4. Security in the possession of health
5. Security in the possession of a sound education
6. Sensitiveness to beauty and order.

These, when they are analyzed are precisely the foundations of abiding culture and civilization. The end, if carried through, would be a radically improved status and acceptance, and in the effort, the weaker group would have the greater spur of deliberate design and intention. The passions conserved might burst forth in creative art and intellectual employments; command of emotions could bring superiority to the silent conflict; security of wealth, by all the economic laws which we worship today, brings respect; security of health brings strength and resistance. This, in its principal outline was actually the social philosophy of Washington.

The setting. Washington was born in slavery, a fact which gave a certain dramatic value to his life and philosophy, as did the similar birth of Douglas and his subsequent flight from the institution. Following his various experiences to manhood now well known through his autobiography, which has been translated into some seventy languages, he emerged from Hampton in 1875. And although his important social career did not begin immediately, the significance of all that was to follow lay in the position of Negroes at that period and their relation to the vast national and sectional changes in process. De Tocqueville pointed out a subtle truth when he observed that the difference between the ancient slave masters and those of the South was that the former kept the bodies of their slaves in bondage but placed no restraint upon their minds, while the Americans employed their despotism and their power against the human mind itself, depriving the slave even of the desire for freedom. Not only had the slave been denied education, but the duration of the system required that he be stripped of his humanity for conscience sake. Theories of an eternal and inescapable inferiority in mind and soul had been established from science, philosophy and Biblical literature. Their ignorance was taken as proof of the eternal fitness of their status. Sympathies for the slave in his hopeless position were dulled by the assurances that the slave neither wanted nor could sustain anything different. The literature painted his happiness and contentment. Even the slave believed. Then came the Civil War, which with a blow swept away the institution without touching the habits of mind which supported it. The revolution of a reconstruction period followed with the sudden rise to power of the despised blacks supported in office by the guns of the North. Passions had been whipped into a delirium of hatred and desire for revenge. However wrong the South had been it had suffered defeat and had had heaped upon its head the bitterest of insults. And when the Army was removed there came the inevitable and cataclysmic recoil. The Ku Klux Klan arose bringing in a reign of terror; the freed Negroes were without property or education or protection; the poor whites who had been held in a poverty and debasement even worse than that of the slave, began to emerge and vent their long suppressed hatred—a hatred stirred deeper by the fear of the competition of Negroes. They began to make laws, repressive laws, beginning first with attempts to render useless the hand of the emancipated slave in competition in the

open labor market. The revulsion against the former slaves was electric. They were pushed not only out of office but out of politics. The
slogans "White domination", white supremacy and "The Solid South",
had their birth. Passions were directed against every symbol of association. Then it was that most talk was heard of deportation, annihila-
tion, segregation. Demagogues like Tillman in South Carolina and
Vardaman in Mississippi arose, and rode to power on the inflamed hatred of illiterate whites. Tillman told them what they wanted to hear:

> *The Negro bears about him a birthright of inferiority that is as unalterable as*
> *eternity. He who in the morning of Creation set the shifting sands as a barrier to*
> *the mad waves of the mighty deep and said thus far, has also set his seal upon the*
> *Negro forever in his black skin, kinky hair, thick lips, flat nose, double layer of*
> *skull, different anatomy as well as analogy from white men. His stupid intellect is*
> *fulfilled in prophesy, uttered thousands of years ago, but no less true today, "A ser-*
> *vant of servants shalt thou be".*

The breaking up of slavery had forced a change in the agricultural
economy; fertile lands were being exhausted and the population was
moving toward new lands. The North, now beginning to feel contrite,
was insisting less and less upon interfering with the South in its handling of what was termed its own "peculiar problem", and, moreover
offered little economic opportunity for the Negroes outside the South.
It was instead, looking to the South as a field for investments when the
fires of anger should finally die down sufficiently to permit them to
enter. The Negroes' struggle was fourfold: against a new economic system, against the revenge of the poor whites, against the scorn of their
former masters and against their own ignorance. This struggle was reg-
istering in increasing ill feeling, repressive legislation and a terrific
mortality. Underneath the whole fabric was one surging passion—that
of fear: fear of the competition of Negroes, fear of an enforced social
equality, fear of political domination, and fear of losing the black labor,
so necessary to the rebuilding of the South. It was then that there appeared also the book called *Ariel;* which attempted to prove that a
Negro was the snake who tempted Eve in the Garden of Eden. And it
was admitted into the libraries.

Into this picture Washington came. It is entirely possible that had it
not been for his famous Atlanta speech, delivered before the Cotton
States Exposition in 1895, he would not have been known for more
than the successful school principal that he was, nor had either the influence or prestige to give weight to his ideas, however worthy; nor to

have faced situations demanding the vital judgments and practice which went into his later career. He had addressed but one other important Southern body and then for only five minutes. He was not known nationally, although he had been working in the South some fourteen years. But Atlanta was making a bid for Northern capital, and to make a show of cosmopolitanism, invited Washington to appear on the program. No one expected him to do anything unusual. Such occasions, however, present at times, the opportunity for the projection of a fortunate philosophy if one has a philosophy to offer. By just such chance incidents are men made.

The author of a recent volume, *Men and Portents* recalls the power of change, clear-cut philosophies in public utterance. The philosophy of Lincoln comes down to us embalmed in the famous sentence, "No nation can long continue to exist, half slave, half free." It was a clarification of a great impending issue. Avistide Briand in London at the signing of the Locarno pact arose to international fame overnight by a fortunate remark which challenged the thought of the world on the action taken there. He gave an ideal plain and unequivocal utterance. Similarly, Coolidge emerged from obscurity by a phrase, while the nation was in the midst of panic over a local situation of vast national implications. He settled fears that were agitating the public mind even tho these fears were as illusory as the racial fears that obsessed the south. In the Boston police strike, when the bug-bear of Bolshevism terrified, and there was alarm, lest, not merely Boston but the country would find itself forced to change its concepts of social order, he brought in the militia, broke the strike and made a speech in which he said: "*There is no right to strike against the public safety by anybody, anywhere, anytime.*" The author, quoting a commentator says, of the speech. "It struck fire from the Americanism of the entire country. Wires relayed it to the remotest regions and it thrilled the United States." He was rewarded with the vice-presidency and moved on up. The same circumstance surrounded Booker Washington in Atlanta. Fears were rampant, segregation laws were the expression of these fears; they were widening in their reach—the schools, transportation, intermarriage laws, and finally they were reaching out for industry threatening the life as well as the manhood of the race. The major part of his philosophy is embodied in that speech. But the phrase that rang over the south and country was this: "*In all things that are purely social we can be as separate as the fingers of the hand, yet one as the hand in all things essential to mutual progress.*"

The effect was electric. It was a solution. Clarke Howell of the Atlanta *Constitution* wired to New York that it was one of the most notable speeches ever delivered to a southern audience; "a revelation, a platform upon which blacks and whites can stand with full justice to each other."

This is as good a point as any to begin a rough classification of his full philosophy and it is stated descriptively and briefly.

He advocated conciliatory rather than aggressive tactics in race relations. The principle has been confused both by his critics and his imitators of less vision and courage. It is not for us to determine whether he was less manly, or wanted less than those who insisted on their full rights immediately. The fact remains that no power within the control of Negroes could have quieted the fears of the white south now gaining the sympathies of the north in its dilemma over the Negro problem, nor saved them from the injury of these fears exploded. Altho the white south received this as a solution for all time, nowhere is it evident that Washington stated this as more than a temporal adjustment. These results were immediate: For the first time the south found itself listening seriously to the voice of the Negro, it was a demonstration of acumen from an unexpected and disarming source; it called attention to Negro progress; it killed the spectre of a fictitious social equality and began the destruction of the vague and mysterious connotations of the other myths and symbols that had been troubling the south, it strategically reversed the position of Negroes in the south from that of a menacing burden to that of a possible ally, and linked the fortunes of Negroes publicly with the fortunes of the south.

All of us are familiar with the interpretations placed upon these doctrines by white persons. Let us consider some of the implications: Social psychologists recognize now the tremendous potency of symbols and illusions. One of the items in the rift between the two sects of Quakers is on the trivial matter of whether or not the hat should be worn in church. Difference is heavily charged with emotion. Wars have been fought over symbols of faith in religion. We are aware how during the World War, men were stirred to cast away their lives on the symbolism of a vague and meaningless phrase "Saving the world for Democracy." Just such a symbol is, "Social Equality," and the wiser social strategy recognizes this as a symbol and treats it so. The inevitable result has been the laying of a foundation beneath tradition for the very social equality which was feared. The paradox is clear when it is observed that Washington himself came to be accorded in recognition of the position to which his power entitled him, a social recognition attained by no rank of his Atlanta audience below that of the Governors.

He advocated the ownership of land and homes and the development of business. The difference between the American Negro and the European peasant is in the ability to own land. It is on the security of income of the masses that the talented tenth must rest. He urged remaining on the farms because whites were leaving them. He urged the establishment of business thus to combine with labor the contribution of capital to their resources. And wisely he refrained them from exploiting the political aspects of economic principles inherent in this program, and from giving it the spectre of a name. In the respect he was more subtle than the Socialists who, by emphasizing the differences in theories without attempting to live their own into execution, surrounded themselves with a conscious resistance which in the end defeated their hopes.

He emphasized the dignity of work. To Negroes this was a kind of treachery, an attitude which had developed from the association of work with the former status of slavery. This, however, was a prop for the broad economic platform which Washington attempted to lay. In this way the tides were turned which were pushing Negroes from their old traditional trades and permitting the revengeful poor whites to come too precipitously to power. The masses of men without philosophy could be stimulated to harder effort when prosaic work itself, so vastly necessary, was surrounded by glamour. One expedient was a fortune phrase, oft repeated, which had the effect of drawing from the work an element of pride which it lacked for so many. "There is a difference between working and being worked."

He advocated beginning boldly at the beginnings with the elements of education. His most effective method of emphasis was ridicule of the thin and crackly veneer of the half-educated. It was the emphasis which developed into the schism between the schools of higher and industrial education. When disgusted with the inadequacies of public provision for elementary training for Negroes in the south, he did not content himself with the virtuous feeling of indignation over the difference per capita spent for white and Negro children in the States. In the mood of the south it was a proportion, which befitted the situation of the two classes—"one civilized; the other incapable of civilization." He interested philanthropy in planting a seed of Negro training which gradually drew white and Negro support and raised the level to a point that would not have been attained in fifty years of distant agitation. The wisdom of this lies in the fact that people, contented in their ignorance can never be expected to want seriously to be educated until a first interest has been stirred. No one can say how much the quiet dissemination of training thruout the rural south was responsible for the discontent which registered in the migration. On the industrial phase, we are just beginning to appreciate the value of the substitutes for apprenticeship which his type of institution provided, now that it has been incorporated into this educational policy of the country.

A recent study of industrial training by Dr. May of the University of Illinois points out the absolute absence of any formal method in our present industrial system for men to move from unskilled to skilled trades, since the break-up of the apprentice system a hundred years ago. Those who have contact with Negro labor know how hopeless is this progression for Negroes where no emergency forces the experiment with Negro labor in new lines. Eighty per cent of the Negro population depends upon labor for its sustenance, and the other twenty per cent is measured in its advance by the stability and competence of the base.

He was an objectivist. People believe what they can see whether they will to believe or not. Instead of giving his whole emphasis to arguing that Negroes are capable of being educated he helped Negroes educate themselves. His vast institution at Tuskegee was indisputable evidence of the capacity of Negroes for managing their own affairs. The principle carried thru his educational practice and the finer elaborations of this practice which have since been developed independently by Dewey and Montessori. His work constituted a contribution to educational theory and practice.

He refused to stress politics. On this point he has received the most persistent criticism from Negroes. But he would have been less astute than his other policies indicate if he had not seen that the agitating for ballots was merely another of the meaningless appurtenances which even the white voters did not take advantage of when the novelty had worn off. As has already happened in many of the southern cities, the enfranchisement of Negroes was forced by the logic of events when it became apparent that there were Negroes who wanted elected men who in character were superior to those who rose to power thru ignorance and chance. And a man who is broad enough to be fair to Negroes is most likely to be the one most social minded, and capable of administering the affairs of a community.

He diverted attention from Negroes by comparing them with other races and cultures—i.e., he lifted them to a new level by finding someone lower. This was the burden of his book "*The Man Lowest Down*," and the comparison was made with an extraordinary sympathy. He rationalized his own status when he said, "You can beat me being a white man but I can beat you being a Negro." It was no different from the present course of the Negro writers and artists who, in their new representations of Negro life are doing the very thing for which he found a phrase.

There is another apt example of his philosophy which would bear quoting: "No man can drag me down by making me hate him. If you hold me in the gutter you must remain there with me." In this there is the subtle directing of attention to the intelligent self-interest of the stronger group. It is an irresistable reminder that the strong cannot abuse the weak without suffering consequences as debasing to itself as it creates for others.

Effort has been made to state this philosophy in the light of its implications for the general development of Negroes in this country. The tremendous advances in understanding evidenced in the south would suggest that many of these policies have worked. Whether this advance would have come without it is worth speculating upon, but there is no pressing indication that it would. Human nature has changed and the response has been to a process of molding, it would seem, rather than to shock. There is still need of a doctrine of work, of self-respect, of creative inspiration, of material development, of friendships that will progressively dispel the fears of one group of what the full manhood status of the other will do to it.

The most effective interest of the present is art, and even of this it may be said that it is but an elaboration of Washington's principles of stressing work rather than the rewards of work. And in any estimate of this philosophy, it should be evident that there is no virtue in the hand that withholds the rewards so that they must be acquired thru strategy even after they are earned.

There is a view which may be taken of this whole setting, which conceives the white south itself as the object of education, and, since it must be untaught the traditions of hundreds of years, and new principles instilled, the Negroes conceived as the teachers. Here then might apply to the Negroes an adage, as aptly as to the martyred old philosopher of whom it was said:

"Woe to him who would teach men faster than they can learn."

THE SPIRIT OF THE KU KLUX KLAN

*In this essay, N.A.A.C.P. official Robert W. Bagnall relates the objectives
and motives behind the spirit and actions of the Ku Klux Klan. This essay
was published in September 1923.*

I

Beginning with silly pranks of young men, there developed in this
country during the days of Reconstruction a murder-band, which
killed and maimed 50,000 people before the government disbanded it.
This was the old Ku Klux Klan and its namesake and successor is worthy of it. Barbaric in form, with silly jargon for a ritual, with masks and
shrouds, dreadful oaths, and weird ceremonies, it yet makes its appeal
to a number of men who have been regarded as decent and sensible.

Appealing to all pet prejudices, it has spread in unsuspected circles
in the North, South, East and West. It makes its members censors of
morals, judge, jury and executioners. It especially seeks to prevent the
rise of Jews, Catholics, foreigners and Negroes. Its weapon is terrorism
and its method—flogging, branding, mutilating, and killing. Its victims
make a formidable list, and in many regions it overrides all law and
order. Witness Oklahoma and Louisiana. Yet it terms itself patriotic
and one hundred per cent American.

Certainly such patriotism is that of which Samuel Johnson spoke,
"the refuge of fools and scoundrels." It seeks to control government—
municipal, state and national, and is no neglible factor in the politics of
many places.

II

The Ku Klux Klan is an astonishing phenomenon. What is its explanation? Is it the savage in man seeking expression in mystery, weird symbolism, and regalia? Is it the brute in man which, made safe by masks, strikes at its enemies? Is it the base prejudices finding in this organization a focal point? Is it the prudence of scoundrels, who realize they are far safer within a censoring organization where they can do the censoring? Is it the American whites inferiority complex in the face of foreigners, Jews, and Negroes? All of these enter, I believe, into the explanation of the phenomenon of the Klan, and in addition, there is something more—a desire to bolster up a waning sense of superiority.

What does it object to in those it opposes? The Klan is against Jews, for it claims that Jews seek to control the finances of the world. It feels that American whites who are non-Jews cannot cope with them in this project,—are their inferiors in financial ability, and, therefore, force and terrorism must be invoked against them. The Klan is against foreigners, for they say these would change our institutions. This presupposes that our institutions are perfect and cannot be improved. It also presupposes that they cannot stand the contest with the newer ideas. Again a sense of inferiority. The Klan is against Catholics because with a strange bigotry it imagines that they seek to suborn the government to their religion. The silliness of this needs no comment. The Klan is against Negroes, hereditarily so, because "this is the white man's country", and the Negro is disposed not "to remain in his place." Here again, we see a sense of inferiority and fear, seeking an explanation in empty myths; the myth that this is only the white man's country, and it follows that the Negro or any other American has or can be made to have a static, caste place.

III

The result of the Klan's teaching is always racial intolerance, religious bigotry, jingoism, obsoletism, lawlessness and violence. If these things are good, then the Klan is good; if they are evil, then the Klan is evil.

However, the spirit of the Ku Klux Klan has been manifested in other than the organization that bears its name. It has been seen even in actions of the government, as well as in private institutions and organizations. Who has forgotten the disgraceful persecutions of the Department of Justice under Palmer; the beating and maiming of innocent men and women, and the wanton destruction of their property because a mad hysteria caused them to be suspected of being communists? And even yet we have fine, splendid men in prison, their pardon refused because these souls were brave enough in a mad world to proclaim that war was evil and should be opposed. Is not this the Klan spirit? And as to private or semi-public groups, there is no lack of examples.

This spirit is being manifested with reference to the Tuskegee Veterans' Hospital by United States Congressmen and Senators and other white citizens in Alabama, who have used or condoned threats and all sorts of pressure, that the privilege of nursing and doctoring black soldiers *at the price of sixty odd thousand a month* may be preserved for whites and denied black physicians and nurses.

A few weeks ago, in a mining town in West Virginia, the school board discharged a Negro principal because he had the temerity to teach his children that no person was better than themselves *simply because of race.* In other words, because he would not teach a lie or keep silent about a truth essential to the self respect of his group, he was forced out of his job.

In New Orleans, a Negro principal, a most efficient teacher, when present at a school board meeting was asked if he thought himself as good as a white man. When he replied that he certainly felt himself as good as any man who was no better in character, mentality, and attainments, the school board discharged him.

In these instances the spirit of the Klan found full expression.

Ludwig Lewissohn in "Upstream" tells how most of the leading colleges of America are determined that *no Jew* shall occupy the chair of English literature. Again, the Klan spirit.

I might multiply these examples, but I have cited a sufficient number to indicate that in this country the spirit of the Ku Klux Klan is wide-spread. Indeed, it is not confined to this country, but I am limiting my observations at this time to the United States.

IV

Back of the spirit of the Ku Klux Klan is that intolerance which regards all contrary opinion as necessarily wrong and its own ideas as divinely inspired. They who hold this spirit are the successors of the Spanish inquisition and believe that those who will not conform should be destroyed, and that force can change opinions. They revert to the assumption that might makes right, and would reduce society to the oneness of belief which characterizes the savage. They would make terrorism—the lash, the knife, the rack, the fagot, and the stake the instruments whereby men should be converted, and not reason. In other words, they are throwbacks to an age of barbarism, if not of savagery. They are anachronisms in a civilized era; an outcropping of the wolf and the tiger in man. And where they are not quite willing to revert to physical violence, they would destroy by social proscription and make the offender an outcast.

If one would sum up what is behind the Klan spirit in this country, he would find that *consciously* there is this credo:

1. The Anglo-Saxon white man (a myth as the term is used in America) is inherently superior to all other whites and to all non-whites. Therefore, he must be provided a superior status and opportunities.

2. All other races must be kept in an inferior position, and most of all the Negro, by force, if necessary.

3. The non-whites must not be permitted to mingle their blood with the whites. (This does not mean that the whites must not be permitted to mingle their blood with non-whites. While it seems the same, it is quite different).

4. Our present government cannot be bettered, but is the acme of perfection.

5. God destined the whites to rule because He made them superior. This superiority is *ipso facto* without any measurements. (How God revealed this remarkable edict is not made clear).

6. This is a white man's country, and all non-whites are in this country on sufferance and must be content with whatever rights the whites choose to give them. This includes the Amer-indian, who has to be naturalized to become a citizen of his own country.

Of course there is not a single proposition here that can be maintained by science or logic.

V

This is the conscious belief behind the spirit of the Klan, but there is an unconscious belief which is the real and motivating one. I have already hinted at it. It is the inferiority complex on the part of whites which gives rise to the spirit of the Klan. When men eternally talk of their superiority, when they use every possible means to emphasize that they are superior, and when they insist on unfair advantages in competition with those they call inferior, one may know that down in the unconscious mind at least there is a feeling that their claim has no basis. This is the case with the American white. He who boasts of his fighting prowess over much is usually a cowardly bully. The man who ever vaunts his honesty, you had best not trust with your money. She who constantly states that she never talks about anybody is usually the town gossip. And the white man who ever proclaims his inherent superiority is often trying to convince both you and himself that his claim is true.

The California white is prejudiced against the Japanese. Because he is unfit? No. Because he is too fit. The whites cannot compete with him. The Japanese is a better farmer. The Japanese can work longer and maintain his health on less food. The Japanese succeeds where the whites fail. He is their superior in these things, and so they would debar him from competition.

The Anti-Semitics inveigh against the Jew. Why? Because the genius of the Jew threatens, in his opinion, to control the money market. The southern white oppresses the Negro. Why? Because he is worthy of oppression? No. Because the southern white depends for his economic life on the Negro. Realizing this dependence, he seeks to maintain it by keeping the Negro in a condition where he can be exploited. Behind this is the inferiority complex that he, without whom the white South cannot get along, may not be the inferior being after all. This, of course, stimulates the endeavor to force an inferior status on the Negro. When one realizes that while the Negro forms two-fifths of the population of the South, he produces three-fifths of its wealth, one sees that this fear may have point. But the remedy is not to be found in the oppression of the Negro but in the bestirring of the white to greater effort.

Lothrop Stoddard, himself a reputed Klansman, well expresses this inferiority complex in his book "The Rising Tide of Color" where he says, "Nowhere can the white man endure colored competition."

VI

The spirit of the Ku Klux Klan is the manifestation of a group mentally sick. It is the evidence of a lack of sanity in the realm with which it is concerned. It is the result of minds dwelling amidst shadows, creating imaginary hob-goblins, and striking in hysterical and maniacal fury at innocent victims. It is the fatal result of a dogma that the human race permanently can be safely divided into groups of tyrant and subject, master and serf. It is the fevered expression of a sick world that must be healed, if it is not to die.

A Note on Negro Education

This essay, published by E. Franklin Frazier in March 1924, analyzes the past and present problems of African-American education in relation to the society in which African Americans live. Frazier discusses an alternative direction for the education of his race.

The aim of this article is to evaluate the past education of the Negro in relation to the culture complex in which he has been placed, and indicate the direction its future development should take. Consequently, we shall not consider those well-known travesties upon education where schools calling themselves universities have conferred imaginary degrees; or where thousands of dollars are spent annually to perfect athletic teams and nothing is expended for library books; or where orating is the chief scholastic effort; or, finally, where quartets are the most prized products. Such instances of short-sightedness and ignorance must find a place in the sadder pages of the history of Negro education. They concern us only as they relate to the theme of this article, namely: How has the education given the Negro so far fitted him for participation in the particular culture complex known as American civilization?

Before considering the question raised above, let us review briefly the main features in the history of Negro education. The fact that strikes us is its missionary and religious nature. Among the pioneers who undertook the education of the Negro, the majority were inspired with missionary zeal. Their aim was primarily religious. Inspired by the missionary endeavors of the nineteenth century to Christianize backward peoples, they sought, on the one hand, to train ministers of the gospel and, on the other hand, to convert Negroes to Christianity. Allied with but somewhat differentiated from the missionary aim was the philanthropic spirit. This was also a product of nineteenth century humanitarian ideals. Those influenced by these ideals endeavored through educating the Negro not only to assist him because he was disadvantaged socially but, in many cases, to fit him for full citizenship in the American commonwealth.

The reaction of the South is too well known to repeat. It is sufficient to say that the South has never seriously opposed giving to the Negro ministers who would prepare him to live in another world so long as it did not interfere with the Negro's working in this world. As long as his leaders unlocked the mysteries of heaven, there was no opposition. It was only when his teachers unfolded the mysteries of this world that the southern white man has objected. A landmark in Negro education, so far as the white man was concerned, was reached when a type of education was discovered that concerned itself with this world and at the same time did not disturb the Negro as a worker. Tuskegee has stood in the white man's imagination as such a reconciliation.

It may be well to restate here the main features of the culture complex in which the American Negro has been placed. According to one student of culture, this complex is characterized by mechanical invention, universal suffrage, and mass education under which religion is included. Such a descriptive formula is acceptable for our purpose. Surely no one can gainsay the dominating role of mechanical invention in our civilization. Not only are we concerned with the more obvious aspects and results of a highly developed mechanical environment, but with those subtler effects which are reflected in the habits of thoughts. With this understanding of our culture complex, we are prepared to evaluate Negro education.

In this connection we must recall the controversy between the proponents of industrial education under the leadership of Tuskegee and the defenders of the so-called higher education. It is strange that in this controversy the fundamental value of industrial education was never mentioned. It was neither the undoubtable value of the inculcation of regular habits nor the boasted achievement of making Negroes industrially efficient. The chief value of this education was psychic. The Negro was brought from a culture in which certain primitive mental habits moulded his environment. His experiences under the slave regime affected these psychic attitudes but slightly. In order for the Negro to participate in spirit as well as in outward practices in American culture, it was necessary for him to acquire the basic mental assumptions of western civilization. Mechanical causation is the basis of our thought life. This is quite different from the habit of primitive minds to be indifferent to secondary causes. The surest way to make this transition from primitive to scientific habits of thought was to place the Negro in an environment which he must manipulate according to the principles of mechanical causes. This was the sure antidote to mystic and invisible forces, omens and divination.

The foregoing does not deny that the so-called higher education did not seek and attain the same ends. Its field of operation was, of course, more restricted. But it was restricted in a more fundamental sense. Higher education was an indirect means by which scientific causal relations were impinged upon the Negro's mind through symbols. That this was a less effective method of displacing certain primitive mental habits cannot be denied. In spite of this disadvantage, higher education did allow its students to drink in spiritual values that all leaders must have. This brings us to the chief indictment against Negro education in the past.

Negro education in the past, to characterize it briefly, has been too much inspiration and too little information. This charge applies equally to all kinds of Negro education. Even that type of education that has claimed to concern itself with the realities of life has wasted much time in giving inspiration. Of course, much of this false emphasis has been due to an erroneous conception of the springs of human behavior. The Negro student has been kept constantly tuned up, so to speak. He has heard inspiring speeches daily from his leaders who bubble over with platitudes. The whole gamut of his emotional nature has been played upon. He has dissipated grand emotional experiences and squandered the stirrings of his soul in inaction. Instead of filling the Negro's mind with knowledge and training him in the fundamental habits of civilization, his teachers have quite often led him from one emotional debauch to another. Surfeited with emotional appeals never resulting in action, the product of Negro education has become a spectator of civilization incapable of participation.

He has been a spectator mainly because he has maintained the attitude of one enjoying rather than one helping to create. The environment in which he has been placed has been one in which rational rather than sentimental attitudes were demanded. Some will assign this to a difference in racial temperament. But the operation of environmental factors can, to a large extent, account for this distinctive difference in reaction to the psycho-social environmental. In this case the type of education given the Negro has produced a sentimental rather than rational attitude towards life. This sentimental attitude displays itself all along the line of Negro life. While it may not be fair to charge it entirely to education, it is true that whether we look back upon fraternalizing of the older generation in their secret societies or the newer generation in their college fraternities, or medical conventions degenerated into social functions, we see the same old emotional or sentimental life of school days.

We come now to an aspect of Negro education that accounts for many of the cultural scarecrows who have been the products of Negro education. In their missionary zeal and philanthropic enthusiasm the early apostles, who carried education to Negroes, called in all who labored and were heavily burdened with ignorance. While, it is true, there did not exist even the present unperfected means of selecting students qualified for different grades of work, some degree of selection was possible. This failure to select students has produced queer schools and queer students. Some schools have been crosses between a reformatory and a school for feeble-minded and an ordinary school. They were true melting pots with religious, or rather emotional, education as the solvent. The products have varied in ignorance of and disharmony with the spirit of western culture. While most of the outstanding products are trained in "turning on" the emotions, there are a few exceptions who possess the spirit and culture of our civilization.

Such has been Negro education in the past. Today Negro education faces a crisis. This crisis is not so much due to the passing of missionary and philanthropic support. It is a spiritual rather than an economic crisis. The old ideals are inadequate. Missionary education might have prepared the Negro to live in heaven, but it did not fit him for the culture complex in which he finds himself. But the old education in its day did give the Negro an objective. Negro education offers no objective to the Negro today. Old ideals have been dissipated. The Negro is either revolting against the old ideals or is adopting a narrow and selfish individualism. Hence the large number of students who are preparing themselves for the professions as a means to wealth and enjoyment, and not as a means for deeper and more responsible participation in our civilization.

What of the new educational ideals? In the first place, the education of the future must make the Negro himself of first consideration. The education of the past did not do this. It must be conceded that in the absence of adequate Negro leadership someone else had to assume the responsibility, and our gratitude for this leadership, that offered itself when a nation shirked its duty and the South determined to keep the Negro in ignorance and economic slavery, can never be too great. Yet this education was to satisfy certain impulses and mould the Negro in accordance with certain prejudices and ideals. This is excellently illustrated by the case of a philanthropic white woman who had given large sums of money for years to the education of Negroes. After these many years of an apparently high appreciation of the Negro, she happened to attend a meeting of Negroes for social development. She came away alarmed and determined not to give another cent for Negro education because she found Negroes as cultured and as intelligent as white people! She felt guilty and dismayed when she beheld the result of her efforts. Her attitude towards Negroes was primarily that of a kindly lady who has sponsored a society for the prevention of cruelty to animals, but naturally resents rescued dogs, for example, assuming roles reserved for homo sapiens; or our general refusal to confer citizenship upon the intelligent ape at Hollywood, however much we are willing to pay for him to do tricks. It is evident that such educational efforts do not make the Negro the center of their aims. They do not represent attempts to develop the Negro into full manhood and afford ample development for a personality that has been abridged. This means that if white people are to assume the direction of Negro education, the older missionary and philanthropic ideals must be abandoned, or Negroes must assume the direction of their education. His educational institutions can no longer be the prizes in church politics or furnish berths for failures in other walks of life. The Negro must be educated for his own sake as a constituent member of American civilization.

The new education must be built upon the sure foundation of sound scholarship. The Bachelor's degree from a Negro school should assure us at least that the holder can read and write English. We should expect this from those of high school standing. Aside from mere technical knowledge, the educated Negro should understand the moral and scientific values afloat in our civilization. Recently the Negro ministers of a large city prided themselves on the fact that they were 100% "strong" in believing in the Virgin birth. Since Negroes cannot boast of superior "spiritual" or "mysterious" insight, this fact can only be a monument to the ignorance of the Negro preacher. The equipment of the educated Negro should represent an attitude determined by a possession of the most advanced knowledge extant in the world. But to achieve this end it will be necessary to select students. However much we may be inclined to excuse the wholesale education of Negroes in the past, with the means available today, there is no excuse whatever for the past indiscriminate education of Negroes which has produced so many scarecrows of culture.

We must hasten to a consideration of moral and religious aspects of the new education before some object to "soulless" scholarship as the ideal in education. The old education of Negroes depended upon the easily communicable emotional states to mould conduct and character. This has been one of the main weaknesses in Negro education generally. Conduct and character are the results of habits. The exploitation of the emotions in the Negro has not built up motor responses but has dissipated itself in the air.

Sound moral education for the Negro must subject him to situations where desirable motor responses will be elicited so as to build up habits valuable for the civilization in which he is placed. If the Negro is endowed with an extra share of emotion so much the better for the desirable habits he has acquired. Negro education has had in this respect the same ill effects that American athletic contests have upon the mob of spectators, who lose themselves in emotional debauches which never result in activity. Negroes must be taught to act as well as feel.

When we consider the place of religion in the education and life of the Negro we are keenly aware of the statement of Dean Kelly Miller, that the religion of Jesus has been interpreted to the Negro through Teutonic eyes and that the Negro must return to the source for inspiration in the future. For people situated as the Negro, in the midst of a militant and overbearing civilization, there could be no better religion than the simple, fundamental principles, taught by Jesus, of the brotherhood of man and the superiority of moral force. As we know, these principles have been ignored by the Teuton and the militant, hypocritical and ceremonial Christianity with its castes, which we behold today has nothing to offer the Negro. His preachers have aped the Teutonic interpretation; but in many cases, it must be said, out of pure ignorance. Some cowardly preachers and leaders have pretended to emulate Jesus' humility and reliance upon moral forces by lying to the white man and bartering away for favors the moral sanctions of justice in the face of an opponent depending upon physical force. Except in a few rare cases the non-resistance of the Negro has never been actuated by the religion of Jesus. His reliance upon moral force has been a cowardly denial of his right to the enjoyment of the same treatment as the white man; and his humility has been lying about his desire for this. If the new education for the Negro includes in its program religious training, let it return to the source as Dean Miller so aptly counsels. Let it avoid both the aimless emotional dissipations of the past and the hypocritical and militant counterfeit Christianity of white civilization.

In the evolution of Negro culture there is one factor making for rational attitudes, namely,—economic development. Business experience for the Negro is proving more fundamentally educative in certain respects than his formal education, because it has put him in contact with an environment requiring less expenditure of emotion and a greater exercise of rational habits. Of course, business has its narrow outlook and restricted aims and can not exercise the influence on the Negro we are seeking.

This brings us to the greatest task of the new education, namely,—the rationalization of the culture process with Negroes. Recently a young European, who visited this country and noted his impressions concerning the Negro problem, was struck by the servile way in which Negroes imitated the white man's ideals and values and his fear of being different. Imitation, of course, is a natural social process and the Negro responds according to the universal laws of imitation. But a group situated as the Negro must avoid the danger of unconsciously assimilating values which either have no meaning for him or which the leaders of thought in the world are trying to replace with higher values. The Negro, rather advantageously situated, should be a pioneer in enunciating values that those overwhelmed by their own culture could never attain. For example, there is no reason for the Negro to be an intense nationalist. When his leaders boasted after the War that there was not one Negro conscientious objector, they reflected the subservient and short-sighted outlook of Negro leaders; and, if the claim were true, the unidealistic mind of the Negro. It is the function of Negro educators to disseminate those desirable values and elements of the environing culture that the Negro is to incorporate into his life. Already the Negro, unguided or rather misguided, has unconsciously drunk in values and ideals that have no meaning to him. The accomplishment of a consciously built up culture will depend upon leaders with a vision and understanding of cultural processes. Nevertheless, spiritual and intellectual emancipation of the Negro awaits the building of a Negro university, supported by Negroes and directed by Negro educators, who have imbibed the best that civilization can offer; where his savants can add to human knowledge and promulgate those values which are to inspire and motivate Negroes as a culture group.

THE GARVEY MOVEMENT

Marcus Garvey (1887–1940) founded the Universal Negro Improvement Association in 1919. Garvey's "Back to Africa" movement attracted a worldwide following. When this essay was published by E. Franklin Frazier in November 1926, Garvey was serving a five-year prison term for mail fraud. In this essay, Frazier discusses why African Americans were attracted to the Garvey movement and its effects on their lives.

Garvey, himself, could not have planned a more strategic climax to his career in America than his imprisonment in Atlanta. The technical legal reason for his incarceration is obscured by the halo that shines about the head of the martyr. There is a sort of justice in this; for if the government were to punish all those who use the mails to defraud, it would round up those energetic business men who flood the mails with promises to give eternal youth and beauty to aging fat matrons, to make Carusos and Galli Curcis of members of church choirs, and to make master minds of morons. Garvey's promises were modest in comparison. And, indeed, what does one ship, more or less, matter in an imaginary fleet of merchantmen?

There are aspects of the Garvey Movement that can not be treated in this cavalier fashion. It is those aspects we propose to set forth here. The writer recalls that when he was a child one could still hear Negroes express the hope that some Moses would appear among them and lead them to a promised land of freedom and equality. He has lived to see such hopes displaced by more prosaic and less fanciful efforts towards social betterment. When Booker Washington first appeared on the scene he was hailed as a Moses. This was chiefly an echo of the white man's appraisal and soon died down when the Negro heard a message of patient industry, unsweetened by any prospect of a glorious future. What has distinguished the Garvey Movement is its appeal to the masses. While Negroes have found a degree of self-magnification in fraternal orders and the church, these organizations have not given the support to their ego-consciousness that whites find in the Kiwanis and especially the Klan. Garvey re-introduced the idea of a Moses, who was incarnate in himself, and with his masterly technic for dealing with crowds, he welded Negroes into a mass movement.

Before considering Garvey and his work, something should be said of the people he had to work with. The social status of the Negro in America should make them fertile soil for a mass movement to spring up in. They are repressed and shut out from all serious participation in American life. Not only does the Negro intellectual feel this repression, but the average Negro, like all mediocre people whose personalities must be supported by empty fictions, must find something to give meaning to his life and worth to his personality. One has simply to note how the superficial matter of color raises the most insignificant white man in the South to a place of paramount importance, in order to appreciate how much support a fiction gives to one's personality. Yet American Negroes have been relatively free, from mass movements. This fact should not be regarded as a further testimony to the Negro's reputation for a policy of expediency in his present situation. There have been other factors to take the place of mass movements.

Many American Negroes have belittled the Garvey Movement on the ground that he is a West Indian and has attracted only the support of West Indians. But this very fact made it possible for him to contribute a new phase to the life of the American Negro. The West Indian Negroes have been ruled by a small white minority. In Jamaica, the Negro majority has often revolted and some recognition has been given to the mulattoes. This was responsible for Garvey's attempt, when he first came to this country, to incite the blacks against those of mixed blood. He soon found that there was no such easily discernible social cleavage recognized by the whites in this country. Yet his attempt to draw such a line has not failed to leave its effect. The fact that the West Indian has not been dominated by a white majority is probably responsible for a more secular view of life. The Garvey Movement would find the same response among the Negroes of the South as among the West Indians, were it not for the dominating position of the preacher, whose peculiar position is symtomatic of an other worldly outlook among the masses. Even in the face of this situation foreign Negroes have successfully converted hard-shelled Baptists to the Movement in spite of the opposition of their ministers. This secular influence in the life of the Negro attains its true significance when viewed in relation to the part that preparation for death plays in the life of the black masses.

The Garvey Movement afforded an asylum, as all mass movements, for those who were dissatisfied with life for many reasons, which could in this case be attributed to their status as Negroes. Although most of his followers were ignorant, we find among them intellectuals who had not found the places in the world that their education entitled them to. Instead of blaming themselves,—and they were not always individually responsible—they took refuge in the belief that in an autonomous black Africa they would find their proper place. The black rabble that could not see its own poverty, ignorance, and weakness vented its hatred upon obscure "traitors" and "enemies," who generally turned out to be Negro intellectuals who had achieved some distinction in American life. There is good reason to believe that Garvey constantly directed the animosity of his followers against the intellectuals because of his own lack of formal education.

We have noted how the Garvey Movement turned the Negro's attention to this world. This was accomplished not only by promising the Negro a paradise in the future in Africa; but through the invention of social distinctions and honors, the Negro was made somebody in his present environment. The humblest follower was one of the "Fellowmen of the Negro Race," while the more distinguished supporters were "Knights" and "Sirs." The women were organized into the Black Cross Nurses and the men into the Great African Army. "A uniformed member of a Negro lodge paled in significance beside a soldier of the Army of Africa. A Negro might be a porter during the day, taking his orders from white men, but he was an officer in the Black Army when it assembled at night in Liberty Hall. Many a Negro went about his work singing in his heart that he was a member of the great army marching to 'heights of achievements'."[1] Yet these extravagant claims were based upon the deep but unexpressed conviction in the minds of most Negroes that the white man has set certain limits to their rise in this country.

In his half acknowledged antagonism towards Negro preachers and the soporific religion they served the masses, Garvey did not ignore its powerful influence. In fact he endeavored to fuse the religious experience of the Negro with his own program. The symbolism associated with Christmas was made the sign of the birth of a Negro nation among the nations of the earth; while Easter became the symbol of a resurrected race. Nor did he overlook the opportunity to make his position appear similar to that of Jesus. According to him, his own peo-

[1] Garvey: A Mass Leader, The Nation, Vol. CXXIII, No 1189, by the writer.

ple, especially the recognized Negro leaders, had incited the American authorities against him just as the Jews had incited the Roman authorities against Jesus. In this connection the idea of gaining a lost paradise appears as it does in most mass movements. The "Redemption of Africa" became the battle cry. To his followers he trumpeted: "No one knows when the hour of Africa's redemption cometh. It is in the wind. It is coming one day like a storm. It will be here. When that day comes, all Africa will stand together."[2]

The messianic element in this movement is not altogether lacking, although it does not stand out prominently. When Garvey entered the prison in Atlanta, besides commending his wife to the care of his followers, he spoke of the possibility of his death as only a messiah would speak. Under the caption, "If I Die In Atlanta," he bade his followers:

"Look for me in the whirlwind or the storm, look for me all around you, for, with God's grace, I shall come and bring with me the countless millions of black slaves who have died in America and the West Indies and the millions in Africa to aid you in the fight for liberty, freedom and life."[3]

By this promise Garvey raised himself above mortals and made himself the Redeemer of the Black World.

Many people are at a loss to understand how Garvey was able to attract supporters to a scheme which was manifestly infeasible and has been discredited by continued exposés of corruption and bickering within the organization. But such tests of reasonableness can not be applied to schemes that attract crowds. Crowds, it has been said, never learn by experience. The reason is clear, for the crowd satisfies its vanity and longings in the beliefs it cherishes. Not only because of their longing for something to give meaning to their lives, but because of the scepticism about them. Negroes do not find the satisfaction that their fathers found in the promise of heavenly abode to compensate for the woes of this world. They therefore offer a fine field for charlatans and fakirs of every description. This Movement has attracted many such men who give the black crowds the escape they are seeking. The work carried on by the National Association for the Advancement of Colored People, which has been the subject of so many attacks by Garvey, has never attracted the crowd because it does not give the crowd an opportunity to show off in colors, parades, and self-glorification. The Association appeals to intelligent persons who are trying to attain

[2] Ibid.
[3] The Negro World, February 14, 1925.

tangible goals through cooperation. The same could be said of the Urban League. Dean Kelly Miller, it is said, once made the shrewd observation that the Negro pays for what he wants and begs for what he needs. This applies here as elsewhere. Those who support this Movement pay for it because it gives them what they want—the identification with something that makes them feel like somebody among white people who have said they were nobody.

Before concluding this brief interpretive sketch, we must add a few observations. Doubtless the World War with its shibboleths and stirrings of subject minorities offered a volume of suggestion that facilitated the Garvey Movement. Another factor that helped the Movement was the urbanization of the Negro that took place about the time. It is in the cities that mass movements are initiated. When the Negro lived in a rural environment he was not subject to mass suggestion except at the camp meeting and revival.

One of the most picturesque phases of the Movement has been the glorification of blackness which has been made an attribute of the celestial hierarchy. To most observers this last fact has been simply a source of merriment. But Garvey showed a knowledge of social psychology when he invoked a black god to guide the destiny of the Negro. The God of Israel served the same purpose. Those whites who said they would rather go to hell than to heaven presided over by a black god, show what relation the average man's god must bear to him. The intellectual can laugh, if he will; but let him not forget the pragmatic value of such a symbol among the type of people Garvey was dealing with.

The question is often asked, "Is Garvey sincere?" The same question might be asked of the McGee brothers of the Kentucky Revival and of evangelists in general. Although Garvey's appeal has been more permanent, his methods have been in many respects those of the evangelist. Just because evangelists as a rule are well fed and free from material wants, it would be uncritical to put them all down as common swindlers. Likewise, with the evidence we have, we can not classify Garvey as such. He has failed to deal realistically with life as most so-called cranks, but he has initiated a mass movement among Negroes because it appealed to something that is in every crowd-minded man.

THE PROBLEMS OF THE CITY DWELLER

When Mary McLeod Bethune published this essay in February 1925, approximately 34 percent of all Americans were living in urban areas. Bethune addresses the problems of black urban life and offers some thoughts on how black city dwellers might be assisted.

It is ever the problem of living a rational, healthy life in the midst of an environment which for the masses is for the most part, unfavorable. It is the problem of fresh air, wholesome food, sunshine and freedom within limits as pitilessly circumscribed as prison walls. It is the problem of making an increased wage, a better school, an easily accessible and cheap means of transportation, electric light, motion pictures, parades and band concerts, a policeman on the corner and propinquitous neighbors, compensate for the sweep of the hill, the greeness of expansive meadows, and the lure of the endless road. It is the problem of getting a chance to live the abundant life, the door to which in our urban centers yields only to the touch of a golden key.

The problem has been greatly intensified in the past ten or twenty years by the rush from the rural districts. This rush has been neither sectional nor racial. Every section of the country has felt it. While there may be specific causes back of the "push" that has moved hundreds of thousands of Negroes from the Southern States to various points in the North-east and middle West, the migration can be truthfully considered as only another phase of the general movement of population from the rural towards the urban centers. In fact, for a long period, preceding the migrations of large bodies of Negroes northward there was a steady and perceptible increase in the Negro population of Southern cities caused by a movement of this element of the population from the country to the city.

"During the past 30 years there has been a great shift of population from the country to the town, and every class of towns, from village to great cities, has grown, whereas the country districts have actually decreased in population. The increase of the Negro urban population in the South in the decade 1910–1920 was 396,444 or 56,000 more than the increase for the same period in the number of Negroes in the North from the South—340,260. More than one-third—34% of the total Negro population is living in urban territory. The census reports show an actual decrease of 234,876 or 3.4% in the Negro rural population of the United States. In 1910 the number of Negroes reported as living in rural territory was 7,138,534. In 1920 the number thus living reported was 6,903,658."

A powerful contributory cause for recent legislation in the restriction of immigration was the alarming extent to which our future citizens were concentrating in the large seaport and manufacturing cities instead of seeking the extensive and unworked agricultural lands of the middle West and the West. It is not necessary for me to worry you with census figures, and other statistics compiled by special investigators to establish the fact that the problem of the city dweller has been greatly intensified by this almost steady and constant movement of the rural dweller to the urban centers. The causes back of this almost universal movement of population cityward are usually conceded to be economic, educational and social.

In spite of the manifold movements, plans and efforts to make Farming and other rural pursuits pay, the country lad still turns his eye towards the city as his El Dorado. He wants a shorter working day; wages that will insure him good clothes and creature comforts; an opportunity to advance in earning power as he increases his ability to be of service in his calling; a fair chance to acquire wealth and become a leader in his community. To the country lad with plenty of time to dream while he plods thru days and days of monotonous routine, this is what the city means. To many an adult, weary of the grind and isolation of wresting a living from the soil, it offers an opening for a new chance, a realized vision. And so they come—young and old—beardless youth and gnarled old age—all expecting that the road to wealth and power and influence lies down the great white way of the modern city.

The cry of the Soul to know has given another push to this modern move towards the city. Longer school terms; better-equipped school buildings; more capable teachers; the broadening influence of lectures; concerts, motion pictures, libraries, parades and festive and holiday occasions, have lured many a grizzled homesteader to abandon home and ancestral acres and move cityward. The widening out and diversification of the modern high school with its facilities for teaching the technique of skilled trades and business, home economics and agriculture, as well as the arts and sciences. The extending of education at the public expense in some cities to include even a college education. The offering of night courses for underprivileged boys and girls, men and women. These are advantages which even the phonograph, the motion picture machine and the radio cannot compensate for in the country.

Then, again, in spite of automobiles, Fords, good roads and the transmission of electric light current over long distances, the country is still a lonely place for thousands and thousands of dwellers. Weary of quilting parties, barnraisings and quarterly meetings, they are impelled cityward by the age-old urge towards companionship and recreation. Happiness is usually a result of a perfect balancing of work-time, play-time and rest-time, and the normal human being is likely to continue to migrate until he arrives at a place where that balance comes nearest to being struck. The city with its socialized Churches, its civic clubs, its parks, its easily accessible amusement resorts and centers, its playgrounds, its bathhouses and skating rinks; its roof gardens, theatres and cabarets exert a pull as mighty as the social push of the rural populations toward the metropolitan centers.

Though not so often mentioned as a cause, the desire for protection has impelled many a rural dweller to move into or nearer the city. This is especially true with Negro rural dwellers in nearly every part of the South, where the lack or indifference of constabulary or police agencies make the possession of property uncertain—often hazardous and the safeguarding of life uncertain. These people turn towards the cities for protection in the exercise of the rights guaranteed them under the constitution, and a half chance to defend themselves should these rights be infringed upon. They also seek the protection from fire and ravages of disease which the superior organization and supervision of city life afford.

Because of these causes—educational—economic—social—the country has been for decades, disgorging itself into the cities and the very obtaining of the advantages it has come to seek presents the biggest problem to the city dwellers. To get wealth when the cost of living keeps pace or a little in advance of increased wages; to enjoy educational advantages when creature needs require the time of all whose strength can be turned into wages; to appreciate recreations that take for all the coin that should be spent for fuel and bread; to have better health and longer life in crowded ghettoes and sunless rooms; to have a neighbor in the man that lives next door and a friend in the thousands that pass unknowing and unknown along a hundred ways; to have children who will not grow to adult life unacquainted with a tree or afraid of a blade of grass; to have counting rooms and generous hearts; great white ways and unstained souls; apartment houses and the spirit of home; this, my friends, in homely, unscientific language, is the problem of the city dweller.

To meet this problem is the social challenge of our generation! To assist the city dweller to make the adjustments necessary to a full possession and enjoyment of the manifold blessings and privileges of urban life is the business of the Church; the mission of the trained social worker; the raison d'être of organized philanthropy and charity. To this task should be applied the earnest and intelligent aid of every group that makes up the population of our cities. It requires cooperation among racial groups widely differing in language, national customs, and color. It requires mutual racial respect and confidence. It requires tolerance and a courageous application to all sorts of unusual maladjustments, of the principle of the Golden rule. Whether the newcomer to the city is from Texas or South Carolina; whether he is from the Steppe of Russia or the sunny Plains of Italy; whether he is of Nordic hue, or wears the "shadowed livery of the burnished sun," his problem is to obtain for himself and family a living wage, and a place to invest it in cleanliness, fresh air, sanitary surroundings and wholesome recreation. Forcing individuals or groups into segregated ghettoes, with poor sanitation, unpaved streets, run-down houses, filthy alleys and surroundings conductive to depravity of both thought and action is neither a scientific nor altruistic approach to the problem of the city dweller. Agencies must be multiplied that can and will bring sufficient pressure to bear upon city governments to insure living conditions that will safeguard the well being of all the dwellers in urban centers, and the self respect of the individual. The work of Americanizing the foreigner thru easily accessible agencies for teaching him the language, customs and traditions of his adopted country, the work of protecting him in industry, educating his children, and drilling him in habits of decent living must be prosecuted with ever increasing earnestness and zeal. The breaking down of racial barriers and the conceding to every man his right to own and enjoy his property wherever his means permit him to own it; the opening up of parks and playgrounds for the enjoyment and development of all citizens alike; the firm but patient tutoring of the uninitiated newcomer in the privileges and obligations of urban life, must still be the foundation of the programme of organizations like the Urban League and other great social agencies whose militant efforts in these directions have made them national in scope and purpose.

The Negro and Economic Radicalism

A. Philip Randolph published this essay in February 1925 while he was the editor of the Messenger *magazine and an organizer for the Brotherhood of Sleeping Car Porters. Randolph underscores the unreasonable working conditions of the porters and the obstacles that prevent them from successfully organizing.*

The term radicalism is a bugbear in these United States of America. So adroitly has it been manipulated in the press that in the mind of the average man it connotes something sinister, terrible. Merely to mention the word makes our so-called respectable gentry feel creepy. Before them lurid visions arise of wild-eyed, hairy men and women, with red bandana handkerchiefs around their necks, daggers between their teeth and flaming torches in hand, stealthily prowling amidst banks, factories and homes, bent upon the destruction of private property. Even common wife-beaters and murderers, from the viewpoint of the 100 percenters, are shining angels of light to the radicals. As the behaviorists would say, this is the result of their language organization or language habit.

But, of course, it is all pure fiction. It does not mean any such thing of the kind. Radicals are not lawless. They are not such ungodly humans. They merely have the courage of their convictions, seeking ever not only to point out social wrongs, but also to indicate the cause and prescribe a remedy. They are seekers after truth. As the word implies, they want to get at the roots of our social problems. It is for this only that they are damned and spat upon, for the nonce.

Now, there are different shades, types and schools of radicals, differing largely in forms of tactics, of methodology, in trying to right our social maladjustments. But all represent a revolt against the old ways of thinking and doing things. Of course, any one who breathes the slightest social, political or economic protest, such as Roosevelt, Woodrow Wilson, Jane Addams or La Follette, is forthwith labelled a radical.

During and since the World War the outcry for economic citizenship, for industrial democracy, has become more insistent and passionate.

Doubtless the war, the dynastic and political revolutions in Russia, Germany and the Balkans, contributed to the growth of radical movements working for the relief of the masses from economic stresses and social injustices.

And out of different social situations have emerged varying forms of radicalism. In India, China, Egypt and Ireland it is nationalistic; in England, France, Germany and Italy, economic; in Russia, politico-economic; among Negroes in America and South Africa, politico-economic and racial.

In these United States of America, among Negroes, the radical form has taken precedence, since the obvious incidence of oppression was racial. The elder race radicals, such as Frederick Douglass, Bishops Daniel A. Payne and Henry McNeal Turner, Monroe Trotter, Kelly Miller, W. E. B. Du Bois, James Weldon Johnson, the Grimkes, T. Thomas Fortune, etc., struck out against the race's detractors of the ilk of former Confederate slave masters, Thomas Dixon, Vardaman and Blease, instead of against the race's exploiters, such as the pawnbrokers, loan sharks, turpentine still and plantation owners who foster peonage and tenant-farming; and the lumber mill and railroad barons who overwork and underpay the black proletariat. This attitude of mind was doubtless due to the fact that they stood under the shadows of the old slave regime and the aftermath, which through vagrancy laws, corrupt court practices, grandfather clauses, the subtle nullification of the 13th, 14th, and 15th amendments to the Constitution, and segregation, well-nigh effectually re-enslaved the Negro. Hence theirs was not an unmerited fight.

Out of this revolt the Niagara Movement, the National Association for the Advancement of Colored People and the Equal Rights League, were formed. They proclaimed a civil rights program. They wanted political citizenship. Of the outstanding Negro leaders, only Archibald and J. Francis Grimke, James Weldon Johnson, W. E. B. DuBois and George E. Haynes seem to have sensed, though lightly and seldom stressing it, that there were other factors in the so-called race problem equation save race; that there was the "nickle under the foot," an economic basis to the conflict of races in America.

Of organizations, in the last two or three conventions, the National Association for the Advancement of Colored People has been definitely adopting a program in the interest of the organization of black workers.

The National Urban League too, in a less militant way, more in the form of surveys and securing new industrial opportunities, has turned its attention to the question of improving the lot of the Negro workers.

In the main, the old crowd leadership damned the detractors and blessed the exploiters of the race, because the former criticized and the latter subsidized the Negro industrial schools and colleges. The elder race radicals, in their heyday, while they did not bless the exploiters of the race, they did not oppose them. They simply thought that the struggle for civil rights was more important. Kelly Miller is a peculiar exception. Though a consistent fighter in the interest of civil rights, he fawns before the altar of big business and glorifies the so-called capitalists' benefactions to the race, apparently unmindful of the service which black labor is to white capitalists.

Only since the war has economic radicalism within the race emerged. Its chief mouthpiece is the *Messenger* magazine, which is more philosophically and less dogmatically radical. It is more pronouncedly labor unionistic. During the hot days of the war and immediately thereafter the outstanding Negro economic radicals were Chandler Owen, Otto Houiswond, Frank R. Crosswaith, Ross D. Brown, Helen Holman, Eugene Moore, W. A. Domingo, Lovett Fort-Whiteman, Hubert H. Harrison and the writer. They were Socialists. The Communists' schism, which grew out of the Russian revolution, split them just as it did the white Socialists everywhere. Today the Negro radicals, like the whites, are few in number and weak in influence. Their movements were well-nigh liquidated by the frenzied persecution under Burleson, Palmer, Daugherty and Sweet, during and after the war. The movement represented by the American Negro Labor Congress is perhaps the strongest, which is not saying anything for it, but a whole lot against it.

However, the Negro radicals have not wrought in vain. It was theirs definitely to shape a working class economic perspective in Negro thought. Booker T. Washington had very masterly stressed the bourgeois side. Negro workers had been viewed as the flotsam and jetsam of the race; for had not even the white workers in the South been dubbed reproachfully as poor trash, while the rich white people were regarded as the Negroes' benefactors?

Booker T. Washington had sought to prepare Negro workers for new industrial and agricultural tasks which grew out of the rapid industrialization of the South, whereas the burden today is securing an adequate reward for the performance of those tasks. This raises the question of the how and wherefore.

It is out of this latter economic concept that the trend of Negro workers into economic organization grows.

Perhaps the most significant manifestation of this trend is the movement to organize the Pullman porters. Of course, this movement is not radical, except in the sense that the whole trade union movement is fundamentally radical. It is not backed by Moscow, nor has it any Communistic connections, as has been falsely charged. It is a simple labor union seeking a living wage and better working conditions. It also has spiritual aims, such as the abolition of professional mendicancy, which is the result of relying upon tips for the means of life—a demoralizing practice. The porters also want a voice in the determination of the conditions under which they work, the abolition of the Pullman feudalistic paternalism, a relic of the old master and servant relationship. They want to maintain their manhood, their self-respect. This can only be secured through organization of, by and for themselves, because organization is the only basis of power. The Brotherhood will not injure the Pullman company; it will help it. It does not counsel insubordination, but efficient discipline.

Specifically, the porters want to raise their wages from $67.50 a month to a point which will enable them to command commodities and services essential to a decent American standard of living, as budgeted by such accredited economic agencies as the U. S. Bureau of Labor Statistics.

They also want pay for preparatory time, or the time from which a porter reports for duty and the train departs. For example, a porter leaving for Washington from New York at 12:30 midnight, any night, reports for duty at 7:30 P.M., works until 12:30 making ready his car and receiving passengers, but his time does not begin until the train leaves the terminal station. In other words, he has given the Pullman Company five hours of his labor for absolutely nothing. On the basis of his monthly wage, $67.50, he receives 25 cents an hour. Five hours of work put in as preparatory time represents $1.25. This the porter is deprived of every night he makes the trip. He makes the trip twelve times a month, which means that he loses in labor values $15 every month, or $180 a year; not an inconsiderable item, this, for a worker whose yearly wage is only $810. There are thousands of porters in the service who thus work without pay, so that, over a period of a year, it would be conservative to estimate the exploitation to trench hard upon a million and a half dollars.

But this is not the only palpable injustice practiced upon the porters.

There are what is known as "in charge" porters, or those that do the conductor's and porter's work combined. But they only receive a porter's pay, plus $10 additional monthly. Since the minimum conductor's pay is $155 a month, the company saves $145 on every porter who runs "in charge." One of the demands of the Brotherhood is: Conductor's pay for conductor's work. The company will not even flatter the porter with the title of conductor. He is titled "in charge."

Perhaps the most unreasonable condition of the porter's work is the requirement that he make 11,000 miles a month, which is nearly 400 hours' work, an inhuman exaction. Upon such a mileage basis, if a porter's train were five or six hours late every trip, he would not get a cent for it, because the time sheet requires that his delayed arrivals be put in the accumulated mileage column, which renders it practically impossible for a porter to make overtime unless he has an extraordinarily long run. The demand of the porters is for 240 *hours or less in regular assignment* as a monthly basis of pay. This is not a revolutionary demand, since the other railroad workers have it, including the Pullman conductors.

It is practically because of these just demands, already possessed by all other railroad workers, that the Pullman company has waged a vicious and relentless war upon the men organizing. Through threats and intimidations it has attempted to force the men to vote for its company union, euphemistically called the Employee Representation Plan, a plan initiated, dominated and controlled by the company and which was designed to impress the men and the public with the idea that the porters have an organization. Under the plan the Assistant District Superintendent, who has the power to recommend the discharge of a porter, sits in the Local Grievance Committee and passes on all cases involving disputes between the porters and the company or porters and passengers. In other words, the local management of the company acts as prosecutor, judge and jury.

In order to prevent the porters from achieving their objective, the company has employed Mr. Perry W. Howard, Negro Special Assistant to the United States Attorney General, and smothered the criticism of several Negro newspapers by placing advertisements with them. Be it said to the credit of the Eastern Negro press that they refused to be bought.

But the company, in utter desperation, did not stop at trying to throttle the Negro press. It reached out for the Negro leaders, and it has not entirely failed.

The conference of fifty Negro leaders recently held in Washington, presumably to discuss matters of segregation, actually engaged only in condemning the movement to organize the Pullman porters. I do not charge, however, that every person in that conference knew that he was being used as a tool to prevent the porters from getting a living wage. But it is difficult to understand their silence after they learned of the corruption of the conference. It is quite significant that a conference called to discuss segregation did not invite the National Association for the Advancement of Colored People, the organization which has most consistently fought the evil. But, of course, the reason was that the N. A. A. C. P. had already officially endorsed the Brotherhood of Sleeping Car Porters, and its speakers, James Weldon Johnson, William Pickens and Robert W. Bagnall, have spoken for the movement throughout the country.

One need not be a prophet to realize that the beneficent consequences of this movement to the Negro are immeasurable. It will awaken the Negro workers everywhere to a sense of their power and rights, and the methods to adopt in order to secure them. It will develop more spirit, manhood and independence in the race. It is a promise of economic and spiritual liberation.

Immunity to Disease Among Dark-Skinned People

Charles H. Garvin, a prominent African-American doctor, explains in this essay why some racial groups are susceptible to diseases. However, Dr. Garvin acknowledges that there is no absolute racial immunity to any disease. This essay was published in August 1926.

The subject of immunity shares with other branches of medical science the difficulties of constantly being subjected to alterations of point of view and concept. Every infectious disease or pathological process is the result of a struggle between two variable factors, the pathological powers of the infecting bacteria or causative agent, on the one hand, and the resistance of the subject on the other hand, each of course modified by variations in the conditions under which the struggle takes place. Again, infectious organisms may be capable of causing a fatal infection in one individual but may be only moderately virulent or entirely innocuous for another and conversely. The physical state or environmental condition under which the invader and the invaded are brought together are determining factors.

The mere fact that animals and man are in constant contact with infectious agencies, many virulent, and do not succumb reveals that there is a defensive mechanism. This is due to the unique modes of defense that we possess. The susceptibility or capacity for resistance on the part of the body to disease, or in a more limited sense to infection we call immunity. Therefore, the conception immunity, resistance and susceptibility are relative terms which can never be discussed without consideration of all the modifying conditions. It has long been known that having suffered from one attack of a certain disease that the individual is more refractory to subsequent infections; generally one attack of small pox, typhoid, mumps, yellow fever, scarlet fever, confers immunity. This is the basis of our sound principles of vaccination. This is acquired immunity. You can no doubt recall epidemics of disease that have swept through a community and have attacked many and yet left others untouched. This we call natural immunity. When this immunity is limited to a particular group or race, we call it racial immunity. When this is limited to one of a race, we call it individual immunity. There are all gradations and divisions of immunity, but we are only concerned with that immunity which depends upon certain racial attributes. This paper was prepared in the hope that a concise statement of the facts and more important hypothesis concerning immunity and resistance to disease of the dark skinned peoples may become known.

There is no doubt that there is a difference in susceptibility between various races of man and there are many interesting factors. It must be remembered that no absolute immunity exists. The highest attainable immunity may be broken down by environmental conditions and physical state. Racial immunity cannot be conclusively proven in man as in animals, because of the racial intermingling that has been going on for centuries and will continue to go one. This is all the more difficult in the American Negro. In speaking of immunity in this paper, I shall only discuss the more common diseases and many of the details and theories of immunity will be brought out in the discussion of the various diseases. It is generally agreed that the Caucasian is less susceptible to tuberculosis than is the Negro, Indian and Eskimo, but that the Negro shows more resistance to yellow fever, malaria and hookworm than does the white man. It is interesting also to note the nearer the Negro is to the equator, the less susceptible he is to yellow fever.

Before going further into the subject, it might be wise to discuss the question of inheritance of disease and immunity. It is a question not definitely decided, whether racial immunity is really an instance of survival of the fittest or whether immunity acquired by an individual can be wholly or in part transmitted to an offspring. There are, however, a number of factors which indicate that inheritance plays an important part. Whether direct inheritance of the individually acquired immunity may be considered at all as a contributing factor is difficult to say. Various experiments permit no doubt as to the validity of this fact. Many regard this so called hereditary immunity as not inherited susceptibility or resistance, but rather as an acquired immunity from a mild infection in childhood. *Some* observers argue that this immunity is dependent upon a gradual elimination as far as reproduction is concerned of those individuals that are more susceptible and by gradual selection a higher racial resistance is gradually developed. Hans

Zinsser[1] believes that an inherited factor plays a big part in immunity. Rosenau[2] believes that there is a certain degree of resistance inherited.

It is apparent and convincing that in the case of many diseases afflicting human beings that infection takes a milder course in those races among which it has long been endemic; whereas the same disease suddenly introduced among a new people is relatively more severe and spreads more rapidly. It is more infectious and virulent in races first attacked than in those from which it comes. The decimation of the population of Ireland after the introduction of measles was one of the horrors of improved communications. Subsequent epidemics have been less fatal. The introduction of syphilis among the American Indians and Negroes showed a virulence unheard among the Caucasian. Syphilis was formerly unknown in regions populated by Negroes which had not been invaded by whites. Syphilis when first described epidemically toward the close of the fifteenth century was certainly more virulent than it is today. The native African when brought in contact with tuberculosis rapidly succumbs. The Negro is certainly less susceptible to tropical fevers than is the Caucasian. They are diseases that he has been fighting for centuries. Many explain this as due to mild infections acquired during childhood. The fact remains the same, nevertheless.

Whether or not direct inheritance of the individually acquired immunity may be transmitted is difficult to say. The immunity transferred to an offspring may be natural immunity or may be an immunity acquired by the parent and transferred to the fetus, because of the presence of factors in the circulating blood of the mother. The Caucasian having been the victim of tuberculosis for many centuries—it is called the "White Plague"—a degree of racial immunity has been established by virtue of the element of the survival of the more resistant individuals. It is also true that there has been an inherited resistance, if only in physical makeup. Tuberculosis is certainly less virulent among them. Some argue that what appears to be inherent characteristics of the race is difference in hygienic conditions and degree of exposure.

Fishberg[3] states that a study of the epidemology of tuberculosis teaches that the danger of tuberculosis infection depends upon the length of time a people have been exposed to the disease. Thus, when primitive peoples, who have never been affected with the disease move into tuberculosis surroundings, they soon become infected and the disease runs an acute and fatal course. This was the case of Negroes brought to America. They acquired tuberculosis easily and succumbed readily. We know that tuberculosis is no respecter of races. The Chinese, even under the worst possible conditions of overcrowding, sanitation and hygiene show no greater mortality tables than do the Caucasian, probably their greater age as a race and longer exposure to infection have built up their resistance in spite of adverse living conditions.

The American Indians coming in contact with whites, and therefore with the tuberculosis germ, were practically decimated by the disease which ran an acute and fatal course as among the American Negro.

In Africa where the Negro lives uncontaminated by white civilization, tuberculosis and syphilis are unknown. Even among the Senegalese the disease is never endemic. Cummins[4] points out that the Sudanese soldiers recruited from tribes among which tuberculosis is practically unknown, were much more liable to tuberculosis than those who have been in contact with it, as have been the Egyptians. Even in past centuries, the Sudanese slaves were the cheapest on the market because it was assumed that a large number would contract tuberculosis and die.

It is a common observation among those that specialize in tuberculosis that the greater number of those with tuberculosis among the dark skinned races have the so-called "young adult type," a very fulminating and virulent type. Paisseau[5] states that tuberculosis in the native African reveals the character of a primary infection similar to that seen in infants infected. Carter[6] of the Virginia Sanitorium has observed this same fact. Most of his cases were between 20 and 30 years of age and the whites were between 28 and 34 years of age. He concludes that this indicates a lessened resistance on account of absence of contact and that it explains the predominance of the "young adult type" of tuberculosis in the Negro. He further observes that the high death rate is due to lack of resistance, due to short periods of contact of the race with the disease rather than bodily weakness and unhealthful surroundings. Grandy[7] also emphasizes this fact and further adds that "where the same type of preventive work is done on both white and Negro the disease will be lessened in the Negro."

Carter[8] observed that the mulatto has better resistance to the disease than does the black. This is undoubtedly true because of the intermixture and thus acquiring of more immunity. His studies show also that while there is lessened resistance the Negro will as rapidly respond to treatment as the white and will remain well just as long.

Borel[9] states that in the areas of Africa that have not had contact with European civilization, tuberculosis is practically unknown. This was proven by the experience of the British army and its African troops when transported to France in 1917–18. The death rate from tuberculosis was 56% against 5.7% for the other British troops. This was in troops who had been subjected to careful and rigid medical examination before leaving Africa and who therefore acquired tuberculosis in France. Borel informs that among French African troops who recently arrived from Senegal only 4% or 5% gave a positive cutaneous reaction—a test that indicates whether one is tuberculous. In these same troops after staying in France the death rate increased to 11.14%. On the other hand the American Negro troops who had been exposed to tuberculosis in the United States did not have an excessive tuberculosis mortality while serving in France in the American army. This same fact is noted among the immigrants to the United States, coming from countries and cities long exposed to tuberculosis. In the Jew the tuberculosis mortality is less. This proves that long contact means heightened immunity. The almost universal decline of tuberculosis in countries where it was formerly epidemic and the decreased incidence of this disease in racial stocks that have been exposed long to civilization and to tuberculosis have in general been due to an increasing immunity acquired by infection. Brolet[10] contends that children of tuberculous parents do not even inherit a predisposition to the disease but an increased degree of immunity to its invasion.

When speaking of race influence on the incidence of tuberculosis the facts mentioned must be borne in mind. Tuberculosis appears not to be a racial problem. There are no races which are more or less vulnerable to the disease because of ethnic peculiarities, such as height of body, color of skin and other morphological traits which distinguish one race from another.

Fishberg[3] states that one human race when first meeting tuberculosis is as vulnerable as another. It is only after they have been exposed for many generations to the disease that they acquire a resistance.

The susceptibility of dark-skinned races to pneumonia is well known. The death rate is very high even in the United States. In 1923 the death rate was 137.8 per 100,000 as against a death rate of 160.8 in 1911. Rosenau[2] points out that pneumonia is particularly virulent among races in which it has not been prevalent. This was the case with the laborers in the Panama Canal and in the diamond mines of Africa. He believes that a certain amount of racial immunity is acquired through long conflict with pneumonia. The Senegalese proved especially susceptible to pneumonia on transporting them to France during the World War, more than 5% succumbing to pneumonia before they had been acclimated. In those that had been in France two or three years the death rate was reduced to two in 7,000. Whether this reduction is due to acclimation or early elimination of the more susceptible is an open and debatable question.

As early as 1894 Dean Ballock[11] of Howard University School of Medicine called attention to three conditions peculiar to dark skinned races—keloid, fibroma and elephantiasis. He affirmed as a pathological axiom that fibrous processes constitute a racial peculiarity and applied the term "fibroid diathesis" to the tendency. Matas[12] of New Orleans a few years later stated that fibroid tumors occur five times more frequent in those of African descent than in the whites. Howard Kelly[13] of Johns Hopkins affirms this. Most observers having a chance to make observation agree that fibroma are more common in the dark skinned races. I am quite positive that a statistical review of the records of hospitals with a large Negro clientele will substantiate this. Most observers point out the frequency of fibroid tumors in native African women and rarity of cancer.

Keloid, which is an excessive growth of fibrous scar tissue, usually resulting in a healing wound is seen almost exclusively in those of African descent, about eighteen times as common as in whites. My own observation bears out the fact that scar formation is much more abundant in dark skinned peoples. In fact, benign fibrous strictures occur about ten times as often in the Negro. Day,[14] investigating the urologic idiosyncrasies of the Negro was also impressed with the presence of a number of fibrous tissue reaction in lesions, strictures, multiple fistulæ resulting from structure and types of gland enlargements. Rosser[15] of Texas also called attention to a large number of benign rectal strictures in dark skinned people.

Matas[12] believes that scar tissue formation is frequent in the Negro because of the syphilis and tuberculosis, but he is in error because fibrous changes, especially keloid is noticed in the nonsyphilized and non-tuberculized African native, who utilize this tendency for purposes of ornamentation and tribal identification. The smallest wound such as ear piercing often results in large fibrous growth. This certainly offsets that theory. Most investigators state that there is no real difference in the histology of the scar tissue in the races. Alexis Carrell in a careful histological study admits that there is a factor in dark skinned folk which causes an exaggerated fibrous tissue reaction but does not know the factor.

There is certainly a fibroplastic diatheses in rectal and unrologic cases, but rectal and genito-urinary cancer is 3 1/2 times more frequent in the white race. According to Royster of St. Agnes Hospital in

North Carolina, a hospital for colored patients, there is no record of a case of rectal cancer. However, U. S. census show that in 1920 the Negro death rate from cancer had risen from 3.8 in 100,000 in 1880 to 50.4 in 100,000. The rarity of melonitic cancer, a type of cancer characterized by an abundant deposit of pigmentation is still a puzzle when we consider the enormous stores of pigment in the skin of Negro that could be made the play of the cancer that is so destructive in white race.

The rarity of cancer among primitive people is noticeable. It certainly is a disease of modern civilization. The rarity of cancer among the native African has been noted by all investigators. M. Guyon, a physician in the French African army says that in the north of Africa and even in tropical Africa it is very rare. A list of the causes of death in Algiers for a number of years showed no death from cancer in the natives.

Rosser[15] believes in the heritability of this diathesis and the possibility of the perseverance of distinct characteristics in dark skinned races. While he discredits the inheritance of disease as such, he believes that the predisposition to certain disease is heritable. Karl Pearson also believes in the heritability of predisposition to disease. Rosser[15] suggests that in the slow and gradual development of the human race from a lower mammalian class, numerous separations and divisions have occurred, some offshoots being stranded in a primitive stage. The Negro division of the human family possessing distinctive anatomical characteristics bearing the unmistakable print of this origin, approaches the anthropoid apes in the esential characteristics in which he differs anatomically from the rest of mankind. This is not the opinion, however, of authorities in anthropology.

Granuloma inguinale, a tropical ulceration usually occurring in the inguinal region is another disease that is seen almost exclusively in the Negro. Nearly every case reported in the United States was in a Negro. In 1923 I[16] made a review of the literature of this tropical disease and found only one case in whites. This is a bacterial disease found mostly in the tropics and why it is found almost exclusively in Negroes has not been determined.

Rickets is another disease that seems to attack Negro children in the United States in very large numbers. The greatest number of cases are seen in Negro and Italian children. This is a deficiency disease seen in city children in crowded tenements, where there is faulty diet and lack of sunshine. In Africa the disease is not seen. There is no racial factor except the poor hygienic surroundings in Negro tenements. Jewish children have fewer cases. I am of the opinion, however, that the deformities of the chest caused by rickets certainly predispose the Negro to tuberculosis and other respiratory diseases. Public health measures are doing a great deal to cut this disease down. This is also a frequent cause of death in childhood, not primarily, but because rickets makes the inroads of other diseases easy. Although the general death rate of the Negro in the registration area is about 15 per cent higher than in the whites, the difference between the mortality rates of the two races in early childhood is most striking. More than one-fourth of all Negro children born alive die before they are five years old. Among the outstanding causes of infant mortality are pneumonia, tuberculosis, syphilis. Syphilis, tuberculosis and pneumonia account for 29 per cent of all infant deaths among Negro children and only 7 per cent among white children.

The Negro has a definite immunity to hookworm. This is a disease that he has had in Africa and he has built up an immunity to it. There are a large number of cases in the American Negro but they are mild and do not make the inroads that it does among the whites in the South. It, however, lowers his resistance and I am of the opinion that it is one of the factors in making the inroads of tuberculosis easy. The Negro seems especially susceptible to smallpox and the mortality is greater. The apparent racial immunity to malaria may be explained by the long contact with the disease and the probability of acquiring immunity during childhood by mild cases.

Dublin of the Metropolitan Insurance Company points out the increase in mortality from the "degenerative" diseases, like cerebral hemorrhage, organic diseases of the heart and kidneys, in the Negro. These are the so-called diseases of civilization. This is not a racial tendency, but the present tendency in all races. The increased incidence is attributed to syphilis and to the fact that the Negro is living longer and these are diseases of advanced life and that he is living better, has more ease, eats more, becomes more obese, and thus holds himself liable as does the white man, to hypertention and diabetes. Diabetes is also on the increase in the Negro.

CONCLUSIONS

There is a difference in susceptibility to disease between races of men, but there is no absolute racial immunity to any disease.

It is apparent that disease takes a milder course among those in which it has long been endemic and a new disease suddenly introduced among a new people is more virulent. One human race or ethnic group is as vulnerable as another to disease. Long contact gives resistance.

The Negro is not more susceptible to tuberculosis because of physical makeup or inherent racial traits, but because his resistance has not had time to develop.

There is no doubt but that dark-skinned races are prone to fibroplastic processes.

· BIBLIOGRAPHY

1. Zinsser: Infection and Resistance. Macmillan Co., N. Y.

2. Rosenau: Preventive Medicine and Hygiene. D. Appleton, N. Y.

3. Fishberg: Pulmonary Tuberculosis. Lea & Febiger, N. Y.

4. Cummins: Tr. Soc. Trop. Med. and Hy., 1911–12, Vol. V. p. 245.
Cummins: *Inter. Jour. of Public Health* 1920, Vol. 1, p. 137.

5. Paisseau: *Bulletins de la Societe Medicel des Hospitaux,* Paris, October, 1924.

6. Carter: Pulmonary Tuberculosis Among Negroes. *Am. Rev. of Tuber.,* Jan. 1926, Vol. VI, p. 11.

7. Grandy: Racial Characteristics as Cause of High Tuberculosis Death Rate Among Negroes. *Am. Rev. of Tuber.,* Nov., 1924.

8. Carter: Further Observations on Pulmonary Tuberculosis in American Negroes. *Am. Rev. of Tuber.,* Jan., 1923, Vol. VI, pp. 1002–1007.

9. Borel: Ann. Inst. Pasteur. 1920, Vol. XXXIV, p. 105.

10. Brolet: Inheritance Factor in Tuberculosis. *Am. Rev. of Tuber.,* Nov., 1924.

11. Balloch, E. A.: Relative Frequency of Fibroid Processes in Dark Skin Races. *Trans. Southern Med. Assoc.*

12. Matas: Surgical Peculiarities of the Negroes. *Trans. Am. Surg. Assoc.,* 1896.

13. Kelley, Howard: *Medical Gynecology.* Appleton, N. Y.

14. Day: Urological Idiosyncrasies of the Negro. *Jour. of Urol.* Vol. V, 1925.

15. Rosser: Proctologic Peculiarities of the Negro. *Am. J. Surg.,* Nov., 1923, Vol. XXXVII, pp. 265–271.
Rosser: Rectal Pathology in the Negro. *Jour. Am. M. Assoc.,* Jan. 10, 1925, Vol. LXXXIV, p. 2.

16. Castelleni and Chalmers: *Manual of Tropical Diseases.*
Mendelsohn: Natural Immunity to Infection and Resistance to Disease as Exhibited by Orientals. *Phill. Jo. of Sc.,* Feb., 1923.

17. Emerson: War Medicine. Vol. II, Pct. 1918.

18. Kolmer: Infection, Immunity and Specific Therapy. Saunders, N. Y.

19. Barker, J. Ellis: Cancer. E. P. Dutton Co., N. Y.

20. Goldstein: Diabetes in Negroes. *N. J. Med. Soc. Jour.* June, 1922, Vol. XIX, p. 6.

LILY-WHITE LABOR

When this essay was published in June 1930, its author, Ira De A. Reid, was Director of Research for the National Urban League. Reid discusses the divergence between the unions' stated policies regarding admitting African Americans and the realities for the masses of black workers.

In 1881, Jeremiah Grandison, a Negro worker of Pittsburgh, Pa., told the Federation of Organized Trades and Labor Unions then meeting in that city, that it would be dangerous for them to exclude from their membership common laborers in general, and Negro workers in particular, lest they "in an emergency, be employed in positions they could readily qualify themselves to fill." At that time the skilled craftsman was supreme. Through his union he sought to protect his skill, which was at a premium, and his craft which was an art. The organization of the unskilled worker was considered ill-advised, for that group then would become dependent upon the skilled workers in the unions. The unskilled worker was to be considered only when the skilled ones "were in danger of losing their advantages and places, due to the unstinted competition of the unskilled."

The Federation of Organized Trades and Labor Unions resolved itself into the American Federation of Labor, which organization attempted to maintain the same liberal membership policy for Negro workers that was fostered by the Knights of Labor. For the first nine years of its existence the pressure of organization routine kept the racial difficulties in the background. It was not until 1890 that the A. F. of L. gave specific attention to the problem of color discrimination. In that year it went on record as looking with disfavor "upon trades unions having provisions in their constitutions which exclude from membership persons on account of race or color." The 1893 convention reaffirmed "as one of the cardinal principles of the labor movement that the working people must unite or organize, irrespective of creed, color, sex, nationality or politics." In substantiation of this avowed policy labor leaders cited the fact that the International Association of Machinists had been refused admission to the Federation because its membership was limited to white persons. In 1897 the Federation finding it necessary to refute charges to the effect that trades unions were obstructing the economic progress of Negroes by refusing them admission to their organizations, declared that "it welcomes into its ranks all labor without regard to creed, color, race, sex or nationality, and that its efforts have been and will continue to be to encourage the organization of those most needing its protection, whether in the North or South, East or West, white or black." When, in 1910, Samuel Gompers was accused of reading the Negro out of the labor movement, he stated that, "instead of reading the Negroes out of the labor movement, my contention, and the contention of the American Federation of Labor is to try to bring them into the organized labor movement in our own country."

For forty odd years such declarations as the aforementioned have been fed to the Negro workers. When the World War ushered in a period of greater industrial inclusion for Negro workers, representatives of Negro organizations petitioned the A. F. of L. to "show a more active interest in the organization of Negro labor." As a result of this overture, the 1918 convention adopted a resolution to the following effect:

"It is with pleasure we learn that leaders of the colored race realize the necessity of organizing the workers of that race into unions affiliated with the American Federation of Labor, and your committee recommends that the Executive Council give special attention to organizing the colored wage workers in the future. We wish it understood, however, that in doing so no fault is or can be found with the work done in the past, but we believe that with the cooperation of the leaders of that race much better results can be accomplished."

When the Communists called the Negro Labor Congress in Chicago in October, 1925, the Federation branded the scheme as deceptive and deserving of the indignation it received. For "It is bad enough to mislead those who have an equal opportunity to know, but *to take advantage of the weakness of those who have a moral right to our special care* is quite outside the pale of decency and ethics. The A. F. of L. offers to Negro wage earners as a substitute for the Communist movement the "protection and the experience of the Trade Union Movement"* (as exemplified by the A. F. of L.).

---

*Editorial—The American Federationist, Vol. 32, No. 10, October, 1925.

Though the American Federation of Labor has uttered pronouncement upon pronouncement favoring the admission of Negro workers,
that body has failed to convince the masses of Negro workers that it is
rendering other than lip service to such expressed policies. For evidence these workers cite the fact that twenty-two national unions,
eleven of which are affiliated to the A. F. of L., exclude Negroes from
their membership through provisions in their constitutions or rituals.

II

In addition to the Brotherhood of Dining Car Conductors, the Order
of Railway Conductors of America, the Grand International Brotherhood of Locomotive Engineers, the Brotherhood of Locomotive Fire-
men and Enginemen, the Neptune Association, the American
Federation of Railroad Workers, the Brotherhood of Railroad Station
Employers and Clerks, the American Association of Train Dispatch-
ers, the Railroad Yardmasters of America, the Railroad Yardmasters of
North America the following unions affiliated with the A. F. of L. exclude Negro workers: The International Brotherhood of Boilermak-
ers, Iron Shipbuilders and Helpers of America, the International
Association of Machinists, the Brotherhood of Railway Carmen, the
Brotherhood of Railway and Steamship Clerks, Freight Handlers, Ex-
press and Station Employees, the Order of Sleeping Car Conductors,
the National Organization of Masters, Mates and Pilots of North
America, the Switchmen's Union of North America, the Railway Mail
Association, the American Wire Weavers Protective Association, the
Order of Railway Telegraphers and the Commercial Telegraphers
Union of America. As a result of the exclusion policy of the eleven
unions affiliated to the Federation not less than 225,000 Negro workers are denied trade union affiliation and its attendant benefits.

Because of the A. F. of L.'s policy that affiliated organizations may
not retain in their constitutions any discriminatory clause or clauses
against the race or color of workers, the Boilermakers and the Machinists accomplish such an exclusion by a pledge which forms a part
of the ritual, and binds each member to propose only white workmen
for membership. Singularly, the Machinists who were refused membership in the Federation until 1895 because the constitution made eligible for membership "white workers" only, were admitted when the
same exclusion was achieved through their ritual. The Negro workers,
however, would have little reason for quarreling with the American
Federation of Labor if that organization did no more than obey the let-

ter of the law. Though some unions not admitting Negro workers have jurisdiction over fields in which few or no Negroes are employed—as the Dining Car Conductors—that exclusion serves to prevent Negro employment in that field. Unfortunately the A. F. of L. has not played fair with itself in this respect, to wit: the cases of the Machinists, the Boilermakers, the Railway Clerks and the Railway Mail Association.

In the case of the Railway and Steamship Clerks, the Federation (1) permitted the union to remain a member and exclude Negro workers (2) organized the excluded workers into local unions subject to the A. F. of L. (3) failed to validate its ruling on discriminatory clauses by permitting the Railway Clerks to retain its affiliation to the A. F. of L. (4) suspended the union because it failed to obey a ruling of the Federation on a jurisdictional dispute arising with the Teamsters' Union (5) permitted the union to reaffiliate upon satisfactory settlement of this dispute without having the clause "all white persons" removed from the constitution.

About fifteen years ago the Railway Mail Association was reported to have two hundred Negro members who were railway postal employees. While a member of the A. F. of L. this body amended its constitution so as to exclude Negroes from membership because "statistics indicate that certain groups of society are a greater risk than other groups. Being chartered as a fraternal organization it was inconsistent for the Association to attempt to carry any group of workers at the expense of others, and this thought possibly had a great deal to do with the amending of the constitution as it was amended." The only Negro members of the Association today are the "hangovers" from the early days.

The American Federation of Labor condones other discriminatory practices affecting Negro workers. The Railway Carmen, for example, limits its membership to "any white person between the ages of 16 and 65 years." In 1921 the Carmen, without changing the aforementioned restriction made a special ruling covering 500 Negro workers employed on railroads in the South. The constitutional amendment on this matter reading:

"On railroads where the employment of colored persons has become a permanent institution they shall be admitted to membership in separate lodges. Where these lodges of Negroes are organized they shall be under the jurisdiction of the nearest white local, and shall be represented in any meeting of the Joint Protective Board Federation, meetings or conventions where delegates may be seated, by white men."

No more definite example of the restriction of free labor is extant than that fostered by the International Brotherhood of Blacksmiths, Drop Forgers and Helpers, affiliated to the A. F. of L. When the Blacksmiths were forced to organize the Negro workers because of the great inroads that group was making into the organized field, the following constitutional qualifications were established:

> "Where there are a sufficient number of colored helpers they may be organized as an auxiliary local and shall be under the jurisdiction of the white local having jurisdiction over that territory. Colored helpers shall not transfer except to another auxiliary local composed of colored members, and *colored members shall not be promoted to blacksmiths or helper apprentices and will not be admitted to shops where white workers are now employed.*"

One of the objects of the Brotherhood of Blacksmiths is "to perpetuate our association on the basis of friendship and justice." What a satisfying creed for 10,000 Negro workers employed in the trades over which this union has jurisdiction!

The analysis may be carried on to include the Brotherhood of Maintenance of Way Employees, with 10,000 Negro members, all of whom are entitled to "all of the benefits and protection guaranteed by the constitution," but not one of whom may represent his lodge in the grand lodge. That privilege is for white men, who shall be selected by their colored brethren. Or, the analysis may include the International Association of Sheet Metal Workers who organize Negro sheet metal workers into segregated unions from which they may not transfer except to another segregated union; or the Hotel and Restaurant Employees who provide in Section 20 of their constitution, that

> "If a colored worker at our craft shall desire to enter a local in a city where only a white local exists, he may be accepted in the International Union as a member-at-large, provided he possesses the necessary qualifications."

or, the National Federation of Rural Letter Carriers who, while accepting Negro members in some states permit only white members to serve as delegates to conventions, and as office holders; or, the Flint Glass Workers who object to Negro workers universally because "the pipes on which glass is blown pass from one man's mouth to another"; or, the Journeymen Plumbers and the Electrical Workers, who, though not restricting membership to white workers by law are generally understood not to admit Negroes. As early as 1903 the editor of *The Electrical Worker* wrote "We do not want the Negro in the International Brotherhood of Electrical Workers, but we think that they should be organized in locals of their own, affiliated to the American Federation of Labor as that organization knows no creed or color."[1]

III

The suggestion of the Electrical Workers that Negroes join local unions affiliated to the A. F. of L. illustrated the effect of the measure adopted by the 1902 convention of the Federation whereby separate units of Negro workers might be organized by that body. It was in 1900 that President Gompers suggested that these separate locals be organized. Realizing that some remedial action had to be taken in the situation produced when thousands of Negro workers were denied union affiliation the 1902 convention amended the Constitution of the A. F. of L. as follows:

> "Separate charters may be issued to Central Labor Unions, Local Unions, or Federal Labor Unions composed exclusively of colored members, where, in the judgment of the Executive Council, it appears advisable and to the best interests of the Trade Union Movement to do so."

By such action the Federation not only recognized the legality of excluding Negroes from organized bodies, but accepted "James Crow" as a full-fledged member of the American Federation of Labor. If the labor leaders of that day had not totally misread the trends in American industrial life, it is doubtful that they would have attempted giving such permanency to the institution of Negro local and federal unions. They, the labor leaders, undoubtedly felt that such an organization was better than no organization. The Negro workers, on the other hand, found that being directly affiliated to the A. F. of L. through the local unions was, in many instances, as good as having no organization at all. Why? Because, instead of removing barriers from the path of Negro workers, it perpetuated an existing one—biracialism; because, it estab-

[1] The Electrical Worker—April 1903, p. 102.

lished a dual system of federation and because the Negro local tended to create for the Negro worker a bargaining power weaker than that of the white worker. With what results? The secretary of Local Union No. 17786 states:

"We do not get the same rights as the white help do in no way. Of course we get 14 days off in the summer months without pay and the whites get it off with pay—14 days. But we pay just as much dues as they do and do more work for the company. We are only getting $3.12 a day for 8 hours, no time and half for overtime."

There is no doubt that the A. F. of L. enjoyed a measure of success in organizing Negro workers through the medium of local unions until 1923. In December, 1911, there were 11 Negro local and federal unions with 309 members affiliated to that body. In 1919, the number of locals had increased to 169. In 1929 there were 21 locals. In 1911 there were three salaried Negro workers employed as organizers; in 1929 there was none. When the National Urban League broached the question of Negro organizers to the Executive Council of the Federation in 1926, that body decided that it was impossible to add a Negro organizer at that time, despite the fact that outside sources were willing to pay half of the salary of such a person. The relative and absolute decline of Negro local unions is shown in the following table:

Local Trade and Federal Labor Unions Composed Exclusively of Negro Workers and Per Cent of Negro Unions in Total for Selected Years— 1919–1929

Year	Total Locals	Negro Locals	Per Cent Negro
1919 (1)	900	169	18.7
1921, Nov. 4	679	141	20.8
1922, Mar. 15	663	131	19.9
1922, June 1	592	108	18.2
1923, Nov. 12	527	79	14.9
1925, Jan. 1	408	41	15.4
1926, Mar. 10	372	38	11.1
1927, Dec. 15	342	23	6.7
1928, Dec. 31	377	23	6.1
1929, Nov. (2)	383	21	5.4

(1) Statement of Samuel Gompers, "Negro in Chicago," p. 403.
(2) Handbook of American Trade Unions, U. S. Bureau of Labor Statistics, Bulletin No. 506, p. 6, November, 1929.

Thus, the one instrument ordained to foster the organization of Negro labor, the Negro local, has shown itself to be incompetent in meeting the situation. Because it lacked a system of control and supervision the Negro local has failed to keep the Negro worker organized on the one hand, and has been negligent in fostering his inclusion in national unions on the other. Furthermore, it has shown that same gap between the Federation's policy and practice, for, despite the fact that each member of a local trade or federal labor union is required to take an obligation to the effect that,

> "I am to be respectful in work and action to every woman, to be considerate to the widows and orphans, the weak and the defenseless, and never to discriminate against a fellow worker on account of creed, color or nationality,"

there are local trade and federal labor unions that unhesitatingly state a violation of that part of the obligation, pertaining to color discrimination. Local No. 10167 of Baggage Messengers does not admit Negro workers on account of its "business transactions with the public, does not regard the organization of Negro workers as essential to the success of the labor movement in its case, and makes no effort to secure Negro membership."

IV

What then is the official policy of the American Federation of Labor toward the organizing of Negro workers? It consists of a number of resolutions urging that Negro workers be organized; generous declarations to the effect that workers should be organized without regard to race, creed or color; protests here, and vacuous decrees there against the organizing efforts of left-wing groups; the segregated organization of Negro workers in certain occupations through local trade and federal labor unions; a few organizing campaigns that died aborning; the employment, at various times, of a few Negro organizers, and a total inability, if not unwillingness, to compel the member International unions to remove from their constitutions Negro exclusion clauses or have their charters revoked.

The A. F. of L. essays certain policies, "stands for" them, realizing they are not being made effective. It has attempted to live up to a philosophy of liberalism without performing the mechanics necessary to make that liberalism a reality. So void and few have been the A. F. of L.'s efforts in behalf of Negro workers, despite its pronouncements, that it has failed to crystallize the opinion of Negro and white workers, and the public to any other effect than that the American Federation of Labor "stands for" the organization of workers, despite their race, creed or color, then, with complacent self-satisfaction sits down, having done actually nothing. In fact, the American Federation of Labor, because of its hands-off policy in the early nineties, because of its failure to maintain the organization of the thousands of Negro workers organized in local trade and federal labor unions from 1917–1922, and despite its Negro membership of 61,032 workers belonging to national unions affiliated to the A. F. of L., has less positive power and influence among Negro workers than at any other time in the last thirty years.

When the Negro worker faces his problems of affiliation to organized labor he expects to find a champion in the A. F. of L. This worker knows that such limitations so far as his being organized is concerned are secondary considerations. The prime factor is that his employment opportunities are restricted to a greater degree, because he is excluded. Therefore, when the American Federation of Labor condones practices similar to the above mentioned, and sugarcoats these practices with its palaver about all workers being organized despite race, etc., etc., etc.,—meanwhile skilfully evading or bluntly ignoring the plaints of the Negro group as expressed to that body by the National Urban League in 1918 and 1926, and the National Association for the Advancement of Colored People in 1924, the Negro worker may justifiably reply "Applesauce."

THE NEGRO IN EUROPEAN HISTORY

In this essay, J. A. Rogers relates the contributions by Africans to European culture and civilization. This exposition was published in June 1930.

As artist, poet, religious and spiritual leader, or conquerer and soldier, the Negro has played an important part in Europe, and now that he is slowly but surely rising into prominence again it may be well to recall some of his history on that continent.

This history, which dates back to the dimmest antiquity, would fill one or more large volumes, and the best that can be done in a short article is to give the barest outlines and to mention some of the leading individuals. So far very little research historic or pre-historic has been done on this matter, nevertheless enough has been done to warrant the conclusion that a Negro race, known as the Grimaldi, played an important part in the artistic development of pre-historic Europe. Discoveries made by Dr. Verneau, Sir Arthur Evans, Schenk and Hervé point, as Sir Harry Johnston says, "to the actual fact that many thousands of years ago a Negroid race had penetrated into Italy through France, leaving traces at the present day in the physiognomy of the peoples of Southern Italy, Sicily, Sardinia, Southern and Western France and even in the western parts of the United Kingdom of Great Britain and Ireland."

In his 1916 address as president of the British Association for the Advancement of Science, Sir Arthur Evans said: "One should never lose sight of the fact that from the earliest Aurignacian period (early Stone Age) onwards a Negroid element in the broadest sense of the term shared in this artistic culture as seen on both sides of the Pyrenees."

Grecian civilization was almost a direct fruit of Egyptian culture, which was Negroid. Negro influence was powerful on both shores of the Mediterranean when Negro Pharaohs like Amunophis III, Amunophis IV, and Tirhaquah sat on the throne. Later Negroes (we use the American acceptation of the word) played an important part in the building of Carthage, and in her struggle with Rome. When Hannibal, the greatest general of antiquity, who, through the centuries, has generally been thought of as black, invaded Rome, he took large numbers of Negro soldiers with him. Massinissa, King of Numidia, as ally of Rome against Hannibal, helped wrest supremacy from Carthage and made Rome master of the world. Another famous general, Metinus, the mulatto, with his Numidian cavalry, came near driving the Romans out of Sicily.

Rome also had a large number of Negro soldiers, who fought her battles as far north as Britain. One of the most noted of her generals was St. Maurice (St. Moor in English). St. Maurice, when brought from Africa by the Emperor Maximian Herculius, with his legions, to attack Christian slaves in Gaul, refused to do so and was killed at St. Maurice-en-Valais, Switzerland. An abbey which still stands was erected there in his honor. A representation of St. Maurice was painted by Grunewald and hung for centuries in front of the altar in the Cathedral of Halle, Germany. It is now in the Old Pinakothek, Munich. St. Maurice, who is one of the leading Catholic saints, is depicted as coal-black.

In parts of Southern Europe, Christ and the Virgin Mary are depicted as black in many cathedrals. This is particularly true of Spain. There are also the Black Virgin and Christ of Siena, Italy; of Myans, Savoie; of Rieux; Vélay, and elsewhere.

Fodere Pierre-Jacques, writing of Notre Dame de Myans in 1619, says: "In this Chapel is the image of Our Lady, black in the form of an Ethiopian woman, holding before her her infant of the same color." (Le Pelerinage de Notre Dame de Myans p. 9). This writer has pictures of these Black Virgins and Christs.

A gold solidus of Justinian II, Roman emperor, circulated about 705 A.D., shows the emperor on one side and a wooly-haired Christ on the other. This coin was the cause of war between Justinian and Abdul Malik, fifth Caliph of the Ommayeds, because Justinian insisted that tribute should be paid in that coin.

The Christian religion came from the East, and it may be mere fantasy on my part, but I believe that the word Christ could be traced to Chrisha, the black Savior of the Dravidians of India.

The Dravidians are a Negroid people, sometimes almost pure Negro, although they have been mixing with the Aryans and Mongolians for thousands of years. The Negroes with the wooliest hair are to be found, not in Africa, but in Asia, on the Andaman Islands, off the coast of India. North Africa also played an important part in the development of Christianity in Europe. St. Augustine, Tertullian, Origen and many other Fathers of the early Church, were born in Africa. At least one of the three African popes was a Negro, Melchiades.

In the Eighth Century A.D. the Moors, a Negroid people, crossed the Straits and became a power in Europe for several centuries, giving it, according to many historians, the finest culture it had had so far. At that time the Mohammedan power centered at Bagdad, and extended as far as the Atlantic on both shores of the Mediterranean. Several of the Caliphs, or rulers, of this empire, were mulattoes. Black women were admitted freely into the harems of the rulers and their sons sometimes mounted the throne.

One whole dynasty of Caliphs were mulattoes, the Abbasides. Perhaps the most famous from an artistic standpoint was Ibrahim al-Mahdi, great-great-grandson of Mohamet. Ibrahim, brother of Haroun-al-Raschid, was the greatest Islamic singer of all time. According to Ibn Khallikan, Arab historian of the 13th Century, Ibrahim's mother was Shiklah, who was a Negro woman, and the daughter of a Persian King.

The Moors, whose Negro ancestry, then, as now, was reinforced by the large numbers of their pure black soldiers, spread into Europe until their defeat at Tours by Charles Martel. Thereafter their power waned.

The next wave of Negro influence came with the introduction of slavery in 1442. Thereafter for more than three centuries Negroes from Guinea poured into Southwestern Europe until today Southern Spain and Portugal are Negroid.

Several important figures arose during this period of whom perhaps the most prominent, but not the greatest, was Alessandro, the Moor, first Duke of Florence, and last descendent of the elder branch of the Medicis.

Alessandro's mother was a humble Negro slave named Anna, while most historians, English and Italian, agree in saying that he was the son of Pope Clement VII, but that the latter passed him off as his nephew. Most writers also say that he was a Negro, of which fact his picture, by Bronzino, in the Uffizi Gallery in Florence, leaves no doubt. Alessandro married the daughter of the Emperor Charles V, the most powerful monarch of his day. The match was arranged to bind a treaty between the Pope and the Emperor.

Two others were Ludovico the Moor, most noted of the Sforza family, and Duke of Milan. Another was Louis, the Moor. So far our researches on these last two are incomplete.

Still another was St. Benedict, the Moor. This man, who came of the humblest slave parentage, was born in Sicily. He lived such a life of piety, devotion and charity that he was canonized by Pope Pius IV.

In Spain, during the 19th Century, two Haitian Negroes rose to high rank, namely, Biassou and Jean-Francois. The former rose to be field-marshal and the latter to general in the Spanish army. Both were comrades of Toussaint L'Ouverture, and had cast in their lot with Spain rather than again side with France.

Going northwards into France one finds that the Negro has played a part no less distinguished. Foremost comes the Dumas family, the founder of which, the general, was the son of a French marquis and a black West Indian woman. General Dumas, who was in all respects a modern Richard of the Lion Heart, rose to be chief commander of the Republican armies of France during the Revolution. It was just by a twist of fate that caused Napoleon to supersede him. Dumas was living on the outskirts of Paris when the Convention wanted a strong man to restore order. Dumas was sent for but before he could arrive things had reached such a crisis that Barras suggested Napoleon, who was accepted. When Dumas did come Napoleon was in power. Later Dumas was Napoleon's chief of cavalry, among those serving under him being General LeClerc, Napoleon's brother-in-law, and Murat, later King of Naples.

The other two Dumases, the great novelist and the famous playwright, are too well-known to need special mention.

Another Negro of great distinction was the Chevalier Georges de Georges, the model of elegance of his day. His father, the Marquis de Langey, one of the greatest men in France, gave him a splendid education. He was the greatest swordsman of his day and an all-round athlete, as well as an accomplished violinist and composer. He was one of the leading courtiers of Versailles and a personal friend of George IV.

Napoleon had seven other Negro generals, namely, Andre Rigaud, Villate, B. Leveille, Alexander Petion, J. P. Belley, Magloire Pelage and Dugommier. The first three were full generals and sailed along with the next two, who were adjutant-generals, on the expedition against Toussaint L'Ouverture. All of these Negro generals were born in the West Indies and had been educated in France.

On that expedition also went three colonels, nine majors and many captains, among whom was Boyer, who later, like Petion, became president of Haiti.

Magloire Pelage commanded a brigade in the Peninsular War, while Dugommier was commander of the Army of the Pyrenees. Two other Negro generals, made by the Convention, were Antoine Cloualette and Martial Besse.

Many other distinguished Negroes of this period could be mentioned like Mentor Sejour, member of the Convention, who captured an English warship, and Victor Sejour, private secretary to Louis Napoleon, and a dramatic author. Space, however, must be reserved for Sister Louise-Marie, daughter of Marie-Theresa of Spain and Austria, wife of Louis XIV. Sister Louise-Marie was known as the Black Nun, and her father was supposed to be a Negro dwarf that was presented to the Queen by an African king. The Black Nun's picture hangs in the St. Genevieve Library, while Voltaire, the Duke of St. Simon and many others of the time, have written about her.

A noted Negro of recent years is Gen. Alfred A. Dodds, who was of mixed white and black parentage on both sides of his family. He was born in Senegal and was perhaps France's best known general prior to the last war. Dodds commanded armies in France, Africa and China, and was for a brief period commander-in-chief of the Allied forces in China during the Boxer rebellion. During the last war he was a member of the War Council.

Another is Col. N. Mortenol, who commanded the Air Defense of Paris during the last war. Col. Mortenol has also been a captain in the navy, and was once commander of the naval fortifications at Brest.

At the present time there are several high posts held by colored men in France. Alcide Delmont, deputy from Martinique, is Under-Secretary of State for the Colonies and is in the present Cabinet, while two other deputies, M. Gratien Candace and Blaise Diagne, as also M. Lemery, Senator from Martinique, hold high governmental positions. M. Isaac, son of ex-Senator Isaac, is first assistant to the Minister of Commerce.

There are also several college professors, heads of government offices, judges and other officials, among whom is M. Hector Simoneau, formerly prefect of a department, and now paymaster-general of the Aube.

In Austria and Germany there have been Angelo Solliman, an exslave, who rose to high favor with the Prince de Lichtenstein, and was personal friend and adviser of the Emperor Joseph II.: Ira Aldridge of

Baltimore, Shakespearean actor, who received more honor from crowned heads and learned European societies than any other American actor before or since. The Czar of Russia, the King of Prussia, the Emperor of Austria, and cities, gave him gold medals, of which the metal alone was valued at $10,000. The King of Prussia had a medal struck especially in his honor, the only others who up to that time had been so rewarded were Lizst, the musician; Spontini, the composer, and Humboldt, the naturalist.

George A. P. Bridgetower, one of the greatest violinists of his day, was a personal friend of Beethoven, and used to accompany Beethoven with his violin at soirees of the élite. Bridgetower was a social lion both on the Continent and in England and was for a time private musician to the Prince of Wales, afterwards George IV.

There has also been a number of learned men, among them being Anthony William Amo, an astronomer, who gave lectures at the University of Wittenberg; Gustavus Vasa, sailor, explorer and agitator for justice for Africans; J. J. Capitein, Latin scholar, and Ignatius Sancho, protege of the Duke of Montague.

Blumenbach, the Father of Anthropology, who had a library filled with the European Negro authors of his day, says:

"Entire and large provinces of Europe might be named in which it would be difficult to meet with such good writers, poets, philosophers and correspondents of the French Academy, and that moreover, there is no savage people who have distinguished themselves by such examples of perfectibility and capacity for scientific cultivation, and consequently that none can approach more nearly to the polished nations of the globe than the Negro."

In Russia the Negro has also played his part. One of them bought or stolen from the harem of the Sultan Selim IV, named Abram Hannibal, rose to be commander-in-chief of the Russian army. Hannibal, who is best known as "The Negro of Peter the Great" was one of the leading engineers of his day. He was the ancestor of Pushkin, Russia's most noted poet, and apostle of liberty.

During the time of the Czars, hundreds of Negroes were taken into Russia and were used as mascots for royalty and the nobility. Catherine the Great, in her portrait by Lampi is shown with one of them, and she had a Negro favorite, according to the Princess Murat, to whom she gave much wealth, including a property with a large number of white slaves. This man Yermeloff, was one of the officers of her guard.

At Catherine's court was a Negro noblewoman, Mlle. de Protassov, who, according to the Countess Golovine, was a relative of the powerful Prince Orloff.

Schuyler, American Consul, writing in the last century, says in his "Life of Peter the Great," "Negroes were in esteem, as indeed they have been of recent years. Volynsky sent from Astrakan a couple in order to ingratiate himself with her."

Peter III had a Negro favorite, named Narcissus, of whom he was so fond that he would even let the ambassadors of great countries wait while he finished his game with him.

In England the Negro has played but a minor part. In addition to Ira Aldridge and Bridgetower, there has been Coleridge Taylor, the prolific and spirited composer. Paul Robeson and Roland Hayes in England are now making their influence felt in Europe.

The subject, as was said, is a vast one, and has been dealt with here but sketchily. Many noted names have been left out, like those of Geoffrey L'Islet, the mathematician, and Tanner, the American Negro artist. Nothing also has been said of the influence of present day Negro art and music, which is considerable, nor of the important part played by Negro soldiers in the last war.

Trained Men for Negro Business

When this essay by John Hope was published in May 1931, he was president of Atlanta University. He discusses the progress of African Americans as entrepreneurs despite obstacles they face because of racial discrimination. He remains optimistic about the future of the race in business considering that blacks are only three generations from slavery.

THE NEGRO AS A BUSINESS MAN

Seventy thousand business enterprises are conducted by American Negroes. By far the greater number of these are small businesses, such as restaurants, barber shops, beauty parlors, grocery stores, transfer agencies and the like, where the relationship between customer and proprietor is immediate and personal, and relatively little capital is required. In addition, moreover, the Negro has shown considerable initiative and a measure of aptitude in the organization of banks and insurance companies. According to the 1930 Negro Year Book there are 51 Negro banking institutions in the United States, which have total resources of $20,000,000 and do approximately $75,000,000 business annually. A survey of insurance companies officered by Negroes shows that 23 of these companies have total resources of $18,445,798, and that twenty of them, in replying to questionnaires, reported a total of $260,000,000 insurance in force.

It is self-evident from these fragmentary facts that the Negro, while he has made a beginning in business, is far from being the master of his economic life. Of the $2,200,000,000 that Negroes expend annually for food and the $1,950,000,000 spent for clothing and shoes, probably not more than five per cent goes into the tills of Negro merchants. One major insurance company carries a billion and a quarter insurance on Negro lives, or about five times the amount carried by the twenty leading Negro insurance companies. If the total deposits in Negro banks were distributed equally among the Negro population, each person would receive little more than a dollar.

When one considers the economic and social handicaps that the Negro faces in venturing into business, the wonder grows that so many had the initiative to do so at all. Moreover, as one realizes the racial discrimination that is evidenced against Negro enterprise, and the obstacles—such as denial of credit—that are deliberately placed in the way of his progress, he cannot but be amazed at the Negro's success.

Negroes, it must be remembered, are only three generations removed from slavery. Since emancipation their progress has been impeded by the ruthless working of social and economic law, and by widespread and deepseated racial prejudice. Tradition has made Negroes laborers and servants, and custom has kept them in their place. Their education has been generally neglected, and such training as their diligence has won for themselves has in the main fitted them for the life of artisans and farmers. There has been little opportunity for the Negro to learn the rudiments of business as a clerk or apprentice. Nor could he absorb the fundamentals of business from his father, as many white boys do, for there has been no tradition of business in his family, or in his race.

All about him the Negro sees business controlled by white men,— the Italian at the corner fruit stand, the Greek at the neighborhood lunchroom, the Jew at the adjoining clothing store and pawn shop, the alert Nordic in the chain grocery, the drug store, and the bank. White men, it seems to him, have a monopoly on business.

To be sure, here and there, he sees a Negro engaged in trade. An occasional lunch counter, grocery store, barber shop or undertaking parlor has a colored proprietor, employs Negro help, and serves the race exclusively. For the most part these establishments, in comparison with their white counterparts, are poorly equipped, and seem ever to be tottering on the edge of bankruptcy. In these ventures the Negro sees little to inspire his confidence in the business ability of his people.

Yet in the face of these conditions there is unmistakable evidence of the emergence of the Negro as a business man. The Negro is becoming a realist, is evidencing serious interest in economic thought, and looking at the situation about him, is asking what is to be done about it. Moreover, he is beginning to act. In the past ten years, more than ever before, Negro men and women have opened retail stores, restaurants, hotels, barber shops, beauty parlors; they have established and today publish more than 300 newspapers; they have built theatres, and other places of amusement; they have gone into manufacturing, and today make sixty different commodities; they have organized 10 national trade associations which operate through 250 local units throughout the country; they have made a distinct contribution to racial solidarity through their banks, insurance companies, and fraternal organizations; recently they have formed a nation-wide chain of grocery stores, comprising 270 separate establishments, one of the most far-reaching and ambitious business enterprises launched by a Negro group; through their thrift 700,000 of their race have become owners of their homes, 232,000 have acquired farms, and their aggregate wealth has reached the immense total of two billion dollars.

In all this development of his business life the Negro has shown the same measure of patience, good humor, diligence and faithfulness that won for him and his father the traditional reputation as good servants and workmen. In addition, he has come to display an unsuspected degree of initiative and resourcefulness, marked ability as a promoter and salesman, a capacity for adaptation to the changing ways of business.

But he lacks one thing,—the technical training that is necessary in these days of keen business competition. The failure of many Negro business projects has been due in great measure to ignorance of business practices on the part of its officers and directors. An official of a large and successful Negro insurance company said recently that it is easy to get young men to do the routine tasks of an agency, but difficult to get those who possess training to handle administrative problems, to organize and direct the work of subordinates, to foresee and prepare for contingencies, to assume responsibilities, and generally to take leadership.

For this leadership in business Negroes look hopefully to the graduates of their colleges and universities. For more than fifty years many of these institutions have been sending out teachers and pastors, who have served their race well. More recently colleges have turned their attention to the training of lawyers, doctors, dentists, and social workers who have won confidence by their skill and understanding. Now the colleges are called on to undertake a new and perhaps more difficult task,—the training of Negro men and women for careers in business.

A SCHOOL OF BUSINESS ADMINISTRATION
FOR NEGROES

Believing that no field offers more striking opportunity for educational service than the training of business men, Atlanta University, chief institution in the far South for the higher education of Negroes, two years ago organized a graduate department of commerce and business administration. The work was inaugurated at a propitious time in that it followed, and was indeed made possible by the affiliation of the University with Morehouse College for men and Spelman College for women. In each of the three colleges there had been established during the last ten years a department of economics and finance. A lively interest in economics has been created, and there has developed a definite turning to business as a profession, and a growing realization on the part of undergraduates, alumni and faculty of the value of sound training in business.

Thus in establishing graduate courses in business administration Atlanta University built on foundations that have been in existence for some time. As early as 1921 Morehouse College, sensing the need for such training, began instruction in finance. When an instructor was sought only one prospect was to be found in Atlanta, a graduate of Brown University and the owner of a successful drug store in the Negro business district, whose only free hour for teaching was from seven to eight in the morning. A course in money and banking was given at that hour, and soon became one of the most popular in the curriculum. The following year a course in accounting was added; in 1924–25 a full department of business administration was organized, half a dozen courses were added to meet the increasing demand, and the staff was augmented by a full-time instructor in economics and a practicing certified public accountant, who was able to divide his time with the college.

In the meanwhile Atlanta University which had limited its work to a single course in elementary economics organized in 1923–24 a department of economics and finance. In the next seven years there was built up a curriculum of fifteen courses in general and applied economics. Spelman College, which in 1924 attained full status as a college, had about the same time made available to its students several basic courses in economics, and engaged the full-time services of an instructor in this department.

By the affiliation in 1929 of the three institutions provision was made for the organization of a graduate department of business administration at Atlanta University, which had become under the terms of the affiliation agreement a graduate institution, and for the continuation and development of strong undergraduate departments of economics and finance at the two undergraduate colleges. Under the working plan of the affiliation the graduate department is closely allied to the departments of economics at Morehouse and at Spelman; members of the Morehouse and Spelman faculties comprise in some measure the teaching staff of the graduate school, and provision is made whereby specially qualified seniors in the colleges may register in senior-graduate courses that the University offers.

Atlanta University in establishing its department of economics and finance has become the first Negro institution to offer graduate work in business. During the past year thirteen courses were given—three of them being graduate courses, and ten senior-graduate courses (that is, courses which are open to graduates and specially-qualified seniors in Morehouse and Spelman Colleges). Of the seven undergraduate courses, five were offered by Morehouse College and two by Spelman College. The total enrollment in these courses was 425—223 during the fall term and 202 during the spring term.

In the diversity and quality of work offered and in the character of teaching the curriculum compares favorably with the courses of study offered in the larger universities of the North and West. In the teaching methods every effort is made to relate the theories of the classroom to the actual problems of business, and to develop in the students a realistic understanding of the working of the economic society in which they live.

Particularly in the courses in accounting, which are taught by Jesse B. Blayton, the only Negro Certified Public Accountant in Georgia, are the students given field experience of a practical character. During the past year eighteen advanced students have been assigned to work under his supervision in keeping the books for Negro business enterprises in Atlanta, and in helping these business men to improve their business practices. These students have worked this year with two coal yards, two barber shops, a printing company, a transfer company, a dry cleaning concern, a grocery, a garage, a candy and notions store, a hospital, a church, a bicycle shop, a drug store, a social club, a realty company, an undertaking establishment and a tailor. In addition men were assigned to look after the finances of the extra-curricular activities office at the college.

"I know of few fields of commercial activity so filled with potentialities as the Negro market," Julius Klein, Assistant Secretary of

Labor, wrote in a recent issue of OPPORTUNITY. "It is capable of great development as the mounting intelligence and rising living standards of the group create demands for a wide variety of commodities. The scope of such business progress is being enlarged as education, the increase of skilled and professionally trained labor and the growth of a dividend-earning class combine to augment the wealth of the particular market."

FUTURE DEVELOPMENT OF THE SCHOOL OF BUSINESS ADMINISTRATION

The expansion of the courses in economics and finance already offered at Atlanta University into a School of Economics and Business Administration offers an opportunity to do an outstanding piece of work for the benefit of the Negro race.

Primarily the School would offer to a group of qualified students a wide variety of theoretical and practical courses, which would serve to give these students sound knowledge of the economic structure of society and the basic principles of business procedure; in addition the School would make available to students of exceptional promise the opportunity to do specialized and closely supervised work in fields of insurance, investments, banking, real estate, merchandising, and the like.

No group in America is more oppressed economically than the Negro. None responds more readily to intelligent measures for his betterment. There is no surer way of improving the social and economic conditions of the colored people than by providing them with educated and conscientious leaders who will be able to direct the economic stabilization of their people. Once the Negro people in America can control and conserve the wealth they are able to create through their energy and their thrift many of their troubles will be at an end. But to do this they must have leaders who are men and women of integrity and intelligence. It is to training of such leaders that Atlanta University with the aid of its generous friends has set itself.

NAT TURNER: FIEND OR MARTYR?

On August 21, 1831, the militant Nat Turner led a dramatic and unprecedented slave revolt. Although Turner was captured on October 30, 1831, and subsequently executed, he had fearlessly devoted himself fully to the cause of his race without any hope to survive. When Rayford W. Logan published this essay in November 1931, he was a doctoral student in history at Harvard University.

Down the River Dundy floated black, bloated corpses, rotting under the African sun. The village of a thousand huts along its banks was no longer filled with the prattle of children—vultures contended with beasts of prey for their tender carcasses. Here Yanee had once loved King Omloo, but a bullet had sent Yanee to Kanno Beyond the Grave and King Omloo was trudging in a slave coffle to the coast.

The White Man had brought his civilization to Africa.

The slaves "were tied to poles in rows, four feet apart; a loose wicker bandage around the neck of each, connected him to the pole, and the arms being pinioned by a bandage affixed behind above the elbows, they had sufficient room to feed, but not to loose themselves. . . . Often did they look back with tears in their eyes." Some went mad and laughed back at the hyenas. Some died under the leash. Others sought certain death through flight or mutiny. Still others refused to die before they had a chance to kill.

Death marched with the Black Ivory—but would it be always to the black man to whom it beckoned?

Death reaped another black harvest in the barracoons and during the embarkation. Some slaves preferred the shark's belly to the journey beyond the seas. Death revelled in the vile ship's hold amid the offal of those dying with dysentery and groaned with those going blind from ophthalmia. It led the slaves to promise not to throw themselves overboard if given a breath of air on deck. They promised—and threw themselves to the sharks.

A ship hails in sight. Is it rescuer or kidnaper? Their ship, every sail gasping for wind, runs away. The sea is becalmed; their pursuer closes. The captain manacles the slaves to the anchor chain on the far side of the ship. Just before the English officers come on board, he cuts the chain and six hundred men, women, and children go to Davey Jones' locker. The captain is not arrested, because there is no "evidence." He returns to Africa and a thousand more children are left orphans, a dozen more wenches are chosen to grace the sailors' bed, and a thousand more men die so that five hundred or four hundred or one hundred may till the fields of the Land of the Free.

> *The skipper on arriving in port closes*
> *". . . the Bible carefully, putting it down,*
> *As though his fingers loved it."*

For two centuries the gentle souls of the Western Hemisphere lolled at their ease on their plantations, their *habitations,* and their *haciendas* while fifty million corpses were rotting in Africa, the depths of the seas, and on the coasts of the western world. The fate of the living was sometimes worse: husband was torn from wife and mother from child. And yet they sang. They had to sing or die or kill.

II

On August 21, 1831 Nat Turner, a deeply religious, highly moral Negro slave belonging to one Travis of Southampton County, Virginia, stopped singing and praying and led an insurrection in which fifty-five white men, women, and children were killed. One white for each million of Africans. Nat was a long way from a reckoning either according to the Bible or the Constitution of the United States which rated five Negroes equal to three white men.

So long as Nat was at large, Virginia shuddered. A thousand troops could not find him. The imagination of the planters heard bare feet gliding on the roof when the autumn leaves fell. In the twilight it saw burly black forms assemble silently behind ghostlike trees. The sighing winds brought chants from Dismal Swamp where the murderers were whetting their axes. From North Carolina came rumors of "Walarums and excursions." The *Macon Messenger* barely got off the press because all the able-bodied men were on patrol. New Orleans trembled at the report that a black man had twelve hundred stand of arms in his cellar. "Pity us!" implored a correspondent from Kentucky. The South was scared—scared as it perhaps never was before or since. The least frightened denied Divine Retribution.

Such terror demanded relief. Since Nat could not be found, any "nigger" would do. One man admitted killing ten or fifteen. General Eppes, commanding the troops, officially denounced the "revolting, inhuman, acts of barbarity." The slaughter continued. At the same time Virginia was praying for further success to the Poles who were reported as having butchered 14,000 Russians.

The coincidences of history afford alluring speculation. November eleventh is now an occasion for rejoicing at the conclusion, stupefaction at the beginning of the greatest holocaust of the modern age, and preparation for the next. To 12,000,000 black folk it should be a day of pride—for on that day one hundred years ago a black man kept his "Rendezvous with Death" rather than live a bondsman. His simple courage surpassed the comprehension of his executioners as did that of the Man of Galilee.

There are those who would have you believe that Nat Turner's Insurrection was a failure. It is true that his executioners divided his remains for souvenirs, thus setting perhaps a precedent for a later American outdoor sport. The punishment meted out to him and to his accomplices effectively discouraged any other insurrections of note. The board of education of a Virginia county recently denied a petition for a colored training school because of the execrable memory of Nat Turner. No monument commemorates his deed. And in 1930 a Negro college professor told a white audience that the Negro will probably be back in captivity in the next twenty-five years.

III

But did he die in vain? By a peculiar and unwitting coincidence the lock and key of the jail in which Nat was confined lie in a case in the Virginia State Library next to the call to arms issued in Lexington County, Virginia, at the outbreak of the Civil War. No one would be foolhardy enough to assert that Nat Turner's insurrection caused the Civil War. One may safely declare, however, that it did reveal the only solution to America's Gordian knot—the sword. Slavery had rung again as "an alarum bell in the night," and some already realized that the "panacea of palaver" was as worthless as all other nostrums.

At first the South sought to repress any other attempts to gain freedom by force. Systematic conversions to the Christian Church taught the proper submission. Dialecticians proved that converting a slave did not make him free. The most rigorous and drastic regulations were enacted to prevent any recurrence of insurrections.

The planters blamed Garrison and his *Liberator* for the insurrection. This accusation is probably unfounded, but who will deny that Nat's effort crystallized the fighting ideals of the Abolitionists? Let him who would be free strike the first blow. Lovejoy and John Brown would not have been ashamed to be called the spiritual descendants of this black slave. Wendell Phillips in eulogizing Toussaint Louverture must have seen in him a kindred spirit. Even the Quakers, who suffered ostracism and imprisonment for their underground activities, must have gained respect for a race that produced men who preferred death to slavery.

And finally, the South erected a gigantic defense mechanism to justify their "peculiar institution." Only savages, they shouted, would revolt against such an idyllic state as slavery. The slave was better off than he would have been in Africa. Had he not come to know the Anglo-Saxon God, and, hence, gained a passport to Heaven? His fate was better than that of white laborers in the North or in Europe, than that of free Negroes. He was sure of his job, was he not? Black mammies, although not allowed to keep their own children, had the privilege and honor of allowing the best blood of the South to suckle at their breasts. Some white men held black wenches in such high esteem that they used them to increase their human stock exactly as they used studs to increase their stables. Though slaves, they were erecting a Kingdom of Cotton that all of Europe would not dare attack. They made possible as fine a breed of gentlemen as ever knew how to ride to hounds, drink mint juleps, betray their wives, turn a "bon mot," dance the reel, carve a wild boar, and amass debts that they could not pay. Had the Roman *latifundia* or the *haciendas* of New Spain created anything finer? Why in the name of an Almighty and Just God should these beasts want to kill fifty men, women, and children?

The dead tell no tales, not even fifty million of them.

No reputable historian doubts that the period from 1831 to 1861 was the most horrible era of slavery. As the abolitionists redoubled their attacks, the South increased its drastic regulations and pious preachments. Driven from post to post, the planters finally proclaimed slavery such a fine thing that it could not, by the laws of man or the will of God, be kept out of the newly acquired federal territory, out of the Carribbean, out of the old Northwest Territory, out of the free states themselves. In 1860 a man practically unknown but destined to become the Greatest American, peculiarly ugly but performing perhaps

the only true "beau geste" in American history, was elected on a platform that declared among other things, the power of Congress to exclude slavery from federal territory. The South, proclaiming "Better
out of the Union with slavery than in it without slavery," placed its
trust in the arbitrament of war and the justice of God. The gallantry of
the South fighting a lost cause is still the theme of poetry and history.
Nat Turner, ignominiously hanged for seeking liberty, is mentioned
only to be execrated as a bloodthirsty beast.

IV

Every one is free to form his own opinion of Nat Turner. It is interesting to note, however, the sentiment of a man still shuddering from the
shock. Samuel Warner, writing in 1831, declared:

"It seems almost incredible that there could be found an individual
of the human species, who rather than to wear the goading yoke of
bondage, would prefer becoming the voluntary subject of so great a
share of want and misery (as that which Nat found in his hiding
place)!—but, such indeed, is the love of liberty—the gift of God!—
and while we shall ever feel it a duty which we owe to humanity to lend
our aid if necessary in suppressing insurrections so fatal to the lives of
our countrymen as the one of recent occurrence in the South when
fifty-five innocent persons were in the space of a few hours most inhu-
manly butchered by a band of ill-advised wretches, who heeded not
the entreaties of the aged and infirmed or the heart piercing screeches
of the expiring infant! yet, we can not hold those entirely blameless
who first brought them from their native plains—who robbed them of
their domestic joys—who tore them from their weeping children and
dearest connections, and doomed them in this 'Land of Liberty' to a
state of cruel bondage!"

Thirty years later Thomas Wentworth Higginson was not afraid to
write:

"Who now shall go back thirty years, and read the heart of this extraordinary man, who, by the admission of his captors, 'never was
known to swear an oath, or drink a drop of spirits;' who, on the same
authority, 'for natural intelligence and quickness of apprehension was
surpassed by few men,' 'with a mind capable of attaining anything;'
who knew no book but his Bible, and that by heart; who devoted himself soul and body to the cause of his race, without a trace of personal
hope or fear; who laid his plans so shrewdly that they came at last with

less warning than any earthquake on the doomed community around; and who, when that time arrived, took the life of man, woman, and child, without a throb of compunction, a word of exultation, or an act of superfluous outrage? Mrs. Stowe's 'Dred' seems dim and melodramatic beside the actual Nat Turner, and De Quincy's 'Avenger' is his only parallel in imaginative literature."

The South no longer shackles black bodies—that is, in general. It has, however, enslaved the minds of black folk just as surely as it once did their bodies. What a glorious task on this, the one-hundredth anniversary of Nat Turner's Insurrection, to dedicate ourselves to the emancipation of the minds of twelve million black folk. One may even hope for some little intelligence from the white master minds. If not, who will dare predict that there will never be another Nat Turner?

Not in the Headlines:

A Story of a Negro Radio Operator

This essay by Elmer A. Carter was published in November 1931. Carter writes about Elmer Smith, a young African American who desires to become a radio operator. Because of obstacles caused by race prejudice, the road to his dream is long and arduous.

I.

The story of Elmer Smith must be set down in three parts. The first part is similar to the story which ten thousand colored boys might tell if they would. He was born twenty-two years ago in Montclair, New Jersey. His father, J. Lansing Smith, was also born in New Jersey at Elizabeth and his mother was born in Warrenton, North Carolina. From the time he was ten years old, Elmer Smith has been interested in radio. Everything he could read on the subject he read. As he became older he constructed sets and finally secured an amateur operator's license. Throughout his high school course he spent all of his spare time tinkering with radio sets and studying technical and theoretical problems as they were presented in various publications—newspapers and magazines. Before he completed his high school course he decided to study the radio for a career. Whereupon he entered the Radio Institute of America in New York City. In six months—half of the allotted time—he had completed the course as a high ranking student. And in 1929 he took the examination and was granted a commercial operator's license.

Then began the search for a job. Day after day he walked the streets of New York, to steamship offices, to radio stores, department stores, electrical shops. He visited over two hundred different businesses with his diploma and the recommendations of his teachers. In each one he was told that they could not employ a Negro. Some elaborated on their refusal. Others were blunt and discourteous. Others dismissed him with a smile.

II.

In Montclair there was a young white lad who shared Elmer Smith's intense interest in radio. And while both were mere lads their common interests created a mutual friendship that became closer as they grew older. Together they entered the Radio Institute of America and together they were graduated. And here for a moment their paths separated. While young Smith was tramping the streets of New York looking for a job, his friend secured one with the Canadian Navigation Company at Belize, Honduras, as a commercial radio operator. They parted, but as the young white lad boarded the train he promised that if he ever got the chance he would send for his chum. Alas, how many such promises have been made in the flush of youth . . . only to be forgotten.

But there are exceptions and this white boy didn't forget. Within six months after his arrival at Belize he summoned Smith and last December Elmer Smith was employed by the Canadian Navigation Company as a commercial radio operator. For about five months he worked as a radio operator. And then because of his efficiency and skill he was promoted to chief technician with eight operators under him. It became a part of his duty to design and install all radio equipment on all the ships of the Canadian Navigation Company. At last he had his chance.

III.

The flags were flying in Belize, picturesque capital of British Honduras. Bands were playing and little children sang and danced in the streets. The cafés were crowded with happy, light-hearted, care free folk. In the harbor the ships of the Canadian Navigation Company listlessly swung at anchor on a sea that was so calm that from shore it seemed like a huge painting suspended between the cloudless ceiling of blue sky and the distant horizon. The holiday spirit was abroad. It was the tenth of September, the 133rd anniversary of the end of Spanish dominion.

Morning passed quickly. The program for the afternoon was scheduled to begin at 2:30. Eager with anticipation the laughing bantering crowds began to assemble for the festivities which had been long in preparation. Worries were forgotten. Holidays did not come often. Why worry?

Of the fourteen thousand souls in Belize there were only two, or possibly three, who were ill at ease. One of these was the superintendent of the Canadian Navigation Company, the ships of which plied between Halifax and Belize, the other was the United States Vice Consul, the third was Elmer Smith, a young man of medium height and unblemished brown skin, chief radio technician of the Navigation Company.

He sat alone in his quarters, ear phones fastened snugly over his head, his eyes intent on a small sheet of paper on which were typed a few laconic sentences. Within arms reach were other sheets which he picked up and studied, then carefully laid aside.

Every morning they came—the weather reports—which were handed to the superintendent who in turn passed the information on to the city and state officials. Ordinarily, it was a routine matter, but for the preceding two days the reports had carried an ominous note.

To those who live in the region of the Carribean the word "storm" is sufficient to create consternation. And that word in the weather report of September 10, 1931 was the cause of an apprehension, which the superintendent, the Consul, and the chief radio technician were unable to shake off, despite the spirit of gayety which pervaded the little city. Strange to say the city officials, who had been immediately warned by the superintendent on receipt of the disquieting news, remained indifferent. Belize had never yet suffered from a violent storm. Had not the report said the storm would pass north of Teia in Spanish Houduras, south of Belize and go inland? And besides, look what a beautiful day, what a glorious holiday morning.

—

It is almost two o'clock. The festivities are about to begin. Young Smith anxiously looks over his radio. It is O. K. In the distance he can hear the band. A surprising gust of hot wind sends him hurriedly to the window. Far on the horizon of the sea there is a dark gray cloud which is spreading rapidly over the sky. The storm is coming. He bends to his transmitter.

Suddenly the sun is blotted out as if in eclipse. There is a terrible thunder clap. Rain begins to fall. The bunting and flags are drenched. Then out of the west comes the wind. It is a moderate gale. Not so bad after all. Just as suddenly the rain stops; the wind dies down; the sun comes out again. The people return to the streets, their ardor un-dampened even though the bright colored decorations are soiled and scattered in the gutters.

Concern for the safety of his young wife and infant daughter urged Smith to return to his home. There all is well, but he decides to move them to the house of a friend where he feels they will be safer. This accomplished he returns to duty.

His watch shows just five minutes after four when as if by some sinister magic the sun again is blotted out. The city is plunged in total darkness and the wind comes shrieking out of the southeast. The crash of thunder is echoed by the sharp crackling of severed telegraph and telephone poles. The velocity of the wind increases—houses are demolished. Trees felled as if by a giant ax. Again and again he tries the transmitter. No response. And now mingled with the roar of the wind are the moans of women and the cries of little children.

Convinced after repeated attempts to get a response that the radio set was completely wrecked. Smith starts for his wife and child. By the aid of continuous lightning flashes he finally reached them. For an hour the wind unleashes its fury against the little city as if bent on utterly destroying it. Finally with a long drawn out warning scream it attains a velocity of 150 miles an hour and in its wake comes a tidal wave, a wall of water ten feet high which picks up four ships in the harbor as if they were match boxes and hurls them into the heart of the city.

———

At last the seemingly endless night passed. With the break of day the appalling catastrophe which had befallen the gay little capital on its holiday was clearly visible. Of the ships left in the harbor there was no trace. The house from which young Smith and his wife and baby had fled in the lull between the storms had been unroofed and carried four hundred yards. Dirty water, waist deep, filled the streets. Everywhere were the dead, the dying, the maimed. In less than twenty-four hours a city of 14,000 happy souls had become a shambles.

As soon as he could see, Smith started on a search for his superior officer, the superintendent of the Canadian Navigation Company. Wading through rivers of muddy water and clambering over piles of rubbish he found him at last alone on the littered water front looking out to sea from whence had come the winds of death. He instructed Smith to transmit messages to the State Department for the American Consul, who was seriously injured, to the offices of his company; to ships at sea; anywhere and everywhere in order to get help.

What an assignment! No current, no radio, no telegraph, the power house in ruins and no ship due for five days. Completely cut off from the outside world Smith knew that unless help could be secured pestilence would begin its ravages among the survivors. But he did not hesitate. With the aid of other employees he began a search for a generator by which current might be developed. Finally on one of the ships cast up they were able to salvage one. He then set to work to build a radio from the broken parts he was able to salvage from the four ships. He repaired the transmitters and receivers, set up an aerial and proceeded to call for help. His first contact was with an amateur operator at Miami, Florida, Ellis McClane, to whom he gave messages for the Secretary of State at Washington. He then called Canadian Navigation boats off the coast of Spanish Honduras and the American Consul at Tela, Spanish Honduras. And thus the world was apprised of the recent disaster in which over 2000 lives were lost and a thousand people injured in the hurricane of September 10, 1931 at Belize, capital of British Honduras.

—

For forty-eight hours Smith remained at his post, relinquishing it only when relief arrived by plane and hospital ship from Nicaragua.

In the dispatches of the daily press recounting the story of the Belize disaster no mention is made of the fact that the radio operator who informed the world of this catastrophe was an American Negro in virtual exile from the land of his birth because of racial prejudice.

His feat is all the more remarkable when it is considered that he was able to establish wireless communication 36 hours before the station of the British Government and the Pan American Radio Company station at Belize.

The other day Elmer Smith began his journey back to Belize after a short leave of absence in Montclair. He was eager to go, and just before he left he modestly exhibited a cablegram which said in effect, Need you. Transportation arranged by plane—Miami-Havana-Belize.

BIOGRAPHICAL NOTES

OF CONTRIBUTORS

ALEXANDER, RAYMOND PACE (1898–1975), lawyer and judge, was born in Philadelphia, Pennsylvania. He received a B.S. degree from the University of Pennsylvania in 1920, and a L.L.B. degree from Harvard Law School in 1923. After serving as counsel to numerous important religious, civic, and government organizations, he became judge of the court on common pleas in Philadelphia in 1959. In 1970, he was appointed senior judge of that court.

AUBREY, JOHN, is a pseudonym for an African-American writer who attended Williams College in Williamstown, Massachusetts. (Source: *Opportunity*, April 1931).

BAGNALL, ROBERT W. (1864–1943), clergyman and civil rights worker, was born in Norfolk, Virginia. He was educated at Bishop Payne Divinity School (Virginia) and was ordained an Episcopal priest in 1903. He served pastorates in Pennsylvania, Maryland, and Ohio. In 1921 Bagnall became Director of Branches for the NAACP. In 1931 he accepted the pastorate of St. Thomas's Episcopal Church in Philadelphia. Bagnall was a man of broad knowledge who possessed great writing and oratory skills. His writings appeared mainly in *The Crisis*.

BENNETT, GWENDOLYN (1902–1981), painter, writer, and educator, was the daughter of a Texas lawyer. She refined her artistic talents through Fine Arts study at Columbia University, Pratt Institute, and in France. Upon her return to the United States, she became assistant editor of the Urban League's *Opportunity.* Bennett contributed short stories and poems to *American Mercury, The Crisis, The Messenger, Opportunity,* and *Fire!!* She taught art at Howard University, and was director of the Harlem Community Art Center from 1937 to 1940.

BETHUNE, MARY MCLEOD (1875–1955), educator and civic leader, was born in Maysville, South Carolina. She attended Scotia College (North Carolina) from 1888 to 1895, and the Moody Bible Institute (Chicago, Illinois) from 1895 to 1897. She founded the normal and industrial school for African-American women at Daytona Beach, Florida, in 1904. The school was renamed Bethune-Cookman College in 1923. She served as president of the college until 1947. Bethune was president of the National Association of Colored Women and founder and president of the National Council of Negro Women (1935–1949).

BONNER, MARITA O. (1899–1971), essayist, poet, and educator, was born and educated in Brookline, Massachusetts. She graduated from Radcliffe College with a degree in English and Comparative Literature. She contributed a number of prize-winning essays to *The Crisis* and *Opportunity.* Following teaching positions at Bluefield Colored Institution in Virginia and Armstrong High School in Washington, D.C., she married accountant William Occomy and moved to Chicago, where she taught at Philips High School and the Doolittle School for the Educationally Retarded.

BONTEMPS, ARNA (1907–1972), poet, librarian, and novelist, was born in Alexandria, Louisiana. He moved with his family at the age of three to Los Angeles. Educated at San Fernando Academy and Pacific Union College, he moved to Harlem in 1924, where he was soon welcomed into the "Talented Tenth" club, was published, received awards for poetry from both *Opportunity* and *The Crisis,* and a Rosenwald Fellowship for Caribbean travel. Following some career-enhancing collaborations with Countee Cullen, Harold Arlen, and Langston Hughes, the renowned novelist-poet-librarian spent his final years as curator of the James Weldon Johnson Memorial Collection of Negro Arts and Letters at Yale University.

BRAWLEY, BENJAMIN (1882–1934), educator and author, was born in Columbia, South Carolina. He received B.A. degrees from Morehouse College (1901) and from the University of Chicago (1906), and a M.A. degree from Howard University in 1908. He taught at a number of colleges and universities, including Howard University, Morehouse College, and Shaw University (Raleigh, North Carolina). His books include *A Short History of the American Negro* (1913); *A Social History of the American Negro* (1921); *The Negro in Literature and Art* (1918); and *A Short History of English Drama* (1921).

BROWN, STERLING (1901–1989), poet, critic, folklorist, and educator, was born in the District of Columbia, where he was graduated from the famed Dunbar High School. He was elected Phi Beta Kappa while earning a B.A. degree from Williams College. He earned his M.A. degree from Harvard University. Following positions at Virginia Seminary, Lincoln University in Missouri, and Fisk and Howard Universities, he published his first book of poetry. Through the greater part of the 1930s he was Literary Editor of *Opportunity* and served as Negro Affairs Editor for the Federal Writers' Project. He was the author of *The Negro in American Fiction* (1937) and an editor of *The Negro Caravan* (1941).

CARTER, ELMER A. (1880–1973), educator, essayist, and editor, received his B.A. degree from Harvard University. He taught in the public schools of Texas before joining the staff of the Urban League. In 1928 he succeeded Charles S. Johnson as editor of *Opportunity*.

COLEMAN, ANITA SCOTT (1890–1960), poet, short-story writer, and essayist, was born in the city of Guaymas in Mexico. Her father, a Cuban, purchased her mother as a slave. She was educated in the school system in Silver City, New Mexico. She published in *The Crisis, Opportunity, The Messenger, Flash,* and other magazines. Under the pseudonym of Elizabeth Stapleton Stokes, she published a book of poems, *Small Wisdom* (1937).

COTTER, JOSEPH S., [SR.] (1861–1949), poet and essayist, was the illegitimate son of a prominent white citizen of Louisville, Kentucky. Cotter spent his early adolescence as poor rag picker, brickmaker, and cotton and tobacco picker. After completing his education during an intense period of night study, he eventually became principal of the local high school. Inspired by poet-scholar Paul Laurence Dunbar, Cotter began to write and publish his own dramatic, autobiographical, and poetic writings in magazines such as *The Crisis* and *Opportunity*.

CULLEN, COUNTEE (1903–1946), poet, essayist, and educator, was the adopted son of the prominent Harlem minister Reverend Frederick Cullen. Born in Lexington, Kentucky, he attended De Witt Clinton High School in New York, where he was editor of the school newspaper. Cullen earned his B.A. degree and election to Phi Beta Kappa at

New York University and his M.A. in English at Harvard University. His first poetry was published at age fifteen, and he received the Witter Bynner Poetry Prize at New York University, the Harmon Foundation Gold Medal Award, *Opportunity* poetry prizes, and was the first African American to receive a Guggenheim Fellowship, in 1928. He taught in the public school system of New York City.

DUNBAR-NELSON, ALICE (1875–1935), author, social worker, and poet, studied at Straight College (now Dillard University), New Orleans, Louisiana; the University of Pennsylvania; Cornell University; and the School of Industrial Arts (Philadelphia); before she married the poet Paul Laurence Dunbar in 1898. Dunbar died in 1904. In 1916, she married Robert J. Nelson. Alice Dunbar-Nelson was a probation and parole officer, served as associate editor of the *AME Review* of the African Methodist Episcopal Church, and was editor of the Wilmington, Delaware, *Advocate*. She was also a weekly contributor to the Associated Negro Press. Her books include *Goodness of St. Rocque*, a book of short stories (1899), and two edited volumes, *Masterpieces of Negro Eloquence* (1914) and *The Dunbar Speaker* (1920).

FAUSET, ARTHUR HUFF (1899–1984), author and educator, was born in Flemington, New Jersey. He received his B.A., M.A., and Ph.D. degrees from the University of Pennsylvania. He was a teacher and principal in the public schools of Philadelphia from 1918 to 1946. His books include *Sojourner Truth: God's Faithful Pilgrim* (1938), a biography, and *Black Gods of the Metropolis: Negro Religious Cults of the Urban North* (1944). He was the brother of novelist Jessie Fauset.

FISHER, RUDOLPH (1897–1934), physician, roentgenologist, musician, and novelist, was born in Washington, D.C., but was reared in Providence, Rhode Island. He graduated Phi Beta Kappa from Brown University. He received his M.D. at Howard University but completed two years of specialized training in biology at Columbia University's College of Physicians and Surgeons. He then moved to Harlem, where he began writing novels, short stories, and essays, which were published in magazines such as *Atlantic Monthly, American Mercury, McClure's, The Crisis,* and *Opportunity*. Fisher also served as an arranger for many years of the Negro spirituals sung by Paul Robeson. He eventually died from the chronic effects of exposure to his own X-ray machines.

FRAZIER, E. [EDWARD] FRANKLIN (1894–1962), educator, sociologist, and author, was born in Baltimore, Maryland. He graduated with honors from Howard University, earned a M.A. in Sociology from Clark University in Atlanta, and received his Ph.D. from the University of Chicago. Frazier taught at Atlanta and Fisk Universities and was Chairman of Sociology at Howard. Though primarily an educator and sociologist, he wrote insightful essays for *The Journal of Social Forces, The Nation, The Crisis,* and *Opportunity.* His books include *The Negro Family in Chicago* (1932); *Traditions and Patterns of Negro Family Life* (1934); *The Negro in the United States* (1949); and his most popular and controversial book, *Black Bourgeoise* (1957).

GARVIN, CHARLES H. (1891–1968), physician, army officer, and civic leader, was born in Jacksonville, Florida. He received a B.A. from Howard University and a M.D. from Howard's Medical School. In 1916 he moved to Cleveland, Ohio, where he began his private practice of medicine and genitourinary surgery. Interrupting his medical practice to join the U.S. Army, he was the first African-American physician to be commissioned. A member of the Cleveland Board of the Urban League, he also contributed to *Opportunity* and medical journals.

GORDON, EUGENE, was a writer for the *Boston Post.* His articles on the Negro press have appeared in such journals as *American Mercury, The Fourth Estate,* and *Opportunity.*

GRIMKE, ANGELINA W. (1880–1958), poet, playwright, and teacher, was born in Boston, Massachusetts. The only child of the noted lawyer and government official Archibald H. Grimke, she graduated from the Boston Normal School of Gymnastics (1902). She taught at the well-known Dunbar High School in Washington, D.C., until 1933. Grimke wrote *Rachel,* a three-act play, which was performed in Washington in 1916. She was active in Washington literary circles but became more reclusive in her final years.

HILL, LESLIE PINCKNEY (1880–1960), educator, poet, and college president, was born in Lynchburg, Virginia. He received a B.A. degree (1903) and M.A. degree (1904) from Harvard University. He taught at Tuskegee Institute, Manassass Industrial Training School, and was president of Cheyney State College (Pennsylvania) for twenty years. He authored *Wings of Oppression (Poem)* and *Toussaint L'Ouverture: A Dramatic History.*

HOLSTEIN, CASPER (1877–1944), businessman, essayist, and philanthropist, was born in the Virgin Islands. He arrived in New York City shortly before World War I and began work as a porter. Dissatisfied with his low wages and threadbare lifestyle, he developed a system for betting on three-digit numbers taken from the daily stock market listings. The odds on betting were six hundred to one. Through his organized gambling enterprise, he became one of the most notorious overlords in Harlem. He was a major financial contributor to *Opportunity*'s annual contests.

HOPE, JOHN (1868–1936), educator, essayist, and college president, was born in Augusta, Georgia. He received a B.A. degree (1894) and a M.A. degree (1907) from Brown University. In 1906 he became president of Atlanta Baptist College. Playing a role in coordinating the six denominational colleges to design the new Atlanta University, he became the institution's president in 1929.

HORNE, FRANK (1899–1974), physician, public official, and poet, was born in New York City. He graduated from the City College of the City University of New York in 1921. Horne received a degree in ophthalmology from Northern Illinois College of Ophthalmology in 1923. He joined the staff of Fort Valley State College as dean and for a time was acting president. Among his publications includes a book of poems, *Haverstraw* (1963).

HUGHES, [JAMES] LANGSTON (1902–1967), poet, playwright, novelist, anthologist, and historian, was born in Joplin, Missouri. His parents separated when he was a child. His maternal grandfather was the abolitionist Charles Langston, who fought with John Brown at Harper's Ferry, and his half-brother was John Mercer Langston, U.S. Congressman from Virginia. Though his rearing was rather peripatetic, his literary talents brought him notice in elementary and secondary schools. As a merchant seaman, Hughes saw much of the world but was "discovered" by poet Vachel Lindsay as a "busboy poet" in Washington, D.C. Having dropped out of college at Columbia, he returned to Lincoln University with the financial assistance of Amy Spingarn, wife of the NAACP Board Chairman J. E. Spingarn. His touching and lyrical poetry won him notice from both jazz and literary patrons, but he began to lose favor when he chose voluntary exile for a time in Cuba, Russia, and Spain. He later collaborated with Arna Bontemps on anthologies and children's works and funded theater groups in Harlem, Chicago, and Los Angeles.

HURSTON, ZORA NEALE (1907?–1960), short-story writer, playwright, and novelist, was born in Eatonville, Florida. Studying under famed anthropologist Franz Boas, she received a B.A. degree from

Barnard College. She wrote three novels, *Jonah's Gourd Vine* (1934), *Their Eyes Were Watching God* (1948), and *Seraph on the Suwanee* (1948). Her autobiography, *Dust Tracks on the Road*, was published in 1943.

JOHNSON, CHARLES S. (1893–1956), social scientist, educator, editor, and college president, was born in Bristol, Virginia. He received his B.A. degree from Virginia Union University in 1916 and a Ph.D. degree from the University of Chicago in 1918. Between 1917 and 1919, he served as director of research and records for the Chicago Urban League. In 1921 Johnson moved to New York to become director of the Urban League's Department of Research and Investigations. Two years later he became editor of the League's new official organ, *Opportunity*. In 1928, he left the Urban League to become chairman of the Social Science Department at Fisk University. In 1946, he became president of Fisk University. His books include *The Negro in American Civilization: A Study of Negro Life and Race Relations in the Light of Social Research* (1930), *Shadow of the Plantation* (1934), and *The Negro College Graduate*.

JOHNSON, GEORGIA DOUGLAS (1886–1966), poet, essayist, and educator, was educated at Oberlin Conservatory of Music and Atlanta University, where she met and married her husband, Henry Lincoln Johnson. They settled in Washington, D.C., where she was employed by the federal government and he became a prominent figure in the Republican Party. Georgia Douglas Johnson was a founder of The First Nighters, a literary club whose membership included Mary Miller, Angelina Weld Grimke, Alain Locke, Jean Toomer, Richard Bruce Nugent, James Weldon Johnson, W.E.B. Du Bois, Jessie Fauset, and Langston Hughes. She was the first African-American woman to be widely recognized as a poet in the early twentieth century, received considerable acclaim as a poet and teacher, and won a first prize in an *Opportunity* contest for one of her plays.

JOHNSON, HELENE (1907–1995), one of the youngest of the Harlem Renaissance poets, was born in Boston, Massachusetts. She attended Boston University and Columbia University. Her poem "The Road" appeared in Alain Locke's critically acclaimed volume *The New Negro*. Her other poems were published in *Opportunity*, *Vanity Fair*, and *Fire!!* Johnson disappeared from Harlem shortly before the literary movement ended.

JOHNSON, JAMES WELDON (1871–1938), poet, educator, novelist, lawyer, diplomat, newspaper editor, and civil rights leader, was born in

Jacksonville, Florida. He attended Atlanta University Preparatory and received a B.A. degree from Atlanta University in 1894. Upon returning to Jacksonville, he accepted a position as principal of Stanton School—the school that he ultimately made the first high school for blacks in the state of Florida. During this time he founded the weekly newspaper the *Daily American* and passed the Florida bar exam. He moved to New York in 1902, where he and his brother, J. Rosamond Johnson, collaborated with musician Bob Cole to produce highly successful light operas, musical comedies, and more than two hundred songs. Johnson authored a number of books, including *The Autobiography of an Ex-Colored Man, God's Trombones: Seven Negro Sermons in Verse, Black Manhattan,* and *Along This Way,* an autobiography.

LARSEN, NELLA (1893–1963), novelist and nurse, was born in Chicago, Illinois. She attended Fisk University and graduated from the prestigious Lincoln Hospital Training School for Nurses (New York City) in 1915. In 1930 she became the first African American to receive the prestigious Guggenheim Award. Her two novels, *Quicksand* (1928) and *Passing* (1929), were widely acclaimed.

LOCKE, ALAIN [LEROY] (1885–1954), philosopher, educator, literary critic, and anthologist, was born in Philadelphia, Pennsylvania. Locke was elected to Phi Beta Kappa and became the first African-American Rhodes Scholar. After two years at Oxford, he studied at the University of Berlin and College de France and, later, earned his Ph.D. in Philosophy from Harvard. From 1912 until his retirement, he taught at Howard University. His best known work is the anthology *The New Negro* (1925).

LOGAN, RAYFORD W. (1897–1982), historian, essayist, and educator, was born in Washington, D.C. Logan received B.A. (1917) and M.A. (1929) degrees from Williams College, and his Ph.D. from Harvard University in 1936. He taught at Virginia Union University and Atlanta University before becoming head of the department of history at Howard University. His books include *Diplomatic Relations of the United States with Haiti* (1941), *The Negro and the Post-War World: A Primer* (1945), and *The Betrayal of the Negro: From Rutherford B. Hayes to Woodrow Wilson* (1965).

McKAY, CLAUDE (1889–1948), author and poet, was born in Jamaica. His initial training was in Agriculture in Tuskegee, from which he later transferred to Kansas State College. Upon his arrival in New York he entered the bohemian and revolutionary lifestyle in Greenwich Village. His first American poetry was published under the pseudonym Eli Edwards. In 1919 McKay moved to London, where he read the works of Marx and Lenin and joined the staff of the communist newspaper *The Worker's Dreadnought.* Disenchanted with America's race relations, with Marcus Garvey's Universal Negro Improvement Association (UNIA), and with editorial politics at *The Liberator,* where he was editor, he traveled to France and North Africa, where he wrote many of his prize-winning works. With the exception of James Weldon Johnson, McKay sharply criticized many senior notables of the Harlem Renaissance.

MATHEUS, JOHN F. (1887–?), short-story writer and educator, was born in Keyser, West Virginia. He received a B.A. from Western Reserve University (1910) and a M.A. from Columbia University (1921). He taught at Florida A&M College and West Virginia Collegiate Institute. His prize-winning short story "Fog" was included in Alain Locke's *The New Negro* (1925).

MILLER, KELLY (1863–1939), educator and essayist, was born in Winnsboro, South Carolina. He received a B.A. degree from Howard University in 1886. From 1887 to 1889 he attended Johns Hopkins University, where he studied mathematics, physics, and astronomy. In 1890 he began teaching at Howard University in the mathematics department. From 1915 to 1925 he taught in the department of sociology. He was chairman of the department from 1925 to his retirement in 1934. He contributed to numerous journals and leading newspapers. During the 1920s he became known as a major intellectual voice in the black press.

MORYCK, BRENDA RAY, essayist and educator, was born in Newark, New Jersey. A graduate of Wellesley College, she taught in the public schools of Washington, D.C., and New York City.

NUGENT, R. BRUCE (1906–1989), poet, essayist, illustrator, was born in Washington, D.C., where he attended public schools. His poems were published in Countee Cullen's *Caroling Dusk* anthology. His illustrations appeared in *Fire!!, Harlem,* and other journals of the time.

POWELL, ADAM CLAYTON [SR.] (1865–1953), preacher, author, and reformer, was born in Franklin County, Virginia. Powell graduated from Wayland Seminary and College (Washington, D.C.) in 1892. While a special student at Yale University's Divinity School in 1895, he accepted a pastorate of Immanuel Baptist Church in New Haven,

Connecticut. He moved to New York City in 1908 and began his pastorate at the Abyssinian Baptist Church. He was the father of the late Congressman Adam Clayton Powell, Jr., who succeeded him as pastor of Abyssinian Baptist Church.

RANDOLPH, A. [ASA] PHILIP (1889–1979), socialist, labor leader, and civil rights activist, was born in Crescent City, Florida. Randolph moved to New York after high school. He worked at a series of odd jobs before he cofounded the socialist weekly, *The Messenger*, in 1917. In 1925 he founded the Brotherhood of Sleeping Car Porters (BSCP), and a decade later the union successfully negotiated a collective bargaining agreement with the Pullman Palace Car Company. In 1957 he was elected vice-president of the AFL-CIO. His socialism toned down, he was a prominent organizer of the 1963 March on Washington. Randolph founded the A. Philip Randolph Institute in New York City, which is dedicated to education and job training.

REID, IRA DE A. [DE AUGUSTINE] (1901–1968), sociologist, educator, and author, was born in Clifton Forge, Virginia. He received his B.A. degree from Morehouse College in 1922, his M.A. degree from the University of Pittsburgh in 1925, and his Ph.D. from Columbia University in 1939. Reid taught at several universities before joining the department of sociology and anthropology at Haverford College (Pennsylvania) from 1947 to 1966. His books include *In a Minor Key: Negro Youth in Story and Fact* (1940) and *Sharecroppers All* (1941) with Arthur F. Raper.

RICHARDSON, WILLIS (1889–1977), playwright, was born in Wilmington, North Carolina, and reared in Washington, D.C. He studied at Dunbar High School. Among those who encouraged and inspired him were his teacher and aspiring playwright Mary Burill, author Angelina Grimke, and W.E.B. Du Bois. From 1910 to 1955 he supported himself as a clerk at the U.S. Bureau of Engraving. His play *Chip Woman's Fortune* opened on Broadway in May 1923. The Howard Players staged his *Mortgaged* in 1924. Other relevant works include *Plays and Pageants of Negro Life* (1930) and *Negro History in Thirteen Plays* (1935).

ROBESON, PAUL (1898–1976), lawyer, actor, singer, and activist, was born in Princeton, New Jersey. He graduated from Rutgers University (New Brunswick, New Jersey) in 1919, and received a law degree from Columbia University. Robeson starred in Eugene O'Neill's Broadway revival of *The Emperor Jones* in 1925. Three years later, he appeared in *Porgy* and *Show Boat*. Making racial history, Robeson starred as Othello at New York's Shubert Theatre. He was an international success as a singer, blending folk music of the world with spirituals, popular music, and classical songs.

ROGERS, J. A. [JOEL AUGUSTUS] (1880–1966), writer and historian, was born in Negril, Jamaica. After arriving in the United States in 1906, he began to write fiction and history. His writings include *Man and Superman* (1917) and *The World's Greatest Men of African Descent* (1931).

SCOTT, CLARISSA M. (1901–1927), poet and educator, was born in Tuskegee, Alabama. The daughter of Emmett J. Scott, secretary to Booker T. Washington, she attended Tuskegee Institute and Wellesley College. She taught at the prestigious Dunbar High School in Washington, D.C. Her poetry has been included in a number of anthologies.

THURMAN, H. WALLACE (1902–1934), novelist, poet, and dramatist, was born in Salt Lake City, Utah. He attended the University of Utah (1919–1920). After enrolling at the University of Southern California, he met fellow writer Arna Bontemps. In 1924 he founded *The Outlet*. The journal folded in 1925 and he moved to New York. He worked for several publications, including *The Looking Glass, The Messenger,* and *The World Tomorrow*. In 1927 he started the magazine *Fire!!*

WALROND, ERIC D. (1898–1956), short-story writer, was born in Georgetown, Guyana. He moved to New York in 1918, and later attended City College and Columbia University. After serving as a staff member of Marcus Garvey's newspaper, *The Negro World,* Walrond joined the staff of *Opportunity* as business manager from 1925 to 1927. He left America for England in 1928 to write a novel about the Panama Canal. For the next twenty-eight years he would remain in England without ever publishing.

WEST, DOROTHY (1908–1998), short-story writer and novelist, was born in Boston, Massachusetts. She attended Boston University and Columbia University. "The Typewriter," a short story, was published in *Opportunity* when she was eighteen years old.

WILSON, FRANK H., singer, playwright, short-story writer, and producer, was born in New York City. After spending twelve years in vaudeville performing as a baritone singer, he created the character Joe in Eugene O'Neill's *All God's Chillun Got Wings*. He wrote and produced numerous plays.

WORK, JOHN W. (1901–1968), composer and educator, was born in Tullahoma, Tennessee. He attended Fisk, Columbia, and Yale Universities and the New Musical Art Institute. Work taught at Fisk University from 1948 to 1957, at which time he directed the world-famous Fisk Jubilee Singers. He was published in a number of scholarly journals, and his well-received *American Folk Songs* was published in 1940.

YOUNG, BENJAMIN, was a short-story writer. He taught high school in St. Louis, Missouri.

Bibliography

Aptheker, Herbert, ed. *A Documentary History of the Negro People in the United States, 1910–1932*, vol. 3. Secaucus, N.J.: Citadel Press, 1977.

Bontemps, Arna, ed. *The Harlem Renaissance Remembered*. New York: Dodd Mead, 1972.

Du Bois, W.E.B. *The Autobiography of W.E.B. Du Bois*. New York: International Publishers, 1968.

Gates, Henry Louis, Jr., and Nellie Y. McKay, eds. *The Norton Anthology of African American Literature*. New York: W. W. Norton, 1996.

Hemenway, Robert. *Zora Neale Hurston: A Literary Biography*. Champaign-Urbana: University of Illinois Press, 1977.

Huggins, Nathan Irvin. *Black Odyssey: The Afro-American Ordeal in Slavery*. New York: Vintage Books, 1979.

———. *Harlem Renaissance*. New York: Oxford University Press, 1971.

Johnson, James Weldon. *Black Manhattan*. New York: Alfred A. Knopf, 1930.

———. *Negro Americans, What Now?* New York: The Viking Press, 1934.

Lewis, David Levering. *When Harlem Was in Vogue*. New York: Oxford University Press, 1981.

———. *W.E.B. Du Bois, a Biography of a Race: 1868–1919*. New York: Henry Holt & Company, 1993.

———, ed. *The Portable Harlem Renaissance*. New York: Viking Press, 1981.

Moses, Wilson Jeremiah. *The Golden Age of Black Nationalism*. New York: Oxford University Press, 1978.

National Association for the Advancement of Colored People. *The Crisis* (1910–1931).

National Urban League. *Opportunity* (1923–1931).

Rampersad, Arnold. *The Life of Langston Hughes, Volume I: I, Too, Sing America*. New York: Oxford University Press, 1986.

Singh, Amritjit, William S. Shiver, and Stanley Brodwin, eds. *The Harlem Renaissance: Re-evaluations.* New York: Garland Publishing, 1989.

Watkins, Sylvestre C., ed. *Anthology of American Negro Literature.* New York: Modern Library, 1944.

Wilson, Sondra Kathryn, ed. *The Selected Writings of James Weldon Johnson,* vols. 1&2. New York: Oxford University Press, 1995.

ABOUT THE EDITOR

DR. SONDRA KATHRYN WILSON is an associate of Harvard University's W.E.B. Du Bois Institute and executor of James Weldon Johnson's literary properties. She has published two volumes of Johnson's writings and *The* Crisis *Reader: Stories, Poetry, and Essays from the N.A.A.C.P.'s* Crisis *Magazine.* Her upcoming works include *In Search of Democracy: The N.A.A.C.P. Writings of James Weldon Johnson, Walter F. White, and Roy Wilkins (1920–1977).*

A NOTE ON THE TYPE

The principal text of this Modern Library edition
was set in a digitized version of Janson,
a typeface that dates from about 1690 and was cut by Nicholas Kis,
a Hungarian working in Amsterdam. The original matrices have
survived and are held by the Stempel foundry in Germany.
Hermann Zapf redesigned some of the weights and sizes for Stempel,
basing his revisions on the original design.